Exploring America Part 2

Late 1800s to the Present

Exploring America Part 2: Late 1800s to the Present (2019 Edition)
Ray Notgrass

ISBN 978-1-60999-999-5
2025 Printing

Previous Page: "A Day to Remember" World Trade Center Tribute in Light, September 11, 2010 (Bob Jagendorf / Flickr / CC-BY-2.0)

Front Cover Images—Top: Statue of Liberty, Photo by Jere Keys (jerekeys / Flickr / CC-BY-2.0); Portraits (L to R): *Bucking Bronco* by Frederic Remington (Library of Congress); Woman Working on an Airplane Motor in 1942 by Alfred T. Palmer (Library of Congress); *Dwight D. Eisenhower* by James Anthony Wills (1967, Eisenhower Library); World War II Veteran (Archangel12 / Flickr / CC-BY-2.0); Astronaut Mark Lee / NASA. **Back Cover Image**—Seattle Skyline (WordRidden / Flickr / CC-BY-2.0). Images marked CC-BY-2.0 are used with the permission of a Creative Commons Attribution License: creativecommons.org/licenses/by/2.0/
Author Photo—Mary Evelyn McCurdy

Cover design by Mary Evelyn McCurdy
Interior design by John Notgrass

Printed in the United States of America

Notgrass History
1-800-211-8793
notgrass.com

Homestake Gold Mine in Lead, South Dakota, 1900

Table of Contents

President Theodore Roosevelt and Family, 1903

20 America and the Great War 551

War Gardeners, 1919

21 America in the Twenties 583

Crowd Outside Bank in New York, 1931

22 The New Deal 615

23 World War II 651

Neil Armstrong took this photo of fellow astronaut Buzz Aldrin during their historic moon walk in 1969 on the Apollo 11 mission. Armstrong's reflection is visible in the center of Aldrin's visor.

Memorial in Boston for the Victims of the 2013 Boston Marathon Bombing

Biltmore House, Asheville, North Carolina

16 The Gilded Age

Rutherford B. Hayes tried to create a more positive atmosphere in Washington than had existed during the Grant years. However, the forces of corruption were strong. Concern by farmers and westerners about the nation's monetary policy, among other factors, led to the formation of the Populist Party. In another development, Darwinian evolution captured the popular thinking of the day and changed how many people viewed themselves and the world around them.

Memory Work

Memorize Genesis 1:24-26 by the end of this unit.

Books Used

The Bible
American Voices
In His Steps

Project (choose one)

1) Write 300 to 500 words on one of the following topics:
   - What can you do to bring about more honesty in government and politics? Identify what you think needs to be done and outline steps to bring it about.
   - Imagine that you are the son or daughter of a struggling Midwestern farmer. Write a letter to your grandfather in Chicago describing the hardships your family is facing.

2) Write a hymn with at least three verses and a chorus extolling God's power in Creation. Counter the theory of evolution in a positive way in your hymn. See Lesson 80.

3) Write a play about political corruption. It can be fictional or based on fact and set in any place and time period you wish. Your play should be at least five pages long. Performing the play is optional but would be fun!

Optional Research Paper: If you plan to write a longer research paper as part of this course, plan with a parent when you will work on it. See pages xii-xv of *Part 1*.

Literature

In His Steps

Charles M. Sheldon was a minister in Topeka, Kansas, who told stories for his Sunday evening sermons to try to increase attendance. One Sunday night sermon series involved several members of a church in the mythical town of Raymond who decided to face every situation in life by asking, "What would Jesus do?" and then taking that action themselves. The series was published in book form in 1896 and has been a Christian best-seller ever since.

In His Steps is a good illustration of what the social gospel was about, but it is also a convicting lesson about how our lives can change if we really try to do in every situation what Jesus would do. The book describes the social changes taking place with increased industrialization and shows how some members of American society were pushed to the fringes. It focuses on some wealthy church members and is admittedly a bit idealistic in what it describes; but Sheldon had some particular issues that he was emphasizing, such as alcohol abuse and life in the slums. The novel is a powerful challenge to anyone who will consider its central idea. The question asked in the book, "What would Jesus do?" was the basis for the WWJD? craze in the 1990s.

Plan to finish *In His Steps* by the end of the next unit.

Inauguration of President Hayes, 1877

Lesson 76

Corruption and Reform

They called her Lemonade Lucy. First Lady Lucy Ware Webb Hayes refused to serve alcoholic beverages at White House functions. Mrs. Hayes wanted to send a strong message to the country about the evils of alcohol. The social events hosted by the Hayes were quite a change from the days of free-flowing alcohol during the Grant Administration. Lucy's husband, President Rutherford B. Hayes, was a teetotaler also. They regularly attended services at an Episcopal church in Washington. Her nickname was kind, however, compared to what opponents called her husband after the controversial election of 1876. One nickname for him was "His Fraudulency."

Republican Rutherford B. Hayes set a new tone in the White House. Hayes was a wounded and honored Civil War veteran and popular governor of Ohio. He had a strong and honest character and intended to govern accordingly. However, the forces of corruption and political division were too strong for him to stop.

The Hayes Administration

The Democrats controlled the House during Hayes' entire term, and they also had the majority in the Senate during his last two years. This created a political stalemate that prevented much significant legislation from being enacted. In addition, the Republican Party had a serious division within its ranks. The Stalwarts, led by New York Senator and political boss Roscoe Conkling, included the Radical element of the party that opposed any significant reforms in government. The Half-Breeds, who included Senators James G. Blaine of Maine and John Sherman of Ohio, were more moderate and favored at least some reforms.

Some of the Cabinet selections made by Hayes, such as liberal Republican Carl Schurz as Interior Secretary and southern Democrat David Key as Postmaster General, angered Republican Party leaders; but Hayes managed to get them approved by the Senate.

The End of Reconstruction

Hayes brought the period of Reconstruction to an end by removing the last Federal troops from the South. This also ended the last chance for Republican domination of Reconstruction governments in the southern states. The President hoped that the Republican Party would become stronger in the South by its own merits and not by being imposed on the people. Hayes wanted to bring the nation together, North and South, black and white. His efforts at reconciliation were genuine, but he was

The Gilded Age is a novel by Mark Twain and Charles Dudley Warner that was published in 1873. The book's title came to be applied to the period of American history that followed Reconstruction. To be gilded means to be covered with gold. The point of the book was that in many ways America seemed positive and forward-looking, but underneath lay corruption and much that was wrong. Twain (center) is shown at left in 1871 with author George Alfred Townsend (left) and newspaperman David Gray (right).

still viewed with suspicion because of the deal that had allowed him to become President.

Policies Under Hayes

Hayes refused to fire Federal employees just to replace them with his political allies. Any dismissals would have to be for the good of the government, he said. He also ordered an investigation of the corrupt Collection Office of the Port of New York. Because of the corruption there, Hayes fired Collector Chester A. Arthur and Naval Officer Alonzo Cornell. This angered Boss Conkling, but Hayes stood his ground and his replacements for these posts eventually won Senate confirmation.

At the same time, Hayes was opposed to the power of organized labor in a period when labor unions were commonly seen as dangerous and promoting anarchy. The President dispatched Federal troops to break up a railroad strike in 1877. He vetoed a bill that would have restricted Chinese immigration, a move which angered the unions who wanted less competition from immigrants for American jobs. Hayes believed the bill violated a treaty that the U.S. had signed with China. He did, however, negotiate a new treaty with China which allowed immigration restrictions to be put in place.

Carl Schurz

Carl Schurz was born in Germany and was a student leader in the revolutionary uprising there in 1848. He later came to the United States and spent his life in politics and public service. Schurz lived in several states during his career. While he lived in Wisconsin, he became a Republican and supported Fremont in 1856 and Lincoln in 1860. Schurz toured the South for President Johnson in 1865 and recommended that blacks be allowed to vote, a suggestion which caused his proposals about postwar policies to lose much support. After moving to Missouri, Schurz became a U.S. Senator and split with Grant over the corruption that was running rampant in government. President Hayes appointed Schurz Secretary of the Interior. He is pictured, second from left, with a delegation of Ute Indians. Schurz later lived in New York, opposed Republican James G. Blaine in the 1884 presidential election, and continued to be a strong advocate for civil service reforms until his death in 1906.

The U.S. Army Corps of Engineers oversaw projects that improved navigation along rivers, including the Muscle Shoals Canal Project in Alabama in the 1870s and 1880s. This photo is from 1881.

A ten-year suspension of Chinese immigration was eventually enacted in 1882. Hayes also vetoed a bill to allow greater coinage of silver, but Congress overrode his veto. The law expanded the money supply and pleased farmers and debtors.

The 1880 Election

Hayes' announcement that he would not seek re-election created Republican in-fighting for the nomination. The Stalwarts tried to regain control of the party by pushing the nomination of former President U.S. Grant. However, James G. Blaine of the Half-Breeds wanted the nomination for himself. The deadlocked convention finally turned to Ohio Senator and Union Army veteran James A. Garfield as its dark horse nominee.

To please the Stalwarts, the convention delegates nominated ousted Customs Collector Chester Arthur for Vice President. The Democrats nominated as its presidential candidate another Civil War veteran, Winfield Scott Hancock, who had commanded Union troops at Gettysburg. Garfield won with an electoral majority of 214 to 155 but with a popular plurality of less than forty thousand votes.

Garfield accepted help from the Republican Stalwarts during the campaign, but when he became President in March of 1881, he nominated Half-Breed leader James Blaine to be Secretary of State and named a Conkling opponent to be Customs Collector in New York. Stalwart leader Boss Conkling and his fellow Stalwart Senator from New York resigned their seats in protest over this appointment.

On July 2, 1881, Garfield was shot by a crazed, disappointed office seeker, Charles Guiteau, as the President was passing through a Washington train station. Guiteau shouted, "I am a Stalwart; Arthur is President now" as he shot Garfield from the back. The President survived for several weeks but finally died on September 19, 1881.

James A. Garfield was an elder and part-time preacher in the Christian Church. When he was elected President, Garfield resigned as an elder in his congregation in Ohio. He said that he was stepping down from the higher office of elder in the church to assume the lower office of President of the United States. Above right is Garfield's 1881 presidential portrait by Calvin Curtis. Above left is a memorial ribbon.

Civil Service Reform

The nation was shocked by this second presidential assassination in sixteen years. The fact that Guiteau had sought a government job brought attention to the problems of the politically-weighted civil service system used to hire government workers. Jobs in the Federal government (called the civil service), most of which are in the Executive branch, had long been seen as one of the prizes for the party that captured the White House. The President was able to hire thousands of workers for the Federal bureaucracy, and he usually gave these jobs to people who had supported his candidacy. Remember, for instance, Andrew Jackson's spoils system and Nathaniel Hawthorne's losing his customs house job when the White House changed hands. In practical terms, it appeared that a Federal worker's ability to do his job well was not as important as his party loyalty. As a result, the level of professionalism and competence among government workers was often quite low.

In 1883 Congress passed and President Arthur signed the Pendleton Civil Service Act, named for Ohio Democratic Senator George Pendleton. The measure created a three-person, bipartisan Civil Service Commission to oversee competitive examinations that were administered to candidates for Federal jobs. This meant that those who scored highest on objective exams would get the jobs, not those who were political supporters of the President. The Pendleton Act was genuine reform, but it was only a start. Only about twelve percent of government jobs were covered by the act; however, the President had the power to increase by executive order the number of positions that were covered. The Pendleton Act also made it illegal for political parties to ask Federal workers for contributions.

Although Chester Arthur had been deeply involved in partisan politics in New York, he rose to the occasion when he became President and provided able leadership. Arthur appointed a reformer to head the Civil Service Commission and expanded the list of jobs that were to be filled by competitive examination. His Administration prosecuted fraud in the Post Office, opposed wasteful spending on public works projects, and encouraged the development of a more modern naval force. Arthur supported a reduction in tariffs; and while the tariff law that passed Congress in 1883 reduced overall rates, duties on some items were increased.

The 1884 Election

President Arthur wanted to serve another term, but leaders in the Republican Party turned away from him and nominated Half-Breed James G. Blaine instead. Blaine was handsome, eloquent, and a strong-willed political fighter. A supporter once called him a "plumed knight" who defended the country and his own honor. The Democrats nominated reform New York governor Grover Cleveland, who had established a record of opposing Tammany Hall and laws that favored special interest groups. Liberal Republicans, including Carl Schurz, opposed Blaine and came out in favor of the Democrat Cleveland. The Liberals advocated continued reforms in civil service but continued to oppose labor unions. A newspaper writer labeled these Republican renegades who supported the Democrat candidate Mugwumps (an Algonquian Indian word) because, with their divided party loyalties, they had their mugs on one side of the fence and their wumps on the other.

President Grant had signed legislation in 1872 designating Yellowstone as the first national park in the United States. It includes parts of Montana, Idaho, and Wyoming. President Arthur visited the park in 1883, as seen below (seated center). He was the first sitting President to visit the western part of the country.

The 1884 campaign was another example of dirty politics. Democrats attacked Blaine for his political maneuverings and for the use of his influence for personal gain. "Blaine, Blaine, James G. Blaine—Continental liar from the state of Maine," ran one Democratic chant. Then late in the campaign, a Protestant minister friendly to Blaine described the Democratic Party as promoting "Rum, Romanism, and Rebellion." The reference to rum was a slam against the use of alcohol in a time when prohibition was becoming an issue. Romanism referred to Irish Roman Catholics who usually voted for Democrats. The minister also recalled the Democrat-led rebellion of the Confederacy. Blaine did nothing to oppose the remark, and his failure to do so hurt him with fair-minded voters.

Cleveland, however, had his own scandals to deal with. In Buffalo, where Cleveland had served as mayor, a newspaper reported that he had engaged in an extramarital affair and had fathered a child in 1874. Cleveland had accepted responsibility for the boy and had helped provide financial support for him, but the boy was placed in an orphanage. Republicans jeered Cleveland with the chant, "Ma, Ma, where's my Pa? Gone to the White House, ha, ha, ha." The choice facing the voters was between Blaine, who had a respectable private life and a tainted public career, and Cleveland, who had a respectable public career and a tainted private life.

The election was extremely close. Cleveland won with 219 electoral votes compared to Blaine's 182, and by a margin of less than 30,000 popular votes. Cleveland carried his decisive home state of New York by less than 1200 votes. His win marked the first time a Democrat had been elected President in 28 years, when James Buchanan had won in 1856. Still, the Cleveland Administration brought no significant changes to national government, as both parties wrestled for political control and wrestled with (or sometimes sidestepped) the issues confronting the nation.

Grover Cleveland, *Eastman Johnson (1891)*

Trust in the Lord and do good;
Dwell in the land and cultivate faithfulness.
Psalm 37:3

⋆ Assignments for Lesson 76 ⋆

Literature Begin reading *In His Steps.* Plan to finish it by the end of the next unit.

Bible The Bible readings this week will prepare you for our study on Evolution and the Bible in Lesson 80. Read Genesis 1.

Start memorizing Genesis 1:24-26.

Project Choose your project for this unit and start working on it.

Student Review Optional: Answer the questions for Lesson 76.

Reception for President Harrison in Santa Ana, California (1891)

Lesson 77

Cleveland and Harrison

"We love him for the enemies he has made," was the remark of one Cleveland supporter in describing the one-time mayor and governor and now Democratic President. What Cleveland lacked in personal charisma—weighing 250 pounds and sporting a drooping mustache—he made up for in determination. He strongly opposed corruption in both government and business. Still, his Administration brought no significant break with past Republican policies. Cleveland was always aware of potential attacks by his political enemies who were ready to swoop down upon any misstep, real or imagined, that he might make.

Steps of Reform

Cleveland doubled the number of Federal jobs on the civil service list. This brought the number of positions protected by civil service regulations to over 27,000. However, the government had about 120,000 office-holders; so the vast majority of them were still subject to political firings. Cleveland gave in to political pressure from party leaders and replaced about two-thirds of the Federal bureaucracy with what he called honest Democrats. These moves in opposite directions (adding to the number of secure positions but replacing an even greater number of workers with political appointments) angered both sides.

Cleveland took other steps toward reform. He recovered about eighty million acres of public land that was being held in violation of the law by railroad companies and lumber and cattle interests. He signed a measure in 1887 that created a Division of Forestry, a major step toward greater conservation of the country's natural resources. The Hatch Act, passed the same year, authorized appropriations for the development of experiment stations and demonstration farms to help the nation's farmers. The Electoral Count Act, also enacted in 1887, was an attempt to prevent problems such as the one that had arisen in 1876. The law required Congress to accept the returns from a state that had been certified by the governor of that state.

One sensitive issue that Cleveland faced was the granting of Federal pensions to Union Army veterans. Congress had authorized the first pensions to disabled veterans and their dependents and survivors in 1862. After the war, many individual veterans were able to get pensions by having private pension bills passed by Congress. Union veterans organized the Grand Army of the Republic in 1866 as a social group that was also a political pressure group to try to get generous pension benefits for all veterans. Cleveland believed that many pension requests were fraudulent, put forth by people who simply wanted to be put on the public dole. He vetoed many private pension bills as well as the Dependent Pension Bill of 1887 that offered more generous benefits to Union veterans. Cleveland's opposition to the pensions antagonized many veterans and many Republicans.

Interstate Commerce

The legislation with the most potential for change that was passed during Cleveland's first term was the Interstate Commerce Act of 1887. Various states had enacted regulations on railroad operations, but the Supreme Court had struck down those laws as an unconstitutional barrier to interstate commerce.

In response, the law passed by Congress required that carriers set "reasonable and just" rates for carrying goods and passengers. Railroad companies were forbidden to fix rates among themselves, give secret rebates to selected shippers, or discriminate against shippers in any way. The Interstate Commerce Commission, which was created by the law, had the power to investigate and prosecute possible violators. Many years passed before the law had much effect on business, but it was a significant change in the direction of government regulation.

Congressional Acts

In 1886 Congress passed the Presidential Succession Act, which was a response to the two assassinations of Presidents in the previous two decades. It called for Cabinet officers to succeed the Vice President to the presidency in the order in which their departments had been created, starting with the Secretary of State. The procedure and the order of succession have been changed several times since then by Federal laws and constitutional amendments. Now the Speaker of the House and the President Pro Tempore of the Senate are in line after the Vice President, followed by the cabinet officers in the order in which their departments were created.

In 1887 Congress passed the Dawes Act, which changed the government's policy toward Native Americans. By that time, most American Indian tribes had been forced to live on reservations, blocks of land set aside for particular tribes. Under the Dawes Act, tribes were no longer autonomous; and tribal lands were divided among individuals, who were forbidden from disposing of their land for twenty-five years. This was to protect the Native Americans from being tricked into making a bad deal and losing their land. Indians who accepted these terms were given American citizenship and the right to vote. The Federal government also began providing funding for Indian schools. The stated goal of government policy was to help the Indians become integrated into American life, but most Native Americans still lived on reservations, tried to maintain their tribal culture, and became dependent on Federal payments. Over the next forty years, the government allowed a significant portion of Indian reservation land to be sold off to white businessmen. Native Americans did not receive citizenship as a group until 1924. Land policy was reversed in 1934 to allow tribes to own their property communally.

Sitting Bull (c. 1831-1890) was a Hunkpapa Lakota leader among the Sioux who resisted the reservation system.

Tariff Reform Attempt

The main issue during Cleveland's last full year in office was tariff reform. The President and many others believed that high tariff rates gave American business unfair protection from foreign competition. This tariff protection, Cleveland charged, encouraged non-competitive practices and drove higher the prices that Americans had to pay. In addition, tariff collections had created a Federal surplus that kept money from being available to the public. Cleveland devoted his entire annual message to Congress in December of 1887 to his request that rates be lowered or eliminated on the 4,000 items affected by import tariffs.

The House passed a measure lowering the average rate from almost 50 percent of the value of the items to about 40 percent, but the bill died in a Senate committee. The tariff debate created the first significant difference between Democrats and Republicans in several years and became a major issue in the 1888 presidential election.

The Election of 1888

The Democrats nominated Cleveland to run for a second term on the record he had made as President. The Republicans passed over more prominent figures and selected Benjamin Harrison of Indiana. Harrison was the grandson of William Henry Harrison and the great-grandson of a signer of the Declaration of Independence, who was also named Benjamin Harrison. He had served in the Union Army during the Civil War and represented Indiana in the U.S. Senate from 1881 to 1887. While in the Senate, Harrison had supported increasing pensions for Union veterans.

The election was extremely close. Cleveland polled about 91,000 more popular votes than Harrison, but Harrison won the electoral count 233 to 168. Harrison was a competent person, but let Congress run the country. He appointed James G. Blaine as Secretary of State; and Blaine, not Harrison, became the most important political figure in Washington during Harrison's term.

Benjamin Harrison regularly taught a Sunday School class at his Presbyterian church in Indianapolis. Harrison was the first President to submit a peacetime Federal budget that totaled one billion dollars. During Harrison's term, the White House was wired for electricity. Unfamiliar with electricity, however, Harrison and his wife were afraid to touch the switches! The 1895 portrait above is by Eastman Johnson.

The Republican Party developed its nickname of the Grand Old Party (GOP) in the 1880s. The party was actually younger than the Democratic Party, but the term was an attempt to recall the days when the Republicans led the grand effort to save the Union. The party is still called the GOP today.

The Republicans controlled the White House and had a majority in both houses of Congress during Harrison's first two years, the only time between 1875 and 1895 that this was the case. The Republicans worked hard at undoing much of what had taken place during Cleveland's tenure. The GOP replaced as many Federal workers as the law allowed with people from their own party. Congress helped Union veterans by passing the Dependent Pension Act, which was largely the same bill that Cleveland had vetoed. The McKinley Tariff of 1890 raised duties on imported goods.

War of the Roses

Brothers Alf and Bob Taylor came from a politically active family. They ran against each other for governor of Tennessee in 1886. Bob ran as a Democrat and Alf as a Republican. The brothers made forty-one joint appearances across the state, as seen in the illustration at right. They played their fiddles and gave good-natured speeches.

The campaign came to be called the War of the Roses after a fifteenth century struggle for the English throne by two related families. The symbol for the York family was a white rose and the symbol for the Lancaster family was a red rose. During the campaign, Bob and the Democrats wore white roses while Alf and the Republicans wore red ones.

Democrat Bob won the election and was re-elected to two more two-year terms. He was chosen as a U.S. Senator from Tennessee in 1906. Alf was elected to a single two-year term as governor in 1920. Both brothers won and lost several other election campaigns, though they never again ran against each other. They toured the country together in the 1890s. They played their fiddles, told stories, and made positive speeches which they titled "Yankee Doodle" and "Dixie." They tried to bring healing to the entire country the way that their gubernatorial campaign had brought healing to Tennessee. Bob and Alf Taylor showed that brothers can differ politically and still be brothers.

The Sherman Antitrust Act

The consensus of political leaders in both parties was that something had to be done to control the growing power of business monopolies and trusts. Sponsored by Ohio Senator John Sherman, the antitrust act that passed in 1890 forbade business combinations or conspiracies that limited trade or that created monopolies in interstate commerce. The measure eventually had an effect on business practices, but the law was poorly enforced in the first decade of its existence.

Another growing controversy involved Federal monetary policy, particularly as it affected Midwestern farmers. One side supported the existing policy of hard money based on the gold standard. The other side advocated increased minting of silver coins and the printing of Treasury notes that could be redeemed in either gold or silver. The Republican Congress enacted the Sherman Silver Purchase Act of 1890, which increased the amount of silver purchased by the Federal government. However, the law did not have the impact that silver advocates desired. The country was heading toward another economic panic, and the currency issue would become even more urgent in 1893.

1890 Mid-Term Elections

The activism of the Republican-led government became the key issue in the mid-term congressional elections of 1890. Voters repudiated the higher tariff, political partisanship in Washington, and the apparent lack of concern for the average citizen demonstrated by the Republicans. Democrats gained an almost 3-to-1 majority in the House and cut the Republican majority in the Senate from 14 to six. Even prominent Senator William McKinley of Ohio went down to defeat in the Democratic landslide. Nine Congressmen affiliated with neither major party were elected from farm states and served notice that the national government was going to have to address the growing crisis in farming.

New Game, New Rules

The changes back and forth between Democratic and Republican Congresses and administrations were an indication of a major upheaval taking place in American life and the inconsistent attempts by both parties to address it. The United States was changing from an agricultural society that had some industry to a society driven by industry with agriculture as a major component. The old economy of subsistence, where most families produced almost everything they needed (but little that was extra), was giving way to an economy of exchange, where people earned money from their jobs and used the money to buy most of the things they needed. Manufacturing plays an important role in an economy of exchange. The old ways of country life were passing, and the new ways of city life were becoming the norm. New industries were being created, and with them came new jobs and new demands on the public and on the government.

With improved modes of transportation, the U.S. was developing a truly national market for manufactured goods and farm products. Huge corporations were changing the face of American business. Technology was affecting the way people lived and worked. Employees were able to produce more, but at the same time the increasing use of machinery threatened the jobs of many workers. With so much attention focused on new industries, people in the farming sector felt pushed aside. Leaders of industry were becoming enormously wealthy; the middle class of wage earners was growing larger; but many immigrants, some farmers, and most blacks were living in poverty.

But God said to him, "You fool! This very night your soul is required of you; and now who will own what you have prepared?" So is the man who stores up treasure for himself, and is not rich toward God.
Luke 12:20-21

★ Assignments for Lesson 77 ★

Literature Continue reading *In His Steps.*

Bible Read Psalm 8.

Work on memorizing Genesis 1:24-26.

Project Work on your project.

Student Review Optional: Answer the questions for Lesson 77.

Workers at the Bureau of Engraving & Printing Drying Printed Currency (c. 1890)

Lesson 78

Money Matters

Each society determines what has value for its people and how that value is expressed. In the past, a carpenter might have set the price for a table as two sheep. A winter coat might have cost a bushel of corn. A sack of seed might have cost one pig.

For thousands of years, people have given special value to gold and silver. People have owned and exchanged these precious metals in the form of nuggets, bars, coins, and jewelry. Societies have often viewed owning a large amount of gold as an indication of being wealthy.

Owning a large amount of land has also long been considered a sign of wealth. This was true when European settlers started coming to America. More people were able to own more land in America than they could own in England and Europe.

The Development of Currency

Trade increased the use of currency. It was easier to pay money for a transatlantic shipment, for instance, than to make payment with a herd of sheep. Gold and silver coins were more convenient than commodities for use in trade, and coins gave a person more flexibility in what he might purchase.

The American colonies and the early states each printed their own paper money, backed by state banks. State regulations varied, so the worth and reliability of the banks and their notes varied as well. Coins were reliable, but paper notes were easier to use. However, notes from an unreliable bank were not worth much. The individual state currency systems made national trade difficult, since a merchant in Boston might not trust paper money from a Charleston, South Carolina, bank he did not know. Continental paper dollars authorized by the Continental Congress were not worth much because they did not have sufficient gold reserves backing them.

As a national economy developed, it needed a reliable national system of money and exchange. More and more people were wage earners who acquired the items they wanted and needed with the money they earned on the job instead of making the items themselves or bartering other goods for them. After earlier attempts at a national bank, the creation of an independent Treasury, and periods of dependence on state banks, Congress passed the National Bank Act in 1863.

This law authorized the chartering of Federal banks. Banks used money that individuals invested in these banks to buy United States bonds. The banks could then issue currency notes that had a total value of up to 90 percent of their bond holdings. This arrangement enabled the Federal government to have the money it needed to conduct the Civil War. It also created a more stable national currency system.

Hard Money Versus Soft Money

The system was more stable, but not very flexible. Experience had shown that a system based strictly on hard money did not allow enough money in the economy to encourage business and facilitate growth. If a few people hoarded gold, money became scarce and conducting business became more difficult. Whenever gold was discovered, more money became available; but depending on gold strikes to grow the economy was an unpredictable system. Besides, people did not want all of their money to be in the form of gold or silver all the time.

By government decree, worth was given to paper money that could be exchanged for gold or silver upon demand. During the Civil War, Congress authorized paper money called greenbacks that could be redeemed for gold. However, the successes and defeats of the Union Army affected the people's confidence in the greenbacks and thus made the value of the paper money fluctuate widely. People feared that they might not be able to redeem their greenbacks for gold whenever they wanted to.

The paper money system encouraged more business activity. People went into debt for their business or their farm, believing that they could pay off the debt with the income they earned. Moreover, businesses thought they could charge higher prices when more money was available. However, the system had the downside of making money less valuable through inflation.

Inflation is a decrease in the value of money. As a result of inflation, prices rise and people have to spend more to purchase items they once could purchase for lower prices. The temptation facing the government was to print more money to keep up with inflation, but this caused the inflationary spiral to go even higher.

Many people still held to a hard money philosophy. After the Civil War, the Treasury started withdrawing greenbacks from circulation by buying them with gold coins. This restricted the money supply, leaving fewer dollars in circulation and making them more valuable. Farmers and debtors opposed this policy because it made money harder to come by while they still had debts to pay. Prices went down as the dollar became more valuable. However, debtors still owed the same number of dollars, and having fewer dollars in circulation made their debt harder to pay off. In 1868, in an attempt to maintain a sufficient supply of money in the economy, the government stopped buying greenbacks.

The Silver Issue

The government had minted silver coins since 1837, but in 1873 Congress ended the minting of silver coins in order to go entirely to a gold standard.

Workers at the Bureau of Engraving & Printing Trimming and Stacking Currency Sheets (c. 1890)

Silver had been minted at a ratio of sixteen to one: sixteen ounces of silver equalled one ounce of gold.

However, for many years silver was scarce. Owners of silver could earn more from their silver by selling it to individuals than by selling it to the government. This is why the government had not been minting much silver money. However, new discoveries of silver in the western United States led those who wanted to see a greater flow of currency to call for a return to the minting of silver coins. They called the cessation of minting silver coins the Crime of '73, even though little silver had been minted for several years before that.

In 1877 Congress passed the Bland-Allison Act, which called for between $2 million and $4 million in silver coins to be minted each month at the ratio of sixteen silver dollars to one gold dollar. President Hayes vetoed the bill, but Congress overrode the veto in 1878 and the bill became law. The measure was seen as a victory for advocates of cheaper, more freely-available money. However, the Treasury only purchased the minimum required by the law, so the new law did not do much to increase the money supply.

After the Panic of 1873, the government had reissued some greenbacks to help stimulate the economy. The Grant Administration proposed that the Federal government resume buying greenbacks with gold beginning on January 1, 1879. Delaying the purchases until then gave the Treasury time to stockpile enough gold to make the purchases.

Rutherford B. Hayes became President in 1877. His Administration stockpiled a considerable amount of gold to purchase the greenbacks as the Grant Administration had proposed. Since people knew their greenbacks would be redeemed at full value, and since the paper money was more convenient, no run on the gold reserve occurred in 1879 and the economy remained relatively stable.

Monetary policy remained largely unchanged throughout the 1880s. The country continued on the gold standard while a relatively small amount of silver was minted each month. The nation finally rebounded from the six-year depression that followed the Panic of 1873. Six new western states joined the Union in 1889 and 1890. The Senators and Congressmen from these states promoted the cause of farmers and silver miners. At the same time,

George T. Morgan worked for the United States Mint and designed the silver coin commonly known as the Morgan Dollar. It was minted from 1878 to 1904 and again in 1921.

Republican leaders in Congress were pushing for higher tariffs. They agreed to support an increase in the minting of silver coins in exchange for western support of higher tariffs.

In 1890 Congress enacted the Sherman Silver Purchase Act. The law required the Treasury to purchase $4.5 million in silver each month and to buy it with paper money that could be redeemed in either gold or silver. The Treasury purchased just about all of the silver mined in the United States. As a result the government more than doubled the production of silver and silver-backed currency. This was an even greater victory for the supporters of cheap money, but many of them wanted the free and unlimited coining of silver at the 16-to-1 ratio, without a monthly or yearly cap.

Charles Broughton drew this image of the scene in the New York Stock Exchange on May 5, 1893, from sketches made on the spot.

The Panic of 1893

Since paper money could be redeemed for either gold or silver, the country was on a two-metal money standard. This was called bimetallism. However, problems developed with the system. So much silver was available that by 1893 the silver in a silver dollar was actually worth only sixty cents. More and more people began redeeming their paper money for gold, and foreign investors began redeeming their investments in gold as well. This led to a serious drain on U.S. gold reserves.

In March of 1893, the Treasury only had about $100 million in gold reserves. Fears arose that the government could not continue to redeem paper money in gold. That summer, the value of silver in a silver dollar fell to forty-nine cents. Runaway inflation threatened the nation, as businesses were having to raise their prices to get enough money to pay the higher prices they were facing. This led to the Panic of 1893.

President Cleveland called for the repeal of the Sherman Silver Purchase Act. Even though the move infuriated farming and mining interests, Congress repealed the measure in the fall of 1893. However, the government's gold reserves continued to diminish as people kept redeeming paper money for gold.

In 1895 the Cleveland Administration made an agreement with a group of bankers led by J. P. Morgan. The bankers said that they would buy U.S. bonds with gold, thus in effect loaning gold to the government. In addition, the group of bankers said that they would not redeem any notes for gold and that they would try to stop gold from going out of the country (such as by ceasing to make payments to foreign banks or companies in gold). This restored the confidence of the public, and the run on gold ended. However, the agreement further angered the silver interests and the cheap money advocates. The bankers had received a generous commission for their work, which to Cleveland's critics sounded like a corrupt deal with Wall Street; but it was actually just another illustration of the process of worth and exchange. The bankers had something that the government needed, and the government had to pay for what it got.

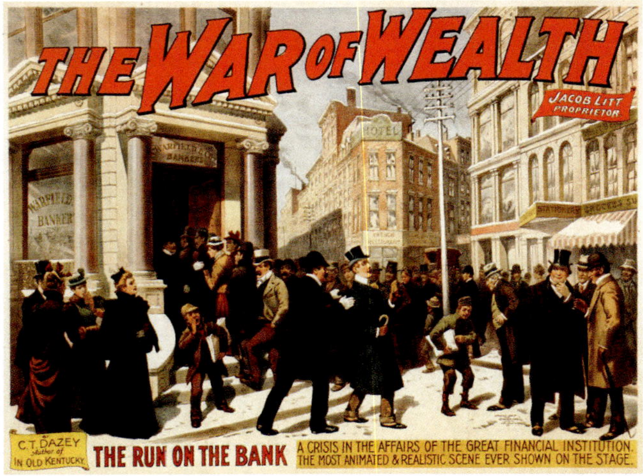

The monetary policy of the government was a central element in the rising tide of discontent many Americans felt. It fueled the Populist movement that swept through American politics in the 1890s.

Charles T. Dazey's play The War of Wealth, *inspired by the Panic of 1893, opened in 1895. This promotional poster claims that it featured "the most animated & realistic scene ever shown on the stage."*

Like apples of gold in settings of silver
is a word spoken in right circumstances.
Proverbs 25:11

★ Assignments for Lesson 78 ★

Literature Continue reading *In His Steps.*

Bible Read Psalm 139:13-14.

Work on memorizing Genesis 1:24-26.

Project Work on your project.

Student Review Optional: Answer the questions for Lesson 78.

People's Party Convention in Nebraska (1890)

Lesson 79

The Populist Revolt

Who is for the farmer? That was the question increasingly voiced by the rural population of America as the nineteenth century was coming to a close. Farmers felt left out of the changes taking place in the country. They felt ignored by the major political parties, and they were having an increasingly hard time making it financially in the changing economy.

Factors in the Crisis

Political Party Makeup. After the Civil War, the two major national parties developed into coalitions of groups that shared enough of the same goals to work together for political power. Many people perceived the Republican Party as the party of big business. Wealthy industrialists gave money to the party's candidates. Party members in Congress generally supported the interests of business by, for instance, voting for high tariffs to protect American business from foreign competition. The party was also popular with Midwestern farmers, blacks, and Union war veterans. The support of these groups came as a result of the days when the Republican Party was seen as working for the preservation of the Union.

The Democratic Party, meanwhile, was a coalition of southern whites, many big city political machines, factory workers, immigrants, small farmers, and businessmen who opposed a high tariff. Obviously, plenty of wealthy people were Democrats, too. Republicans did not have a monopoly on big contributors. Both parties stood for certain principles, but they were also interested in power and the benefits that come from being in power.

Domination of Industry. The late nineteenth century witnessed the growth of American industry. The money that talked loudest in those days came from industrialists. The government was concerned with making business conditions better for the growing industrial segment of the economy. High tariffs helped manufacturers. Railroads got sweet deals from the government to build lines. The Interstate Commerce Act and the Sherman Antitrust Act were only enacted after businesses began growing and exerting economic and political influence. Companies suspected of violating these laws were not actively prosecuted for several years after the laws were put on the books.

The Farmers' Plight. The group that felt most left out of the picture were Midwestern and southern farmers. The government only seemed to care about business, and business only seemed to care about profits. The average farmer did not receive much attention. Laborers were in a similar dependent

An idyllic view of "The Great West" by Gaylord Watson, published in New York around 1881.

position. They formed unions to strengthen their hand against management. Farmers, on the other hand, had a whole array of opponents to fight: bankers, millers, railroad companies, and middlemen, not to mention the vagaries of the weather and insect invasions. Small farmers were concerned about rising land prices and lower crop prices; sharecroppers and tenant farmers wondered whether they could ever own land at all.

Organizing farmers for greater economic and political power was not as easy as organizing factory workers. Farmers were traditionally independent. Most farmers in the Midwest lived several miles apart from each other, while thousands of factory workers lived in the same city.

At the heart of the farmers' complaint was falling crop prices. Between 1870 and 1897, the price of a bushel of wheat fell from $1.06 to 63 cents; corn from 43.1 cents to 29.7 cents per bushel, and cotton from 15.1 cents per pound to 5.8 cents. Moreover, even at these rates, the farmers only got a portion of the price they were paid since transportation expenses had to be taken out of what they received. Kansas farmers could only get 10 cents for a bushel of corn in 1889, so many of them simply used their corn for fuel. Coupled with falling prices was the pressure of debt that the farmer carried on his land and equipment. With money hard to come by, many farmers wanted to see more money in circulation. The back-and-forth monetary policy of the Federal government, culminating in the repeal of the Sherman Silver Purchase Act in 1893, left farmers frustrated and fearful.

The reasons for the farmers' distress were complicated. When farmers did a good job and produced more crops, the increased supply drove down the price they received. Thus, when farmers were successful at what they did, they got less for it. Railroads charged high fees for transporting farm products because the rail companies had no competition. Farmers had little influence on the prices they had to pay for equipment and other necessities. High tariffs raised the prices of the goods that farmers wanted and needed to buy. The tariffs also discouraged foreign buyers from purchasing American farm products, since America was not importing many goods from other countries. The farm production of other countries increased during this time, which also cut into the world market for American farmers.

Searching for Solutions

The Grange. In 1867 former Minnesota farmer Oliver Kelly organized the National Grange of the Order of the Patrons of Husbandry, commonly called the Grange. When Kelly toured the South in 1866, he was struck by the plight and isolation of farmers. The Grange began as a way for farmers to enjoy time together and to benefit from agricultural education. The effort then moved on to organizing farmers into buying cooperatives. It eventually exerted influence in state politics, especially in pressuring legislatures to regulate the prices charged by railroads and grain elevators. The regulation of warehouses by state governments was upheld by the 1877 *Munn v. Illinois* U.S. Supreme Court decision. At its highest point in 1874, the Grange claimed 1.5 million members. By 1880, however, the twenty thousand local chapters had dwindled to four thousand. The novelty of it wore off, and the Grange did not prove to be the cure-all for the farmers' woes.

The Greenback Party. The Greenback Party was formed in the mid-1870s to advocate more paper money, lower interest rates, and lower taxes. It was begun by eastern laborers, but farmers took over the organization after they began feeling the effects of the Panic of 1873. Fifteen Greenback Congressmen were elected in 1878, but after that high point the party died out by 1888.

Farm Alliances. The next effort by farmers was the formation of regional alliances. The largest and most influential of these were the Northwestern Alliance in the Midwest and the Southern Alliance in the South. The Southern Alliance had three million members in 1890, and another one million blacks were part of the parallel Colored Alliance. Membership in the alliance was available to all farming men and women sixteen or older who were industrious, were of good moral character, and believed in God.

This 1875 image takes inspiration from the motto of the Grange, "I pay for all."

Women were heavily involved in the membership and leadership of the alliances. The groups formed buying cooperatives and attempted to exert political influence. The two largest alliances pursued many of the same goals, but an attempt to merge them in 1889 failed. Southerners wanted to keep blacks out of the white organization and also wanted to maintain a degree of autonomy.

Social functions were nice, and cooperative buying efforts were noble (although largely unsuccessful); but farmers still saw no significant change in national policy toward farmers, which meant no change in their basic condition. To top it off, a ten-year drought began on the Great Plains in 1886, ruining crops and sending many farmers back east to try another line of work.

The Populist Party

Western farmers organized themselves into political parties in several Midwestern states. They called themselves the People's Party or the Populist Party (*populus* is the Latin word for the people).

Congressman Jerry Simpson

The groups controlled a few state legislatures and elected a governor, a few U.S. Senators, and several Congressmen. Among the leaders in Kansas were Mary Elizabeth Lease, one of the first female attorneys in the state and a dynamic speaker, and "Sockless" Jerry Simpson. During Simpson's 1890 campaign for Congress, his Republican opponent was a wealthy railroad executive. Simpson described him as an aristocrat with "silk hosiery." In trying to put Simpson down, the Republican said that it was better to wear silk socks then none at all (which, he implied, was what Simpson did). Simpson picked up on this, quit wearing socks for the rest of the campaign, took the nickname "Sockless Jerry," and won the election.

Southern farm advocates generally worked within the Democratic Party and won several elections. Among the agrarian leaders in the South were Tom Watson of Georgia and "Pitchfork Ben" Tillman of South Carolina. Tillman was the uncouth boss of South Carolina politics. He promised, if elected to the U.S. Senate, to jab his pitchfork into President Cleveland's ribs. Tillman became a Senator in 1895 and remained in the Senate until his death in 1918, but he did not jab any Presidents with a pitchfork.

After state Populists enjoyed several victories in the 1890 congressional elections and received pledges of support from some Democrats and Republicans in Congress, agrarian leaders met in Cincinnati in 1891 and formed the national Populist Party. They held their 1892 national convention in Omaha.

The party's platform called for the free and unlimited coinage of silver at the ratio of sixteen to one; restrictions on immigration; government ownership of railroads, telephone, and telegraph systems; the direct election of U.S. Senators (instead of their being chosen by state legislatures) and other electoral reforms; and a graduated income tax (one that required those with higher incomes to pay a higher percentage in taxes, which was seen as a way to milk the rich and redistribute wealth). The party also called for shorter working hours for industrial

What Else Was Happening?

1877 Thomas Edison invents the phonograph, which plays sounds recorded on cylinders wrapped in foil.

1879 Frank W. Woolworth opens his first Five Cent Store in Utica, New York. It fails, but another in Lancaster, Pennsylvania, succeeds. Almost 600 F. W. Woolworth Five-and-Ten stores open by 1912.

1879 A saloon manager invents the cash register to guard against employee theft.

1879 Thomas Edison successfully uses a carbon filament of scorched cotton thread in his electric light bulb.

1879 Frank and Jesse James rob a train in Glendale, Missouri.

1880 The frankfurter is invented in St. Louis. At first it has no bun, but the creator starts using buns when customers don't return the gloves he gives them to use. The photo at right shows a frankfurter stand in New York around 1906. The price is three cents each or two for five cents.

1881 Russian Tsar Alexander II is assassinated by members of a radical group. Tsar Alexander III uses a new secret police force to rule more oppressively. Since one of the radicals was a Jew, violence breaks out against Jews in 200 Russian cities. These attacks are called pogroms.

1881 Louis Pasteur develops a weak strain of anthrax bacteria to use in vaccine.

1881 Sheriff Pat Garrett kills Billy the Kid (William Bonney) in Fort Sumner, New Mexico.

1883 The Brooklyn Bridge is completed. It is the world's longest suspension bridge at the time and the first to use steel cables.

1883 Buffalo Bill Cody's Wild West Show debuts in North Platte, Nebraska.

1884 Ottmar Mergenthaler invents a machine that sets a full line of type for printing. Previously, each letter had to be put in place by hand. Because of what it produces, the machine is called a linotype.

1885 Gottlieb Daimler and Karl Benz, independent of each other, build the first practical automobiles.

1886 The Statue of Liberty is dedicated in New York harbor as a gift from France.

1886 James Pemberton, a pharmacist in Atlanta, sells to Asa Candler an interest in his medicinal drink called Coca-Cola (which started out with cocaine but now does not include the drug).

1887 Sir Arthur Conan Doyle writes the first Sherlock Holmes story.

1888 George Eastman introduces the first pushbutton camera. He develops celluloid film the next year.

1889 The Eiffel Tower, built by Alexandre Eiffel, is completed in Paris. Standing at 984 feet, it becomes the tallest structure in the world.

1890 The World Building opens in New York with sixteen stories. It is called a skyscraper.

1890 Navy wins the first Army-Navy football game 24-0.

1891 Carnegie Hall opens in New York City.

1892 Ellis Island opens as a facility to process immigrants from Europe.

Frank Steunenberg was elected to the Idaho state legislature in 1890 supported by both the Democratic and Populist Parties. He was elected governor in 1896. Steunenberg was favorable toward labor unions, but he declared martial law when a mine strike became violent. After Steunenberg left office, he was killed by a man who worked for a labor union. The monument at left honoring Steunenberg was dedicated in front of the Idaho State Capitol in Boise in 1927.

laborers. The convention nominated for President James B. Weaver, a former Union general who had been the Greenback candidate in 1880. The party's vice presidential nominee was James G. Field, a former Confederate general.

The Republicans in 1892 renominated incumbent Benjamin Harrison, while the Democrats gave the nod to former President Grover Cleveland. Cleveland gained only 46 percent of the popular vote, but he had a clear majority of the electoral vote. Weaver received just over one million votes (8.5% of the turnout) and 22 electoral votes. Populists were elected to ten House seats, five Senate positions, three governorships, and 1,500 seats in state legislatures. The Populist Party fared poorly in the South, where white voters feared that splitting the Democratic vote would return Republicans to power. The agrarian cause was not completely lost in the South, however, since many southern Democrats held populist positions.

No third party had ever done so well just one year after its formation. The success of the Populists sent a message to the Democrats and Republicans that many voters were not satisfied with the status quo. The Populist surge helped to define politics in the 1890s.

Know well the condition of your flocks, and pay attention to your herds; for riches are not forever, nor does a crown endure to all generations.
Proverbs 27:23-24

★ Assignments for Lesson 79 ★

American Voices — Read the Populist Party Platform of 1892 (pages 254-257).

Literature — Continue reading *In His Steps.*

Bible — Read Romans 1:16-25.

Work on memorizing Genesis 1:24-26.

Project — Work on your project.

Student Review — Optional: Answer the questions for Lesson 79.

Cumberland River, Tennessee

Lesson 80 - Bible Study

Evolution and the Bible

The theory of evolution as propounded by the Englishman Charles Darwin has had a profound impact on the way people see themselves and their world and what they think about God. Darwin's ideas swept across American society in the late nineteenth century.

Darwin's Theory

Charles Darwin published *The Origin of Species* in 1859. His book was an attempt to give a scientific explanation for why varieties or differences exist in the species of living things. Darwin proposed that these variations were hereditary. All living things are in a struggle for existence, he said, and only the strongest or fittest variations survive. This process, which Darwin called natural selection, means that some species disappear while others adapt and survive. It seemed to Darwin that life had evolved from simple to complex forms over a long period of time and that humans were the pinnacle of the process. Darwin had no hard evidence to support his hypothesis. It was simply a guess he made based on his observations of living things. In *The Descent of Man* (1871), Darwin extended his hypothesis to claim that man adapted morally to his environment as well as physically.

In its broadest terms, "evolution means a process whereby life arose from non-living matter and subsequently developed by natural means" (Michael Behe, *Darwin's Black Box*, New York: The Free Press, 1996, pp. x, xi). This is sometimes called macro-evolution, or change involving all living things across species. Change within a species is referred to as micro-evolution. Darwin was not the first person to propose the theory of evolution, but his presentation of it captured the minds of the public as no one else's had. However, Darwin did not provide the last word on the subject. The generally accepted theory of evolution has gone through several changes since he published his book.

The Influence of Evolution

Almost all scientific and popular thinking has been affected by the theory of evolution. It is commonly accepted as an assured fact in the scientific world and by the general public. To quote Scott Huse:

> The theory of evolution has dominated our society for about a century, especially in our educational institutions. The media has been most influential in promoting the "fact" of organic evolution with some

Light Over the Atlantic Ocean, New Smyrna Beach, Florida

> television programs and magazine editorial sections loyally devoted to the evolutionary viewpoint. Usually this indoctrination is obvious and insistent; but even when it is more subtle, it is nevertheless unmistakably effective. (*The Collapse of Evolution*, Grand Rapids: Baker, 1993, p. 11)

Although the evidence that would prove evolution with finality does not exist and much that disproves it does exist, the idea has carried the day in scientific study and in society. To question the reality of evolution is seen in most academic and popular circles as equivalent to questioning gravity.

Evolution has influenced other fields of study besides the physical sciences. In the 1880s, William Graham Sumner applied Darwin's ideas to sociology and called it Social Darwinism. Sumner held that "survival of the fittest" applied not only in the physical realm but also in society. Sumner said that this is why some people are successful and others fail.

In addition, evolution has influenced many believers in their understanding of how God created the world. Some believers have adapted Darwin's ideas and have proposed God as the first cause in the evolutionary process. This hypothesis is sometimes called theistic evolution. These people do not question many of Darwin's claims; instead, they accept them as true and adapt their understanding of God and the teachings of the Bible to them.

Evolution has even influenced how some people think the Bible was written. The documentary hypothesis of the Pentateuch, which is popular among liberal theologians, holds that the first five books of the Bible evolved in the hands of generations of editors who used source documents (called J, E, P, and D) as they were handed down and edited through the generations. In addition, the four New Testament gospels, many scholars believe, are the result of the evolution of an early document of sayings of Jesus (a document which is called "Q" for the German word *quelle* or source, but which has never been found) combined with other sources that were available to the writers/editors of the gospels. Even religion itself has been seen as having evolved from primitive forms to more developed forms, with Christianity being merely one form of religion and certainly not the authoritative one.

Implications of Darwin's Theory

The debate over evolution does not just involve differing ideas on how physical processes take place in our world. Accepting evolution has serious consequences. For instance, the theory of evolution leaves no place for God. As an entirely material process, evolution recognizes no absolutes and no eternal destiny for human life. The question of where the universe came from is largely left unanswered, although the assumption many evolutionists make

Ocean and Sky, Huntington Beach, California

Dry Land and Plants, Madeline Island, Wisconsin

is that it could not have been God. According to most evolutionists, the only processes involved in the world are material. Scientists might speculate about the origins of the universe, but they do not really deal with the question of how physical things came into existence in the first place.

I was once in England doing some evangelistic canvassing. The young woman who came to the door at one house told me, when she learned why I was there, that she didn't believe at all in God. I said that I wondered where the world came from if God did not exist. She replied, "Well, it's all evolution, isn't it?"

Evolution reduces the value of man. Rather than being a special creation of God as taught in the Bible, according to the theory of evolution man is merely the most fully-developed species currently on earth. The idea of a soul or an eternal realm of life has no place in evolution. Man has value in an evolution-based world only as he contributes to the physical well-being of the world. Any spiritual longings or thoughts that people might have are just superstitions that mankind has developed.

Evolution brings into question the very nature of the world. Isaac Newton believed that God created the world to be guided by fixed, unchanging laws that produce dependable results. Darwin, on the other hand, believed that natural law produces variation and change. The issue is whether the world is dependable and knowable or undependable and unknowable.

Many of our current social and moral problems are a result of the humanistic philosophy which evolutionary thinking encourages. The so-called new morality we are presently witnessing is actually no morality. It is the inevitable result of atheistic, evolutionary philosophy that denies any eternal truth.

Challenges to Evolution

Darwin proposed evolution as the explanation for the variety of living things (thus his book attempted to explain "the origin of species"). Since Darwin, most scientific research has been undertaken and interpreted with the assumption that evolution is true. The problem with this approach is that when you go looking for something, you are likely to find it whether the evidence bears it out or not. Here are some problems with the theory of evolution.

First, the clear evidence to support macro-evolution does not exist. Modern evolutionary theory is based largely on logical assumptions about how different fossils might be related to each other and how organisms might develop new attributes. Many scientists want to believe in evolution, despite its recognized flaws, because they do not have another theory available—besides Creation.

Second, changes that occur from one generation to the next, called mutations, are usually harmful to an organism, not beneficial changes that help a variation survive.

Third, the well-known and widely accepted geologic column outlining the Paleozoic and Mesozoic eras and the Jurassic, Triassic, and Mississippian periods, and so forth, is a theoretical construct. It has not been found to exist anywhere on the earth. Bits of evidence have been discovered in different parts of the world; and, using the assumption of evolution, it has been put together to create the theoretical column.

Fourth, the theory of evolution changes to fit the latest thinking or to try to deal with valid challenges. When scientists realized that the kind of variations required to go from amoeba to humans required more time than any interpretation of evolution allowed, advocates of evolution changed their argument to say that variations occurred not gradually but by huge, quick leaps of change. More recent theories have suggested the possibility of "intelligent matter" or a "life force" in organic material as a way to try to get around the problem of how the universe began and how change could have taken place without God.

Fifth, the laws of thermodynamics do not support the idea of evolution. If matter has existed forever (that is, if the Creation had no beginning point) and the laws of thermodynamics applied to matter in the past as they do now, matter should have wound down and ceased to exist long ago.

Sixth, a qualitative difference exists between man and the rest of Creation that cannot be bridged by evolution. As G. K. Chesterton noted, someone might have: "dug very deep and found the place where a man had drawn the picture of a reindeer. But he would dig a good deal deeper before he found a place where a reindeer had drawn a picture of a man" (G. K. Chesterton, *The Everlasting Man*, originally published 1925; this edition San Francisco: Ignatius, 1993, p. 33). He continues:

> Monkeys did not begin pictures and men finish them; Pithecanthropus did not draw a reindeer badly and Homo Sapiens draw it well. The higher animals did not draw better and better portraits; the dog did not paint better in his best period than in his early bad manner as a jackal; the wild horse was not an impressionist and the race-horse a Post-Impressionist. . . . We cannot even talk about (all this) without treating man as something separate from nature (pp. 34-35).

Moon Jellyfish, Kill Devil Hills, North Carolina

Running From God?

Darwin cannot bear all the blame for the way that evolution has become accepted theory. Some blame must be reserved for those who have accepted his theory, developed it, and promoted it. Perhaps one reason that the theory of evolution became so popular is that people considered it a convenient excuse not to have to deal with God any longer. In the theory, God is not the Maker and Judge to whom

Bald Eagle Fishing, Homer, Alaska

we owe allegiance and obedience; He simply either does not exist or He does not matter. What really matters, in evolutionary thinking, is survival of the fittest in physical terms. Many people would rather be their own lord than have to answer to Another. Religious faith is thus relegated to the realm of opinion. If someone wants to believe in God, a modern thinker might say, "That is his option, but enlightened people deal only with facts." Actually, evolution is the idea that is not based on fact. The truth is that everyone will have to deal with God one day (Hebrews 9:27).

Squirrel, Dixon, Illinois

In the beginning God created the heavens and the earth.
Genesis 1:1

⋆ Assignments for Lesson 80 ⋆

American Voices Read "When I Heard the Learn'd Astronomer" by Walt Whitman (page 187).

Literature Continue reading *In His Steps.*

Bible Recite or write Genesis 1:24-26 from memory.

Project Complete your project for the unit.

Student Review Optional: Answer the questions for Lesson 80 and take the quiz for Unit 16.

Milling District, Minneapolis, Minnesota (c. 1907)

17 The Business of America

The major challenge that America faced as it approached the end of the nineteenth century was managing growth and change in a way that helped as many Americans as possible. Business enterprises became larger and larger. Meanwhile, many workers struggled to make ends meet with the relatively low wages they received. Changes came to the South, the West, and to the major cities. Social Darwinism was an attempt to explain (and perhaps to justify) the emerging social order, while the social gospel was a belief system that encouraged helping those negatively affected by social change.

Memory Work

Memorize 1 Peter 2:19-21 by the end of this unit.

Books Used

The Bible
American Voices
In His Steps

Project (choose one)

1) Write 300 to 500 words on one of the following topics:

- Write an essay on the significance of the city in American life. Include your thoughts on at least three issues related to cities, which could include: how the city has changed the American economy, how the city has played a role in including immigrants in American life, how the city has been a laboratory for testing new technology and inventions, and how urban life challenges family life and traditional morality. See Lesson 84.

- What is your opinion on entertainment? How is it helpful and how is it a distraction? What forms of entertainment are inappropriate for Christians? Why is immorality passed off as art? What will you want your children to watch and participate in?

2) Memorize Matthew 25:31-46. If you choose this project, you should recite or write the verses from memory at the end of the week.

3) Make a portfolio profiling large and small businesses that operate in your area. Profile at least three large, nationwide businesses (restaurant chains, mobile phone companies, discount stores, etc.) and three small, local businesses (with less than twenty-five employees). If possible, talk to someone who works with each business. Include photos, print advertising, and a summary of the history and product or service offered by each business in your portfolio. Your portfolio should contain at least two pages for each business.

Staff of the Western Union Office in Key West, Florida (c. 1898)

Lesson 81

The Growth of Big Business

In the late 1800s, the United States recovered economically from the Civil War and in many ways developed a new national identity. One of the major changes in the U.S. during this time was the rapid increase in manufacturing and the growing predominance of business in the American economy. This can be demonstrated with a few statistics.

During the last three decades of the 1800s, the American population doubled and farm production also doubled; but the value of its industrial output increased sixfold. In 1890 the value of domestic manufacturing output surpassed the value of farm output for the first time. By 1900, only ten years later, the value of industrial production was twice that of agriculture. This growth of business not only affected the American economy; it impacted the social fabric of the nation.

Reasons for the Growth

Three major changes in technology and resources enabled this growth, which has been called the Second Industrial Revolution (the first was centered in Great Britain in the late 1700s). First, the development of a national rail transportation system and a national communication system utilizing the telegraph and telephone created a national market for manufactured goods. Advances in steamships and the transoceanic telegraph cable helped to expand America's global market.

Second, the development of electrical power enabled industry to produce more. Although only two percent of American industry was powered by electricity in 1900, electricity was the power source of the future. In addition, public utilities and electric-powered streetcars allowed factories to locate anywhere that power could be sent through transmission lines. Electrical power also allowed workers to live anywhere they could catch the streetcar to work. This was one way in which the Second Industrial Revolution changed the fabric of American society, in that cities became larger and more spread out.

Third, the period saw a remarkable output of inventions, advances in technology, and the application of these advances to industry. Improvements in the refining of petroleum; advances in the production of steel; and inventions such as the typewriter, sewing machine, and electric light made it possible for businesses to do more things and to produce more products. We will talk more about some of the inventions that were developed during this period in a later lesson.

Charles Alderton of Waco, Texas, created the soft drink Dr. Pepper in the 1880s. It became a national brand in the early 1900s. This advertisement is from Comanche, Oklahoma.

Business Organization

The way that large American businesses were organized during the late 1800s enabled companies to utilize the advances being made in communication, transportation, energy, and technology. Business organization underwent a significant change during this period.

The simplest kind of business is an individual proprietorship, such as John Jones making wooden tables or Susie Smith selling pies. If the business gets big enough, John or Susie might employ workers to help; but the business still belongs to one person. Almost all American businesses before the Civil War were small proprietorships, and most business owners knew all of their workers personally.

The next step in complexity is a partnership, in which two or more individuals put their resources and talents together and share in the profit or loss of a business. A partnership makes more business activity possible; but the business is still dependent on a few people, all of whom share all of the liability of the business.

The third level of business organization is the corporation. Individuals apply to a state legislature for a charter to engage in a certain kind of business as a corporation. The corporation, which is run by a board of directors, can sell stock in the company to investors or stockholders, who put money into the business with the hope of sharing in its profit. In the eyes of the law, a corporation is considered to be a legal person, with an identity separate from its partners. As a legal person, the corporation is able to conduct business, make contracts, and sue in court. A corporation has access to much greater amounts of money than an individual usually does, and the corporation can continue even if one participant (whether a director or a stockholder) dies or leaves the business. In addition, no one person is legally responsible for the entire corporation. A stockholder can only lose what he has invested, and a director can keep his personal assets separate from the assets of the business. In the period after the Civil War, the corporation became a much more common form of business organization in the United States.

A further step that some corporations took in the late nineteenth century and early twentieth century was the formation of combinations of companies in a particular field. Such combinations could get lower prices on raw materials, spend less on advertising, and avoid competition that cut into profits. Business combinations took several forms. One combination that was practiced in the late 1800s was a pool, in which corporations made an informal agreement to divide a market among themselves or to charge a fixed price for goods or services. Because these agreements were made informally, they were not subject to prosecution in court until they were declared illegal in 1887.

Another combination was the trust. A trust was created when the stockholders of several corporations agreed to let their companies be run as one large company. The trust could gain a monopoly in an industry and charge higher prices without fear of competition. Trusts were established in several industries, including oil, steel, and sugar refining.

Still another form of business combination popular after 1890 was the holding company. A holding company is a financial investment company created for the purpose of controlling the stock of other companies that actually produce goods and services. Holding companies have to be chartered by a state and are liable for the illegal actions of their subsidiaries, but around the turn of the twentieth century convictions for wrongdoing by companies were hard to obtain.

Yet another combination was the interlocking directorate, in which some or all of the board of directors of one company were on the boards of other companies. This enabled companies to share inside information and make secret agreements. They risked prosecution for conspiracy to restrain trade, but evidence of secret agreements was hard to obtain and difficult to present effectively in court.

The Shape of American Business

Corporations and other business arrangements that concentrated power and wealth in the hands of a relatively few people came to dominate American business. Huge corporations were able to respond to the rapidly growing national market faster than small, family-owned businesses could. Big businesses were able to use mass production and distribution techniques and to capitalize on technological advances. The more investment capital a company had available, the more technology it could utilize. In addition, companies benefited from few government regulations on their activities, from a protective tariff that kept out foreign goods or made them expensive, and from politicians who were willing to be paid off to keep their noses out of questionable activities. Single companies sometimes organized all aspects of an industry, from obtaining raw materials to production to distribution, into one enterprise. Larger combinations, such as pools and trusts, came to dominate entire industries.

The majority of the American people, the American government, and the major American political parties were decidedly pro-business. The reigning philosophy held that government should take a hands-off approach to business. However, advocates of this so-called free market approach did not want government to take absolutely no action with regard to business. They actually wanted government to provide help for business, including tariff protection, tax breaks, and looking the other way when questionable practices occurred. Business leaders also wanted the government to pass laws that prohibited the formation and activity of labor unions. The hands-off approach that was widely encouraged was understood to mean active assistance from government but no restraining interference from government in what businesses did.

The first big business was railroading. Total investment in railroads increased from one billion dollars in 1860 to $10 billion in 1900. Railroad employment grew from 1.3 million in 1860 to 5.3 million in 1900. Many railroad companies were formed, but the relatively few that survived were the ones that were big enough to last through slow starts and hard times, that got the most government assistance, or that took over smaller lines and

Executives of Midvale Steel Company in Nicetown, Pennsylvania (c. 1887)

The Illinois Central Railroad, chartered in 1851, was one of the earliest and longest-surviving railroad companies in North America. It eventually connected Chicago and New Orleans with several additional lines on both sides of the Mississippi River. This print illustrates the company's operations around 1882. John Luther "Casey" Jones, who died in a 1900 train wreck made famous in song, was an engineer on the Illinois Central.

developed regional monopolies. The trend toward fewer railroad companies made for better, cheaper, and less complicated scheduling and traveling. However, the trend also made rail company owners extremely rich and it hindered competition. By 1900 two-thirds of the track in the country was controlled by only six business groups. Some heads of companies, such as Jay Gould, Diamond Jim Fisk, and Daniel Drew, were not above using bribes, deceit, intimidation, and any other means to accomplish their goals. Other businessmen watched what happened with the railroads and applied the lessons they learned to other fields.

Courts Support Business

A growing concern by many citizens and elected representatives over the power of big business led to the passage of regulatory laws. In 1890 Congress passed the Sherman Antitrust Act. The law forbade any contract, combination, or trust, including monopolies, that restrained trade (lessened free competition) in interstate or foreign commerce. The law, however, did not define such terms as monopoly, trust, or combination. Few prosecutions took place to break up trusts and monopolies; and when cases were taken to court, the decisions usually went in favor of the companies rather than the government.

Two decisions by the U.S. Supreme Court illustrate the situation. In 1895 the Supreme Court ruled in the case of *U.S. v. E. C. Knight Company* that, even though the sugar trust controlled 98% of the sugar refining business in the country, a monopoly itself did not necessarily restrain interstate trade. This gave industrialists the signal that they could proceed with forming trusts in various industries because restraint of trade would be hard to prove in court. The formation of trusts actually increased after the Sherman Antitrust Act was passed.

In the *Smyth v. Ames* decision of 1898, the Supreme Court interpreted the 14th Amendment in an unexpected way that also gave support to big business. The 14th Amendment guarantees persons due process of law. The original intent of the amendment was to protect individuals from having their property seized or from having other

Ohio Republican Senator John Sherman, for whom the Sherman Silver Purchase Act and the Sherman Antitrust Act were named, was the younger brother of Union General William T. Sherman. This photo shows Senator Sherman in his office in 1894.

rights violated. In this decision the Court said that corporations were persons and thus were guaranteed the right of due process. The decision struck down any law that prohibited a corporation from making what the Court termed a reasonable profit. This verdict made it almost impossible to enforce any law that attempted to regulate business.

Robber Barons or Captains of Industry?

The growth of big business was a mixed blessing. More products, and more kinds of products, became available to the American public. Some products and services became more affordable. Many people who had lived in poverty and many immigrants were able to find work. On the other hand, the lack of competition drove some prices higher and lowered the quality of some products.

The heads of companies became more and more wealthy while their employees toiled away at low wages and often in poor working conditions. Workers felt as though they were being used by the few who had money and power. Employees began organizing into labor unions to gain more power for working people against company owners. As we shall see, labor and management were involved in several fierce and sometimes bloody showdowns in the late 1800s.

The men who led the huge new corporations were skillful, ambitious, and sometimes ruthless entrepreneurs. They envisioned what was possible and were willing to go beyond where business had gone previously. These men came mostly from lower or middle class families, had little formal education, and were denominational Protestants. Their supporters praised them as captains of industry, while critics dubbed them robber barons for the tactics they used to acquire wealth and power. These men took different directions with their lives and left different legacies, but without a doubt they were the most prominent men of their day. We will look at a few of the better known business leaders of the era.

Cornelius Vanderbilt
Nathaniel Jocelyn (American, 1846)

Cornelius "Commodore" Vanderbilt (1794-1877)

Cornelius Vanderbilt was born on Staten Island in New York. He left school when he was 11 years old. At sixteen he borrowed money from his parents to buy a ferry boat that he piloted in New York harbor between Staten Island and New York City. In 1829 he formed a steamboat company and ran successful routes up and down the Hudson River. This is how he earned the nickname Commodore. Vanderbilt expanded his shipping business to ports in the Northeast, and he was a millionaire by 1846.

In the 1870s Vanderbilt expanded his empire to include railroads. He organized the New York Central Railroad by consolidating several smaller lines. The New York Central cut fares, improved service, and established the first regular routes between New York and Chicago. When Vanderbilt died in 1877, his estate was worth $100 million dollars. His gifts to Central University in Nashville, Tennessee, led to the school being renamed Vanderbilt University (and their sports teams are called the Commodores).

Commodore Vanderbilt's only son, William Henry Vanderbilt (1821-1885), was at first not thought to have as much business savvy as his father; but he managed to expand the family railroad empire such that, when he retired in 1883, he had almost doubled his father's fortune. William cared little about legal regulations or about the public his companies served. He died only eight years after his father's passing.

William Henry Vanderbilt had three sons. Cornelius (1843-1899), named for his grandfather, took over the family business and later endowed the Vanderbilt Clinic as part of the Columbia University Medical School in New York City. William Kissam Vanderbilt (1849-1920) was mostly interested in social and yachting activities. George Washington Vanderbilt (1862-1914) built the Biltmore estate near Asheville, North Carolina.

John D. Rockefeller (1839-1937)

John David Rockefeller grew up in Cleveland, Ohio. He became interested in the oil business as a result of wells that were drilled in western Pennsylvania in the late 1800s. In the early days, oil was used for lubrication or refined to produce kerosene, but Rockefeller's company was in a good position to make immense profits when the gasoline refined from oil later came to be used for America's growing number of automobiles. In 1870 Rockefeller formed the Standard Oil Company of Ohio. He bought out or forced out most of his competitors in Ohio, and by 1879 Standard Oil controlled over 90 percent of the oil refined in the country.

Standard Oil took over almost every aspect of oil production: drilling, refining, pipelines, making oil drums, and whatever else it could. Rockefeller made or forced special deals with railroads to get a good price for shipping his oil. The company was one of the first to combine its various enterprises into a trust. In 1892 the Ohio Supreme Court ordered Standard Oil to be broken up into various companies that would be independent of each other. As time went on, some of these companies were SOHIO (Standard Oil Company of Ohio), SOCONY (Standard Oil Company of New York), and ESSO (from the initials of Standard Oil). In the mid-1970s, Esso became the Exxon Corporation.

John D. Rockefeller Sr. and Jr. (c. 1915)

Rockefeller was a religious man and strict in his personal habits and schedule. Though his business practices drew sharp criticism from some observers, he seemed not to be overly concerned about any discrepancy between the Biblical principles he studied and espoused and his method of gaining wealth. He considered his wealth to be a gift from God. Rockefeller was a generous philanthropist who sought carefully to give money to worthy causes.

One of John D. Rockefeller's grandsons, Nelson Rockefeller, was Republican governor of New York and later Vice President under Gerald Ford. A great-grandson, John D. (Jay) Rockefeller IV, served as Democratic governor of West Virginia from 1977 to 1985 and then as U.S. Senator from that state.

Andrew Carnegie (1835-1919)

Andrew Carnegie was born in Scotland. His family emigrated to the United States when he was twelve. Andrew worked in a textile mill making $1.20 per week. After the Civil War, Carnegie became interested in bridge building, which developed into an interest in producing iron and steel. As steel became the construction material of choice, Carnegie invested heavily in it, grew his company, and wiped out his competitors. In 1901 Carnegie sold his steel interests for about $500 million and retired to devote himself to philanthropy. He gave $350 million to various causes, including public libraries and universities.

Carnegie believed that God had ordered the arrangement of society such that some have wealth and others do not. As a result, he said, the wealthy have a duty to be generous to others. The accumulation of wealth brought the opportunity to do great good for mankind, in Carnegie's thinking. Carnegie did not marry until his mother died and he was in his fifties.

John Pierpont Morgan (1837-1913)

J. P. Morgan was born to a wealthy Connecticut family. He expanded his father's banking enterprise by investing in various businesses. Morgan did not own a company that produced a commodity; instead, he pioneered in the field of finance capitalism by managing investments in successful production companies. Controlling this investment capital gave Morgan and other finance capitalists great power in what companies produced and how they were run. Morgan made a large fortune in railroads. He also created the United States Steel Corporation when he bought out Andrew Carnegie in 1901.

Morgan's activities exemplify how big money came to dominate big business. In 1893 twelve large U.S. companies had a total worth of about one billion dollars. By 1904 318 industrial combinations had a combined capitalization of $7.25 billion and operated over 5,000 production facilities.

Richard Sears and Alvah Roebuck

In the past, when you wanted to buy something, you went to the store to get it. Traveling salesmen took retailing to a new level by going to the customers in their homes, but such salesmen could only carry a relatively few items with them. In the spirit of the entrepreneurial age, a few individuals envisioned a new way to market and sell. Their system became part of the American and world economy.

Aaron Montgomery Ward of Chicago decided that he could reach more people by mail than on foot, so he began sending out a catalog of goods that people could order from him by mail. Richard Sears and Alvah Roebuck, also based in Chicago, picked up the idea and carried it even further than Ward did. The 1897 Sears and Roebuck catalog contained almost 800 pages. It appeared in German and Swedish editions for the immigrant population. The company offered an amazing variety of goods, including clothes, farm equipment, school textbooks, and even kits to build complete houses.

This 1903 photo shows Andrew Carnegie (in center wearing top hat) at the laying of the foundation stone for a library in Waterford, Ireland.

SEARS, ROEBUCK & CO.

WE SELL EVERYTHING BY MAIL ORDER ONLY. YOUR MONEY WILL BE PROMPTLY RETURNED FOR ANY GOODS NOT PERFECTLY SATISFACTORY AND WE WILL PAY FREIGHT OR EXPRESS CHARGES BOTH WAYS

A 7944.

OUR 40 ACRE NEW HOME - THE LARGEST MERCANTILE PLANT IN THE WORLD

BOUNDARIES: KEDZIE AVE HARVARD ST. CENTRAL PARK AVE. AND CHICAGO TERMINAL TRANSFER R.R.

CABLE ADDRESS: SUPPLY CHICAGO. DIRECT WIRE WITH WESTERN UNION AND POSTAL TELEGRAPH CO'S. LONG DISTANCE PHONE KEDZIE 2500 WITH PRIVATE EXCHANGE TO ALL DEPARTMENTS.

OUR MAMMOTH CATALOGUE CONTAINS OVER 100,000 ILLUSTRATIONS AND QUOTATIONS MAILED TO ANY ADDRESS FREE ON APPLICATION. THIS BIG BOOK NAMES THE LOWEST PRICES ON EVERYTHING WRITE FOR IT TODAY. WE CAN SAVE YOU MONEY ON ANYTHING YOU WANT TO BUY.

REFERENCE BY SPECIAL PERMISSION. FIRST NATIONAL BANK CHICAGO. CORN EXCHANGE NAT'L BANK CHICAGO. NATIONAL CITY BANK NEW YORK. NATIONAL SHAWMUT BANK BOSTON.

Sears, Roebuck & Co Letterhead, 1907

Sears and Roebuck kept a close eye on inventory and cut their expenses by eliminating the middleman in getting the goods to their customers directly. Federal mail delivery directly to rural addresses began in 1896, which encouraged mail-order businesses even more. Through mail order catalogs, people on isolated farms and in small communities had easy access to the same goods that were available in cities. Modern commerce on the Internet and delivery by UPS, the U.S. Postal Service, and other carriers are an extension of what Montgomery Ward and Sears and Roebuck started in the late nineteenth century.

For the love of money is a root of all sorts of evil,
and some by longing for it have wandered away
from the faith and pierced themselves with many griefs.
1 Timothy 6:10

⋆ Assignments for Lesson 81 ⋆

Literature Continue reading *In His Steps.* Plan to finish it by the end of this unit.

Bible This week we will be looking at how God's people should respond to the needs of people and the economic realities of the world. Read Leviticus 19:9-37.

Start memorizing 1 Peter 2:19-21.

Project Choose your project for this unit and start working on it.

Student Review Optional: Answer the questions for Lesson 81.

Labor Committee at the Botany Worsted Mills, Passaic, New Jersey (c. 1912)

Lesson 82

The Rise of Organized Labor

The big business ventures of the nineteenth century involved the collection of raw materials; the production of goods; and the transportation, advertising, and selling of those goods. All of that could not have happened without one key factor: the human element of workers. When companies emphasize bigness, money, efficiency, and power, the individual persons (both employees and customers) who are involved in the process can come to feel unimportant and used. This is how many workers in American factories felt in the late nineteenth century. Many workers responded to the growth of industry by trying to take back a degree of power and protection for themselves.

Conditions

Huge factories required many workers. The demand was met in part with the labor of immigrants, including women and children. This dramatic increase in the number of wage earners affected the quality of life for many Americans. Most workers no longer knew their employers personally. The increased impersonalization made it easier for employers to use their workers without compassion and for workers to see employers as their enemy.

The workers had jobs, but many jobs did not pay well. In 1900 the average wage was 21.6 cents per hour and the average annual income was under $500. Moreover, working conditions were poor. The average work week was 59 hours; steel workers often put in twelve-hour days, sometimes seven days per week. In 1913 25,000 factory deaths were reported and 700,000 work-related injuries occurred that required at least a month of disability (and workers generally did not receive disability payments). Some workers were able to save money, earn promotions, and improve their lot; but many lived out their lives working in the same jobs and living in crowded, unsanitary tenements.

Still, the average American was becoming more prosperous. The middle class was increasing, made up largely of professionals, industrial managers, and skilled laborers. Many workers received more income than they had earned before. The overall status of Americans was improving, but industrial workers were still on the lower end of the scale and many struggled to keep up.

Difficulties in Organizing Workers

The one tool that workers had which could give themselves some power against the demands of management was their labor. Providing their labor to companies made the owners wealthy; withholding their labor, they believed, could draw management's attention to their needs and could fulfill their desire to have a bigger share of the American dream. An individual worker refusing to work in a factory would not make much difference; he would simply be fired and replaced. However, if all the workers at a factory refused to work (a labor stoppage which came to be called a strike), management might take notice. At least, this was labor's theory.

Organizing laborers into effective unions was no easy task. One factor was sheer numbers. A meeting of ten corporate presidents had more impact on business than a meeting of a hundred workers, and the presidents' meeting was easier to arrange. Second, since many Americans wanted to be independent, they shied away from organizations that took away the freedom for each man to act as he saw fit. Third, immigrants often spoke little or no English and resisted being controlled by others. It was because of this kind of control in their homelands that many immigrants had come to America, the land of the free. Fourth, many workers lived in the hope that their current job was temporary until they found something better. They did not see it as being in their long-term interest to devote time to labor activities and risk unemployment just to try to change the working conditions where they were.

This photo, taken about 1900, shows a garment presser who had worked at the same shop for about 40 years, since he was 18.

In addition, the labor union movement was viewed with suspicion by a large part of the American public, including by many workers themselves. Many people saw unions as potential troublemakers. All of the talk about workers uniting sounded to many people like the radical and decidedly un-American socialist and Communist thinking that had been emerging in Europe. Many workers wanted no part of it.

Labor Disturbances

The problems that could come as a result of workers protesting their work conditions were proven to many people by early, unorganized labor actions. In 1874 and 1875 some Irish coal miners organized a terrorist group called the Molly Maguires that intimidated, beat, and killed coal mine owners in Pennsylvania because of unsafe working conditions. Twenty-four of the group were convicted in 1876, and twenty of them were hanged. Wages in the mines were reduced as a result of the disturbances as a warning against any future protest actions by laborers.

Following the Panic of 1873 and the resultant economic depression, railroads cut wages twice. After the second cut in 1877, workers in Martinsburg, West Virginia, walked off their jobs. Some of the unorganized protesters turned to violence against railroad property. Sympathy strikes spread across the country. Scattered violence left one hundred people dead, and millions of dollars worth of property was destroyed. Public opinion supported the strikers at first, but the violence turned people against the workers' grievances. It reminded them of similar unrest that had occurred in Paris, France, in 1871. The striking workers eventually went back to work. The work stoppage had failed.

During the rail strikes, a gathering of workers in the Sand Lot in San Francisco resulted in violence being committed against some Chinese people who happened to pass by. The American workers saw

This 1883 cartoon by Friedrich Graetz in Puck *magazine illustrates the conflict between labor and big business.*

the Chinese as being responsible for their labor difficulties because they thought that the Chinese took jobs away from Americans and because they thought that the Chinese were willing to work for lower wages. Anti-Chinese violence spread and erupted in several West Coast cities. In the political realm, industrial workers had an impact in California, as Workingmen's Party candidates won some elections. The longest-lasting result of the California labor activity was that in 1882 Congress banned Chinese immigration for ten years.

The National Labor Union was formed in Baltimore in 1866 and lasted until 1872. It successfully influenced Congress to set a maximum eight-hour day for Federal workers and for workers on Federal contracts. The group also helped convince Congress to repeal the Contract Labor Law that had been enacted in 1864. Under the law, employers paid the passage for immigrants to come to America with the understanding that the immigrants would work for the company. The immigrants were willing to work for low wages, which American workers resented. Contract labor arrangements also commonly took advantage of immigrants, and many American laborers believed that such arrangements hurt all workers.

A larger labor organization, the Knights of Labor, began in 1869. At its high point in 1886, it claimed over 700,000 members. The organization's best-known president, Terence Powderly, generally tried to avoid labor strikes and preferred using arbitration to settle disputes. A strike against railroad lines owned by Jay Gould in 1885 that was supported by the Knights resulted in Gould rescinding pay cuts for his workers. The influence of the Knights was not consistent, however. A tragic 1886 confrontation in Chicago permanently weakened the organization.

The Haymarket Riot

In May of 1886, several unions went on strike to demand the eight-hour day. International Harvester hired other workers in an attempt to break the strike and continue production. Striking workers attacked strikebreakers at the International Harvester plant in Chicago, and the strikers were in turn confronted by police. One striker was killed. A small anarchist group called a protest meeting for the next night in Haymarket Square. Near the end of the series of speeches, police moved in to order the crowd to disperse. Someone threw a bomb into the police, killing one and wounding others. The police opened fire on the crowd and several people were killed.

Eight anarchists were convicted in an atmosphere of hysteria, although the identity of the bomb-thrower was never determined. Seven of the eight were sentenced to death, while the other received fifteen years in prison. Four were hanged, one committed suicide in prison, and the other three were eventually pardoned by the governor of Illinois. One of those convicted was a member of the Knights of Labor. This forever associated the Knights with violence and anarchism, and many Americans turned away from the organization on the basis of guilt by association.

The American Federation of Labor

The labor movement was divided over the best way to organize workers. Craftsmen preferred to organize by profession (creating different unions for carpenters, plumbers, pipefitters, and so forth, regardless of where they worked), while many unskilled workers wanted to organize by industry (having unions for all those who worked in steel mills, all who worked in railroading, and so forth, regardless of their specific job). Craft unionists feared that their specialty (and higher pay) might get lost in the crowd of unskilled workers. Unskilled workers believed that they had the most power if they could shut down an entire factory or even an entire industry. The Knights of Labor were organized by industry.

In 1886 representatives of several craft unions formed the American Federation of Labor (AFL). The AFL was an umbrella organization for several specialty unions. Samuel Gompers was the president from its inception until his death in

Anarchism was a political philosophy that opposed any government whatsoever. Anarchists used acts of violence to attack the system that they saw as the cause of many contemporary ills. Anarchism was mostly a negative movement. How people were supposed to live together in society and govern themselves without a formal government was not a point on which anarchists had much to say. This 1894 illustration is by British artist Walter Crane, a socialist who was sympathetic to those convicted after the Haymarket Riot.

1924. Gompers was a practical, plain-spoken leader who concentrated on economic issues and ignored politics and philosophy. He was willing to use the strike to improve workers' conditions but preferred to negotiate agreements with management. The AFL had a half-million members in 1900; by 1920 its numbers had grown to four million. Even so, the AFL accounted for only about fifteen percent of non-farm workers, and the total of all unionized workers was only about eighteen percent of the non-farm workforce. This was significant growth, but still far from a majority of workers.

The Homestead and Pullman Strikes

Two violent work stoppages in the 1890s hurt the cause of union labor. In 1892 the Carnegie steel factory in Homestead, Pennsylvania, was planning job cutbacks to save money and to break the influence of the union. The company locked out unionists and hired 300 agents from the Pinkerton security company to protect the men hired as strikebreakers.

As the armed Pinkertons moved up the Monongahela River on barges toward the factory, armed workers who had lost their jobs manned smaller boats on the river and hid behind iron barricades on shore. Someone fired the first shot; and in the ensuing battle, sixteen people were killed.

Samuel Gompers (1850-1924)

The state militia arrived the next day to protect the strikebreaking workers at the plant, and the union was defeated. The cause of labor was not helped when the president of the plant was shot and wounded by an anarchist.

Two years later, the American Railway Union went on strike against the Pullman Railroad Car Company near Chicago. Pullman workers had been required to live in company housing (for which they paid rent) and to buy from the company store. The community of company homes was attractive, but many workers felt trapped by the arrangement. After the Panic of 1893, George Pullman laid off half of his employees and cut wages for the rest; but he did not lower rent or other expenses charged to the workers.

This 1894 illustration shows three men involved in the Pullman Strike. From left to right are George Pullman; Senator Cushman Davis (R-MN), who objected to the strike; and union leader Eugene Debs. The bottom picture shows railroad cars blocked in Chicago.

Looking Backward

Edward Bellamy (1850-1898) was a socialist who published Looking Backward: 2000-1887. *In the book, a man who is receiving medical treatment in a basement is trapped while he is asleep. He wakes up in the year 2000 to find a radically different America, the country Bellamy hoped America would become—a utopian world no longer crippled by cut-throat competition and abject poverty.* Looking Backward *is fiction, but it is more than just an attempt to tell a story. The book is a novel designed to promote a particular cause. In this way, it is like* Uncle Tom's Cabin.

Bellamy advocated the nationalization (that is, the operation by the government) of all industry and the equal distribution of wealth. He called his system Nationalism. He avoided the term socialism because of the negative associations it had with Communism and anarchism. Looking Backward *sold over a half million copies and was translated into twenty languages. Nationalist clubs were formed across the country, and Nationalist publications promoted public (that is, government) ownership of railroads and utilities as well as other progressive changes.*

Bellamy was the son of a Baptist minister, but during his life he moved away from traditional Christian beliefs (in the book, many people in the year 2000 stay home from church and listen to services transmitted over telephone lines). Bellamy died of tuberculosis in 1898.

The leader of the union, Eugene V. Debs, asked for a settlement by arbitration; but Pullman refused. Union workers then stopped handling Pullman cars. Within a few weeks railroads in 27 states and territories were affected, disrupting the economy on a wide scale. Railroad owners brought in strikebreakers, and special deputies were sworn in to provide protection. Debs' call for a peaceful boycott was ignored, and clashes occurred between strikers and the deputies. Eventually President Cleveland sent in Federal troops to keep the trains moving. Pullman cars were intentionally connected to U.S. Mail cars; so interference with Pullman cars meant interfering with the mail, which was a Federal offense.

The conflict came to an end when a Federal court issued an injunction forbidding any action that interfered with delivery of the mail or that negatively affected normal trade. The same day, Debs was sentenced to six months in jail for violating the injunction. This was an example of how the courts turned the restraint of trade clause of the Sherman Antitrust Act against unions instead of against business. Debs became a socialist and was the Socialist Party candidate for President several times.

The Wobblies

The Industrial Workers of the World was formed in 1905 to rekindle the drive to organize unions by industries instead of by crafts. Union leaders spoke openly about class struggle and used other terms that reflected socialist thinking. The IWW (called

This man wears an IWW hat card that says "Bread or Revolution" (1914).

the Wobblies by detractors for their W's and their wobbly philosophy) was strongest in the lumber and mining industries in the West. The union had a poor rate of success in confrontations with management, and its strong anti-government views cost it support during World War I.

The Effect of Early Labor Organizations

The labor movement of the late nineteenth and early twentieth centuries was a response to a perceived need for fairer treatment for workers. Management held most of the advantages in the on-going conflict. Management's tools included blacklisting workers who tried to organize unions, insisting on so-called "yellow dog" contracts in which workers promised not to join a union, hiring strikebreakers to do the work, ordering lockouts that attempted to force strikers back, and seeking court injunctions that forbade strikes as a restraint of trade.

The power of labor was limited because of difficulties in organizing workers, negative public opinion toward unions, and incidents of violence and extremism. Some workers had legitimate complaints about working conditions, and some business owners failed to accept responsibility for those conditions; but labor organizers faced an uphill struggle to right these wrongs, and they sometimes hurt their own cause by taking extreme action.

Mary Harris "Mother" Jones (c. 1837-1930) was born in Ireland and immigrated with her family to Canada during the potato famine. She moved to the United States as a young woman and married George Jones. A yellow fever epidemic killed George and the couple's four children in 1867. Mary established a dressmaking shop in Chicago, but it was destroyed in the Great Fire of 1871. She became an active promoter of the labor movement for the rest of her life.

In November of 1909, some 20,000 young women who worked in New York's shirtwaist industry went on strike for eleven weeks. This photo shows workers volunteering for picket duty during the strike. This strike helped lead to a strong union presence in the garment industry.

***By the sweat of your face you will eat bread,
till you return to the ground, because from it you were taken;
for you are dust, and to dust you shall return.
Genesis 3:19***

⋆ Assignments for Lesson 82 ⋆

American Voices Read the hymns by Philip P. Bliss (pages 237-238).

Literature Continue reading *In His Steps.*

Bible Read Isaiah 1:10-20.

Work on memorizing 1 Peter 2:19-21.

Project Work on your project.

Student Review Optional: Answer the questions for Lesson 82.

Farm Owned by African Americans in Georgia (c. 1900)

Lesson 83

New South, New West

In the 1880s, Henry Grady, editor of the *Atlanta Constitution*, became a major proponent of what he called the New South, a South that would be open to industry, that would involve all of its citizens and all of its natural resources, and that would not be as dependent on cotton farming alone. While many white southerners looked back wistfully and hoped that "old times there are not forgotten," a growing minority wanted to look forward to develop wealth in new ways and to help the region recover economically after the devastation of the Civil War. In many ways, a new day was indeed coming to the South. Some aspects of southern life, however, were disturbingly familiar.

Changes in Agriculture

The old plantation system of agriculture was gone. Many planters were in desperate financial shape and others had simply abandoned their land when they left the South. Many large plantations were broken up and sold as smaller farms. Despite these structural changes, cotton was still the chief crop of the region; and production of it grew after the Civil War. By 1871 the South's cotton production surpassed that of 1860. Additional land in the Southwest region of the country was also devoted to cotton growing. In 1900 Texas alone produced one-third of the nation's cotton output.

However, diversity was coming to southern agriculture. Tobacco, which had been the mainstay of southern farming before the invention of the cotton gin, was revitalized, especially in Kentucky, North Carolina, and Virginia. Fruit growing increased dramatically. The expansion of railroads and the invention of refrigerator cars enabled the development of a national market for the fruits and vegetables produced during the long southern growing season. Railroad access and the overall national economic expansion encouraged the use of the South's large forests for lumber and other wood products. States opened agricultural colleges that taught the latest and most effective farming methods. Agricultural output in the region increased because of advances in farm machinery and the use of fertilizers. However, extensive tree-cutting and the use of fertilizers sometimes had a negative impact on the environment.

One factor that limited southern agricultural progress was the continued dependence on tenant and sharecropper farming. These farm workers provided the necessary labor for production on larger farms, but the system left them living at a subsistence level and extremely dependent on the landowner's fortunes. When farm workers, along with factory workers, could not afford to buy the products they helped to produce, this limited economic growth. A few tenants and sharecroppers were able to save enough to purchase their own land, but the use of tenants and sharecroppers kept the region dependent on single-crop farming (such as cotton or tobacco). Sharecropping and tenant farming continued in widespread use until the agricultural reforms of the 1930s. Those reforms included the change to paying wages to farm workers and the increased utilization of farm machinery.

Changes in Industry

An even greater change took place in southern manufacturing, especially textile production. Rather than continue to ship cotton to northern mills, southerners built their own mills to produce cotton fabric. The number of mills in the South increased from 161 in 1880 to 400 in 1900. Some northern investors helped with this growth, but the majority of the money came from southerners. Single investors, small groups of investors, and sometimes entire communities put up the money to build the factories. However, southern mill workers faced the same struggles that northern industrial laborers did. When a family or a small group owned the mill, workers were forced to be dependent on the owners. Employees had to make purchases in the company store and were required to live in company-owned housing.

Mill Workers in Macon, Georgia (1909)

Southern manufacturing was helped by the rapid expansion of railroads in the region. In 1890 the railroad track mileage in the South was double what it had been in 1860. Southern manufacturing output in 1900 was four times what it had been in 1860. A related development was the growth of several large southern cities. Richmond, Virginia; Nashville, Tennessee; Durham, North Carolina; and Atlanta, Georgia, grew rapidly during this period. The huge coal reserves in the Appalachian Mountains from West Virginia to northeastern Alabama were tapped for energy needs. Birmingham, Alabama, was founded in 1871 and quickly became the "Pittsburgh of the South" because of its iron and steel facilities.

Changes in Education

One important element of the New South agenda was the improvement of educational opportunities. Proponents of change believed that better education would prepare people for the factory and office jobs that they thought held the key to the broad economic transformation of the region. The South benefited from generous contributions from northerners such as George Peabody and John Slater. The Peabody Education Fund, for instance, supported the development of the George Peabody College for Teachers in Nashville, Tennessee. Many

The Duke Family

The story of the Duke Family combined agriculture and industry. In the years following the Civil War, Washington Duke went from having almost nothing to producing 125,000 pounds of bright-leaf tobacco every year. His son, James Buchanan (Buck) Duke, grew the business by investing heavily in advertising and by undercutting the prices of competitors.

In 1890 Duke brought his and other smaller companies together to form the American Tobacco Company, which controlled about ninety percent of the country's cigarette production. The Supreme Court ordered the company to break up in 1911. A small college in Durham, North Carolina, was renamed Duke University in 1924 in honor of the Duke family for its financial assistance to the school.

Statue of James Duke on the Duke University Campus

other trade schools and training institutes for whites and blacks began during this time.

Funding for grade schools by state governments was slower in coming, however, because public support for education was not a cherished and long-standing practice. Many schools were small, private efforts. Few communities had schools that went beyond the eighth grade. State and county governments usually resisted significant increases in funding for public education, especially for blacks. A few cities responded to calls for improved public education, but it would be the early twentieth century before major changes took place.

Southern Politics

Most southerners were Democrats. Before the Civil War, the Whig Party had a respectable presence in the South; but after the collapse of the Whig Party, few southerners became Republicans because of that party's clear position against slavery. The Republican-led state governments that existed in southern states after the Civil War were largely imposed on the states by Congress. This drove even more southerners into the Democratic Party. As interest in the South's recovery from the Civil War lessened in Congress and the rest of the nation, the Democrats were able to regain power. Soon after the end of Reconstruction in 1877, the Democratic Party once again controlled all of the state governments in the former Confederate states.

Oakwood University in Huntsville, Alabama, was founded as Oakwood Industrial School in 1896 by the Seventh-Day Adventist Church. It is one of about one hundred historically black colleges and universities across the country.

Southern Democrats were led by wealthy planters and merchants. They called themselves the Redeemers because they believed that they had redeemed the South from Republican and Yankee control. Their opponents called them Bourbons after the reactionary royal family of France that was the target of the French Revolution. These opponents said that the Bourbon Democrats wanted to return the South to the days of control by a small elite of wealthy and influential whites.

The Redeemers supported the change to a new, industrial South; but they opposed changes in social policy. In an effort to cut government spending, these Democrats often reduced state education budgets and repudiated debts incurred by previous Republican-led state governments. To increase revenue, the Redeemers engaged in convict-leasing, a policy which loaned convicts as workers to private businesses such as coal mines. The company paid a modest fee to the government for this service. Convict-leasing provided cheap labor for the businesses and allowed the state to make some money off of the men's work. The convicts were often not treated well in these arrangements.

The Changing West

Open-range cattle drives were threatened in the 1880s by the arrival of ranchers and farmers who wanted to fence in their land. Conflicts arose between cattle drivers on one side and ranchers and farmers on the other. These conflicts sometimes resulted in violence. Eventually the fencing of the land led to the end of the cattle drives. Some ranches were huge, up to 100,000 acres.

Water was relatively scarce in many places, and water rights became a major issue for western settlers. (It is still a major issue for many living in the

In 1889 President Harrison opened the Oklahoma District for settlement. On the appointed day, April 22, between 50,000 and 100,000 people were packed along the boundary line. When a shot was fired at noon, the prospective settlers rushed in to claim land for homesteading. All available land was taken within a few hours. Some people had sneaked into the territory sooner than the law allowed to stake out a claim; these were called Sooners. Oklahoma was organized as a territory the next year and became a state in 1907. This painting of the Land Rush by John Steuart Curry (American, 1939) decorates the U.S. Department of the Interior building in Washington, D.C.

West, where some areas receive only 10-20 inches of rainfall per year, much of that in the form of snow.) Well-digging became an important profession, and windmills were developed to make access to water easier. Trees were scarce, so settlers made their first homes out of blocks of sod (this and their plowing techniques led to their being called sodbusters). Fence posts were often stone pillars. Life on the plains was not easy, but homesteaders continued to move west and establish new lives.

Settlers in Custer County, Nebraska, built many sod houses. The Dowse Sod House was built in 1900 and was used as a residence until 1959. All of the surrounding farm buildings—barn, chicken house, hog house, and windmill—were destroyed by a tornado. The house was restored and opened as a museum in the early 1980s.

American Literature In This Period

A popular kind of writing that was read by millions in this era were the rags to riches stories by Horatio Alger and Oliver Optic (pen name of W. T. Adams). They showed how young people of the city overcame obstacles to achieve success. These were the best examples of the many paperback dime novels published during this era.

Another trend of the times was local color writers, who told vivid stories about the regions they knew best. Most successful of these was Mark Twain, who wrote much about what he knew of life on the Mississippi River. Sarah Orne Jewett (pictured at right) told stories from Maine, George Washington Cable wrote about the South, and Bret Harte told stories from the rugged West. Henry James wrote probing novels about upper class life. William Dean Howells, editor of Atlantic Monthly *and later a writer for* Harper's Monthly, *was a friend of Twain and was considered the leading literary figure of the age.*

Lesson 88 mentions the muckrakers, who criticized big business and other aspects of American life. In addition to those mentioned there, Thorstein Veblen indicted the well-to-do in The Theory of the Leisure Class *(1899).*

As white settlers spread across the western U.S., opportunities for Native American tribes to practice their traditional ways of life continued to diminish. Edward S. Curtis traveled across the West in the early 1900s to capture Native American culture in photographs. Over 2,000 images were published in twenty volumes over a period of several years in The North American Indian. *This photo shows the frame of a sweat lodge built by the Cheyenne.*

In all labor there is profit,
But mere talk leads only to poverty.
Proverbs 14:23

⋆ Assignments for Lesson 83 ⋆

American Voices Read "The Significance of the Frontier in American History" by Frederick Jackson Turner (pages 258-273).

Literature Continue reading *In His Steps.*

Bible Read Isaiah 58 and Mark 10:17-31.

Work on memorizing 1 Peter 2:19-21.

Project Work on your project.

Student Review Optional: Answer the questions for Lesson 83.

Great Hall at Ellis Island (2012)

Lesson 84

Life in the City

As America became an increasingly urban nation, life in the city became more diverse and challenging. Eastern cities grew rapidly; but many cities in the West, such as San Francisco, Los Angeles, Kansas City, and Denver, grew at an even faster rate.

One way that cities grew was by more and more people leaving farms and small towns and heading for metropolitan areas. They were pushed from the farms because of unstable and often hard economic times. They were pulled to the cities by the attraction of steady work and by the variety of activities and opportunities there. An even bigger factor in the growth of the cities was foreign immigration.

The "Huddled Masses"

By 1900 thirty percent of city dwellers were foreign born. Most of this post-Civil War immigration came from Southern and Eastern Europe, from countries such as Italy, Hungary, Russia, Poland, and the Slavic nations in the Austro-Hungarian Empire. They were pushed from the old countries by disease, economic distress, lack of opportunity, and political and religious persecution. They were pulled to the new world by the opportunity for jobs and land and the promise of personal, political, and religious freedom.

Many Europeans responded to advertising by railroad companies that promoted America as a land of opportunity. The ads were evidence of the companies' desire to sell the land that the companies had received from the government in building the railroads. Some Europeans were persuaded to sign contracts with American businesses that called for the company to pay their passage in return for the immigrant going to work for the company. Unfortunately, companies often paid low wages and took the cost of the fare out of the workers' paychecks. This practice, called contract labor, was permitted through a law passed in 1864. The law was repealed in 1868, and the practice of contract labor was specifically forbidden by an 1885 law.

The stream of immigrants was constant. During the 1870s, three million people entered the country. In the 1880s, the total rose to five million. The 1890s, beset by economic depression, saw only 3.5 million come; but in the first decade of the twentieth century, 8.8 million immigrants entered the U.S.

The Way In

For years many immigrants entered through the Castle Garden processing facility in New York City, which was run by the state of New York. However, Castle Garden was rife with corruption:

moneychangers cheated the immigrants, railroad agents overcharged for tickets, and baggage handlers blackmailed the bewildered newcomers. The facility was closed in 1890.

The Federal government took over the processing of immigrants and funded the construction of a new immigration center on tiny Ellis Island near the Statue of Liberty in New York harbor. The statue, "Liberty Enlightening the World," had been dedicated in 1886 as a gift from the people of France to the people of the United States commemorating the friendship between the two countries. When the Ellis Island center opened in 1892, the statue was a symbol of the new life of freedom that millions of immigrants anticipated.

Federal immigration workers at Ellis Island asked the arriving immigrants a series of questions, including whether they had a job or relatives in the U.S., whether they had a criminal record, and what money they had with them. Immigrants who were financially self-supporting had an easier time getting into the country. The newcomers were given a cursory medical examination to check for insanity or infectious diseases. If an immigrant was ill, he or she might be quarantined on the island for a period of time. Only about two percent of immigrants were sent back to their native land because of health or other reasons. At its busiest, the center processed one million people in 1907, or an average of about 5,000 per day. Between 1892 and 1954, approximately 70% of European immigrants came through Ellis Island. Most of the others came through Boston, Philadelphia, Baltimore, and New Orleans.

New Realities

Immigrants often took low-paying or dangerous jobs, such as those in mines or sweatshops. Poor arrivals in the big cities lived in crowded tenement buildings that had only outside toilets or only a few indoor communal facilities. Foul odors and infectious diseases were rampant. Immigrants usually wanted to live near people from their home country, so districts such as Little Italy and Chinatown became common.

The newcomers provided cheap labor for the American economy, but their presence also created tensions. Some Americans believed that foreigners took jobs away from other Americans. The presence of so many Catholic and Jewish newcomers stirred up anti-foreigner, anti-Catholic, and anti-Jewish (often called anti-Semitic) sentiment among some

Children Playing Ball in a City Alley

Americans. Some Americans also were afraid that dangerous new political ideas might be entering the country; and enough radicals were found among the immigrants to justify, in the minds of many Americans, fears about all immigrants. Chinese immigrants on the West Coast were subjected to anti-foreigner as well as racial prejudice. Chinese immigration was restricted in 1882, and the restrictions were not removed until 1943. Some Chinese (such as students and persons with a Chinese-American parent, for instance) were allowed to enter even during the time of restrictions. Angel Island, six miles offshore from San Francisco, was the West Coast equivalent to Ellis Island.

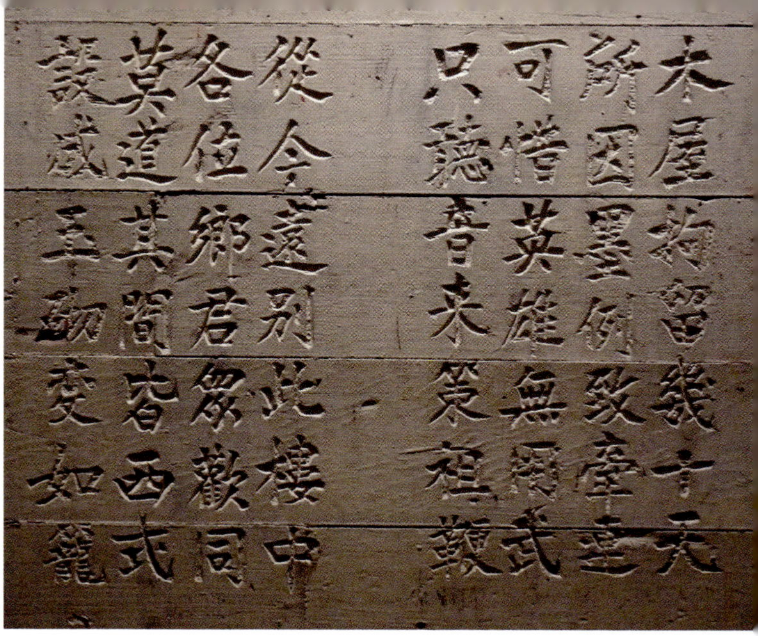

Angel Island operated as an immigration station from 1910 to 1940. Many of the immigrants who came there, particularly those from China, were detained for months or even years. Some were finally allowed to enter the United States, while others were deported. Detainees left inscriptions on the wooden walls in their native languages. Numerous original poems written in Chinese, such as the one above, have survived.

Other Aspects of City Life

Innovations changed the face of American cities. Steam heat generated from a central boiler and sent through pipes and radiators meant that each apartment in a tenement building did not need its own fireplace. Before the Civil War, few buildings were more than three or four stories high. Cast-iron and steel frame construction techniques developed in the 1880s made taller buildings possible, with some skyscrapers going as high as eighteen or twenty stories. Elevators (invented in 1889) helped move people up and down inside these taller buildings.

The Gilded Age was known for excessive decorations and elaborate designs on buildings. A new school of architecture, led by Louis Sullivan and Frank Lloyd Wright among others, offered more sleek lines. The rebuilding of Chicago after the 1871 fire provided a laboratory for new architectural concepts. The neoclassical structures used in the 1893 Chicago World's Fair inspired people from many cities to duplicate their style.

Cities offered the good and the bad to its residents. City parks, typified by Central Park in New York, brought an oasis of God's Creation to the inner city. Meanwhile, saloons were commonplace, with New York City offering 10,000 such watering holes in 1900. Streetcars (steam-powered until the 1890s and electric after that) and automobiles moved the growing city population faster and over wider areas. Middle- and upper-class residents moved to the suburbs, leaving the inner city to the poorest and newest city dwellers.

A New View of Government

America had been built on the idea of limited government. British control of the colonies sent the country into a revolution for freedom. Alexander Hamilton's program of a national bank and government assistance to manufacturers ran into stiff opposition from those who continued to believe in limited government. Andrew Jackson believed that the national bank was unconstitutional. Neither the state nor the national government was seen as a source of assistance to people in need.

With the growing urban population, the increasing power of big business (and government's helpful attitude toward it), and the needs of millions of people who were new to these shores, many

Woman and Children Making Artificial Flowers for Sale at Home

Americans looked to the government to provide more services. The ideals of the free market and American individualism were being challenged by the realities of poverty, the advantages awarded to the politically influential, and the demands of urban life. Farmers also wanted more help from government.

Entertainment

Although wages were generally low, especially by modern standards, a greater percentage of Americans were better off financially than had been the case in previous decades. The increasing standard of living enjoyed by many Americans made leisure activities a bigger part of life. With more people working in hourly jobs and pay scales increasing, and with fewer people tied to the seasonal farming schedule, a larger segment of the population had leisure time on their hands. Well-to-do families engaged in leisure activities at home, including board games and the new stereopticon, which used two pictures and a special personal viewer to create three-dimensional scenes. People enjoyed croquet, tennis, and riding the newly improved device called the bicycle. Women took part in these activities, wearing split skirts and bloomers when riding bicycles.

When people went out, they often attended political rallies or to hear speakers on various topics. Speeches were well attended and were considered an enjoyable form of entertainment. Labor unions sponsored educational programs for members and their families. Americans also began attending showings of motion pictures ("movies") in theaters. Thomas Edison is credited with inventing motion pictures, although many people had experimented with motion photography before him. The first movies could only be seen by one person at a time using a special viewing box. Thomas Armat invented a movie projector in 1895 which Edison refined and debuted in a public performance the next year.

The 1903 film "The Great Train Robbery" showed that movies could go beyond being merely a curiosity to present a real story. Early movie making was based in Chicago and New York, but the sunny climate of southern California attracted many producers. William Selig set up the first movie studio in Los Angeles in 1907 and built the first permanent studio there in 1911. D. W. Griffith's epic "Birth of a Nation" in 1915 was three hours long and terribly racist, but it was immensely popular and demonstrated the possibilities for storytelling with movies. Movies were without sound. When they played in theaters a live piano player provided background music, changing tune and tempo as the action changed on the screen.

Circuses toured both large cities and small towns with their collection of acrobats, animal trainers, and sideshows. The most famous Wild West show was the touring company headed by William ("Buffalo Bill") Cody. Cody was born in Iowa and reared in Kansas. His life was the classic western adventure story. Cody was a Pony Express rider, a Union scout during the Civil War, and then a buffalo hunter to help feed railroad construction crews. It was this work that gave him his nickname. He also was a scout for railroad crews and received the Medal of Honor for service in the Indian Wars.

A writer published a series of novels based loosely on Cody's life. In 1883 Cody used the publicity he gained to organize a western show that included sharpshooter Annie Oakley and featured wild animals. Cody also hired Native Americans, including Sitting Bull, to take part in the shows. The Indians staged attacks on innocent settlers and re-enacted the Battle of the Little Bighorn that involved George A. Custer. In these productions, whites were always the innocent victims and the Indians were always the aggressors. Cody died in 1917 and his show folded, but western entertainment lives on in the form of the modern rodeo.

Vaudeville was a common form of entertainment in many cities. Vaudeville was a variety show that often lasted several hours. The program included singers, comedians, jugglers, gymnasts, and many other entertainers. Vaudeville started in saloons to draw in customers, and it developed a (justifiably) bad reputation at first. However, when theaters were built to attract families and other paying customers, the entertainers had to clean up their act.

This 1907 stereoscopic image shows cowboys at dinner in the "Wild and Wooly West" of Arizona.

Music

John Philip Sousa (1854-1932), the "March King," was in his heyday during this period. Born in Washington, D.C., the son of a Portuguese father and German mother, Sousa wrote 140 marches, including "Semper Fidelis" (1888; the official Marine Corps march), the "Washington Post March" (1889), and "Stars and Stripes Forever" (1896). He led the Marine Corps Band for twelve years and later toured the U.S. and the world with his own band. He directed military bands during the Spanish-American War and World War I. Later in his career, Sousa wrote comic operas.

George M. Cohan (1878-1942) was born on July 3, 1878 (not the Fourth, as the song claims) into an entertainment family. He joined the family vaudeville act while he was still a child. Cohan became a success on Broadway in 1904 and wrote several popular musicals. In a 1906 performance, he carried an American flag around on stage while singing its praises, and this became his trademark. He wrote "Over There" as a tribute to the United States' involvement in World War I, and he was awarded the Congressional Gold Medal in 1940 for his patriotic songs. Other popular Cohan songs include "Yankee Doodle Boy," "You're a Grand Old Flag," and "Give My Regards to Broadway."

George M. Cohan Statue in Times Square

"When Johnny Comes Marching Home" was written during the Civil War, but it became well-known nationally during the Spanish-American War. The period saw many new sentimental popular songs, including "Sidewalks of New York" (1894) and "In the Good Old Summertime" (1902). When carmaker Ransom Olds sent two Oldsmobiles on a difficult cross-country trip from Detroit, Michigan, to Portland, Oregon, for the Lewis and Clark Centennial Exposition in 1905, the song "In My Merry Oldsmobile" was written in tribute.

Sports and Leisure

Greater leisure time led to an increase in spectator sports. Horse racing and prize fighting had been around for a long time, but team sports were an important addition during this period. College football and basketball and professional baseball had enormous popularity. Better transportation made inter-city rivalries possible, and the growing interest in sports led newspapers to begin having sports pages. Gambling on the outcome of games was commonplace.

Alexander Cartwright (not Abner Doubleday) developed the game of base, or baseball, in New York City in 1845. Early players set the bases 90 feet apart and positioned the pitcher 45 feet from home. Pitching at first was done underhanded. When the pitching mound and overhanded throwing were introduced, the pitcher was moved back to 60 feet, 6 inches from home plate. (It was supposed to be just 60 feet, but the first plans had an error in them). The first professional team organized in Cincinnati in 1869. The National League was founded in 1876,

Carlisle Indian Industrial School was a boarding school in Pennsylvania for Native American children from 1879 to 1918. The school fielded a football team from its beginning, as pictured above left. One star Carlisle player in the early 1900s was Jim Thorpe. Thorpe went on to be an Olympic champion in track and field and a professional football (above right photo, c. 1915) and baseball player.

and the American League went into operation in 1901. The first World Series was played in 1903.

The first football game, developed from English rugby, was played between Rutgers and Princeton in 1869. It had twenty-five men to a side, and the ball was literally kicked down the field. The game was a favorite with college men. Play was rough in its first few years—eighteen people were killed and 150 seriously injured in football games in 1905. Controversy over the sport led to the founding of the National Collegiate Athletic Association in 1910.

James Naismith developed basketball for the YMCA in Springfield, Massachusetts, in 1891, as a sport to play between the fall football and spring baseball seasons. He nailed two peach baskets to the gymnasium balcony (which happened to be ten feet high), and he had students throw a soccer ball into them. Vanderbilt fielded the first college men's basketball team in 1893.

World Expositions

America and the world took entertainment and enlightenment to new heights during this period with several expositions or world fairs. The first such event was the Crystal Palace Exposition in London in 1851. There the British put their newest technology on display for the world to see. An exposition in Paris followed in 1867. Then Philadelphia hosted a Centennial Exposition in 1876, in honor of the one hundredth anniversary of the country's beginning. An estimated ten million people attended the fair over the months it was open. Following two more expositions in Paris, Chicago hosted the World's Columbian Exposition in 1893, celebrating (a year late) the 400th anniversary of Columbus' historic voyage to the New World. The city also wanted to display its recovery from the devastating fire of 1871. Some 27.5 million people attended the fair in Chicago.

The Louisiana Purchase Exposition of St. Louis was held in 1904 and hosted 19.7 million visitors. That fair inspired the song that said, "Meet me in St. Louis, Louis/Meet me at the fair." San Francisco put on the Panama-Pacific International Exposition in 1915, a year after the opening of the Panama Canal and nine years after the city suffered a horrendous earthquake. About nineteen million people came to the fair. World's Fairs presented displays of culture and technology from many different nations as well as rides and other forms of entertainment.

This official Louisiana Purchase Exposition postcard features the Palace of Manufactures.

The Lord is high above all nations;
His glory is above the heavens.
Psalm 113:4

⋆ Assignments for Lesson 84 ⋆

American Voices Read the hymns by Fanny J. Crosby (pages 241-242).

Read "The New Colossus" by Emma Lazarus (page 246).

Read "Casey at the Bat" by Ernest Lawrence Thayer (pages 251-252).

Literature Continue reading *In His Steps.*

Bible Read Matthew 25:31-46.

Work on memorizing 1 Peter 2:19-21.

Project Work on your project.

Student Review Optional: Answer the questions for Lesson 84.

Raising Funds for the Salvation Army (c. 1912)

Lesson 85 - Bible Study

Social Darwinism and the Social Gospel

Two philosophical trends of the late nineteenth century offered differing belief systems regarding human society. Social Darwinism applied the theory of evolution to social interaction; the social gospel involved the application of Christian faith to social action.

Social Darwinism

Charles Darwin theorized that living things adapted to their environment by the survival of the fittest: the stronger varieties survived and flourished while the weaker strains died out. Darwinian evolution so swept human thought in the last half of the 1800s that it influenced several spheres of study. One field was the examination of human society. Those who applied Darwin's theories to society were called Social Darwinists.

The English writer Herbert Spencer (1820-1903) actually coined the phrase "survival of the fittest." Spencer's earliest work predated Darwin's publications, but he used similar assumptions. Spencer believed that the government should protect the natural rights of persons but should otherwise leave society alone. Society—and especially economics—would evolve, he said, by the survival of the fittest: financially adept people and institutions would survive, and those that were weak would fall by the wayside.

Social Darwinists in America used Spencer's ideas to justify big business and fabulously wealthy individuals as simply examples of the survival of the fittest. They said that government intervention interfered with natural selection. As a result, Social Darwinists opposed a higher income tax rate for the wealthy, sanitation codes, and laws that protected people against business fraud. All of these, Social Darwinists claimed, helped the unfit to survive. Social Darwinists saw business as the engine of social progress, and they saw business failures as simply the result of the process of natural selection. Adherents to this philosophy opposed the efforts of social reformers.

One of the leading proponents of Social Darwinism was William Graham Sumner (1840-1910), a professor of sociology and economics at Yale University. Sumner gave many speeches and published several essays promoting Social Darwinism. In "The Concentration of Wealth," Sumner wrote:

> The millionaires are a product of natural selection, acting on the whole body of men to pick out those who can meet the requirement of certain work to be done.

> In this respect they are just like the great statesmen, or scientific men, or military men. It is because they are selected that wealth—both their own and that entrusted to them—aggregates under their hands. Let one of them make a mistake and see how quickly the concentration gives way to dispersion. They may fairly be regarded as the naturally selected agents of society for certain work. They get high wages and live in luxury, but the bargain is a good one for society (*Social Darwinism: Selected Essays of William Graham Sumner*, Englewood Cliffs, New Jersey: Prentice Hall, 1963, p. 157).

Sumner also spoke up for the one he called "The Forgotten Man," the average middle-class worker who wants the freedom to do as he wishes, who contributes to the welfare of society and benefits from the same, and who is hampered by undue government regulation and interference.

Other writers took a different view of how society worked. Lester Frank Ward, for instance, believed that cooperation, not competition, brought more progress in society.

Social Gospel

Mainline Protestant denominations, especially their large congregations attended by the socially prominent, generally defended the status quo in society. Their members often tried to keep their distance from the poor, and they considered the "unwashed" as unworthy of their attention. As social ills became more pressing, however, a few urban Protestant clergymen called for believers to attend to the physical needs of those around them as a way to fulfill the mission of the church. Churches built gymnasiums and libraries to attract members of the working class to their buildings. Two examples of Christian social activism were the Young Men's Christian Association (or YMCA, begun in England in 1844 and developed in America starting in 1851) and the Salvation Army (organized in England in 1878 from previous social mission efforts and begun in the U.S. in 1880).

Proponents of the social gospel moved away from teaching the gospel to the lost and from emphasizing the individual believer's relationship to God. They believed instead that the mission of Christ was to help alleviate the physical suffering of mankind. Church members became involved in campaigns to pass child labor laws and to enact worker's compensation benefits for those injured on the job. A leading spokesman for the social gospel was Walter Rauschenbusch (1861-1918), who was a minister in a German Baptist Church in the tenements of New York City for a number of years. In 1902 he became a professor of church history at Rochester (New York) Theological Seminary. During his time in Rochester he published *A Theology for the Social Gospel*, which was based on a series of lectures he gave in 1917. The book presented his theological basis for the social gospel.

Rauschenbusch believed that the world was suffering from collective sins such as capitalism and the exploitation of workers. In response, the church was to be an organization of unselfish service to the world. Regeneration in Rauschenbusch's mind involved a renewed concern for other people, and salvation was "the voluntary socializing of the soul" (this edition Nashville: Abingdon, 1945, p. 99). Central to Rauschenbusch's theology was his view

YMCA Building in Keene, New Hampshire (c. 1900)

Walter Rauschenbusch

of the kingdom of God, which to him involved creating a better life for people on earth. He rejected individual theology and individual salvation as inappropriate responses to Christ. Rauschenbusch claimed that his views were Christ's original intent, reflected in His actions and His teachings, and that this intent became lost as the church became more inwardly and other-worldly focused.

For a long time, advocates of the social gospel made up only a minority of church membership and clergy. The majority of members maintained the traditional understanding of Christian doctrine. The social gospel movement did have influence, however, on how churches saw their mission. Eventually, especially among mainline denominations, the social gospel became mainstream.

God has always cared about how His people treated others. He has always commanded that kindness be shown to the poor and fairness be the standard in business (see, for example, Leviticus 19). Jesus spent much of His earthly ministry tending to the physical needs of those around Him. The early Christians more than once assisted those in financial distress (see, for example, Acts 11:27-30). All of this concern, however, was to be a reflection of a Christian's relationship with Christ and not the sum total of what it means to be a Christian.

Evangelicals and other conservative Christians long resisted involvement in social improvement programs because they considered such efforts to be a distraction from the central mission of teaching the gospel. However, efforts undertaken by conservative Christians in recent years such as marriage seminars, pro-life rallies, and campaigns against gambling show that these believers want their faith to make a difference in everyday life.

People living in Colorado faced hard times in the 1890s. Droughts and harsh winters hurt agriculture, and political changes affected the silver mining industry. As the major city in the region, the capital of Denver (pictured below in 1898) drew many people struggling to get by. Thomas Uzzell was a leader of the People's Tabernacle in Denver from 1885 until his death in 1910. That church established numerous outreach programs in the community, including a medical clinic, a "store" offering second-hand goods at no charge, summer camps in the mountains, night schools, and classes for immigrants.

Bramwell and Evangeline Booth, children of Salvation Army founder William Booth, visited the United States in 1913 for a Salvation Army convention. A parade through New York escorted them back to their ship. Bramwell was the second General of the Salvation Army (1912-1929), and Evangeline was the fourth General (1934-1939).

Social Darwinism reflected Darwin's belief in an entirely material process of evolution. Social Darwinists used Darwin's ideas to justify what was happening in the American economy. They wanted society to be left alone so that the fittest would survive. Social gospel advocates, on the other hand, sought to improve the way society worked to ease the hardships that many faced.

The King will answer and say to them, "Truly I say to you, to the extent that you did it to one of these brothers of Mine, even the least of them, you did it to Me."
Matthew 25:40

⋆ Assignments for Lesson 85 ⋆

American Voices Read "O Master, Let Me Walk With Thee" by Washington Gladden (page 244).

Literature Finish reading *In His Steps*. Literary analysis available in *Student Review*.

Bible Recite or write 1 Peter 2:19-21 from memory.

Project Complete your project for the unit.

Student Review Optional: Answer the questions for Lesson 85 and for *In His Steps* and take the quiz for Unit 17.

U.S. Navy Cruisers New York *and* Brooklyn *With a Fishing Boat (c. 1898)*

18 Beginnings of the Modern Age

As the nineteenth century came to a close, Democrats and Republicans continued to battle for political predominance while the Progressive Movement picked up the reform mantle of the Populist Party and urged even more sweeping changes. The United States became an important player on the world scene. The work of Sigmund Freud brought changes in how people see themselves and differed from the traditional understanding of human nature that is taught in the Bible.

Memory Work

Memorize 2 Corinthians 5:20 by the end of this unit.

Books Used

The Bible
American Voices
Up From Slavery

Project (choose one)

1) Write 300 to 500 words on one of the following topics:
   - Write a newspaper editorial either supporting or condemning the Spanish-American War as if you were writing in that day.
   - How has Freud and psychoanalysis helped people, and how has it hurt? In what ways does it challenge Biblical teaching? What is a good balance between using what Freud and other students of human behavior have said and relying on the Bible to be the source of our solutions?
2) Interview someone who administers a charitable organization in your area about how he or she became involved in the work, their goals for the organization, disappointments he or she has experienced, and some memorable successes. Compose at least ten questions ahead of time. You can conduct your interview by phone or in person. Be respectful of your interviewee's time and keep the interview within an hour. If possible, make an audio recording of the interview. See Lesson 88.
3) Write a poem of at least twenty lines about race relations in the United States, either past, present, or both. See Lesson 87.

Literature

Up From Slavery

Booker T. Washington (1856-1915) was born as a slave in Virginia. After getting an education during the Reconstruction period, he led the Tuskegee Institute in Alabama from its founding in 1881 until his death. Washington believed that the best hope for blacks was not to cause political agitation but to accept their inferior social status and try to improve themselves through education and economic growth. He published his autobiography, *Up From Slavery*, in 1901. Plan to finish the book by the end of this unit.

History Class at Tuskegee Institute Studying Captain John Smith (1902)

The Loser of a Political Bet Pulls the Winner in a Cart After the 1892 Election, Joseph Klir (1893)

Lesson 86

Politics in the 1890s

In the 1892 election, Democrat and former President Grover Cleveland defeated the incumbent Republican Benjamin Harrison to win another term. Voters were unhappy with the way that the Republicans had reversed previous changes that had taken place under the Democrats. Benjamin Harrison's wife died on October 25, 1892, near the end of the campaign; and this might also have had an impact on the outcome of the election. Populist candidate James B. Weaver polled over one million votes and got 22 electoral votes. Over 700,000 more people voted in 1892 than in 1888, which is probably an indication that the Populist cause drew more people to the polls, but not enough to carry the election.

The Panic of 1893

The Panic of 1893, as we discussed previously, hit soon after Cleveland took office again. It was the most severe economic panic and depression to that point in the nation's history. Numerous banks failed and some 15,000 businesses filed for bankruptcy. Factories and mines closed, four million people were thrown out of work, and prices for farm products fell even further.

President Cleveland, along with most people in his day, did not believe that it was the role of government to help people who were hurt by economic reversal. In his 1893 inaugural address, as trouble was looming on the horizon, Cleveland said

Grover Cleveland

Grover Cleveland received a plurality of the popular vote in each of his three presidential contests. He is the only man to serve two non-consecutive terms as President. Cleveland is officially listed twice in the roster of Presidents, as both the 22nd and the 24th President.

After 1892 the Democrats did not win another presidential election until 1912, when Woodrow Wilson was elected with 42% of the vote in another three-man race.

that the people should support the government but that the government's "functions do not include the support of the people."

Cleveland blamed the depression on the Sherman Silver Purchase Act and the resulting cheap money that had come into the economy. Late in 1893, Cleveland put together a coalition in Congress of Republicans and Democrats who supported the gold standard; and Congress repealed the Sherman Silver Purchase Act. This widened a growing split within the Democratic Party, as few southern and western Democrats in Congress voted with the President. Unfortunately, the return to the gold standard did not ease the depression. It was only when a group of bankers agreed to pump more gold back into government reserves by buying bonds with gold that the economy regained strength. By 1897 the economic crisis had passed.

The Tariff Issue

Another divisive issue during Cleveland's second term was the tariff. The Democratic Party campaigned in 1892 on a pledge to reduce tariffs. However, the Wilson-Gorman Tariff that passed Congress in 1894 lowered average rates only a small amount. During the debate on the measure in Congress, rates on hundreds of items were toyed with as lobbyists representing many industries tried to influence Senators and Congressmen. Cleveland was furious with Democrats who supported the bill, and he refused to sign the measure; but it became law over his pocket veto. The differing views within the Democratic Party concerning the tariff was another factor in widening the split within the party. In the congressional elections of 1894, the Republicans took back control of the House and the Democrats barely held on to the Senate.

The American Protective Tariff League published this card in 1906. It is critical of how Cleveland and the Democrats handled of events leading to the Panic of 1893.

To make up for what was expected to be lost revenue, the tariff bill included a clause creating a two-percent tax on income over $4,000 per year. The Supreme Court ruled that the income tax was unconstitutional in 1895, since it was a direct tax not apportioned among the states by population, something prohibited in Article I, Section 9 of the Constitution. The income tax had already become a political issue and would become even more of one in the years ahead. The Supreme Court's ruling led supporters of the income tax to press for a constitutional amendment that would allow it. Such an amendment was ratified in 1913.

The 1896 Election

As another presidential campaign approached in 1896, the Republicans were somewhat more unified than the Democrats. They nominated former Ohio Congressman and governor William McKinley, appraised by most observers as a kind and decent man. McKinley and the Republicans were indecisive on the money issue, although the party convention adopted a platform that included a plank supporting the gold standard.

The Democratic convention, on the other hand, was held amid serious party discord. Cleveland was severely criticized by western, silver, and agricultural interests as caring too much for business interests and too little for the common man. After the party's losses in 1894, farming interests had taken over almost all of the state Democratic Party organizations; and they were spoiling for a fight to control the party at the national level. They hoped that by doing so they could win the Populists back into the party's fold.

At the convention, a thirty-six-year-old attorney and former Congressman from Nebraska, William Jennings Bryan, electrified the crowd with an eloquent speech supporting the coinage of silver and denouncing the gold standard as unfair to the common man. He concluded the speech by announcing, "You shall not press down upon the brow of labor this crown of thorns; you shall not crucify mankind upon a cross of gold." The leading candidate for the Democratic nomination going into the convention had been Congressman Richard Bland of Missouri; but Bryan captivated the delegates and was nominated on the fifth ballot. The nomination looked like a surprise; but Bryan had actually been gathering support among farm Democrats for several years, and his speech at the convention was the culmination of his quiet campaign for the presidency. His running mate was Arthur Sewell of Maine.

This 1896 campaign poster shows William Jennings Bryan and his family with the text of his "Cross of Gold" speech.

Next came the Populist convention, where the party was in a dilemma. If they nominated their own candidate, they feared that he might split the anti-Republican vote and allow McKinley to win. If they nominated Bryan, many Populists feared that their identity would be swallowed up by the more numerous and more powerful Democrats. The convention chairman (who was from Nebraska) informed the delegates that the Democrats would replace Sewell with a Populist leader, Tom Watson of Georgia, if they nominated Bryan. On this basis the Populists nominated Bryan, but the Democrats did not remove Sewell from the ticket. The chairman's announcement had either been misleading or mistaken.

McKinley's personal campaigning consisted largely of delivering prepared speeches from the front porch of his Ohio home which were reported in newspapers across the country. The real political work was carried out under the direction of his campaign manager, Mark Hanna. While Bryan raised about $300,000, Hanna raised over ten times as much, which earned him the nickname of "Dollar Mark" Hanna. Republican surrogates launched vicious attacks on Bryan. Meanwhile, Bryan himself engaged in unprecedented campaigning for a presidential nominee. He visited over twenty states, logged 18,000 miles, and gave six hundred speeches. It is estimated that he spoke to five million people during the campaign.

This colorized 1897 photograph shows Chief Justice Melville Fuller (left), who was nominated by President Grover Cleveland during his first term. Fuller is swearing in William McKinley (center) as President while outgoing President Grover Cleveland stands nearby.

Out of 13.6 million votes cast, McKinley received 51.1% and had a 610,000 vote margin. He won the electoral college 271 to 176. The Republicans carried the Northeast, the states of the Midwest east of the Mississippi, and California and Oregon, while Bryan carried the South and the plains states. The Democrat Bryan did not make many inroads among laboring men. They probably did not identify with his farming background, and much of the nation blamed the recent recession on Cleveland and the Democrats. In addition, according to informal reports, some Republican factory managers told workers when they were paid on the Saturday before the election that if Bryan won they would no longer have jobs.

The Republican victory in 1896 returned the party to another period of national political power and broke the Populist movement. The Dingley Tariff of 1897 raised rates to their highest level in history, an average of 52 percent of the value of imported goods. The Gold Standard Act of 1900, which declared that the country would permanently be on the gold standard, ended any realistic hope by silverites or those favoring bimetallism.

The Election of 1900

McKinley had run on domestic issues, but the last part of his first term was engulfed in international affairs as the United States fought a war on foreign soil and began to develop a world empire. We will study these developments later in this unit. Both McKinley and Bryan were renominated by their respective parties in 1900. Vice President Garret Hobart died on November 21, 1899, so the Republicans nominated New York governor Theodore Roosevelt to take the second spot on the ticket. The popular understanding at the time was that the reform-minded Roosevelt had so angered Republican Party leaders that they decided to get rid of him by kicking him upstairs to the vice presidency. They hoped that he would be forgotten and that he would not be able to bother them any longer. The nation's prosperity, along with the victory in the Spanish-American War, gave the incumbent McKinley a strong advantage. Bryan tried to raise the silver issue again, but it did not catch on with voters. McKinley was re-elected and got slightly more votes than in 1896, while Bryan got slightly less. The Populist Party was out of the picture by 1900.

The Wonderful Wizard of Oz

L. Frank Baum published The Wonderful Wizard of Oz *in 1901. An illustration from the first edition of Dorothy meeting the Cowardly Lion is shown at right. Baum's introduction claimed that the book "was written solely to please children of today."*

Baum was an astute political observer who had a keen sense of humor. American history teacher Henry Littlefield suggested in a 1964 essay that Baum's story was a parable of populism. This interpretation has been hotly debated and widely criticized. However, numerous parallels can be seen between the story and the politics of the 1890s. Here is one way to look at the story:

Dorothy Gale represents the typical woman who deserved more rights. The cyclone was the storm (the Gale) out of the west that swept away everything in its path—in other words, victory by Bryan. The Wicked Witch of the East killed by Dorothy stands for the moneyed Eastern Establishment. The munchkins represent everyday folks—the little people. The Wicked Witch of the West represents the lumber and mining barons who made life difficult for the little folks.

In the book, Dorothy is given silver slippers (not the red ones that are in the movie). Silver (i.e., the free and unlimited coinage of silver at the ratio of 16 to 1) is her key to success as she travels along the Yellow Brick Road (gold is often formed into yellow bricks). Dorothy's dog Toto stands for Prohibition forces (teetotalers). The scarecrow is the American farmer who needs help. The tin man is the American worker who needs oil to be freed from his bondage and suffering. The lion represents Bryan, who needs support to be successful.

The Emerald City stands for Washington, D.C. (which at one time was called Federal City). The Wizard of Oz (oz is the abbreviation for ounce, which is how silver and gold are measured) is President McKinley, who appears powerful but who is actually (in Baum's portrayal) only a charlatan. Dorothy kills the Wicked Witch of the West by pouring water on her. Rainfall in the West in the 1890s made western farmers more prosperous, cutting the power of the moneyed interests. The Good Witch of the North stands for northern voters, whom Bryan had to win over in order to achieve victory. In the end, Dorothy, the lion, and her friends demonstrate their courage, expose the wizard's weakness, are honored in the Emerald City, and return home triumphant.

A good name is to be more desired than great wealth,
Favor is better than silver and gold.
Proverbs 22:1

⋆ Assignments for Lesson 86 ⋆

American Voices Read "America, the Beautiful" by Katherine Lee Bates (page 274).

Read the excerpts from the "Cross of Gold" speech by William Jennings Bryan (pages 278-282).

Literature Begin reading *Up From Slavery*. Plan to finish it by the end of this unit.

Bible In the Bible study lesson for this unit, we will look at the ideas of Sigmund Freud and how they differed from the Biblical understanding of man. To prepare for that lesson, read Romans 7:8-8:13. Here Paul provides the insight that two competing spiritual forces, the way of God (righteousness) and the way of Satan (sin), seek to influence us. The apostle teaches that each person is responsible for his sin; this is why he exhorts people to make the decision to follow Jesus and to keep deciding this day by day. He does not blame his parents or society or his unconscious drives. He recognizes the influences on him but takes the responsibility for his actions. A person overcomes the influence of sin by relying on the saving work of Jesus Christ. In Christ, a person is to set his mind on the things of the Spirit and by the Spirit put to death the deeds of the flesh.

Start memorizing 2 Corinthians 5:20.

Project Choose your project for this unit and start working on it.

Student Review Optional: Answer the questions for Lesson 86.

Feeding Chickens in Georgia (c. 1900)

Lesson 87

Race Relations

Not every American shared in the good life that the changing American culture was offering. Blacks were for the most part unable to enjoy the benefits that were available to whites because of laws and customs that enforced racial segregation and discrimination.

Life for Southern Blacks

In the late 1800s, whites were clearly in control in the South. The Bourbon Democrats who ruled allowed only limited participation by blacks in the political process. Some states had a few black legislators, and various black Congressmen served in Washington until 1900. Blacks in most states were able to vote, but intimidation and unfair application of voting laws limited their turnout in many localities. Although blacks participated to some degree in politics, the line of racial segregation in schools, neighborhoods, rail cars, and hotels was clearly drawn.

The Populist movement of the 1890s frightened southern whites, who feared that a divided white vote would give blacks more power. White politicians began calling for the vote to be taken away from blacks. This could not be done on the basis of race because of the 15th Amendment, but whites found other methods. Residency requirements eliminated migrant farmers who moved often as they were looking for a better life. Conviction for petty crimes meant the loss of the right to vote in some states. States also imposed a poll tax, which had to be paid for a man to be able to vote. The tax was due early in the year, which meant that blacks often did not have the money; or the record of payment could be lost before election day. Voters were required to pass literacy tests to the satisfaction of the registrar, who could apply the law unfairly to blacks. Many states instituted Democratic Party primaries, which allowed only party regulars to vote. Since the whites controlled the party, and since Republican opposition was weak or non-existent in the general election, this was another way to take blacks out of the political process.

These methods took the vote away from many blacks, but they also served to disenfranchise a significant number of poor whites. In 1898 Louisiana introduced the grandfather clause as another way to control who had the right the vote. This law said that, even if a man was illiterate, he could vote if he or his father or grandfather had been eligible to vote on January 1, 1867. Many poor whites qualified under this provision; but since blacks by and large could not vote in 1867, they were not allowed to vote in 1898. Black voter registration fell significantly in the 1890s and early 1900s.

Segregated Society

Blacks faced difficulties in the South, but they were also treated unfairly across much of the country. Racial prejudice was the norm among most white Americans. Most northern cities had laws that kept blacks from living in white neighborhoods and that enforced racial segregation throughout society.

Discrimination by state governments on the basis of race was outlawed by the 14th Amendment. However, corporations and individuals practiced racial segregation on a wide scale. In an 1883 decision dealing with a cluster of civil rights cases, the U.S. Supreme Court ruled that the 14th Amendment applied only to state action and not to individual actions. The Court thus ruled that segregation in the private sector was legal.

Another reality in many states was the practice of providing so-called separate but equal facilities for blacks and whites. Even though the races were segregated, blacks supposedly had equal facilities and opportunities. Many blacks, however, did not accept this arrangement. Homer Plessy, who was one-eighth black, refused to leave a railroad car in Louisiana that was designated as being for whites. He was arrested, and his case eventually came before the Supreme Court. In 1896 the Court ruled in *Plessy v. Ferguson* that maintaining separate facilities for the races was an appropriate policy by state governments in carrying out its police powers. States applied the separate but equal doctrine to restaurants, hospitals, streetcars, and schools. The justification given for this was that blacks had access to their own restaurants, streetcars, and other public facilities and thus should not mix with whites. However, besides the discrimination involved, most black facilities were not equal to facilities available to whites.

One further activity in which some whites participated and which many other whites condoned was the lynching of blacks. Lynching is an execution carried out by a mob outside of the legal system. About two hundred blacks were lynched every year in the 1890s, and about one hundred per year were killed in this way in the first decade of the 1900s. Lynching was a way to intimidate blacks and to punish those whom whites believed had gotten out of line. It was not a big step from believing that all blacks were inferior to believing that certain blacks did not deserve to live.

"Jump Jim Crow" was a song and dance developed in the 1820s by a white comedian who performed in blackface. During the 19th century, "Jim Crow" became a derogatory name for African Americans. Thus "Jim Crow Laws" became the name for the legal segregation of whites and blacks. This 1913 cartoon from Puck *magazine illustrates how the idea of "separate but equal" tended to work in reality.*

Black Response

The black population was not, as a whole, willing to speak out or act against such discrimination and violence. Most blacks were willing to accept their lot, to do the best they could to provide for their families, and to live within black society. Of the blacks who were willing to speak out, two represented differing views.

Booker T. Washington, born before the Civil War as the child of slaves in Virginia, later obtained an education at Hampton (Virginia) Institute. In 1881 Washington helped to found Tuskegee Institute in Alabama. Washington believed that blacks could best help themselves by getting an education, pursuing a trade, and contributing to society in a positive way. He believed that it was more important for a black person to be able to earn a dollar in a factory than to have the right to spend a dollar in an opera house. Washington lamented segregation, but he accepted it. He encouraged blacks to do what they could to improve and advance themselves within the system rather than spend time and energy trying to change the system. He believed that this would be the best course for blacks in the long run. As blacks devoted themselves to good work and good citizenship, Washington believed, they would be accepted by black society and eventually by white society.

W. E. B. Du Bois, on the other hand, was a more radical reformer. A native of Massachusetts, Du Bois was educated at Fisk University in Nashville and at Harvard University. He chafed at the segregation imposed upon blacks, and he urged direct protest and political involvement. Du Bois did not want to accept less than the highest ideals of life, and he believed that blacks deserved true equality in American society. He was willing to agitate for such political and social equality. Du Bois strongly denounced what he called Booker T. Washington's accommodation to the status quo.

W. E. B. Du Bois (1918)

Booker T. Washington (c. 1910)

Both Washington and Du Bois had valid points. Washington, a man of the soil, was concerned with how the individual black might improve his lot. He believed that taking time to agitate for voting rights might not produce any significant change in a black person's life. He also believed that blacks had enough doors open to them to improve themselves and their conditions. However, Du Bois, a man of ideas, was also correct that institutionalized discrimination will not usually go away by itself without being challenged. Washington believed that change would come eventually, step by step. Du Bois wanted immediate and significant change, even if it meant challenging the status quo.

The generation of blacks that grew to maturity after the Civil War learned for themselves that slavery was over but that the effects of slavery and discrimination were still very much a part of American life. This was true in the North as well as the South. It was an issue that would arise again at various times in the twentieth century and is still a factor to some degree today.

These photographs are among the hundreds of portraits which W. E. B. Du Bois presented at the Paris Exposition in 1900. His purpose was to counteract the stereotype of blacks being a poor, uneducated people.

In everything, therefore, treat people the same way you want them to treat you, for this is the Law and the Prophets.
Matthew 7:12

★ Assignments for Lesson 87 ★

American Voices Read Booker T. Washington's "Speech Before the Atlanta Cotton States and International Exposition" (pages 275-277).

Read "Of Booker T. Washington and Others" by W. E. B. Du Bois (pages 285-292).

Read "Sympathy" by Paul Laurence Dunbar (page 283).

Read "Songs for the People" by Frances E. W. Harper (page 184).

Literature Continue reading *Up From Slavery.*

Bible Work on memorizing 2 Corinthians 5:20.

Project Work on your project.

Student Review Optional: Answer the questions for Lesson 87.

Workers at a Tobacco Company in Connecticut, 1917

Lesson 88

The Progressive Movement

By 1900 the Populist movement was dead. Despite its successes, the Populists never captured enough support among Republican and Democratic voters to become a viable political party. However, many people still wanted government to be responsive to the needs of the people. The group that picked up the mantel of reform came to be known as the Progressives. The Progressives achieved what the Populists did not.

A Middle-Class Response

The Progressive movement was largely an uprising by the middle class against what they perceived as evils around them. As a group, Progressives were younger than the average American, so they brought youthful energy to their activism. Progressives were generally more educated and more urban than the Populists and had a stronger appeal to the growing numbers of urban voters than the Populists did. Progressives were on the whole more politically aware and involved than many of those who supported the Populists, and the new movement cut across party lines.

This is not to say that the Populists were bad and the Progressives were good; these are just some of the reasons why the Progressives were able to get much of their agenda enacted into law whereas the Populists did not. No doubt part of the Progressives' success came from their being able to build on the inroads that the Populists had made in American thought.

It is important to remember that, at the time, American society and politics were dominated by big business, its standards, and its money. City politics had become corrupt in many places. Many working men and women received low wages and lived in poor conditions. Hardly any laborer had a pension program or benefited from worker's compensation in the event of an injury on the job. Two million children worked in American factories, many of them at night. One percent of American families owned seven-eighths of the nation's wealth, while ten million Americans lived in poverty. Many people resented the poor level of urban services, the presence of powerful monopolies, and the collusion between business and politics.

Progressives felt within themselves a moral imperative to pursue justice in society. They believed that things could truly be different. They wanted government to take a more active role in defending the average citizen, and they were willing to work to see that their goals were accomplished politically.

The Progressive Agenda

A major interest of Progressives involved how elections and government were conducted. It had become a tradition for political parties to print their own ballots on colored paper. In an election, a voter asked for the ballot of a party and put it in the voting box. It was thus easy for others to see how someone voted. Poorly-qualified candidates were often elected simply by being listed on the winning party's ballot. The secret ballot was developed in Australia and put all candidates on a single sheet which voters marked in secret. Progressives favored this voting reform as well as the practice of direct primaries, in which candidates for political office were chosen by popular elections rather than by a small group of party leaders. Processes called initiative and referendum gave voters the chance to propose and vote directly on new laws. A petition drive with a certain number of signatures could put a measure on the ballot by initiative, and then people would vote on it in a referendum. The recall (pronounced RE-call) allowed the removal of an elected official by a petition drive and then a vote on whether that person should continue in office.

Other election reforms proposed by Progressives included the election of U.S. Senators by popular vote instead of by state legislatures. This became law with a constitutional amendment in 1913. Off-year elections put state and local campaigns in years when a national election was not being held. The thinking of Progressives was that the national campaigns overshadowed local elections and prevented sufficient attention from being given to local candidates. This reform was enacted in many states, but the result was often that local elections drew far fewer voters than the number which participated in national election years. It was a simple fact that the publicity of national elections brought many more voters to the polls. A further Progressive reform proposal was for women to be able to vote (called women's suffrage). This became law in fifteen states before a constitutional amendment was passed in 1920 that established it nationwide.

The Progressives urged changes in local government. The mayor-city council format was replaced in many cities by a commission, in which each commissioner was responsible for a particular area of service (such as police, sanitation, and so forth). The first city to adopt a commission form of government was Galveston, Texas, which was devastated by a hurricane and tidal wave in 1900. The city created the commission form of government because the existing city government did not respond well to the disaster. The commission form made the heads of departments more responsive to the people and made inside dealings by a local political machine more difficult. Another change was the city manager form of local government, where an elected city council hired a professional city manager to carry out the operation of the government. The formation of the National Association of City Managers in 1914 indicated the growth of this approach.

The San Francisco school board voted in 1906 to segregate the city's 97 Japanese students (along with its Chinese and Korean students) away from the Anglo-Saxon students. Japan was insulted by this decision, and President Roosevelt called it "a crime against a friendly nation." He summoned the school board to the White House, and the board later agreed to rescind the order if Japan agreed to limit emigration of peasants and laborers to the United States. Japan agreed to do this. The photo below of a Japanese Tea Garden in San Francisco was taken in 1904.

The Jane Addams Hull-House Museum is housed in two of the original buildings, the Hull-Home (pictured above) and the Residents' Dining Hall. The museum is located on the campus of the University of Illinois at Chicago.

Social and Business Reforms

Progressives pressed for regulations to be enacted regarding child and female labor. One event that propelled this need into the national consciousness was a devastating fire in 1911 at the Triangle Shirtwaist Company in New York. One hundred forty-six people, most of them young women, died in the upper stories of the building because the structure did not have adequate exits. Progressives also sparked movements for limiting normal work days to ten hours and for the creation of a required minimum wage for workers. They called for regulation of business practices, especially the practices of monopolies (since breakup of the monopolies was so hard to achieve), and government regulation or takeover of municipal utilities.

Many people were moved to help those living in crowded tenements. Jane Addams was involved in the founding of Hull House in Chicago in 1889, where people could gather for educational and social events. Similar centers (called tenement houses) were begun in other cities. Addams was also involved in child-labor reform and the promotion of world peace. She won the Nobel Peace Prize in 1931.

Another growing cause during this period was for the prohibition of alcoholic beverages. Temperance groups had been active to some degree for decades, but the movement gained new life because of the devastating effect that drinking had on families, factory workers, and increasingly crowded city neighborhoods. The Women's Christian Temperance Union had been formed in 1874; but the Anti-Saloon League, founded in 1893, was more successful in pressing the issue in states and cities. Congress passed the prohibition amendment in 1913 and it was ratified in 1919; but by the time it became part of the Constitution, prohibition had already been established by state law for three-fourths of the nation's population.

Leading Progressive Spokesmen

One of the foremost champions of the Progressive cause in the early twentieth century was Robert M. ("Fighting Bob") LaFollette of Wisconsin. LaFollette was born in a log cabin, but he graduated from the University of Wisconsin in 1879. Fighting Bob was a Republican who achieved political success in his home state outside of the political machine that controlled politics and favored the lumber and railroad industries. LaFollette was elected governor of Wisconsin in 1900. He broke the power of the machine and oversaw the enactment of new regulations and taxes on railroads and utilities. LaFollette called his approach the Wisconsin Idea, and it gained attention nationwide. LaFollette was elected to the U.S. Senate in 1906 and served there until his death in 1925. He sought the presidential nomination of the Progressive Party in 1912 but lost out to Theodore Roosevelt. He did run as a Progressive in 1924 and received 16.6% of the popular vote and thirteen electoral votes.

Other Progressive leaders included Charles Evans Hughes in New York State, Hiram Johnson in California, and Joseph W. Folk in Missouri. The man who probably did the most to further the Progressive cause nationally was Theodore Roosevelt. Known as a reformer in New York State, where he had been elected governor in 1898, Roosevelt as President brought to the national stage his energy for the causes he championed.

The Muckrakers

The Progressive cause was furthered by journalists and authors who wrote about what they saw as the underside of American life. Theodore Roosevelt gave them their name by comparing them to a character in *Pilgrim's Progress* who could only look down because he had a muckrake in his hands. Muckraking authors investigated scandals and emphasized what was wrong in the United States. Their persistent reporting made many Americans aware that all was not good in American life and business, even though their reporting was not always accurate.

Robert LaFollette Giving a Radio Speech (c. 1922)

Jacob Riis, an immigrant from Denmark, revealed how terrible life was in the slums in *How the Other Half Lives* (1890). Perhaps the first author who could be described as a muckraker was Henry D. Lloyd. Lloyd published *Wealth Against Commonwealth* (1894), a critique of the Standard Oil Company and other monopolies. Ida Tarbell gave a more detailed expose than Lloyd's in *The History of the Standard Oil Company* (1904). Lincoln Steffens described corruption in city governments in *The Shame of the Cities* (1904). Upton Sinclair's novel, *The Jungle* (1906), drew attention to unsanitary conditions that existed in the meat packing industry. Popular magazines that went into millions of homes published articles exposing corruption in government and business.

Efficiency Principles

The adoption of efficiency principles in business was an element of Progressive thought during this time. Frederick W. Taylor pioneered the scientific study of work activity to help companies save money and produce more. His goal was to help employees be more productive and strive to achieve above average results. Management loved efficiency principles, but many workers feared that they would be pressured to work harder than they were able or would be replaced by machinery.

Frank Gilbreth was an internationally-known efficiency expert who tried to apply his scientific principles to his family of twelve children. The book Cheaper by the Dozen, *written by two of his children and published in 1949, describes their family up to the time of their father's death in 1924. After Frank died, his wife, Lillian, pictured at left, took up her husband's cause and became a leading industrial engineer in her own right. She died in 1972.*

This 1906 cartoon from Puck *portrays muckraking journalists as an army of Crusaders. It depicts many prominent authors from the period carrying banners with the names of magazines that featured their articles.*

What Else Was Happening?

1896 *The first modern Olympics are held in Athens, Greece.*

1896 *Adolph Ochs buys the ailing* New York Times. *His motto is, "All the news that's fit to print."*

1897 *William Randolph Hearst authorizes the first comic strip, the Katzenjammer Kids, originally drawn by Rudolph Dirks. A frame from 1901 is shown at right.*

1899 *The Bronx Zoo, largest in the world, opens its gates.*

1900 *Vladimir Lenin, in exile from Russia for revolutionary activities, begins a newspaper to promote his brand of Marxism.*

1900 *The zeppelin airship is unveiled.*

And if you give yourself to the hungry and satisfy the desire of the afflicted,
Then your light will rise in darkness and your gloom will become like midday.
Isaiah 58:10

⋆ Assignments for Lesson 88 ⋆

American Voices Read "Standing on the Promises" by R. Kelso Carter and "Leaning on the Everlasting Arms" by Elisha Hoffman (pages 248-249).

Literature Continue reading *Up From Slavery.*

Bible Work on memorizing 2 Corinthians 5:20.

Project Work on your project.

Student Review Optional: Answer the questions for Lesson 88.

U.S. Soldiers Meet with Local Leaders in the Philippines (c. 1900)

Lesson 89

American Empire

Expansion has been part of American life since the British colonies began. After the founding of the United States, that expansion focused on the North American continent. For over a century, America was not greatly interested in colonies because America had once been a colony herself; and the country stood for the principles of independence and democracy. Besides, the territories in the western part of the country appeared to provide the U.S. with all of the land it would ever need.

In the mid-1800s, however, American interest began to turn to lands beyond its borders. Secretary of State William Seward had a great desire for expansion. It was during his tenure under President Andrew Johnson that the United States purchased Alaska and took over the Midway Islands in the Pacific. Social Darwinists justified colonization as an example of the survival of the fittest on a world scale.

Paralleling this economic and political interest, many Christians felt a missionary zeal to teach the gospel to the lost in every nation. Missionaries were sent out in large numbers in the late 1800s. Congregationalist minister Josiah Strong wrote *Our Country: Its Possible Future and Its Present Crisis* in 1885. Strong proposed that, as Anglo-Saxons, Americans had a divine mission to teach a pure Christianity and to be their brother's keeper around the world. By 1900 an estimated 18,000 American missionaries were serving around the world.

In 1890 Captain Alfred T. Mahan published *The Influence of Sea Power upon History, 1660-1783*, in which he argued that, historically, national greatness depended upon a powerful navy and merchant marine. Such a navy, he said, needed secure fueling ports around the world. Mahan believed that an American naval force would be especially strengthened by a greater presence in the Caribbean. In the 1880s and early 1890s, the U.S. government took steps to build up its fleet of warships.

The United States was not alone in developing an interest in a world empire. During the latter half of the nineteenth century, several other nations, including Great Britain, Germany, the Netherlands, Spain, Belgium, and Japan, expended great resources in building or strengthening foreign empires. Many people believed that the possession of colonies was an indication of national greatness.

Probably the greatest impetus toward involvement in foreign affairs was economic. The U.S. (along with other empire-building nations) was experiencing phenomenal industrial growth. The increasing number of factories created an immense demand for raw materials that could be used to produce finished goods. In addition, manufacturers looked for new markets for their finished products. Secure foreign colonies seemed to offer that possibility. The American public for the most part supported this increasing push for building a foreign empire.

Early Forays

American interest in Pacific trade increased after completion of the transcontinental railroad in 1869. The U.S. government and private companies negotiated for a naval base and refueling station on the island of Samoa, but Great Britain and Germany also wanted access to the island. After many years of jockeying for control, the U.S. and Germany divided the island while Great Britain took the Gilbert and Solomon Islands.

Statue of Queen Liliuokalani, Hawaii State Capitol

Another target of American interest were the Hawaiian Islands, then an independent country. American businessmen had developed sugar cane and pineapple industries on the islands, and many American missionaries were present. The Americans on the islands had a sizable influence in Hawaiian political affairs. In 1887 the U.S. obtained the rights to maintain a naval base at Pearl Harbor near Honolulu. However, the Hawaiian government was unstable and inconsistent in its treatment of American interests. In 1892 Queen Liliuokalani revoked the special privileges that whites enjoyed. The Americans on the islands responded by overthrowing the queen and her government early the next year with the support of the American minister and a unit of U.S. Marines stationed on a ship nearby.

The new American-controlled government of Hawaii asked that the U.S. annex the islands, hoping to avoid a tariff on sugar and other products sent to the U.S. President Cleveland refuse to agree to the annexation, and the debate over what to do continued until 1898. Many saw Hawaii as providing a crucial base for strengthening American operations in the Pacific. Many newspapers supported taking over the islands. Bryan endorsed it in 1896. McKinley opposed annexation during the campaign but changed his mind once in office. The islands were finally annexed in July of 1898 after the Spanish-American War had demonstrated the benefits of an American presence in the Pacific.

Cuba

Closer to home, the island of Cuba had suffered under years of misrule by Spain as a last vestige of Spain's world empire. The Cubans attempted to revolt from time to time, only to be cruelly suppressed by Spain. At the same time, American interest in the island grew, particularly because of Americans' involvement in sugar-growing and mining. The 1890 McKinley Tariff allowed Cuban sugar to be

The life and newspaper career of William Randolph Hearst inspired Orson Welles' classic 1941 film Citizen Kane. *The photo of Hearst above is from 1906.*

imported duty-free, but the 1894 Wilson-Gorman Tariff tacked on a 40% tariff, which severely hurt the sugar industry. As sugar piled up in Cuban warehouses and as poverty on the island increased, so did revolutionary unrest. An 1895 revolt gained wide support in America, influenced by an effective propaganda operation conducted by the Cuban Revolutionary Party that was based in New York City. Sympathetic newspapers such as the *New York World* and William Randolph Hearst's *New York Journal* played up the unrest and the suffering endured by impoverished Cubans under Spanish rule. This kind of reporting that advocated a cause was called yellow journalism.

The Spanish response to the revolt included sending General Valeriano ("Butcher") Weyler to Cuba, who rounded up civilians and put them in detention camps that had poor food and unsanitary conditions. American public opinion increasingly supported the revolutionaries and favored American military involvement. President McKinley resisted for as long as he could the rising tide of public opinion calling for American intervention. The President put diplomatic pressure on Spain, which recalled Weyler and promised to give Cuba the same autonomy that Canada had in the British Empire.

Pressure for War

In early 1898, Hearst published a letter from the Spanish minister in the U.S. to a friend in Cuba, in which he criticized McKinley as a weak leader. The letter had been stolen from the mail by a Cuban spy. To show that the U.S. was serious about bringing about a settlement to the Cuban situation, McKinley sent the battleship USS *Maine* to Havana harbor.

Evangelina Cossío y Cisneros, involved in the Cuban resistance, was imprisoned by the Spanish. Hearst sent one of his reporters, Karl Decker, to Cuba to secure her release. Working with U.S. and Cuban authorities, Decker helped the young woman escape from prison and come to the United States in 1897. Hearst played up the story, which helped sway American opinion against Spain.

A few days after the letter was published, the *Maine* blew up, resulting in the loss of 266 men (eight others died later from injuries they had received). The explosion of ammunition on the ship caused it to sink. The explosion might have been accidental, but many in the U.S. blamed Spain. Pressure for war with Spain grew intense as newspapers called on the nation to "Remember the Maine!" McKinley wanted to avoid war, but his political advisors doubted that he could be re-elected if he continued to resist the war fever.

In late March, the President demanded an armistice in the on-going fighting in Cuba between rebels and loyalist forces. McKinley also called for the closing of detention centers and for Cuban independence. The President was drafting a war message to send to Congress when Spain agreed to the first two demands. Spain was not, however, willing to agree to independence for Cuba. On April 20, 1898, Congress passed a joint resolution declaring Cuba to be independent and authorizing the use of force to remove the Spanish from Cuba. The Teller Amendment to the resolution pledged that the U.S. would withdraw from Cuba when independence had been established. McKinley ordered a naval blockade of Cuba. In response, Spain declared war on the U.S; and then the United States declared war on Spain.

"A Splendid Little War"

Assistant Secretary of the Navy Theodore Roosevelt had earlier taken advantage of the absence of his boss to order Commodore George Dewey in the Pacific to attack the Philippines, another Spanish possession, if war erupted. Responding to the official declaration of war, Dewey sailed into Manila Bay on April 30, 1898, and quickly destroyed the Spanish fleet. However, he had no land invasion force at his disposal; so he had to wait for troops from the U.S., who brought about the surrender of the Philippines on August 13.

Meanwhile, American forces prepared to invade Cuba. The standing American Army consisted of about 30,000 men who were poorly equipped and scattered throughout the country. Numerous volunteers swelled the Army's numbers. The volunteers included Roosevelt, who resigned his post in the Navy Department to lead a unit of Rough Riders into Cuba. The American assault on Santiago, Cuba, included the taking of San Juan Hill (led by Roosevelt), which gave the Americans a strong position overlooking the harbor. The Spanish fleet tried to escape but was decimated by American firepower on July 3. The Spanish garrison at Santiago surrendered on July 17. The U.S. also took Puerto Rico from the Spanish.

The photo at left below shows the crew of the USS Maine *before its sinking. At right below is the telegram sent to the Secretary of the Navy notifying him of the explosion and destruction of the ship.*

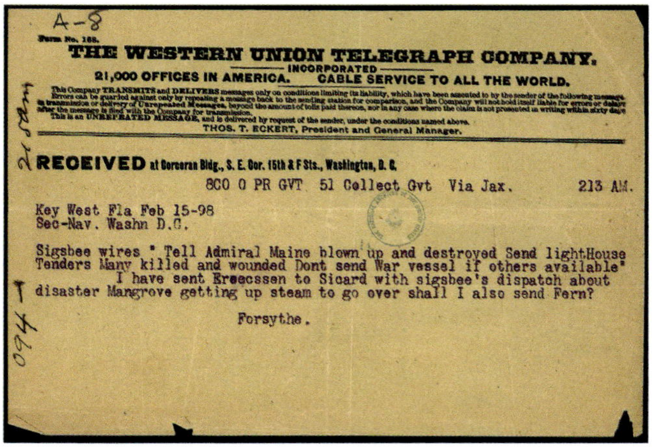

A-8

Form No. 168.

THE WESTERN UNION TELEGRAPH COMPANY.

INCORPORATED

21,000 OFFICES IN AMERICA. CABLE SERVICE TO ALL THE WORLD.

This Company TRANSMITS and DELIVERS messages only on conditions limiting its liability, which have been assented to by the sender of the following message. Errors can be guarded against only by repeating a message back to the sending station for comparison, and the Company will not hold itself liable for errors or delays in transmission or delivery of Unrepeated Messages, beyond the amount of tolls paid thereon, nor in any case where the claim is not presented in writing within sixty days after the message is filed with the Company for transmission.
This is an UNREPEATED MESSAGE, and is delivered by request of the sender, under the conditions named above.

THOS. T. ECKERT, President and General Manager.

RECEIVED at Corcoran Bldg., S. E. Cor. 15th & F Sts., Washington, D. C.

8CO 0 PR GVT 51 Collect Gvt Via Jax. 213 AM.

Key West Fla Feb 15-98
Sec-Nav. Washn D.C.

Sigsbee wires " Tell Admiral Maine blown up and destroyed Send lightHouse Tenders Many killed and wounded Dont send War vessel if others available"
I have sent Ereecssen to Sicard with sigsbee's dispatch about disaster Mangrove getting up steam to go over shall I also send Fern?

Forsythe.

The Rough Riders, *Mort Künstler (American, 1984)*

An armistice was signed on August 12. The Treaty of Paris that officially ended the war was signed in late 1898. Spain gave the United States Cuba and Puerto Rico in the Caribbean as well as Guam and the Philippines in the Pacific Ocean. The United States agreed to pay Spain $20 million. During the hostilities, American forces had also landed on and claimed Wake Island in the Pacific. Future Secretary of State John Hay, who helped negotiate the treaty that ended the conflict, wrote to Theodore Roosevelt, "It has been a splendid little war." American casualties included 450 killed in action and another 5,200 who died of disease.

American policy toward Cuba was determined by the Teller Amendment, but the question of what to do with the Philippines was still open. American businessmen pressed for taking control of the country as a base for Pacific trade and military operations. McKinley agonized over what to do; but finally, he said, he went to his knees in prayer and determined that God's will was for the U.S. to protect, train, and convert the Philippine people (even though the majority were already Catholic). Spanish rule in the Philippines had actually been more harsh than in Cuba. McKinley tested public opinion before instructing the treaty negotiators to demand complete control of all the islands.

The Treaty of Paris was ratified by the Senate in 1899 on a close vote. Democratic Senator William Jennings Bryan urged approval of the treaty in the hope that Cuba and the Philippines would one day be independent. He believed (incorrectly) that imperialism would be a major issue in the 1900 presidential campaign. America took over the Philippines, but it encountered continued resistance to foreign rule by many of the people there. Filipinos fought a costly war against American troops until 1902. An American government was set up on July 4, 1901, with William Howard Taft as civil governor. The Philippines were granted independence in 1946.

Puerto Rico was given a civil government in 1900. Its people became American citizens in 1917. Puerto Rico became America's only commonwealth in 1952. It rules itself as long as it creates no conflict with the U.S. Constitution.

Cuba benefited from the American presence there, especially in terms of improved public health and education. The U.S. moved toward granting independence to Cuba, but the Platt Amendment to a 1901 Army appropriations bill attached strings to that independence. The Platt Amendment required that Cuba could never impair its independence by making a treaty with a third nation. Cuba had to allow American intervention to protect Cuban independence, and Cuba was also required to sell or lease land for an American base on the island. This allowed for the creation of the U.S. base at Guantanamo Bay, which the United States still owns.

The U.S. began 1898 with the Midway Islands as its only overseas possession. A year later, it owned a worldwide empire and began to feel the benefits—and headaches—of being a developing world power. During this period the country also extended its interests into other areas, especially in Asia. Over a period of about ten years, the United States went from a nation mostly content within

Milkman in Cuba (c. 1905)

Frank S. Nicholson created this promotional poster around 1940 as part of a Federal art project started during the Great Depression.

itself to a nation with the second-largest navy in the world and a significant presence in Asia and Central America. Involvement in Europe would come in the second decade of the twentieth century. The events of this period made the United States a major player in international relations, a role that continues to this day.

Herbert and Lou Hoover married on February 10, 1899, in California. The next day they sailed for China, where Herbert began working for the Chinese government in the mining industry. The next year they were among the international residents caught in the crossfire of the Boxer Rebellion. Later, when Herbert became President of the United States, they spoke to each other in Mandarin Chinese when they did not want others to eavesdrop on them.

China

The United States had been a trading partner with China since 1784, and the two countries had grown especially close since the 1840s. During the last half of the nineteenth century, European nations seeking to build empires (notably Great Britain, Germany, France, and Russia) as well as Japan had operated in mutually-recognized spheres of influence in China for their respective benefit.

In 1899 Great Britain began refusing to pay export tariffs to China. This refusal threatened the revenues of the already-weak Chinese government. The United States feared that if the Chinese government fell, European nations would carve up China as pieces of their respective empires and push the U.S. out of the picture. America insisted that all nations respect the rights of China and of each other. Fearing any imbalance of power, all the nations involved agreed, with the exception of Japan. The United States was not interested in controlling any area of China, but the American government wanted to protect its economic interests and trading rights with the country. The American position was announced by Secretary of State John Hay and became known as the Open Door policy because it encouraged an open door to all nations wanting to do business with China.

Meanwhile, a group of ultranationalist Chinese attempted to drive out the presence and influence of all of the "foreign devils" who had taken control of their country. In the spring of 1900, the Boxers, as westerners called the group, attacked and killed some 300 foreigners in northern China. They then besieged the foreign settlement in Tientsin and the British legation in Beijing. The foreign nations involved in China rushed troops to the area. This included some 2,500 American troops. The combined forces rescued the besieged foreigners, although 65 of them were killed in the conflict.

This Japanese print from 1900 illustrates the eight nations allied against the Boxers in China: Japan, Britain, Russia, France, Germany, Austria-Hungary, Italy, and the United States.

Troop L of the 6th U.S. Cavalry at the Great Wall (1900)

The colonial powers in China wanted to take control of the situation lest something worse occur, but the United States insisted on protecting Chinese territorial integrity. No land was taken over by a foreign power, but China was required to pay about $333 million in damages to the foreign countries who claimed losses as a result of the rebellion. This included about $24 million to the United States. The U.S. turned most of this money over to citizens who had lost property in China and returned the rest to China. China in turn used the money to send thousands of students to American colleges.

He says, "It is too small a thing that You should be My Servant
To raise up the tribes of Jacob and to restore the preserved ones of Israel;
I will also make You a light of the nations
So that My salvation may reach to the end of the earth."
Isaiah 49:6

⋆ Assignments for Lesson 89 ⋆

American Voices Read "Anywhere With Jesus" by Jessie Brown Pounds and "Faith Is the Victory" by John Henry Yates and Ira D. Sankey (pages 250 and 253).

Literature Continue reading *Up From Slavery.*

Bible Work on memorizing 2 Corinthians 5:20.

Project Work on your project.

Student Review Optional: Answer the questions for Lesson 89.

1911 International Psychoanalytic Congress (Freud in Center)

God and Freud

Just as Charles Darwin's theories changed the way people look at the world around us, the work of Sigmund Freud (1856-1939) changed the way people look at the world within us. Freud was a medical doctor in Vienna, Austria, who specialized in treating nervous diseases. His studies of patients led to the founding of the modern practice of psychoanalysis. He published *The Interpretation of Dreams* (1899) and several other books.

Elements of Freud's Theories

Freud believed that an individual's personality is divided into three parts. The *id* is the "want to" part, which expresses the desires of the person. The opposite of the *id* is the *superego*, which is the "ought to" aspect of a person's thinking. Freud believed that the *superego* is not a God-given conscience guided by eternal truth, but instead consists of the moral expectations imposed on individuals by society. Mediating between the "want to" and the "ought to" is a person's *ego*, which is a person's awareness of reality.

In a challenge to the accepted Enlightenment view of man as essentially reasonable, Freud said that man is essentially irrational, guided by subconscious mental processes. Freud believed that mental actions were merely physical, biological mechanisms. He did not recognize the spiritual realm (Dan Blazer, *Freud vs. God*, Downers Grove, Illinois: Inter-Varsity, 1998, p. 65). Although he was reared in a practicing Jewish home, Freud was convinced that religion had no objective validity and that no evidence of a transcendent reality existed (ibid., p. 67). Religion in Freud's judgment was merely a result of human needs and desires. To Freud, God was a human mental construct, the longed-for father. In other words, man created God, not the other way around.

Psychiatry and psychology have moved beyond Freud as other theories, such as behaviorism, have been proposed. Not many psychiatrists and counselors today see themselves as pure Freudians, just as not many scientists see themselves as pure Darwinians. Nevertheless, the work of Freud is still the starting point for much of the study, discussion, and treatment of disorders of the mind.

The Impact of Freud's Theories

As with Darwin, Freudian theory has changed the playing field on which humans operate. Many of Freud's ideas have come to be accepted as unquestioned assumptions. The revolution that Freud began has created a new vocabulary and thought structure in which believers and unbelievers alike operate, almost without thinking about it (unconsciously if not subconsciously!). Religion once taught people to think in terms of sin, guilt, responsibility, demons, and forgiveness. Secular psychiatry and psychology, on the other hand, uses terms like depression, schizophrenia, neuroses, and chemical imbalances. Even the fields of Christian psychiatry and psychology have taken many Freudian constructs and adapted Biblical and traditional Christian teaching to them.

Freudian theory has also changed how we determine responsibility for a person's actions. Psychological struggles that a person has within himself are explained as his parents' fault or perhaps as society's fault. This tends to remove from an individual the responsibility for his actions. Religion, with its teaching of individual moral responsibility, is often seen as a cause of the problem, not the solution.

Sigmund Freud, About Age 16, With His Mother Amalia (1872)

Another result of Freud's influence is that Christians often go to the Bible to find answers for questions it does not address. For instance, the Bible does not use such terms as personality, self-image, and depression. The Bible might talk about them in some way, but not in the terms and constructs used today. If trying to use the Bible to address modern psychological problems sometimes seems a bit forced, it could be because we are approaching it with assumptions that come not from Scripture but from Freud and Freudian-influenced modern thinking.

Freudian psychiatry can even affect how we look at history. William Bullitt, an advisor to President Woodrow Wilson during the negotiations on the Treaty of Versailles that ended World War I, wrote a book that psychoanalyzed Wilson's actions regarding the treaty. The opening essay in the book was written by Sigmund Freud, who explained his ideas not as theories but as facts. When Bullitt described Wilson's words and actions regarding the treaty, not too surprisingly he saw them as evidence of the supposed subconscious forces Bullitt was looking for!

Challenges to Freud

The perspective of faith holds that God is real and that we are made in His image as spiritual beings. Religion is not a human construct but is the reality of man approaching his God. The spiritual realm does exist. We are responsible before God for how we live our lives. We have a conscience, a God-given capacity to know right and wrong. The conscience must be trained, and the beliefs and practices of others influence the conscience; but humans are answerable to more than just the standards of society. The Christian faith holds that belief in God and obedience to His way are the answer to one's problems and inner turmoil.

Freud's House and Office in Vienna, Austria, Now Houses a Museum

We can easily see the impact of home and early childhood experiences on a person's behavior. Parents do have a profound effect on the lives, minds, and well-being of children. This confirms what the Bible says about training up a child in the way he should go (Proverbs 22:6) and about the sins of the father being visited on the children to the third and fourth generations (Exodus 34:6-7). However, each person has the responsibility to overcome his background and environment and to be responsible before God for his or her own actions (Ezekiel 18:4, 2 Corinthians 5:10).

Yes, much wrong has been done in the name of religion. Many children have been taught to feel excessive guilt because of overbearing parents who used religion as a club for discipline. Exceptions and imperfect human practice, however, are not a basis for determining God's truth and how it applies to our lives.

Freudian psychiatry affects how we view God and how we view ourselves. If your goal is only to be the best you can be on earth, you will probably be influenced by society's standards of right and wrong. If this is your goal, you will be guided by self-interest: what works for you and what brings you pleasure. If, on the other hand, you live on earth with the goal of reaching heaven, you will be guided by God's standards, which teach us to do what is best for others even at one's own expense.

Another Attempt to Eliminate God

One appeal of the ideas of both Darwin and Freud to many people is that they seem to eliminate the need for God. In their theories, everything can be explained scientifically and materially without recourse to a Creator. This takes away personal responsibility and any morality that is based on eternal truth. People often don't want to think about God or to be responsible for their actions. Darwin and Freud gave people encouragement to do this. Their theories say that it is healthier and more correct not to think about God.

Everything that is true comes from God, whether it is discovered or published by a believer or by an infidel. We can learn from and be helped by many different sources without taking them as the final authority. The Christian's task is not to filter the Bible through modern psychiatry but to filter modern psychiatry and every other field of human study through the Bible. We need to remember that God's teachings have been guiding people effectively and creating happy, well-adjusted, purposeful, fulfilling lives for thousands of years, while Freud's teachings have been around for just over one hundred years and have already been challenged and amended. Theories come and go and are repeatedly modified, "but the word of our God stands forever" (Isaiah 40:8).

God created man in His own image, in the image of God He created him;
male and female He created them.
Genesis 1:27

⋆ Assignments for Lesson 90 ⋆

Literature Finish reading *Up From Slavery.* Literary analysis available in *Student Review.*

Bible Recite or write 2 Corinthians 5:20 from memory.

Project Complete your project for the unit.

Student Review Optional: Answer the questions for Lesson 90 and for *Up From Slavery* and take the quiz for Unit 18.

New York, *George Bellows (American, 1911)*

19 The Triumph of Progressivism

Theodore Roosevelt was a progressive Republican who wanted to use the power of the Federal government for the good of the nation. The trend of reform continued into the Taft and Wilson Administrations. The late nineteenth century and early twentieth century was a period of tremendous innovation and change. One key example of this was the construction of the Panama Canal. The division in society between conservative and liberal, traditional versus modern, extended into churches, with the result that several groups suffered splits and Christendom became even more divided.

Memory Work

Memorize 1 Timothy 6:20-21 by the end of this unit.

Books Used

The Bible
American Voices
Mama's Bank Account

Project (choose one)

1) Write 300 to 500 words on one of the following topics:

- What is the Christian's responsibility toward the environment? What is the proper Biblical balance between taking God's Creation for granted and worshiping it as a deity? See Lesson 92.

- Express your own beliefs about one of the religious liberal/conservative debates discussed in Lesson 95.

2) Create a sculpture that celebrates the age of invention as discussed in Lesson 93.

3) Create a magazine as if it were published in 1900. Choose the audience for your magazine—women, men, youth, young children, ministers, farmers, homemakers, etc. Create a variety of illustrations, features, fiction, poetry, articles, and advertisements that reflect life in 1900. Your magazine should be a minimum of ten pages, including a cover. See the discussion of magazines in Lesson 91.

Literature

Mama's Bank Account

In *Mama's Bank Account*, Katherine Forbes tells stories about a Norwegian immigrant family in San Francisco in the early 1900s. The incidents that Forbes relates are funny, touching, and thought-provoking; but they always weave their way back to Mama. We see something of the subculture in which immigrants lived as they tried to make a new life in America. The book was published in 1943. It was adapted into a Broadway play the next year and made into an excellent movie in 1948. The theatrical and movie versions were entitled *I Remember Mama*. Plan to finish the book by the end of this unit.

State Street, Chicago (1900)

Lesson 91

America in 1900

As the nineteenth century came to a close in 1900, the United States stretched from coast to coast and consisted of forty-five states. Utah was the last state to have entered the Union, having been admitted in 1896. Oklahoma, Arizona, New Mexico, Alaska, and Hawaii were still territories. The U.S. census and other sources of statistical information offer us some insights into the nature of American life in that landmark year.

Population

The official population of the United States in 1900 was 76,212,168. A century earlier, the nation had been home to about 5.3 million persons. Today, over three hundred million people reside in this country.

The 1900 population figure was an indication of the period's rapid growth. The 1900 number reflected a 21% increase over the 1890 census. The 1890 total was 25% higher than the 1880 count, which in turn was 26% more than the 1870 figure. This growth was based primarily on three factors: more women were giving birth to babies, more of those babies survived infancy, and the influx of immigrants into the country was significant. The racial makeup of the American population included 66.8 million whites and 8.8 million blacks. Just under a quarter million residents were Native Americans, and about 115,000 were of Asian descent.

About one-third of the U.S. population in 1900 was either foreign-born or the children of those who were born in another country. Some 13.6% of the population (or about one out of every seven persons) had been born in another land. This indicates the profound impact that immigration was having on the nation.

In 1900 the United States was still predominantly a rural nation. Sixty percent of the population lived in communities of 2,500 or less. The population of five states was over 90% rural. However, as we indicated in an earlier lesson, cities were becoming the defining feature of American life. This can be seen by the fact that in 1860, 83% of the population had lived in communities of 2,500 population or smaller. Between 1880 and 1900, the country's rural population increased by just under ten million persons, while urban population during the same period increased by over sixteen million.

Only three U.S. cities had a population greater than one million in 1900. The five largest cities were New York City (3.4 million), Chicago (1.7 million), Philadelphia (1.3 million), St. Louis (575,238), and Boston (560,892). Los Angeles registered 102,479 residents in the 1900 census.

California Ranch Family (c. 1900)

The life expectancy for the average American in 1900 was only 47.3 years, which reflects the significant impact of disease, infant mortality, and dangerous work conditions. The life expectancy in America today is about 78.6 years. In 1900 about 4% of the population was 65 and over. Today that figure is 13%.

The Working World

In 1900 the United States had the largest industrial output of any country in the world. The nation had achieved this status in 1894, having grown rapidly since the end of the Civil War. A major factor in this growth was the production of steel, which proved to be a superior product to iron. Steel was important in many aspects of the growing American economy, including the building of railroads (both rail lines and rail cars), girders for the construction of buildings, and the rapidly expanding market for urban streetcars. In 1865 the country had about 35,000 miles of railroad track. By 1900 that total had increased to 193,000 miles. In 1920 the total track mileage in the country reached its high point of 260,000 miles.

Another growing industry was petroleum. Oil drawn from the ground was refined to produce kerosene, a widely-used lighting and heating product. In the early twentieth century, the combination of steel production, the refining of gasoline from oil, and the manufacturing of automobiles would bring about explosive growth in these and related industries.

The barons of industry profited greatly from this growth in the American economy. The opportunity for work and the average wage that workers earned were increasing in the boom. The standard of living was getting higher for many Americans. However, the workers did not share in the bounty as much as they would have liked. It was not uncommon for steel mill workers to put in 84-hour weeks (working six days per week, fourteen hours per day). Other factory workers usually worked twelve-hour days and 60-hour work weeks. Construction workers usually were expected to work 48 hours per week.

Despite these long hours, the average annual income for non-farm workers was $490.00. This average includes clerical and all other positions, many of which paid less than factory jobs. The cost of living in 1900 was about one-twentieth what it is today, so a $490.00 annual income in 1900 would be approximately the same as an income of $9,800.00 in today's dollars. This is about what the Federal government today considers the poverty level to be for an individual, and it is about one-half of the current poverty level income for a family of four.

Workers in a New England Cotton Mill (c. 1900)

Compare this turn-of-the-century image of Manhattan with the one on page 420 to see how New York City had changed over a period of 25 years.

In addition, workers in 1900 had few benefits. Social Security did not exist, and practically no companies offered retirement plans or health insurance benefits for the average worker. This meant that many families faced hard decisions. Either they did without, or the father worked two jobs, or the wife and children had to contribute to the family's income. Unions had not become strong enough to have much of an impact on the pay and working conditions of most Americans.

Education

Americans showed an increased interest in public education during this period. The push was influenced by the desire to teach new immigrants and to prepare the next generation for the changing world around them. The biggest change came with the increase in the number of public high schools. Before 1900 most public schooling ended with the eighth grade, and high schools were rare. State funding for public education was the exception, not the rule. During the early twentieth century, state funding for education became the norm.

Students Cutting Paper into Leaf Shapes (c. 1900)

An emerging leader in this new push for education was John Dewey. Dewey was born in 1859. He received a doctorate from Johns Hopkins University in 1884 and began teaching at the University of Chicago in 1894. In 1904 he began a career at Columbia University in New York. His first major work on education was *The School and Society*, published in 1899. Many Americans at the time were attracted to the philosophy of pragmatism, which holds that people should do whatever works in order to achieve their stated goals. The more extreme proponents of pragmatism reject absolute truth and believe that whatever works should be considered true. John Dewey wanted to move education away from classical academic studies and to make more of a connection between education and life because he believed that this was pragmatically the best thing to do given that day and time. Dewey was one of the first proponents of a school-to-work approach to education. The traditional educational approach attempted to prepare a person for living a well-rounded, values-based, responsible adult life. Dewey's method was based more on expedience. A major emphasis among educators became the designing of pragmatic educational programs that would equip students to hold jobs in the American workplace rather than to teach students to think for themselves and to become independent businessmen, civic leaders, and homemakers. Dewey's philosophy had a profound influence on American education in the twentieth century.

The Chautauqua Auditorium in Shelbyville, Illinois, is a twenty-sided wooden building 150 feet in diameter. Built in 1903, it has a special roof truss system that does not require any interior columns. Even with a full house of 6,000 people, every audience member had a clear view of the stage.

The increased demand for more and better trained public school teachers was an impetus for the founding of more colleges and universities. Before this time, most universities had specialized in teaching the classic liberal arts curriculum that nearly all students at the university took. Now, colleges broadened their offerings; and students created their own programs of study by choosing electives. Women were permitted to enroll in more colleges, and universities specifically for women were begun.

Graduate education also received increased attention, based largely on the model of German universities. Johns Hopkins University, which opened in 1876, was dedicated to research and graduate studies. Colleges also began professional training programs in fields such as medicine and architecture. These programs helped the public identify professionals who had received adequate training. They also helped professionals by controlling the number of people who entered those fields.

The Chautauqua Movement and efforts similar to it brought education to the general public. In the summer of 1874, a businessman and minister organized a two-week program of sermons, Bible lessons, and uplifting messages for Sunday School teachers at Lake Chautauqua in New York State. The event was so popular that it was repeated in succeeding years and expanded to include presentations on science, economics, and literature. The Chautauqua Reading Circle became a national organization, and Chautauqua speakers and similar programs spread around the country. By 1900 some 200 groups sent speakers into many communities, where people eagerly turned out to hear lectures on various subjects or to be entertained with humor and music.

Newspapers and Magazines

The total circulation of newspapers increased faster than the growth of the population during this period. Inventions such as the linotype machine and improved printing presses as well as businesses wanting to advertise their products in newspapers helped spur the growth. Joseph Pulitzer built a financially successful newspaper chain that specialized in playing up sensational human interest stories and scandals. News services such as the Associated Press supplied national and world news to local papers.

Popular magazines such as the Atlantic Monthly *and* Ladies' Home Journal *also grew in circulation. In 1900* Ladies' Home Journal *became the first magazine to have 1,000,000 subscribers. Edward Bok, a Dutch immigrant, edited the magazine from 1889 to 1919. His autobiography,* The Americanization of Edward Bok, *is a fascinating account of life in America and Bok's correspondence and encounters with many famous Americans. His book received a Pulitzer Prize, first awarded in 1917 based on the instructions Joseph Pulitzer left in his will.*

The fear of the Lord is the beginning of knowledge;
Fools despise wisdom and instruction.
Proverbs 1:7

⋆ Assignments for Lesson 91 ⋆

American Voices Read "This Is My Father's World" by Maltbie Babcock (page 284).

Literature Begin reading *Mama's Bank Account.* Plan to finish it by the end of this unit.

Bible In the Bible study lesson for this unit we will consider the conflict between liberal theology and traditional theology that affected American Christianity around the beginning of the twentieth century. Read 2 Timothy 1.

Start memorizing 1 Timothy 6:20-21.

Project Choose your project for this unit and start working on it.

Student Review Optional: Answer the questions for Lesson 91.

President Theodore Roosevelt (1907)

Lesson 92

T. R. and Taft

Six months after William McKinley's second inauguration, the President visited the Pan-American Exposition in Buffalo, New York, which was a celebration of the new century. As he received visitors at a reception on September 6, 1901, an anarchist, Leon Czolgosz, approached. His heavily bandaged right hand concealed a gun, and Czolgosz shot McKinley twice at close range. After the shooting, McKinley saw people subduing his attacker and called out, "Don't let them hurt him." The President died eight days later.

For the third time in thirty-six years, America was plunged into mourning over the assassination of a chief executive. The new President, Theodore Roosevelt, was forty-two years old when he took office, the youngest man ever to do so. He continued the Republican dynasty; but his personality, policies, and perspectives brought a new style to Washington and ushered in the heyday of the Progressive Era.

Roosevelt's Background

Theodore Roosevelt was born in 1858 to a wealthy family in New York City. Sickly with asthma as a youth, he built up his physical strength by the strength of his will. He studied at Harvard and became fascinated with history and politics. Roosevelt eventually wrote several books on those subjects. While he was serving in the New York state legislature, tragedy struck. Within hours, in the same house, his mother died and then his wife died after giving birth to a daughter. Roosevelt's father had died while Theodore was a student at Harvard.

Roosevelt left it all and lived on a cattle ranch in the Dakota Territory for most of the next two years, enjoying the strenuous life he yearned for and idealized. He then returned to New York, remarried, ran for mayor of New York City, and lost. President Harrison appointed him to the U.S. Civil Service Commission. Following this, he was New York City Police Commissioner (when he would sometimes roam the streets with police patrols at night in a dark cloak) and then became Assistant Secretary of the Navy. Roosevelt left his job in the Navy Department in 1898 to organize the Rough Riders cavalry unit that fought in Cuba during the Spanish-American War.

Later in 1898, Roosevelt was elected governor of New York. In 1900 the Republican Party tapped him to be William McKinley's running mate as their vice presidential nominee. In September 1901, Roosevelt became President upon McKinley's death.

Roosevelt was energetic, eloquent, bold, and zealous for what he believed to be right. He was also a classic politician who was willing to compromise to get at least half a loaf rather than nothing. His presidency gave the Progressive movement a strong national leader.

Labor Unions

Less than a year after Roosevelt took office, the United Mine Workers (UMW) union struck coal mines in Pennsylvania and West Virginia. They demanded a nine-hour workday (down from the prevailing ten hours), a 20% wage increase, better working conditions, and the right to be recognized and negotiate contracts as a union. Management, however, refused to negotiate.

As the strike dragged on through 1902, many Americans feared a coal shortage for the coming winter. The price of coal went from $5.00 per ton to $30.00 per ton. The President came under intense pressure to break the strike with Federal troops the way Cleveland had handled the Pullman Strike in 1894; but Roosevelt refused. Instead, he called both sides to the White House to suggest binding arbitration to settle the dispute. The management representative refused to speak to the union representative, which infuriated Roosevelt. The President threatened to send in Army troops, not to break the strike but to operate the mines for the good of the nation. With that threat, management finally agreed to negotiate. Mine owners accepted the nine-hour workday and offered a 10% raise, but they refused to budge on other demands. The union accepted the offer and went back to work.

The significance of the coal strike settlement was that, for the first time, the Federal government had acted on behalf of union interests as well as on behalf of management. Roosevelt's summoning of the UMW representative to the White House was tacit recognition of the union's right to exist.

Working Americans made definite progress during the Roosevelt years. Between 1897 and 1914, wages rose 37% and the average workweek fell from sixty hours to fifty. However, unions did suffer some defeats. For instance, the hatters union called for a nationwide boycott against a hatmaker in Danbury, Connecticut. The company sued the union, saying that the boycott was a restraint of trade and violated the Sherman Antitrust Act. In 1908 the U.S. Supreme Court said that the boycott did indeed restrain trade and ordered the union to pay damages to the company.

The American Federation of Labor was strongly opposed by the National Association of Manufacturers, which was made up mostly of smaller companies who wanted to resist hiring union workers. Some companies even used intimidation and violence to limit the influence of unions. Labor unions wanted the protection of Federal law to organize and to engage in other tactics, but such legislation was not forthcoming.

This 1902 cartoon portrays Roosevelt at "The Washington Schoolmaster" lecturing the mine owners.

Business

Meanwhile, business also suffered some setbacks. The Elkins Act (1903) made it illegal for a company to accept a rebate from a railroad. The Supreme Court in 1904 said that the Northern Securities Company, a holding company for three railroads between Lake Michigan and the Pacific Northwest, was an illegal restraint of trade and ordered that it be broken up. The next year, the Court said that the Swift Meat Company held an illegal monopoly in the meat packing industry. Previously, the Court had said that a particular industry was generally intrastate commerce since it was located within a state. With the Swift ruling, however, the Court established the stream of commerce doctrine that said the Swift company controlled too many aspects of the entire process (production, shipping, distribution, etc.) and thus did restrain interstate trade.

Encouraged by the Northern Securities decision, Roosevelt went after other trusts by having the Justice Department file lawsuits that were called trust-busting efforts. Not all of these came to trial, however, and heads of corporations still made secret gentlemen's agreements to avoid having legal action taken against them. Roosevelt tried to apply the rule of reason to his trust-busting activities. He said that big was not necessarily bad. His test was whether a monopoly or trust had a negative effect on business and the public. He preferred greater government regulation over trying to break up monopolies altogether.

Inauguration of Theodore Roosevelt (1905)

In 1903 Congress created the Department of Commerce and Labor as a new part of the President's Cabinet. Whenever a new Cabinet-level department is created, this means that the Federal government is giving increased attention to a subject. Since these two areas (commerce and labor) were often in conflict, the department divided in 1913 into the separate Departments of Commerce and of Labor.

1904 Re-Election

Roosevelt was eager to be elected in his own right in order to continue the program he had begun. He was opposed by conservatives within the Republican Party but easily won renomination. Roosevelt promised a square deal for every American. The Democrats nominated Alton Parker, chief justice of the New York State Supreme Court. Parker had ruled for labor in some cases that came before him, but he supported the gold standard and had other conservative positions. The Democrats tried to portray Parker not as more progressive than Roosevelt but as more conservative and reliable. It didn't work. Roosevelt got over 57% of the popular vote, a 336 to 140 electoral majority, and carried every state outside of the South, including Missouri, which had not voted for a Republican presidential nominee since 1868.

On election night, Roosevelt accepted victory and pledged that he would not run again. This was a decision he later regretted. It weakened his position as President and ran against his competitive spirit.

Second Term Reforms

Roosevelt had to fight against the conservative Old Guard Republicans in Congress who thought he went too far as well as Progressives who thought he didn't go far enough. Despite his announcement that he would not seek re-election in 1908, Roosevelt had enough influence to see significant changes take place in the first part of his second term. His cause was helped by several muckraking writers who exposed corruption and betrayal of the public trust by various industries. The 1906 Hepburn Act gave more power to the Interstate Commerce Commission by allowing it to investigate railroad rate fixing and to take other steps to regulate business practices.

Another area of concern was the packaging of food products and the manufacture and promotion of drugs. In 1906 Upton Sinclair published *The Jungle*, his shocking novel that described unsanitary practices in the meat packing industry. He wrote, among other things, that the processing plants were dirty and used spoiled meat in what they packaged and sold. Roosevelt read the pre-publication proofs of *The Jungle* and ordered an immediate investigation. Another commission reported that patent medicines were often either ineffective or harmful. The result of these investigations was the passage, on the same day in 1906, of the Meat Inspection Act and the Pure Food and Drug Act. Meat packers had opposed any regulation; but after sales dropped in Europe following publication of the investigation, the processors decided to support legislation.

Swift & Co. Packing House, Chicago (c. 1906)

Conservation

During the increased industrialization of the late nineteenth century, little had been done to regulate the use of natural resources or to protect the environment and natural beauty of the country. Businesses, as well as many Americans, assumed that the supply of natural resources was endless and that the environment was not an issue.

Logging companies cleared lands of forests without any thought of replanting or of the environmental impact of what they did. By 1900 only about one-fourth of the country's virgin forests remained (200 million acres out of a previous total of 800 million acres). Eighty percent of the timber was owned by private companies or individuals. The government had given away huge amounts of public lands to railroads and had sold still more land to other businesses. Cattle ranchers overgrazed semiarid lands, creating huge dust bowls. Coal companies often took the coal that was easiest to mine and then abandoned the site. Natural gas was allowed to escape into the air, and cities had badly polluted air and streams.

A few steps were taken in the late 1800s when some forest lands were made into public reserves and the Forest Service was created within the Agriculture Department in 1887. Theodore Roosevelt, with his love of the outdoors and his experiences on the western plains, wanted to protect the land and insure that its benefits would be available to later generations. Roosevelt helped the American public become more aware of the need for conservation.

The President appointed activist Gifford Pinchot as head of the Forest Service. Roosevelt withdrew forest land and coal and phosphate mines from sale; he vetoed the private development of a dam and hydroelectric plant at Muscle Shoals, Alabama; and he urged Congress to create more national parks and wildlife sanctuaries. During his tenure five national parks were created (doubling the number in existence), along with sixteen national monument areas and 51 wildlife refuges.

In 1902 the Newlands Reclamation Act (named for a Senator from Nevada) authorized money from the sale of public land to be used for irrigation projects in western wastelands. Twenty-eight such projects were begun by 1906. The Shoshone Dam in Wyoming and the Roosevelt Dam in Arizona were completed by 1911, the latter enabling the irrigation of 200,000 acres of desert.

Roosevelt also used what he called the "bully pulpit" of the presidency to convene conservation conferences, appoint investigative commissions, and influence public opinion. His was an activist presidency, during which he pushed hard for causes in which he believed.

Japan

Theodore Roosevelt faced issues on the international scene as well. The island nation of Japan lived in virtual isolation from the world until 1853, when American Commodore Matthew Perry sailed into Japanese waters and demanded to meet with government officials. This contact led to a treaty of friendship and trade between the U.S. and Japan. The American visitors introduced Japan to the latest technological advances, including the railroad, modern guns, and the telegraph. A group of younger Japanese wanted to modernize the country as rapidly as possible to benefit from western inventions and manufacturing.

This introduction to the world outside of Japan led to a desire within Japan for more raw materials to use in manufacturing than could be found within its own borders. In addition, as Japan had contact with other nations, it saw the efforts of European nations in colonizing China and wanted a piece of the action to improve life for its growing population. Japan attacked China in 1894 and began the Sino-Japanese War (Sino is from the French word for China). Japan acquired the island of Taiwan, the Korean peninsula, and other land from China as a result of the war.

Conflicting interests between Russia and Japan led to the Russo-Japanese War of 1904-05, fought in China and on the Pacific Ocean. The war threatened the stability of China and American trading interests there. President Theodore Roosevelt warned Germany and France not to get involved in the

Roosevelt Foreign Policy

In a speech at the Minnesota State Fair in 1901, Roosevelt said, "There is a homely adage which runs, 'Speak softly and carry a big stick; you will go far.' If the American nation will speak softly and yet build and keep at a pitch of the highest training a thoroughly efficient navy, the Monroe Doctrine will go far." Roosevelt's foreign policy was often summarized by the statement, "Speak softly and carry a big stick."

In 1907 President Roosevelt sent the entire American naval fleet on a tour around the world. The trip was intended to show American power and America's willingness to fight anywhere its interests might be threatened. Roosevelt especially wanted to rattle a saber at Japan. The fleet, which was the second largest in the world behind Great Britain's, was welcomed warmly everywhere it docked. The photo at right shows its arrival in Rio de Janeiro, Brazil. The fleet returned to the United States in early 1909, just before Roosevelt left office.

war. He said that the U.S. would enter the war on the side of Japan if those nations helped Russia. Roosevelt called representatives from Russia and Japan to a meeting at Portsmouth, New Hampshire, in 1905 that resulted in an end to the war. Japanese authority over Manchuria, Korea, and the southern half of Sakhalin Island was recognized; but Russia refused to pay a cash indemnity to Japan. Roosevelt received the 1906 Nobel Peace Prize for his efforts in negotiating the treaty that ended the war.

The Roosevelt Corollary

The Monroe Doctrine had declared that European countries should stay out of the western hemisphere, but the doctrine had only been seriously tested twice since it was announced in 1823. Napoleon III of France attempted to create a French empire in Mexico in the 1860s, but the attempt was short-lived. Then Great Britain and Venezuela had a boundary dispute in 1895 concerning British Guyana, and the British government eventually accepted American arbitration to help resolve the matter instead of taking direct military action against Venezuela.

Although European countries did not become militarily involved in the western hemisphere, they did became economically involved there. Part of that involvement included making loans to poorer nations. In the early 1900s, the United States wanted to prevent European nations from taking action against Caribbean nations that defaulted on loans. Great Britain and Germany blockaded the Venezuelan coast in 1902 in response to such a default. Roosevelt insisted that the countries involved submit to arbitration, which they did. In his annual message to Congress in 1904, President Roosevelt declared that if intervention were needed in any Latin American country, the U.S. would do it instead of a European country. He claimed the right of America to exercise "an international police power" in such situations. This statement of policy was called the Roosevelt Corollary to the Monroe Doctrine.

This handkerchief commemorates Roosevelt's military exploits in the Spanish-American War and his peace efforts at Portsmouth. The words in the heart are those bestowed before on George Washington: "First in War, First in Peace, First in the Hearts of His Countrymen."

The first test of the Corollary came in 1905. European nations demanded that the Dominican Republic either arrange for the payment of its debts or face an invasion. The republic turned to the U.S. for protection. Roosevelt agreed to defend the territorial integrity of the Dominican Republic, but for this protection the republic had to agree to let the U.S. collect customs duties and apportion it among the Dominicans and its creditors.

The Dominicans wanted to end the protectorate in 1916; but the United States was not ready to do so at that point. The U.S. dispatched an invasion force there, suspended the Dominican legislature, and ruled by military dictatorship until 1924. The American military was removed that year, but the Dominican Republic remained a U.S. protectorate until 1940. A similar intervention by the U.S. occurred in Haiti in 1914.

Speaker "Uncle Joe" Cannon presides over the House of Representatives in 1906.

The Tenure of Taft

In 1908 Theodore Roosevelt hand-picked his good friend and Secretary of War William Howard Taft to be the Republican presidential nominee. Taft's first love was the law. He spent many years in public service, first in his native Ohio and then as U.S. solicitor general, arguing the government's cases before the Supreme Court, and as a Federal circuit judge. He was named as civil governor of the Philippines when that country was taken over from Spain after the Spanish-American War, and his work in that role was exemplary. Theodore Roosevelt named him as his Secretary of War, and as such Taft was Roosevelt's troubleshooter and close advisor.

Taft was elected over the Democratic candidate, William Jennings Bryan, though his margin of victory was smaller than Roosevelt's had been in 1904. The Republicans also maintained control of Congress as a result of the election. The American Federation of Labor broke with its previous neutrality and endorsed Bryan in the campaign, but this support did not make the difference Bryan needed.

William Howard Taft was intelligent, good-humored, and generally sympathetic to Progressive ideas. He was a capable and dedicated public servant. However, he had the misfortune of serving as President directly after the activist Theodore Roosevelt. Taft did not have the energy, skill, and boldness that Roosevelt did. Moreover, Taft was not a political man and he hated political battles. He was more concerned with the strict legal aspects of issues than with molding public opinion and breaking new ground. Taft saw his role as consolidating the changes that had taken place under Roosevelt, not striking out on new initiatives. Because of this, he was generally perceived as being more conservative than Roosevelt. His record in office was better than he is often given credit for, although it was not what Roosevelt and other Progressives would have liked.

During the 1908 campaign, Taft promised to push for tariff reductions. He called a special session of Congress less than two weeks after he was inaugurated to push for the reductions. A bill cutting tariffs easily passed the House; but the Senate made some 800 changes, many of which raised rates on some items. Taft at first wanted to see the bill defeated; but then he backed down and accepted a compromise that was far from what he had originally proposed. When he signed the Payne-Aldrich Tariff, he called it the best tariff that Republicans had ever passed. This hurt Taft's popularity with the Progressive wing of the party.

Another political battle erupted in the House of Representatives when insurgent Republicans sought to curtail the power of the Speaker of the House, Joe Cannon of Illinois. House rules had allowed the Speaker to become a virtual dictator in naming the Rules Committee, deciding what legislation would be considered on the floor of the House, and even in recognizing members to speak. The first attempt at curbing the powers of the Speaker failed in 1909; but after a fierce debate, enough Democrats joined with progressive Republicans in 1910 to make rule changes that lessened the Speaker's authority. Taft did not endorse the insurgents' effort, which also cast him as a supporter of the Old Guard.

New Rules and Regulations

However, the Taft Administration oversaw several reforms that embodied Progressive ideals. The Mann-Elkins Act of 1910 put telephone, telegraph, and cable services under the Interstate Commerce Commission. The next year, Congress made it illegal to use false labels on products being sold in interstate commerce. Another law made the eight-hour day mandatory for workers on Federal projects. (Such laws about Federal working conditions have often set the standard for the rest of working Americans.) New legislation required political parties to make public the sources of their contributions and the amounts of their expenditures. President Taft added many Federal jobs to the list of those protected by civil service regulations.

Congress created the Bureau of Mines in the Interior Department and the Children's Bureau in the Department of Labor. Under Taft, the Justice Department actually initiated more antitrust suits than were begun under Roosevelt. Congress created the postal savings system, which made every local post office a savings bank, and parcel post delivery, which made more accessible a service that had previously been carried out by private companies. The 16th Amendment to the United States Constitution, allowing a Federal income tax, and the 17th Amendment, calling for the popular election of U.S. Senators, both of which were major Progressive issues, passed Congress during Taft's term; and both were ratified in 1913.

The Supreme Court in 1911 ordered the Standard Oil Company and the American Tobacco Company monopolies to be broken up. The Court decided that these companies were unreasonable combinations that restrained trade—monopolies that had a negative effect on the public.

William Howard Taft, *Anders Zorn (Swedish, 1911)*

First Lady Nellie Taft loved the cherry trees that she saw in Japan on her family's travels. After a suggestion from Eliza Ruhamah Scidmore, Mrs. Taft was responsible for cherry trees being planted by the Tidal Basin in Washington, D.C. The trees were a gift from the City of Tokyo, Japan. The National Cherry Blossom Festival is held in Washington every spring. The photo at left is from 2012.

Conservation Controversy

Taft was more cautious than Roosevelt regarding conservation issues, although he limited access to more Federal land than Roosevelt did. Again, Taft was more concerned with the letter of the law; and he opposed what he saw as Roosevelt's fast and loose approach. Interior Secretary Richard Ballinger returned to public sale some water-power sites that Roosevelt had withdrawn because he believed that the former President had acted illegally. Forest Service chief Gifford Pinchot protested the move. Taft sided with Pinchot, and the land was returned to the forest reserve.

Later, some public lands in Alaska were made available for sale to private interests under questionable circumstances. Pinchot again protested, but this time Taft fired him. Ballinger resigned in 1911, and a congressional investigation found no evidence of wrongdoing. The land in question was returned to the government's forest reserves by the new Interior Secretary, but the public perception was that Taft had backed away from Roosevelt's commitment to the environment.

Do not judge according to appearance, but judge with righteous judgment.
John 7:24

⋆ Assignments for Lesson 92 ⋆

American Voices Read the excerpts from the Roosevelt Corollary to the Monroe Doctrine (page 293).

Literature Continue reading *Mama's Bank Account.*

Bible Work on memorizing 1 Timothy 6:20-21.

Project Work on your project.

Student Review Optional: Answer the questions for Lesson 92.

First Successful Flight of the Wright Flyer (1903)

Lesson 93

A Time of Invention

The telephone.
Recorded sound.
The light bulb.
The automobile.
Coca-Cola.
Aspirin.
Radio.
The airplane.
The chocolate candy bar.

These are things that we take for granted today. When they were invented, however, each of them was the cause for a revolution in science, business, and American life. Even more amazing is the fact that all of the inventions listed above, along with many others, came onto the American scene within a generation, over a period of less than thirty years, between 1876 and 1903.

Much has been said about the amazing changes that took place in our world between 1900 and 2000, but almost equally amazing were the changes that took place between 1800 and 1900. As the twentieth century began, technology was advancing at a rapid rate. New inventions were changing the lives of millions of Americans.

Before the steamboat, the railroad, and the telegraph were invented in the first half of the nineteenth century, people, goods, and information could be moved from one place to another only as fast as they had ever been carried throughout history: by horse, the human foot, wagon, and water transportation. With the coming of the transcontinental railroad and telegraph, people could go from one coast to the other in days instead of weeks, while information could travel that distance almost instantaneously. Other inventions improved the quality of life for almost all Americans, whether they traveled or stayed at home.

Many factors came together to make this explosion of inventions possible. First, that generation stood on the shoulders of all previous generations; and the accumulated knowledge of mankind reached a point where material progress in many areas of life was possible at about the same time. Second, the technology involved in producing needed materials and the availability of electrical power made rapid development possible. Third, the U.S. and the world had the wealth necessary for the production and widespread distribution of these products. Inventors and manufacturers had to have wealth to produce the goods, and the public had to have enough wealth to create a market for the goods. Fourth, the U.S. and the world enjoyed relatively peaceful conditions in which a great many people were able to enjoy life and did not have to be so concerned about merely surviving.

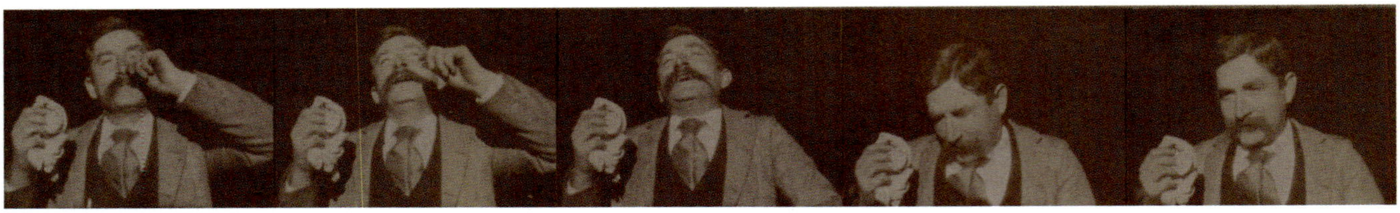

These frames are from Edison's Kinectoscopic Record of Sneeze. Received in 1894, it is the oldest surviving "motion picture" registered with the U.S. Copyright Office.

Thomas Alva Edison (1847-1932)

Thomas Edison symbolized this period of American history in many ways. Edison was an inventive genius and shrewd entrepreneur. He patented over one thousand inventions, and his work helped begin several major industries (such as electric utilities and motion pictures). Edison received only three months of formal schooling. He was an experimenter and independent businessman from his teen years.

Edison invented the phonograph (1877), the incandescent light bulb (1879), the motion-picture camera (1891) and projector (1896), and many other items we use every day. He also took the first steps in the production and distribution of electricity to serve a wide area.

Other inventors, Nikola Tesla and George Westinghouse, developed and promoted the alternating current system of electrical power that replaced Edison's direct current format. This allowed even wider distribution of electric current.

Alexander Graham Bell With his Wife Mabel and Their Daughters Elsie (far left) and Marian (c. 1885)

Alexander Graham Bell (1847-1922)

Alexander Graham Bell was not a dedicated inventor the way that Edison was; but his interests led him to use the technology of his day to invent one device, the telephone, that changed the world. Bell's interest was in speech and in the transmission of sound along wires. His grandfather and father were actors, and his father became a speech teacher. Alexander's father developed a system of written symbols to illustrate verbal sounds that he used in teaching the deaf. Alexander also became a teacher of the deaf. While experimenting with a device called a multiple telegraph (which was intended to send telegraph signals to several receivers at once), Bell hit upon a way to send sounds along electrical wires. Thus the telephone was born in 1876.

The device caught on when Bell presented a series of public demonstrations in which he sent and received vocal sounds to and from a remote location. Bell established a company to build the devices and to string connecting wires between subscribers. The company began the practice of renting telephones to subscribers instead of selling them outright, a practice that telephone companies continued until late in the twentieth century. Bell separated himself from direct involvement in the business fairly soon, but the Bell Telephone System became an American institution.

Bell's wife, who had been one of his students, was deaf. Mrs. Bell was never able to use her husband's invention directly. She always had to have someone listen on the telephone and communicate to her what the person on the other end was saying.

The Automobile

Automobiles, or horseless carriages, were developed by several different inventors about the same time. Brothers Frank and Charles Duryea built the first successful gasoline-powered car in the U.S. in 1893. They began producing it commercially in 1896, the same year that Henry Ford unveiled his first successful model.

Ransom Olds introduced mass production to the automobile industry in 1901. His company made 400 cars the first year, and they sold for $650.00 each. Henry Ford developed mass production techniques after founding the Ford Motor Company in 1903. General Motors was organized in 1908. The Ford Model T went into production in 1908, and more than 15 million were sold over the next twenty years.

This photo from a campout in 1921 shows Henry Ford, Thomas Edison, President Warren Harding, and Harvey Firestone, a leading tire manufacturer.

Model T's Coming Off the Assembly Line at the Highland Park Ford Plant in Michigan (c. 1913)

The simple car (you could get any color you wanted, as long as it was black) furthered auto driving and road building more than any other single factor.

Names that have endured in the automotive industry for decades were part of its early history. David Buick built his first car in 1903. Louis Chevrolet started his motor car company in 1911. Horace and John Dodge made bicycle parts before founding the Dodge Motor Company in 1914. Other innovators, such as the Studebaker brothers and Charles Nash, started companies that lasted for a time but no longer exist.

In 1914 Henry Ford made nationwide news when he announced that he was going to raise the salary of the assembly line workers at his company to the unheard of rate of five dollars per day, almost double what they had been getting. When he did this, he encouraged the workers to invest some of their earnings in the company. This gave the employees a reason to stay with Ford, and it also gave back to the company a significant amount of the salary increase in the form of employee investments.

In 1900 some 8,000 automobiles were in use in the United States. By 1920 Americans owned 8.1 million cars and 1.1 million trucks. Improvements in related industries such as rubber production and petroleum refining also helped spur the industry. In turn the increasing number of car owners helped bring about a demand for better and safer roads.

A Reproduction of the Wright Brothers' Shack at Kill Devil Hills, North Carolina

The Ferris Wheel at the 1893 World Columbian Exposition in Chicago carried almost 1.5 million passengers. It was reused at the Louisiana Purchase Exposition in St. Louis in 1904 before being scrapped.

Other Inventions

Man took flight with the Wright Brothers' airplane on December 17, 1903. Orville and Wilbur Wright designed and built their flying machine in their bicycle shop in Ohio. Orville flew the first heavier-than-air machine 120 feet in twelve seconds along the windy Outer Banks seacoast of Kitty Hawk, North Carolina. Progress in flying proceeded rapidly. In 1919 a Navy plane crossed the Atlantic by way of the Azores, and that same year a two-man crew flew non-stop from Newfoundland to Ireland.

The Italian Guglielmo Marconi sent the first wireless telegraph signal by radio in 1895; in 1901 he sent and received messages across the Atlantic. Three years later, voice and music were broadcast by radio for the first time. Marconi won the Nobel Prize in physics in 1909. Radio came into widespread use in the 1920s.

The following list shows how rapid and widespread the inventive impetus was:

1873 *Mass production of typewriters*

1886 *Coca-Cola*

1887 *The player piano (for saloons in the American West, where human piano players were scarce)*

1893 *Ferris Wheel (by George Ferris)*

1894 *The chocolate candy bar (by Milton Hershey)*

1894 *Practical production of artificial silk, later called rayon*

1895 *The first flaked cereal (by William and John Kellogg)*

1895 *The discovery of x-rays (by William Roentgen)*

1899 *Aspirin perfected*

1899 *Condensed soup (by John Dorrance of the Campbell Preserve Company)*

This steady stream of practical inventions began to make life in America look more like what we know today than what it had been a hundred years earlier. Automobile and airplane travel, rapid electronic communication, improved health care, a wide variety of packaged and prepared foods—the kind of life we know in America began to take shape in the late nineteenth and early twentieth century.

All of these inventions were amazing. But the blessings that God has in store for His people are even more amazing.

Every prudent man acts with knowledge,
But a fool displays folly.
Proverbs 13:16

★ Assignments for Lesson 93 ★

American Voices Read "His Eye Is On the Sparrow" by Civilla Martin and Charles Gabriel (page 294).

Literature Continue reading *Mama's Bank Account.*

Bible Work on memorizing 1 Timothy 6:20-21.

Project Work on your project.

Student Review Optional: Answer the questions for Lesson 93.

The Pacific End of the Panama Canal (2009)

Lesson 94

The Panama Canal

It's a story that has it all: grand plans made against overwhelming odds, tragic defeat and magnificent triumph, political intrigue and scandal, personal and national achievement, and a literal life and death struggle. It involves science, geography, technology, medicine, and compelling human interest. It is an event that literally changed the world.

American Interests

People had dreamed of a water route through Central America since the early 1500s, when Spanish explorers crossed the forty-mile wide land bridge that connects North and South America and that separates the Atlantic and Pacific Oceans. They understood that such a passage would be invaluable to world exploration, travel, and trade.

In 1846 the United States concluded a treaty with the country of New Granada (later known as Colombia, of which Panama was a province) that gave the U.S. the right to build a means of transit across the Isthmus of Panama. The Senate ratified the treaty in 1848. The matter held little interest to most Americans until gold was discovered in California that year. Then it became a matter of huge interest.

Thousands of people wanted to go from the eastern U.S. to California, but no easy route existed. They had the choice between a difficult journey across the western U.S. territories or a difficult voyage around South America. Both routes were expensive and required weeks of travel. In 1850 an American company undertook to build a railroad across Panama. It was completed in 1855 and was an immediate financial success. However, no one devised a workable plan for a canal until the late 1800s; and the inspiration came from a Frenchman, Ferdinand de Lesseps.

De Lesseps' Dream

De Lesseps was a diplomat and promoter whose vision led to the building of the Suez Canal between Egypt and the Suez peninsula. The Suez project was completed in 1869. The Suez Canal was the fulfillment of another dream. It eliminated the need for ships to sail around Africa to reach India and the Far East. The Suez Canal was universally hailed as a triumph of planning, engineering, and construction; and the people of France took understandable pride in the accomplishment.

Then de Lesseps turned his attention to Central America and the digging of another canal, one that, along with the Suez Canal, would complete a naval pathway around the globe and bring the people of the world closer together. However, the task of building a canal across Central America would be more difficult than at Suez. In Suez the terrain was flat and sandy, so all that was needed there was a big, long ditch dug at sea level. By contrast, Central America had jungles and mountains. Suez was hot; but Central America was hot and rainy and known for deadly diseases such as yellow fever, typhoid, and malaria. De Lesseps was undaunted. He was sure that a canal could be built, and he devoted himself to raising money and putting together a team that could do the job. De Lesseps obtained the rights from New Granada to build a canal.

Construction began in 1881. The organizers and leaders of the work were French, but most of the laborers were black men from islands in the Caribbean. The work was difficult if not disastrous from the start. First, de Lesseps' idea of a sea-level canal was simply not workable given the terrain in Panama. Second, the technology that was available was inadequate for the task. Third, work-related accidents and tropical diseases took a heavy toll among the workers. The French did not keep exact records, but it is estimated that as many as 20,000 people died during the French-directed efforts. Fourth, it was revealed later that the project suffered from the misappropriation of funds, much of which had been raised by bonds authorized by the French government and purchased by average French citizens. Some of the money, for instance, had been paid to newspapers to get them to report glowing accounts of the project to the French people even as the work was progressing poorly. The company that oversaw the project went bankrupt, and construction halted in 1887.

Illustration of French Work on the Canal (1885)

There the situation remained for over a decade. The French did not have the heart to take on another attempt, and the only other country that entertained even the possibility of doing the work was the United States. A canal would be of great assistance to the U.S. with its two-coast geography. However, American interest in undertaking the work was not great. In addition, American opinion was divided over whether to build a canal in Panama or to select a route further north in Nicaragua. The total mileage across Nicaragua was greater; but Nicaragua had more gentle terrain, natural waterways that could be used to connect parts of a canal, and a lower risk of tropical diseases. In addition, the distance from the U.S. to Nicaragua was considerably less than it was to Panama.

Renewed American Interest

American interest in a Central American canal increased dramatically because of the Spanish-American War in 1898, when matters in the Caribbean became of great concern to Americans. When the war erupted, the battleship *Oregon* took six weeks to go from California around South America to the Caribbean. Newspapers reported the ship's progress every day, and this drama convinced most Americans of the need to build a canal.

In 1901 the United States and Great Britain signed a treaty that gave the U.S. the right to build a canal across Nicaragua. The two countries had previously agreed to build and operate a canal together, but the U.S. now wanted sole control of the project and Great Britain was ready to let go of its interests. However, the United States soon thought it had a better deal than the Nicaraguan route. The French company that had overseen the failed effort in Panama offered to sell its canal rights there to the

U.S. for $40 million. America was ready to snap up the offer, and it also offered to pay Colombia a lump sum of $10 million as well as $250,000 in annual rent to Colombia for a six-mile wide canal zone. However, Colombia balked at the offer in the hope of getting more money.

Revolution in Panama

President Theodore Roosevelt and many other Americans were furious at this insult by the Colombian government. Fortunately for the United States, the leaders of the province of Panama chafed at Colombia's rule and resented Colombia's refusal to accept the American offer. Panamanian leaders envisioned their land being the crossroads of international trade and did not want to let the opportunity slip away. Panamanian representatives secretly went to Washington, D.C., to inquire about the possibility of American assistance if a revolution in Panama created a separate nation there. The request was officially refused, but representatives of the American government indicated that America would not interfere if a revolution got underway.

Word got out that an American warship would be in the area of Panama on November 2, 1903. The gunboat *Nashville* did arrive in Panama on that day, but a Colombian boat also landed that day with a detachment of troops headed for Panama City. Panamanians seized and imprisoned Colombian officers. With this the revolution began and the insurrectionists soon declared victory. (In 1921 the United States paid Colombia $25 million to settle any outstanding issues and resentments from the events of November 1903.)

President Roosevelt on a Steam Shovel in Panama

Panamanians organized a new government on November 4, and the U.S. recognized it on November 6. The United States and Panama signed a treaty on November 18, giving the U.S. a 99-year-lease for a ten-mile-wide strip on which it would build a canal. America pledged to pay Panama $10 million as well as $250,000 a year for the lease. Exemplifying the deeply intertwined maneuvers in the Panama deal is the fact that the representative for the new Panamanian government who concluded the treaty with the U.S. was Philippe Buneau-Varilla, a French engineer who had worked for the French company that originally made the offer to the United States.

America Builds the Canal

American-led work in Panama began in 1904. After the first leaders of the work resigned following brief stints, Roosevelt put Army engineering officers in charge of the work since, as he put it, they could not resign. American technology and engineering made the work feasible. Little of what the French had done was of much use to the Americans. The American plan involved using and diverting existing waterways as well as building locks that could be closed around ships to raise and lower them as needed along the canal route. As with the earlier French project, the large majority of laborers were black men from the Caribbean who came to Panama seeking jobs. President Roosevelt paid a brief visit to the work site, thus becoming the first U.S. President to leave the country while in office.

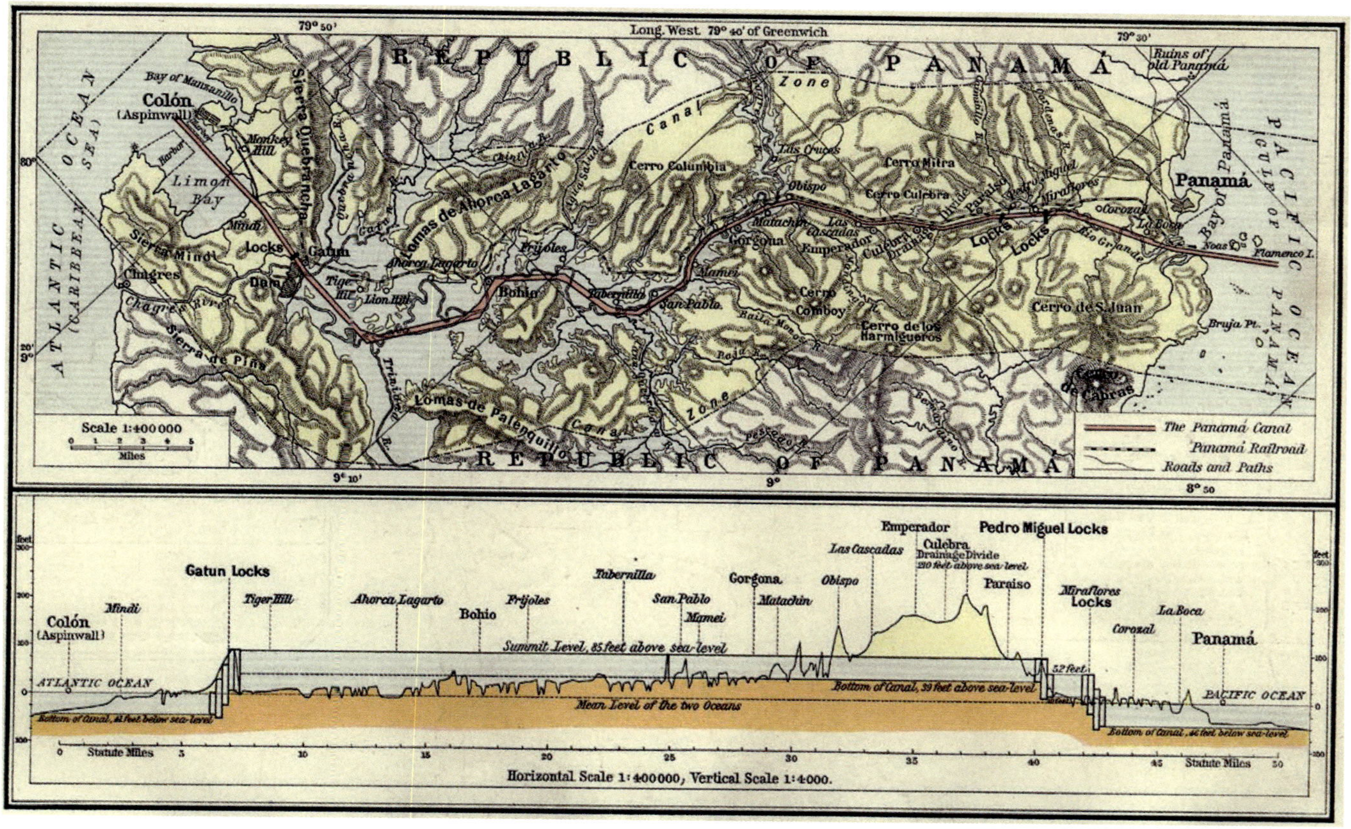

These overhead and side views of the Panama Canal are from William R. Shepherd's Historical Atlas *(1911).*

One development that made the Panama Canal possible was the conquering of yellow fever and other jungle diseases that had made the area inhospitable. Few people at the time believed that mosquitoes had anything to do with transmitting disease. Most thought that "vapors" rising from the damp ground were the cause. However, Dr. Walter Reed proved shortly after the Spanish-American War that yellow fever was transmitted by mosquitoes. His research taught the world that getting rid of mosquitoes greatly reduced the incidence of yellow fever. Other researchers and physicians led the efforts in Panama to drain standing water and to do away with other breeding areas for mosquitoes. These improvements radically transformed the region and largely eliminated the diseases that had taken many lives.

This 1904 cartoon in Judge *magazine pictures Theodore Roosevelt and describes the Panama Canal as "a crown he is entitled to wear." In 1911 Theodore Roosevelt, commenting on his desire to take decisive action, remarked in a speech, "I took the Isthmus, started the canal and then left Congress not to debate the canal, but to debate me."*

What Else Was Happening?

1901 *Harry Houdini, pictured at right, builds an international reputation for making daring escapes.*

1901 *Queen Victoria dies after reigning since 1837.*

1902 *A New York toymaker displays a political cartoon of Theodore Roosevelt refusing to shoot a bear cub next to a toy stuffed bear that he calls a Teddy Bear.*

1904 *The New York City subway begins operation.*

1905 *Albert Einstein publishes his special theory of relativity and develops the equation* $e=mc^2$.

1906 *The Muslim League is formed to protect the rights of Muslims in the mostly Hindu nation of India. The League eventually helps bring about a division of India to form the Muslim country of Pakistan.*

1907 *The* Lusitania *makes its maiden voyage, crossing the Atlantic in 5 days and 54 minutes.*

1907 *Hans Geiger develops the first machine to measure radioactivity, the Geiger counter.*

1908 *The Gideons begin their program of placing Bibles in hotel rooms in Iron Mountain, Montana.*

1908 *James Spangler invents the vacuum cleaner. He sells the rights to W. H. Hoover.*

1908 *Sir Robert Baden-Powell founds the Boy Scouts in Britain. The Boy Scouts of America begin in 1910. The Girl Guides begin in Britain in 1910. Juliette Low begins Girl Scouts in the U.S. in 1912.*

1909 *The first synthetic plastic (Bakelite) is produced by Leo Baekeland.*

1911 *The first airmail delivery in America takes place when a biplane carries mail a few miles between two points near New York City.*

1911 *The first transcontinental airplane flight takes 82 hours and 4 minutes (the flight is not non-stop).*

1911 *A revolution in China topples the Ch'ing Dynasty. A republic ends 3,000 years of monarchy.*

1912 *The separable fastener is developed. It becomes known as the zipper.*

1912 *American Indian athlete Jim Thorpe wins gold medals in the pentathlon and decathlon at the Stockholm Olympics, but he is stripped of them a year later because he played semipro baseball in 1909 and 1910. The medals are restored posthumously in 1982.*

1912 *The supposedly unsinkable* Titanic *strikes an iceberg on its maiden voyage and sinks off Newfoundland.*

The Panama Canal was an astounding engineering accomplishment. It was opened to the commerce of all nations on August 15, 1914, at a cost of about $350 million. About 5,600 workers (most of whom were black) lost their lives during the ten years that the U.S. oversaw the work.

The trip between New York and San Francisco was cut from 13,932 miles around Cape Horn to 6,059 miles through the canal. Unlike the French debacle, the American effort came in under budget without any financial scandal and was completed about six months ahead of schedule.

The United States operated the canal peacefully and profitably through times of war and peace. However, the American presence there came to be seen as a vestige of American imperialism. During the tenure of President Jimmy Carter, the U.S. Senate ratified treaties that gave legal control of the canal to Panama in the year 2000 and permanently guaranteed the canal's neutrality.

You make him to rule over the works of Your hands;
You have put all things under his feet, all sheep and oxen,
and also the beasts of the field,
The birds of the heavens and the fish of the sea,
whatever passes through the paths of the seas.
O Lord, our Lord, how majestic is Your name in all the earth!
Psalm 8:6-9

★ Assignments for Lesson 94 ★

American Voices	Read "I Stand Amazed" by Charles Gabriel (page 295).
Literature	Continue reading *Mama's Bank Account.*
Bible	Work on memorizing 1 Timothy 6:20-21.
Project	Work on your project.
Student Review	Optional: Answer the questions for Lesson 94.

Billy Sunday

Lesson 95 - Bible Study

Liberal and Conservative

Change in Christian America took two different directions in the late nineteenth and early twentieth centuries. Each change was in some sense a reaction to the other, and each continues to have an impact today. Like most other aspects of life, religion was caught up in the ferment of change in America at the turn of the century. Some believers absorbed the materialistic spirit of the age while others reacted to the age by searching for a deep, personal, guiding faith.

Theological Liberalism

Developments in American theological studies showed a strong influence from the trends of the world. German schools of theology began raising doubts about the inspiration and authority of Scripture in the first part of the 1800s. This was hastened by the influence of Darwinian thought in the latter half of the century.

In this rejection of the authority of Scripture, theologians began asking questions about whether and how the Scriptures were inspired by God. Some believed that the Scriptures as we have them are merely a product of evolutionary change. They said that early writings were pulled together and edited to produce the final product that we have today. As a result, these scholars saw the Bible as one expression of faith but not more authoritative for all times and places than anyone else's expression of faith. They said that the Bible contains the Word of God (the message God wanted to convey to the world) but that it is not the Word of God (final, authoritative, and without error). But if such were true, how could the average person determine what is truth and what is error? One supposes that these scholars were the ones who would have to interpret the Scriptures and convey that word to us, since in their view the message had become clouded by error and tradition.

A key battleground in this war of interpreting Scripture was the Creation account in Genesis. The traditional view held that God created the world in six literal twenty-four-hour days. Liberal interpreters believed that Genesis had to fit the theory of evolution; so they began interpreting Genesis 1-2 as describing seven long periods of time or as a merely poetic account that was not intended to have historical or scientific accuracy.

Liberal theologians also raised questions about the words and deeds of Jesus. More extreme scholars doubted whether Jesus was actually divine, whether He actually performed miracles, and whether He really was raised from the dead. Their assumption was that, if there is a supernatural realm, it does not invade the temporal realm. With that assumption, the miracles of the Bible are automatically cast into doubt. Liberal theologians also rejected the traditionally accepted dates for when the Biblical books were written. They suggested much later dates than the traditionally understood ones, since they believed that the ideas in the books were the result of the evolution of thought. Many also questioned the authorship of some of Paul's letters.

Some liberals even questioned whether Christianity could be accepted as the one exclusive pathway to God and the truth. They thought it was arrogant to say that only one belief system was right. Such scholars believed that, if God could be known at all, he was certainly not a God of judgment.

Many schools of theology suffered serious division as these ideas became accepted. The influence of these ideas extended beyond the seminary because theologians teach ministers and ministers teach the people in the pew. The Princeton School of Theology and the Presbyterian Church as a whole were a major theological battleground.

If the liberals were right, the value of Christianity was not that it was the way to find God, but that it offered a helpful perspective on truth and morality. They said that Jesus was a great, perhaps the most perfect, example of an ethical man, and that His importance was not His substitutionary atonement for sin but His example of a good life.

Conservative Reaction

Meanwhile, and partly in reaction, conservative religious activity increased. The period around the turn of the twentieth century was the day of huge evangelistic crusades in big cities with preaching by men such as Dwight L. Moody (1837-1899). Moody established the Chicago Evangelization Society in 1886 to help train people for city mission work. It became the Moody Bible Institute after his death.

Billy Sunday (1863-1935) was a professional baseball player who began a career with the Chicago White Stockings in 1883. Three years later he had a religious conversion, and in 1891 he quit baseball to go into full-time evangelistic preaching. Sunday was known for his dramatic and often theatrical messages. The country witnessed numerous revival meetings in the twenty years before the Great War.

Dwight Moody (pictured below with beard) saw the need for mission work among all segments of society. He established a Sunday School in one of the worst neighborhoods of Chicago in the 1850s. President-elect Abraham Lincoln visited and spoke at the school before he went to Washington, D.C.

Emily Hartwell (far left) was born in China to missionary parents in 1859. After studying in the United States as a young woman, she returned to China and served there for over 50 years. This photo was taken in 1902.

Missionary societies increased their activity in other countries. As advances in travel and communication helped Americans become more aware of the world, believers sought to respond to Christ's Great Commission to go into all the world and teach the good news. Missionaries went to Africa, Hawaii, and other foreign lands as well as to the Indian tribes in the American West.

John Darby (1800-1882) and Cyrus Scofield (1843-1921) popularized the method of Biblical interpretation known as dispensational premillennialism. This was an attempt to apply the message and prophecies of the Bible to world history. Dispensational premillennialism holds that mankind's time on earth is divided into seven dispensations: innocence, conscience, human government, promise, law, grace, and kingdom. It says that we now live in the sixth dispensation and that the next period will be the millennium when Christ will reign on earth. Classic dispensationalism held to Bishop Ussher's dating of the earth's Creation around 4000 BC and expected the millennium to begin around 2000 AD. The Scofield Reference Bible, published in 1909 and revised in 1919, has copious notes interpreting all of Scripture from the perspective of dispensational premillennialism.

Yet another trend from this period was the Holiness movement that arose primarily in the Methodist Church. This teaching held that Christians were perfected by a second work of grace called entire sanctification. The Church of

Cyrus Scofield (c. 1920)

Division in the Restoration Movement

The churches of the Restoration Movement, begun a century earlier as a result of the Second Great Awakening, suffered a division that reflected the divergent views of the day. Many members wanted their churches to stick to what they saw as the old paths of Biblical teaching and patterns. Others accepted practices not specifically authorized in the New Testament, such as the use of mechanical instruments in their assemblies and the creation of missionary societies separate from the local church.

The Restoration Movement did not see itself as a denomination in the usual sense, so no official division took place. However, a 1906 religious census taken by the U.S. Government (something not done now) revealed that the more conservative congregations were generally called Churches of Christ while those accepting newer practices were often called Christian Churches.

The Christian Churches suffered another division later in the twentieth century as more conservative congregations separated from the group that has come to be known as the Disciples of Christ. Christian Churches/Churches of Christ continue to be generally conservative and congregationally autonomous while the Disciples see themselves as a mainline denomination. These divisions were repeated in many religious bodies throughout the country during this period.

Christian Church in Plantersville, Alabama (1896)

the Nazarene was formed by Holiness believers who came out of the Methodist Church in 1908. A branch of Holiness called Pentecostalism also arose in the early 1900s. This movement, which holds that miraculous gifts are still practiced today, gave rise to denominations such as the Assemblies of God.

While all of the theological debates and all of these actions and reactions were taking place, a group of wealthy businessmen funded a publication project that proposed to set out the basic tenets of traditional, conservative Biblical interpretation. The effort utilized some of the best-known conservative scholars of the day. The material appeared in a series of booklets called *The Fundamentals* starting in 1910. About three million copies were sold over a three-year period. The series was ended by the coming of the Great War. The title of the series and the conservative orientation of the teaching in the booklets led to those who held to these beliefs being called Fundamentalists.

Believers were also involved in the drive to outlaw the sale of alcoholic beverages. Some secularists recognized the damaging effect of alcohol on individuals and families, but by far most of the energy and numbers of the prohibition movement came from Christian people. Unfortunately, a fair number of Protestants were also involved in anti-Catholic and anti-Jewish activities as increasing numbers of Catholic and Jewish immigrants came to America from Eastern and Central Europe.

Beloved, while I was making every effort to write you about our common salvation, I felt the necessity to write to you appealing that you contend earnestly for the faith which was once for all handed down to the saints.
Jude 3

⋆ Assignments for Lesson 95 ⋆

American Voices Read "Softly and Tenderly" by Will L. Thompson and "Give Me the Bible" by Priscilla Owens (pages 245 and 247).

Literature Finish reading *Mama's Bank Account.* Literary analysis available in *Student Review.*

Bible Recite or write 1 Timothy 6:20-21 from memory.

Project Complete your project for the unit.

Student Review Optional: Answer the questions for Lesson 95 and for *Mama's Bank Account* and take the quiz for Unit 19.

U.S. Navy Recruiting Poster (1917)

20 America and the Great War

Woodrow Wilson expanded the Progressive reforms that had begun with Theodore Roosevelt and William H. Taft. However, the country became engulfed in the growing conflict in Europe known as the Great War. The long and difficult peace treaty negotiations were highlighted by Wilson's insistence on including a League of Nations in the treaty. This issue, however, led to the Senate's rejection of the treaty. U.S. involvement in the Great War made Americans more aware of the peoples of different lands.

Memory Work

Memorize Micah 4:1-2 by the end of this unit.

Books Used

The Bible
American Voices
Miracle In the Hills

Project (choose one)

1) Write 300 to 500 words on one of the following topics:
   - Write a letter from an American soldier in France to his family back home, describing what it was like to fight in the Great War. See Lesson 97 and 98.
   - Write an editorial about America's entry into the League of Nations as if you were writing during the heat of the debate in 1919. Take a definite stand on one side or the other of the issue. See Lesson 99.
2) Memorize Micah 4:1-5. If you choose this project, you should recite or write the verses from memory at the end of the week.
3) Create a propaganda poster for the World War I era. Choose an appropriate message (e.g., staying out of the war, encouragement to enlist, women's services in the war) and design your poster in the style of the times. See the examples in this unit or look for other examples. Make your poster about the size of a piece of posterboard.

Literature

Miracle In the Hills

Eustace and Mary Martin Sloop were both physicians. They married in 1908 and moved to the mountains of western North Carolina to serve the people in that isolated region. The Sloops were an amazing couple. They worked to overcome the poverty, illiteracy, superstitions, and lack of health care that they found there. The Sloops were instrumental in bringing electricity, paved roads, and a hospital to the town of Crossnore. Mrs. Sloop established a weaving room that helped to rekindle interest in Appalachian crafts. In 1913 they founded Crossnore School, an institution that still exists today and is on the National Register of Historic Places. In 1951 Mrs. Sloop was named American Mother of the Year. Their son and daughter went to medical school and returned to serve the people of the region as a dentist and a physician, respectively.

Miracle in the Hills is Mrs. Sloop's 1953 memoir of her remarkable life, written with North Carolina journalist and author LeGette Blythe. The book is full of stories of surgery performed under an apple tree, overcoming opposition to the school and other changes they brought to mountain life, and the great faith that motivated all they did. Mrs. Sloop once said, "Beyond all else, Crossnore is the product of prayer."

Mrs. Sloop died in 1962, less than a year after her husband passed away.

1912 Campaign Poster Showing Roosevelt, Wilson, and Taft

Lesson 96

Wilson's Domestic Agenda

Republicans controlled the national government for many years, but controversy over tariff rates and conservation policies cost the party much public support. In the 1910 congressional elections, the party lost control of the House of Representatives to the Democrats for the first time in sixteen years. Theodore Roosevelt, back from an African safari, was distressed at the inconsistent pattern he saw in the Taft Administration. In 1910 Roosevelt presented a major speech in which he proposed a series of reforms he called the New Nationalism, including a graduated income tax, workmen's compensation, child labor laws, tariff reforms, and greater regulation of corporations.

The 1912 Election

The Progressive wing of the Republican Party became increasingly dissatisfied with Taft and looked for another standard-bearer for the 1912 election. The leading candidate was Wisconsin Senator Robert M. LaFollette, who campaigned for the nomination but could not garner enough support. A number of Republicans urged Theodore Roosevelt to make another run, which he finally agreed to do.

In states that held Republican Party primaries, Roosevelt won big; but Taft controlled the party machinery and received the nomination at the convention. About 300 Roosevelt delegates accused Taft of steamrolling the convention and walked out. They reconvened six weeks later as the Progressive or Bull Moose Party and nominated Roosevelt for President.

The Democrats meanwhile found their own progressive candidate in Woodrow Wilson, governor of New Jersey. Wilson was highly moralistic and idealistic, and he believed strongly that government should act for the public good. His New Freedom platform spoke out strongly against business trusts. His progressive record as governor convinced enough delegates at the convention that he was the party's best choice for President.

The campaign, which featured two clear Progressives and one at least semi-Progressive, was the high-water mark for the Progressive movement. However, in terms of politics the campaign was unusually intense. Roosevelt issued bitter attacks against his old friend Taft, and Taft eventually responded in kind. The former President was shot and wounded by a would-be assassin in Milwaukee, but he insisted on giving his speech before getting medical attention. Wilson made several speaking tours into various regions of the country.

Wilson benefited from the division within the Republicans. The New Jersey governor received only 42% of the vote, but with the Republicans split he carried forty states and received 435 electoral votes. Roosevelt finished second with 27.4% of the popular vote and 88 electoral votes, the best showing of any new third party in American history. Taft came in third with 23.2% and won only two states and eight electoral votes. Adding to the mix, Socialist Eugene Debs received just over 900,000 votes, or six percent of the total votes cast. The Democrats also won control of both houses of Congress for the first time since 1893.

Political control of Washington changed hands with Wilson's election; but the Progressive Era continued during his first term, until the country became embroiled in the Great War in Europe.

Wilson's Background

Thomas Woodrow Wilson was born in 1856 in Staunton, Virginia, the son of a Presbyterian minister. His family moved to Georgia when he was one year old. From his childhood, Tommy was intensely dedicated to the rightness of what he believed. Wilson received a degree from the College of New Jersey (which later became Princeton) and briefly studied law at the University of Virginia. After an unsuccessful attempt to establish a law practice in Atlanta, he earned a Ph.D. from Johns Hopkins University. His dissertation was published as a book, *Congressional Government*, in which he argued that the strict separation of powers made the

Roosevelt and Taft

Theodore Roosevelt maintained an active life after the 1912 campaign, even though the bullet from the assassination attempt was never removed. The photo below left shows him discussing his 1913-1914 expedition to Brazil. Injury and illness on that trip greatly affected his health. Roosevelt was eager to enlist for service in the Great War but was never called. He and Taft were able to reconcile their relationship before Roosevelt's death in 1919.

After his presidency, William H. Taft became a professor of constitutional law at Yale University. In 1921 President Warren G. Harding chose Taft to be Chief Justice of the U.S. Supreme Court. Taft's swearing in ceremony is shown below right. Taft was better suited to be Chief Justice than to be President. He served until just before his death in 1930 and garnered praise even from those who had been his political opponents. Members of the Taft family continued in public service in Ohio and at the national level.

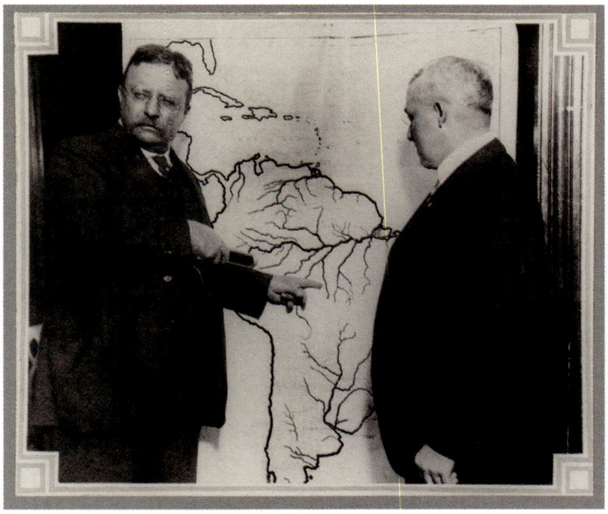

American government less effective than it could be. He argued for an activist executive, which is what he became.

Wilson taught at several colleges, including Princeton, and served as president of Princeton from 1902 to 1910. In that year he ran for governor of New Jersey and was elected. He did not depend on the regular state Democratic political machine but instead appealed directly to the voters. Once in office, he gained the attention of the national Democratic party and was nominated as their progressive hope in 1912.

The United States had become a world power during the McKinley and Roosevelt Administrations, but few issues involving foreign affairs arose during Taft's term. The 1912 election focused on domestic issues and the extent to which the Progressive movement could achieve its goals. In his first term, President Wilson oversaw the enactment of the greatest Progressive legislative program to date.

Tariff Reform

Wilson and most other Progressives believed that high tariffs gave an unfair advantage to American businesses by reducing competition and allowing higher prices. At the same time, however, tariff protection helped to insure American jobs and higher wages than workers in similar jobs received in Europe. Tariff reform was so important to Wilson that he called a special session of Congress right after he was inaugurated and took the unusual step of addressing Congress in person, something that had not been done since the days of Thomas Jefferson.

The Democratic Congress responded to Wilson's leadership by enacting the Underwood Tariff of 1913. The new law reduced rates to a fifty-year low, cutting the average rate from around 40% to 29%. To replace the lost revenue, Congress also passed an income tax, something that had been enabled by the recently ratified 16th Amendment. The income tax law set rates of one to six percent on incomes over $3,000 per year. The graduated income tax had been a

Woodrow and Ellen Wilson With Their Daughters Jessie, Margaret, and Eleanor (c. 1912)

Populist and Progressive proposal for many years, on the assumption that those with higher incomes had more discretionary income and could pay a higher rate than those with less income. The immediate effect of the lower tariff rates was hard to gauge since regular trade was interrupted by the war in Europe and because the war brought about a boom in the U.S. economy with increased production of many goods related to the war effort.

Banking Reform

The nation operated under a banking system that had been created during the Civil War. Most observers felt the need for reform, but opinion was divided on whether the government or private bankers should have the greater amount of control. The Federal Reserve Act of 1913 was something of a compromise. It is the banking system the nation uses today. The new law divided the country into twelve Federal Reserve districts, each with a Federal Reserve Bank. The reserve banks are overseen by the Federal Reserve Board. All Federally chartered banks are members of the Federal Reserve, and state chartered banks are allowed to join if they meet certain criteria.

The Federal Reserve Board (often called the Fed) deals with member banks, not individual depositors. Federal Reserve Banks take loans made by member

Graduated vs. Flat Tax

The graduated income tax has been the policy of the Federal government ever since the income tax was enacted in 1913. Some opponents of the graduated tax favor what they call a flat tax, which involves everyone paying the same percentage of tax regardless of income. Flat tax proponents say that it is more fair to tax everyone at the same rate, just as rich and poor alike pay the same sales tax when they make a purchase, rather than "soaking the rich" with a higher tax rate, as some put it. Most flat taxers propose protecting income up to a certain amount from any income tax as a way to help the poor.

Wealthier Americans, who pay higher rates but who also have more clout in Washington, have countered the graduated rate structure by influencing Congress over the years to pass a dizzying number of tax exemptions and loopholes that have made the current tax law overwhelming in size and confusing to just about anyone who pays income tax. Flat taxers want to eliminate almost all of the exemptions and special provisions in the tax code. They say that, with a flat tax, Americans could complete a tax return on a postcard. Opponents of the flat tax say that the wealthy should pay more taxes and would get most of the benefit of a flat tax. They also say that a flat tax would bring in less revenue. Flat taxers answer by saying that the government doesn't need as much money as it now gets. A drastically simplified tax code would be difficult to pass in Congress because of all the special interests that have gotten protective provisions written into the tax law that they don't want to lose.

This November 1913 *Puck* cartoon shows men cutting pieces from a turkey labeled "Income Tax Litigation" with the caption: "Lawyers at least have plenty to be thankful for."

banks as collateral, in return for which they send currency to member banks, which then enables member banks to make more loans. The Fed can transfer money from one region of the country to another when it is needed and can order more or less currency when such is needed during the year (for instance, when farmers need money for spring planting and fall harvesting). The board also adjusts its discount rate, which is the interest rate it charges member banks for money, to stimulate or slow down the economy as it determines what is needed. If the board believes that more business activity is needed, it will cut the discount rate, which lowers the interest rate for customer loans. This in turn encourages more business activity (in the form of home loans and business loans, for instance).

Antitrust Reform

The Clayton Antitrust Act of 1914 was stronger than previous antitrust legislation against monopolistic practices of business, even though enforcement was still difficult because of court rulings. The law restricted trade practices that led to monopolies; for instance, it outlawed interlocking directorates for companies capitalized for $1 million or more. The act also removed labor unions from antitrust restrictions and said that strikes, boycotts, and picketing were legal actions. Court injunctions against strikes could be used only if persons or property were threatened. Despite these provisions, courts still frequently ruled against unions when suits were brought before them.

Congress also created the Federal Trade Commission (FTC), which oversees the activities of companies involved in interstate trade. Companies have to submit annual reports to the FTC, and the commission is empowered to investigate business activities and to order companies to stop certain business practices such as the mislabeling of products. Both the FTC and a company it investigates can appeal an issue to the courts.

Other Legislation

The Smith-Lever Act of 1914 provided Federal aid to rural education by funding demonstration agents who showed farmers improved techniques in agriculture. The program was administered by land grant universities. The Smith-Hughes Act of 1917 provided money for vocational education in public high schools.

The Federal Farm Loan Act of 1916 made it easier for farmers to borrow money. The Adamson Act of the same year provided for railroad workers to receive the same pay for an eight-hour workday that they had been getting in a ten-hour day. The immediate impetus for this law was a threatened rail strike that would have been devastating to the country's preparation for possible involvement in the war in Europe. Congress also authorized Federal aid for highway construction, reversing the Jacksonian tradition of the national government not funding internal improvements. Renewal of the program in 1921 led to the numbered system of U.S. highways that we still use today.

President Wilson at first opposed a child labor reform bill because he believed it to be a matter for state regulation. Congress did eventually pass and the President did sign a law outlawing products from interstate commerce if they had been made by children under fourteen years of age, but the Supreme Court ruled that the law was unconstitutional. The Court said that work conditions in a factory were not subject to regulation as a part of interstate commerce.

Though Wilson established the most progressive record of legislation in the nation's history, the record of the Wilson years was not consistently progressive. Wilson did not support a constitutional amendment giving women the right to vote. He also held and demonstrated prejudiced attitudes toward blacks, and no effort was made to eliminate racial segregation in American life. Five of Wilson's ten Cabinet members were from the South, and Secretary of State William Jennings Bryan was widely revered in the South. This tended to limit the progressive tone of Wilson's Administration. However, Wilson did appoint Louis Brandeis as the first Jewish Justice to the U.S. Supreme Court.

Louis Brandeis (1856-1941) earned his law degree from Harvard before he turned 21. He often donated his legal services to causes he believed in. Brandeis served on the Supreme Court from 1916 to 1939.

Mexico

President Woodrow Wilson and Secretary of State William Jennings Bryan supported the Roosevelt Corollary by favoring U.S. intervention in Latin American countries in circumstances that would promote democracy. The tumultuous situation in Mexico put this commitment to the test.

Much of the wealth in Mexico was owned by the United States, Great Britain, and the Roman Catholic Church, while many of the people of Mexico lived in abject poverty. Porfirio Diaz had ruled as dictator since 1877. In 1910 the Mexicans revolted and Diaz escaped to Europe. Francisco Madero became president, but he could not control the guerrilla forces that were still active. In 1913 Madero was assassinated and Victoriano Huerta seized power.

Wilson refused to recognize Huerta and persuaded Great Britain to withdraw its support of the Huerta government. The President then offered to help Huerta's chief rival, Venustiano Carranza. In 1914 Wilson ordered American forces to take control of the Mexican city of Vera Cruz to prevent the unloading of a German shipment of arms intended for Huerta. This act of American aggression angered many Mexicans, including Carranza. The U.S. agreed to arbitration by the ABC powers (Argentina, Brazil, and Chile), who arranged for Huerta to resign in favor of Carranza.

Wilson shifted his support to Pancho Villa, a Mexican leader with his own army. Carranza defeated Villa's forces; and the U.S. recognized Carranza's government in late 1915. Villa then attacked Americans in 1916 in an attempt to regain power by inciting an American response. His men killed fifteen American engineers in northern Mexico and seventeen more in New Mexico. Wilson sent troops to secure the border and ordered a military expedition against Villa's forces into Mexico that was largely unsuccessful. The growing conflict in Europe in 1917 led Wilson to withdraw the American forces involved on the Mexican border.

All of these forays into foreign relations helped the United States to become a greater international power, but they were merely precursors of the huge involvement by the United States in the Great War in Europe.

1916 Election

In the 1916 presidential election, the Republicans nominated Charles Evans Hughes to oppose Wilson. Hughes had been a reform governor of New York before Taft named him to the Supreme Court in 1910. He resigned in 1916 to run for President. The Progressive (Bull Moose) Party renominated Theodore Roosevelt, but Roosevelt refused the nomination and gave his support to Hughes. This effectively ended the life of the Progressive Party. The Democrats trumpeted Wilson's record of reform legislation. As war engulfed Europe, the President's supporters could say, "He Kept Us Out of War."

This American plane is carrying messages in Mexico during the 1916 campaign against Pancho Villa.

Wilson himself conducted a front porch campaign from his New Jersey home.

The election was surprisingly close. Late on election night, Democrats conceded defeat; but even later returns from California gave Wilson the victory. Wilson won the state by less than four thousand votes. He won the popular vote nationwide by about 600,000 (9.1 million to 8.5 million, or 49.4% to 46.2%) and carried the electoral college 277 to 254.

President Wilson was able to focus on domestic issues and keep the country out of war during his first term, but world events drew the United States into war and dominated the President's second term.

Charles Evans Hughes was Secretary of State under Republican Presidents Warren G. Harding and Calvin Coolidge. He then served on the World Court for a time. In 1930 Herbert Hoover nominated Hughes to be Chief Justice of the U.S. Supreme Court, a position in which he served until 1941. This portrait is by Thomas C. Corner.

But flee from these things, you man of God,
and pursue righteousness, godliness,
faith, love, perseverance, and gentleness.
1 Timothy 6:11

⋆ Assignments for Lesson 96 ⋆

American Voices Read "Love Lifted Me" by James Rowe (page 296).

Literature Begin reading *Miracle In the Hills.* Plan to finish it by the end of the next unit.

Bible Start memorizing Micah 4:1-2.

Project Choose your project for this unit and start working on it.

Student Review Optional: Answer the questions for Lesson 96.

Ruins of Vaux, France (1918)

Lesson 97

Trouble in Europe

He wanted freedom for his people after years of foreign oppression. He was willing to risk everything, even his life, to help his cause. He met with a few people who believed as he did, and they developed a plan. On the fateful day, he took his gun and went out to the parade.

Gavrilo Princip lit the spark that ignited World War I, but the entire continent of Europe was a powder keg waiting to explode. Princip committed his deed in the Bosnian capital of Sarajevo, but the result of his deed was that 32 nations engaged in a four-year war which cost the lives of eight and one-half million Europeans.

Background Factors

Several factors contributed to building the powder keg. The first was the policy of imperialism that many nations followed. As we discussed in an earlier lesson, the way that many countries built their wealth, prestige, and power was by developing empires. Great Britain, Germany, and France had done it; and other nations wanted a piece of the action. One such country was Austria-Hungary, and one area it wanted was the Balkan peninsula to its south. The Balkan region was home to a mixture of Slavic peoples in Serbia, Bosnia, Herzegovina, and other nations. Austria-Hungary annexed Bosnia and Herzegovina in 1908.

A second and conflicting factor contributing to war was nationalism. While some countries wanted to take over other countries, people in the threatened countries resisted being ruled by foreigners and wanted to exert their own identity. The people of the Balkans had been a political football for centuries. They resented being dominated by the Austrians and wanted to be independent.

The third factor was the rivalries of various states for power and sometimes for the same land. European nations entered into alliances in order to strengthen their positions against possible enemies. Germany and Austria-Hungary were in an alliance because of their common Germanic heritage and because Germany, as the stronger partner, posed a threat to Austria if it didn't go along. Italy was also a part of this Triple Alliance because it had designs on part of the Balkans and Italian leaders thought aligning their country with Germany was the best way to get it.

France to the west and Russia to the east were threatened by Germany's power, so they developed an alliance to resist any German aggression. England sided with them, and the three countries were known as the Triple Entente, also called the Allied

Powers, to resist German aggression anywhere it might occur. These alliances created a delicate balance of power as each side hoped that its strength would discourage aggressive moves by the other side. What is more, Russia and Austria-Hungary faced the threat of political revolutions within their own borders. The leaders of these countries thought that they could call on their allies to help quell domestic disturbances if the need arose.

The Spark

The heir to the Austro-Hungarian throne, Archduke Francis Ferdinand, and his wife visited Sarajevo, Bosnia, on what he called a goodwill visit. It also served to remind the Bosnians who was in charge. On June 28, 1914, the archduke and his wife rode through the streets of Sarajevo. Serbian nationalist Gavrilo Princip, who had slipped across the border into Bosnia, fired from the crowd and killed them both. He wanted to strike out against Austria-Hungary, which he saw as threatening Serbia and all of the Balkans.

Japan, which had its eyes on German possessions in the Pacific, declared war on Germany on August 23. The Japanese print below shows Japanese troops in action. Turkey allied itself with the Central Powers. Italy stayed out of the conflict for a while; and when it did come in, it did so on the side of the Allied Powers.

Franz Ferdinand and His Wife, Sophie

Following the assassination, Austria-Hungary made a list of ten demands on Serbia, mostly having to do with stamping out anti-Austrian propaganda. The demands as a whole were impossible to meet, but the Serbian government agreed to try to follow eight of them. This was not good enough for Austria-Hungary, which declared war on Serbia on July 28, 1914, and began a military move toward Serbia.

The Dominoes Fall

This triggered a response from Russia, which mobilized its forces to help Serbia. Russians and Serbians are both Slavic peoples, and Russia wanted to help its ethnic relatives against aggression by the Triple Alliance. To protect its alliance, Germany declared war on Russia on August 1, 1914, and on France two days later. France then declared war on Germany. Germany planned to knock out France quickly, then move all its forces against Russia. The French had built a strong defensive line on its eastern border with Germany, so the Germans moved through neutral Belgium to get to France.

This violation of Belgian neutrality led Great Britain to declare war on Germany on August 4. The Belgians put up a noble resistance which held up the German forces and gave French and British armies time to reach the area to strengthen Allied resistance to German aggression. The two sides dug in to their positions along a 600-mile front across Europe. Most of the rest of the war involved terrible fighting along this front, with one side or the other making occasional advances.

Great Suffering

All war is terrible, but the death and destruction brought about in the Great War was especially costly. The two sides traded attacks using new military technology, including machine guns, aerial bombing, poison gas, land mines, and armored tanks. Many of the infantrymen spent much of the war in trenches along the front, emerging to attack and then either returning to the trenches or digging new ones. Conditions in the trenches were awful, especially in the rain and mud. Flooding and unsanitary conditions cost many lives. The exchange of shelling obliterated large areas of European landscape. In the Battle of the Somme, 20,000 British soldiers were killed and 40,000 were wounded in one twenty-four-hour period.

Soldiers in France from the French Colony of Senegal

The novel All Quiet on the Western Front *by Erich Maria Remarque recounts the awful realities of trench warfare during World War I. Remarque tells the story from the German side, but conditions were much the same for both sides. The book includes some rough language and graphic battle scenes. The German soldier above was photographed in 1916.*

American Neutrality

President Wilson committed the United States to a position of neutrality when the war erupted. He and most other Americans believed and hoped that the isolation afforded to the United States by the Atlantic Ocean would keep the U.S. out of direct involvement in the European conflict.

Nevertheless, feelings ran high among Americans about the countries involved in the conflict. Historically and culturally, most Americans felt drawn to support Great Britain. The historic friendship with France dating back to the American Revolution strengthened American support for the Allied forces. In addition, most Americans had an uneasy feeling about German aggression and the consequences of a German victory. On the other hand, the eight million German immigrants and German-Americans had strong feelings for their fatherland. The four and one-half million Irish in America had an historic hatred of Great Britain, which pulled them toward opposing the Allies. Polish and Jewish Americans disliked Russia.

The practicalities of neutrality were hard to balance. Germany wanted to control more land and Great Britain wanted to control the seas. Both of these policies affected American trade. A strict embargo on American foreign trade would hurt Great Britain, but helping the Allies would hurt Germany. Exports to Allied countries helped the American economy, a benefit that was difficult to give up for the principle of neutrality. Many daring Americans left the country to fly in the new Canadian or French air forces.

Wilson accepted British control of the seas, high-handed as it was at times. He also permitted trade that helped the Allies, although he forbade the making of loans to combatants so that the American gold reserve could remain strong. Wilson changed this policy in 1915, when the J. P. Morgan bankers were allowed to make a $50 million loan to France; and the ban on loans was lifted that summer. The President also rejected a proposal by German-Americans to halt all sales of arms to the warring countries.

German Aggression on the Seas

America was pulled into the war mostly by the provocations of Germany on the high seas. On February 4, 1915, Germany declared a zone of attack around the British Isles. It said that all ships were subject to attack without warning by German submarines or U-boats (*unterseebooten*). This was a major change from the traditional rules of war which allowed for safe passage of non-military vessels. President Wilson warned Germany that it would be held to strict accountability for any actions that harmed American ships and lives.

Three Americans died in two separate incidents in the spring of 1915. Then on May 7, 1915, German torpedoes sank the British passenger liner *Lusitania* off Ireland, with the loss of 1,198 lives including 124 Americans. Germany had issued warnings in the United States against traveling on the vessel. Despite these losses and despite Wilson's warnings to Germany, many Americans still wanted to avoid involvement in the war.

Wilson sent a series of messages to Germany warning her of the consequences of continued aggression. The second of these notes was so strongly worded that Secretary of State Bryan resigned out of fear that it would provoke a German declaration of war. Germany did, however, promise the safety of unarmed passenger liners.

Meanwhile, the U.S. began a slow program of preparedness by strengthening the Army and Navy. Many opposed such a program as the first step toward war, but conservatives generally supported the program. To finance the buildup, Congress increased income tax rates; and about $21 billion was raised through the sale of war bonds.

This 1915 song by Alfred Bryan (lyrics) and Al Piantadosi (music) was popular among the large portion of Americans who opposed entering the war.

Following Wilson's re-election in 1916, he urged the combatants to pursue a negotiated peace; but the replies he received from the nations involved showed coolness to his idea. He addressed the Senate on January 17, 1917, to state his general desires for peace. Wilson said that he wanted to see "a peace without victory" and that "only a peace between equals can last." He urged all nations to avoid entangling alliances, to guarantee the freedom of the seas, and to support government by the consent of the governed.

Two weeks later, Germany resumed unrestricted submarine warfare, revoking its earlier promise regarding passenger ships. In response, Wilson severed diplomatic ties with Germany. America's neutrality would not last much longer.

The Great War was a complex global conflict. A British propaganda office in China published the poster shown at right. It warned Muslims in China not to trust Germans, referencing a German official in Africa who had issued regulations against Islam.

The righteousness of the upright will deliver them,
But the treacherous will be caught by their own greed.
Proverbs 11:6

⋆ Assignments for Lesson 97 ⋆

American Voices Read "A Beautiful Life" by William Golden (page 304).

Literature Continue reading *Miracle In the Hills.*

Bible Work on memorizing Micah 4:1-2.

Project Work on your project.

Student Review Optional: Answer the questions for Lesson 97.

Woodrow Wilson Asks Congress for a Declaration of War

Lesson 98

America Goes "Over There"

The United States had watched from a distance the European conflict erupt and begin to take its terrible toll. The Wilson Administration had tried to maintain neutrality toward the belligerent nations, although most American sympathies and what little aid was given were directed toward the Allied Powers of Britain, France, and Russia. Germany had caused the loss of innocent American lives by its submarine attacks on passenger ships. For a while, in response to sharp American demands, Germany had ceased firing on non-military shipping; but in early 1917 that practice resumed. This was seen in America as an insult, especially in the face of Wilson's pleas for a peace without victory and a peace among equals.

Further German Insults

Then came another blow. On February 25, 1917, the German foreign minister Arthur Zimmerman sent a telegram to the German ambassador in Mexico, instructing the ambassador to approach the Mexican government about a possible alliance with Mexico if Germany went to war with the United States. Among other things, the note suggested that such a move might help Mexico win back "the lost territory in Texas, New Mexico, and Arizona." The telegram was intercepted by British intelligence and made public in America on March 1. Once again the American public was outraged. Wilson then asked Congress for authority to arm American ships. When the request was blocked, Wilson found the authority in existing legislation and ordered it anyway.

The Germans sank three American ships in March 1917. That same month, a liberal revolution ousted the tsar from power in Russia. This made all of the Allies appear to be fighting for democracy. On the battle front, meanwhile, the Allied position seemed increasingly desperate in several areas.

Declaration of War

On April 2, 1917, President Wilson asked Congress for a declaration recognizing that a state of war existed between the United States and Germany. He said the world had to be made "safe for democracy." Congress voted overwhelmingly in favor of the declaration on April 6. Nearly three years had passed since the war began in Europe. Continued aggressive actions of Germany toward the United States finally pushed America into the war. British propaganda about the war and American economic interests played a role in shaping American opinion, but when principles that America held dear were repeatedly violated, Congress and the Wilson Administration believed they had no choice but to go to war.

America entered into intense war preparations. The most significant early assistance that the U.S. gave the Allied cause was in naval escorts of Allied shipping. This dramatically cut the number of losses from German submarine attacks. In addition, General John Pershing led a 14,500 man contingent to France in June of 1917. His judgment after arriving was that the Allies were unable to mount a significant offensive on their own, and he requested that Wilson send a million American troops to Europe by the spring of 1918. The Army then directed its efforts toward meeting that goal.

America at War

When the United States entered the war, its Army numbered 379,000 troops. A month after entering the war, the government instituted a draft (called Selective Service) to register men between 21 and 30. Later the range was expanded to include men between the ages of 18 and 45. The first men were drafted in July. The Army grew to about 3.7 million men. Of those, about two million eventually went to Europe, where 1.4 million saw combat. The recruits were ushered into hastily built training camps, most of which were in the South because of better weather conditions there.

The nation also mobilized its domestic resources to help in the war effort. The War Industrial Board led by industrialist Bernard Baruch had oversight of all industrial production and could order the specific use of raw materials and other resources it saw fit to help the war. The government created other wartime agencies, including the Food Administration overseen by Herbert Hoover.

Hoover was a millionaire mining engineer who had guided relief efforts for embattled Belgium and who then returned to the U.S. when it entered the war. Hoover managed food production and usage to help the armed forces. His agency encouraged people to have Meatless Tuesdays, Wheatless Wednesdays, and Porkless Saturdays and to grow their own gardens in order to make more food available for the troops. The Food Administration did not have to use rationing. The Fuel Administration introduced Daylight Saving Time and encouraged Heatless Mondays. When labor issues arose in the factories, the government usually supported labor in order to keep production going.

Many southerners moved north to work in factories and to escape their rural poverty. This included many blacks, and the black exodus to the North continued into the 1920s. People in the north, however, often did not welcome African Americans kindly. Race riots broke out in St. Louis, Chicago, and elsewhere as whites committed violence against the blacks they didn't want around and who they saw as a threat to their jobs.

When General John Pershing arrived in Paris, he went to the tomb of General Lafayette, French hero in the American Revolution. A war correspondent reported that he heard Pershing say, "Lafayette, we are here," indicating that now it was time for America to come to the aid of France. In his memoirs of the war, Pershing said that he did not remember saying it and that another American officer used the line in a speech in Paris on July 4, 1917.

This American officer is in an observation balloon near the front lines in France (1918).

Women went to work in greater numbers as millions of men joined the Army. After the war, most women returned home. Unions generally opposed women being in the workforce. Their stated reason was that women's place was in the home, but they probably also feared that their jobs might be given to women who were paid less. The changed role of women in society did lead President Wilson to come out in favor of women's suffrage by 1918.

The Supreme Court upheld the Espionage and Sedition Acts just after the war in its decision in the case of Schenck v. United States *(1919). Justice Oliver Wendell Holmes Jr. said that speech could be limited when a "clear and present danger" exists. Holmes said that the right of free speech does not, for example, extend to someone falsely shouting "Fire" in a crowded theater and thus causing panic. His ideas have been accepted as limits on free speech ever since. Jane Addams and Helen Keller (pictured at right) were two vocal opponents of the war who were not prosecuted.*

The Battle for American Hearts and Minds

The Administration also engaged in a certain amount of information and speech control to encourage the war effort. Journalist George Creel was appointed head of the Committee on Public Information, which turned out to be the government's propaganda operation. It kept the public informed of Allied war aims with speakers and pamphlets and sought to influence public opinion in enemy countries. The government also limited domestic free speech in opposition to the war with laws such as the Espionage Act, the Trading with the Enemy Act, and the Sedition Act, which attempted to suppress criticism of the war effort and of government leaders.

A significant portion of the American public opposed the war, and many prosecutions took place under the legislation. Over one hundred leaders of the Industrial Workers of the World were convicted for opposing the war effort. Socialist Eugene V. Debs also was against American involvement in the war. He was sent to jail for encouraging men to resist the draft. While in prison, he received over 900,000 votes for President in 1920.

Because of Germany's aggressive actions, things with German connections fell into disrepute. Some people with German ancestry felt the need to change their last names. Familiar terms of German origin were also changed. Hamburger (named for Hamburg, Germany) became Salisbury steak (named for a town in England). Frankfurters became hot dogs. In England, the royal family changed its name in 1917 from the German-sounding House of Hanover to the English-sounding House of Windsor. In addition, many Americans opposed labor strife because it reminded them of Bolshevik (Communist) unrest in Russia.

Wilson's Fourteen Points

In Russia, the Bolsheviks staged another revolution in November of 1917 and took control of the country. The new government made a separate peace treaty with Germany and pulled out of the war. On January 8, 1918, President Wilson outlined his vision for world peace in his Fourteen Points speech before Congress. He laid out what he saw as essential steps to bringing about a just peace, including "open covenants" arrived at "in the public view," free navigation of the seas, impartial settlement of colonial claims, and the addressing

Alvin C. York

The greatest American hero of World War I was a quiet, thirty-one-year-old man from rural Tennessee, Alvin C. York. York had led a wild life before his conversion at a revival in 1914. When he was drafted for military service, York asked not to serve because of his objections to war; but his request was denied. He eventually agreed to go into battle to help stop others from killing.

In October of 1918, Corporal York's unit of eighteen men was ordered to take a railroad line in the Argonne Forest. They misread their map and wound up behind enemy lines. A German officer surrendered even though he had the Americans outnumbered. German machine guns opened fire on their own men who had surrendered, killing nine Americans in the process. York, an expert marksman, was ordered to take out the machine guns, which he did. Eventually 132 Germans were captured by the nine remaining Americans. York never claimed to have acted alone, but only two other soldiers were ever decorated for their part in the encounter.

News of York's heroism eventually made its way to the American military command. York received the Medal of Honor, was promoted to sergeant, and was welcomed back to the U.S. as a national hero. Tennessee civic clubs raised money to buy York and his new wife a house, but they were only partly successful and York had to take out a mortgage for the rest. York dedicated his life to helping educate the children of his area. He founded and raised money nationwide for the York Institute, which eventually became a high school and vocational school. York never tried to make money off of his heroism. He resisted Hollywood offers to make a movie based on his life until World War II began. York then agreed to a movie deal to encourage young Americans to support their country in that effort. The movie Sergeant York *starring Gary Cooper is a good representation of York's life through his return to Tennessee.*

Americans Celebrating in Philadelphia After Announcement of the Armistice

of border questions involving European nations. He also called for national self-determination in the Balkans, Turkey, Poland, and other areas. The fourteenth point was a call for "a general association of nations" to guarantee independence and territorial integrity to all people. This became Wilson's proposal for a League of Nations.

Armistice

The peace settlement with Russia enabled Germany to concentrate its efforts on the western front, but it was too late. American forces began having a real impact in the war in the summer of 1918. Decisive American offensives in September drove German armies into retreat and brought a request from the German high command for terms for an armistice with the Allies. Austria-Hungary dropped out of the war in the fall. On November 9, 1918, the German Kaiser abdicated his throne. An armistice was signed that went into effect at the eleventh hour on the eleventh day of the eleventh month, November 11, 1918. The armistice was signed by German and Allied officials in a railroad car.

This documentary film described the Allied effort to defeat Germany by France, Britain, Italy, and the United States. Originally intended as a propaganda piece, it was released six days after the Armistice with an edited ending about the end of the war.

This photo shows the Aisne-Marne American Cemetery and Memorial in Belleau, France, decorated for Memorial Day in 2013. The cemetery has 2,288 graves with headstones shaped either as Stars of David or crosses. The cross in the foreground has this inscription: "Here rests in honored glory an American soldier known but to God."

In all, 61 million people served in the military around the world. Eight and a half million Europeans died as a result of the war, including two million Germans and about 1.7 million each from France and Russia. Nineteen million people were injured. American casualties included 114,000 dead.

International efforts that had for so long been directed toward war now turned to the task of creating a just and lasting peace. These efforts created a different kind of conflict among nations. They led to an unsatisfactory peace in many ways and left the door open for further conflict later in the century.

Too long has my soul had its dwelling with those who hate peace.
I am for peace, but when I speak, they are for war.
Psalm 120:6-7

⋆ Assignments for Lesson 98 ⋆

American Voices Read Woodrow Wilson's War Message to Congress and the excerpts from his "Fourteen Points" speech (pages 297-302 and 305-306).

Read "Over There" by George M. Cohan (page 303).

Literature Continue reading *Miracle In the Hills.*

Bible Work on memorizing Micah 4:1-2.

Project Work on your project.

Student Review Optional: Answer the questions for Lesson 98.

Hall of Mirrors at the Palace of Versailles

Lesson 99

An Imperfect Peace

With the approach of peace, Woodrow Wilson felt the highest calling of his life. He was determined to use every ounce of skill and every resource at his disposal to create a better and safer world. After the war to end all wars, he wanted a world safe for democracy. Wilson's idealism might have helped to create a peace that was better than it otherwise would have been. However, Wilson faced difficulties in implementing his plan; and his uncompromising devotion to his vision created resistance from others involved in the peace process.

Partisan Missteps

During the congressional election campaign of 1918, Wilson appealed to the American public to return a Democratic Congress that would support him in his efforts for peace. This blatantly partisan call in the midst of war backfired, and the Republican Party won enough seats to gain control of both the House and the Senate. Wilson decided to attend the peace conference at the palace of Versailles, just outside of Paris, France. The conference lasted over a period of six months, and Wilson was there for almost all of it.

Wilson's determination to go to the conference showed his commitment to his plan for peace. However, while he was gone his Administration lacked leadership in generating public support for his plan and furthering the work of government as the nation wound down from its war effort. In addition, Wilson did not name a single Republican to the peace delegation. Republicans in Congress considered this an insult and another example of Wilson's partisanship, and they resolved to oppose Wilson's plan when it came before them.

Wilson in Europe

When Wilson arrived in Europe, he was wildly welcomed by the people of France, Great Britain, and Italy as a hero and savior. Some homes had Wilson's picture placed behind candles, as though it were an icon. This popular reception increased his sense of mission for the treaty negotiations. He sat down with Prime Minister David Lloyd George of Great Britain, Premier Georges Clemenceau of France, and Premier Vittorio Orlando of Italy with the purpose of crafting a new world order with the United States as the moral power behind it. Representatives of all the nations that had declared war on or broken diplomatic relations with Germany were present, but the meetings were dominated by the Big Four countries and their leaders. Then things started caving in.

The Big Four at Versailles: David Lloyd George, Vittorio Orlando, Georges Clemenceau, and Woodrow Wilson

First, Wilson had to deal with the expectations that had been created by previously made secret treaties. When the Bolsheviks had taken over Russia, they had published the contents of secret treaties made by the Allies at the start of the war. These treaties called for the victor nations to carve up parts of Germany and Austria-Hungary and to take over Germany's overseas colonies. England, France, and Italy expected those agreements to be honored; but Wilson had strong objections to such actions, especially since they had been made in secret.

Second, the American President came with high ideals for molding a world of peace without the sense of winners enjoying the conquest of losers. However, the European leaders had seen their countries devastated by war; and they wanted Germany to pay for the damages. Lloyd George had just won an election in Britain with his party using the slogans "Hang the Kaiser" and "Make Germany Pay." He had no intention of being kind to Germany or risking Britain's dominance at sea. Clemenceau had seen France suffer long enough under the threat of German military power, and he wanted to crush Germany's might. Orlando's main interest was in acquiring a portion of the Balkans that Italy had been promised in 1915 when it had come into the war on the Allied side.

Finally, Wilson's primary goal was the formation of a League of Nations, which he believed could prevent or limit future wars. He wanted this so badly that he was willing to compromise on many other points in order to get the League included as part of the final treaty. The treaty called for the demilitarization of the west bank of the Rhine and the giving of the coal-rich Alsace-Lorraine region to France. German colonies were to be given to victor nations and administered by a mandate program under the auspices of the League of Nations. Many other changes were made in the map of Europe. Slavic peoples were given their own countries: Czechoslovakia and, in the Balkans, Yugoslavia. Poland was re-established from the eastern part of the German empire. Finland, Estonia, Latvia, and Lithuania were created to give other ethnic groups their own countries. Italy received the corner of the

A massive influenza epidemic struck in 1918. Estimates of the worldwide death toll are at least 20 million. American soldiers returning from Europe brought the disease into the country with them, and the eventual death toll in the United States alone was a half million people. Ten thousand Americans died in September of 1918. From then until June of 1919, about one-fourth of the American population had the flu. The photo below shows volunteer Red Cross nurses tending patients in the Oakland (California) Auditorium.

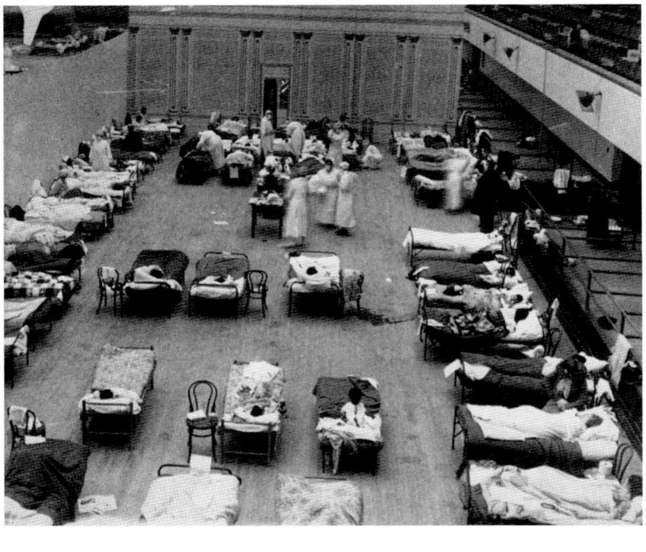

Balkans that it was hoping for. Austria and Hungary were made into separate nations.

In the most controversial part of the treaty, Germany (not Austria-Hungary) was made to accept the blame for the war and was ordered to pay huge sums in reparations to the victor nations. The German military was reduced to a tiny force. The United States joined Britain and France in a defense pact against any future German aggression.

Wilson did not like the imposing of war guilt and reparations on Germany, but he was forced to accept these provisions so that the other leaders would accept the League of Nations. As drawn up in the treaty, the League would be overseen by a secretary-general. It would have a general assembly of one representative from each member nation. The real power would reside in a council, which would have the United States, Great Britain, France, Italy, and Japan as permanent members and other nations rotating on for periods of time. Any of the five permanent members could veto any resolution or action of the council. Other agencies were included in the League's operations as well. The League was well-intentioned, but it had weaknesses. No member state was compelled to act against an aggressor nation that invaded another member state. The veto power of the permanent council members stymied the chances for almost any significant action. Finally, the League simply did not have much power to end a conflict that might erupt.

The treaty was presented to representatives of the German government, who objected strongly to its punitive provisions. However, under threat of an Allied military invasion, Germany signed the treaty on June 28, 1919.

The Battle for the Peace

Wilson came home in July of 1919 to a nation divided over the Treaty of Versailles. The German-American community and the influential Hearst newspapers didn't like the harsh terms imposed

The Signing of Peace in the Hall of Mirrors, Versailles, 28th June 1919, *William Orpen (Irish, 1919)*

on Germany. The Irish didn't like that fact that no provision was made for an independent Ireland. Italian-Americans didn't believe that Italy had gotten enough in the settlement. More important politically, many Republicans in the Senate, including a group of isolationists called "The Irreconcilables," pledged themselves to defeat the treaty. Their main reason for opposing the treaty was the League of Nations, which they felt created a permanent entanglement of the United States in foreign affairs which the U.S. was not free to control. Partisanship also played a significant role in the Republicans' opposition. Still, a large number of Americans supported at least the general terms of the treaty and the concept of an international body to maintain peace.

Senate Foreign Relations Committee Chairman Henry Cabot Lodge drew up a list of reservations that he wanted attached to the treaty before he would approve its passage. One reservation said that the U.S. would not be obligated with regard to any

Violence in Ireland escalated during and after World War I as many Irish fought for the independence of their country. During the conflict, the British stationed thousands of constables in Ireland, many of them veterans of the Great War. Because of their uniform colors, they were called the Black and Tans. Ireland eventually became independent of Great Britain through a long series of steps, including the ratification of a new constitution in 1922. The northern counties on the island remained with Great Britain and became Northern Ireland.

League of Nations action without a joint resolution of Congress specifically supporting it. Wilson refused to accept any reservations, and the battle over the treaty boiled down to a standoff between Wilson and Lodge.

Wilson tried to go directly to the American people to gain support for the treaty. He went on an exhausting speaking tour informing people about the treaty and attempting to get the public to share his vision for creating the means of maintaining world peace. The response he received was strongly positive. However, seven days after giving a speech in Pueblo, Colorado, the President suffered a serious stroke that paralyzed his entire left side. Robbed of its most effective supporter, the treaty appeared headed for defeat. Lodge presented the treaty with reservations to the Senate. Wilson, dogmatic to the last, urged his fellow Democrats to vote against it; and the treaty was defeated in November of 1919. However, this did not settle the question of how officially to end the war. The country had enough support for the treaty and the League that the treaty was brought up for a second vote in March of 1920, but again it fell short of the majority it needed. A change by seven Democrats would have been enough to ratify it. Wilson then asked that the 1920 election be a "solemn referendum" on whether the United States would fulfill its role on the world stage or retreat into isolationism.

On May 20, 1920, Congress passed a joint resolution declaring the war over. Wilson vetoed it. Another joint resolution passed July 2, 1921; and with the signature of Republican President Warren G. Harding, the state of war was finally ended. The United States concluded separate treaties with Germany and with Austria-Hungary in October of 1921.

The Recovery Stumbles

While the political turmoil was going on in Washington, more immediate pressures were facing many Americans. Soldiers returned from Europe and began looking for work just as war production

1919 Cartoon from Punch *Magazine*

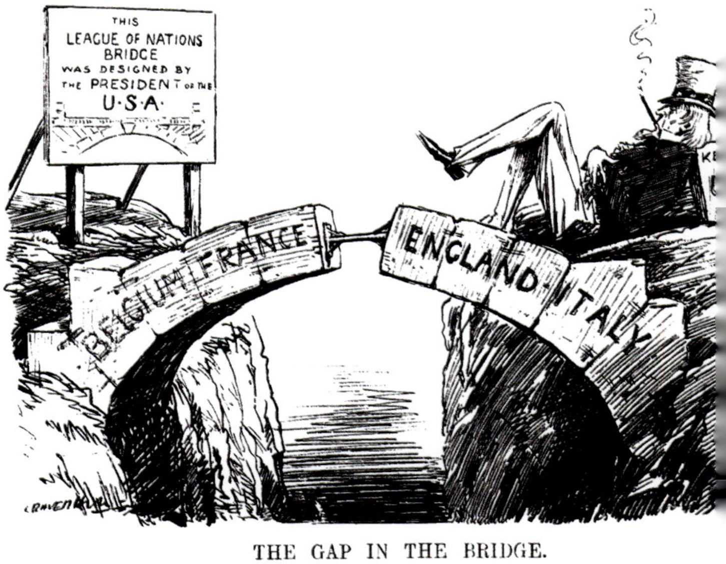

THE GAP IN THE BRIDGE.

ceased and the need for workers fell. Farm prices also decreased as European nations began to rejuvenate their domestic agriculture and didn't need American imports. Labor unions resorted to strikes to try to improve their members' lot. During 1919 a total of four million workers were on strike at one time or other. Some of the strikes became violent. When the Boston police went on strike, the city's mayor and Massachusetts governor Calvin Coolidge called out the National Guard to maintain order. The police then announced their intention to return to work, but the mayor refused to accept them and announced his plans to hire a new force. Governor Coolidge supported the mayor and declared, "There is no right to strike against the public safety by anybody, anywhere, any time." Coolidge's stance gained him national attention and helped him receive the Republican vice presidential nomination in 1920.

Another upsetting factor in post-war America was the fear of Communist revolutionaries in the country that came to be called the Red Scare. The Bolshevik Revolution in Russia in November of 1917 caused many Americans to believe that a similar attempt was possible in this country. Indeed, thirty mail bombs were discovered, including some addressed to Cabinet members and a Supreme Court Justice. A bomb exploded on Wall Street at noon on September 16, 1920, killing 38, injuring hundreds, and causing hundreds of thousands of dollars worth of damage.

Attorney General A. Mitchell Palmer arrested hundreds of suspected radical agents and had many deported without a trial. The young J. Edgar Hoover was put in charge of building files on suspected radicals. Palmer received criticism for some of his actions, which included making some raids without search warrants. The uneasy atmosphere of the Red Scare was widespread. The New York State legislature expelled five Socialists who had been fairly elected because their ideas were deemed not in the best interests of the country. Americanism became a cause that lasted well into the 1920s and resulted in immigration restrictions and other actions against those whose loyalty some Americans questioned.

The fighting had ended, but tensions were not completely gone in either Europe or in the United States. Different battles emerged during the period of the 1920s.

Wilson's first wife, Ellen, died on August 6, 1914, just as war was brewing in Europe. The President married Edith Bolling Galt, a Washington widow, on December 18, 1915. It is generally believed that Edith maintained a tight control of Wilson's activities following his stroke and might even have been involved in making policy decisions while he was recovering. This 1920 photo shows Edith holding a document for the President, paralyzed on the left side, to sign. Woodrow Wilson died in 1924.

What Else Was Happening?

1914 *The first transcontinental telephone line is completed.*

1914 *Work begins on the Lincoln Highway, which will eventually carry auto traffic from coast to coast.*

1914 *The first signal light to regulate traffic (red = stop, green = go) is installed in Cleveland, Ohio.*

1915 *The Corning Glass Works markets the first cookware made from heat-resistant glass.*

1917 *Congress passes the 18th Amendment outlawing the making, selling, or transporting of alcoholic beverages. It is ratified by enough states in January of 1919 and goes into effect one year later. The Volstead Act, passed in 1919 over Wilson's veto, outlaws any beverage with more than .5% alcohol.*

1918 *British women over the age of thirty are given the right to vote.*

1919 *British violence against unarmed Indian protesters causes Mohandas Gandhi to begin a campaign for Indian independence.*

1919 *Karl Barth publishes his commentary* Epistle to the Romans.

1919 *The Weimar Republic begins in Germany.*

1919 *The Cincinnati Reds defeat the heavily favored Chicago White Sox in the World Series, five games to three. It is later revealed that several White Sox players were paid by gamblers to play poorly on purpose to try to lose the games, thus increasing the payout on bets made on the underdog Reds. It becomes known as the Black Sox Scandal. Shoeless Joe Jackson and other players are banned from baseball. Players taking bribes from gamblers has been commonplace since salaries are so low. The first commissioner of baseball, Judge Kennesaw "Mountain" Landis, is appointed to clean up major league baseball.*

Deceit is in the heart of those who devise evil,
But counselors of peace have joy.
Proverbs 12:20

⋆ Assignments for Lesson 99 ⋆

American Voices Read "Wonderful Grace of Jesus" by Haldor Lillenas (page 307).

Literature Continue reading *Miracle In the Hills.*

Bible Work on memorizing Micah 4:1-2.

Project Work on your project.

Student Review Optional: Answer the questions for Lesson 99.

Church Service in N'Gaoundere, Cameroon (2007)

Lesson 100 - Bible Study

From Every Nation, Tribe, and Tongue

The involvement of the United States on the world stage made Americans more aware of the peoples of different lands, especially those who were different from them in terms of skin color, language, culture, and religion. This is therefore a good time to consider what the Bible says about the nations of the world and how Christians should think of them.

Nations in the Bible

After the great flood that is described in Genesis, the children of the sons of Noah spread out over the face of the earth and gave rise to the nations of people who inhabit the earth (Genesis 10). At first all the people used the same language; but when some people attempted to build a tower to the heavens, God confused their language in order to keep them from accomplishing their goal (Genesis 11). Thus the different languages of the world began.

The Bible does not place a great emphasis on what we call the racial divisions of mankind. However, Scripture does take note of various nations. In the Old Testament, nations and people groups that are mentioned include: Canaanites, Hittites, Amorites, Perizzites, Hivites, Jebusites, Ammonites, Edomites, Moabites, Gileadites, Egyptians, Philistines, Assyrians, Babylonians (Chaldeans), Persians, and Israelites. The New Testament refers to the Jews (descendants of people from the tribe of Judah who returned from captivity in Babylon), Romans, Greeks, Syrophoenicians, Ethiopians, Scythians, the geographic regions of Spain and the area on the Balkan peninsula called Illyricum.

The Jews, generally speaking, saw the world as divided into two kinds of people: Jews and Gentiles. The Jews saw themselves as God's special, chosen people; and they saw Gentiles as dirty dog sinners with whom Jews were not to associate. Among the unacceptable people in the Jews' minds were the Samaritans. Samaritans were descendants of the intermarriage of two groups: the pagan Assyrians who were brought in to repopulate the Northern Kingdom after the Northern Kingdom was taken into captivity, and the pagan Northern Israelites who remained in the land. These pagan people received some instruction about serving the Lord, so as a result the Samaritans "feared the Lord and served their own gods" (2 Kings 17:24-41). The Samaritan religion accepted only the Pentateuch, the first five books of the Old Testament.

Jesus' View of the Nations

Jesus taught His disciples to look at others without the stereotypes and prejudices that people often have. Jesus spoke freely with a Samaritan at the well—indeed, He spoke there with a Samaritan woman, thus pushing aside two social taboos at once (John 4:7-9). Every Roman centurion who is mentioned in the New Testament is discussed in a positive way (for example, Matthew 8:5-10). Jesus told His disciples that He had "other sheep, which are not of this fold" (John 10:16). This is usually understood to refer to His followers who are not Jews.

In the Great Commission, Jesus instructed the apostles to "make disciples of all the nations" (Matthew 28:19). The Greek word for nation is *ethnos*, from which we get the word ethnic. The meaning of the Greek word is closer to the English term people group than it is to how we use the word nation today. Today we think of a nation as a geographic area with defined political boundaries, but often a modern nation will encompass many ethnic groups. The Kurdish people in Iraq, for instance, are a distinct ethnic group. Native American nations are ethnically different from European-Americans who live in the United States. The aborigines in Australia are a separate ethnic group. Large countries, such as Russia and China, have many different ethnic groups within their borders. Many African nations encompass a number of tribal groups. There are about two hundred nations in the world today; but there are hundreds if not thousands of distinct ethnic groups and language groups in the world.

After World War I, the Young Women's Christian Association offered help to immigrants seeking to understand American culture and establish new lives in their new country.

When Christians seek to fulfill the Great Commission, they need to realize that Jesus' call goes beyond simply entering a political nation. It includes the ethnic groups within each nation. Reaching the predominant ethnic group in a country is not necessarily the same as reaching every *ethnos* in that country.

The Nations Hear the Gospel

The first step in taking the gospel to all the nations took place on the day of Pentecost, when Jews from many different countries heard the message of Jesus for the first time (Acts 2:1-11). Later, God used persecution in Jerusalem to nudge Christians into the mission field; and Philip proclaimed the gospel in Samaria (Acts 8:1-8). Then God forced Peter to get out of his comfort zone by leading him to teach about Jesus to Cornelius, a God-fearing Roman centurion (Acts 10). Because of this experience, Peter had the earth-shattering realization that, "In every nation the man who fears Him and does what is right is welcome to Him" (Acts 10:35), a shocking idea for someone who had been a faithful Jew. In Antioch, Christians from Cyprus and Cyrene shared the gospel with Gentiles, and many of them turned to the Lord (Acts 11:19-21). On Paul's first missionary journey, when Jews rejected his message,

This 1903 photo shows the Christian Mission School in Nablus, Palestine. Today Christians in Palestine are among the most active worldwide in sending out international evangelists.

Paul declared that he was going to teach the Gentiles. Many Gentiles responded joyfully (Acts 13:46-48).

Some Jewish Christians opposed bringing Gentiles into the faith. When Peter returned to Jerusalem after entering the home of the Gentile Cornelius and teaching him, Peter had some serious explaining to do (Acts 11:1-18). Some time later, a heated discussion took place in the church in Jerusalem about whether Gentiles had to be circumcised and had to obey the Law of Moses in order to be faithful Christians (Acts 15:1-35). The problem was that many Jewish Christians believed that a person had to become a Jew in order to become a Christian. Paul understood that this was not the case.

Inspired by the Holy Spirit, Paul grasped a worldview-changing truth. The gospel made national differences inconsequential. Referring to Jews and Gentiles, Paul said that Jesus "made both groups into one and broke down the barrier of the dividing wall . . . so that in Himself he might make the two into one new man, thus establishing peace" (Ephesians 2:14-15). In Christ "there is neither Jew nor Greek" (Galatians 3:28). In other words, the important fact about Christians is not that they are Jewish, Greek, French, American, or Kenyan. The important fact is that they are Christians, period. This is the most important distinguishing trait of God's people, wherever they live and whatever their national or tribal background might be.

In the thrilling description in the book of Revelation of the throne of God, John tells of seeing "a great multitude which no one could count, from every nation and all tribes and peoples and tongues, standing before the throne and before the Lamb, clothed in white robes, and palm branches were in their hands" (Revelation 7:9). The separation and scattering of people because of sin as described in Genesis is reversed through the blood of Christ. In Christ the nations of the world are truly made one.

Taking the Gospel to Other Lands

In the nineteenth and early twentieth centuries, British and American Christians took seriously Christ's call to fulfill the Great Commission. Missionaries went to many lands to preach the gospel. Their lot was often difficult. Many people responded; but many times the missionaries and their message were rejected, sometimes violently.

Missionaries are most effective when they make a distinction between the cultural traits of a people that should be respected and the aspects of the people's lives and cultures that need to be changed in order for the people to be submitted to Christ. However, many times missionaries took not simply Christianity but the form of Christianity they had known in their home countries. It seemed as though tribesmen in Africa or villagers in Japan were expected to become British or American in order to become Christians. Missionaries did not understand that such people did not need hymnbooks, pews, organs, clergy vestments, and other elements of western Christian practice in order to be faithful to God.

Mosque and Church in Ferizaj, Kosovo

In addition, Americans have tended to be condescending toward people of other nations and other ethnic groups. It was common for Americans to refer to the people of the Philippines, for instance, as "our little brown brethren" or to use other such belittling phrases. Many mission efforts tried to keep control of their work in the hands of western missionaries, who were thought to be more intelligent or more reliable than the native peoples. In more recent times, missionaries have concentrated on training local men to be preachers who can take the gospel to their own ethnic groups; and this approach has generally been more effective in reaching the lost.

Americans need to remember that Jesus, ethnically, was a Jew. The first Christians were Jewish and non-Jewish people of the Mediterranean world. Many years passed before the gospel made significant inroads into western Europe, and hundreds of years passed before the first believers that we know about came to the western hemisphere. We are all dependent on someone else teaching us the gospel. The gospel that we share with others did not originate with us; it is only the message that we received from someone else.

"The earth is the Lord's, and all it contains; the world, and those who dwell in it" (Psalm 24:1). God is moving powerfully in many places on the globe, separate from American presence or influence. The following sections give two examples of God's work in other nations today: a survey of the Christian faith in Communist China, and an incident in Nigeria that shows how God can use even a little thing like pencils to further His cause.

The Christian Faith Is Alive in Communist China

The government of the People's Republic of China is officially atheist. The Chinese Constitution guarantees freedom of religious expression, but this provision has been violated frequently. Believers have often been subjected to fierce persecution by Communist officials because of the believers' supposedly unpatriotic or imperialistic activities.

China does, however, have an official church. It is called the Three Self Patriotic Movement or the Three Self Church. Because western missionary efforts in China in the 1800s were closely associated with western economic abuse of China, many Chinese are skeptical of western missionaries. The Three Self Church is an attempt to have a Christian church led by the Chinese that is subject to the Communist government. The Three Self Movement encourages churches to be self-governing, self-supporting, and self-propagating. Three Self Church leaders are considered government employees and, for the most part, parrot the official government position on all questions. The Catholic Church in China is also allowed to function because it has aligned itself with the Communist government. Officially, the Catholic Church in China does not answer to the Pope in Rome.

However, genuine Christian faith is alive and growing in China primarily due to a huge underground house church movement. Millions of Chinese assemble regularly in homes all across China, in large cities and in small villages. Secret training programs equip Chinese preachers and evangelists to work in and to begin house churches. Most of this activity takes place without any involvement by Americans, although some Americans have helped from time to time.

A Chinese Christian Pastor and His Family (c. 1900)

The policy of the Chinese government toward house churches has been inconsistent. At times the government has beaten and imprisoned house church leaders. At other times, government officials have turned a blind eye to religious activities. Even some leaders and members in Three Self churches do not go along with Communist doctrine, and they have sometimes been allowed to operate relatively freely. It appears that a major factor in the nature of official actions toward churches and church leaders is the attitude of local government bureaucrats. If those bureaucrats choose to ignore Christian activity, the churches can function with little interference. If, on the other hand, local officials decide to crack down on Christians in their district, life for believers can be made miserable.

Right under the thumb of a Communist government, Christianity is thriving and growing. Xiao Min (pronounced *see-ow meen*) is a Chinese believer. She received no formal music training, but she has written over one thousand hymns that beautifully convey the Christian faith using phrases and ideas that communicate well to the Chinese mind and heart. A published collection of her songs is called *Canaan Hymns*.

Chinese Christians have even been leaving China to serve as missionaries in other countries. The picture of faith in China is complicated because China itself is complicated; but God is definitely moving in the People's Republic of China.

God Used Pencils to Save Lives

Healing Hands International (HHI) is a Christian relief ministry based in the United States. It provides food, clothing, medical supplies, and other assistance to people who have been affected by droughts, floods, and other disasters. A few years ago, HHI received a large donation of pencils. The organization sent some of the pencils to a contact in Nigeria. A part of that shipment was then sent to Simon Dabish, a Christian preacher who lives in a predominantly Muslim part of Nigeria.

Simon and his wife decided to distribute the pencils to the families in their community for the children to use in their schools. School supplies are not easily obtained where they live. Mr. and Mrs. Dabish dressed in their traditional Muslim-style attire and went house to house, giving pencils to the children. The families they visited were grateful for the pencils, but beyond that their efforts seemed to have little impact.

One day a riot erupted among the Muslims in their village, and the object of their wrath was the Christians. The mob decided to burn down every church building. One of the Muslim leaders gained the attention of the mob and announced, "It is good for us to teach the Christians a lesson, but there is one church that must not be touched. They are the ones that gave our children the pencils."

Simon and his family watched from the doorway of their church building as the mob burned all the other church buildings in town. As this was happening, several Muslim children stood around the Dabishes' church building and shouted, "This is the church that is not to be touched!"

A few months later, another riot erupted. This time Simon was not at home with his family. He was away preaching in a nearby village. As he was walking home, some of the angry Muslims recognized him as a Christian preacher. They seized Dabish and planned to execute him. Then the Muslims summoned one of their leaders to carry out the murder.

The leader they called was the same man who had led the previous disturbance. When he saw that the man the mob was holding was Dabish, he told the crowd, "We will not kill this man. This is the same man who gave pencils to our children!" Simon was released and taken home to his terrified family, who had been informed that Simon had already been executed.

God used pencils to save a preacher's life and to continue the work of the kingdom.

After these things I looked, and behold, a great multitude which no one could count, from every nation and all tribes and peoples and tongues, standing before the throne and before the Lamb, clothed in white robes, and palm branches were in their hands.
Revelation 7:9

⋆ Assignments for Lesson 100 ⋆

Literature Continue reading *Miracle In the Hills.*

Bible Recite or write Micah 4:1-2 from memory.

Project Complete your project for the unit.

Student Review Optional: Answer the questions for Lesson 100, take the quiz for Unit 20, and take the fourth history exam, English exam, and Bible exam.

Advertisement for a 1922 Movie

21 America in the Twenties

After the Great War, many Americans wanted a return to what Warren G. Harding called "normalcy"; but the 1920s brought the country anything but that. America withdrew into isolationism and took little interest in activity beyond its shores. The robust economy of the decade came crashing to a halt with the Great Depression that started in 1929. The Twenties saw cultural changes and serious social issues. The Scopes Evolution Trial in 1925 symbolized the great divide in American thinking and demonstrated the increased influence of modernism and religious skepticism.

Lesson 101 - Return to Normalcy?
Lesson 102 - The Roaring Twenties
Lesson 103 - Prohibition, Race, and Skepticism
Lesson 104 - Hoover and the Great Depression
Lesson 105 - Bible Study: The Scopes Trial

Memory Work Memorize Mark 12:29-31 by the end of this unit.

Books Used

The Bible
American Voices
Miracle In the Hills

Project (choose one)

1) Write 300 to 500 words on one of the following topics:

- Write an essay on the role that religion should play in the life of an elected official. Do you want an elected official to vote on the basis of his or her faith? Might a person's religious beliefs cause you not to vote for him or her?

- Select one of the innovations of the 1920s (e.g., automobiles, movies, radio, consumerism) and describe how it has affected our lives for good or ill. Give specific reasons for your answer.

2) Write and illustrate a children's book that explains the Great Depression and its impact. Your book should be a minimum of fifteen pages. You might need to do research outside the information found in this unit. See Lesson 104.

3) Write a play that relates to the Scopes Trial. You could dramatize the trial itself; explore a different angle, such as the experience of the people of Dayton, Tennessee, during the trial; or focus on an individual involved. You could also concentrate on how the Scopes Trial influenced American thought. You might need to do additional research. Your play should be at least five pages long. Performing the play is optional but would be fun! See Lesson 105.

Warren and Florence Harding and Grace and Calvin Coolidge

Lesson 101

Return to Normalcy?

Woodrow Wilson's idealism gave way to the harsh realities of postwar America. The country had suffered through the horrors of war, a postwar economic downturn, and concerns about radical revolutionaries at home. Despite the accomplishments of the Progressive movement earlier in the twentieth century, the country still faced serious issues.

Democrats were divided over whether to continue Wilson's quest for international engagement. The party convention used forty-four ballots to nominate former Ohio governor James Cox. His running mate was Franklin D. Roosevelt. Roosevelt was serving as Assistant Secretary of the Navy, the same job once held by his fifth cousin, Theodore Roosevelt.

Votes for Women

Though several states had already approved women's suffrage, the 19th Amendment made it a national right. The amendment needed approval by thirty-six states to become part of the Constitution. Thirty-five states had ratified it when it came before a special session of the Tennessee legislature in August of 1920. Vocal representatives of both sides of the issue gathered in Nashville to influence legislators. Supporters believed that women deserved the right to vote because they were just as much American citizens as men. Opponents said that women belonged in the home and that men should take care of a family's political business. Supporters hoped for change and opponents feared change if women got the vote. The Tennessee state senate passed the amendment easily, but the state house of representatives was evenly divided. During the deliberations, the youngest member of the house got a telegram from his mother which said, "Don't forget to be a good boy" and urged him to support ratification. He voted for the amendment, and it passed 50 to 49. In the first presidential election in which women across the country could vote, the conservative Republican Warren Harding was elected. Harding, by the way, carried Tennessee.

Meanwhile, the Republicans were hoping for a change. They already controlled Congress, and they believed that the disillusionment in the country with Wilson and the Treaty of Versailles meant a new chance for winning the White House. The Republican presidential nomination went to Ohio Senator Warren G. Harding. The convention nominated for Vice President Calvin Coolidge, the Massachusetts governor who had won national fame for his strong stand against the Boston police strike.

Harding set the tone for his campaign when he said that what America needed was "not heroics, but healing; not nostrums, but normalcy; not revolution, but restoration." His words captured the American mindset that had experienced world war and now wanted to settle back into domestic comfort. Harding defeated Cox with 16.1 million votes to 9.1 million votes and a 404-127 electoral landslide. Only about half of eligible voters participated, which suggests that many women, who had gained the right to vote with the 19th Amendment, did not take advantage of the opportunity. Cox did not carry any state outside of the heavily Democratic South. Republicans increased their majority in both houses of Congress.

Radio station KDKA in Pittsburgh reported 1920 election returns in the nation's first regularly scheduled broadcast. In 1938 the "tomato can" microphone used for that broadcast was donated to the Smithsonian Institution, as seen above. KDKA is still on the air.

The Harding Scandals

The new President was an easy-going man who liked to play cards, have some illegal liquor, and apparently indulge in frequent extra-marital affairs. He also liked to do favors for his friends, and this is what created scandals for his Administration. Some of his appointments were excellent, such as Charles Evans Hughes as Secretary of State, Herbert Hoover as Commerce Secretary, and Andrew Mellon to oversee the Treasury. Others, such as Interior Secretary Albert Fall and Attorney General Harry Daugherty, wound up in deep trouble. Daugherty headed up what was called Harding's "Ohio Gang," a group of political cronies who took advantage of their friend being in the White House to profit handsomely at the public's expense.

It was revealed in 1923 that the head of the new Veterans Bureau was robbing the government of medical supplies. He resigned and fled to Europe. Two men either in or close to the Administration committed suicide when questionable dealings started to surface. Attorney General Daugherty barely escaped indictment over mishandling German war reparation payments. The biggest scandal involved government-held oil deposits in a place in Wyoming called Teapot Dome. Interior Secretary Fall allowed private companies to tap into the deposits secretly without making competitive bids for the rights. Fall's personal standard of living dramatically improved while this was going on, and he eventually went to jail for taking bribes even though he always denied that he had done anything wrong. Many of the scandals that took place during Harding's tenure only came to light after the President's death.

Return to Prosperity

The Republican Congress cut income tax rates and increased tariffs. Some of what people saved in taxes was invested in the stock market, causing an upsurge in stock prices. The new heads of regulatory agencies were more lenient toward big business than the Democrats and Progressives had been.

Commerce Secretary Hoover encouraged trade associations, in which businesses shared ideas about cost-cutting, marketing, and other activities. The Supreme Court, led by Harding-nominated William Howard Taft, struck down a Federal law regulating child labor and ruled against some of the Federal regulatory agencies. However, Mellon did balance the Federal budget and decrease the national debt. The overall trend was toward a stronger national economy.

Many of the nation's workers shared in the prosperity. Non-farm income rose 20% between 1921 and 1928, while farm income rose only 10%. Mining and textile workers, however, faced increased layoffs due to the use of new labor-saving machinery. Unions also had a hard time sharing in the greater prosperity. The postwar Red Scare left the impression that union activity could lead to political revolution. Companies began sweetening the pot of benefits for non-union workers. Union membership decreased about thirty percent over the decade.

Warren Harding in Alaska (1923)

Thaddeus Caraway, pictured below, was a U.S. Senator from Arkansas and a leader in the investigation of the Teapot Dome scandal. After Senator Caraway died in 1931, his wife, Hattie, became the first woman elected to the U.S. Senate.

In July of 1923, Harding went on a trip to the West for speech-making and to visit Alaska. He suffered food poisoning in Seattle and died of apoplexy on August 2 in a hotel in San Francisco. In the early morning hours of August 3, 1923, Justice of the Peace John Coolidge administered the presidential oath of office to his son, Vice President Calvin Coolidge, in Plymouth, Vermont, where Calvin had been visiting his father.

Silent But Determined Cal

Coolidge's style was a marked change from the loose-living Harding. He was known as a man of few words and strong integrity. Coolidge encouraged the growth of business as the best way to help the most Americans. Business mergers increased and the nation's economy enjoyed robust growth.

In 1924 the Republicans nominated Coolidge for a full term. The Democrats, still divided between urban and rural elements of the party, took 104 ballots to select Wall Street lawyer John Davis. A coalition of farm and labor interests gave rebirth to the Progressive Party and selected Robert LaFollette as their candidate. LaFollette was also supported by the Socialists and the American Federation of Labor.

Coolidge focused most of his comments during the campaign on the dangers he saw with LaFollette's proposals. Davis won the South, LaFollette won Wisconsin, and Coolidge won everything else. A majority of voters decided to follow the President's campaign slogan and "Keep Cool with Coolidge." He carried the popular vote 15.7 million to 8.4 million for Davis and 4.8 million for LaFollette. The turnout was slightly smaller than it had been in 1920.

Farm Policy

Farmers suffered from low commodity prices through most of the 1920s. They tried to help themselves by investing in modern machinery, organizing into marketing associations that signed contracts with processors, and handling their farms along the lines of business. Western Republicans and southern Democrats in Congress tended to vote as a bloc on farm legislation. They helped enact laws that exempted farm cooperatives from antitrust action and that created credit banks which made loans to farm associations and cooperatives.

The McNairy-Haugen Bill was introduced in 1924 and finally passed Congress in 1927. It proposed a parity pricing system, in which commodity prices would be set by government decree to give farmers the same purchasing power they had in the better times of 1909 to 1914. Coolidge vetoed the bill as unconstitutional price fixing. The bill passed Congress again in 1928, and again Coolidge vetoed it. The idea of parity, however, had been introduced into the national debate and would be heard again.

Isolationism

After World War I, the attention of the United States turned toward domestic issues and away from involvement in world affairs. This tendency is called isolationism. Most Americans believed that the country had paid a heavy price for participation in the Great War, and they believed that continued international involvement would be an unwelcome burden for the country.

In the decade after the war, the U.S. raised tariff rates on foreign imports. The government set severe restrictions on immigration from other countries. In the face of the Red Scare, calls for "one hundred percent Americanism" came as a result of a widespread suspicion of people with international connections.

Stories abound regarding Coolidge's use of few words. After attending a church service, Coolidge allegedly was asked what the preacher's sermon was about. "Sin," Coolidge replied. What did the preacher say about it? Coolidge answered, "He said he was against it." Supposedly on one occasion a dinner guest sitting next to him told the President that she had made a bet with someone that she could make him say three words. "You lose," he told her. A saying attributed to him explained, "If you don't say anything, you won't be called on to repeat it."

This 1932 portrait of Calvin Coolidge is by Charles Sydney Hopkinson.

Foreign Relations

The United States did not distance itself completely from the League of Nations. The Harding Administration sent official observers to League meetings. By 1924 U.S. representatives were participating in League conferences that addressed specific issues. Nevertheless, the United States never officially joined the League of Nations.

United States policies toward Latin American countries became more friendly during the 1920s. The American government took fewer opportunities to invoke the Roosevelt Corollary and enter into troubled nations. American presence in several nations was cut back or withdrawn altogether. President Coolidge met with President Gerardo Machado of Cuba in Washington, D.C., in 1927, as seen in the photo above. Coolidge visited Cuba the next year to speak at a Conference of American States (meaning nations in the Western hemisphere).

In the 1930s, President Franklin Roosevelt announced his intention to follow a policy of being a good neighbor to Latin American countries as opposed to being the hemisphere's policeman.

Wilson wanted the 1920 election to be a solemn referendum on the League and his peace efforts, so the Republican victory that year was seen as a rebuff to Wilson and internationalism. Nevertheless, some efforts were made in the 1920s to address world issues, even though the results of these efforts were merely some noble-sounding agreements which had little practical effect in stopping war. The reality was that the United States was an international trading partner and held several colonies around the world, so complete isolation from the world was impossible.

War Debts and Reparations

The international financial entanglements resulting from World War I were a continuing issue that was never resolved satisfactorily. During and after the war, Allied nations had borrowed about $10 billion from the United States. Repayment of these debts depended on two factors: (1) Reparation payments by Germany, which was continually behind in making the payments, and (2) the Allies selling their imports to the U.S., which was made difficult by America's high tariffs.

Resentment grew among both the Allies and Germany about paying these debts. Many Allied government leaders believed that the U.S. should simply cancel the debts and write them off as having been part of America's war effort. The Allies had paid a greater price than the U.S. in terms of lives lost and economic hardship, so they thought it was only fair that the U.S. help out by canceling the debts.

Germany, on the other hand, suffered under the reparations plan set out in the Treaty of Versailles. Complicating the issue was the way that money flowed through the various countries. The U.S. made loans to Germany, which used much of the money to make its reparation payments to the Allies, who then used that money to repay the United States. The U.S. probably did not profit much overall because of the loan and repayment methods followed.

Germany's continued failure to make reparation payments led to a series of renegotiations among Germany and the Allies. The original $33 billion payout demanded in the treaty was cut by 1929 to about $2 billion. Meanwhile, Allied loan repayments to the United States dwindled. In 1931 President Herbert Hoover declared a one-year moratorium on all war debts. However, Germany never made another reparation payment.

Disarmament

Several years before the war, the United States had embarked on a construction program that eventually made it the second largest naval power in the world. Great Britain and Japan built up their navies after the war, and an alliance between them made their combined force especially strong. Moreover, Japan gave indications that it was willing to move aggressively in several areas of the Pacific. In the context of the recent world conflict, peace advocates believed that the arms race increased the likelihood of another war.

The United States invited several nations to the Washington Armaments Conference in 1921 to discuss relevant issues. Secretary of State Charles Evans Hughes opened the conference with a surprise proposal that the participating nations cut back their navies and promise to limit future construction. This was a call for a policy of voluntary disarmament. As a result of the Washington Conference, three treaties were signed.

The Five-Power Treaty committed the United States, Great Britain, Japan, France, and Italy to limiting their naval power to agreed levels (which meant the destruction of some existing ships). These countries also committed to building no new battleships for ten years and to making no improvements in fortifications that each nation had in the Pacific. The Nine-Power Treaty committed the five powers plus China, Belgium, Portugal, and the Netherlands not to divide China into spheres of influence and to respect the territorial integrity of China. This was a follow-up to the Open Door policy set forth by the United States some years earlier. The Four-Power Treaty said that the U.S., Great Britain, Japan, and France would respect the Pacific territories of each other and would consult with each other on any disputes that arose.

These agreements sounded good, but they had little clout. The construction of battleships was banned but not the construction of other fighting naval vessels or other forms of military buildup. The pacts spelled out no consequences for failing to live up to their terms. In addition, the effect of the treaties was to enhance Japan's power in the Pacific.

The photo below left shows American and French officials at the Washington Conference in 1921, flanked by Secret Service agents. The poster below right was created that year by the National Council for Limitation of Armaments, a network of groups promoting international peace.

Authors from This Period

The 1920s and 1930s were a fertile time for American literature. F. Scott Fitzgerald (his full name was Francis Scott Key Fitzgerald) portrayed in his books the worldly and empty lifestyles of those caught up in the new morality of the time (which was really old immorality). Sinclair Lewis ridiculed the materialism and hypocrisy of American life. Lewis was awarded the Pulitzer Prize for literature in 1926 but refused to accept it. He did accept the Nobel Prize for literature in 1930 and was the first American to receive the Nobel literature award. Willa Cather wrote about the challenges of life on the Plains.

Two writers who were beginning to be recognized in the 1920s were William Faulkner and Ernest Hemingway. Faulkner (1897-1962) lived in Oxford, Mississippi, which was portrayed as the town of Jefferson in Yoknapatawpha County in many of his novels. Hemingway (1899-1961) was typical of what was called the Lost Generation of writers who were embittered and disillusioned by the Great War. Hemingway had been an ambulance driver during the war.

Black writers during the 1920s, such as Claude McKay, James Weldon Johnson, and Langston Hughes (pictured at right), brought about what has been called the Harlem Renaissance, which celebrated African American life. Black writers had not been given much attention by the general public in the U.S. before this period.

This period also saw the emergence of some of America's best-known poets. Edward Arlington Robinson (1869-1935) was a descendant of Puritan poet Anne Bradstreet. He often expressed a hardened, cynical view of the America he saw. Robert Frost (1874-1963) expressed a gentler view of America in his poetry based on life in his native New England. His struggle to decide whether to live in England or America is reflected in "The Road Not Taken." He decided to return to America, at the time the "road less traveled by" in terms of literature. Carl Sandberg (1878-1967) from Illinois was the son of Swedish immigrants. His free verse celebrated the robust life of the prairie and the city life of Chicago. He also became a renowned scholar on Abraham Lincoln and wrote a multi-volume biography (for which he won a Pulitzer Prize) as well as a single-volume biography of him.

Thomas Stearns (T. S.) Eliot (1888-1964), born in St. Louis, is claimed as an American poet although he went to study in Oxford, England, in 1913 and decided to live in England. He eventually became a British citizen. Eliot's best-known work describes the moral aimlessness of modern society, but he laments it from the perspective of a believer. "The Love Song of J. Alfred Prufrock" (1915) describes a superficial man in a superficial world who is afraid to do anything significant and who fritters his life away instead. "The Waste Land" (1922) expands on this theme. "Four Quartets" (1943) is often considered to be his best poetic work. Eliot wrote several plays, including Murder in the Cathedral *(1935) about the killing of Thomas à Becket by supporters of the King of England in 1170. Eliot received the Nobel Prize in Literature in 1948 and was awarded the Medal of Freedom by U.S. President Lyndon Johnson in 1964.*

Kellogg-Briand

In 1928 Frank Kellogg, American Secretary of State, and Aristide Briand, French foreign minister, initiated the Treaty of Paris. The U.S. and France committed themselves to abstaining from war as an acceptable method of foreign relations. They invited other countries to agree to the pact, and eventually 62 nations became signatories. However, the treaty was widely seen as simply an attempt to appease peace advocates. The treaty allowed war in the case of self-defense, which is a common claim even when a country initiates conflict. The United States approved the treaty with the reservation that the Monroe Doctrine still applied in the western hemisphere. In addition, no consequences were given for violating the terms of the treaty. As we will see, the desire for peace and the efforts to lessen the chances for war crumbled with events in the early 1930s.

And He will judge between many peoples
And render decisions for mighty, distant nations.
Then they will hammer their swords into plowshares
And their spears into pruning hooks;
Nation will not lift up sword against nation,
And never again will they train for war.
Micah 4:3

⋆ Assignments for Lesson 101 ⋆

American Voices Read the excerpts from "The Destiny of America" by Calvin Coolidge (pages 308-312).

Literature Continue reading *Miracle In the Hills.* Plan to finish it by the end of this unit.

Bible The Bible study lesson for this unit is a look at the 1925 Scopes evolution trial in Dayton, Tennessee. The trial pitted the traditional, Biblical view of Creation against the theory of evolution. Read Mark 12:28-34. What are three things a Christian should keep in mind as he studies science?

Start memorizing Mark 12:29-31.

Project Choose your project for this unit and start working on it.

Student Review Optional: Answer the questions for Lesson 101.

Ray Miller and His Orchestra (c. 1924)

Lesson 102

The Roaring Twenties

The United States recovered from the Great War and entered into the bustle of an ever-changing world in the 1920s. The country took on more aspects of modernism. Many people enjoyed material prosperity even while aching questions arose about the meaning and purpose of life. The decade ended with the catastrophic Great Depression that exploded the myth of never-ending and always-increasing prosperity.

Population Changes

The 1920 census revealed that the population of the country was about 106 million. For the first time, urban population was greater than rural population. By 1930 the population had grown to 123 million, and the gap between rural and urban population had widened. In addition, the number of people living on farms decreased during the decade. Even the rural population was becoming centered in small towns as opposed to isolated farms.

Cities grew larger and apartment buildings became more common. Women were liberated from some of the drudgery of housework by labor saving devices, processed foods, and ready-made clothing. Many women used their time to become involved in civic causes, political organizations, and church and social groups. Even farming areas were affected by the changes in technology and energy. Many farm families had electricity, radios, appliances, and cars; and farmers invested in new farm equipment for their work.

Immigration Changes

Long the haven for the huddled masses of foreign countries, the United States effectively closed its gates to immigrants in the 1920s. This was in response to several trends of public opinion. First, a general fear and distrust of internationals arose after the war and with the eruption of political revolution in Russia. Second, labor unions did not want immigrants to compete for their jobs and to accept lower pay than Americans did. At the same time, employers no longer needed as much cheap labor as they had when railroads were being built and industrial growth was booming. Finally, many resisted newcomers who did not speak English and who did not blend in easily with the American culture.

In 1921 Congress enacted a quota system for European immigrants. The number of newcomers from a specific country in a given year could not exceed three percent of the people from that country who lived in the U.S. in 1910. The law also restricted total annual immigration to about

350,000. Three years later, the quota was cut to two percent and the base year was changed to 1890. This severely limited the number of immigrants who could come from Southern and Eastern Europe, since immigration from these areas had occurred primarily after 1890. The base year was changed to 1920 in 1929 legislation, but the total number of immigrants allowed was cut to about 150,000. Immigration from countries in the western hemisphere was not affected.

The new policy embittered first and second generation Americans and aroused resentment in the foreign countries affected by the restrictions. Foreign nationals who were unemployed or oppressed had once looked to the United States as their chance for a new start, but now for most people that chance was gone.

Business and Labor

American business grew with the spread of assembly lines and improved machinery. Over one thousand business mergers took place in the decade, consolidating effort and expense. By 1930 half of the nation's corporate wealth was held by two hundred companies. The country tapped new sources of energy to power its factories, homes, machines, and automobiles. Coal consumption fell by about 20% over the decade, while petroleum production doubled and natural gas production increased 150%. By 1930 the U.S. was using more electricity than all the other countries of the world combined.

American workers in general were better off in 1929 than they had been in 1920, but labor unions were not. Employers encouraged workers to stay out of unions. Some organized company unions within plants that were controlled by management. Because of the perception of unions as potential troublemakers as well as the improved standard of living that made the need for collective bargaining seem less pressing, union strength declined during the 1920s from twelve percent of the work force in 1920 to seven percent in 1930.

American Aviators

In May of 1927, Charles Lindbergh became the first person to fly solo across the Atlantic Ocean. His single-engine plane, Spirit of St. Louis, *took a little less than 34 hours to fly from New York to Paris, France. Lindbergh had no radio and battled fog, wind, and sleepiness on the flight. "Lucky Lindy" became an international hero and was welcomed home with a huge parade in New York City. Lindbergh promoted aviation for the rest of his life. The movie* Spirit of St. Louis *with Jimmy Stewart is a good dramatization of Lindbergh's heroic flight.*

Amelia Earhart became the first woman to fly solo across the Atlantic in 1931. Six years later, Earhart's plane went down in the Pacific while she was trying to fly around the world (not non-stop) accompanied only by a navigator, Fred Noonan. A massive sea and air search at the time failed to find information about what happened.

Advertisement from the 1920s

The Consumer Culture

The Twenties saw an increased emphasis in marketing and advertising, especially in newspapers and magazines and in the new medium of radio. The growth in production of consumer goods, such as automobiles, appliances, and clothes, gave companies a reason to encourage Americans to buy.

Automobile ownership increased from eight million in 1920 to 23 million in 1930. The latter figure meant an average of one car for every six people. Cars replaced horse-drawn vehicles and significantly decreased the use of trolleys and railroads. At the same time, 40,000 city buses around the country replaced streetcars. Industries related to vehicle manufacturing, such as glass, steel, and rubber, grew accordingly, as did the demand for more and better roads. By the end of the decade, automobile manufacturing was the largest industry in the country.

The decade of the Twenties saw the emergence of radio. The first commercial station, KDKA in Pittsburgh, signed on in November of 1920. By 1929 radio sales totaled $400 million, 600 stations were on the air, and a third of American homes owned at least one receiver. Radio brought news, entertainment, information, political speeches, and advertising into American living rooms. National broadcast networks brought the country together as people everywhere listened to the same programs.

This 1925 ad shows film actress Clara Horton with the latest in decorative radio sets. The photos on the radio are of actresses Corinne Griffith and Colleen Moore.

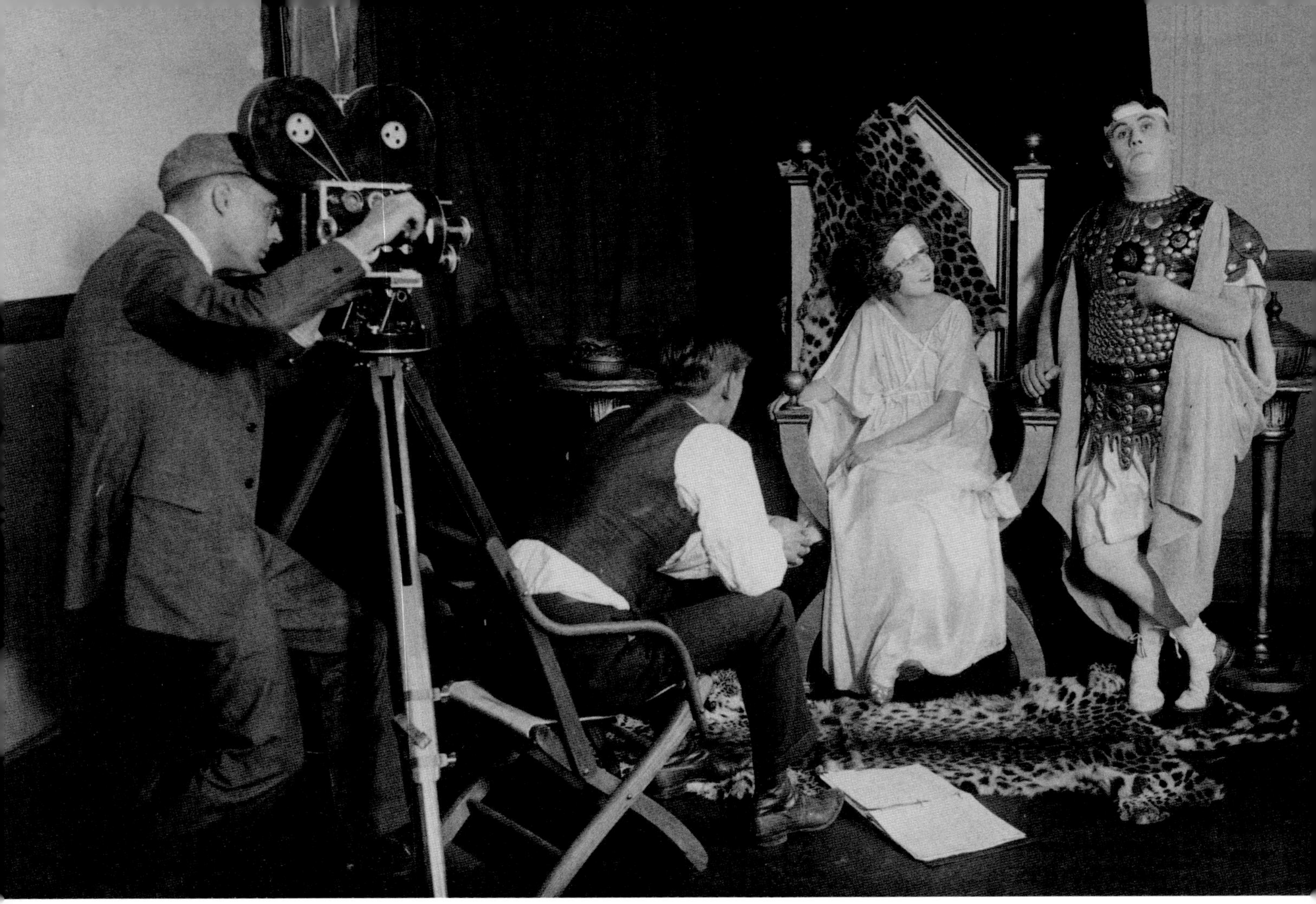

A group of businessmen in Atlantic City, New Jersey, organized a beauty pageant in 1921 that became known as the Miss America pageant. Margaret Gorman of Washington, D.C. was the first winner. This 1922 photo shows her filming a burlesque on the Burning of Rome. A burlesque is a comic theatrical production, often mocking a serious subject.

Military and airline use of radio helped improve safety and service. In 1927 Congress created the Federal Radio Commission to regulate the broadcast industry. The title and function of the agency was broadened in 1934 to the Federal Communications Commission.

The decade also saw phenomenal growth in the movie industry. By 1927 America had 20,000 movie theaters, and millions of people went to the movies every week. The first motion pictures did not have sound. *The Jazz Singer*, starring popular actor and singer Al Jolson, was the first "talkie." It debuted in 1927.

Recreation and spectator sports continued to grow in popularity. Nine to ten million people watched major league baseball each year. Fans followed the exploits of their favorite players and teams. Babe Ruth became the first superstar, astounding the sports world by hitting an amazing sixty home runs in 1927. Boxing was also widely popular, as were college and professional football. In those wild and crazy days, fads such as sitting atop flagpoles for long periods, doing the Charleston dance, and wearing shocking fashions (with skirts all the way up to the knee) swept the country.

Enrollment in high schools and colleges grew. A better educated public with more free time offered a bigger market for magazines. *Reader's Digest* began in 1922, *Time* magazine was founded the following year, and many other periodicals appeared during the Twenties.

What Else Was Happening?

1920 *Hermann Rorshach, a psychiatrist, begins showing his clients inkblots and asking them what they think they might be.*

1922 *Benito Mussolini becomes the Fascist leader of Italy.*

1922 *Turkish leader Kemal Ataturk abolishes the Ottoman throne (in existence since 1300) and establishes the Turkish republic the next year.*

1922 *A British archaeologist discovers the tomb of Tutankhamen in Egypt.*

1923 *Adolf Hitler attempts to take over Germany, but he fails and is sentenced to prison. While there, he writes* Mein Kampf ("My Struggle").

1923 *Yankee Stadium opens in New York. It is called "The House that Ruth Built" because of ticket sales to people wanting to watch new star Babe Ruth. Ruth had been bought from the Boston Red Sox in 1920 for $125,000. He had been an outstanding pitcher, but he was such a good hitter that he was moved to play right field so that he could play every day. The photo below shows Opening Day on April 18.*

1924 *Soviet leader Vladimir Lenin dies, leaving a power vacuum in the Communist Party. Leon Trotsky and Joseph Stalin battle for control, with Stalin winning out by 1929.*

1924 *Astronomer Edwin Hubble explores the universe with the new 100-inch telescope in an observatory on Mount Wilson in California.*

1924 *George Gershwin's* Rhapsody in Blue *combines jazz and orchestral music into one composition.*

1924 *At the Olympic Games in Paris, British athletes Harold Abrahams and Eric Liddell win the 100 meter and 400 meter races respectively. Liddell went on to be a missionary in China and died there in 1945. (The accomplishments of Abrahams and Liddell are featured in the 1981 movie* Chariots of Fire.*)*

In the 19th century, Hot Springs, Arkansas, became a popular destination for vacationers and people with ailments who hoped that the waters would provide relief. Professional baseball teams also used Hot Springs as a site for spring training until Florida and Arizona became more attractive in the 1920s. The Quapaw Baths, shown above, were built in 1922. After a period of disuse, the building was reopened as a bath and spa in 2008.

A generation goes and a generation comes. . . .
Ecclesiastes 1:4

⋆ Assignments for Lesson 102 ⋆

Literature Continue reading *Miracle In the Hills.*

Bible Read Matthew 5:43-48. List three assurances a Christian should remember if he or she is ridiculed for believing in the Genesis account of Creation.

Work on memorizing Mark 12:29-31.

Project Work on your project.

Student Review Optional: Answer the questions for Lesson 102.

From a Drawing of Pennsylvania Avenue in Washington, D.C. by Susan Brown Chase (American, c. 1925)

Lesson 103

Prohibition, Race, and Skepticism

The 1920s were not just a time of new gadgets, new cars, and new pastimes. Serious issues confronted the American people, and not all of them were handled well.

Prohibition

What Herbert Hoover called the noble experiment of prohibiting the manufacture, distribution, and sale of alcoholic beverages lasted throughout the 1920s. Federal Prohibition culminated decades of efforts by church, women's, and civic-minded groups to eliminate the problems caused by drinking. Unfortunately, the law only drove the manufacture, distribution, and sale of alcoholic beverages underground. It was smuggled into the country and distilled by bootleggers all over the nation. Secret bars (often not-so-secret) served liquor regularly. Such taverns were called speakeasies because one had to speak easy (that is, quietly) to the man at the door in order to gain entrance.

Criminals such as Al Capone in Chicago took over the alcohol business, and it became the basis for gang wars and further illegal activity, including gambling and racketeering. One common racket was for a gang to demand payment from businesses for "protection," meaning that if a business didn't go along with the gang, bad things would mysteriously start to happen to the business.

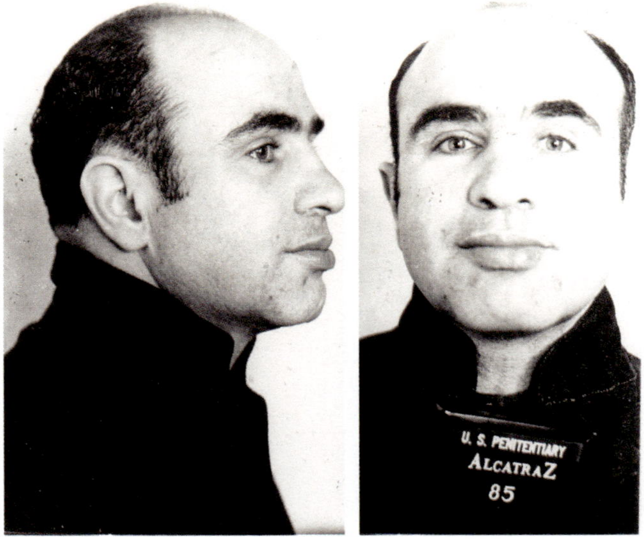

"Scarface" Al Capone created a lavish and well-protected lifestyle for himself by his involvement in bootlegging and other aspects of organized crime. After an agent for the Treasury Department infiltrated his gang, Capone was eventually sentenced to eleven years in prison for tax evasion. The mug shots at right are from his time at the new Federal Penitentiary of Alcatraz. He was released in 1939 and died in 1947.

This 1921 cartoon by Ralph Barton illustrates prohibition. A Puritan has buried John Barleycorn (a personification of alcoholic beverages), but an armed criminal has driven the Puritan away.

Prohibition laws were widely ignored. Some law enforcement officials took bribes from criminals and bootleggers to look the other way. Politicians began speaking openly about repealing Prohibition. Al Smith lost the presidential election in 1928 partly because of just this position, but Franklin Roosevelt stood for repeal in 1932 and won. The 21st Amendment, ratified in 1933, repealed the 18th Amendment that had made Prohibition a national policy. Control of the liquor business was returned to the states.

Race and the Klan

The black population in America became significantly less rural and more urban during the Twenties. The migration of blacks to northern factory cities, which had begun during the Great War, continued through the decade. Many more blacks came to be employed as clerical workers and in civil service jobs. Tens of thousands owned their own businesses. However, blacks were usually met with discrimination and hatred as they tried to live in their new communities.

Many African Americans took pride in their ethnic culture and pressed for better treatment in American society in general. The National Association for the Advancement of Colored People (NAACP) was founded in 1910. W. E. B. Du Bois was one of its early leaders. The group focused its efforts on outlawing lynching and on the enforcement of laws that guaranteed equality.

A more extreme response to the conditions of African Americans was the black nationalism promoted by Marcus Garvey. Garvey wanted blacks to separate from white society, a position that Du Bois and other black leaders condemned. The solution Garvey proposed was for blacks to set up their own country in Africa. His United Negro Improvement Association claimed six million members. In 1925 Garvey was convicted of mail

Marcus Garvey is pictured below in 1924. This park in Harlem was renamed the Marcus Garvey Park in 1973.

fraud and sent to prison, though his prosecution might have been politically motivated. President Coolidge pardoned Garvey in 1927 but deported him to his native Jamaica. Garvey died in London in 1940.

One menacing problem for blacks as well as for other Americans was the rebirth of the Ku Klux Klan. A Georgia man began the Klan anew in 1915, not to raise up the old Confederacy but to defend what the group defined as pure Americanism. The Klan targeted not just blacks but Catholics, Jews, foreigners, and anyone else who did not measure up to their definition of what was 100% American. Many Klan chapters formed in the North and Midwest.

Klansmen were known for wearing white robes and hoods and for intimidation and violence against those whom it opposed, such as the burning of crosses in private yards and during their meetings. They put on a 40,000-man march in Washington, D.C., in 1925. Claims about the Klan's membership during the decade vary from 3 million to 8 million. Legislation restricting immigration caused the Klan's appeal to diminish, as did the fact that people got tired of the Klan's use of fear and violence. Factional differences within the Klan led to its breakup into several competing groups, each claiming to be the true Klan.

The Pillar of Fire Church was an anti-Catholic and anti-Semitic organization that promoted the Ku Klux Klan. This illustration from their 1926 book Klansmen: Guardians of Liberty *portrays the KKK as "the defender of the 18th amendment."*

A Changing Outlook

The Great War touched off attitudes of despair and disillusionment in many of the younger generation of the 1920s. The world was no longer on what seemed to be a steady march of progress. Instead, mankind had demonstrated the willingness to use horrific weapons such as machine guns and mustard gas on each other. Many apparently decided that the best use of life was pursuing pleasure. They came to be called the Lost Generation.

"The Jazz Age," as F. Scott Fitzgerald called the period, not only had new kinds of music and dance clubs; it also brought about changes in personal morality. Many women cast off restraints and took up drinking, smoking, and immorality, although the trend was probably not as widespread as publicity suggested. The trend declined in the 1930s as Americans discovered that such a lifestyle bore bitter fruit.

The world was experiencing dramatic change with new technologies, new means of transportation and communication, and new challenges to accepted standards. Freudian psychoanalysis changed the way people understood human behavior. Authors and artists explored new avenues of expression. Painters such as Picasso, Cezanne, Van Gogh, and Gauguin reflected this new and uncertain perspective of

Crime and Punishment

Two trials typified the tense times of the Twenties. Nicola Sacco and Bartolomeo Vanzetti were arrested in 1920 in a Boston suburb and charged with murder and robbery. The trial raised as many issues about their nationality and political beliefs as it did about the crimes themselves. The judge privately called them anarchists. Sacco and Vanzetti were found guilty. Despite many appeals for mercy and demonstrations on their behalf around the world (the 1921 photo at right is from London), they were electrocuted in 1927.

In 1924 two young men, Nathan Leopold and Richard Loeb, were tried in Chicago and found guilty of a murder that they committed apparently just to see how it felt to kill someone in what they hoped would be the perfect crime. Their defense attorney was Clarence Darrow, who managed to get them sentenced to life in prison instead of the death penalty. The men's attitude was an extreme example of the aimlessness and disillusion that affected many people in the 1920s.

reality in their work. Meanwhile, some reacted to the changes by focusing on (and insisting on) traditional standards and what they understood to be traditional Americanism.

The theory of relativity and the quantum theory of physics challenged the way people understood the physical universe. Scientists suggested that the world was not as neat and orderly as had once been thought. Albert Einstein suggested that as matter approached the speed of light, measurements would become shorter and clocks would slow down. Max Planck's quantum theory showed that atoms were complex structures.

Werner Heisenberg published his uncertainty principle in 1927, which stated that one could not know exactly where electrons were at any given moment. Such theories were difficult for many people to understand, and the way they were presented in the media led people to believe that the natural laws described by Isaac Newton were no longer adequate for explaining the world in which they lived.

As a scientist exploring fundamental aspects of the universe, Albert Einstein believed in a basic order of things. "I shall never believe that God plays dice with the world," he wrote in response to the idea of uncertainty in the physical world. "I want to think God's thoughts," he once said. "The rest is details." Though Einstein was ethnically Jewish, the "God" he talked about was in his mind an impersonal deity, not the personal God described in the Bible.

What Else Was Happening?

1925 *Scottish inventor John Baird transmits the first television image of a human face.*

1925 *Clarence Birdseye develops a means of quick-freezing food to preserve its taste.*

1927 *Opposing groups battle in China, with the Nationalists led by Chiang Kai-Shek winning control. The Communists led by Mao Zedong escape into the countryside for years of training and preparing for a new assault.*

1928 *"Steamboat Willie," a new cartoon by animator Walt Disney, introduces the character of Mickey Mouse.*

1928 *Station WGY in Schenectady, New York, begins regular 90-minute television broadcasts three days per week.*

1930 *The planet Pluto is discovered. In 2006 it is demoted to a dwarf planet by a vote of the International Astronomical Union.*

1931 *Japan invades Manchuria, a province of China, and begins a pattern of imperialism in the Far East (see photo at right).*

1931 *The Empire State Building is completed in New York City. At 1,250 feet, it is the world's tallest building.*

1932 *The infant son of Charles and Anne Morrow Lindbergh is kidnapped on March 1. The family pays a $50,000 ransom, but the child is found dead on May 12. Bruno Hauptmann is convicted of the crime and is executed in 1936.*

If the dead are not raised, let us eat and drink, for tomorrow we die.
1 Corinthians 15:32b

⋆ Assignments for Lesson 103 ⋆

Literature Continue reading *Miracle In the Hills.*

Bible Read 1 Peter 3:13-17. What are three things you can do to be better prepared to give an answer for your faith if anyone asks you about your belief regarding the Creation versus evolution issue?

Work on memorizing Mark 12:29-31.

Project Work on your project.

Student Review Optional: Answer the questions for Lesson 103.

President Coolidge in Cowboy Costume With Photographers in South Dakota (1927)

Lesson 104

Hoover and the Great Depression

While President Calvin Coolidge was visiting the Black Hills of South Dakota in August of 1927, he distributed a typically terse written statement to members of the press covering his trip: "I do not choose to run for President in 1928." This opened the Republican nomination to a large field of candidates. By the time of the 1928 Republican convention, Commerce Secretary Herbert Hoover was the clear choice of the party.

Hoover had never held elected office. He was a mining engineer by training and profession and had become wealthy by managing mines in China and Australia. He gave years of his life in public service as director of relief for Belgium after the German invasion of 1914, then as head of the U.S. government's Food Administration during the war, and finally as Secretary of Commerce under Harding and Coolidge. In many ways he fit the thinking of the times: a successful businessman guiding the work of government, first in relief and then in prosperity.

The Democrats in 1928 had a hard time finding an issue that resonated with the voters during the Republican-led prosperity. The party nominated New York governor Alfred E. Smith, who said that he stood for price parity for farmers and greater governmental regulation of utilities. A much larger issue developed, however, when Smith revealed that he favored either cutting back or eliminating Prohibition. This touched on a sensitive issue for many Americans and positioned Smith as too liberal for their comfort.

Another major question about Smith was the fact that he was a Roman Catholic. No Catholic had ever been nominated for President by a major party, and anti-Catholic bias against Smith arose in many parts of the country. Opponents feared that Smith would have more loyalty to the pope than to the United States. As a final blow, Smith was associated with the Tammany Hall political machine of New York.

Hoover rode the wave of prosperity and anti-Smith bias to victory, receiving a 21.4 million to 15 million popular majority and a 444 to 87 landslide in the electoral college. Smith carried only Massachusetts, Rhode Island, and six states in the Deep South. Hoover even carried Smith's home state of New York. With no Progressive candidate, Smith did, however, almost double the vote that Democrat John Davis received in 1924. The New York governor's candidacy helped build the urban base of the Democratic Party that it has today, and the next Roman Catholic nominated for President by a major party, John F. Kennedy, won his election in 1960.

Good Times for Business

Hoover encouraged business activity. He believed that government should help business but not individuals. He stressed "rugged individualism" and feared that government assistance would weaken individual initiative. However, Hoover did favor tax relief for low-income Americans. His mining and relief experience caused him to see value in limited government planning. In a departure from typical Republican policy, Hoover sought to help farmers with the Agricultural Marketing Act of 1929. The law created a $500 million fund to help cooperatives store and market crops in order to provide price stability. Co-ops could buy grain when prices were low to hold it off the market so that prices might rise with increasing demand.

In his inaugural address on March 4, 1929, Hoover said, "I have no fears for the future of our country." Seven months later, the future of the country looked bleak indeed.

Operators at the Cheasapeake and Potomac Telephone Company (1927)

Clouds on the Horizon

During the 1920s America enjoyed a long period of prosperity. Wages, profits, stock values, and investment dividends all increased. The segment of the economy involving consumer goods and retail sales grew dramatically. Businesses invested a good portion of their profits back into the production of more goods.

Land Speculation in Florida

The expression, "If you believe that, I've got some swampland in Florida to sell you," arose from one of the speculative manias of the 1920s. The population of Miami more than doubled between 1920 and 1925. Real estate prices skyrocketed as the automobile made Florida more accessible, and promoters around the country encouraged the dream of quick wealth in the land of sun and sea.

People bought land they saw only on maps with as little as ten percent down. They hoped that the value of the land would increase and then they could sell it at a profit. Some of the land was in swamps, but many thought such land could be reclaimed or made into an American Venice. The Venetian Causeway, shown at left, was built in Miami in 1925-1926.

Then reality struck. By 1926 and 1927, prices started falling. Local governments were often unable to collect taxes. Speculators began counting their losses as they could not find buyers for land in Florida any longer.

At the same time, investment in stocks continued to grow as investors speculated (gambled) on a continued economic expansion. The wealthiest five percent of Americans had one-third of the nation's income. This level of income allowed their savings to increase, and a good portion of it was invested in stocks. The more typical American also was encouraged to invest in the market by buying stocks on margin. This meant that they could buy stocks by putting down only about 10-25 percent of the face value. The broker would loan the investor the rest of the money with the expectation that they would both make money as the stock increased in value. About a half million people bought stocks on margin, and about 1.5 million Americans had accounts with stock brokers. In general, many Americans came to believe that panics and depressions were a thing of the past and that prosperity was a permanent fixture in American life. Even President Hoover spoke of being nearer than ever before to the complete elimination of poverty in America.

The economy did have some negatives, however. Some people lost their jobs because of improved machinery or because their skills became outdated (although this is always a risk in a changing economy). Farmers still had a hard time because of low commodity prices. If they increased production, it only made prices go down further. Much of the agricultural South was struggling long before 1929.

Signs of trouble increased in the latter years of the decade. The zeal to produce more goods finally outpaced consumer demand, and sales dropped off. Wages did not keep pace with increased production, so people did not have the buying power to keep making as many purchases as they had been making. The creation of capital goods (large investments such as factories and machines) decreased in the last half of the decade as production slowed.

The Crash

Some investors began selling off their stock in the summer of 1929 because they believed that stocks were valued higher than their real worth. However, the bull market stumbled on into late October, when a series of sell-offs sent the market plummeting. Tuesday, October 29, 1929, was the worst day in the history of the stock exchange to that point, when the market lost 13 percent of its value in one day.

Crowd Outside the New York Stock Exchange After the Crash (1929)

Sellers could not find any buyers interested, and stock values continued to fall. Those who had bought on margin could not recover their investment, let alone pay off their brokerage loans. The market lost 40% of its value by the end of November. Total losses in the market have been estimated at $30 billion.

Even with such losses, the recession was mild at first. The Federal Reserve Board lowered its discount rate to member banks to make loans cheaper and more readily available. The government provided some emergency help to farmers. Unemployment was not much above what had been typical rates. Administration officials expressed confidence that the economy was fundamentally sound and that the worst would be over soon. The nation had endured many such panics in its history and had weathered all of them.

Worsening Conditions

In 1930, however, things got much worse. Congress passed the Hawley-Smoot Tariff, which raised tariffs to their highest level in history. Businesses said that they needed this protection from foreign competition. Hoover had reservations about the bill, but he signed it into law. Not only did it limit imports, but it also hurt trade with other countries as they refused to accept goods if they could not send goods to America. A major New York bank failed in December of 1930, which caused a ripple effect with other banks. The Federal Reserve did not act to make more money available, and this restriction of currency added to the problems. In the summer of 1931, banks in Europe began to fail. This was when Hoover proposed suspending debt and reparation payments to help ease the crisis. By this point the depression was becoming worldwide.

Unemployment in the U.S. rose from between six and seven million in 1930 to 12 million by 1932. This meant that at least 25% of the nation's work force was out of a job. Many of those who continued working had their wages and hours cut. Between 1929 and 1932, personal income fell just over 50%.

Dorthea Lange photographed this woman in 1936. Widely known as the "Migrant Mother," she was a thirty-two-year-old mother of seven. Her family was living in a makeshift tent and scrounging for food in California when the photo was taken. Her face has come to epitomize the terrible hardship endured by many during the Great Depression.

More unemployment meant fewer people were able to buy goods. This led to a cut in production, which resulted in more unemployment. Some 9,000 banks closed their doors because they were unable to collect on loans. Between 1930 and 1934 about one million farms went into bankruptcy. Stock values in 1932 were about 20% of what they were in 1929 before the crash.

The Republicans lost their majority in the House of Representatives in the 1930 congressional election and only barely maintained a majority in the Senate. The general philosophy of Hoover and the Republicans was that direct relief to individuals was a function of local and state governments, not the

The Hoovers Visit with Wounded Veterans at the White House (1931)

Federal government. Congress did create the Farm Board, which offered loans to farm cooperatives. Federal public works projects increased, but employment in these projects might have been offset by declines in projects funded by state and local governments. In 1932 Congress created the Reconstruction Finance Corporation, which made loans to banks and large businesses in order to keep them afloat. The Home Loan Bank Board helped banks with short term loans so that they would not have to file as many foreclosures on mortgages.

By 1932 the situation was critical. Thousands of people had lost their homes, farms, and jobs. Lines formed daily outside of soup kitchens sponsored by churches and other relief agencies. People who had lost their homes sometimes settled in groups of makeshift shelters called Hoovervilles. Some 15,000 unemployed veterans of World War I gathered in Washington in the summer of 1932 to demand immediate payment of a bonus that had been promised to them in the form of life insurance set to mature in 1945.

When the bill to make the payments failed to pass Congress, many of those in the Bonus Expeditionary Force went home. Many of the rest moved into temporary shelters in Anacostia Flats in the District of Columbia. Congress then voted to buy tickets for the men to return home, and all but about 700 left. In late July, Hoover ordered the huts torn down.

Bonus Army Camp at the Anacostia Flats (1932)

General Douglas MacArthur, assisted by Dwight Eisenhower and George Patton among others, led a force of troops into the settlement that drove out the Bonus Army and their families and burned down the shanties. The image of soldiers using tanks and other military force against fellow Americans only highlighted the nation's plight and made Republican chances for victory in the fall election even more remote.

Herbert Hoover was a good, generous, and sympathetic man. He gave many years of his life in public service. Hoover was President during the country's most challenging economic crisis, and his vision of what the Federal government should do in that crisis seemed to fall short of what was needed. In the 1932 election, the people looked elsewhere for the leadership that they hoped would bring the nation out of the Depression.

Do not weary yourself to gain wealth, cease from your consideration of it. When you set your eyes on it, it is gone, for wealth certainly makes itself wings like an eagle that flies toward the heavens.
Proverbs 23:4-5

★ Assignments for Lesson 104 ★

Literature Continue reading *Miracle In the Hills.*

Bible Work on memorizing Mark 12:29-31.

Project Work on your project.

Student Review Optional: Answer the questions for Lesson 104.

Dayton, Tennessee (1925)

Lesson 105 - Bible Study

The Scopes Trial

Change. It is a word that can either cause excitement or strike fear. Some changes are good, such as a move toward more racial equality. Other changes are bad, such as the increasing acceptance of abortion. The standard for determining what are good changes and what are bad changes has to be the Word of God.

Defend. This is another word that can be either positive or negative. It is good and right to defend the truth. It is not good to defend what violates the truth. Again, we must use God's Word to determine what we should defend.

The period of the 1920s was one of strong challenges to accepted beliefs and strong defense of traditional beliefs. This is the essential context for understanding the dramatic battle that was played out in a small-town Tennessee courtroom in 1925.

Changes and Defense

America witnessed great changes in the Twenties, and many people believed that the country as they had known it was disappearing. For instance, in reaction to the rising tide of immigration, the painful foreign involvement during the Great War, and the fear of radical revolutionaries infiltrating the land, the United States government drastically limited immigration and engaged in a crackdown on those whose ideas were different and new. In reaction to the growing numbers and influence of foreign-born, non-Protestant individuals, the Ku Klux Klan arose to defend what it saw as pure Americanism. In an attempt to control the evils of alcohol, the United States enacted prohibition laws.

As a reaction to the attack on the foundations of traditional Christian doctrine, conservative believers mounted an active campaign against evolutionary thought and theological liberalism. Princeton Bible scholar J. Gresham Machen published *Christianity and Liberalism* in 1923, denying that liberal theology could even be considered as an expression of Christianity. The conservative faculty at Princeton Theological Seminary separated from the institution in 1929.

The Legal Background

In the context of these changes and perceived threats to traditional Christianity, and in an attempt to limit the influence of the theory of evolution, state legislatures considered laws that would ban the teaching of evolution in schools. Oklahoma passed such a law in 1923, and a few other states enacted similar laws during the decade.

Tennessee was one of the liberal-conservative battleground states. In 1924 William Jennings

Bryan gave a speech in Nashville entitled, "Is the Bible True?" Bryan affirmed his belief that it is. Copies of the speech were given to every Tennessee state legislator during its 1925 legislative session held in the spring. During that session, the Tennessee General Assembly passed the Butler Act (named for its sponsor, John Washington Butler). This Act made it illegal for any teacher in a public school "to teach any theory that denies the story of the Divine Creation of man as taught in the Bible, and to teach instead that man has descended from a lower order of animals."

The Challenge

The American Civil Liberties Union (ACLU), a national liberal group, advertised in Tennessee that it would defend in court anyone who was charged with violating the Butler Act. In other words, they were willing to make a test case to determine if the law was constitutional.

A group of businessmen in Dayton, Tennessee, a small town about an hour north of Chattanooga, saw the ACLU advertisement and decided that having a trial on evolution and Creation in Dayton might bring the community and the area national publicity. They believed that people from all over the country would come to Dayton, see the beauty there, and want to move there; and the local economy would benefit.

The high school coach, John Thomas Scopes, agreed to be arrested for the test case. He had substituted for the science teacher for a couple of weeks; and although he couldn't say for sure that he had taught evolution, he thought that he might have. The people who organized the trial wanted to bring two high-profile lawyers to Dayton to argue the case.

The prosecution invited William Jennings Bryan, a three-time presidential candidate, former Secretary of State, and well-known and widely respected defender of traditional Christian teaching. Clarence Darrow agreed to donate his time for Scopes' defense. Darrow was perhaps the best-known defense attorney in the country and widely known to be a religious skeptic. Each side had several other attorneys who worked on the case with Bryan and Darrow.

Religious Activities in the 1920s

The Twenties were a time of intense religious activity. Revivalists, sometimes flamboyant, drew large crowds during the period. Perhaps the best-known religious figure of the day was Aimee Semple McPherson, a woman who began the International Church of the Foursquare Gospel. Her first husband, a missionary, died in Hong Kong in 1910. She left her second husband, Harold McPherson, to begin her own preaching and faith-healing ministry. Mrs. McPherson built a 5,000-seat arena in Los Angeles and began a radio station, Bible school, and magazine. Mrs. McPherson disappeared in 1926 only to emerge five weeks later claiming to have been kidnapped. She was accused of perjury in the matter but was found innocent. Mrs. McPherson died in 1944.

The biggest-selling religious book of the decade was Bruce Barton's The Man Nobody Knows, *published in 1925. Appropriately for the era, Barton portrayed Jesus as the consummate businessman. Sinclair Lewis wrote a scathing novel about a hypocritical evangelist,* Elmer Gantry, *in 1927.*

The Trial

Scopes was well-liked in the community and never went to jail. When people from out of town began arriving for the trial, Scopes was among those welcoming them. Local businessmen created a festival atmosphere for the event, although calling it a carnival or circus is somewhat extreme. The trial was held from July 10 to July 21, 1925, in the Rhea County Courthouse. Dozens of reporters came to cover it. Radio station WGN of Chicago broadcast the trial live.

The case was presented as a battle between those who held traditional Christian beliefs and those who held modern, evolution-based ideas about man and the world. Twelve scientists and theologians submitted statements that were included in the record of the case, but none was cross-examined. The prosecution tried to show that Scopes had indeed violated the Butler Act. Scopes himself did not testify.

John Scopes

The highlight of the trial came when Clarence Darrow questioned William Jennings Bryan, who took the witness stand as an expert on the Bible. Bryan did a good job of standing up for the Bible, even though Darrow tried to make Bryan's beliefs look silly. Darrow's questioning of Bryan concluded the testimony in the trial. Darrow surprised the courtroom by urging the jury to find Scopes guilty. He said that he planned to appeal the case. Bryan had prepared to give a long closing speech, but Darrow's request that Scopes be found guilty made that impossible.

Because of intense heat inside the courtroom, part of the trial was held outside. This photograph shows Clarence Darrow, standing at center, questioning William Jennings Bryan, seated opposite him.

The jury found Scopes guilty, and the judge set his fine at $100, the minimum allowed by the law. Two years later, when Scopes was in graduate school at the University of Chicago, the Tennessee Supreme Court ruled that the Butler Act was constitutional, but it reversed Scopes' conviction on a technicality. The state constitution said that any fine greater than fifty dollars was to be set by the jury, not the judge.

Aftermath

After the trial, Bryan made some speeches in the Dayton area and worked on a printed form of the closing speech he had planned to give in the trial. He talked with supporters in Dayton about starting a college there that would teach fundamental Christian beliefs, and he offered money to help get it started. Bryan died in his sleep five days after the trial ended. William Jennings Bryan University, now called Bryan College, opened in Dayton in 1930.

Dayton and Tennessee did receive extensive publicity during and after the trial, but much of it was unkind. Many newspaper and magazine articles at the time, as well as books written later, made the people of Tennessee appear to be opposed to progress and education. Many of the wrong ideas about the trial that are current today stem from the 1956 play *Inherit the Wind* and the movie version that appeared a few years later. Much of what was said in the production about the town, the people, and the trial was not accurate. It presents those who believe the Bible as hateful, ignorant, and prejudiced. The play was written to criticize the atmosphere of intolerance that the authors saw around them in the 1950s, not to present a fair account of the Scopes Trial.

The trial was not a bitter event that divided the community of Dayton. Scopes left Dayton only because he wanted to attend graduate school. Bryan was a kind and intelligent man. He had earlier supported such reforms as women's suffrage and the creation of a Cabinet-level Department of Labor. He had resigned as Secretary of State under Wilson because he feared that one of Wilson's letters to Germany during the submarine crisis was too strongly worded and might bring about war. Bryan even offered to pay the fine for Scopes.

The Rhea County Courthouse in Dayton, Tennessee, has a museum dedicated to the trial, and the second-story courtroom looks much as it did in 1925. A Scopes Trial Play and Festival is held in Dayton each July. Portions of the trial are re-created from the transcript of the proceedings.

The trial is sometimes called the Monkey Trial because the theory of evolution says that man evolved from monkeys. Some school systems were afraid to teach evolution because they did not want to go through a trial like the one that had occurred in Dayton. Textbook publishers removed any mention of evolution in many school books. The Butler Act stayed on the books until the Tennessee legislature repealed it in 1967.

The Creation-evolution debate continues today, along with the debate over the inspiration and authority of the Bible. The Scopes Trial was a dramatic event in American history that propelled each side to believe in its position more strongly.

Christian people need to be fair in considering the evidence of Creation and kind toward those who disagree. We must not lower ourselves to the tactics of those who ridicule belief in the Creator and in the Biblical account of Creation. The best way to change minds is to present the proof and the logic of Creation in a respectful and consistent manner.

Some of the information on the Scopes trial in this lesson was taken from "The Myth of the Scopes Trial" by John Clayton in Does God Exist? *January-February 2000, pp. 4-10.*

In 1936, eleven years after the trial, a government photographer captured this shot of a church in Dayton on a Sunday morning. The photographer described the town as the scene of the "famous Scopes trial."

If you are reviled for the name of Christ, you are blessed, because the Spirit of glory and of God rests on you.
1 Peter 4:14

⋆ Assignments for Lesson 105 ⋆

Literature Finish reading *Miracle In the Hills.* Literary analysis available in *Student Review.*

Bible Recite or write Mark 12:29-31 from memory.

Project Complete your project for the unit.

Student Review Optional: Answer the questions for Lesson 105 and for *Miracle In the Hills* and take the quiz for Unit 21.

Detail from WPA Mural at the Fisher Federal Building in Trenton, New Jersey
Charles Ward (American, 1935)

22 The New Deal

The crisis of the Great Depression brought Franklin Roosevelt to the White House and the social experiments of the New Deal to the nation. The Federal government implemented many programs, but only the stimulus of war production brought the nation out of the economic depression. Many Americans in the Thirties suffered from abject poverty while the glamor of Hollywood and radio was increasing. As the decade progressed, ominous developments in Europe and Asia pointed toward a coming world conflict. The Depression reminds us that when we face suffering and hardship in this world, we can look to the Bible for understanding, comfort, and hope.

Lesson 106 - Happy Days Are Here Again
Lesson 107 - The New Deal Runs Aground
Lesson 108 - Life in the Thirties
Lesson 109 - War Clouds Build
Lesson 110 - Bible Study: The Dilemma of Suffering

Memory Work

Memorize Romans 8:28-30 by the end of this unit.

Books Used

The Bible
American Voices
To Kill a Mockingbird

Project (choose one)

1) Write 300 to 500 words on one of the following topics:
   - What do you think was the overall effect of the New Deal? Did it provide the critical difference in helping the nation survive the Depression, or did it begin an unhealthy dependence on the Federal government? What elements of the New Deal were constitutional or unconstitutional? Give reasons from the Constitution for your answer. See Lessons 106-108.
   - Write a summary of your understanding of the dilemma of suffering and the best way to approach it in faith. See Lesson 110.
2) Memorize Romans 8:26-39. If you choose this project, you should recite or write the verses from memory at the end of the week.
3) Create an audio recording of a fictional call-in radio talk show as if it were taking place in the 1930s. Write an outline of what the host and callers will say. Have callers who support and others who oppose the New Deal, sharing their own experiences with the Depression and the New Deal. Recruit friends or family to portray the callers if possible, while you portray the host (or use different voices yourself). Your radio program recording should be at least fifteen minutes long. See Lessons 106-108.

Literature

To Kill a Mockingbird

To Kill a Mockingbird by Harper Lee is a sensitive description of life in a small southern town in the mid-1930s. The story is told from the perspective of Scout Finch, a young girl being reared by her widower father, attorney Atticus Finch. The storylines of Scout's childhood, the mysterious Boo Radley, and the realities of racial prejudice come together in the trial of a black man accused of assaulting a white girl.

The book portrays the innocence of children in sharp contrast to the prejudice of adults. People discover the truth about Tom Robinson in spite of their prejudice, and Scout discovers the truth about Boo Radley despite her prejudice. The full impact of the events is understated by the author, as a young girl would do. Scout won't really understand what it all means until she is much older.

The book won the Pulitzer Prize for Literature in 1961. An excellent movie version starring Gregory Peck appeared in 1962. Harper Lee was born in a small town in Alabama in 1926. Her mother's maiden name was Finch, and her father was an attorney. A childhood friend was the author Truman Capote, who was the inspiration for Dill. *To Kill a Mockingbird* is Harper Lee's only novel.

Plan to finish the book by the end of the next unit.

Breadline Statue at the FDR Memorial in Washington, D.C.

Lesson 106

Happy Days Are Here Again

The nation was in the grip of the worst depression in its history. President Hoover blamed the depression on international economic conditions, and he expressed confidence that his policies would eventually bring about recovery. Meanwhile, millions were out of work. Families were losing their homes because they could not make rent or mortgage payments. Banks and factories were closing. The programs enacted by the Federal government following the 1929 crash had not ended the decline. At the 1932 Republican convention where Hoover was renominated, few delegates expected an easy time at the polls in the fall.

By contrast, the Democrats gathered with the belief that they would select the next President. Their choice was the buoyant and positive governor of New York, Franklin Delano Roosevelt (often abbreviated as FDR). Born into a wealthy family and a cousin of Theodore Roosevelt, Franklin attended Harvard and then Columbia Law School. He married his cousin Eleanor, who was a niece of Teddy. In 1920 Franklin Roosevelt was the Democratic nominee for Vice President.

In 1921 Franklin was stricken with polio. Thereafter he was unable to walk without crutches and leg braces. However, he did not let his physical handicap hold him back from public service. Roosevelt was elected governor of New York in 1928 (when fellow New York Democrat Al Smith lost the state to Herbert Hoover in the presidential election), and he was re-elected in 1930 by a record majority. Roosevelt was a smooth politician who had a knack for effective public speaking. He was willing to use people and to sacrifice anything in order to achieve his political ends, and his ultimate political goal was winning the presidency.

Landslide

When Roosevelt accepted the Democratic nomination, he blamed Republican policies for the depression and promised a "new deal" for all Americans. The New Deal program was not well-defined, but Roosevelt did promise aid for individual Americans, a program of public works to put people back to work, and better safeguards for stock investors and bank depositors. Voters were swayed not so much by the specifics of his proposals as by his positive spirit and his commitment to do something to help the country. Roosevelt's optimistic campaign theme song was "Happy Days Are Here Again."

Roosevelt won the election in a landslide: 22.8 million votes to Hoover's 15.8 million. Roosevelt carried all but six states and secured a 472 to

59 electoral triumph. Democrats swept to huge majorities in both houses of Congress.

The worst period of the Depression was during the four months between the election and Roosevelt's inauguration the following March. Hoover believed that he had been repudiated, the lame-duck Congress did nothing to help ease the nation's economic woes, and Roosevelt kept to himself and planned what he would do once in office. At its worst, about one-fourth of the nation's workers (fourteen million people) were unemployed. Eighty percent of the nation's financial institutions were closed. People could not get their money, write checks on their accounts, or have any confidence that they could ever get their money out of a bank.

The New Deal Begins

The new President had no carefully devised plan to stimulate the economy. He gathered around him advisors who were largely academics and intellectuals (nicknamed the brain trust) and explored ideas about what might work. FDR was willing to experiment, keep what worked, and discard what did not. The roots of his philosophy of government activism lay in Theodore Roosevelt's Square Deal, Populist and Progressive reforms, emergency government agencies that had operated during World War I, and the experience of other countries that were also attempting to cope with the worldwide depression. The New Deal developed three areas of attack: relief (immediate help), recovery (longer-term assistance), and reform (to prevent future depressions).

Immediately upon his inauguration, Roosevelt called a special session of Congress and imposed a bank holiday. Congress responded by passing over a dozen pieces of legislation during Roosevelt's first hundred days in office. The new laws and the Federal agencies they created were known by their initials, creating what observers called an alphabet soup of bureaucracies.

The 20th Amendment to the U.S. Constitution, ratified in February of 1933 and taking effect later that year, changed the inauguration day for the President and Vice President from March 4 to January 20. It also changed the opening day of Congress from December of the year following the election to January 3 after the election (almost an entire year sooner). The previous dates reflected an era when communication and transportation were much slower. Now the country did not want or need to wait four months to see the newly-elected President inaugurated or almost an entire year for the newly-elected Congress to convene. The photo below shows President Roosevelt watching the parade on the day of his inauguration—March 4, 1933.

Polio

Poliomyelitis (usually called polio) is a disease of the nervous system that is caused by a viral infection. It can cause partial or complete paralysis. Its most common occurrence is in children ages five to ten, when it is called infantile paralysis. The disease has no known cure.

With President Roosevelt's support, his friend Basil O'Connor organized fundraisers on the President's birthday to support medical care for polio patients, as seen in the poster at left. These balls evolved into the National Foundation for Infantile Paralysis, now known as the March of Dimes.

This organization funded research that led to preventative vaccines. In 1954 Jonas Salk developed an inoculation that used polio viruses grown in the laboratory. Albert Sabin later produced a vaccine that can be given orally. The oral vaccine was licensed in 1963 and largely replaced the Salk injection. Because of the work of Salk and Sabin, polio has been almost completely wiped out.

Banking And Money

The Emergency Banking Relief Act was passed March 9. Banks were not allowed to re-open until they proved their soundness to the Treasury Department. By March 15, banks that held ninety percent of the nation's deposits were open once again. Roosevelt then decided to take the country's currency off the gold standard, a move that he announced in April. All gold coins and gold certificates were called in, and the hoarding of gold became a crime.

Roosevelt continued the Reconstruction Finance Corporation, which was founded under Hoover. Also in 1933, Congress created the Federal Deposit Insurance Corporation. Banks could purchase insurance from the FDIC that protected customers' deposits from loss. The maximum FDIC coverage for each account has risen over the years to keep pace with the needs of depositors.

Congress strengthened the Federal Reserve System to protect against bank instability. In 1934 the Securities and Exchange Commission was created to govern the buying and selling of stock. Regulations were put in place to oversee stock trading, to avoid the problems associated with buying on margin, to protect against insider trading (buying or selling stock using information not generally available), and to make sure that investors have accurate information about stocks.

The first chairman of the Securities and Exchange Commission (1934-1935) was Joseph Kennedy (center below), father of President John F. Kennedy and Senators Robert Kennedy and Ted Kennedy.

When Roosevelt took office, about 1,000 homeowners per day were losing their property to foreclosure because of an inability to make the mortgage payments. The Home Owners Loan Corporation (HOLC, 1933) enabled owners to refinance their mortgages. An estimated one million homes were saved from foreclosure by this measure. The Federal Housing Authority (FHA, 1934) insured banks against loss for granting mortgages for the building or repairing of homes that met FHA standards.

Relief and Recovery

The Roosevelt Administration wanted to put people to work as soon as possible. The Federal Emergency Relief Administration (1933) distributed $3 billion to states, which then directed the money to about eight million families in various ways. FERA programs included the construction of bridges and public buildings and providing aid to college students.

The Civil Works Administration (CWA, 1933) put four million people on the Federal payroll in about four months. However, the program was wasteful and poorly managed. People were saved from idleness and hunger, but some jobs involved little more than leaning on a shovel. The CWA was dissolved in April of 1934. The Public Works Administration (PWA, 1933), led by Interior Secretary Harold Ickes, built bridges, government buildings, hospitals, and other facilities in hundreds of communities.

Roosevelt believed that the Federal government should be actively involved in the recovery, but he preferred creating work relief jobs to giving out welfare checks. The Civilian Conservation Corps (CCC, 1933) employed 500,000 men between the ages of 18 and 25 in two thousand work camps across the country. The men cleared forest land, built state parks, helped with construction of dams, and carried out many other jobs. The men were given food, clothing, and shelter; and they received a salary which they were expected to share with their families back home. As progressive as the CCC was, the camps were still racially segregated. An off-shoot of the CCC was the National Youth Administration (NYA, 1935), which paid 400,000 students to perform work around many of the nation's schools.

Perhaps the best known New Deal recovery program was the Works Progress Administration (WPA, 1935), which replaced FERA. Overseen by Harry Hopkins, the WPA cooperated with state and local governments in building or repairing 6,000 schools, 5,000 sewage plants, and 128,000 miles

First Lady Eleanor Roosevelt (1884-1962) was an active political figure in her own right. After she discovered Franklin's affair with her personal secretary in 1918, Eleanor continued to support Franklin's political goals, but she also pursued her own agenda. She made speeches that addressed issues of public policy, wrote a newspaper column, and invited representatives of black and women's groups to the White House. She was the first woman to address a national political convention.

Following Franklin's death in 1945, Eleanor helped start the liberal Americans for Democratic Action. From 1945 to 1953, she was a delegate from the U.S. to the United Nations. Eleanor is pictured at left with singer Frank Sinatra in 1947. He is holding a statue of her late husband.

of road. In addition, many writers, musicians, and artists found work through WPA projects that were created to allow them to use their artistic abilities. In 1936 some four million people had work through the WPA.

Reform

In 1933 Congress passed the National Industrial Recovery Act (NIRA), which set up the National Recovery Administration (NRA). The law enabled industries to create their own codes of fair practices, with approval from the NRA. Among other things, these codes regulated production levels, prices, work hours, and wages. The law also gave unions the right to engage in collective bargaining with employers. It established the National Labor Relations Board to oversee union organizing and bargaining. Many businesses opposed the NRA as inappropriate meddling in business and because it gave rights to unions. Nevertheless, stores and factories across the country began displaying the NRA blue eagle logo in their windows, indicating their participation in the program.

The Farm Credit Administration (FCA, 1933) made loans to farmers for mortgage payments or to buy supplies they needed. In a more radical move to raise farm prices and thus energize the entire economy, Congress passed the Agricultural Adjustment Act (AAA, 1933). This law created a bureaucracy to set limits on agricultural production in the hope that a lower supply would cause prices to rise. Taking the plan a step further, the AAA paid farmers subsidies for not growing certain crops.

The money for the payments came from a tax imposed on food processing companies. As a result of the AAA, crops were plowed under and livestock was slaughtered while millions were going hungry. However, prices for farm products did rise. The taxes imposed on processors were passed on to consumers, raising prices even further. The AAA plan helped farmers but made it harder for city dwellers to buy farm products. Actually, the program mostly helped large farmers, not smaller ones. As production was reduced, the first land set aside was often that worked by tenants and sharecroppers, who then lost the work they were doing. The Federal bureaucracy created by the AAA was a source of frustration for both farmers and consumers.

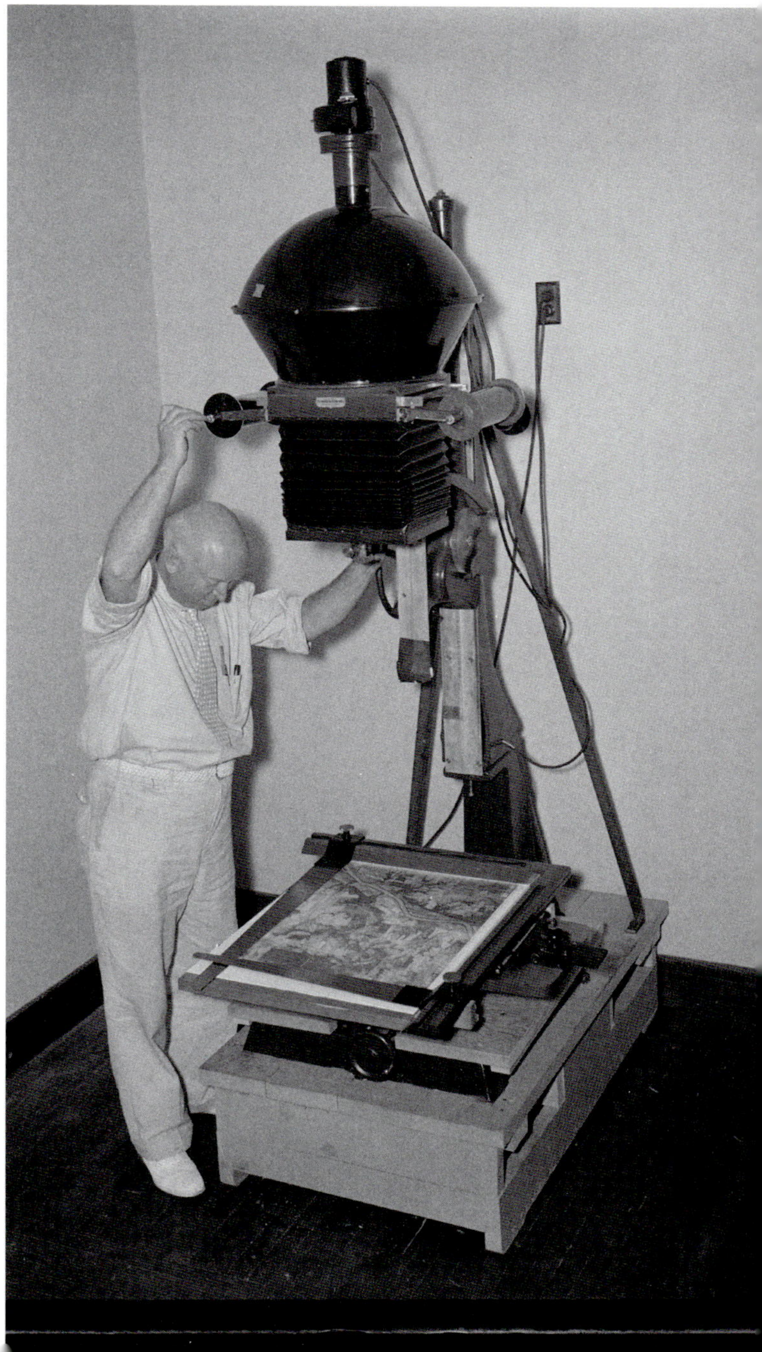

One project of the AAA involved taking aerial photographs of about one-third of the United States to document the country's farmland. This AAA worker is preparing prints for publication.

Literature from the 1930s

Pearl S. Buck (1892-1973, pictured below left) was the daughter of American missionaries and lived in China until 1933. She wrote many books about China and its people, including The Good Earth *(1931), which received the Pulitzer Prize. Buck was awarded the Nobel Prize for Literature in 1938.*

Perhaps the best-known book from the 1930s is Gone With the Wind *(1936) by Atlanta journalist Margaret Mitchell (1900-1949, pictured above right). This is the saga of Scarlett O'Hara in the Civil War years and later. It received the 1937 Pulitzer Prize. The film version (1939) continues to be immensely popular. The book is more risque than the movie, and the book also contains many more curse words.*

The leading American novelists during the 1930s were William Faulkner, Ernest Hemingway, and John Steinbeck. Much of their work contains foul language and, especially in the case of Hemingway and Steinbeck, a neutral presentation of moral wrong. Shown at right is one of William Faulkner's typewriters on a desk at his home in Oxford, Mississippi.

As America tried to cope with the Depression, some looked for answers outside of the American mainstream. Some artists and writers either joined or were attracted to the Communist Party. It is a testimony to the strength of the American system that during such a difficult time more people did not try to find answers in extreme movements.

President Roosevelt put his eloquence to good political use in his fireside chat radio addresses to the nation. Thirty times while he was President, Roosevelt spoke to the American people as though he were sitting with them next to the fireplace. This helped the office of the President seem less distant and made many people believe that they had a true friend in the White House.

The New Deal revolution took the Federal government further into the lives of Americans than it had ever gone before. Beyond simply regulating business, the government became involved in social planning and in giving direct assistance to individuals. The next lesson gives further examples of New Deal programs but also tells how the Roosevelt Administration began to encounter roadblocks.

If there is a poor man with you, one of your brothers,
in any of your towns in your land which the Lord your God is giving you,
you shall not harden your heart, nor close your hand
from your poor brother.
Deuteronomy 15:7

★ Assignments for Lesson 106 ★

American Voices Read Franklin D. Roosevelt's First Inaugural Address (pages 314-316).

Literature Begin reading *To Kill a Mockingbird.* Plan to finish it by the end of the next unit.

Bible The Bible study lesson for this unit is on the subject of suffering. List three common questions that people ask about the problem of suffering.

Start memorizing Romans 8:28-30.

Project Choose your project for this unit and start working on it.

Student Review Optional: Answer the questions for Lesson 106.

Workers at Norris Dam in Tennessee (1933)

Lesson 107

The New Deal Runs Aground

As the 1930s progressed, the Roosevelt Administration achieved other landmarks in its New Deal programs. It also stumbled due to poor judgment and to reversals in court.

Tennessee Valley Authority

In 1933 Congress created the Tennessee Valley Authority (TVA) as an experiment in the unified planning and development of an entire region. The government had operated hydroelectric power plants and nitrate factories (for dynamite and fertilizer) at Muscle Shoals on the Tennessee River in northern Alabama since the Great War. Nebraska Senator George Norris had long resisted attempts by the government to turn the Muscle Shoals facilities over to private companies. Norris wrote the legislation creating the TVA as an independent public corporation whose mission was to expand on the beginning made at Muscle Shoals and develop several aspects of the seven-state Tennessee River Valley region, one of the most economically depressed areas of the country.

The TVA was given the authority to build dams on the Tennessee River and its major tributaries to power hydroelectric power plants, to provide flood control, and to improve navigation on the Tennessee River. The agency also became involved in soil erosion and conservation projects and other aspects of life in the region. The dams created a system of lakes that were used for recreation and became known as the Great Lakes of the South. The cheaper electricity and improved quality of life made the region attractive for industrial development.

TVA provided electricity on a broad scale to local utility systems at low cost in a region that was behind the national rate of electrification. If any question remained on whether the individual American home would be a good customer for electricity, the TVA resolved it. Flood control, recreation, and other benefits have helped the Tennessee Valley. However, the improvements did not come without cost. Small power companies, many of which had already built dams on various rivers, resented what they saw as TVA's unfair advantage in the power business with its government subsidies and tax exemptions. Many people lost their homes and property and historic sites were permanently covered with water as a result of TVA projects.

Building on the TVA, the Rural Electrification Administration (REA) was created in 1935 to generate and distribute electricity to rural areas. After the TVA was declared constitutional by the Supreme Court in 1936, Roosevelt asked for six more regional development agencies for other parts of the country, but Congress refused. By then, the economy was doing better, the areas involved were not as isolated as the Tennessee Valley, and many observers believed that private developers could do the job better in those other areas.

In 1936 the first TVA dam began operation north of Knoxville, Tennessee. It was named Norris Dam after Senator George Norris; the town of Norris was also founded nearby.

Social Security

In 1935 Congress created the Social Security Administration to provide a broad range of personal benefits to millions of American individuals, including unemployment insurance, assistance to persons with disabilities, and retirement benefits. Social Security and the TVA are probably the two New Deal programs that continue to have the broadest impact in American life today.

Unemployment assistance was to be financed by a payroll tax on business. Pensions for retired workers were to be covered by a payroll tax paid by employers obtained by deductions (forced savings) from workers' paychecks. The retirement stipends were not intended to provide all the income that a retired worker would need but rather a safety net of less than $100 per month (the amount varied depending on how much one paid into the system). Pensions were to begin being paid in the early 1940s.

Social Security was the result of planners who wanted to respond to a crisis in the American economy by having government be involved in more aspects of everyday life. Many Americans were not covered under the original law, including public workers, farmers, church and charity workers, and domestic servants (many of whom were minorities). From its inception until now, Social Security has been a political battleground, and the Social Security program has been changed on numerous occasions. Social Security is one program that has led to an increasing dependence on the Federal government.

Fortunes and Misfortunes

The Roosevelt Revolution got off to a fast and almost unhindered start. In the 1934 congressional election, the Democrats accomplished a rare feat and actually increased their majorities in Congress (the party out of power usually gains in off-year elections). When the year's elections were over, only seven Republicans held governorships.

New Deal programs were having an impact, but the depression still had a firm grip on the country. In 1935 the unemployment rate was 20%, meaning ten million Americans were still out of work. Also in 1935, the Supreme Court weighed in and began striking down one piece of New Deal legislation after another. The Court decided against the Administration in seven of nine cases that it heard.

1935 Poster Announcing the Social Security Program

In *Schechter v. the U.S.* (1935), the Supreme Court declared the National Industrial Recovery Act unconstitutional because it delegated too much power to the executive branch. It said that the industrial codes could not be legally binding and that the government could not control business in the way that the law called for. Then in *U.S. v. Butler* (1936), the Court struck down the Agricultural Adjustment Act, declaring that Congress had no power to impose controls on agricultural production. Agriculture was to be regulated by the states since growing crops and livestock did not involve interstate commerce.

These were stinging defeats for the popular Democratic President. Roosevelt believed that government action to help suffering Americans was being held back by the decisions of what some called the nine old men of the Supreme Court who did not share his views. Despite these setbacks, Democrats faced the 1936 election with confidence. Personal income was rising and unemployment had fallen to nine million workers. About three and a half million Americans were on some kind of government relief. Several businessmen and bankers opposed Roosevelt, but their influence was not enough to stop the tide of popular opinion.

Roosevelt was renominated by the Democrats. The Republicans selected Kansas governor Alf Landon as their candidate. Landon did not call for the dismantling of all New Deal programs. He said that government spending was too high and that some programs were poorly administered. Roosevelt's popularity meant that Landon's "me too,

Congress passed a second Agricultural Adjustment Act in 1938 to replace the one struck down by the Supreme Court. Farmers were again paid for not growing crops. The government set the amount of crops to be marketed. A new feature was that the government held surpluses of commodities and granted farmers commodity credit loans with surplus crops as collateral. The loan amounts were just below the parity price. If prices stayed below parity, farmers could keep their loans. If prices rose above the parity level, the farmer could sell his crop that was held in surplus and pay off the loan. As seen in this photo, not all American farmers supported these agricultural changes.

just not as much" approach did not resonate with the voters.

In the election, FDR swamped Landon with 27.5 million votes to 16.7 million votes and received an even more impressive 523 to 8 electoral college victory. Landon only carried Maine and Vermont. Democrats held a 77 to 19 majority in the Senate, a 328-107 margin in the House, and all but six governorships.

The election cemented the new Democratic coalition of the South, the cities, labor, those helped by government programs (including a fair number of formerly Republican farmers), and, in the biggest change, African American voters. Blacks had traditionally supported Republicans as the party of Lincoln and the party that withstood Democratic control in the South, but no more. The great majority of blacks felt that the Republican Party had abandoned them and that the Democratic Party was now more sympathetic to their needs.

Court Packing

Roosevelt took his huge win in 1936 as a mandate to try two bold political steps, both of which backfired. The first involved the Supreme Court. Roosevelt was frustrated that so many New Deal programs had been overturned by the Court. In February of 1937, Roosevelt announced a plan to reform the Federal judiciary. He proposed fifty new Federal judgeships and a remake of the Court. His idea was to create a new seat on the Court for every Justice who did not retire at the age of seventy, up to a maximum of six new seats. The court packing plan, as it came to be called, was a blatant political move to create a Court more to Roosevelt's liking. The President did not consult with congressional leaders before announcing the plan. It also insulted some of the older justices, who actually supported New Deal legislation.

Predicting Election Results

The Literary Digest *magazine conducted a poll of over two million Americans in the weeks prior to the 1936 election and predicted a Landon victory. The reason that its survey was so badly wrong was that it polled people who owned automobiles and telephones. These were generally middle to upper class people who were more likely to vote Republican. The discredited magazine went out of business soon after the election.*

On the other hand, a new polling company led by George Gallup correctly predicted the outcome of the election by conducting a poll of only 50,000 Americans. Gallup's company quickly became a leader in the conduct of scientific polls.

Maine used to conduct its balloting in September, several weeks earlier than the rest of the country. Often the results in Maine were an indication of how the rest of the nation would vote. An old saying was, "As Maine goes, so goes the nation." With the 1936 results, many people paraphrased the saying to, "As Maine goes, so goes Vermont."

Alf Landon, pictured above, retired from public life after his term as governor of Kansas. His daughter, Nancy Landon Kassenbaum, was a U.S. Senator from Kansas in the late twentieth century. She later married former Senate Majority Leader Howard Baker.

Chief Justice Charles Evans Hughes spoke to a joint session of Congress in 1939, commemorating the 150th anniversary of Congress. Other Supreme Court justices are seated in the front row.

The proposal got nowhere in Congress and cost the President considerable public support. However, Roosevelt still got a measure of what he wanted. The Court began supporting the Administration in its decisions that were announced after Roosevelt made his court packing proposal. The Court upheld the National Labor Relations Act, the Social Security Act, and a Washington state minimum wage law that was quite similar to a New York law that the Court had struck down earlier. In addition, by 1941 Roosevelt had seen seven of the "nine old men" replaced by his own nominees.

Purging the Party

Roosevelt's other major misstep came in 1938. He wanted to rid the Democratic Party of those who did not go along with his agenda, and he campaigned for liberal Democrats in several states. His attempt to purge the party of those who did not toe the Roosevelt line, however, was another miscalculation of the public will. Democrats did not like the President telling them which Democrats to support. Perhaps it reminded them too much of the dictators in Europe they had been hearing about. In the 1938 election, the Democrats lost over half of their majority in the House as well as fourteen seats in the Senate.

Another problem for the Roosevelt Administration was that after several years of recovery, the economy slumped into another recession in 1937. Factories began closing again and unemployment rose. The culprit appeared to be Roosevelt himself. New Deal programs had rung up a significant Federal deficit, and in 1937 the Administration began cutting back on expenditures. However, the economy had not recovered enough to continue growing without Federal aid; and thus the economy suffered a relapse. With new banking regulations and new projects priming the economic pump, the economy was doing better by the end of 1938. However, with the reversals that Roosevelt suffered after 1936 and the growing attention demanded by events in Europe, the wind had gone out of the New Deal sails. Few new programs were introduced after 1939.

Labor Activity

Stimulated by the problems of the Depression and by the belief that the Democrats were sympathetic to their cause, organized labor became more active in the Thirties. John L. Lewis, for instance, led the growth of the United Mine Workers from 150,000 members to a half million. The American Federation of Labor (AFL) increased its membership, but it suffered an internal split during the period.

The AFL emphasized the smaller and more skilled craft unions, while Lewis and others wanted unions organized by industry regardless of what specific jobs members held in those industries. The advocates of industrial unions formed a Committee for Industrial Organization within the AFL in 1935. Craft union workers feared that they would be overshadowed by the larger industrial unions, and a power struggle ensued. The AFL expelled the industrial unionists in 1936, who began their own group, eventually called the Congress of Industrial Organizations (CIO).

The CIO targeted the automobile and steel industries for organizing workers. The United Auto Workers (UAW) staged a new tactic at General Motors in 1937. Workers simply sat down in front of their machines and refused to leave, making production impossible. Their wives organized efforts to bring them food. Management tried threats and intimidation and asked for Federal troops to be brought in, but they could not break the strike. Finally the company agreed to recognize the UAW and to engage in collective bargaining with the union as representative of the workers. Other auto makers made similar agreements, and steel industry workers were soon organized in like fashion.

The CIO grew to be about the same size as the AFL. Overall labor membership increased in the decade from about three million in 1933 to almost nine million by 1940. In 1939 the U.S. Supreme Court said that sit-down strikes were an illegal restraint of trade. The Court, by striking down the National Industrial Recovery Act, also struck down a provision in the law guaranteeing unions' right to collective bargaining; but that right was restored in a later law.

These CIO organizers are campaigning among harbor boatmen before a union election in 1937.

Frances Perkins was Roosevelt's Secretary of Labor throughout his Administration. She was the first female Cabinet member. She is shown here arriving for a meeting at the White House in 1938.

The Fair Labor Standards Act of 1937 (also called the Wage and Hour Law) established standards for businesses engaged in interstate commerce, which quickly became the standard throughout the nation. The law set a national minimum wage of 25 cents an hour in 1938, to increase to 40 cents an hour by 1940. It made the standard work week forty hours, with overtime work to receive time and a half pay. The legislation also said that children under sixteen could not be employed in industries engaged in interstate commerce.

Two other New Deal laws worth noting were the Food, Drug and Cosmetic Act (1938), which established guidelines for testing, labeling, and advertising products, and the Hatch Act (1939), which forbade putting pressure on government workers to contribute to a political party or to vote in a certain way.

American Political Parties

The American political party system has undergone several changes over the years. During the 1790s, two opposing factions developed: the Federalists, who generally supported a stronger central government, and the Republicans, who generally supported a weaker central government. This is often called the first two-party system in American politics because party organization and expectations of party loyalty developed during this time.

After 1812 the Federalists gradually faded from the scene. By 1828 the Republican Party had divided into National Republicans (led by Henry Clay and John Quincy Adams, among others) and Democratic Republicans (led by Andrew Jackson). The Jackson group became known simply as Democrats. Around 1833 the National Republicans and others who were opposed to Jackson and the Democrats became known as the Whig Party. This was the second two-party system.

In the early 1850s, the Whig Party splintered largely over slavery. In 1854 antislavery Whigs and other opponents of slavery formed the Republican Party, which had the same name but was not really the same party as the one that had opposed the Federalists in the early 1800s. Since 1854 the two-party system in American politics has consisted of the Democratic Party and the Republican Party.

From time to time other parties have been organized. Before the Civil War, the Anti-Masonic Party, the American or Know-Nothing Party, and the Free Soil Party each existed for a few years. After the Civil War, the Greenback Party (1874-1884), the Populist Party (1889-1896), and the Progressive Party (early twentieth century) arose and later dissolved. During the twentieth century, many parties existed from time to time, including the Socialist Party, the Dixiecrats led by Strom Thurmond in 1948, the American Independent Party led by George Wallace in 1968, the Reform Party founded by Ross Perot, the Green Party (with which Ralph Nader was sometimes associated), the Libertarian Party, and the U.S. Taxpayers' (later renamed Constitution) Party. An April 15, 2010, rally in St. Paul, Minnesota, is pictured at left.

The New Deal Legacy

The government got the money to pay for New Deal programs in several ways. One was by raising taxes. Another was the printing of more money, which caused inflation. A third way was by deficit spending, with the government going into long-term debt to have the money it wanted immediately.

America is still influenced by the New Deal. Some specific programs, such as Social Security and the TVA, are part of American life. Regulations enforced by the Securities and Exchange Commission have prevented another stock market crash with the consequences of the one that occurred in 1929. More generally, the U.S. has been influenced by the legacy of the Federal government continuing to take a more active role than just regulating business. The Federal government is involved in managing the economy, and Congress passes laws that deal with many aspects of American life. The regulations set by the bureaucracy of the executive branch have the effect of law.

The New Deal did not fully accomplish its goal of restoring the American economy. In 1939 unemployment was still at 17%, which meant that nine and a half million people in the labor force were out of work. Only the stimulus of wartime production in the early 1940s brought the economy to full recovery. The reasons given for this failure are as numerous as the commentators giving them. Some say that Roosevelt tried to do too much, others claim that he did too little. Conservatives say that business investment was not encouraged. Liberals say that wealth was not redistributed from the rich to the poor enough to make a real difference.

The New Deal brought changes for good and ill to the American system, changes with which we all have to live. Despite Roosevelt's liberalism, one area in which his Administration failed to act in any significant way was in social issues. The civil rights of blacks and the problem of racial segregation were not addressed by the Democratic majority, in large part because Roosevelt did not want to risk losing the support of white southern Democrats.

WPA Recreation Project Poster (1939)

Every person is to be in subjection to the governing authorities. For there is no authority except from God, and those which exist are established by God.
Romans 13:1

⋆ Assignments for Lesson 107 ⋆

Literature Continue reading *To Kill a Mockingbird.*

Bible Read Hebrews 12:1-13 and James 1:1-8. What are three lessons that these passages teach us about suffering?

Work on memorizing Romans 8:28-30.

Project Work on your project.

Student Review Optional: Answer the questions for Lesson 107.

Huey Long (1935)

Lesson 108

Life in the Thirties

His nickname was the Kingfish, from a character on the *Amos 'n' Andy* radio program. Huey Long, boss of Louisiana, held tight control over Democratic politics and government in the state. Long was elected governor in 1928, then resigned to become U.S. Senator in 1932. Long worked for better roads and free school textbooks, two of the many social programs he advocated in Louisiana.

As he rose to national prominence, Long advocated a "Share Our Wealth" program, which proposed to tax the rich in order to give to the poor. Part populist, part demagogue, Long aroused intense loyalty and intense hatred. He had his eyes on running for President, but he was assassinated in 1935 by the son-in-law of a political enemy. Robert Penn Warren's 1946 novel, *All the King's Men*, is loosely based on Long's life.

Huey Long was one of the more colorful figures of a decade that produced many fascinating characters and movements. Some involved politics, while others touched on various aspects of life in America.

Politics

Franklin Roosevelt and the New Deal had many opponents. Some believed that Roosevelt was too conservative, and they wanted to see even more government programs. Many more thought that FDR was too liberal, and these opponents wanted less government involvement in American business and life. The Liberty League was formed in 1934 by Republicans and conservative Democrats to oppose what they saw as the New Deal's threat to American liberty. Among those participating were former Democratic presidential candidates John Davis and Al Smith.

The hard times of the Thirties brought out advocates of many radical ideas. In 1934 Dr. Francis Townsend in California began advocating a plan to stimulate the economy by giving all retirees sixty and over $200 per month, provided that they not work and that they spend the money within the month. A Townsend newsletter and Townsend Clubs in hundreds of American cities and towns promoted the idea, even though it was shown to be fiscally impossible.

Charles Coughlin was a Catholic priest in Michigan who had a regular radio program on which he pushed his own political agenda. He especially emphasized the problems he saw in America and came close to engaging in anti-Jewish hate speech. Gerald L. K. Smith was a Shreveport, Louisiana, minister who lent his support to Huey Long.

America in the Depression

The decade of the 1930s was filled with sharp contrasts. Millions of Americans lived in poverty. Bread lines and soup lines were common sights in larger cities. Homeless men and families wandered the streets and countryside. Hobos bummed rides on trains. An area of western Kansas and Oklahoma called the Dust Bowl was especially hard hit economically, particularly after a drought there between 1932 and 1935. Many families left the area and moved to California, trusting in the reports of work opportunities in that land of plenty. Some settled in the cities of Los Angeles, San Francisco, and San Diego, but about half of the Okies went to the agricultural region of the San Joaquin Valley to find employment. There they had to compete with Hispanics for low-paying farm work and had to deal with ugly prejudice directed against them.

At the same time, the glamor of Hollywood was in its heyday. Even with the hard times, millions of people went to the theaters every week and paid twenty-five cents to see entertainment on the big screen. It was the time of gangster movies, elaborate musicals starring singer and dancer Fred Astaire, comedies with the Marx Brothers, and "shorts" with the Three Stooges. Actors Clark Gable, Spencer Tracy, Shirley Temple, and Bette Davis were in their prime. Walt Disney amazed theater-goers with animated features such as *Snow White and the Seven Dwarfs* (1937). *Frankenstein* (1931) and *King Kong* (1933) terrified millions. Charlie Chaplain lampooned the industrial age in *Modern Times* (1936). Director Frank Capra created several memorable movies still worth watching, including *Mr. Deeds Goes to Town* and *You Can't Take It With You* (the latter voted Best Picture of 1938). The decade ended with several movies released in 1939 that have come to be classics, including *Gone With the Wind*, *Stagecoach*, *The Wizard of Oz*, and *Mr. Smith Goes to Washington* (the latter directed by Frank Capra and starring Jimmy Stewart).

At home radio was king. About eighty percent of American homes had at least one radio by 1940. Millions tuned in each week to hear the continuing adventures of the Lone Ranger, Superman, and the Shadow, the antics of George Burns and Gracie Allen, the stereotypical humor about blacks on *Amos 'n' Andy* (originally played by white actors), variety shows hosted by such popular singers as Bing Crosby, and tear-jerker soap operas broadcast each day. Many programs made the switch to television when that medium developed in the late 1940s and early 1950s. In the latter half of the Thirties, Americans could browse the new magazine *Life* (begun in 1936), that emphasized pictures of newsmakers and news events and spawned several imitators.

Will Rogers from Oklahoma was the leading American humorist of the day. He started out with a vaudeville act in which he twirled a lasso and commented on the news of the day. Rogers later made personal appearances, spoke on the radio, appeared in movies, and wrote a newspaper column, offering gentle but stinging barbs about politicians and human foibles. Rogers was killed in a plane crash in 1935.

New York City Mayor Fiorello La Guardia Delivering a Radio Message, 1940

The profound impact of the Depression caused many people to realize their need for God's help and to rethink what was truly most important in their lives. Conservative churches such as the Church of the Nazarene and the Assemblies of God had dramatic increases in membership, while liberal denominations suffered declines. Many churches helped those in need with free meals and other services.

New York City hosted a World's Fair in 1939 and 1940. The displays featured the latest technological advances from countries around the world. The opening ceremonies, including a speech by President Roosevelt, were televised live to the few hundred television sets in operation around New York. The fair emphasized the promise that the future offered; but ironically another world war was even then erupting in Europe and Asia.

What Else Was Happening?

1933 *Adolf Hitler becomes de facto dictator in Germany; the next year, he takes the titles of chancellor and president.*

1933 *The first major league All-Star baseball game is played at Comiskey Park, Chicago.*

1935 *The musical play* Porgy and Bess *by George Gershwin opens in New York.*

1935 *Jews in Germany lose their citizenship.*

1935 *The first night baseball game is played in Cincinnati.*

1935 *The magnetic tape recorder is invented.*

1935 *The parking meter is introduced in Oklahoma City.*

1936 *African American Jesse Owens wins four gold medals in track and field at the 1936 Summer Olympics held in Berlin, defying Hitler's claim of Germanic white racial superiority. The photo at right shows the medal ceremony for the long jump. Jesse Owens, the gold medal winner, is in the center. Behind him is silver medalist Lutz Long of Germany. In front of Owens is bronze medalist Naoto Tajima of Japan.*

1936 *The first modern helicopter is invented.*

1937 *Joe Louis becomes the first African American to hold the world heavyweight boxing championship title.*

1937 *The crash of the airship* Hindenberg *at Lakehurst, New Jersey, is described by an announcer covering the event on the first nationwide radio newscast.*

1938 *The radio broadcast on October 30 of the play* War of the Worlds *by Orson Welles, describing an invasion from Mars, is misunderstood to be a news report and causes panic among thousands.*

1938 *Hosiery made from the synthetic fiber nylon goes on sale. Recycled stockings, as seen at left, were used to make parachutes and other war materials.*

1939 *The first FM radio station is built.*

1938 *American Chester Carlson invents the photocopier using a technology that comes to be known as xerography.*

As the decade of the Thirties ended, America was challenged to look beyond its twenty years of isolation from the rest of the world and once again to become involved in an armed conflict far away. In the 1920s and 1930s, the United States had been able to concentrate on its own good times and bad times. The country's participation in World War II and international relations after the war caused isolationism to be left far behind.

The Merchant Marine Act of 1936 led to the creation of the United States Maritime Service in 1938. As the threat of war loomed, it recruited men to operate and protect American cargo ships.

And turning His gaze toward His disciples, He began to say,
"Blessed are you who are poor, for yours is the kingdom of God.
Blessed are you who hunger now, for you shall be satisfied.
Blessed are you who weep now, for you shall laugh."
Luke 6:20-21

⋆ Assignments for Lesson 108 ⋆

American Voices Read the hymns by Tillit S. Teddlie (page 313).

Literature Continue reading *To Kill a Mockingbird.*

Bible Write a paragraph of about 100 words on how you or someone you know has grown in faith because of personal suffering or by serving someone else who was suffering.

Work on memorizing Romans 8:28-30.

Project Work on your project.

Student Review Optional: Answer the questions for Lesson 108.

The 1934 Purim Carnival in Tel Aviv, Israel, included a float mocking Hitler.

Lesson 109

War Clouds Build

Looming over domestic economic recovery during the 1930s was a growing international crisis that eventually led to the Second World War. The United States remained neutral for as long as it could, but aggression by other countries led the U.S. to offer help to nations who were opposing the aggression. Eventually the United States itself entered the war.

Early Roosevelt Foreign Policy

Before the Communist revolution in 1917, Russia was an independent country, as were nearby countries such as Ukraine, Uzbekistan, Armenia, and Kazakhstan. The Communists took over these and other nations to form the Union of Soviet Socialist Republics (U.S.S.R., or the Soviet Union). Since Russia was the largest and most dominant of the Soviet Republics, the name "Russia" is often used to refer to the U.S.S.R. in the period from 1917 to 1991.

In 1933 the U.S. gave official recognition to the Communist government of the Soviet Union. America had resisted offering legitimacy to the Communist regime because of the strong disagreement many Americans had with Communism. However, Roosevelt believed that replacing diplomatic isolation with normalized relations was in America's strategic best interest. Two immediate and practical reasons were behind the move. First, the U.S. hoped that the Soviet Union might become a lucrative trading partner. Second, America believed that better relations with Russia might help stop Japanese aggression in Asia and the Pacific.

Deputies to the Supreme Soviet (c. 1935)

As the U.S. considered extending diplomatic recognition to Communist Russia, the Soviets promised to stop pro-Soviet propaganda in the U.S. However, Russia proved to be an unreliable friend. The propaganda did not stop. In addition, among the complicated treaties and alliances leading up to World War II, Japan and Russia signed a mutual non-aggression treaty. Moreover, no significant trade developed between the United States and Russia.

Roosevelt also pursued an easing of relations with other nations in the Western Hemisphere. He backed away from the role of policeman and moved toward being a good neighbor and a partner with the nations of Central and South America. The U.S. withdrew its troops from Haiti, signed a promise not to intervene in the domestic affairs of Panama, and gave up the Platt Amendment which had allowed American intervention in Cuba. This change combined noble principle with practical necessity. The United States wanted to increase trade with its hemispheric neighbors to help alleviate the effects of the Depression. In addition, the U.S. hoped that better relations would lessen the risk of countries in the Americas aligning themselves with the dictatorial powers that were gaining strength in Europe.

The most favored nation status of Communist China was a hot topic in the 1990s. Opponents of extending MFN status cited human rights violations in China and did not want to reward China when its government was oppressing its own people. Those favoring MFN said that positive engagement with China gave the U.S. its best chance of influencing the Chinese government to change its domestic policies. The U.S. eventually granted MFN status to China, and the two countries are now major trading partners. Sea containers like those pictured below transport billions of dollars worth of goods each year between the two countries.

The United States still controlled the Philippines during the Great Depression. This photo shows Roosevelt signing an agreement in 1935 that called for a ten-year period of transition. During this time the Philippines were a U.S. commonwealth. On July 4, 1946, the Philippines formally became an independent nation.

The Reciprocal Trade Agreements Act of 1934 brought a new day to American tariff laws and to trade relations with other countries. Rather than the U.S. setting overall tariffs on all imported goods, the law authorized the Administration to make separate trade agreements with individual countries. The President could increase or decrease tariff rates with other countries by as much as 50% without Congress needing to take any action. Secretary of State Cordell Hull actively pursued these reciprocal trade agreements, and twenty-two were signed by 1940. The act created the status of most favored nation (MFN), which meant that a country with MFN status could receive the best terms that the U.S. gave any nation provided that the country did not discriminate against the United States in setting its own tariff rates.

Tariffs are not usually thought of as an exciting topic, but South Carolina almost seceded over the issue of tariffs in the 1830s. Tariffs and MFN status are factors that influence what we can buy in stores and how much we have to pay for what we buy. Tariff policy makes a difference to American companies and, directly or indirectly, to almost all Americans.

Problems in Europe and Asia

The uneasy and fragile world peace that followed the Great War broke down during the 1930s for a number of reasons. First, the framework for peace created after the war was not strong and provided for no recourse against aggressor nations. Second, turmoil within Germany, Italy, and Japan opened the door for dictatorial, militaristic, and aggressive governments to form in these countries. Adolf Hitler used the oppressive terms forced on Germany in the Treaty of Versailles as a rallying point to rebuild German military strength.

Benito Mussolini

Third, the alliance among Great Britain, France, and Russia was an uneasy one because of historic distrust among those countries. The Soviet Union had not been a party to the Treaty of Versailles, and its intentions toward Germany and other western nations were often in question. Fourth, France and Britain had allowed their military strength to slip while German power increased. Fifth, the United States removed itself as a player in the international scene after World War I and was perceived as posing little threat to aggression. Sixth, the isolationist and pacifist movements in the U.S., France, and Britain were vocal enough to make any move toward increasing armaments within those countries politically risky. Finally, a complicated web of treaties and alliances drew countries into war when their treaty partners were attacked. This caused war to escalate quickly whenever one event took place.

The Rise of Dictators

A frightening pattern of dictator governments coming to power affected several nations. All of these dictatorships scorned democracy as a weak form of government and bragged that the new, autocratic state was the source of real power and control. Benito Mussolini seized control of Italy in 1922. The previous Italian government had been ineffective, and the country had not gained much from its involvement in the Great War. Mussolini called his approach Fascism, from the Latin word *fasces*, a bundle of rods that was a symbol of strength in ancient Rome.

In actions that became the pattern for what happened in many countries, Mussolini demonstrated a show of strength and claimed to be the country's savior; and the people endorsed his seizure of power. The government under Mussolini took over almost every aspect of business and life in Italy, the military became of central importance, and all opposition and dissent were ruthlessly oppressed. Many Italians cheered Mussolini's rise until they became victims of his lust for greater power.

Militarists rose to power in Japan in the late 1920s. Using a variety of pretexts to cover their aggression, Japan invaded the Chinese province of Manchuria in 1931. The League of Nations stood by helplessly. The next year Japan bombed the Chinese city of Shanghai. When the League of Nations protested Japan's actions in 1933, Japan simply withdrew from the League.

Adolf Hitler gained complete control of Germany in 1933. As in Italy, the sitting German government was weak; and Hitler's National Socialist (Nazi) Party was able to take over with a combination of popular support and strong-arm tactics. Hitler played on German resentment toward its weakened military position and the requirement of making war reparation payments, both called for in the Treaty of Versailles. He also found a convenient scapegoat by blaming the Jews for what he saw as the country's economic and social problems.

Joseph Stalin consolidated his power as leader of the Soviet Union in the 1930s. Americans suspected and feared tactics the Communists used to maintain control, but American criticism was muted because Russia was seen as a potential helper against German aggression. Only in later years was the truth revealed about the millions of people that Stalin killed in his political purges and in his cruel suppression of dissent.

In Spain Fascist General Francisco Franco revolted against the elected government in 1936 and began a civil war. Stalin gave some assistance to the government forces, but Germany and Italy helped Franco to a much greater degree. This made Spain something of a trial run for the forces that would oppose each other in the coming world war. Franco gained control in 1939, and he kept Spain out of World War II.

It Can't Happen Here, a 1935 novel by Sinclair Lewis, describes an American President who becomes a Hitler-style dictator. A New Deal program funded performances of the theatrical version across the country.

Franco is shown at left (second from right) meeting with Nazi officials in 1940. Franco ruled Spain until 1973, when he resigned as premier but remained head of state. He died in 1975; and his hand-picked successor, Juan Carlos, grandson of the former Spanish king, became monarch. Spain is now a constitutional monarchy with an elected prime minister.

Aggression Increases

In 1935 Italy invaded the African nation of Ethiopia. The Italians with their modern tanks and weapons slaughtered the Ethiopians, who were mounted on horses and armed mostly with spears. Ethiopian emperor Haile Selasse (HIGH-ly se-LASS-y) pled in vain for help from the League of Nations. Meanwhile, Japan withdrew from the Washington Armament Conference agreements and began building up its navy.

In March of 1936, Germany stationed military forces in the Rhineland, the western province situated along the Rhine River and next to France, in direct violation of the Treaty of Versailles. That fall Germany and Italy signed a military pact. Mussolini said that Rome and Berlin formed the new axis around which the world turned. Italy and Germany came to be called the Axis Powers. Japan joined the Axis in 1937. In July of that year, Chinese armies clashed with the Japanese forces trying to gain further control of China. This is often seen as the start of World War II in Asia.

Hitler became increasingly aggressive in Europe as he saw potential enemies doing nothing to stop him. He believed that the German people were the superior race and were destined to rule the world. His excuse for invading other countries was to unify all Germanic people and to provide more *lebensraum* (living space) for them. In March of 1938, Hitler invaded and annexed Austria. He then threatened to take the Sudetenland, the western territory of Czechoslovakia which had a large German population. The Sudetenland had been made a part of Czechoslovakia in the Treaty of Versailles.

Neville Chamberlain, British Prime Minister, met with Hitler in Munich, Germany, in September of 1938 and reached an agreement. Hitler said that he would end his aggression if he were allowed to take the Sudetenland. By appeasing (giving in to) Germany's desire for the Sudetenland, Chamberlain hoped to end Hitler's desire for more conquests.

Chamberlain returned to England, held the signed agreement aloft as he got off the airplane, and stated that he believed that they had achieved "peace for our time." Chamberlain was wrong. In March of 1939, Hitler took the rest of Czechoslovakia. At the same time, Mussolini invaded Albania.

The photo at left below shows Chamberlain (left) with Hitler (center) during their meeting in Germany. The photo at right below shows Chamberlain after his return to England.

American Isolation

While all of these events were taking place, the United States struggled to maintain its position of official neutrality and its isolation from foreign entanglements. Many in the U.S. were disillusioned by the horrors of the Great War and by the fact that it had not brought about an end to war and the triumph of democracy. Wilson's vaunted League of Nations, seen as the best hope for world peace, was powerless.

Meanwhile, a Senate investigation into financial arrangements made during the Great War revealed that some bankers and munitions producers had made enormous profits from the tragedy of war. Americans were not anxious to create another opportunity for what some called the "merchants of death." In addition, many Americans simply did not see the need to become involved in a European or Asian war. The country was protected by its geographic isolation, the needs at home were great, and many simply wanted to avoid all war. The arguments were similar to those made before the U.S. entered the Great War, except that German and Italian aggression was so blatant that most American public opinion was now clearly against them.

Congress passed and Roosevelt signed a series of Neutrality Acts, which said that the U.S. could not sell arms to belligerent nations and could sell those nations only a restricted list of other goods. In addition, Americans were forbidden from traveling on the vessels of nations at war. At the same time, Roosevelt and many other Americans were concerned about the world situation and wanted to take a stand against aggression.

U.S. Senator Gerald Nye, a Republican from North Dakota, chaired the Special Committee on Investigation of the Munitions Industry. The businessmen who profited from the Great War were labeled "merchants of death."

The America First Committee (AFC), founded in 1940, was the largest group that advocated keeping the United States out of the war in Europe. Its most well-known spokesman was Charles Lindbergh. After the Japanese attack on Pearl Harbor, the AFC closed its operations and called on Americans to support the war effort.

In October of 1937, Roosevelt delivered a speech in which he said that aggressor nations should be "quarantined" so that their attacks would end:

> It seems to be unfortunately true that the epidemic of world lawlessness is spreading. When an epidemic of physical disease starts to spread, the community approves and joins in a quarantine of the patients in order to protect the health of the community against the spread of the disease. It is my determination to pursue a policy of peace. It is my determination to adopt every practicable measure to avoid involvement in war. It ought to be inconceivable that in this modern era, and in the face of experience, any nation could be so foolish and ruthless as to run the risk of plunging the whole world into war by invading and violating, in contravention of solemn treaties, the territory of other nations that have done them no real harm and are too weak to protect themselves adequately. Yet the peace of the world and the welfare and security of every nation, including our own, is today being threatened by that very thing.

The threat to American interests was demonstrated in December of 1937 when the U.S. gunboat *Panay* was attacked by Japanese forces in Chinese waters with several American casualties. While following an official policy of neutrality, Roosevelt sought funding for a build-up of American military forces and looked for ways to help Great Britain and other countries that were committed to resisting Nazi aggression.

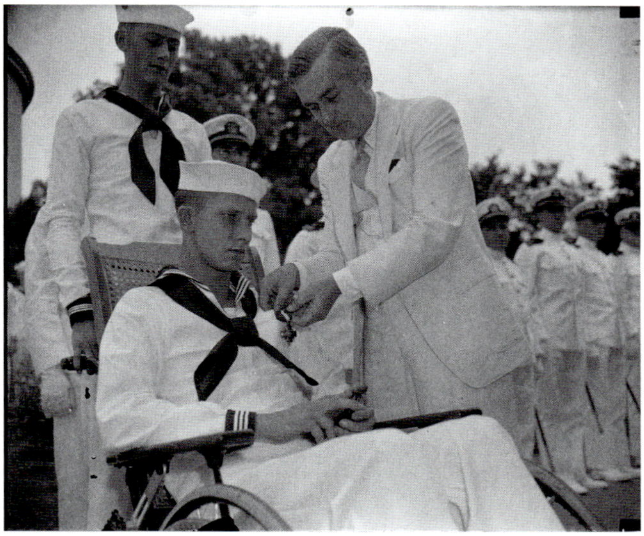

John L. Hodge of the U.S. Navy is shown here receiving the Navy Cross while recovering at the Naval Hospital. Even though he was wounded in the attack on the USS Panay, *Hodge assisted in putting out a fire and performed first aid on wounded Americans and Chinese.*

War in Europe

Great Britain and France knew that Germany had its eyes on Poland to its east. They declared that any attack on Poland would bring about a state of war with Germany. The two countries hoped that the Russian presence east of Poland would keep Germany from making an attack. However, in August of 1939, the world was shocked when Germany and the Soviet Union announced the signing of a mutual non-aggression pact. What was not announced was an agreement between the two countries on how to partition Poland between them.

On September 1, 1939, Germany launched a massive invasion of Poland using *blitzkrieg* (fast war) tactics. The Soviet Union moved into Poland from the east to claim its share. Two days later, Britain and France declared war on Germany. The Second World War had begun. In response the United States began moving away from its position of neutrality. Congress lifted the arms embargo, and the United States began selling weapons to Great Britain. However, following the invasion of Poland, Europe was calm for a time. Skeptics scoffed that it appeared to be a *sitzkrieg* (sitting war). The reality of the continuing German menace would be revealed in 1940 as the U.S. drew ever closer to direct involvement.

Members of the British Auxillary Territorial Service process and check weapons sent under Lend-Lease.

***Or what king, when he sets out to meet another king in battle,
will not first sit down and consider
whether he is strong enough with ten thousand men
to encounter the one coming against him with twenty thousand?
Luke 14:31***

⋆ Assignments for Lesson 109 ⋆

Literature Continue reading *To Kill a Mockingbird.*

Bible Work on memorizing Romans 8:28-30.

Project Work on your project.

Student Review Optional: Answer the questions for Lesson 109.

London Children Made Homeless by German Bombing (1940)

Lesson 110 - Bible Study

The Dilemma of Suffering

The realities of suffering, whether it be personal suffering, suffering by the innocent, or national suffering as experienced during the Great Depression, can challenge the belief that God is just and loving. For years people have used the reality of suffering to question the existence or goodness of God. If we are trying to look at history from the perspective of faith, we must consider whether the suffering that history has recorded renders faith in God an invalid option.

If God does not exist and everything that occurs is merely the random effect of billions of atoms that happen to join into brains that make and use guns against other people or into hurricanes and tornadoes that destroy lives and property, faith in God will not help us understand history. On the other hand, if the God of the Bible does exist, He can help us understand the meaning of suffering in our world.

Consider It Logically

The idea that suffering proves that God does not exist is a reaction based on little thought. The following ideas help us approach the question of suffering with careful, faith-centered thinking.

1) A rational world could not be the product of an irrational process. (See C. S. Lewis, *Miracles*, originally published 1947; this edition Washington, D.C.: Canon Press, 1969, pp. 219-220). While not everything in the world is rational and orderly, how could anything rational and orderly result from chance creation and mindless evolution? Some might suggest that the world is the result of a chance process that we simply do not understand yet. However, we do know that a rational process results in creation. We see it every time an inventor creates a gadget or a writer creates a story.

Whether you believe that the world was created by God or created by chance, you are accepting something on faith: either faith in God, or faith in irrationality, or faith in an unknown rationality. Given our current understanding of the world, it is more likely that something was created from nothing by an Intelligence behind it all than by irrationality. Since this is the case, those who believe in God do not have an irrational belief. Faith in God is the more rational and more likely position.

2) God is either in charge or he is not. Either the God of the Bible rules the universe or He does not. One of these is true, regardless of what we believe about it. If God does not rule the universe, it might be because He does not exist, or because He exists but lacks control, or because He does not care to control the universe.

If a loving and all-powerful God is in control, one wonders why pain and suffering exist in His world. But if God were not in control, many more disturbing questions would arise. Did He once have control and subsequently lose it? Does He control the world for some people but not for others? How and why would we pray to God if He did not control the world?

The Bible helps us deal with questions such as these. Christians trust that God is in control, even though they don't understand everything that happens; and they trust that He is working to accomplish His will and to do good, even through the suffering that occurs. Once again, with whatever choice you make, you have a faith system.

3) This world, not an imaginary one, is where we have to live. If this world is amiss, would you prefer one in which God turns bullets into feathers and stops hateful thoughts before they lead to action? Would we not feel physical pain when we touch something hot? As inviting as such a world might sound, two problems emerge in envisioning it:

First, such a world would never offer an occasion for someone to show courage, perseverance, and joy amid suffering. Some of the noblest and most important human characteristics develop as a result of suffering. A world in which people did not have to struggle and grow would not be good for us.

Second, such a world is not the one in which we live. You would be saying that you could do a better job of creating the world than the One who did create the world, and yet you are totally incapable of creating such a world. How do you know it would be better? If humans would be different in such a world and not need to develop courage, perseverance, and so forth, how can we say that such a world would be better for us? In such a world, we would not be us. We would be something else, and that seems to beg the question. What is the best world for us to live in? We are in it.

4) People are able to believe in God even when they suffer. Helen Keller had multiple disabilities, yet she believed in God. Corrie Ten Boom endured the horrors of Nazi concentration camps and emerged a believer. Although some people caring for a loved one with Alzheimer's Disease become embittered against God, many others serve in such trying situations with great love, they experience spiritual growth, and they receive invaluable lessons from God throughout the experience.

Medical Supplies Being Distributed in Ethiopia After the Italian Invasion (1935)

Job and Joseph: Can You Trust God?

Since faith in God is the more reasonable position even with the reality of suffering, we can look to the Bible to find God's answers about suffering. The Old Testament book of Job provides one perspective of faith concerning the issue of personal suffering. In the book, Satan believes that Job is faithful to God because God has blessed him. God, on the other hand, believes that Job will be faithful regardless of what happens to him.

In the story, Job loses first his possessions, then his family, and finally his health. He agonizes over his losses. Three friends come to comfort him. The friends say, in one way or another, that Job has suffered because he is guilty of sin and that he needs to repent. Job denies this and says that he wants to make the case before God that he doesn't deserve what has happened to him. A fourth friend appears and suggests that God has brought suffering onto Job in order to teach him a lesson. If this is true, one wonders why righteous Job needed such a severe lesson. Neither Job nor those who spoke to him about his plight know about the conversations between God and Satan in the first two chapters of the book.

Then God comes onto the scene. For the most part, He simply asks questions. The questions all seem to be asking in one way or another whether Job and his friends really know what they are talking about. They claim to know the mind of God, but they don't even know how the world operates. Time and again, when God asks Job if he understands a given process or reality in nature, Job has to say, as would we all, "No."

God's questions to Job lead to a more basic question: Can you trust the God who is? Belief is a conviction based on things that a person does not understand or see in the physical sense (Hebrews 11:1). Job realizes that, even with all that he does not know or understand, he can still trust the God who exists. Job was able to believe in God in spite of his suffering.

The story of Joseph in the book of Genesis is an example of how God used wrong to bring about good. Joseph irritated his brothers, and they responded with cruelty to him. He was treated unfairly more than once when he was in Egypt, but God eventually placed him in a position of authority that enabled him to save the lives of his family and many others. After Joseph's family had arrived safely in Egypt, his brothers begged Joseph to show them mercy. Joseph replied, "Am I in God's place? As for you, you meant evil against me, but God meant it for good in order to bring about this present result, to preserve many people alive" (Genesis 50:19b-20). It was hard for Joseph to endure what happened to him, but in the end he saw that God was working through it all.

Civilians in Shanghai, China, Seeking Refuge During Battle Between the Chinese and Japanese (1937)

The New Testament's Message: Suffering Helps Us Grow

The message of the New Testament regarding suffering is that the followers of Jesus can grow spiritually as a result of it. Paul said that tribulation builds character, which gives us a hope that will not disappoint (Romans 5:3-5). For this reason, we can rejoice even when we are facing hard times because we know we will be better for it.

The writer of Hebrews warns his readers not to give up in the face of suffering because of the terrible consequences of doing so (Hebrews 10:23-39). He encourages them to look at Jesus, who endured much worse suffering than they are going through. Hebrews explains what is happening to them as the discipline of a loving Father: painful at the moment, but necessary in order for them to live well (Hebrews 12:1-11).

James tells his readers to consider it joy when they encounter trials. Such trials produce endurance which helps the believer be spiritually mature (James 1:2-4). Those who endure trials are blessed. Even in the face of suffering, we can know that the Lord is compassionate and merciful (James 5:10-11). We might wonder sometimes what we have done to deserve the difficulties we face; but when we think of how sinful we really are, we understand that we get much better than we deserve based on our actions.

Peter wrote his first epistle to assure fellow Christians that the persecution they were enduring helped their faith grow (1 Peter 1:6-7). They were enduring nothing more than what Jesus had to go through, and as He made it through to a glorious end so could they (1 Peter 4:12-19). In fact, Jesus left us an example that we should follow (1 Peter 2:21-25).

Habakkuk on National Suffering: Live By Faith

The prophet Habakkuk agonized over what he saw among the unrighteous people of Judah. He wondered how these things could happen among God's people. He asks God:

> Why do you make me see iniquity,
> And cause me to look on wickedness?
> Yes, destruction and violence are before me;
> Strife exists and contention arises.
> Therefore the law is ignored,
> And justice is never upheld.
> For the wicked surround the righteous;
> Therefore justice comes out perverted.
>
> Habakkuk 1:3-4

In response, God reveals to Habakkuk that He is raising up the Babylonians to punish Judah and take many of them captive (Habakkuk 1:6). Whatever human motivations might have been in Nebuchadnezzar's mind when he attacked Jerusalem, from God's perspective this was the real reason for what happened. However, God's explanation only raises another question for Habakkuk. He asks God how He could ever use pagan Babylonians to punish His chosen people. Habakkuk wonders:

> Your eyes are too pure to approve evil;
> And you can not look on wickedness with favor.
> Why do you look with favor
> On those who deal treacherously?
> Why are you silent while the wicked swallow up
> Those more righteous than they?
>
> Habakkuk 1:13

The Royal Castle in Warsaw, Poland, After a German Attack (1939)

God has an answer for this question also. He says that in due time the Babylonians will get their own punishment (Habakkuk 2:4-19), which they did at the hands of the Persians. God then explains how someone should look at the historical events that unfold around him. "The righteous will live by his faith" (Habakkuk 2:4). It takes faith to believe in God even though events seem out of control.

What To Do About It: Work the Works of God

Jesus tells us what to do with suffering when we encounter it. Once when Jesus was with his disciples, they saw a man blind from birth. The disciples asked Jesus whose fault it was that the man was blind. Had he sinned or had his parents? Their question assumes that suffering is the result of sin. However, Jesus says that this is not the issue. His reply was, "It was so that the works of God might be displayed in him" (John 9:3).

Jesus did not directly answer the disciples' question of why the blindness had occurred. He simply said that since it had occurred, it was an opportunity to do the work of God in the man's life. Jesus was not so much interested in discussing the cause of the suffering as in dealing with the effect of it. The Lord gave a similar answer concerning a political execution and an accident. When commenting about Pilate killing some people who had been making sacrifices and about eighteen people who had been killed by a falling tower, Jesus denied that they deserved such a fate because of their sins. They weren't necessarily any worse sinners than anyone else who had lived and died. The lesson He took from it was a warning: "Unless you repent, you will all likewise perish" (Luke 13:1-5).

Some people look at the suffering that exists in the world, fail to find a reason for it, and end up doing nothing. The eye of faith, however, sees suffering as an opportunity to do the work of God's mercy for those who are suffering. Faith sees the suffering in the world as a miniature portrait of what it would be like not to follow God. A person with such faith responds positively to the warning.

Alabama Sharecropper Frank Tengle Singing Hymns with His Family in the Midst of the Great Depression (c. 1935)

Groaning As In Childbirth: This World Is Not My Home

Paul comes closest of all writers in Scripture to giving an explanation for suffering. "We know that the whole creation groans and suffers the pains of childbirth together until now" (Romans 8:22). Suffering exists because the world is going through childbirth, preparing for something better. It exists because this world is broken. We need to be attuned to something beyond the suffering of this world. C. S. Lewis said that pain is God's megaphone to rouse a deaf world (*The Problem of Pain*, originally published 1940; this edition New York: Macmillan, 1962, p. 93). Just as physical pain tells your brain that something is wrong in your physical body, the presence of suffering in the world is a message to our hearts that something is wrong here.

It is significant that, when Jesus came into the world, He came as a physical human who was just as capable of suffering as everyone else. He redeemed suffering by entering into the realm of suffering and using it for God's glory. Because Jesus suffered in the world, Jesus' followers should not be surprised if they suffer in the world also.

What It Means

The existence of pain and suffering in the world does not prove that God does not exist. It does not prove that He doesn't care or that He is weak. When we see evil and suffering in the world of whatever nature—natural disaster, disease, terrorist attacks, or automobile accidents—we can and should still believe that God is in control. Suffering is evidence that this world is no place to spend eternity and that a better one is coming. Suffering is an opportunity to do the work of God in caring for those who are suffering.

Jewish Inmates at a German Concentration Camp in Latvia (1941)

Consider it all joy, my brethren,
when you encounter various trials,
knowing that the testing of your faith
produces endurance.
James 1:2-3

⋆ Assignments for Lesson 110 ⋆

Literature	Continue reading *To Kill a Mockingbird.*
Bible	Recite or write Romans 8:28-30 from memory.
Project	Complete your project for the unit.
Student Review	Optional: Answer the questions for Lesson 110 and take the quiz for Unit 22.

National World War II Memorial, Washington, D.C. (2006)

23 World War II

The conflagration that had been spreading across the globe finally swept up the United States. The U.S. had been a non-belligerent partner with the Allies for some time, but Pearl Harbor led the country into war against the Axis. The Allies had a difficult time for the first part of the war, but eventually American manpower and resources turned the tide that led to an Allied victory. The American home front was very much a part of the story of success. We look at the war through the experiences of one individual soldier. In the Bible study, we remember that Christians today need to be aware of the spiritual war being waged within us and around us.

Lesson 111 - America Enters the War
Lesson 112 - America At War
Lesson 113 - Victory!
Lesson 114 - One Soldier's Story
Lesson 115 - Bible Study: Don't You Know There's a War On?

Memory Work Memorize Ecclesiastes 3:1 and 3:7-8 by the end of this unit.

Books Used The Bible
American Voices
To Kill a Mockingbird

Project (choose one)

1) Write 300 to 500 words on one of the following topics:

- Write a letter home as someone in military service in Europe or Asia during World War II. Remember that your letter will be censored by American officials so that you do not give away any information that might be helpful to the enemy.

- Write your view on whether or not the United States should have used atomic weapons against Japan. See Lesson 113.

2) Research recipes that were created during World War II to help families conserve rationed foods such as meat, sugar, and fats. Prepare some of these recipes and serve a "Victory Dinner" to your family.

3) Create a model of a weapon or vehicle (tank, jeep, plane, ship, etc.) that helped the Allies win World War II. You will need to do research and locate photos to guide your planning. Make your model as close to scale as you can and from the material of your choice (e.g., wood, cardboard, clay, STYROFOAM™, LEGO® bricks).

U.S. Naval Base at Pearl Harbor, Hawaii, October 30, 1941

Lesson 111

America Enters the War

Germany's invasion of Poland on September 1, 1939, is considered the beginning of World War II in Europe. Because of this attack, Great Britain and France declared war on Germany. In April of 1940, Germany invaded and seized Denmark and Norway. The next month, Hitler turned his attention to France. Following the Great War, France had built a series of forts called the Maginot Line along its border with Germany. To invade France, German forces simply went around the line by going through the Netherlands, Belgium, and Luxembourg.

The onslaught of the German army trapped a force of about 300,000 mostly British troops against the English Channel at the town of Dunkirk in northern France. The British government called for every available ship and boat in Britain to go to Dunkirk to rescue the troops. The evacuation at Dunkirk was one of many courageous acts that the British people performed during the war.

German troops advanced on Paris and took the city in June of 1940. Italy, seeing how the conflict was going, declared war on France and Great Britain. Hitler forced France to sign an armistice surrendering to Germany on June 22, 1940. The vengeful Hitler made French officials surrender to him in the same railroad car at the same spot where Germany had signed the armistice ending World War I. Germany set up a puppet French government loyal to Germany in the French town of Vichy.

This left Great Britain as the only declared enemy of Germany still able to fight. Newly installed prime minister Winston Churchill vowed that Britain would never surrender. In the summer of 1940, Hitler's *Luftwaffe* (air force) began a fierce attack on the island nation that came to be called the Battle of Britain. Air raid sirens and the need to take shelter became daily occurrences. German bombers targeted the major cities and especially strategic factories. Between a third and a half of London was destroyed.

However, the Royal Air Force (RAF) performed brilliantly and was able to knock out many German planes. This significantly weakened Hitler's air power. In addition, the British government and the British people refused to bow to Hitler. The air attack was supposed to be a prelude to a German invasion of Britain, but the air campaign was not successful and Hitler called off the invasion.

In September of 1940, Germany, Italy, and Japan signed an agreement which said that if war were declared against any one of them, the other two would join forces and declare war on the opposing nation.

A Third Term for Roosevelt?

Meanwhile in America, 1940 brought another presidential campaign. The Republicans were in some degree of disarray about whom to nominate. Their convention selected Wendell Willkie, a Wall Street lawyer who had spoken up for private power companies against the TVA. Willkie had been a lifelong Democrat and in fact had voted for Roosevelt in 1932, but since then he had seen dangers in the New Deal and had changed his party registration to Republican.

The big question in everyone's mind was whether Roosevelt would run for an unprecedented third term. Republicans and some disaffected Democrats made noises about a constitutional amendment setting a two-term limit for a President. FDR discussed his thinking on the issue with practically no one, and in the end he accepted a well-orchestrated first ballot nomination at the Democratic convention. The justification the Democrats gave was that Roosevelt's continued leadership was essential because of the mounting war in Europe. The Vice President, John Garner, had fallen out of favor with the President. Garner opposed deficit spending and the sit-down strike tactic of unions that FDR refused to condemn. Garner even campaigned briefly for the presidential nomination himself that year. Roosevelt picked his Secretary of Agriculture, Henry Wallace, a former Republican, to be his running mate.

During the campaign, Willkie charged that the New Deal was inefficient and too expensive; but he did not challenge the basic idea of an activist Federal government. When this approach did not catch on with the voters, Willkie began asserting that Roosevelt was a warmonger who would lead the U.S. into another world conflict. The President assured the public, "Your boys are not going to be sent into any foreign wars." Apparently Roosevelt believed that if the United States were attacked, the conflict would no longer be a foreign war. Willkie's charges and Roosevelt's denials were both a bit of campaign theater, since both men supported giving aid to Great Britain and knew the threat that Hitler posed.

1940 Presidential Campaign Billboard

Roosevelt won the election, which brought out more voters than ever before in an election; but he had a smaller margin of victory than in his two previous triumphs. The President enjoyed a 27.3 million to 22.3 million popular vote victory and a 449-82 win in the electoral college. The third term issue being settled, Roosevelt once again turned his attention to the war.

Further War Preparations

While the political campaign was going on, the U.S. gave additional assistance to Britain and took another major step toward preparing for direct involvement. On September 3, Roosevelt announced that the United States had given fifty older naval destroyers to Britain in exchange for the right to use certain navy and air bases in Britain's possessions in the western hemisphere. Two weeks later, the government instituted its first peacetime draft registration for all men aged 21 to 35.

In 1941 Germany and Italy took control of Greece, Hungary, Romania, Bulgaria, and parts of northern Africa. Almost all of Europe was now under Axis control. In response, America increased its level of assistance to the Allies. Britain's military supplies were dangerously close to depletion. The President proposed to Congress that the U.S. lend or lease military supplies to Britain and any other country resisting Hitler. In a fireside chat to the American people, Roosevelt said that the U.S. had to be the arsenal of democracy to help Britain. The lend-lease proposal aroused a storm of controversy. Supporters said that it was America's best chance at avoiding direct involvement in the war, while opponents claimed that it would clearly lead the country into war by giving support only to one side. The plan passed Congress in March of 1941, and aid started flowing to Britain. When Germany invaded Russia in June of that year, the U.S. extended lend-lease assistance to the Soviets.

During the spring of 1941, German and Italian submarines began attacking Atlantic shipping routes. The U.S. began providing assistance to British ships by locating enemy subs, and U.S. troops occupied Iceland to keep the Germans from taking it. In September Roosevelt gave "shoot on sight" orders to American ships regarding any enemy vessel. U.S. ships began escorting British vessels, and Congress voted to let American ships enter combat zones. The President ordered such ships to be armed.

In August of 1941, President Roosevelt and Prime Minister Churchill met off the coast of Newfoundland on a heavily protected warship to discuss joint Allied goals for the war. Roosevelt and Churchill issued the Atlantic Charter, which stated such shared principles as an end to aggression, self-determination for the governments of all nations, and freedom from the fear of attack. The United States was still not technically a belligerent, but it was coming as close as it could short of a formal declaration of war.

Jeanette Rankin (1880-1973) was the first woman to serve in the U.S. House of Representatives. A Montana Republican, she served two terms in Congress: 1917-1919 and 1941-1943. Both times she ran as a pacifist. She voted against American entry into World War I, and in 1941 she was the only member of either house to vote against American entry into World War II.

Problems in the Pacific

Japan and the Soviet Union signed a non-aggression treaty in April of 1941. This allowed Russia to concentrate on the German threat in Europe, but it gave Japan a free hand to escalate the war in Asia. In June of 1941, Japan seized French Indochina (the area that later became Vietnam). The U.S. responded by ending almost all trade with Japan and freezing Japanese assets in the States. America also sent a lend-lease package to China.

Seeing that the U.S. was becoming more involved in the conflict, Japan took a two-pronged approach. It sent a peace mission to Washington in November while preparing for a full-scale attack on U.S. possessions. Japan insisted that the U.S. release Japanese assets that had been frozen, supply Japan with all of its demands for gasoline, and end all aid to China. The United States refused to accept these demands. On the morning of December 7, 1941, the Japanese government sent a secret message to its delegation in Washington to break off negotiations. The message was to be presented to the American government just before the attack on Pearl Harbor, but delays prevented it from being delivered until after the attack had begun.

December 7, 1941

The day was a Sunday. Millions of Americans attended church services that morning knowing that war was raging around the world and wondering when it might engulf their own country. Professional football teams played that afternoon. In the early morning hours in the territory of Hawaii, the Japanese launched a massive surprise air assault on the American naval and air bases at Pearl Harbor. In two hours the Japanese destroyed about 150 American planes and eight battleships and inflicted other severe damage on the installations. Some 2,400 enlisted personnel and civilians were killed and another 2,000 were wounded. That day the Japanese also attacked American bases at Wake Island, Midway Island, Guam, and the Philippines, along with British positions in Hong Kong and the Malay Peninsula.

Historians have long debated what the United States government knew and when. It is easy from hindsight to suspect conspiracies and to charge dereliction of duty. The American government was apparently aware that a large Japanese buildup was underway, but U.S. officials assumed that the main target was going to be in Asia.

At left below is a photograph taken from a Japanese plane during the attack on Pearl Harbor. At right below U.S. Navy personnel rescue a survivor from the water near the heavily damaged West Virginia *battleship.*

American intelligence intercepted the December 7 message to the Japanese delegation in Washington. A non-specific warning that something was about to happen was sent to American bases, but the warning arrived in Hawaii too late.

The Japanese missed two important targets. They did not hit oil storage tanks at Pearl Harbor, which gave the American Pacific fleet a fuel supply closer than supplies on the West Coast of the United States. Also, American aircraft carriers had put out to sea some days before, which gave the U.S. an important weapon in the Pacific theater for the days ahead.

The day after the attack, President Roosevelt addressed Congress and asked for a declaration of war. Congress responded that day with only one dissenting vote. Germany and Italy declared war on the United States three days later. The conflagration had indeed become a world war, and America was now directly involved.

Virginia Young (right) lost her husband in the attack on Pearl Harbor. She joined the war effort by finding living quarters for female workers like Ethel Mann, who moved from out of state to work at the Naval Air Base in Corpus Christi, Texas.

A time to love and a time to hate; a time for war and a time for peace.
Ecclesiastes 3:8

★ Assignments for Lesson 111 ★

American Voices Read the Atlantic Charter and Franklin Roosevelt's Declaration of War speech (pages 317-319).

Literature Continue reading *To Kill a Mockingbird.* Plan to finish it by the end of this unit.

Bible The Bible study for this unit considers the spiritual warfare taking place between God and Satan and how each person is a part of the battle. Paul often uses battle imagery in describing the Christian life. Read 2 Corinthians 10:3-6. List three non-material weapons to which you think Paul is referring in this passage.

Start memorizing Ecclesiastes 3:1 and 3:7-8.

Project Choose your project for this unit and start working on it.

Student Review Optional: Answer the questions for Lesson 111.

Working on an A-31 Bomber at the Vultee Plant in Nashville, Tennessee (1943)

Lesson 112

America at War

America's entry into the war was the decisive factor in the ultimate Allied victory, but the tide that brought this about did not turn for some time. Through most of 1942, the Axis powers advanced and the Allied forces retreated in both the Atlantic and Pacific.

In 1941 and 1942, the Japanese overran Allied positions throughout the Asian rim of the Pacific, including American and British possessions and countries that had joined with the Allies. The American commander in the Pacific, General Douglas MacArthur, was ordered out of the Philippines in late December of 1941. As he was leaving, he declared, "I shall return." The Japanese advance in the Pacific was not halted until mid-1942. In the naval battles that took place in May in the Coral Sea north of Australia and at Midway Island in June, American forces defeated the Japanese and inflicted heavy losses on the Japanese fleet. These losses weakened Japanese naval power for the rest of the war.

The German army, having taken almost all of the other countries in Europe, concentrated on an invasion of Russia beginning in June of 1941. Hitler's forces covered a wide area and caused considerable damage, but they failed to take Moscow by the end of 1941. As Napoleon had found out over one hundred years earlier, the Russian winter is a merciless foe. The Germans bogged down in 1942 without conquering Russia. Meanwhile, German and Italian submarines in the Atlantic wreaked havoc on American shipping. Over 400 vessels were sunk in American coastal waters, some within sight of the mainland.

Turning Point

The beginning of Allied success in both the European and the Pacific theaters of operation came in November of 1942. In that month, American forces began attacking the Japanese position on the island of Guadalcanal in the Solomon Islands northeast of Australia. Although the assault took six months, the Americans eventually cleared the Japanese from the island.

Through the rest of 1943 and into 1944, Allied Army, Navy, and Marine forces conducted slow, often costly sweeps of Japanese positions in the Pacific. The Allied goal was always to be moving toward Tokyo. The Allies did not try to take every island held by the Japanese. They leapfrogged over some islands, leaving Japanese forces on them cut off from supply lines. The scattered units eventually had to surrender. (For many years after the war, Japanese soldiers who had not heard—or not believed—that the war was over were found on remote islands.)

In Europe in late 1942, the Russian army assumed the offensive against the invading Germans. At the same time, Allied forces moved against German positions in northern Africa. America, Britain, and Russia had debated long and hard about where to mount the first major assault against Germany and Italy. Russia wanted it to be on its own turf, where it could help to push the German forces back toward Germany. Finally, however, the decision was made to launch a coordinated attack on German forces in North Africa. From there the armies of freedom could strike Italy, which Churchill called the soft underbelly of the Axis. British and American forces in northern Africa moved from opposite directions against the German army led by Erwin Rommel. The British under Bernard Montgomery headed west from Egypt, and the Americans under Dwight Eisenhower moved east from Morocco and Algeria. The Allies caught the Germans in a giant pincer, and Rommel's forces surrendered in Tunisia on May 13, 1943. The Allies then controlled northern Africa.

British and American forces invaded and took control of the island of Sicily in July of 1943. The move surprised the Italians and knocked Mussolini out of power. The new Italian government indicated its willingness to surrender and even switch sides to join the Allies. Negotiations between Italy and the Allies dragged on until September, by which time German troops had considerably strengthened their positions in Italy. The Allies finally invaded Italy at Salerno on September 9, 1943. The fighting that winter was extremely difficult in mountainous terrain during terrible weather. The Allies prevailed and began moving toward Rome. Americans took Rome on June 4, 1944, two days before D-Day.

Americans With a Fruit Vendor in North Africa (c. 1942)

A Truck Driver and Mechanic Stationed at Fort Knox, Kentucky (1942)

Meanwhile, Axis attacks against Allied shipping in the Atlantic were brought under control by May of 1943 with improved radar, better intelligence on submarine positions, and the use of convoys to protect vessels taking supplies to Europe. Also during 1943 and into 1944, Allied bombing of Germany took a heavy toll. The American Army Air Force attacked specific targets such as industrial complexes during the day, and British RAF bombers blanketed selected cities in nighttime raids. The Allies lost many planes, but the damage to Germany was considerable. One specific reason for the air attacks was to weaken Germany in preparation for the upcoming invasion of Europe along the north of France.

The Tehran Conference

In November of 1943, Russian premier Joseph Stalin, British prime minister Winston Churchill, and American President Franklin Roosevelt met in Tehran, Iran, to discuss mutual war aims. Roosevelt and Churchill had conferred several times before, but this was the first meeting of all three leaders. At the conference, the Big Three discussed the coming invasion of northern France and the Soviet offensive against Germany from the east.

What Else Was Happening?

1941 *The movie* Citizen Kane *is released.*

1941 *New York Yankee Joe DiMaggio has a 56-game hitting streak.*

1941 *The aerosol spray can is first marketed.*

1942 *The movie* Mrs. Miniver, *portraying English life during the Battle of Britain, wins the Academy Award for Best Picture.*

1942 *Self-contained underwater breathing apparatus (scuba) gear is invented.*

1942 *James Paul McCartney, future member of The Beatles, is born in Liverpool, England, on June 18.*

1943 *The movie* Casablanca *with Humphrey Bogart, showing life in wartime North Africa, wins Best Picture.*

1943 *The Broadway musical* Oklahoma! *debuts.*

Roosevelt got Stalin to commit to entering the war against Japan two or three months after Germany was defeated. As it turned out, Russia's help was not needed against Japan; but getting the promise of Russia's assistance seemed important at the time. The Big Three also discussed how to govern a defeated Germany and how to create an effective international organization to maintain peace after the war.

Robert F. Sargent, Chief Photographer's Mate in the U.S. Coast Guard, took this photo on D-Day as soldiers were leaving his landing craft. Two-thirds of the men in that company were killed or wounded that day.

D-Day

The Allies agreed that Germany had to be defeated before Japan. Military planners decided that the major thrust to accomplish this would come through a massive invasion along the northern coast of German-occupied France. The Allied armies would then retake Paris, move east through Belgium, and strike Germany itself. About one million American troops were sent to Britain during 1943 and early 1944 to prepare for the assault, code named Operation Overlord. Dwight Eisenhower was named commander of Supreme Headquarters, Allied Expeditionary Forces (SHAEF).

The German army had heavily fortified the northern French coast with machine gun positions, minefields, and barbed wire. Hitler expected a landing somewhere; but he thought that it would come at Calais, where the English Channel was most narrow. Eisenhower sent a decoy maneuver there, but the main landing actually took place to the west at Normandy Beach and other nearby locations. Air cover and paratroopers moved in early to soften the German resistance. Early on June 6, 1944, 4,000 ships carrying 150,000 troops (about a third of them Americans) began landing in northern France. Bad weather hampered air cover operations and caused rough seas for the landing craft. German resistance was stout, and about 5,000 Americans were killed or wounded that day. However, the beaches were taken; and within two weeks a million Allied soldiers had invaded occupied France and were moving inland.

As the Allied assault advanced, some in the German high command saw the beginning of the end and tried to persuade Hitler to sue for peace. The stubborn German leader refused. A few officers tried to assassinate Hitler by planting a bomb in his fortified bunker, but the attempt failed. Paris was liberated on August 25, 1944; and the Americans turned east to chase the retreating Germans back into Germany. Meanwhile, another Allied force landed in southern France and began heading north.

Parade in Paris After Liberation from the Germans

1944 Presidential Election

As the war seemed to be heading for an Allied victory, America headed into a presidential election. Roosevelt was tired and ill, but he allowed himself to be nominated for a fourth term. The real contest was for the second spot on the ticket. Henry Wallace was too liberal for southern Democrats; and many saw Roosevelt's own choice, James Byrnes, head of the Office of War Management, as too conservative. Roosevelt and party leaders compromised on Missouri Senator Harry S. Truman. Truman was a World War I veteran and former men's clothing store operator. As a Senator, he had supported the New Deal; but he had also helped uncover waste in the government's war effort.

The Republicans chose New York governor Thomas Dewey. Dewey had achieved prominence as a prosecuting attorney who took on racketeering activities which involved illegal businesses and operations involving organized crime. When Dewey was elected governor of New York in 1942, he was the first Republican to hold the office since 1920. Dewey had made a run for the Republican nomination for President in 1940.

Republican gains in the 1942 congressional election gave the party hope that they might finally be able to defeat FDR, but it was not to be. Roosevelt won, though he received his smallest margin of victory: 25.6 million to 22 million popular votes, and a 432-99 electoral margin. The Democrats also continued to control Congress.

Shortly after D-Day, Germany began using a new weapon, the V-1 rocket. It had a small jet engine and was often called the buzz bomb. When the device ran out of gas, the buzzing engine stopped and the rocket fell to earth. Though not very accurate, it caused considerable casualties and damage. During the last few months of the war, Germany introduced the more powerful V-2 rocket. It flew faster than sound and could not be intercepted. These weapons caused significant damage, as seen in this photo of London; but they had little effect on the outcome of the war.

Allied efforts in the Pacific continued to go well in late 1944. In October MacArthur was indeed able to return to the Philippines. The Battle of Leyte Gulf in the Philippines was the largest naval engagement of the war. Some Japanese pilots made kamikaze suicide crashes into American vessels. The American fleet won despite heavy losses.

Battle of the Bulge

In Europe the Allied advance toward Germany bogged down before reaching the German border. In December of 1944, a German force broke through the Allied line and made a fifty-mile bulge in Belgium back toward Paris. The Battle of the Bulge was fought during some of the coldest weather Europe had seen in many years. The Allies were forced to fall back, but the Germans overextended their supply lines and could not maintain their strength. The battle was a setback for the Allies, but it only delayed and did not stop their advance.

As the Americans raced toward the German capital of Berlin from the west, Russian troops were advancing on the German capital from the east. The contest was not simply a friendly challenge between allies. Both sides knew that whoever controlled Berlin would hold a powerful position in post-war Germany. Despite Churchill's urging of Eisenhower to take Berlin, the Allied commander chose instead to concentrate on the destruction of the remainder of Germany's army. The Americans backed off and allowed the Russians to get to Berlin first.

During the Battle of the Bulge, Germans surrounded the American position at the town of Bastogne. When the Germans demanded a surrender, American General Anthony McAuliffe replied with one word: "Nuts." On December 26, 1944, American planes dropped supplies for the besieged troops in Bastogne. American reinforcements eventually arrived, and the Germans were pushed back.

Finally, be strong in the Lord and in the strength of His might.
Ephesians 6:10

⋆ Assignments for Lesson 112 ⋆

Literature Continue reading *To Kill a Mockingbird.*

Bible Read Ephesians 6:10-20. List the specific elements of God's armor that Paul describes.

Work on memorizing Ecclesiastes 3:1 and 3:7-8.

Project Work on your project.

Student Review Optional: Answer the questions for Lesson 112.

Americans in Paris Celebrate the End of the War, August 15, 1945

Lesson 113

Victory!

Yalta

In February of 1945, Roosevelt, Churchill, and Stalin met at Yalta on the Crimean Sea. There Roosevelt made significant concessions to Stalin to insure Russia's aid against Japan and its participation in the post-war United Nations. The President agreed to a Soviet sphere of influence in Eastern Europe. This meant that the Russians would oversee the installation of new governments in Poland, Czechoslovakia, Hungary, and other countries, which in turn meant that those governments would be Communist.

The leaders agreed to partition Germany into British, American, Russian (and later French) zones of control. The Russians also received certain islands from Japan and areas of China over which it claimed control. To Roosevelt these were minor concessions that he could make on points that were, in his mind, foregone conclusions, in order to obtain the greater goals he wanted to achieve.

A New U.S. President

On March 7, 1945, Allied troops entered Germany from the west by crossing the bridge over the Rhine River at the town of Remagen. The defeat of Germany seemed to be only a matter of time. Then on April 12, Franklin Roosevelt lived his last day on earth. He was having a portrait painted while in Warm Springs, Georgia, where he often visited to swim in the warm spring water to get relief from the physical pain he suffered as a result of his paralysis. Roosevelt complained of a severe headache, collapsed, and died of a cerebral hemorrhage. Later that day, Harry Truman was sworn in as the new President. Victory in Europe was less than a month away.

Crowd Outside the White House on the Evening of April 12, 1945

The Holocaust

Before the war, the Nazis instituted a program of systematic persecution and murder of those deemed "inferior." Some evidence had leaked out of Germany during Hitler's reign of terror, but the outside world generally met the reports with disbelief or indifference. As Allies took control of Germany, the horrors of the Nazi concentration camps become known. This period of brutal violence is called the Holocaust, from the Greek for "sacrifice by fire."

During the Holocaust, victims were taken from their homes and sent to camps to work as slave labor or to be killed. Jews were a major target. About six million Jews died in the camps by the end of the war. An estimated five million other victims killed by the Nazi regime included Christian leaders, Roma people (Gypsies), people with disabilities, homosexuals, and political dissidents.

A memorial at the Dachau Concentration Camp is shown above. Martin Niemoeller was a German Lutheran minister arrested by the Gestapo, sent to Dachau in 1938, and freed by the Allies in 1945. Niemoeller said:

> *"In Germany, the Nazis first came for the Communists, and I didn't speak up because I wasn't a Communist. Then they came for the Jews, and I didn't speak up because I wasn't a Jew. Then they came for the trade unionists, and I didn't speak up because I wasn't a trade unionist. Then they came for the Catholics, but I didn't speak up because I was a Protestant. Then they came for me, and by that time there was no one left to speak for me."*

V-E Day

Mussolini was captured and murdered by Italian partisans on April 28. Two days later, Adolph Hitler married his mistress and they both committed suicide. The German high command asked for surrender terms on May 2 and on May 7 agreed to an unconditional surrender. May 8 was celebrated as V-E Day (Victory in Europe).

Advances on Japan

In February of 1945, American troops landed on and eventually took the island of Iwo Jima at a cost of 20,000 casualties, including 7,000 dead. Iwo Jima was only 750 miles from Japan and provided an important staging point for a final assault on Japan. The island of Okinawa fell to the Allies in June. With the end of the German threat, the Allies wanted to find the best way to defeat Japan quickly. Allied air attacks and sea-based bombardments were taking a toll on Japan, but military planners feared that an all-out invasion of the island nation might cost a quarter million American lives or more.

During the fierce Battle of Okinawa, these American soldiers heard the radio broadcast about V-E Day.

The A-Bomb

In July the leaders of the Big Three Allies met at Potsdam, Germany. Harry Truman, who had only been Vice President for three months and had rarely even met with Franklin Roosevelt, now led the strongest country in the world. Winston Churchill came from Great Britain, but an election campaign was taking place in Britain. Churchill brought his opponent, Clement Atlee, with him to Potsdam. The voting took place during the conference; and Atlee was elected as the new prime minister of Great Britain, with the Labour Party defeating Churchill and the Conservatives. Only Joseph Stalin remained from previous Big Three summit meetings. During the talks, Truman revealed to Stalin and the British that the United States had the capacity to use an atomic bomb on Japan.

In 1939 Albert Einstein had written President Roosevelt to inform him that he thought it was possible to split an atom and thus release an enormous amount of energy. He also said that he believed the Germans were pursuing research on the process of atomic fission for the purpose of developing an atomic weapon. Roosevelt quietly instituted the Manhattan Project for the U.S. to develop its own nuclear capabilities. The project was so secret, in fact, that Truman did not know about it until he became President. In December of 1942, scientists in a secret laboratory under the football stadium at the University of Chicago instituted the first successful controlled nuclear chain reaction. Following that, the government began a program of assembling the materials for a nuclear weapon. Secret laboratories in Oak Ridge, Tennessee, and Hanford, Washington, developed the materials to be used in the bombs.

The first device was exploded at Alamogordo, New Mexico, on July 16, 1945. Truman received word of it while he was at the Potsdam Conference.

This war bond poster printed near the end of the war featured the iconic image of U.S. Marines raising the American flag on Iwo Jima.

Photo of the First Atomic Bomb Test

No one really knew what the potential destructive power of the bomb was, but Truman gave the approval for production to continue. Serious discussion ensued within the American government on how and whether to use the new device. One plan that was considered involved taking world leaders to the Pacific and detonating the device in a place where no loss of life would occur in order to show its fearsome potential and to convince Japan to surrender. However, this idea was scrapped, and plans moved ahead to use the atomic bombs on strategic Japanese cities. Experts estimated that about 20,000 deaths might occur with the use of one of the bombs.

The first atomic bomb was dropped on Hiroshima on August 6, 1945. Eighty thousand people were killed immediately, and the toll rose to 140,000 before the year ended. Russia came into the war against Japan on August 8. The next day, Americans dropped the second and last atomic bomb on Nagasaki with similar destruction. Japan surrendered unconditionally on August 14 (V-J Day); and the formal surrender took place on September 2, 1945. The long, costly war was finally over.

Japanese Officials at the Surrender

How We Did It

The courage and sacrifice of the American armed forces were matched by the service and sacrifice displayed on the home front. In all about 15 million enlisted men and women served during the conflict. The folks back home clothed, fed, and armed these personnel and sent many supplies to other Allied forces as well. The turnaround of Allied fortunes on the battlefields was due in great measure to American military power and the amazing production capacity of American industry.

Such a massive undertaking required considerable planning and coordination. The country had to set production priorities, manage raw materials, provide an adequate labor force, and convert civilian industries to military output (such as changing the automotive industry to one making jeeps and trucks).

The War Production Board (WPB), created in January of 1942, oversaw the transition to military output. The Office of Price Administration (OPA) regulated the economy by setting prices and determining the rationing policy for goods in short supply, such as tires, gasoline, meat, coffee, and sugar. The government attempted to offset some shortages by encouraging rubber drives, scrap drives, and other collection programs to recycle needed materials. The Office of War Management (OWM), set up in May of 1943, coordinated the work of several wartime agencies. Meanwhile, the demands of war, Republican gains in Congress, and the presence of more conservative Democrats in Washington led to the elimination of several New Deal programs, including the WPA, the CCC, and the National Youth Administration.

Economic Recovery

Wartime production was the tonic that finally helped the country recover from the Depression. The gross domestic product doubled between 1940 and 1945. Unemployment fell from 9 million in 1940 to less than one million in September of 1943. The problem was no longer finding jobs for workers but finding workers to fill the jobs needed by the war industries. The fastest growth in the country was in the West, where defense contractors offered good-paying jobs but housing was in short supply. With so many men on active duty, one major solution to the domestic labor shortage was provided by six million women, many of them married, who took jobs outside the home. By 1944 women made up one-third of the domestic labor force. Wages increased dramatically, faster than the increase in prices caused by inflation. Life for many Americans improved significantly during the war, even with the rationing of several items that had been common in households but were now needed in the war effort.

Labor union membership increased from 9 million in 1940 to 15 million in 1945. The Roosevelt Administration generally protected union rights during the war, but a few industries were taken over by the government when strikes hampered production. Public opinion was strongly against unions engaging in strikes during war time.

Nothing of value, however, is free. All of this production had to be paid for. The two main methods used were increased taxes and greater deficit spending. The government sold about $150 billion in war bonds to the American people, which helped the total Federal debt rise to about $260 billion.

About 200,000 women served in the armed forces as WACs (Women's Army Corps) and Navy WAVES (Women Accepted for Volunteer Emergency Service). Dan Smith painted this image of a WAC Air Controller in 1943.

Racial Woes

One million African Americans served in the armed forces, most of them in segregated units. Ugly racial incidents did occur occasionally. Two hundred thousand Mexicans were hired from Mexico to work the farm fields of the West with the promise that they would not be drafted. They got work, but they also found hardened prejudice against them. Some 25,000 Native Americans in the military were not segregated into separate units. Many of them served as code talkers, who used their tribal languages to create codes for classified documents and radio transmissions.

Navajo Code Talkers

The owner of this store in Oakland, California, had Japanese ancestry. The day after the attack on Pearl Harbor, he put this sign outside his store. He was one of the thousands of Japanese Americans interned during the war.

Nearly all of the soldiers in the U.S. Army's 442nd Regimental Combat Team were of Japanese ancestry. A squad leader is shown above right watching for Germans in France. This unit served with great distinction in Europe, even though the men had family members who were interned back in the United States.

Another sad demonstration of prejudice during the war was the internment of 100,000 Japanese Americans in relocation camps during 1942. People of Japanese descent, even if they were American citizens, were the subject of fierce hatred, especially in the West where they lived in greater numbers. Sixty percent of those placed in camps were American citizens, and a third were under nineteen years old.

All evidence indicated that Japanese Americans were as loyal to the U.S. as members of other ethnic groups; but because of fear and prejudice they were removed from their homes and herded into camps that had been constructed in wilderness areas. In 1988 the United States government issued an apology for the policy of Japanese American internment. Cash reparations of $20,000 each were given to the 60,000 victims still living.

The Cost and the Benefits

Almost 300,000 Americans died in combat during World War II, and another 100,000 died from other causes. As significant as this was, it was far less than what many other countries suffered. It has been estimated that fifty million people, military and civilian, lost their lives during the war. Russia alone grieved over 13 million dead. In addition, the United States mainland did not receive the damage wrought by the war on countries such as France, Great Britain, Italy, and Germany.

The war brought about social, technological, and political changes. The Jewish people have sworn that they will never forget what happened in Nazi Germany. American women and blacks experienced a different world from the one they had known before the war, and many of them were not willing to go back. Changes in submarines, computers, and rockets paved the way for modern technology. Prosperity returned to the United States and has remained to a greater or lesser degree ever since. The reach of the Federal government into more and more aspects of life has become a fixture on the American scene.

Lesson 113 - Victory!

New international alignments affected world events and American foreign policy for decades. The threat of atomic war hung over American life and much of the world for the rest of the twentieth century. Only a tiny fraction of the American people ever again considered isolationism as a real option. The United States, only fifty years after acquiring the beginnings of a world empire, emerged from the war as the strongest nation on earth.

Before 1940 the U.S. military did not allow African Americans to become pilots. Black organizations sought to change this as America prepared for war. Formed at the Tuskegee Institute in Alabama, the Tuskegee Airmen were a group of pilots, navigators, bombardiers, mechanics, instructors, and other support personnel who made valuable contributions to the Allied victory.

These things I have spoken to you, so that in Me you may have peace.
In the world you have tribulation, but take courage;
I have overcome the world.
John 16:33

⋆ Assignments for Lesson 113 ⋆

Literature Continue reading *To Kill a Mockingbird.*

Bible Read 1 Timothy 6:3-16. List three ways you personally can fight the good fight of faith.

Work on memorizing Ecclesiastes 3:1 and 3:7-8.

Project Work on your project.

Student Review Optional: Answer the questions for Lesson 113.

Wesley Notgrass (far left, second row) Overseeing Delivery Boys at The Daily Herald *(c. 1935)*

Lesson 114

One Soldier's Story

The American men and women who fought in World War II have been called the greatest generation. They were, for the most part, citizen soldiers, not career military personnel. They were civilians before the war, then they enlisted or were drafted for service, and afterwards they returned to civilian life.

Every soldier's story is unique, but most of those who fought shared some common experiences. This is the story of one citizen soldier from that generation: my father, Wesley Biddle Notgrass. Other men had more difficult experiences during the war, but our family knows this story best. All of the images in this lesson are from Dad's collection of photographs and memorabilia.

Greetings From the President

Dad was born and grew up in Columbia, Tennessee. He was 26 years old in the spring of 1941 and working for *The Daily Herald* newspaper in Columbia when he received a notice from the Army inviting him to enlist in the Army before he was drafted. He entered the service in June of 1941. Dad expected to be in the Army for one year, as did most other new recruits. Popular songs of the day included, "Goodbye Dear, I'll Be Home in a Year" and "I'll Be Back in A Year, Little Darling."

Along with other recruits from the southeastern United States, Dad was inducted into the Army at Fort Oglethorpe, Georgia. He was asked which job he would like to have. Answering that he did not know one from another, it was suggested that he go with the group heading for Camp Lee, Virginia, to enter the Medical Corps. The decision to put Dad in the Medical Corps meant that he would not carry a gun.

Basic Training

Dad went through basic training at Camp Lee. He learned how to take care of wounds, deliver babies, and perform other medical procedures. After basic training, the new soldiers got their assignments. They were told that they would be stationed near their homes. Dad listened as everyone's name was called but his. He went to the officers to tell them he had been missed. They told him that he would go to Fort Dix, New Jersey (which is not exactly near Columbia, Tennessee). Soldiers from Fort Dix were on maneuvers in South Carolina, so Dad traveled alone by train to join them.

During maneuvers, Dad's job was to work night duty KP (kitchen patrol). When the maneuvers were completed, he and the rest of his unit traveled to Fort Dix. They arrived on a Saturday and were told they would all receive ten-day passes. The next day was December 7, 1941, the day Japan attacked Pearl Harbor. The news from Pearl Harbor that day changed everything for the Army and for Dad. He didn't get the ten-day pass, and he wasn't out of the Army after one year.

Governor's Island, New York

Dad was next assigned to Governor's Island in New York City harbor. He was chosen to be part of the office staff of the Medical Corps, Headquarters Company, First Army. The job required a security clearance, so FBI agents went to Columbia and interviewed his preacher, his high school principal, and his employer.

Since war had been declared against Japan and Germany, the First Army prepared to go to Europe to fight Hitler's forces. Dad was stationed on Governor's Island for almost two years as preparations were made. Dad had never been "up north" before. He thoroughly enjoyed his time in New York, where he could see the Statue of Liberty from the window in his barracks. Dad saw every movie and Broadway play that came to New York. He went to hear the Big Bands and saw many famous performers, including Bing Crosby, Tommy Dorsey, Glenn Miller, and Frank Sinatra.

Soldiers almost always got in free to all events. Once Dad was standing near Madison Square Garden on the night of a big Joe Louis boxing match. A man asked him, "Soldier, do you want to see the fight?" Dad answered, "I sure do." The man took him in to see the fight. Dad even went to Times Square on New Year's Eve—once.

Dad enjoyed taking advantage of this once-in-a-lifetime opportunity. He basically worked an eight-to-five shift and then enjoyed seeing the sights. Things changed dramatically when the time came to go to Europe.

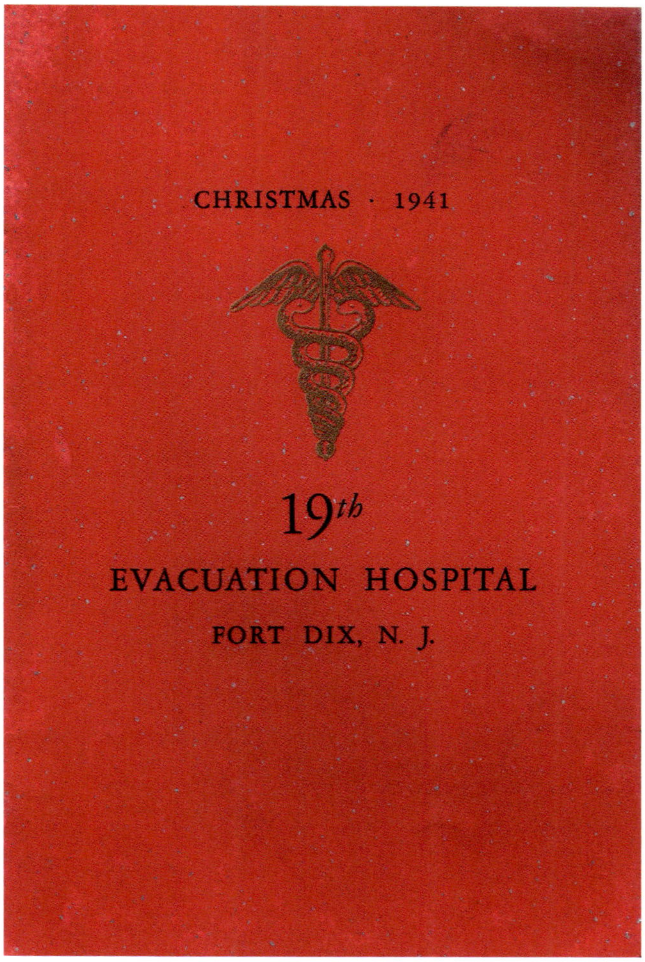

Decorative Menu for Christmas Dinner, 1941

Dad attended Game Three of the 1942 World Series. The St. Louis Cardinals shut out the New York Yankees 2-0, and went on to win the series four games to one.

To England

Dad's unit shipped out for England in October 1943. He was one of 15,000 men making the five-day trip across the Atlantic on the huge passenger ship *Queen Elizabeth*. The *Queen Elizabeth* zigzagged across the Atlantic so it would be harder for German submarines to attack it. Some ships had escort ships to travel with them, but the *Queen Elizabeth* was too fast for the escorts.

Dad and five other men shared a room below deck that was designed for two people. They had bunks stacked three high. When in their room, they took turns standing up since it was hard for all of them to be out of bed at the same time. They did not have to bother getting dressed each morning, however, because they slept in their clothes. The men on the *Queen Elizabeth* could not take a bath for the five days they traveled across the Atlantic. Dad tried taking a bath one day, but after he got wet all over, he found that soap does not lather in salt water.

The soldiers ate two meals a day. Each man was part of the A group, the B group, and so forth. Someone on the loudspeaker would announce, "B group, form your lines," and they would line up to eat. The dining room where some of the men ate was the swimming pool room of the ocean liner. Boards were put over the pool and tables were placed on top for eating.

Dad at Clifton College

MESSING CARD

"A" MESS HALL

2 SECTION

FIRST MEAL 8-00 a.m.

SECOND MEAL 5-00 p.m.

Messing Card from Dad's Trip on the Queen Elizabeth

In Bristol

Five days after leaving America, the ship landed in Glasgow, Scotland, away from the German attacks on England. Then they traveled by train to Bristol. Dad's unit was stationed at Clifton College, a boys' preparatory school next to the Bristol Zoo. The unit took over the whole school. Clifton College became like an army base with soldiers working, eating, and sleeping in the school's many buildings. Officers had one place to eat, privates another, and corporals and sergeants another. By then Dad was a sergeant. As in New York, the men worked regular shifts and had free time to enjoy their stay in England.

The Germans bombed Bristol heavily because the Rolls Royce factory there made airplane engines. Dad's sleeping quarters were in a three-story house near the school campus. Each night the men were required to place blackout covers on the windows. The covers had wooden frames and fit snugly on the windows. Blackout covers made the city dark, thus making it more difficult for the German bomber pilots to hit targets. Air raids were common. One thing Dad noticed about the many nights of bombing was the reaction of the lions and tigers in the zoo across from the school. The animals screamed so loudly that he thought it would hurt their throats.

Dad attended Whiteladies Road Methodist Church in Bristol. There he met a beautiful sixteen-year-old English girl, Joan Kathleen May Clark. At the time, Dad was 28. Dad enjoyed happy times in Joan's typical English home, a small, three-story townhouse on Brighton Road. She lived with her father, step-mother, great-grandfather, younger sister Audrey, and younger brother Geoffrey. Her older brother, Bernard, was away from home serving in the war. Dad was able to meet Bernard when he came home on leave. Great-grandfather Jefferson would greet Dad with the question, "Is this one of our gallant defenders?"

Joan's family worked in the war effort, too. She and Audrey were members of the Auxiliary Territorial Service. The ATS was a women's corps that performed services such as operating telephones and spotting German planes. Her brother Bernard served in the Royal Navy on a submarine and also made several trips to America working for the British merchant marine. Merchant marines served the war effort by shipping supplies through oceans teeming with dangerous German submarines. Joan's dad, Frank Clark, was an air raid warden. His job was to make sure citizens were safe during an air raid. Dad and Joan fell in love and planned to get married. However, Dad and the other soldiers had a little business on the continent to take care of first.

Bombed Church Building in Bristol

Joan Clark (1944)

D-Day

One day while still in Bristol, Dad picked up a piece of paper on a desk. It was the top secret orders for D-Day. Dad quickly put it down, and when an officer came in and saw him, he told Dad not to tell anyone. The soldiers found out that they would go to Europe soon, with the initial force landing in France on D-Day. Other members of Dad's unit would go the day after on D-Plus 1. Still others would go on D-Plus 30. Dad hoped to go on D-Plus 30, but he was selected to go on D-Plus 1.

Finally, his day came. They were awakened in the middle of the night and fed breakfast at 2:00 a.m. The soldiers got in trucks and headed south. Dad thought they would leave from Southampton; but as they traveled through the dark without headlights, they went by a statue honoring early American settlers John and Priscilla Alden. He knew then that they were leaving from Plymouth.

Dad crossed the English Channel in a transport ship. The transport next to his in the Channel hit a mine. Because it was filled with tanks, it sank quickly. Only two men on it survived. The First Army landed on Utah Beach in the Normandy area of northern France. The First Army infantry was on the front line, behind them was the field artillery, and behind them was the Headquarters Company with its Medical Corps. The Medical Corps took care of men who were wounded in the fighting. The men who needed to go to a hospital were taken to a hospital ship in the English Channel. Dad's responsibility in the office was keeping records about the wounded soldiers.

Normandy

During the Normandy campaign, the Medical Corps worked in apple orchards. They put up tents in which they did their work during the day. At night they slept in the foxholes they had dug. Each man slept with his helmet next to his head in case he needed it during the night. During the many weeks they spent in the apple orchards while the infantry was fighting, German planes came over every night (except when it was raining) to drop bombs. As soon as the German planes were heard, the American anti-aircraft guns started shooting. If Dad was sleeping next to an anti-aircraft gun, he had to sit up and put his helmet on because of all the spent ammunition casings falling from the gun.

While they were in the apple orchards of Normandy, Allied battleships were firing over their heads from the English Channel. The force of the gunfire from the battleships was so strong that it blew a piece of paper out of one's hand. Soon after the Allies arrived in France, Hitler's forces began using rockets against England. Now the Germans could fire on England without losing planes. Conquering Germany became even more urgent. Normandy was finally freed from the Germans after many weeks of fighting. This ended Dad's time of sleeping in foxholes. From then on, his unit was able to sleep in tents, abandoned buildings, stables, train stations, and other sheltered places.

At one point in the campaign, a USO (United Service Organization) show came to Dad's area to perform. Dinah Shore (a famous singer) and Edward G. Robinson (a famous actor) were in the show. Afterwards, Miss Shore was talking to some of the soldiers near Dad and mentioned that she was from Tennessee. Dad called out, "I am, too!" Miss Shore broke through the crowd and gave Dad a big hug, which made the other GIs quite jealous. Dinah Shore and Dad talked about Tennessee and another Tennessean they discovered was a mutual friend.

These GIs are setting up a command post near Omaha Beach. GI stands for Government Issue, referring to the uniform and equipment that all soldiers were given. The abbreviation came to be used for the soldiers themselves.

Watching the USO Show Featuring Dinah Shore and Edward G. Robinson

Northern France and Paris

After the Allies took Normandy from German control, they headed further into northern France. Dad always knew when they were going to have to move because the field artillery would start firing non-stop for hours. During the northern France campaign, Paris was freed from German control. Dad got to go into Paris soon after the Allies drove the Germans out. The streets were filled with happy civilians celebrating their freedom. French women grabbed Dad and other soldiers and kissed them. Dad and a friend decided they wanted to see Notre Dame Cathedral. They had to push their way through the large crowd in front of the cathedral. Dad thought that many people would be inside saying prayers of thanks for the liberation of Paris, but the two soldiers walked quietly through the cathedral and did not see another person.

Battle of the Bulge

After the Allies took northern France, they entered Belgium. In December 1944, the Germans counterattacked and broke through the Allied line in the Battle of the Bulge. It was snowing and bitterly cold, about twelve degrees below zero. Dad's unit had to pull back (he was told not to say retreat). The Germans were soon stopped and the Allied forces continued to move toward Germany.

The Beginning of the End

The soldiers were told not to sleep near train tracks because they were likely targets for German bombers. Dad and some others decided one night to do it any way. A German plane dropped a bomb that nearly hit the railroad ticket office where they were sleeping. For some reason the explosion made the light bulb above their heads come on. Lights were dangerous at night because they created an easy target for bombers. Several of the soldiers threw their shoes at the light bulb. The shoes knocked out the light successfully, but it was not a pleasant experience for the man sleeping under the bulb when he got a shoe shower.

Dad called this photo of him in France, "A Study In Shadows."

At one place in Belgium, Dad looked out of the building he was in to see American anti-aircraft guns firing at an American plane. Curious, he went outside on a balcony to find out what was going on. A German pilot had stolen the American plane and was attacking the Americans with it. The German flyer saw Dad and started shooting directly at him. Several bullets went just over his head.

Occasionally a lull occurred in the fighting and the men could have some fun. One day some soldiers, Dad included, found a big haystack and were having a good time sliding down it. The next day they were told to stay off the haystack because German hand grenades had been found in it. Dad's unit had enjoyed playing softball in New York, and the men had brought their equipment with them to Europe; but finding a place to play was hard because the ground was full of bomb craters. Also while in Belgium, Dad ran into a friend from Columbia. After Dad's unit entered Germany, they crossed the Rhine River on a bridge made of pontoons next to the old bridge that had been blown up.

Back to England

After taking the Rhineland region of Germany, the Allied forces headed for Berlin. Germany would soon surrender and the war in Europe would be over; but first, Dad had something to take care of in England. Dad got a pass to go back to England and marry Joan. Dad was thirty and Mother was eighteen. They met in London and rode a train to Bristol. They were married on April 19, 1945, in the church where they had met.

Dad received the Bronze Star for his service during the war. A treasured family possession is a photograph of General Courtney Hodges pinning the Bronze Star on him in Euskirchen, Germany.

After a short wedding trip to Weston-Super-Mare on the west coast of England, Dad had to go back to Germany to rejoin his outfit. He was able to find a spot on a cargo plane heading for Europe. On the plane were supplies for General Dwight Eisenhower, including a case of horseradish. Dad was told that if the plane was too heavy, he would have to get off. He was able to make the flight sitting on the case of horseradish, but it occurred to him that he might have been outranked by a case of horseradish.

Dad and Mother in Columbia

The War Is Over

After Germany surrendered, the Army prepared to send troops from Europe to Japan. However, men who had seen as much action as Dad were discharged and did not have to go. Dad returned to the United States in June, and he was discharged from the Army on August 1, 1945, four years, one month, and seven days after he had enlisted.

Mother was not able to come to the United States until several weeks after Dad returned. Thousands of American soldiers met and married women in Europe. These women were called war brides, a term my mother hated. Dad and Mother settled in Columbia, and Dad went back to work for *The Daily Herald*. My brother was born in 1947, and I was born in 1952.

The American men and women who fought in World War II have been called the greatest generation. I agree with this appraisal.

My thanks to my wife Charlene for her help in writing this lesson.

But now faith, hope, love, abide these three; but the greatest of these is love.
1 Corinthians 13:13

★ Assignments for Lesson 114 ★

Literature Continue reading *To Kill a Mockingbird.*

Bible Read 2 Timothy 2:1-7. List three illustrations Paul uses in this passage to describe the Christian's commitment to the Lord.

Work on memorizing Ecclesiastes 3:1 and 3:7-8.

Project Work on your project.

Student Review Optional: Answer the questions for Lesson 114.

Scrap Rubber Collection (1942)

Lesson 115 - Bible Study

Don't You Know There's a War On?

"Don't you know there's a war on?" During World War II, Americans often asked this question of someone who wasted precious resources, complained about inconveniences, or otherwise acted in a way that disregarded the war effort. Vigilant Americans knew, for example, that talking about sensitive information unthinkingly could endanger our fighting men because "A slip of the lip can sink a ship" (if important information leaked into the hands of the enemy). Of course, everyone knew that a war was going on. Sometimes, however, people forgot the significance of that fact and let selfishness take over.

Christians today need to remember that there's a war going on, a war between the people of God and the forces of evil. When Peter says, "Prepare your minds for action" (literally, "Gird up the loins of your mind," 1 Peter 1:13), he is using war talk. Christians should carry no worldly encumbrances and should always be on active duty, constantly vigilant for God. Since a war is going on, believers should live in a way that does not give aid and comfort to the enemy.

Clear Loyalty

To engage in the war successfully, a Christian needs to have clear loyalty. Any person, especially in wartime, has to act in keeping with his citizenship or he will be considered a traitor. Paul says, "Our citizenship is in heaven" (Philippians 3:20). Our loyalty belongs to a kingdom that is not of this world. A Christian must be sure that his life demonstrates loyalty to the kingdom of God; otherwise, he will be a traitor to the cause of Christ.

God's kingdom is not in peaceful co-existence with the world. There's a war going on. The prizes of this war are the hearts and souls of you and your loved ones. Because the stakes are so high, the Christian must make sure that his loyalty to Christ is clear.

This war allows no conscientious objectors. You didn't start the war and you might not want to be in it, but you are in it nonetheless. The enemy will not leave you alone. If you do not fight for the Lord, you will be conquered by the world and find yourself fighting for the enemy. Jesus drew a clear line when He said, "He who is not with Me is against Me" (Matthew 12:30).

The enemy has no reservations about using any tactic in the attempt to capture your soul. He follows no rules of war, no Geneva Conventions in this battle. Jesus said that Satan is "a liar and the father of lies" (John 8:44). Paul said that Satan "disguises himself as an angel of light" (2 Corinthians 11:14). Because of the nature of this war, Christians must know whose side they are on and act accordingly.

The Battlefields

The war takes place on a number of fields of battle. The first battlefield of this war is your own soul. Peter says that we should "abstain from fleshly lusts which war against the soul" (1 Peter 2:11). Any desires that compromise your loyalty to Christ are from the enemy. The apostle John calls them the lust of the flesh, the lust of the eyes, and the pride of life (1 John 2:16). Peter adds malice, hypocrisy, drinking parties, and the like (1 Peter 2:1 and 4:3). Such things are places of battle because they are attractive to us. We must wage war against these fleshly lusts because they are the devil's assaults against our weaknesses.

A second battleground, sadly, is often the fellowship of believers. The admonitions in 1 Peter 3:8-12 apply to relationships within the church. Christians sometimes think that God's prohibitions against resentment, gossip, and unkindness do not apply in the fellowship. However, these sins actually make you an enemy agent in the midst of the home front, destroying God's kingdom from within.

A third field of conflict emerges when Christians are reviled by the world (1 Peter 3:16). People who have taken seriously the call of Christ have never been universally popular. Simply living the Christian life is a threat to many unbelievers. Those in the world might speak of you as evildoers, mistreat you, or think you strange. The government might enact policies that tear at your soul and threaten your freedom to practice your faith. This was certainly true in Peter's day. The temptation is strong to fight back, to return reviling for reviling, and to try to put your opponents in their place. However, the Lord's strategy is for believers to continue to do good. Jesus set us the example in doing this so that we could follow in His steps (1 Peter 2:21-23).

WPA Poster Created by Al Doria (c. 1942)

The Christian's Battle Plan

The Christian can live with confidence even in the face of opposition. However, our confidence should not be in our own intelligence, knowledge, or cunning. Our only effective battle plan is to sanctify the Lord God in our hearts (1 Peter 3:15-16). To sanctify means to set apart or make holy. The Christian must exalt the Lord as king in his or her heart, giving Him the complete loyalty that He deserves.

Setting apart the Lord in your heart is your best defensive strategy against enemy attacks. Unwavering loyalty to the Lord will keep you from falling prey to that which is merely attractive or popular. Sanctifying the Lord in your heart also provides your best offense. Our offense does not involve attacking people or being offensive. Instead, our offense takes the form of trusting the Lord, doing good, and responding in love and gentleness to those who question our loyalty (1 Peter 3:14-16). The opposition will never be able to stand against such an invasion of good in a world of evil.

Wesley Notgrass and Other Soldiers Attending a Sunday Service During the Allied Advance Through France (1944)

We must remember that we are not fighting against people, even though it is through people that the enemy most often attacks us. The enemy is not other people, but the enemy is still real. Our hope, of course, is that some who are fighting for the enemy will be brought over to the Lord's side (1 Peter 2:12, 3:16).

The Battle Is the Lord's

Nobody likes war, especially those who have been involved in it. Some causes, however, are worth fighting for. There is a spiritual war going on, and the outcome is certain. The battle is the Lord's, and He will have victory. We must decide whether or not we are going to be on the winning side.

Fight the good fight of faith;
take hold of the eternal life to which you were called,
and you made the good confession
in the presence of many witnesses.
1 Timothy 6:12

⋆ Assignments for Lesson 115 ⋆

Literature Finish reading *To Kill a Mockingbird.* Literary analysis available in *Student Review.*

Bible Recite or write Ecclesiastes 3:1 and 3:7-8 from memory.

Project Complete your project for the unit.

Student Review Optional: Answer the questions for Lesson 115 and for *To Kill a Mockingbird* and take the quiz for Unit 23.

WWII Veteran Chuck Yeager Flew Faster than Sound (Mach 1) in 1947

24 Postwar America

The Cold War between the United States and the Soviet Union persisted for over forty years, and the influence of Communism in America was a concern for many. The Korean War is sometimes called the forgotten war because it was not a declared war and was relatively indecisive in its outcome. Harry Truman's 1948 victory was a stunning political upset. Spiritual issues affecting the nation during this period included the establishment of modern Israel and Supreme Court decisions related to questions about the freedom of religion under the First Amendment.

Memory Work Memorize Romans 10:11-13 by the end of this unit.

Books Used The Bible
American Voices

Project (choose one)

1) Write 300 to 500 words on one of the following topics:

- Write an assessment of Joseph McCarthy, including the good and the bad effects of what he did. See Lesson 117.

- What should the policy of the United States be toward Israel? Should the U.S. seek good relations with Arab states in the Middle East? Should America's policy be based on a particular interpretation of Scripture or only on the political realities of today? Write a paper presenting your ideas. See Lesson 120.

2) Use one of the photographs in this unit as a springboard for a painting or drawing in the style and medium of your choosing. You can create a photograph-like copy or create an abstract interpretation.

3) Create a sculpture honoring one of the American heroes discussed in this unit. Your sculpture can represent the person or objects or places connected with that person. Use the medium of your choice (e.g., wire, wood, cardboard, soap, found objects, clay, or STYROFOAM™).

Flags at the United Nations Headquarters (2010)

Lesson 116

The Cold War Begins

The end of World War II brought a new kind of peace and a new kind of war. Even though the country was once again at peace, the U.S. was permanently involved in international affairs. This led to the U.S. having a military presence in several tension spots around the world over the next few years. Along with the uneasy peace came a continuing confrontation with the other superpower in the world, the Soviet Union. It was not a hot war with military engagements; instead, it was a "cold war" with near confrontations, actual fighting by allies of each country, and always the threat of direct—even nuclear—war.

The United Nations

On January 1, 1942, the nations at war with Germany, Italy, and Japan published a declaration of their war aims. These included full cooperation with each other, no separate peace, and a commitment to the Atlantic Charter. The 26 countries (many of which were in the British Commonwealth) who cooperated on the document called themselves the United Nations.

During the war, both Democrats and Republicans in the U.S. expressed support for some sort of international organization to help maintain peace after the war ended. In the summer and fall of 1944, representatives from the U.S., Great Britain, the U.S.S.R., and China met at Dumbarton Oaks, a private estate in the District of Columbia, to discuss the nature of such an organization.

The Soviet representative wanted each of the Soviet Socialist Republics to have its own seat in the General Assembly, even though they were governed by Moscow and would never vote independently of Moscow. The meetings also highlighted disagreements over how the Security Council, the most powerful part of the organization, would function.

In April of 1945, delegates from fifty nations met in San Francisco to write a charter for the United Nations. The United States Senate ratified the charter on August 9, 1945, by a vote of 89 to 2. This was a major change from the Senate's opposition to the League of Nations 26 years earlier. On October 24 of that year, the U.N. came into existence when enough countries had ratified the charter. The League of Nations disbanded and turned its resources over to the United Nations, which is headquartered in New York City.

Each member nation has one vote in the General Assembly of the United Nations. The real power in the U.N. is the Security Council. It has five permanent members: the United States, Russia (formerly the Soviet Union), Great Britain, France, and China. The Nationalist Chinese government of Taiwan was an original member, but in 1971 the U.N. voted to expel Taiwan and admit the People's Republic of China in its place. Other countries rotate onto the Security Council for a period of time. Each of the permanent members has a veto power over any resolution that comes before the Security Council. The U.N. also has several agencies, such as the International Monetary Fund, the World Court, and the United Nations Children's Fund (called UNICEF because it was formerly known as the United Nations International Children's Emergency Fund).

The United Nations now has 193 members. It has served as a forum for international debate on many topics. It has not prevented all war, but it has occasionally been able to act as a body in the name of peace. The various agencies have worked to help the world's population. However, the U.N. is heavy with bureaucracy and often takes a decidedly anti-U.S. slant. One-world ideas (often liberal and idealistic) dominate the thinking of the organization.

Conflicting World Views

The Cold War between the United States and the Soviet Union came about as a result of two different and contrasting visions of how human society ought to operate. The United States stood for freedom and democracy; the Soviet Union stood for control. The United States wanted to protect human rights; the Soviet Union was willing to suppress human rights for what its leaders said was the good of the state. The United States did not want to dictate the governments and policies of other nations; the Soviet Union wanted puppet regimes in other countries that would follow orders from Moscow.

The United States was founded on belief in God and stood for freedom of religion; the Soviet Union was founded on atheism and suppressed religious expression. Both countries wanted to influence the nations of the world that were less developed economically and politically. These less-developed nations came to be called third world countries. Because of their differing outlooks and conflicting goals, the U.S. and the U.S.S.R. looked at each other with suspicion.

The Communist government of the Soviet Union believed in state control of the economy and of individual lives. The official Communist line was that the workers of the world should form

Karl Marx (1818-1883) wanted the workers of the world to rise up in revolution against capitalist business owners. He did not count on the formation of labor unions that could work within the capitalist system to bring about a better life for workers. Most workers in free societies want to work within their system and want to maintain personal and political freedom. Communists, however, have often been actively involved in seizing power and in ruthlessly exterminating all opponents. Communism is not just an economic theory. It is a political philosophy that involves controlling people. Russian sculptor Lev Kerbel unveiled this memorial to Karl Marx in Moscow in 1961.

Joseph Stalin was born in 1878 and led the Soviet Union from 1922 until his death in 1953. This rug depicting Stalin is from Armenia, one of the Soviet Socialist Republics.

their own governments instead of the bourgeois (French word for middle class) capitalists who had for so long controlled the world and its economy and taken advantage of the average worker. In the theory of Karl Marx, workers would form their own government and the state would melt away. In practice, a ruling elite controlled the Soviet Union and other Communist countries. The elite abused and took advantage of the mass of workers. Not everyone in the Soviet Union was a member of the Communist Party, yet it was the party machinery, supported by the military, that controlled the government and the country. The "workers' paradise" that Communism was supposed to create was misery for all but the elite ruling class.

Communists wanted to bring about this kind of state-controlled government and life in all the countries of the world. Communism was the declared enemy of free capitalist economies. They took advantage of weak governments and unstable conditions in several countries to move in and take control. Combined with this offensive Communist philosophy was Russian defensiveness after World War II. Russia had fought two costly wars with Germany within thirty years. Its losses during World War II were far greater than those of the United States. The Russians wanted protection from another invasion. They also believed that they deserved some of the spoils of war that were due to the victor. To the Soviets, the control of Eastern European countries was logical and necessary.

The United States also wanted to influence the world. America wanted to promote freedom and opportunity, but the Soviets believed that they had just as much right to influence others and that they had sufficient proof that the capitalist system degraded people. Each side had its own motives for not leaving the rest of the world alone. The United States saw that if it turned away from involvement in the world, the Communists would take over more and more countries, and the U.S. would have more enemies to fight.

Soviet Aggression

Evidence began to appear soon after the end of World War II that the U.S.S.R. posed a threat to the freedom and stability of other countries. The Soviet Union used force to install puppet Communist governments in Poland, Hungary, Bulgaria, Czechoslovakia, and other formerly independent countries. The Soviets put pressure on Turkey to give them access through the Dardanelles, the strait that connects the Black Sea with the Mediterranean. Russia had long wanted control of a warm-water outlet for its military and merchant ships.

In 1946 Communist rebels fought to take control of Greece from the government that was supported by Great Britain. The next year, Britain said that it could not assist Greece any longer. Great Britain and other victorious European nations were economically devastated as a result of the war, and the Communist Party in those countries (especially France and Italy) had a significant and growing influence. The Russians already controlled the eastern part of Germany. In some of the colonies held by European countries, independence movements arose that led to political instability and the possibility of Communist influence in those dependent nations. India and Pakistan gained their independence from Great Britain in 1947, but democracy was not a strong tradition in those countries and the Communist threat there was real.

The development that heightened American concern about the Soviet threat the most was the revelation in 1949 that the Soviets had detonated their own atomic bomb. Russia did not make an official announcement of it; the news came through intelligence data gathered by the U.S. Now the United States was not the only nation with nuclear capabilities; what was worse, the other country with such capability was fast becoming America's primary enemy. The Truman Administration responded to the news by ordering development of the hydrogen bomb, a weapon even more powerful than the atomic bomb, and by increasing conventional military preparations. Russia resisted efforts to place atomic research under an international agency of the United Nations.

The Soviet Union was not the only Communist threat worrying the United States. Chiang Kai-Shek had ruled China since the mid-1920s, but Communists led by Mao Zedong threatened Chiang's leadership for many years. In 1949 Mao took control of several major cities and Chiang fled to the island of Taiwan (also called Formosa). Chiang still claimed to be the legitimate ruler of China, but in October of 1949 the Soviet Union recognized Mao's Communist regime.

For years after 1949 the Nationalists on Taiwan talked about invading the mainland, and the United States continued to recognize the Chiang government; but as time went on, Communist control of the mainland grew stronger. Thus another Communist government came to power in a large country, and U.S. concerns about Communist influence increased.

Containment

Since Communists supported by the Soviet Union had shown themselves to be willing to use force in order to gain control of other countries, the United States developed a policy aimed at the

The Iron Curtain

On March 5, 1946, Winston Churchill gave a speech at Westminster College in Fulton, Missouri, in which he warned, "From Stettin in the Baltic to Trieste in the Adriatic an iron curtain has descended across the Continent. Behind that line lie all the capitals of the ancient states of Central and Eastern Europe. Warsaw, Berlin, Prague, Vienna, Budapest, Belgrade, Bucharest and Sofia; all these famous cities and the populations around them lie in what I must call the Soviet sphere, and all are subject, in one form or another, not only to Soviet influence but to a very high and in some cases increasing measure of control from Moscow." This is the origin of the phrase Iron Curtain to describe the boundary behind which lay the Soviet Union's sphere of influence.

Bust of Winston Churchill Located Beside the British Embassy in Prague, Czech Republic containment of Communist influence. Communists were not willing to play by the rules of democracy and let the majority rule. The United States had to stand up to Communist aggression; otherwise, Communists would have been able to take over more and more of the world.

President Truman asked Congress in March of 1947 for $400 million in both military and economic aid for Greece and Turkey. In his address, the President stated his belief that the United States should help support free people who were resisting aggression from without or subversion from within. This principle became known as the Truman Doctrine, the first specific element of the policy of containment. With American assistance, Turkey recovered economically and as a result did not give in to Russian pressure. The Greek government defeated the Communist insurgents in 1949.

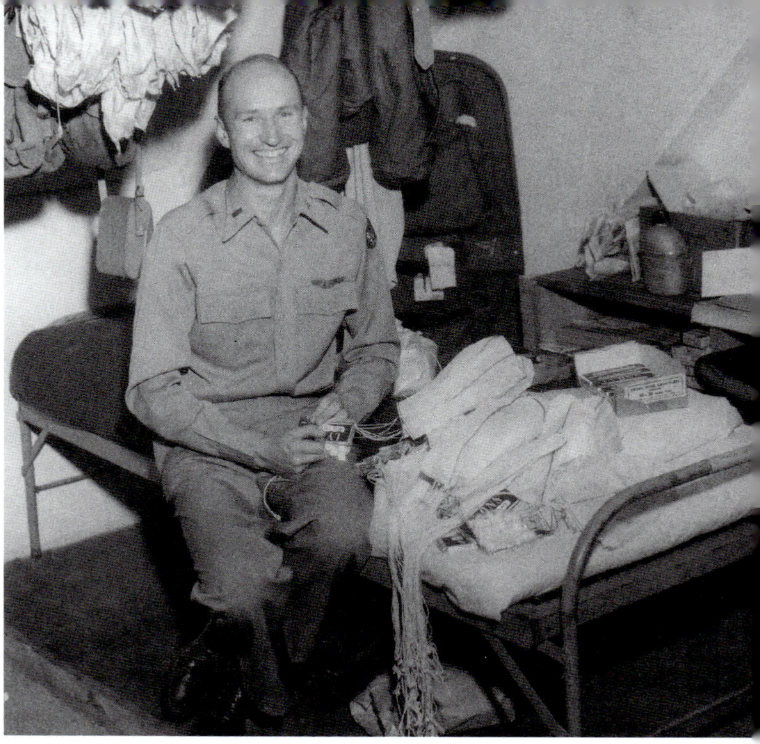

During his flights in the Berlin airlift, American pilot Gail Halvorsen began dropping candy attached to handkerchief parachutes. Other pilots joined the effort and American companies donated tons of candy. It became known as Operation Little Vittles.

The Marshall Plan and the Berlin Airlift

Not only were the economies of western Europe hard hit by the war, but a postwar depression accompanied by bad weather left those nations on the brink of collapse by 1947. Secretary of State George Marshall, who had been Army Chief of Staff during the war, announced a plan to help the countries of western Europe rebuild their economies and resist Communist influence. The plan was approved by Congress, and by 1951 some $13 billion dollars had been approved to help the Europeans. The nations of Europe learned the value of cooperation and eventually formed the European Economic Community, also known as the Common Market.

The Marshall Plan helped Europe recover from the war economically and politically. After World War I, Germany was forced to pay war reparations, and its economy struggled. Hardship in Germany followed that war and paved the way for Hitler's rise to power. The assistance provided by the Marshall Plan helped to prevent another authoritarian leader like Hitler from arising to take advantage of economic hardship and seize power after World War II in Germany or another European country.

The U.S. overcame a Communist confrontation in Germany. The country had been divided after the war into an Eastern zone controlled by the Soviets and a Western zone divided among the British, French, and Americans (these zones were merged into one in 1948). The historic German capital of Berlin, well within the Eastern zone, was itself divided into a Communist controlled eastern sector and a free western part. West Berlin was connected to West Germany by a travel corridor through East Germany. This arrangement worked well enough until 1948, when the Soviets decided to close the corridor to cut West Berlin off from the outside world in an attempt to bring it under Communist control. The Truman Administration decided not to challenge the land blockade but instead airlifted tons of food and other supplies to the isolated western sector of Berlin. The Berlin Airlift operated from June of 1948 until May of 1949, when the Russians lifted the blockade.

This VC-54C, nicknamed the Sacred Cow, *was the first military aircraft specially equipped to carry the President of the United States. It carried President Roosevelt to the Yalta conference and then served President Truman. Truman signed the National Security Act of 1947 onboard this plane. The War Department was replaced in the Cabinet with the less aggressive-sounding National Military Establishment (soon renamed the Department of Defense). The Joint Chiefs of Staff, begun during the war, became permanent. The National Security Council and the Central Intelligence Agency were also formed to centralize and coordinate security and intelligence efforts.*

West Germany became an independent country, the German Federal Republic, in 1954, with its capital in Bonn. East Germany was called the German Democratic Republic.

NATO

The crisis in Berlin was one factor that led to the creation of the North Atlantic Treaty Organization (NATO). Twelve nations bordering on or close to the North Atlantic joined together in an alliance for mutual defense in 1949. The member nations of NATO pledged that an attack on one country would be seen as an attack on all of them. General Dwight Eisenhower was named NATO commander in 1951. The Communist countries of Eastern Europe within the Soviet sphere joined together in the Warsaw Pact in 1954 as a response to NATO.

Other nations have been admitted to NATO since its formation. NATO now consists of 26 countries, including former Communist bloc members Hungary, Poland, and the Czech Republic (part of the former Czechoslovakia). The headquarters for NATO is in Brussels, Belgium.

Point Four

President Truman announced a final element of the American policy of containment in his 1949 inaugural address. The President said that resisting Communism should involve the use of the United Nations, NATO, the Marshall Plan, and, as Point Four, a coordinated program of technological and industrial assistance to third-world countries.

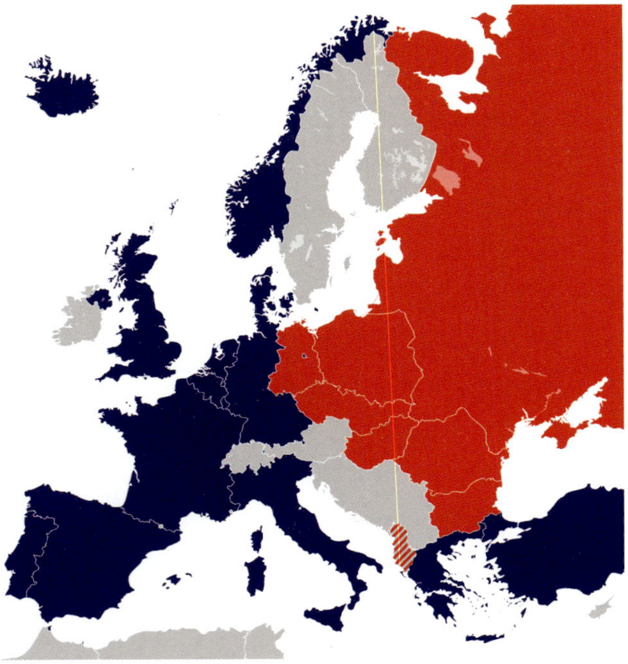

This map of Europe shows NATO countries (blue) and Warsaw Pact countries (red) in 1973.

The program was stymied by developments such as the Korean War; but the idea of continuous foreign aid, both from private sources and from the American government, entered into American thinking. Over succeeding decades, the United States was largely able to contain Communism as American influence grew in developing countries.

In 1950 the United States began extending assistance to the French-backed government of Bao Dai in Vietnam, also called Indochina, just south of mainland China. The U.S. did this to help Dai resist the guerrilla fighters who were led by Communist Ho Chi Minh. Guerrilla is French for "little war." Guerrillas are those who fight for a cause in small groups with hit-and-run tactics as opposed to a traditional war with declared enemies and identifiable front lines. This photo shows French troops operating a U.S.-made M24 tank.

Redeem me from the oppression of man,
That I may keep Your precepts.
Psalm 119:134

⋆ Assignments for Lesson 116 ⋆

Bible Start memorizing Romans 10:11-13.

Project Choose your project for this unit and start working on it.

Student Review Optional: Answer the questions for Lesson 116.

Actor Lionel Stander Testifying Before the House Un-American Activities Committee (1953)

Lesson 117

Communism in America

The United States experienced another Red Scare after World War II, similar to the one that developed after the first World War. The Soviet Union was growing in power, and its aggression was becoming evident to more and more people. It became increasingly apparent that Communists wanted to dominate the world and that they were willing to use undercover and deceitful practices to do so. It was also a fact that a Communist Party existed in the United States, but its size and influence were a matter of speculation. It was not against the law to be a Communist.

The Hollywood Ten

Concern about Communists in the United States affected several walks of life. Labor unions required that their officials take an oath declaring that they were not members of the Communist Party. Loyalty oaths became required for government workers and for professors at several colleges and universities. Many in the entertainment industry were suspected of being Communists. In 1947 the House Un-American Activities Committee (HUAC) subpoenaed nineteen Hollywood actors, producers, and writers to appear before it. The committee wanted to uncover any evidence of a Communist presence in Hollywood.

Only ten of those called to testify actually appeared before the committee, and all ten of them refused to answer the question, "Are you now or have you ever been a member of the Communist Party?" They appealed to the First Amendment freedom of speech and said that party affiliation was a private matter. The Hollywood Ten were found in contempt of Congress and sentenced to a year in prison. In addition, they were blacklisted in Hollywood and were not able to find work because others in the industry feared that any association with the ten would make them suspect in the minds of the public and the government. As it turned out, all ten had been members of the Communist Party.

In 1950 a ring of spies was uncovered that included British and American citizens. Those in the network had passed secrets of American atomic research to the Russians. Among those arrested were Julius and Ethel Rosenberg, who were executed as spies in 1953. Also in 1950, Congress passed the McCarran Internal Security Act over Truman's veto. It required Communist organizations and those secretly assisting Communists (called front organizations) to register with the Justice Department. The law forbade any foreign national who was or had ever been a Communist from being admitted to the United States.

The Hiss Case

The biggest concern involved the presence of Communists in the government. Amid all of the charges, fears, and suspicions, one specific case stood out. Alger Hiss, the president of the Carnegie Endowment for International Peace, had been an attorney in the State Department and in other Federal departments and had also been secretary-general at the conference that organized the United Nations. In 1948 Whittaker Chambers, an editor with *Time* magazine, appeared before the HUAC. He said that he had been a Communist in the 1920s and 1930s and had collected secret information to pass along to the Soviets. One of those with whom he had worked was Alger Hiss, who had given Chambers copies of classified government documents in 1938.

Hiss denied the charges and challenged Chambers to repeat the accusations when he could be sued for libel. Chambers did so on radio and in newspapers, whereupon Hiss sued him for slander. Chambers produced microfilm copies of documents from the State Department and other government agencies which apparently had Hiss' handwriting on them. Chambers had hidden the microfilm inside a hollowed-out pumpkin on his property, and the materials thus became known as the Pumpkin Papers. As a result of a Justice Department investigation, Hiss was indicted for perjury. The statute of limitations had run out on any espionage activities that old, but since Hiss denied under oath that he had engaged in espionage, the charge against him was perjury.

Ethel and Julius Rosenberg after being found guilty of espionage in 1951.

The public battle between Hiss and Chambers pitted insiders versus outsiders. Hiss was a dapper figure, respected and well-liked by many in government. President Truman called the whole matter a red herring, meaning that it diverted attention from the legitimate effort to identify real Communists. Secretary of State Dean Acheson pledged never to turn his back on Hiss. Chambers, on the other hand, was a loner and an outsider. He was overweight and his clothes were often rumpled. Chambers was a former atheist and an admitted former Communist.

The first Hiss trial ended in a hung jury, but he was convicted in a second trial and served time in prison. Whittaker Chambers published an excellent book on the case, *Witness* (1952). Hiss published his defense in *The Court of Public Opinion* (1957). To his death, Hiss maintained his innocence. In a by-product of the Hiss Case, a young Congressman from California, Richard Nixon, who was a member of the HUAC, pursued the case doggedly and used the publicity surrounding it to help him win election to the Senate in 1950.

McCarthyism

In the late 1940s, an atmosphere of fear and suspicion hung over the Federal government and the public. Where might Communists be lurking and working? Who could be trusted? Was our government secure, or were many others like Alger Hiss undermining it?

What Else Was Happening?

1946 *Scientist Percy Spencer notices that a chocolate bar in his pocket melts when he stands in front of a radar transmitter. He guesses that microwaves from the electronic tube in the device caused the melting. The microwave oven is patented in 1946 and becomes available for home use in 1955.*

1947 *Researchers invent the transistor, a tiny device that can amplify a signal 100 times. The transistor becomes the heart of a revolution in communication and entertainment. The Regency TR-1 pocket radio (shown at right), released in 1954, was the first commercially-successful product built with transistors.*

1947 *Otto Frank publishes the diary kept by his daughter Anne while they hid from the Germans in Amsterdam. Otto survived his concentration camp experience, but Anne died at Bergen-Belsen.*

1947 *A shepherd boy discovers ancient scrolls in a cave near the Dead Sea. The Dead Sea Scrolls provide a wealth of information about a Jewish sect that was active around the time of Christ. The scrolls also include at least portions of every Old Testament book (except Esther) as well as other writings from the period. A commentary on the book of Habakkuk is shown below. They give scholars knowledge of the Old Testament text that is a thousand years older than what had been previously available. The similarity between the Dead Sea Scriptures and later, previously-known manuscripts is remarkable.*

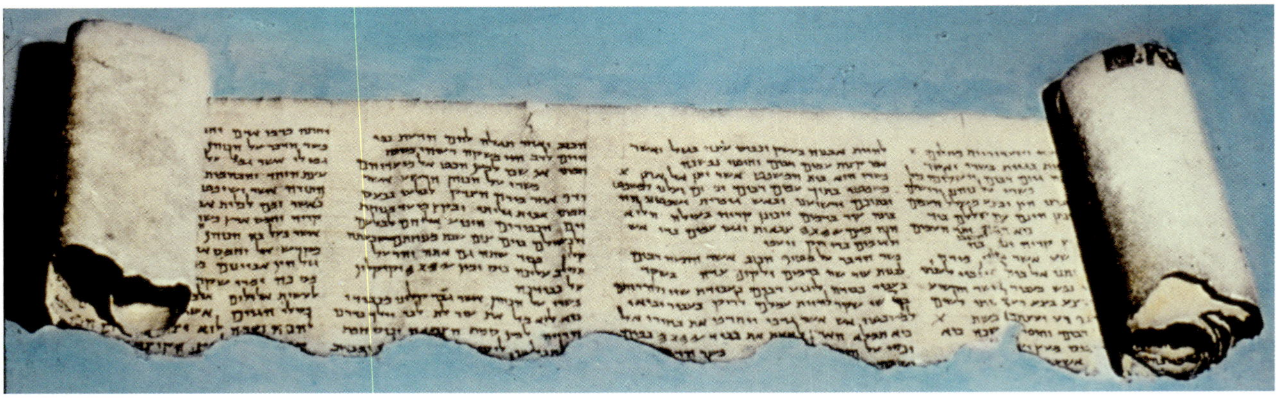

1948 *CBS Records introduces the LP (long-playing) vinyl record that allows the recording and enjoyment of longer pieces or collections of music.*

1949 *The big bang theory of the origin of the universe is published.*

1950 *The Diner's Club Card is the first general purpose credit card.*

1951 *Scientists Presper Eckert and John Mauchley unveil the UNIVAC I, the first digital computer made for commercial uses.*

One politician who seized on the fear of Communists for his own benefit was Joseph McCarthy, Republican Senator from Wisconsin. McCarthy had been elected to the Senate in 1946. Apparently he was looking for an issue to build momentum for his re-election in 1952 when he hit upon the Communist threat. In a 1950 speech in Wheeling, West Virginia, McCarthy claimed that the State Department was infested with Communists and that he had a list of them. Reports of what he actually said in the speech varied. Some said he claimed that over 200 Communists were in the State Department, others that he said about fifty, and still others said that he gave no exact number. McCarthy himself never made his charges specific.

McCarthy's attack seemed to strike home with many people as he repeated the general charges in speeches and statements many times. Finally, McCarthy was challenged to produce the name of one Communist in the State Department. He named Owen Lattimore, but a Senate committee could find no evidence to support the charge. Even this did not stop McCarthy. After the Republicans gained control of the Senate in 1953, McCarthy chaired a special investigative subcommittee that interrogated many witnesses. McCarthy used heavy-handed tactics, badgering and intimidating witnesses. The Senator's accusations played on the fear of Communism to such an extent that, in the minds of many, to be accused by him was equal to being guilty until proven innocent. To disagree with McCarthy made one appear to be treasonous or soft on Communism.

Eventually McCarthy went too far. In 1951 he questioned the loyalty of former Secretary of State George Marshall and even General Dwight Eisenhower. Three years later he made charges against the Army of hiding subversive agents. In reply Army officials accused McCarthy and his aides of using improper influence to gain favors for an enlisted man who was a friend of Roy Cohn, a McCarthy advisor. McCarthy's subcommittee voted to investigate the charges and McCarthy temporarily suspended his chairmanship.

The Army-McCarthy hearings lasted for thirty-six days and were broadcast on national television. McCarthy repeatedly interrupted the proceedings by saying, "Point of order, Mr. Chairman, point of order." His abuse of witnesses and his vague accusations became a source of irritation to many Americans. The turning point was the testimony of Army counsel Joseph Welch, whose soft and often humorous answers deflated McCarthy's wrath. The Senator was thoroughly discredited. Later that year, sixty-seven Senators voted to censure McCarthy for his actions, the harshest punishment the Senate can inflict on one of its own short of expulsion.

This 1947 comic book, published by the Catechetical Guild Educational Society of St. Paul, Minnesota, described a Communist takeover of the United States. Some four million copies were distributed.

Senator Joseph McCarthy (1954)

McCarthy died in 1957 without uncovering a single Communist. The tactics of Joseph McCarthy are an example of taking a bad approach to fix a bad situation. Communists were working in the American government in the late 1940s and early 1950s, but McCarthy's intimidating style and wild accusations were not the best solution.

O Lord, who may abide in Your tent?
Who may dwell on Your holy hill?
He who walks with integrity, and works righteousness,
And speaks truth in his heart.
He does not slander with his tongue,
Nor does evil to his neighbor,
Nor takes up a reproach against his friend.
Psalm 15:1-3

⋆ Assignments for Lesson 117 ⋆

Bible Work on memorizing Romans 10:11-13.

Project Work on your project.

Student Review Optional: Answer the questions for Lesson 117.

Soldiers of the U.S. 2nd Infantry Division in Korea (1950)

Lesson 118

The Korean War

The peninsula of Korea juts from the Chinese mainland off the province of Manchuria and lies just to the west of Japan. The Koreans are ethnically distinct from both the Chinese and the Japanese people. Japan took control of the peninsula at the end of the Russo-Japanese War in 1905. The Korean people always resented Japanese rule and earnestly wanted their independence.

When Japan was defeated in World War II, the Soviet army was in control of northern Korea and American forces held the southern half of the peninsula. The Allied powers oversaw the creation of two separate governments in the different regions. The uneasy division in Korea was similar to that in Germany after the fighting stopped. What happened on the Korean peninsula beginning in 1950 was the first major military confrontation following World War II between the forces of Communism and the forces of freedom. The Cold War became hot.

The Shooting Starts

On June 25, 1950, North Korean troops invaded the South in an attempt to unify the peninsula under Communist control. World governments understood that Stalin and the Soviets supported this aggression by North Korea.

The United Nations Security Council passed a resolution condemning the invasion and asking for troops to repel the invaders. The resolution succeeded only because the Soviet ambassador was boycotting the Security Council meeting to protest the fact that the Nationalist Taiwan government, not the Communist government, was the official Chinese representative at the U.N. The United States committed about 350,000 troops, and nineteen other countries sent a total of 50,000. South Korea matched these commitments with a force of 400,000 of its own. The supreme commander of the Allied forces was Douglas MacArthur. American involvement was officially described as a police action taken in response to the request by the United Nations. It was the largest commitment of U.S. troops without an act of war being passed by Congress that had occurred in American history to that point.

Inchon

The war went badly at first for the Allies. North Korean forces, aided by Russian troops, drove the U.N. armies to the southeast tip of the peninsula. Then on September 15, 1950, MacArthur led a daring and brilliant amphibious landing at Inchon on the western Korean coast, far behind enemy lines, which cut the Communist supply routes. At the same time, the embattled forces in the southeast managed to break out of their entrapment and push the invaders north. The Communists were driven back into North Korea, and the U.N. forces pursued them. President Truman saw the success of the U.N. forces as an opportunity not only to contain Communism but to defeat it in the North where it had already taken hold.

MacArthur wanted to pursue the war even further by bombing China, where supplies and other support for the North Korean army were located. The Truman Administration feared further Soviet intervention and the possibility of Communist China becoming involved in the fighting. If U.N. forces attacked China, the conflict in Korea could escalate into another world war, pitting America against the main Communist powers. Since the Soviet Union had test-exploded its first atomic bomb in 1949, a nuclear confrontation was a real possibility. Therefore, Truman prohibited MacArthur from bombing China.

Escalation

On November 25, 1950, thousands of what the Chinese Communist government called volunteers poured over the North Korean border from China. The Chinese pushed the U.N. armies far to the south, where they regrouped in the area of the 38th parallel of latitude. MacArthur complained that he couldn't win the war because he was not allowed to bomb China or use Taiwanese troops.

President Truman offered to begin negotiations with North Korea to re-establish the border between North and South. At the same time, General MacArthur offered a public warning that the Chinese needed to accept terms of peace or be attacked. In a letter to a Congressman that was made public, MacArthur criticized the Administration's attempt to fight the war with diplomats instead of arms. While the Administration weighed the political cost of further fighting and the military risks involved with invading China, MacArthur boldly stated, "There is no substitute for victory."

Douglas MacArthur

Douglas MacArthur (1880-1964), pictured at left with his trademark corncob pipe, was the son of a Civil War veteran. He graduated from West Point in 1903 and achieved the rank of general during World War I. MacArthur returned to West Point as superintendent from 1919 to 1923. He received criticism for his rough handling of the Bonus Army in 1932.

MacArthur spent many years in the Philippines before World War II. After being forced out of that country early in the war, he led the retaking of several Philippine islands that the Japanese had seized. MacArthur accepted the official surrender of the Japanese government aboard the USS Missouri *on September 2, 1945. He then oversaw the transformation of Japan by demilitarizing it, preparing a new constitution for the country, and liberalizing its laws and customs. The country became more westernized in many ways, and American assistance helped the nation rebuild economically.*

Truman Fires MacArthur

MacArthur's position was supported by a majority of the American people, who shared his frustration over trying to fight a limited war. Truman, on the other hand, saw MacArthur's comments as an act of military insubordination against the civilian commander in chief. On April 11, 1951, Truman fired MacArthur as commander of American and U.N. forces. The general returned to the States for the first time since 1937 and received a warm and tumultuous welcome. He addressed a joint session of Congress to mark the end of his military career. In his speech, he described himself by recalling an old tune which said that old soldiers never die, they just fade away.

Public opinion strongly favored MacArthur over Truman in the days following the old soldier's return. However, a Senate committee investigated the issue over the next several weeks and concluded that MacArthur's plans would have involved the United States in "the wrong war, at the wrong place, at the wrong time, and with the wrong enemy." In other words, the United States did need to help stop Communist aggression in Korea but didn't need to go to war against Communist China.

MacArthur went on a speaking tour that looked like a campaign to win the 1952 Republican presidential nomination, but his speeches were unconvincing and his arrogance became obvious. Over time more people began to see that MacArthur had been wrong and that Truman had been right.

This M24 tank in Korea had a crew from Mississippi (top), Kansas (center), and New Jersey (bottom).

Cease-Fire

By June of 1951, it was clear that U.N. forces could not take North Korea and reunite it with the South. Truman returned to his policy of containment rather than outright defeat of Communism. Talk of a cease-fire arose on both sides, but discussions on the subject dragged on for over two years. Not until July 27, 1953, after Truman had left office, was a truce signed. The opposing armies were facing each other near the 38th parallel of latitude, and that line became the border between North and South Korea.

Generals from the U.S. and North Korea Signing the Armistice Agreement

The Korean Conflict and Korea Today

- *The Korean conflict saw the first engagements of supersonic fighter planes. Russian-built MiG fighters did not venture below the 38th parallel but did control the North Korean skies for a time. To disguise their involvement, Soviet fighter pilots wore Chinese uniforms and used Chinese phrases in their radio communication. The U.S. responded with F-86 Sabres. Russian air losses were considerably greater than those of the Americans over the course of the war.*

- *About 36,574 Americans were killed in the Korean War, and over 100,000 more were wounded or missing. South Korea suffered about 1.3 million casualties, including over 400,000 killed. The combined North Korean, Russian, and Chinese losses totaled between 1.5 and 2 million.*

- *After the armistice, a de-militarized zone (DMZ) about 2.5 miles wide was created along the border between North and South Korea. The DMZ was intended to keep the opposing armies away from each other and thus decrease the risk of confrontations and the resumption of hostilities, though several violent confrontations have taken place. A conference building was constructed in the Korean town of Panmunjom. Representatives of North and South Korea have met occasionally since 1953, but no peace treaty has ever been signed. The police action is still technically going on. The conference table that negotiators use is situated directly astride the 38th parallel. North Korean delegates sit on the North Korean side, and South Korean representatives sit on the South Korean side.*

- *South Korea, aided by the United States, has made a great recovery economically from the war; but the damage to North Korea under Communist rule is impossible to calculate. North Korea has one of most repressive regimes and its people are among the poorest in the world. Millions have starved while the country has built up its military power. Kim Jong Un came to power in North Korea in 2011. He has made a series of threats against South Korea and the United States, declaring that the 1953 armistice is no longer in effect. The photo below is from a "Victory Day" parade in North Korea on July 27, 2013.*

President Truman ordered the integration of the U.S. military in 1948, which took place over the next few years. Men from Puerto Rico formed the United States 65th Infantry Regiment, the only active duty segregated unit of Hispanic soldiers. While stationed in Korea in 1951, the unit was ordered to capture two hills near Seoul occupied by Chinese troops. On February 2, the unit launched the last recorded large-scale bayonet charge in U.S. history and forced the Chinese to flee. This 1992 painting by Dominic D'Andrea commemorates that event.

How blessed is he who considers the helpless;
The Lord will deliver him in a day of trouble.
Psalm 41:1

★ Assignments for Lesson 118 ★

American Voices	Read "Old Soldiers Never Die" by General Douglas MacArthur (pages 320-322).
Bible	Work on memorizing Romans 10:11-13.
Project	Work on your project.
Student Review	Optional: Answer the questions for Lesson 118.

Boys Playing Marbles in Kentucky (1946)

Lesson 119

Life in Postwar America

In 1945 the United States was ready to transition from war to peace. Demobilization of the millions of citizen soldiers progressed rapidly. By 1947 the number of personnel in the various armed services was down to 1.7 million. In early 1950, only about 600,000 persons remained on active duty.

Postwar Adjustments

GI Bill. Once out of the service, veterans went to work and to school. They filled millions of jobs in the growing economy. Many veterans took advantage of the Veterans Readjustment Act of 1944 (also called the GI Bill or GI Bill of Rights). The law provided assistance to veterans who wanted to go to college or vocational school, offered low-cost medical care, granted unemployment benefits, and enabled easy access to home mortgage loans. This law was the beginning of the major commitment that the Federal government has continued to make to military veterans.

Clerk Writing Up a Grocery Bill (1948)

Baby Boom. The country experienced a population explosion as men came home and returned to their families or started families. The population grew twice as fast in the 1940s as it had in the 1930s. The extraordinary number of babies born in the years after the war is called the Baby Boom. Baby Boomers are officially those children born in America between 1946 and 1964. In or around 1964, women who were about twenty years old at the end of the war were nearing the end of their child-bearing years; and the first Baby Boomers began having their own children. About 40 million children were born during this eighteen-year period, accounting for a thirty percent increase in the nation's population.

Inflation. America made the transition from a wartime to a peacetime economy. Many (but not all) women retired from the work force and went back home to their families as returning soldiers looked for work. A significant feature of the postwar economy was inflation, which is a lowering of the value of the dollar and an increase in prices. Several factors drove the inflationary trend. First, wartime rationing and the limited production of many consumer goods such as cars and appliances had allowed many families to save their money but made many items scarce. This drove up prices. After the war, wages paid to employees were generally good. As a result, many people had money and were ready to buy. A willingness to spend and a limited number of goods added up to an increased demand, which led to an increase in industrial production.

Second, businesses had been under profit controls during the war and were now ready to cash in on the boom in sales. Third, unions began demanding higher wages. They wanted to make up for the sacrifices they had made during the war, and they wanted to keep up with everyone else. Rail workers, for instance, threatened a strike that would disrupt service unless they received a generous new wage deal. In response President Truman threatened to draft the rail workers into the Army and operate the railroads as a nationalized service. The workers and rail owners finally came to a settlement.

During the postwar years, the United States could largely set the terms of international trade because the U.S. had the strongest economy coming out of the war. The upward spiral of better wages, increased demand, and the willingness to spend led companies to increase their prices. Price inflation hounded the American economy to a greater or lesser extent into the 1990s. Attempts to control inflation constituted a major effort of the Truman Administration.

Civil Rights

When African American soldiers returned to the United States, they had a new understanding of the world. They had fought just as hard as white soldiers to maintain freedom. They had seen the horrors of racism in Germany. Then they came back to a society that practiced segregation, racial discrimination, and sometimes even violence against people of color. Many decided that they wanted to see changes.

The two top movies of 1946 were The Best Years of Our Lives, *a three-hour drama about the difficulties of postwar readjustment for both soldiers and civilians, and* It's A Wonderful Life, *a warm story starring Jimmy Stewart (a WWII bomber pilot, as seen above) and directed by Frank Capra in which a man learns what is really important in life.* The Best Years of Our Lives *was named Best Picture for 1946.* It's A Wonderful Life *has become a Christmas classic.*

Harry Truman was the first modern President to take decisive steps toward providing greater civil rights for African Americans. He named the first Civil Rights Commission to investigate alleged civil rights violations, and he appointed other task forces to study different aspects of the issue. By executive orders that he issued in 1948, Truman banned racial discrimination in the hiring of Federal workers and racial segregation in the military.

The Supreme Court also had an impact on the changing attitudes about race relations. In 1896 the Court had declared in *Plessy v. Ferguson* that separate but equal facilities met constitutional requirements. States went to great lengths to keep the races segregated. However, in reality the separate facilities for blacks were hardly ever equal. Much of the attention in civil rights cases during this period focused on education. Missouri, for instance, gave financial assistance for black law students to attend law school out of state rather than provide a law school for blacks within the state or integrate the state's public law school. In 1938 the Court struck down this practice as unconstitutional. In a 1950 decision, *Sweatt v. Painter*, the Court under Chief Justice Fred Vinson took matters a step further by ruling that a separate Texas law school for blacks within the state violated the equal protection clause of the 14th Amendment. The smaller school, implied the Court, did not provide an education that was truly equal to that received by whites.

Jackie Robinson (1950)

The most dramatic and public change in the treatment of blacks during this period came in major league baseball. In 1947 Brooklyn Dodgers owner Branch Rickey signed Negro League star Jackie Robinson to a contract. Rickey believed that Robinson had the skills and the character to break the color line of major league baseball. When Robinson was in Brooklyn's opening day lineup, it was the first time that a black man had played major league baseball in the modern era. The change, however, was not easily accepted. Robinson was booed and heckled by fans wherever he played. Opposing players and some of his own teammates abused him. Runners tried to spike him as they rounded the bases. Robinson was not allowed to stay in the same hotels and eat in the same restaurants that the rest of his team patronized. Hate mail poured into the Dodgers' office by the bagful. Robinson proved himself, however, by his excellent play and his patient character. At the end of the season, Robinson was voted National League Rookie of the Year. Over the next several years, major league baseball and eventually all sports became fully integrated.

Some five million blacks migrated from the rural South to large cities in the North. This changed the predominant black American experience from one of rural life to one of life in the city. Those who made the move hoped to find work in northern factories. Most found work, but it was often low-paying. In addition, they were met with frequent and sometimes violent racial discrimination. Blacks still had to attend segregated schools and colleges. The growing economy helped some African Americans, but overall the economic gap between the average white family and the average black family increased.

Politics

As the 1946 congressional elections approached, Republicans smelled victory. The transition from war had not been easy (it never is). Price controls remained in place on rent and many commodities. Both liberals and conservatives were critical of

Strom Thurmond

Strom Thurmond (born in 1902, pictured at right in 1997) was Democratic governor of South Carolina from 1947 to 1951. He was elected to the U.S. Senate in 1954 and re-elected in 1960. In 1957 Thurmond filibustered for just over 24 hours against civil rights legislation. In 1964 he switched to the Republican Party in support of GOP presidential nominee Barry Goldwater. Thurmond was re-elected to the Senate every time he ran. Thurmond's final Senate term expired in January of 2003, shortly after he turned 100; and he died later that year. Thurmond holds the record for being the oldest person ever to serve in Congress; and, for a time, he held the record for the longest tenure of service in the Senate. After he died, the public learned that Thurmond had fathered a child out of wedlock when he was twenty-two years old by a sixteen-year-old black maid who worked in his family's house. Thurmond maintained contact with this daughter, Essie Mae Washington Williams, though he did not publicly acknowledge her. She died in 2013.

Truman's handling of the presidency. The plain-spoken Truman did not have the majestic public style and charm that Roosevelt had. Republicans campaigned against the long dominance of the Democrats with the slogan "Had Enough?" Apparently the voters had, because the Republicans swept to majorities in both Houses of Congress for the first time since the 1928 election.

The new party in power wasted no time in changing the tone of political business in Washington. First, Congress passed and sent to the states the 22nd Amendment to the U.S. Constitution, limiting a President to two elected terms in office. This was generally recognized as an attempt to prevent another Franklin Roosevelt, who was elected to four terms. The amendment was ratified in 1951 but did not apply to President Truman.

A second major act of the Republican Congress was the Taft-Hartley Act of 1947 that limited the power of labor unions. Many Americans believed that unions had come to have too much power, with their ability to control their members and to call or threaten a strike and potentially paralyze an industry or even the entire economy. The Taft-Hartley Act, which passed over Truman's veto, banned the closed shop, a practice which allowed only union workers to hold jobs in a given plant or industry.

The law also allowed the President to call for a sixty-day cooling off period before a strike took place in order to give labor and management more time to reach an agreement. The measure outlawed contributions by unions to political campaigns and limited the check-off (automatic paycheck deduction) method of collecting union dues. Unions were forced to make their financial statements public. Union leaders were required to take an oath that they were not Communists. The Taft-Hartley Act is still law, standing as a statement that unions, like management, need to be regulated for the public good.

The Republican engine seemed to be rolling toward a victory in 1948. Few observers believed that Truman had much of a chance of getting elected in his own right. The President still had enough control of the party to be nominated on the first ballot of the convention, but the Democrats' house was not in order. The party platform had a strong statement in favor of greater civil rights for blacks. This angered many southern delegates, who walked out and formed the States' Rights Democratic Party, also known as Dixiecrats. They nominated South Carolina governor Strom Thurmond for President.

Thomas Dewey (Center) During the 1948 Campaign

Meanwhile, the liberal wing of the party was also dissatisfied with Truman; and a new Progressive Party was formed that nominated former Vice President Henry Wallace. With the Democrats so divided and Truman so unpopular, a Republican victory seemed assured. The GOP once again nominated Thomas Dewey, their 1944 standard-bearer. His vice presidential nominee was California governor Earl Warren. Dewey ran a smooth, cautious campaign; his victory seemed assured.

Truman, however, was not out yet. His acceptance speech at the Democratic convention was especially fiery, a tone people hadn't often seen in Truman. In the speech, he said that he planned to call the Republican Congress back into special session to consider several pieces of legislation. The special session took place, but Congress took no significant action. The President then embarked upon a 31,000 mile "whistle stop" campaign train trip, blasting what he called the "Do-Nothing Congress." The polls, however, showed that Truman still seemed to be fighting a losing battle.

On election night, the returns were extremely close. It appeared that Dewey was going to win. *The Chicago Tribune* printed an early edition with the huge headline DEWEY DEFEATS TRUMAN. However, when all the votes were counted, Truman had won in what is considered one of the biggest upsets in American election history.

The opinion polls that had showed Dewey ahead of Truman were apparently accurate, just out of date. The last polls were taken a few weeks before the election. Truman's campaign developed increasing momentum as Election Day neared, and the opinions of enough voters changed in the days right before the voting took place to give Truman the victory.

Truman won with 49.5 percent of the popular vote to 45.1 percent for Dewey and a 303-189 electoral win. Thurmond and Wallace each got about one million votes. Thurmond carried four southern states, but Wallace won no electoral votes. In addition, Democratic majorities were elected to both Houses of Congress.

A victorious Truman holds the newspaper announcing his defeat the day after the election.

In his 1949 State of the Union Address, President Truman called for several new laws that he said would give a Fair Deal to every American. He called for a higher minimum wage (to 75 cents per hour), continued farm price supports, more public housing, and increased funding for TVA and rural electrification. All of these Congress enacted. However, Congress rejected other proposals that Truman made, including a civil rights bill, national health insurance, Federal aid to education, and repeal of the Taft-Hartley Act.

During the period of transition after World War II, the Truman years provided the first indications of the major changes that were to occur in the United States in coming decades.

Harry Truman with His Wife Bess and Daughter Margaret (1946)

For the word of the Lord is upright,
And all His work is done in faithfulness.
He loves righteousness and justice;
The earth is full of the loving kindness of the Lord.
Psalm 33:5

⋆ Assignments for Lesson 119 ⋆

American Voices Read Harry S. Truman's Farewell Address (pages 323-328).

Bible Work on memorizing Romans 10:11-13.

Project Work on your project.

Student Review Optional: Answer the questions for Lesson 119.

Pro-Israel and Pro-Palestinian Groups in San Francisco (2006)

Lesson 120 - Bible Study

Religious Issues

The Bible study for this unit looks at two different kinds of religious issues that arose during and after World War II. One involved an international development, while the other concerned the relationship between public policies and religious activities within the United States.

The Founding of Modern Israel

When God took Abraham to Canaan, He told him, "I will give to you and to your descendants after you, the land of your sojourning, all the land of Canaan, for an everlasting possession; and I will be their God" (Genesis 17:8). This was the same Promised Land to which God led the Israelites after their period of slavery in Egypt. The Kingdom of Israel ruled the land until Northern and Southern Israel went into captivity in 721 BC and 606 BC respectively.

The Lord brought a remnant of Judah (the Southern Kingdom) back after seventy years of captivity in Babylon. From the time of captivity, the area of Israel was always under the rule of foreign powers except for about a century under the Maccabees shortly before the time of Christ. Rome took over in 63 BC; then when the Roman Empire divided, the Byzantine or Eastern Roman Empire ruled until 638 AD. In that year, Muslim invaders conquered the area, which is also known as Palestine (a name derived from the ancient Philistines). Muslim rule continued in one form or another for the next 1300 years. The Turkish Ottoman (Islamic) Empire controlled the area beginning in 1517 and continued until 1917 except for a brief period of Egyptian rule (1831-1840). By the early twentieth century, Ottoman rule over Palestine was weak.

The push for a renewed, independent homeland for Jews in Palestine (called Zionism), based on God's promise to Abraham, was begun in 1897 by Theodor Herzl in Basel, Switzerland. He encouraged

A Christian Family in Ramallah, Palestine (c. 1905)

Theodor Herzl and His Children (1900)

Jews to move to Palestine in order to increase their numbers and political strength there. Only a few thousand Jews lived in Palestine in 1900, but that number grew to 84,000 by 1922. Most of those who went were from Europe and North America. The large majority of people in Palestine at the time were Muslims, although some Christians lived there also.

The Zionist movement gained the endorsement of Great Britain, which wanted the support of Jews in the Great War against Germany. In 1917 British foreign minister Arthur Balfour expressed his backing for an official Jewish homeland in Palestine. Great Britain received a mandate from the League of Nations in 1922 to administer Palestine and help the Jewish people secure a homeland. Jewish settlement increased significantly over the next several years. Many came from Europe as they fled Hitler's aggression. The Jews in Palestine began a form of self-government among themselves.

The Arab peoples, meanwhile, trace their lineage from Ishmael, Abraham's son by Hagar, Sarah's handmaiden. Arabs who lived in Palestine in the early 20th century believed that the land on which they lived belonged to them. They opposed Jewish immigration and British rule there. From 1936 to 1939 Palestinian Arabs attempted a revolt against British rule and the increased Jewish presence there.

Revelations of the Nazi Holocaust increased the demand for an independent Jewish state and intensified opposition to British rule of the area. After World War II, Britain was ready to be relieved of the oversight of Palestine, and it turned the matter over to the United Nations. In 1947 the U.N. announced a plan to partition Palestine into Jewish and Arab states and to make Jerusalem an international zone. Arab residents of Palestine revolted and attacked the Jewish settlements. Great Britain then withdrew its presence in the region. The Jews in Palestine declared themselves to be an independent state on May 14, 1948. The United States was the first country to extend diplomatic recognition to Israel. Neighboring Arab states immediately joined with Palestinians in attacking the Jews. Israeli soldiers held their own, and Israel was admitted to the United Nations on May 11, 1949.

The new Jewish state announced a policy of welcoming Jews from anywhere in the world. Meanwhile, Palestinian Muslims who had been living in the area claimed by Israel left or were forced out and became refugees on the West Bank of the Jordan River and in neighboring Arab countries. Israel and the Arab states have fought several wars in the decades since Israel's founding, and in between those wars significant tension and terrorism have continued.

Many Bible believers hold that the modern re-creation of Israel is part of God's plan for the Jews and for an earthly millennial reign of Christ. They believe that God's promises to Israel continue to

The Or Torah Synagogue in Acre, Israel, was built in 1955 by Jews who had immigrated from Tunisia.

apply into the Christian dispensation. Others hold that God's covenant with physical Israel has been replaced by the spiritual covenant established in Christ (Hebrews 8:7-13). They note that modern Israel does not claim to be led by God the way Old Testament Israel did.

Modern Israel is a nation founded on political and cultural Judaism and not the religion of Judaism. Only a small percentage of modern Israelis are active Jews religiously. No Jews today follow the law of Moses completely because they are denied access to the site of the temple in Jerusalem where animal sacrifices were made. Muslims constructed a mosque on the site in 691 AD.

The descendants of Abraham through Isaac and the descendants of Abraham through Ishmael continue the strife that those two half-brothers had when they were alive.

As late as 1942, as seen in this Connecticut photo, some schoolchildren recited the Pledge of Allegiance using a raised-arm salute named the Bellamy Salute after Pledge author Francis Bellamy. A similar salute was adopted by the Italians and Germans before World War II. On December 22, 1942, Congress decided that the Pledge of Allegiance should be recited with the right hand over the heart.

Supreme Court Decisions

The U.S. Supreme Court issued several rulings during this period that addressed religious practices in the country.

Religious Expression. West Virginia had a law requiring school children to salute the flag (raise their right hands) and recite the Pledge of Allegiance. Members of the Jehovah's Witnesses group refused to let their children do so because they believed it violated the Second Commandment against making a graven image (Exodus 20:4). Failure to salute the flag resulted in children being counted absent or being expelled.

In 1940 the Court upheld the West Virginia regulation. Writing for the majority, Justice Felix Frankfurter said that "national unity is the basis of national security," and that a required flag salute helped bring about national unity. However, the Court reversed itself three years later in *West Virginia Board of Education v. Barnette* (1943). Justice Robert Jackson said that the flag salute was a form of utterance protected by the First Amendment and therefore could not be compelled.

Transportation Reimbursement. The Court also dealt with questions involving the meaning of the First Amendment prohibition against the establishment of religion and its guarantee of the free exercise of religion. New Jersey allowed local school boards to reimburse parents who provided transportation for their children to attend school. This reimbursement was made whether the children attended public or private schools. The law was challenged as an establishment of religion, but the Court in *Everson v. Board of Education of Ewing Township* (1947) upheld the practice.

Justice Hugo Black in his majority opinion reviewed the historical situation at the time of the founding of the country and the passage of the First Amendment. The people of America had been used to an established state church in Europe, and this was what the First Amendment sought to avoid. Black quoted the words of Thomas Jefferson in a

The best-selling religious book of the 1950s was The Power of Positive Thinking *by clergyman Norman Vincent Peale, published in 1952. Peale chose various passages from Scripture and tied them to real-life anecdotes to show how a positive personal attitude can made a difference. In his book, Peale left aside matters of sin and judgment. The heir to this kind of religion in later years was Robert Schuller with his emphasis on Possibility Thinking.*

private letter which said that "a wall of separation [existed] between church and State." However, the New Jersey law, Black said, helped parents, not a church. Government-supported traffic police assigned to a private school zone, according to Black's opinion, constituted the same kind of acceptable public assistance. Forbidding the New Jersey reimbursement program "is obviously not the purpose of the First Amendment. That Amendment requires the state to be neutral in its relations with groups of religious believers and non-believers; it does not require the state to be their adversary. State power is no more to be used so as to handicap religions than it is to favor them."

Released Time Religious Instruction. Public schools in early America unashamedly taught religion. As America became more secular, religious instruction was moved to the side. Many school districts offered released time programs in which students could be released from the regular school schedule in order to receive religious instruction during school hours if parents approved. The Champaign, Illinois, school system had a program in which such religious instruction was held during school hours, in school facilities, with teachers responsible to the superintendent. In 1948 the Court struck down the practice as violating the establishment clause of the First Amendment.

Four years later, the Court considered a similar but sufficiently different case. New York City schools had a released time program in which students left the school grounds to receive religious instruction. The Court upheld this practice since neither public money nor public facilities were used.

Evangelist Billy Graham began holding large city-wide crusades in 1949. His Los Angeles crusade drew huge crowds and made national news. Graham held more crusades in America and spread his ministry to England and other countries. Graham has probably spoken in person to more people than any other person in history. He has met personally with every President since Harry Truman and has been a spiritual advisor to many of them.

Justice William O. Douglas wrote for the majority, "We are a religious people whose institutions presuppose a Supreme Being. . . . When the state encourages religious instruction or cooperates with religious authorities by adjusting the schedule of public events to sectarian needs, it follows the best of our traditions. For it then respects the religious nature of our people and accommodates the public service to their spiritual needs."

William O. Douglas is shown at left with his son William Jr. after his appointment as a Supreme Court Justice in 1939. Douglas served until 1975—the longest term of any Supreme Court Justice.

Woe to those who go down to Egypt for help and rely on horses,
and trust in chariots because they are many
and in horsemen because they are very strong,
but they do not look to the Holy One of Israel, nor seek the Lord!
Isaiah 31:1

⋆ Assignments for Lesson 120 ⋆

Bible Recite or write Romans 10:11-13 from memory.

Project Complete your project for the unit.

Student Review Optional: Answer the questions for Lesson 120 and take the quiz for Unit 24.

Testament: Little Rock Nine Memorial, *John and Kathy Deering (American, 2005)*

25 The 1950s

Dwight Eisenhower, the first Republican President in twenty years, did not roll back New Deal reforms, which meant that they were here to stay. The push for civil rights that characterized the 1960s had its beginnings in the 1950s. America dealt with several international incidents, but relations with the Soviet Union were the main cause for concern. The space race changed American education, technology, and military priorities. The 1950s, long considered the golden age of American society, had serious cracks in its foundations that would have an even greater impact in later decades.

Memory Work Memorize Romans 12:1-3 by the end of this unit.

Books Used The Bible
American Voices

Project (choose one)

1) Write 300 to 500 words on one of the following topics:

- Is it better to influence another nation by engagement or by boycott? The United States has tried boycotting Cuba but is engaged in trade and dialog with Communist China. Does trading with China endorse its violations of human rights, use of low-paid labor, and poor environmental standards? Or is engagement the best way to have influence with the Chinese government? See Lesson 123.

- Summarize the spiritual blessings and problems of the 1950s. In what ways were they the good old days, and in what ways were they not? What would you have liked about living during that time, and what would you have found difficult to accept?

2) Write a poem of at least twenty lines in rhyme or free verse about one or more ways that American life changed during the 1950s.

3) Make a space race board game, card game, or strategy game to play with your family. Incorporate information about the early days of space exploration into your game. Be creative! See Lesson 124.

Jackie Robinson, President Eisenhower, and Actor/Comedian Joe E. Brown (1957)

Lesson 121

We Like Ike!

Both major parties faced difficult decisions about their presidential nominations in 1952. Although Harry Truman could have run despite the two-term limitation of the 22nd Amendment, he opted out in March of that year. With economic troubles, the Korean War, and charges of corruption and Communists in government, Truman would have faced a difficult campaign. After being President since 1945, he was ready to go back home to Independence, Missouri. The Democratic convention on the third ballot drafted Illinois governor Adlai Stevenson, who was willing to run but who had not been an active candidate for the nomination. To try to bring back the liberal and southern wings of the party that had left in 1948, the vice presidential nod went to a liberal southerner, John Sparkman of Alabama.

The favorite of many Republican Party regulars was Ohio Senator Robert A. Taft. The son of President William Howard Taft, "Mr. Republican" had been passed over in favor of Thomas Dewey in 1944 and 1948. He believed that 1952 was his year. However, Taft's conservatism and his reservations about international involvement seemed out of step with the times. The name that kept coming up with enthusiasm among Republicans was that of Dwight David (Ike) Eisenhower.

The World War II hero was born in Texas in 1890, grew up in Abilene, Kansas, and attended West Point. He held several posts in the Army before being named Supreme Commander of the Allied forces during World War II and overseeing the D-Day invasion and subsequent defeat of Germany. Following the war, he was named Army Chief of Staff and then retired from the military to become president of Columbia University. Eisenhower went back into military service as commander of NATO in 1951. He had not shown much interest in politics, but he had been courted by both major parties because of his fame as a war hero and his personal appeal. Most comfortable as a moderate Republican, he agreed to run for that party's nomination.

Senator Taft did not have the broad appeal that Eisenhower did, and the former general edged out Taft for the nomination. The vice presidential nomination went to Senator Richard Nixon of California, who was much younger than Eisenhower and who appealed to the conservative wing of the party because of his tough anti-Communist stand.

Nixon's Checkers Speech

On September 18, a newspaper revealed that individual contributors had created an $18,000 fund for Nixon to help with expenses involved in his political work. It appeared to be a fund that could be used for undefined purposes and one for which no one was accountable. As criticism of the fund mounted, newspapers and Democrats across the country suggested that Nixon withdraw from the ticket. Eisenhower was in a dilemma. He wanted to support his running mate but he did not want to court disaster by ignoring a political liability. Ike said that he wanted a full accounting from Nixon and would accept nothing but the truth.

Nixon decided to go on national television and explain his position in a thirty-minute presentation paid for by the Republican National Committee (RNC). On the evening of September 23, the vice presidential nominee defended the fund as legal; but most of his speech was about himself and his family. Nixon made reference to one contribution from a supporter, the family dog Checkers, that he planned to keep. He said that his wife Pat didn't have a mink coat but wore a good Republican cloth coat. The embattled Nixon concluded his speech by asking people to write or wire the RNC their opinion on whether he should stay on the ticket. He promised to abide by this expression of the popular will.

Nixon received an overwhelmingly positive response. Letters, calls, and telegrams to the RNC ran 350 to 1 in favor of Nixon staying on. People also wrote to the television networks, General Eisenhower, and any other address they could think of (Nixon had not provided the address for the RNC in his speech). Eisenhower was moved by Nixon's courage and accepted his continued presence on the ticket. Nixon and Eisenhower began drawing large crowds to their campaign appearances.

Labor's Committee for Stevenson and Sparkman Poster

Eisenhower During the 1952 Campaign

Though Stevenson was an eloquent and effective speaker, the lingering issue of Korea turned the tide to the former general, who defeated Stevenson 33.9 million to 27.3 million in popular votes and 442 to 89 in the electoral count. Eisenhower was the first Republican President in twenty years. He even carried some traditionally Democratic southern states. Stevenson only carried Kentucky, West Virginia, and seven states in the Deep South. The victory was mostly a personal one for Eisenhower and not a wide Republican sweep. Democrats held most governorships; and the Republicans had only a slim majority in Congress, which they lost in the 1954 mid-term elections.

Ike in Office

Eisenhower proved to be a quiet leader who worked in the background to form a consensus. He encouraged the growth of private business, as demonstrated in his favoring a private power company over TVA in one decision and supporting private development of atomic energy in another. Eisenhower chose businessmen to serve in his Cabinet, including Charles Wilson, former head of General Motors, as Secretary of Defense. Wilson once said, "What was good for our country was good for General Motors, and vice versa." This was usually misquoted as "What's good for General Motors is good for the country." Cynics quipped that the Cabinet was made up of eight millionaires and a plumber (the Secretary of Labor was the former head of the plumbers' union, and he resigned a few months after taking office).

The new President was a fiscal conservative and worked hard to achieve a balanced budget (something that was accomplished in 1956, although deficits returned in later years). He vetoed wage hikes for Federal workers and tax cuts passed by Congress to stimulate the economy during a recession. Inflation was kept low despite two mild recessions during his term (1953-54 and 1957-58).

The basic structure that had developed in the New Deal of an active Federal government went largely unchallenged. More workers were added to Social Security coverage. The Federal Security Agency was remade into the Cabinet-level Department of Health, Education, and Welfare. Farmers continued to receive payments for not growing certain crops. The government continued to provide price supports for farmers by buying crops when prices fell below about 90% of parity.

Interstate Highways

By 1955 Americans owned 61 million automobiles and trucks. The best roads in the country were two-lane Federal highways which ran directly through towns and cities and which had private driveways and business entrances entering onto them. In 1919 Dwight Eisenhower had participated in a cross-country excursion of tanks and other military equipment on the Lincoln Highway which dramatized the need for better roads. By contrast, when Eisenhower was in Germany at the end of World War II, he admired the Autobahn system that made travel and troop movements easy.

During Eisenhower's term, two final states joined the Union, the only ones that do not share a border with other states. Alaska was admitted as the 49th state on January 3, 1959; and Hawaii as the 50th state on August 21, 1959. The tallest peak in North America is Alaska's Denali, or Mount McKinley, shown at left. Hawaii consists of hundreds of islands spread across a distance of 1,500 miles. The photo at right shows the main islands from space.

The St. Lawrence Seaway was completed in 1959. This joint project of the United States and Canada enabled seagoing vessels to reach the Great Lakes. The Eisenhower Locks at Massena, New York, are part of the Seaway system. The photos above show the U.S. Army Herald Trumpets performing there at the opening in 1959 and again on the 50th anniversary in 2009.

President Eisenhower pressed for a system of wide, limited-access Interstate highways to facilitate travel by the public and to make military transportation easier in times of national emergency. The Federal Highway Act, passed in 1956, created a 42,000 mile Interstate system. The Federal government paid for 90% of the cost, with states picking up the rest. Interstates are now the backbone of vehicle traffic in America. Repair and widening work continues to the present, and new Interstates and connecting routes are occasionally created. Taken as a whole, the Interstate and Defense Highway System is the largest peacetime project ever undertaken in the U.S.

Labor

In 1950 a special Senate committee chaired by Tennessee Democrat Estes Kefauver held hearings on organized crime in several cities across the country. Some of the sessions were televised. The hearings revealed, among other things, that labor unions were often involved in criminal activities. One result of the Kefauver Committee hearings was the Labor-Management Reporting and Disclosure Act of 1959, usually called the Landrum-Griffin Act, which continued the trend of tightening restrictions on unions. The law protected union members from pressure by leadership, required disclosure of the salaries and expenses of union leaders, forced regular elections for union officials, and outlawed excessive charges for routine work (a practice known as a shakedown).

The American Federation of Labor (AFL) and the Congress of Industrial Organizations (CIO) merged in 1955 to become the AFL-CIO. The CIO had resulted from a split in the AFL in 1938, and rivalry between the two organizations had actually increased total union membership. However, with anti-labor sentiment growing in the country, the two groups decided that merging would give them greater power. The AFL-CIO represented about 15 million industrial workers but not all of the unionized laborers in the country. The nation suffered through a major steel strike in 1959 that shut down almost all steel production. It was not settled until early in 1960.

Ike's Second Term

Eisenhower suffered a major heart attack in September of 1955 and was incapacitated for about two months. He recovered well but did not decide until February of 1956 to run for a second term. Nixon was again the choice for second spot. The Democrats re-nominated Adlai Stevenson, who was a more willing candidate this time. In a highly unusual move, Stevenson threw open the vice presidential bid to the convention, which chose Senator Estes Kefauver. Kefauver had been a candidate for the presidential nomination in the Democratic primaries of 1952 and 1956. His choice as the vice presidential nominee was largely the result of the reputation he had gained through his investigation of organized crime and because he did not sign the Southern Manifesto against the integration of public schools (the next lesson will have more information on this). The convention chose Kefauver over a young Senator from Massachusetts, John F. Kennedy.

The nation continued to like Ike, as he rolled up a 457-73 electoral majority and a 35.6 million to 26 million popular vote victory. However, the Democrats still controlled Congress. Eisenhower was the first candidate since 1848 to be elected President but fail to carry at least one house of Congress with him. The Democratic majority increased in each house with the 1958 elections.

Farewell

Three days before he left office, Eisenhower made a nationally televised farewell speech. In it, the former general and the encourager of business warned against the power of the "military-industrial complex." He said that he regretted not being able to insure peace, but he was thankful that he had not been forced to face another war.

Upon retiring from the presidency, Eisenhower moved to a farm near the town of Gettysburg, Pennsylvania. He wrote several books, was often consulted as an elder statesman, and pursued his hobby of painting. Despite his world renown, he and his wife, Mamie, led a simple life that can be seen by visiting their farm house.

Eisenhower died on March 28, 1969. Speaking at his funeral was the man who had been Eisenhower's Vice President and who was then the recently-inaugurated President, Richard Nixon.

Eisenhower Home in Gettysburg, Pennsylvania

Richard Nixon's daughter Julie married Dwight Eisenhower's grandson David in December of 1968. They first met at Ike's second inauguration in 1957 when they were eight years old, but they didn't see each other for several years. They began dating in 1966 while they were attending different colleges a few miles apart. They are pictured above left in 1971. The presidential retreat in Maryland, begun by Franklin Roosevelt, was renamed Camp David by Dwight Eisenhower in honor of his father and grandson, both named David. David was photographed at the camp in 1960.

First of all, then, I urge that entreaties and prayers, petitions and thanksgivings, be made on behalf of all men, for kings and all who are in authority, so that we may lead a tranquil and quiet life in all godliness and dignity.
1 Timothy 2:1-2

⋆ Assignments for Lesson 121 ⋆

Bible Start memorizing Romans 12:1-3.

Project Choose your project for this unit and start working on it.

Student Review Optional: Answer the questions for Lesson 121.

School Integration in Clinton, Tennessee (1956)

Lesson 122

Civil Rights

Relations between blacks and whites in the United States have been difficult since the first Africans were brought to the Jamestown colony in 1619. Slavery ended with the Civil War, but it was replaced with systematic and institutional segregation as well as individual and social prejudice by whites against blacks. African Americans were treated as second-class citizens for decades.

Though the 1896 *Plessy v. Ferguson* Supreme Court decision had declared that separate but equal facilities for the different races were acceptable, facilities for blacks were rarely equal to those available to whites. However, the black community did not have enough power or enough white supporters to bring about a change.

"Negro School" in Georgia (1941)

This did not stop the efforts of some blacks to challenge the treatment of African Americans. The NAACP had resolved in the 1930s to challenge the separate but equal doctrine by means of lawsuits. The Supreme Court decisions during the Truman Administration regarding state law schools had been the first successful challenges. Then the advocates of integration turned to public schools.

Brown v. Board of Education

The Supreme Court considered a group of cases involving racially segregated school districts in Kansas, South Carolina, Virginia, and Delaware (note that only two of the states were in the former Confederacy). Those bringing the suits challenged the practice of separate schools for blacks under the 14th Amendment right of equal protection under law. They claimed that the black schools were not equal and that, even if they were academically equivalent, the fact that they were required to be separate made them unequal to what white children had available to them.

On May 17, 1954, the Court issued a unanimous verdict, centering on the case from

The Chief Justice of the Supreme Court and the man who wrote the Brown *decision was Earl Warren (above left). When Warren had been governor of California he was considered a moderate conservative. During his tenure as Chief Justice, however (1953-1969), Warren led an activist Court that changed many aspects of American life. One of the attorneys who argued the* Brown *case before the Supreme Court was Thurgood Marshall. Marshall is pictured above right in 1967, when he became the first African American named to the Supreme Court.*

Topeka, Kansas. The Court noted that public education was not a major concern at the time the 14th Amendment was adopted in 1868 or at the time of the *Plessy v. Ferguson* ruling in 1896. By 1954, however, the Court said that public education was perhaps the major function of state and local governments. The separate but equal doctrine, the Court ruled, has no place in public education. "Separate educational facilities are inherently unequal," the court opinion said. Lower courts were required to work out solutions for local situations.

The Supreme Court's decision was intended to bring about a revolution in educational and political policy and thus in American life in general. However, local school boards, especially in the South, responded with a firm resistance to such changes. In 1955 the Court ordered that school districts implement desegregation plans "with all deliberate speed." Intended to quicken the pace of integration, the phrase gave school boards an excuse to delay taking any significant action toward integrating public schools. In 1956 about one hundred U.S. Senators and Congressmen expressed their opposition to court-ordered desegregation by signing a Declaration of Constitutional Principles Since all the signers were from southern states, it became known as the Southern Manifesto.

Attempts to integrate local schools sometimes led to violence. Blacks in Clinton, Tennessee, had sued in 1950 to have the local schools desegregated. It was not until 1956, however, that a judge ordered the Clinton High School to admit blacks. When school opened that fall with twelve black students enrolled, about 1,500 white adults gathered at the courthouse to protest. Some of them had come from as far away as New Jersey and Alabama. About eighty reporters from around the country came to cover the incident. Tennessee governor Frank Clement ordered 600 National Guardsmen to go to Clinton to maintain order. The integration proceeded, and Bobby Cain Jr. was the lone black senior to graduate in the spring of 1957. Over a year later, in October of 1958, a bomb exploded at Clinton High School on a Sunday morning. The whites who planted the bomb wanted to stop integration, but the effect of the incident was to make more people in Clinton want to stop the violence.

The Little Rock Nine

An integration effort that attracted more national attention took place in Little Rock, Arkansas. A Federal court ordered the desegregation of Central High School in 1957, and nine black students were enrolled. However, Governor Orville Faubus called out the National Guard to prevent the enrollment from taking place. President Eisenhower met with Faubus, but the meeting did not help. A court ordered the governor to remove the troops and allow the students in, but a mob of whites posed such a threat that the black students were withdrawn.

The Little Rock Nine Meeting New York City Mayor Robert Wagner (1958)

Eisenhower then sent in 1,000 paratroopers to protect the students who re-entered the school; and the President federalized the Arkansas National Guard, who stayed at the school for the entire school year. Ernest Green, one of the Little Rock Nine, became the first black student to graduate from Central High School in 1958.

The use of force to accomplish integration hardened white opposition. White Citizens Councils were organized in many cities, and southern political leaders spoke of "massive resistance" to integration orders. Token integration (such as that in Little Rock) was implemented in a few cities. By 1963 only about one-half of one percent of black students in the South attended integrated schools. Not until the U.S. Justice Department began filing legal suits in the 1960s did significant changes take place. By then the civil rights battle had widened to state universities and to society at large.

Governor Faubus closed the Little Rock high schools for the 1958-1959 school year to keep from integrating them. While the schools were closed, some students watched classes broadcast on television. The schools re-opened in 1959.

The Montgomery Bus Boycott

Like many cities, Montgomery, Alabama, had an ordinance in the mid-1950s that required black riders on city buses to give their seats to whites who asked. On December 1, 1955, seamstress Rosa Parks refused to give up her seat when asked to do so. The bus driver had her arrested. Black leaders met the next night to organize a boycott of the city bus system. Martin Luther King Jr., a young minister in Montgomery, led the boycott. Blacks in the city walked, carpooled, and found other ways to get around while the bus system lost money. Finally in November of 1956, the Supreme Court upheld a lower court ruling declaring segregation in city bus systems to be unconstitutional. King and other blacks boarded Montgomery buses the next day.

Civil Rights Legislation

During President Eisenhower's second term, Congress passed two civil rights laws, in 1957 and 1960, primarily intended to support the right of blacks to vote. It became a Federal crime to interfere

From left to right are four leaders of the NAACP, Henry L. Moon, Roy Wilkins, Hebert Hill, and Thurgood Marshall.

with anyone's ability to vote. Local election officials were required to keep voting records for 22 months after elections, for evidence in case any charges of voting interference were filed. The 1960 law made it a Federal crime to cross state lines while fleeing prosecution for "hate bombing" or other destructive acts.

Oversight of elections had historically been a state jurisdiction, but the Federal government became involved when states were not protecting the rights of blacks. Likewise, the fugitive flight clause of the 1960 law allowed the Federal government to become involved in criminal investigations when state officials were not prosecuting crimes against blacks. Unfortunately, the two civil rights laws did not have much effect in ensuring that blacks were allowed to vote.

The civil rights movement gained momentum in the 1960s, as we will see in the next unit. Racial segregation, discrimination, and violence were present in the North also. Schools in the North were largely segregated also, mostly because of residential patterns which were the result of segregation laws or unofficial discrimination against blacks. In other words, in most communities blacks were not allowed to live in white neighborhoods; and thus they did not attend neighborhood schools with whites. Black schools in the North were usually not as well equipped and maintained as white schools. One reason for this was that blacks did not have the political power to force improvements. White politicians had little to fear if they had the support of white voters.

During the 1950s, millions of blacks left the rural South and moved to northern cities, hoping to find jobs and escape the poverty and discrimination they had known in the South. However, many of them were charged high rent for poor quality apartments and houses, they were discriminated against by employers and labor unions, and occasionally they were the targets of racially-motivated violence.

Pursue peace with all men,
and the sanctification without which
no one will see the Lord.
Hebrews 12:14

★ Assignments for Lesson 122 ★

American Voices Read the excerpts from the *Brown v. Board of Education* Supreme Court decision (pages 329-332).

Bible Work on memorizing Romans 12:1-3.

Project Work on your project.

Student Review Optional: Answer the questions for Lesson 122.

President Eisenhower Waves During a Parade in Rio de Janeiro, Brazil (1960)

Lesson 123

Eisenhower's Foreign Policy

Dwight Eisenhower had been a military officer during two world wars and the commander of NATO. He understood the dangers of war and the complex forces at work in world affairs based on his first-hand knowledge and experience. He also understood the Soviet threat and wanted to limit Soviet power and influence. Yet Eisenhower, like almost all military leaders, was a man who preferred peace to war. He wanted the United States to remain engaged in world events as a force for good.

Relations with the Soviet Union

The overriding foreign policy issue during the Eisenhower years involved America's relations with the Soviet Union. Less than two months after Eisenhower took office, Joseph Stalin died on March 5, 1953. A power struggle ensued within the Soviet Communist Party, and Nikita Khrushchev emerged as leader of the party later that year. He was declared premier of the government in 1958. Khrushchev was a personal and political enigma. He could be charming and friendly but also angry and confrontational. In 1955 he denounced the crimes of the Stalin era, when millions of so-called enemies of the state were killed in the Soviet Union; but the next year, he ruthlessly crushed a freedom movement in Hungary. He said that he favored what he called peaceful coexistence with the West, but he was also willing to go to the brink of war.

The United States exploded the first H-bomb, also called a thermonuclear device, in 1952. It was much more powerful than the bombs dropped on Japan in World War II. This time, however, the Soviets did not have to wait for years to match the U.S. as they had with the atomic bomb. The U.S.S.R. detonated a similar thermonuclear device the next year. These developments increased the fear around the world of catastrophic war.

In July of 1955, Eisenhower, Khrushchev, and the leaders of France and Great Britain gathered in Geneva, Switzerland, for a summit meeting. President Eisenhower surprised the conference attendees by proposing that the United States and the Soviet Union exchange what he called blueprints of their respective military systems and allow surveillance flights by each other's planes. It was a bold move designed to ease tensions, but the Soviets did not accept the "open skies" idea.

Vice President Nixon visited Russia in July of 1959 during a United States National Exhibition in Moscow that displayed the latest developments in American life. In the display of a model American kitchen, Nixon and Premier Khrushchev got into a pointed and sometimes heated debate about the

In keeping with his campaign promise, Eisenhower went to Korea in December of 1952 to encourage the peace efforts there. A cease-fire was declared the following July. One especially thorny issue was the fate of prisoners of war. Many North Koreans held in the South did not want to go back to the Communist North, but North Korean negotiators insisted that all prisoners be returned regardless of their personal wishes. The final truce settlement did allow prisoners to have their wishes respected regarding their being returned to their home country.

merits of their respective political and social systems. They exchanged challenging words but then moved on to tour the rest of the exhibition in peace.

Eisenhower and Khrushchev agreed to make reciprocal visits to their respective countries. Khrushchev came to the United States in 1959. He toured Disneyland, Iowa farmland, and a Pittsburgh factory, and made speeches in large cities. He ended his trip by visiting with the President at the Camp David retreat.

President Eisenhower went on a highly successful tour of Europe and Asia in 1959, concluding with a summit meeting in Paris with the leaders of Great Britain, France, and West Germany. They agreed to hold another summit in May of 1960 and to invite Premier Khrushchev. However, a few days before the 1960 meeting, the Soviet Union shot down an American spy plane that had secretly been taking photographs of Soviet military installations. At first the Eisenhower Administration said that the aircraft was a weather observation plane that had gotten off course. When the Russians displayed the U-2 plane and its captured pilot, Francis Gary Powers, the Administration reversed its stance and admitted the plane's spy mission. As the summit meeting began, Khrushchev angrily denounced the U.S. and then left. The summit meeting was canceled and Khrushchev canceled the invitation for Eisenhower to visit the Soviet Union.

Khrushchev Viewing Wreckage of the U-2 Plane

In the early fall of 1960, the United Nations observed its fifteenth anniversary. President Eisenhower made a conciliatory speech calling for continued efforts at disarmament and assistance to underdeveloped nations. Khrushchev, on the other hand, was confrontational in his remarks. As he listened to other speakers, the Soviet premier often interrupted and pounded the table with his fist and sometimes with his shoe.

Europe

Relations with the Soviets influenced other foreign policy engagements during the Eisenhower years. Khrushchev indicated that he might allow some degree of autonomy in Communist countries that were under Soviet influence. When a moderate Communist leader came to power in Poland, it appeared that this might be the case.

In 1956 a moderate Communist was chosen to lead Hungary. The new Hungarian leader indicated that Hungary might withdraw from the Warsaw Pact. In response, Soviet tanks rumbled into Hungary and crushed opposition freedom fighters. The Russians defended their actions by saying that they were called in by the legitimate Hungarian government to suppress internal rebellion. The moderate leader was replaced, taken to Moscow, and executed in 1958. One reason why Hungarians had attempted the move for greater freedom was statements made on American radio broadcasts into Hungary encouraging them to revolt against Russian domination. However, when Hungarians took the step, the United States did nothing to help them.

The Middle East

The Arab-Israeli conflict in the Middle East has always necessitated delicate moves when dealing with any country in the area. In 1956 Egyptian president Gamal Nasser wanted help in building a dam on the Nile River at Aswan for irrigation and for generating hydroelectric power. The United States, wanting to maintain good relations with Egypt, offered to make a loan for this purpose; but this offer displeased Israel. Egypt was officially not aligned with either the United States or the Soviet Union, and Nasser wanted to get all he could from both sides. Nasser then sought to increase trade with the Soviets; and the U.S. canceled its loan offer, as did Great Britain. In response, Nasser seized control of the Suez Canal, which was being operated by the French and British, and planned to use canal revenues to finance the dam.

Port Said, Egypt, on the Mediterranean Sea, is the northern entrance of the Suez Canal. The city was badly damaged during the 1956 conflict.

Israel, France, and Great Britain then attacked Egypt in what became known as the Suez War. In reaction, Egypt moved further toward friendly relations with the Soviets, which raised the specter of greater Soviet influence in the already troublesome Middle East. The Eisenhower Administration called for a cease-fire and for Egypt's attackers to withdraw. A United Nations resolution called for this also, which Britain, France, and Israel accepted.

In response to the Suez crisis, the U.S. announced in 1957 a policy known as the Eisenhower Doctrine. It said that the United States would help any country in the Middle East that was threatened by Communist aggression from within or from without. The doctrine was called into play the next year in Lebanon. Syria, which was known to be a friend of Nasser and the U.S.S.R., threatened to attack the pro-Western government of Lebanon. Eisenhower sent 5,000 American troops to the Beirut airport as a stabilizing presence. The crisis was averted and the American troops returned home.

Vietnam

Developments during the Eisenhower years slowly but surely led the United States into greater involvement in Southeast Asia. Communist leader Ho Chi Minh declared a new government in the northern part of Vietnam in 1945. The United States, which had wanted to limit Japanese influence in the region during World War II, welcomed the move. The next year, France recognized Ho's government as part of its colonial empire but tried to establish a separate regime in the south of the

Clockwise from top left, these photos show President Eisenhower with King Saud of Saudi Arabia and Vice President Nixon in Washington D.C. (1957), with South Vietnam's President Ngo Dinh Diem in Washington (1957), with Republic of China President Chiang Kai-shek and Madame Chiang in Taiwan (1960), and with King Zahir Shah in Bagram, Afghanistan (1959).

country. The United States supported France in this move. Ho, becoming more dependent on Soviet and Chinese Communist aid, wanted to take all of Vietnam. The government in the south that France supported, led by Ngo Dinh Diem, proved to be corrupt and tyrannical. Ho aided the Viet Cong, a group of Communist insurgents in the south who were attempting to overthrow the Diem regime. In May of 1954, at the Battle of Dien Bien Phu, Ho's army defeated a French force sent into the northern part of Vietnam.

A conference held in Geneva, Switzerland, in July of 1954, involving Russia, Communist China, France, Great Britain, and the governments of Indochina, agreed to partition Vietnam at the 17th parallel of latitude. North Vietnam was accepted as Communist; and South Vietnam, Laos, and Cambodia were recognized as non-Communist. The United States supported the non-Communist nations and helped to form the South East Asia Treaty Organization. SEATO was not as strong as NATO, since member nations were only committed to consult with one another in the event of an attack and since the largest nations in the region, India and Indonesia, did not participate. The U.S. had assisted France with weapons in its fight against the Communists and was now committed to resisting Communist aggression in Indochina.

Cuba

Late in his term, Eisenhower had to deal with trouble much closer to home. On January 1, 1959, rebels led by Fidel Castro ousted a corrupt dictator and seized power in Cuba. The United States gave cautious support to Castro at first; but then the new Cuban leader confiscated American and other foreign property in Cuba, savagely executed his opponents, and established close ties with the Soviet Union. Thousands of refugees fled from Cuba to south Florida. The United States instituted a trade embargo and eventually broke off diplomatic relations with Castro's government.

This tense arrangement continued for decades. President Barack Obama restored diplomatic relations with Cuba in 2015 and began to normalize economic relations between the two countries. Fidel Castro died in 2016.

The American Society of Newspaper Editors invited Fidel Castro to visit the United States in April of 1959. President Eisenhower refused to meet with him.

Keep the commandment without stain or reproach
until the appearing of our Lord Jesus Christ,
which He (God) will bring about at the proper time—
He who is the blessed and only Sovereign,
the King of kings and Lord of lords.
1 Timothy 6:14-15

⋆ Assignments for Lesson 123 ⋆

Bible Work on memorizing Romans 12:1-3.

Project Work on your project.

Student Review Optional: Answer the questions for Lesson 123.

Launch of Explorer 1 *on January 31, 1958*

Lesson 124

The Space Race Begins

America had long prided itself on being the most advanced nation in the world. It had the strongest economy and a well-established tradition of democratic freedoms. The United States benefited from advanced technology; a communication system that brought television, radio, and telephones into virtually every home; and the ability to provide the vast majority of homes with the latest consumer appliances and products. Americans believed that its education system, from grade school to graduate school, was the envy of the world. Its military had been the deciding factor in two world wars and its armed forces ringed the world in defense of freedom.

Dawn of the Space Age *by Gregory R. Todd, a representation of* Sputnik *in orbit commemorating the 50th anniversary of its launch (2007)*

Sputnik

It came as a shock to the American ego, therefore, that on October 4, 1957, the Soviet Union successfully launched the first artificial satellite into orbit around the world. It was called *Sputnik*, which in Russian was an acronym for traveler going with a traveler. The satellite was 22 inches around, weighed about 184 pounds, and circled the earth five hundred miles up at a speed of 18,000 miles per hour, completing an orbit every 90 minutes. It transmitted data back to earth by radio.

Political, military, and scientific leaders in the U.S. expressed deep concern about what Soviet leadership in space science and possibly other fields might mean for America and the world. At the time, the U.S. only had the capability to launch a rocket that could travel 500 miles. If Russia could put a satellite into space, it could conceivably put a nuclear weapon onto a rocket and hit the United States.

American embarrassment did not end with *Sputnik*. On November 3, the U.S.S.R. launched *Sputnik II*, which weighed over 1,100 pounds. It orbited as much as 1,000 miles above the earth, was loaded with scientific equipment, and carried a live dog as an experiment leading toward a manned space flight.

American Response

The American military, then in control of rocket and satellite development, went into high gear. Unfortunately, the effort encountered a series of failures as rockets exploded or failed to get off the ground. The American space program was carried out in full view of the world, whereas the Soviets kept their program secret. Americans did not know how many times the Russians failed attempting to launch satellites. On January 31, 1958, the *Explorer* satellite was finally launched from Cape Canaveral, Florida. It weighed only thirty pounds, but it restored a measure of American pride.

Then, however, embarrassment came to the U.S. again in September of 1959, when the Russians hit the moon with an unmanned craft named *Lunik*. In 1961 the Soviets became the first country to send a man into space.

The United States government decided to make space research and rocket and satellite development a top priority. It was not entirely clear what purposes earth orbit and space travel might serve, but the United States did not want to risk being left behind in this potentially important field. At the very least, the U.S. wanted to be on par with the Russians for whatever military uses might be found for rockets and satellites.

The National Aeronautics and Space Administration (NASA) was organized in 1958 to coordinate the American space program and remove it from military control. The 1957-58 Federal budget included the largest peacetime

At the beginning of the space race, the word "computer" was still used to refer to a person who performed mathematical calculations. NASA employed a staff of female computers to calculate satellite trajectories and other problems—by hand.

On August 3, 1958, the American nuclear-powered submarine USS Nautilus *became the first sub to travel under the North Pole. This accomplishment helped to rebuild American morale after the* Sputnik *debacle. The* Nautilus *commander, William Anderson, later retired to his home state of Tennessee and became a four-term Congressman. The submarine is open to visitors at the Submarine Force Library & Museum in Groton, Connecticut.*

military spending program in the nation's history. America developed new weapons to strengthen its conventional war capabilities. The U.S. developed both medium range missiles and long range, intercontinental ballistic missiles (ICBMs), capable of carrying conventional or nuclear warheads. Another significant development was the capability to fire a Polaris missile from a submarine at sea.

The missile race developed into one of the major issues in American-Soviet relations in addition to the space race. Most people recognized that each country was capable of sending multiple nuclear warheads by missiles into the other country. Each side wanted to develop not only first-strike capability but also the capacity to respond with total destruction of the attacking country. This would make first-strike capability less attractive. Throughout the 1960s and into the 1970s, both the U.S. and the Soviet Union built up huge arsenals of missiles with nuclear warheads. The United States placed many missiles in fortified underground silos so that they would remain operational even if the Soviets struck first.

This 1963 photograph shows (from left to right) Yuri Gagarin, first man in space; Pavel Popovich, another cosmonaut; Valentina Tereshkova, the first woman in space; and Soviet Premier Nikita Khrushchev.

ICBMs at the National Museum of the Air Force in Dayton, Ohio

Missile defense became a major military concern. The U.S. developed NORAD (North American Air Defense), a radar system that kept watch for incoming missiles over the North Pole, the likely route for any Soviet attack. In addition, research went into anti-missile missiles that could shoot down incoming missiles in the air.

Education Funding

Many Americans believed that the Soviets had achieved rocket and space superiority because the Soviet education system emphasized science and mathematics more than American schools had been doing. The U.S. had become complacent about its educational system. In 1958 Congress passed the National Defense Education Act, which provided almost $900 million for math, science, and foreign language instruction in public schools, college loans, and grants for graduate studies. This was the first significant Federal assistance to education since the Morrill Land Grant Act of 1862, and it opened the door for additional Federal funding of education in later years.

What Else Was Happening?

1952 The first issue of Mad *magazine is published.*

1953 Edmund Hillary and his assistant Tenzing Norgay (pictured at left) reach the summit of Mount Everest, the tallest mountain in the world.

1953 Cambridge University researchers James Watson and Frances Crick discover the structure of DNA, calling it a double helix.

1955 Jim Henson debuts his Kermit the Frog Muppet in a five-minute television program.

1955 Actor James Dean is killed in an automobile accident.

1956 Actress Grace Kelly marries Prince Rainier of Monaco. They are pictured at right visiting the White House in 1961.

1956 Television programs are first presented on tape rather than being broadcast live.

1956 The last confirmed Civil War veteran, Albert Woolson, dies at the age of 106. President Eisenhower says, "His passing brings sorrow to the hearts of all of us who cherished the memory of the brave men on both sides of the War Between the States."

1957 After the end of the baseball season, the Brooklyn Dodgers move to Los Angeles and the New York Giants move to San Francisco to become the first major league teams to be located on the West Coast. Dodger Stadium, built between 1959 and 1962, is one of the oldest professional sports facilities still in use.

Lesson 124 - The Space Race Begins

On November 7, 1957, President Eisenhower made a radio and television address to the nation about "Science in National Security." He displayed the nose cone of an experimental missile that had been sent into space and come back to earth. The President described technological advances that the U.S. military had made since World War II and outlined his plans for continued research and development. He concluded:

> *"What the world needs today even more than a giant leap into outer space, is a giant step toward peace. Time and again we have demonstrated our eagerness to take such a step. As a start in this direction, I urge the Soviets now to align themselves with the practical and workable disarmament proposals, approved yesterday by a large majority in the United Nations.*
>
> *"Never shall we cease to hope and work for the coming of the day when enduring peace will take these military burdens from the back of mankind, and when the scientist can give his full attention, not to human destruction, but to human happiness and fulfillment."*

Who has measured the waters in the hollow of His hand,
and marked off the heavens by the span,
and calculated the dust of the earth by the measure,
and weighed the mountains in a balance
and the hills in a pair of scales?
Isaiah 40:12

⋆ Assignments for Lesson 124 ⋆

American Voices	Read Dwight D. Eisenhower's Farewell Address (pages 333-336).
Bible	Work on memorizing Romans 12:1-3.
Project	Work on your project.
Student Review	Optional: Answer the questions for Lesson 124.

Eisenhower Family Birthday Party for Granddaughter Anne (1956)

Were They Really the Golden Days?

American Christians, often looking back at the 1950s with nostalgia, see the era as the good old days. Families were intact, moms stayed at home, decent programs were broadcast on television, good movies were produced, and church membership increased. All of these things were true. However, some of the goodness was only superficial. Beneath the gleaming exterior lay serious problems.

Thankful for the Good

Materially, the 1950s were good times for many Americans. The world war was past, the economy was booming, and jobs were plentiful. New homes were built at a record pace. Home construction is an important indicator of the strength of the economy because of the many factors involved in it, such as building materials, furniture and appliances, and labor. Some people who could remember the Depression had lingering fears about it happening again, but most Americans were confident that prosperity was here to stay.

Greensburg (Kentucky) Baptist Church, Built in 1956

Americans were moving. About 20% of the population moved every year—not a huge jump in the long-term national average but still significant. The warm weather climates of the South and Southwest (which together are often called the Sunbelt), helped by the development of air conditioning, saw huge growth. Many families moved to new suburban developments. Easy mortgage terms with the Federal Housing Authority and the Veterans' Administration allowed families to move into homes with five percent or less down payment. The thirty year mortgage made payments low. Meanwhile, the farm population continued to decrease.

Church membership was rising. Church affiliation rose from 55% of the adult population in 1950 to 69% in 1960. In a 1957 survey, 96% of those who responded gave a specific affiliation when asked what their religion was. Churches spent hundreds of millions of dollars on new construction projects each year, primarily for facilities in the suburbs where the population was exploding. In 1954 Congress added the phrase "under God" to the Pledge of Allegiance. Two years later, "In God We Trust" became the official national motto, a phrase that had been used on U.S. coins since the nineteenth century.

Motion picture epics with religious themes were popular. *The Robe* (1953) was based on a novel that described the transforming power of Christ's garment that a Roman soldier won while gambling at the foot of the cross. Charlton Heston established his reputation for Biblical epics by starring as Moses in *The Ten Commandments* (1956) and as the title character in *Ben-Hur* (1959), which was set during the time of Christ. A dramatized movie portrayal of the founding of modern Israel, *Exodus*, premiered in 1960 (based on an historical novel published in 1957).

In the majority of white American families (though by no means all), wives did not have employment outside of the home. They were busy maintaining the household and engaging in social, civic, and church activities. The baby boom added to the sense of bliss at home. Divorce was relatively rare in middle class families. Women who did work outside the home were often teachers and secretaries.

Those Were the Times . . .

It was the age of television. The U.S. had 7,000 sets in 1946. By 1960 that number had grown to fifty million, and ninety percent of homes had at least one. Almost all of these displayed only black and white pictures; color television became more common in the 1960s. *TV Guide* was the fastest growing new magazine of the decade. American families increasingly looked to television for news, cultural and educational offerings, and daily entertainment.

The time that had been spent reading books, visiting with neighbors, or engaging in conversation became devoted to sitting passively in front of the television. Even family meals were affected. In 1954 the frozen TV dinner was introduced, pre-packaged and ready to be warmed and eaten. A set of TV trays became a standard purchase for families that owned a television.

It was the age of the automobile. Production increased from two million per year in 1946 to eight million per year in 1955. Automobile registrations increased from 40 million in 1950 to 61 million in 1960, over a fifty percent increase. People could live in the suburbs and drive to work, to church, and to shop. Long distance vacations became more practical. The automobile changed many things about American life.

It was the age of advertising. America developed into a consumer culture for all the things that American industry was producing. Television became an important advertising medium. Television commercials told Americans what they needed to buy in order to have the good life. Buying became easier with credit cards and the greater accessibility of shopping outlets. The consumer culture was reflected by the much lower rate of personal savings than had previously been the norm. Why save when you could buy now on easy terms and have what you wanted in your home?

It was the age of the youth culture. Rock and roll music exploded onto the scene in the 1950s. American youth had more money and time available, and they used a good part of it buying and listening to records. Whites picked up what

1956 Chevrolet 150

had been known as rhythm and blues music, which was popular in the African American community. At first white artists recorded their own versions of what was called "race music" (a practice called covering a song). Soon white teenagers were buying the records of the original artists, and black singers such as Chuck Berry, Fats Domino, and Little Richard made the crossover to the white market. Home record players and inexpensive transistor radios made rock and roll music available almost everywhere. The cutting edge 1953 movie *Blackboard Jungle* portrayed the rebellious youth culture. Its sound track was made up of rock songs, such as "Rock Around the Clock" by Bill Haley and the Comets.

In 1954 a former truck driver from Tupelo, Mississippi, named Elvis Aaron Presley made his first record in Memphis, Tennessee. It wasn't long before Presley's blend of country and western music with rhythm and blues made him the first rock superstar. Adoring fans went wild at his concerts. When Presley was drafted into the Army (the draft was still in effect), American teens watched him closely. He was stationed in Germany, but the Army made sure that he stayed out of harm's way.

Trouble in Paradise

Things were not, however, as good as they appeared. The prosperity that America enjoyed led to widespread materialism, as people came to define who they were by what they owned, especially as they compared themselves to other people. As blacks moved from the South to northern cities, whites moved out of the cities to the suburbs (a process

Elvis Presley appeared on The Ed Sullivan Show *in 1956, which increased his national popularity. Presley is shown below left in a promotional shot for his 1957 movie* Jailhouse Rock. *The photo below right shows teenage girls writing on a movie poster of Presley. In addition to his rock and roll music, Elvis Presley recorded three albums of gospel songs. His backup singers for many of his rock hits were the Jordanaires, who were gospel singers.*

called white flight). These changes maintained racial segregation in living patterns. Blacks were routinely discriminated against in new residential developments. Regulations in many of the new suburbs forbade home ownership by anyone who wasn't Caucasian. Resistance to court-ordered school desegregation was widespread around the country. Urban areas came to account for two-thirds of American population, but people knew their neighbors less and less. Americans were becoming, as one book called them, the lonely crowd.

The increase in church membership was not the same as an increase in discipleship. Church membership was often something people did to blend in with others in society. Suburban churches heard fewer sermons about sin and judgment and more about positive attitudes and comfortable Christianity. Some of the most rabid segregationists were staunch churchgoers who believed that they were defending the Christian way of life.

The rise of television made it easy for people to turn their minds off and be entertained. Countless episodes of situation comedies were based on some deception that a husband, wife, or child tried to put over on the rest of the family. What makes for popular television is not necessarily what is right, best, and upbuilding. In 1957 a scandal rocked television when it was revealed that a popular quiz show had been rigged to make it appear more dramatic. Contestants had been given answers and had been instructed to look nervous and be slow in answering. Others were told to miss questions on purpose. It was also revealed that some popular radio disc jockeys (DJs) were being paid by record companies to promote certain songs and to play them more often.

The teenage rock culture developed into a subculture of its own, consciously separate from (and in many ways rebelling against) the standards of the adult generation. Actors James Dean and Marlon Brando portrayed angry young men determined to rebel against the authorities and the older generation. Beat generation writers Jack Kerouac and Allen Ginsberg openly flouted social standards. Novelists John Updike and J. D. Salinger described alienated and disaffected youth and young adults. Meanwhile, busy parents didn't spend enough time teaching God's way to their children or modeling the Christ-like life, but instead these parents pursued more possessions.

Watching Television (c. 1958)

Conclusion

The problems that existed during the 1950s were real. Materialism was growing. Racial prejudice was commonplace. The desire for social conformity influenced decision-making. Many in the younger generation did not have a clear purpose and direction for their lives. A significant number of Americans believed that no one should impose standards of right and wrong on others and that if you could get away with something, that made it acceptable.

On the other hand, family values pervaded society much more than in recent decades. These values were honored in public, in the media, and in schools. Many Americans still wanted to honor God with their lives. Like any period in American history, the 1950s were a mixture of good and bad.

Watching the St. Patrick's Day Parade in New York City (1953)

Do not say, "Why is it that the former days were better than these?" For it is not from wisdom that you ask about this.
Ecclesiastes 7:10

⋆ Assignments for Lesson 125 ⋆

Bible Recite or write Romans 12:1-3 from memory.

Project Complete your project for the unit.

Student Review Optional: Answer the questions for Lesson 125, take the quiz for Unit 25, and take the fifth history exam, English exam, and Bible exam.

Civil Rights Leaders Meet With President Kennedy After the 1963 March on Washington

26 The Turbulent Sixties

The election of John F. Kennedy as President brought a new generation to political leadership. His assassination began a period of disillusionment for the nation. Lyndon Johnson led a great expansion of Federal programs while the Vietnam War overshadowed his presidency and eventually ended it. The civil rights issue took center stage on the domestic front, and 1968 in particular was a year of enormous upheaval. While thinking about the development of the social counterculture, we should remember the One who brought the real counterculture to the ways of the world, Jesus.

Memory Work Memorize Luke 4:16-19 by the end of this unit.

Books Used The Bible
American Voices

Project (choose one)

1) Write 300 to 500 words on one of the following topics:

   - Discuss the impact of the Supreme Court's decisions on prayer and Bible reading in public schools. Discuss the role of religion in the public arena and what constitutes a "law respecting an establishment of religion." See Lesson 127.

   - How do you think Jesus was a countercultural leader? Explain how Jesus challenged the religious and societal structures of His day and how He challenges those same structures today. See Lesson 130.

2) Create a book, using quotations from Martin Luther King's "I Have a Dream" speech as the text and your own drawings, paintings, photographs, or a combination thereof as the illustrations. Create your book intentionally and artistically, and make it inspirational for the continuation of the ideals that King expressed. Your book should be at least fifteen pages in length.

3) Create a portfolio of at least ten protest signs addressing issues that Americans dealt with in the 1960s. Your signs can be the size of a regular piece of paper. The photos on pages 744 and 772 show real protest signs from this era. Research some other examples from the era. Make your signs in the same style. Be thoughtful and original in the messages you place on your signs.

President Kennedy Speaking at American University (1963)

Lesson 126

The New Frontier

The decade of the 1960s seemed to bring more changes than ten years could or should. The period began on a high note of hope and ended amid tragedy and confusion. It was a time of profound upheaval in American society when this country suffered many great losses and when even the victories came at great cost.

The 1960 Election

1960 brought a new generation of leaders. Harry Truman had fought in World War I, and Dwight Eisenhower had been a general in World War II. The two major party candidates in 1960, by contrast, had both been young officers during World War II. They were 23 and 27 years younger than Eisenhower, young enough to be Ike's sons.

Richard Nixon grew up in a relatively poor Quaker family in Whittier, California. He made a name for himself by sheer strength of will, graduating third in his class from the prestigious Duke University Law School. He served in World War II and then was elected to Congress as a Republican from his home district in California, unseating an incumbent from his own party. Nixon took hold of the domestic Communist issue and rode it to a Senate seat in 1950. He was a rising star in the Republican Party and was tapped to be Eisenhower's running mate in 1952. Nixon was a highly visible Vice President, making several overseas trips to represent the administration. As Vice President, he was heir apparent to the general's mantle as leader of the GOP; he faced no serious opposition for the Republican nomination. Veteran politician and statesman Henry Cabot Lodge of Massachusetts was the vice presidential nominee. Lodge had lost his Senate seat in 1952 to a young Congressman named John Fitzgerald Kennedy.

Kennedy was born into a wealthy Boston family and attended Harvard University. While he was in World War II, he displayed great heroism by rescuing several crew members when a Japanese vessel rammed the PT-109 torpedo boat of which he was skipper. In the accident, Kennedy sustained a serious back injury which caused him considerable pain for the rest of his life. Like Nixon, Kennedy was elected to the House of Representatives in 1946; he won a Senate seat in 1952. Kennedy received the Pulitzer Prize for *Profiles in Courage* (1956), a collection of biographical sketches of Senators throughout American history who faced difficult decisions and put principle ahead of politics.

Kennedy had attempted to win the Democratic vice presidential nomination in 1956. In 1960 his two main rivals for the Democratic presidential nomination were Minnesota Senator Hubert

John Kennedy Visits With Eleanor Roosevelt Before the 1960 Election

Humphrey and Texas Senator and Senate Majority Leader Lyndon Johnson. Kennedy received the nomination, and he surprised many by asking Johnson to be his running mate. Johnson surprised many more by accepting. The two men were of different personal and political philosophies. The decision was intended to help the Democratic ticket win in the South. Kennedy was the first Roman Catholic to be a major party nominee since Al Smith in 1928. He had to deal with some of the same suspicions that Smith had faced, but his assurances that the Pope would not be running America appeared to satisfy most voters.

As the campaign began, Nixon had the advantage because of his much greater national name recognition and the positive feelings that most of the country had toward Eisenhower. The two candidates did not have markedly different campaign positions. Kennedy came across as moderately liberal and Nixon as moderately conservative. The difference in the race might well have been the first-ever televised presidential debates. Nixon agreed to the debates, even though as front-runner he had the most to lose. In the first debate, Nixon was recovering from an illness and rejected make-up that might have hidden his tired and somewhat stern features. Kennedy, on the other hand, was well-rested and appeared much more youthful and vigorous. Apparently appearance made the difference. Most of those who watched the first debate on television believed that Kennedy had

won, while most of those who listened to it on radio believed that Nixon had won.

The election outcome was one of the closest in American history. Kennedy had a margin of less than 120,000 votes out of 68 million cast, although the electoral count was a clear 303 to 219 victory for the Democrat. One big factor in the outcome was the Democratic majority in Chicago delivered by mayor and political boss Richard J. Daley that helped Kennedy win the state. It was widely believed that Daley's machine rigged the outcome in Kennedy's favor. Nixon probably had legitimate grounds to challenge the Illinois returns, but he decided not to do so. Almost 63% of eligible voters turned out, a percentage not since equaled in presidential elections.

The New Frontier

Kennedy's inauguration on a cold January 20, 1961, excited many in the country. At 43 he was the youngest man ever to be elected President. He and his attractive wife seemed to capture the hearts of the nation. Kennedy's inauguration address was eloquent, bold, and forward looking. He declared that the torch of leadership had passed to a new generation, and he challenged his listeners, "Ask not what your country can do for you; ask what you can do for your country."

President Kennedy with His Wife Jackie and Their Children Caroline and John Jr. (1961)

The new President surrounded himself with bright young intellectuals as aides, advisors, and Cabinet members. Just as Eisenhower had done, Kennedy selected an automobile executive as his Secretary of Defense: Robert McNamara, who had recently been named president of Ford Motor Company. This move (as well as Eisenhower's) suggested the important role that car manufacturers played in American society and in the economy. Kennedy named his younger brother, Robert, as Attorney General.

Kennedy called his vision and program the New Frontier. Despite the optimistic beginning, Kennedy had a hard time getting much legislation through Congress, even though Democrats held the majority in both houses. Influential southern Democrats felt no need to respond to Kennedy's proposals. Some laws were passed, however. A program of urban renewal put millions of Federal dollars into rebuilding the nation's inner cities. Kennedy implemented an expanded foreign aid package, the intention of which was to help and influence other countries. Another major initiative was the Peace Corps, which trained and sent out thousands of teachers, agricultural workers, and others to third world countries to help people there improve their standard of living. Congress also cut tariffs on foreign imports. However, Congress rejected Kennedy's ideas for medical care for the elderly, Federal aid to education, and tax cuts to stimulate the economy (the cuts finally passed in 1964).

The Bay of Pigs

The greatest foreign challenge Kennedy faced was in his relations with Russia, especially with regard to Cuba. When Kennedy took office, he learned of a secret plan already underway in the U.S. to train 1,500 anti-Castro Cuban immigrants, who hoped to invade the island and remove Fidel Castro from power. Kennedy endorsed the plan with reservations, but he wanted direct U.S. involvement to be as small as possible.

Khrushchev and Kennedy Meet in Austria (1961)

The Cuban freedom fighters landed at the Bay of Pigs in Cuba on April 17, 1961, and were quickly defeated by Castro's forces. One crucial factor was the lack of air cover by American planes that could have made the difference. Kennedy took personal responsibility for the failed invasion attempt. The incident further chilled American-Cuban and American-Soviet relations.

Kennedy met Khrushchev later that year while touring Europe, and the young President was put off balance by the aggressive Soviet leader. A short time later, the Russians erected the Berlin Wall to divide the eastern, Communist sector from the free, western part of the city. The wall became a symbol of tense East-West relations and of the fact that the Communists had to hold people under their rule by force. East German guards killed many people as they tried to climb over the wall. Kennedy visited West Berlin in 1963, and in sight of the wall declared solidarity with the people of the city who wanted freedom. "Ich bin ein Berliner," Kennedy declared ("I am a Berliner").

The Cuban Missile Crisis

In 1962 Cuban leader Fidel Castro asked the Soviet Union to install nuclear missiles in Cuba that could strike targets in the United States. Castro did this to have a way to respond to any future American invasion of Cuba. It also served Soviet purposes because it was a reply to American missiles based in Turkey that could hit the Soviet Union.

Members of the group Women Strike for Peace held these signs near the United Nations building in 1962.

American high altitude photography over Cuba revealed that missile sites were being built. The Kennedy Administration decided to set up a naval blockade around Cuba to stop any Soviet ships from bringing missiles or related materials to Cuba. Khrushchev threatened not to stand for the blockade, but the U.S. Navy did turn back some ships headed for Cuba.

It was a tense showdown between the United States and the Soviet Union. The U.S. demanded and the Soviet Union refused. The U.S. warned the Russians, and the Russians threatened to retaliate. Both countries believed that their prestige and national security were on the line. Finally, an agreement was reached. The Soviet Union agreed to remove missiles from Cuba, and the U.S. agreed not to invade Cuba. As one American official put it, "We stood eyeball to eyeball, and they blinked." America stopped the immediate threat by giving up the long-term possibility of another invasion. The United States also removed some older missiles from Turkey and Europe.

The U.S. and U.S.S.R. agreed to a nuclear test ban treaty in 1963, which forbade any further testing of atomic weapons in the atmosphere. Underground testing was still allowed, and no provision was made for on-site inspection in either country by the other. A direct telephone line, the "hot line," was installed between Washington and Moscow, to improve communication and to lessen the risk of misunderstanding in the future.

Friday, November 22, 1963

Many Americans remember exactly what they were doing when they first heard what happened on this date. President Kennedy was preparing for his 1964 re-election campaign, and he was in Texas to win greater support among Democrats in the state. The President made a morning appearance at one gathering and then traveled in a motorcade, riding in an open-top limousine, to a luncheon gathering where he was scheduled to give a speech.

Three Kennedy brothers were photographed at the White House in August of 1963. Robert is on the left; John is on the right. In the center is Edward (Ted), who was elected to the United States Senate from Massachusetts in 1962 to fill John's unexpired term. He continued to hold that Senate seat until his death in 2009.

The Kennedys Arrive in Dallas, Texas

As the motorcade passed through Dealy Plaza in downtown Dallas, shots rang out from the sixth floor of the Texas School Book Depository building. Kennedy was struck twice in the head and neck. The President slumped onto his wife. As people began realizing what had happened, the motorcade picked up speed to get to a hospital. Mrs. Kennedy climbed onto the trunk of the limousine to help a Secret Service agent get into the car. The President was declared dead soon after reaching the hospital.

That afternoon, police arrested Lee Harvey Oswald in a Dallas movie theater. Oswald was a loner and former Marine sharpshooter who had spent time in the Soviet Union, married a Russian woman, had demonstrated on behalf of a Fair Play for Cuba committee, and worked at the School Book Depository. Also that afternoon, on the presidential plane preparing to take Kennedy's body back to Washington, Lyndon Johnson was sworn in as the new President. His wife as well as Mrs. Kennedy, still wearing the blood-stained suit she had been wearing in the motorcade, were at his side.

On the following Sunday, as Americans watched on television Kennedy's body being taken to lie in state at the Capitol in Washington, coverage switched to Dallas, where Oswald was being transferred to another jail. As the suspect was led through a crowd of reporters and onlookers, Dallas nightclub owner Jack Ruby stepped out and shot Oswald at point-blank range. Oswald died soon after.

Oswald's guilt or innocence was never established in court. In December President Johnson named a commission headed by Chief Justice Earl Warren to find out all it could. In its report issued several months later, the Warren Commission declared that Oswald had acted alone. This did not satisfy many Americans, and conspiracy theories abounded. Some people said that they had heard shots from other places in Dealy Plaza, while others believed the CIA, Fidel Castro, or other forces were behind the assassination. Many people are attracted to conspiracy theories and want to believe that the real truth is more complicated than what is known on the surface. The discussion surrounding Kennedy's assassination continues today, but the issue is not as hot as it has been at times in the past. Sufficient credible evidence has never been uncovered to prove that a conspiracy existed.

Mrs. Kennedy and Her Children Leave President Kennedy's Funeral Service at the U.S. Capitol (1963)

The New Frontier had begun as a new day for America. Not everyone in the country approved of Kennedy's political agenda; but his youthfulness, intelligence, and wit had won the hearts of many Americans. Kennedy was frequently unfaithful to his wife, and he was not above using base political tactics to get what he wanted. Regardless of how they felt about him personally or politically, however, Americans did not want to see the President, father of two small children, struck down in his mid-40s by an assassin's bullet.

A wave of disillusionment swept over much of the younger generation of America. If this is what happens to positive, idealistic leaders, they thought, why bother? Kennedy's death was not the last political assassination that took place in the 1960s. At times the violence, both in America and overseas, seemed out of control. The country recovered, however, just as it has from all previous presidential assassinations, because America is built on something larger and more permanent than the life and ideas of one man.

As for the deeds of men, by the word of Your lips
I have kept from the paths of the violent.
Psalm 17:4

⋆ Assignments for Lesson 126 ⋆

American Voices Read John F. Kennedy's Inaugural Address (pages 337-339).

Bible One feature of American society during the 1960s was the growth of what was called the counterculture: people who chose to live counter to the prevailing ways of their culture. Most of this movement involved a rejection of traditional values and practices. The teachings of Jesus ran counter to much of the culture and traditions of His day; but He called people to a better way of life, one that was in keeping with God's will. Read Matthew 5:21-42. List three examples in this passage in which Jesus challenged how things were done and called people to a higher standard.

Start memorizing Luke 4:16-19.

Project Choose your project for this unit and start working on it.

Student Review Optional: Answer the questions for Lesson 126.

Lyndon Johnson Taking the Presidential Oath of Office, November 22, 1963

Lesson 127

The Great Society

Lyndon Baines Johnson was a Texas political operator from way back. He was elected to Congress in 1937 but was defeated in a U.S. Senate race in 1941. Johnson finally won a Senate seat in 1948 by eighty-seven votes, in an election where allegations of vote fraud abounded. He became Senate majority leader in 1955; he ran for the Democratic presidential nomination in 1960. Johnson accepted the second spot on the Democratic ticket that year, but he hated being Vice President and still had his sights on becoming the chief executive.

Johnson was a New Deal liberal in the populist tradition. As a skilled and experienced politician, President Johnson put pressure on Congress to support his legislative program, which at first was mostly Kennedy's program. In 1964 Congress passed significant tax cuts, the Economic Opportunity Act to retrain jobless workers, a package of aid to higher education, and a sweeping civil rights measure.

Johnson called his agenda the Great Society. He believed that the Federal government should guide American life and create opportunities for all Americans. Congress passed literally hundreds of measures during Johnson's tenure in the White House, many of them after he and the Democrats won a huge landslide victory in 1964.

Civil Rights Act

The 1964 Civil Rights Act was the most comprehensive Federal guarantee of individual rights in the nation's history. It outlawed racial discrimination (as well as discrimination on the basis of religion, sex, and nationality) in housing, public accommodations (such as hotels, restaurants, and unions), and hiring practices. States that continued to practice segregation would lose Federal funding for schools, hospitals, and other programs. The law stated that anyone with a sixth-grade education was presumed literate and could not be denied the right to vote by failing a state-imposed literacy test. The Federal government was given the power to initiate school desegregation suits, which quickened the pace of school integration in the South. Congress passed a Voting Rights Act the following year, which gave Federal officials the right to register voters in counties where less than fifty percent of eligible voters participated in elections.

War on Poverty

As part of his Great Society agenda, Johnson declared war on poverty; and Congress responded by spending billions of dollars on new Federal programs.

The Job Corps helped the unemployed get training and jobs. Head Start provided daycare for children from poor families. VISTA (Volunteers In Service To America) was presented as a domestic Peace Corps. The Medicare program involved the Federal government in health care for the elderly, while Medicaid provided health care for low-income Americans. Congress also approved increased funding for education, projects to help the Appalachian region, and housing and urban development. The Department of Housing and Urban Development was added to the Cabinet in 1965.

The downside of the numerous Great Society programs was that, with so much money available, mismanagement and fraud were commonplace. At first, for instance, Medicare provided no incentives to hold down prices. Whatever a doctor, hospital, or laboratory billed was pretty much what was paid. As a result, medical costs skyrocketed. Stricter rules have since been put in place, but the major increase in medical costs since Medicare began can be traced in large part to the government getting involved in it. Reports of welfare fraud also abounded. A new bureaucracy sprang up to administer the Great Society programs, and that bureaucracy was not always efficient.

Congress also passed a new immigration law in 1965, something that President Kennedy had wanted. The new regulations set a limit from each hemisphere and a maximum of 20,000 newcomers from any one country. Immediate family members of those already living in the U.S. were not subject to quota limits. The effect of the law was that many persons from Hispanic and Asian countries were admitted to the U.S. This changed the immigration picture from earlier in the century when newcomers from Eastern Europe predominated.

Politicians who oppose different kinds of programs use similar arguments to attack their opposition and defend themselves. For instance, a long-standing complaint by liberals about military spending is that a great deal of money is wasted on bureaucracy, fraud, and unnecessary programs. Conservatives say that this is not good, but it is the price we have to pay for military preparedness. Conservatives, meanwhile, decry the fraud and waste in social programs; while liberals say that such is not good but it is the price we have to pay for providing help to those in need. Both sides rationalize money spent on what they support and criticize money spent on what they oppose.

The Personality of the President

Johnson brought a different personality and approach to the White House than had been present with Kennedy. Instead of playing touch football and keeping company with upper class Bostonians, Johnson reveled in barbecues on his Texas ranch. Johnson was homey and plain in his speech and interests. After an appendicitis operation, Johnson pulled up his shirt to show reporters his scar. On another occasion (see right), Johnson playfully pulled the ears of his hound before reporters. Despite the dog's howls (and the howls of animal cruelty opponents), Johnson insisted that the dog was not hurt. One could not imagine the Kennedy clan engaging in such activities. Johnson always felt a degree of personal inferiority with regard to the Kennedys, as though he was standing as President in their disapproving shadow.

The 1964 Election

The Democrats faced no question about who would be their presidential nominee in 1964. For Johnson personally, this was his chance to become President on his own, not as the result of any accident or tragedy. He chose liberal Minnesota Senator Hubert H. Humphrey to be his vice presidential running mate. Johnson ran on the promises to continue the Democratic agenda begun by Kennedy and to keep American boys out of any land war in Asia, referring to Vietnam.

The Republicans, however, were a different story. Conservative Republicans believed that the party had for too long been under the sway of what it called the liberal Eastern Establishment. Eisenhower, Dewey, and many other leaders in the party were not conservative enough for them. They believed that the party leadership had accepted the trend of increased government spending and control begun with the New Deal, and that a position of "me too, just not as much" was a weak campaign stance that denied voters a choice.

Arizona Senator Barry Goldwater was the leading spokesman for the conservative wing of the party. His supporters captured the party organization and enabled Goldwater to receive the nomination. The Arizona Republican had a tendency to speak his mind forthrightly and thus unsettle voters, at least in the way that his remarks were communicated by the media. In his acceptance speech at the Republican convention, Goldwater said, "I would remind you that extremism in the defense of liberty is no vice. And let me remind you also that moderation in the pursuit of justice is no virtue." Goldwater criticized the no-win policy being followed in Vietnam and urged all-out bombing and a commitment to total victory over North Vietnam and the Viet Cong. He sharply criticized Johnson's Great Society programs as wrong and wasteful. Goldwater campaign slogans told voters, "In your heart, you know he's right," and that Goldwater offered "A choice—not an echo."

Democrats were all too happy to portray Barry Goldwater, pictured above, as trigger-happy. One controversial Democratic television ad showed a little girl counting flower petals, and this scene segued to the countdown of a nuclear blast. The suggestion was that Goldwater would risk nuclear war at the expense of our children. The ad ran only once, but the publicity about it was enormous.

Many southern Democrats rejected Johnson's liberalism and his progressive stance on civil rights. He received little help from state Democratic Party organizations in the South, and in Alabama he was not even listed on the ballot (the Democratic Party simply listed unpledged electors). In the end, however, Goldwater came across as too conservative for the majority of Americans; and Johnson was seen as carrying on the slain President's cause. Johnson won in the biggest popular landslide to that date, with 61.1% of the vote (43.1 million) compared to 38.5% and 27.1 million for Goldwater. The electoral college went for Johnson 486 to 52. Goldwater only carried Arizona and five states in the Deep South. In addition, the Democrats won better than 2-to-1 majorities in both houses of Congress, which enabled Johnson's Great Society programs to move through Congress with little opposition.

Shirley Chisholm of New York was a co-founder of the National Organization for Women and the first African American woman elected to Congress.

Social and Political Activists

Many special interest groups came into existence during the 1960s. Some Native Americans sought greater rights and respect through the American Indian Movement (AIM). The National Organization for Women (NOW) was formed in 1966 to promote such causes as equal pay for women in the workplace, increased availability of child care, and greater access to abortion services. Cesar Chavez organized the United Farm Workers, many of whom were Hispanic, in order to give them greater power in negotiating work agreements with growers. The Gay Liberation Front was organized in 1969 to influence society on behalf of homosexual rights.

Constitutional Amendments

The U.S. Constitution was amended three times during the 1960s. In 1961 the 23rd Amendment gave the District of Columbia three electoral votes in presidential elections. Prior to this, residents of the District had not been able to vote for President. Three years later, the 24th Amendment outlawed the poll tax for Federal elections (and thus in practical terms for all elections). Some southern states had continued to require payment of a poll tax, but its removal by constitutional amendment took away one more tool that whites had used to keep blacks from voting.

In 1967 the 25th Amendment became part of the Constitution. Congress passed this amendment in response to the death of President Kennedy. It made clear that the Vice President becomes President when the presidency becomes vacant. A vacancy in the office of Vice President is to be filled by a presidential appointment to be confirmed by a

In 1967 Katherine Switzer was the first woman to run as a numbered entry in the all-male Boston Marathon. She finished despite the attempts of officials to keep her out. In 1972 women were officially allowed to compete in the race. Switzer's autobiography Marathon Woman *was released in 2007.*

majority of both houses of Congress. This procedure was used in 1973 when Spiro Agnew resigned as Vice President and Richard Nixon appointed Gerald Ford to the office, and again the next year when Nixon resigned as President and his successor, President Ford, named Nelson Rockefeller to serve out the remainder of the term as Vice President.

Supreme Court Decisions

The Supreme Court handed down several landmark decisions in the 1960s that continue to have an impact today.

Reapportionment for Elections. Several states had not redrawn their electoral districts to reflect population changes for many years. This resulted in a lack of political power for the growing urban areas and relatively greater power being held by rural areas. Tennessee, for example, had not reapportioned its legislature since 1901. The courts had stayed away from ruling on reapportionment cases because they did not believe they had jurisdiction in political questions.

However, the U.S. Supreme Court said that the political process had not resolved the issue and had not provided equal protection for all Americans. *Baker v. Carr* (1962) was a suit charging malapportionment in Tennessee's legislative districts. The Court said that states were answerable to the courts in providing equitable reapportionment every ten years following the U.S. census. The Supreme Court's verdict in *Reynolds v. Sims* (1964) said that both houses of a state legislature had to be based on population. The upper house could not, for instance, be composed of one member from each county. States could not extend the pattern of Congress to their legislatures.

Today the party in power in each state when legislative and congressional districts are redrawn generally tries to adjust the lines to favor their own party, and the other party routinely files suit to challenge some part of the reapportionment; but at least population changes must now be taken into account every ten years.

The shooting of an African American teenager by a policeman in New York City on July 16, 1964, prompted several days of rioting. Here armed police officers are seeking to maintain order.

Rights of the Accused. The Court rendered several verdicts that affected the way police and prosecutors conduct criminal investigations and interrogations. *Mapp v. Ohio* (1961) said that evidence taken without a search warrant could not be used in state courts. Such a ban had already been in place in Federal courts. *Gideon v. Wainwright* (1963) declared that an accused person has the right to an attorney. Other decisions elaborated on this right. *Escobedo v. Illinois* (1964) said that an accused person could not be denied the presence of an attorney during police questioning and that suspects had to be informed of their constitutional rights. This was confirmed and made more specific in *Miranda v. Arizona* (1966).

After the *Miranda* ruling, arresting officers had to read a suspect his "Miranda rights": a suspect has the right to remain silent; anything the accused says can and will be used against him or her in a court of law; the suspect has the right to the presence of an attorney; and if the suspect cannot afford an attorney, one will be appointed by a court at no charge. This created the position of public defender, an attorney paid by the state to represent indigent suspects during questioning and in court.

A public outcry arose as a result of these decisions, to the effect that the Supreme Court was coddling criminals. The Court was attempting to protect the accused against the power of the state. It is hard to know how many forced confessions have convicted innocent people, but it is also impossible to know how many guilty persons have been let go because of a legal technicality unrelated to the person's guilt or innocence. The overall result of these rulings is that it is now somewhat more difficult to get a conviction, but convictions are now more fairly obtained.

School Prayer and Bible Reading. The New York State Board of Regents, which oversees public education in the state, adopted the following prayer:

> Almighty God, we acknowledge our dependence upon Thee, and we beg Thy blessings upon us, our parents, our teachers and our country.

The Board required the prayer to be said aloud by each public school class in the presence of the teacher at the beginning of each school day. The Board was sued on the grounds that the prayer violated the First Amendment prohibition against the establishment of religion. In *Engle v. Vitale* (1962), the Court ruled that the required prayer did violate the First Amendment. The Court's opinion outlined American colonial history, noted how settlers came to America to escape the established religion of England, and said that the First Amendment was written to guard against such practices as government-sponsored mandatory prayer. The Court said that, "A union of government and religion tends to destroy government and to degrade religion."

Children Entering a School in Farmville, Virginia (1963)

The following year, the Court in *Abington Township v. Schempp* ruled that required Bible reading in public school classrooms was also a violation of the establishment clause of the First Amendment. These two decisions created another uproar among many Americans who believed that the First Amendment was never intended to outlaw reference to God in the public forum but was instead designed to prevent one particular church or faith from being the official religion of the country. The Court interpreted the First Amendment narrowly and said that any official religious activity that was required in a public school was tantamount to the establishment of a religion.

This teacher poses with recent Chinese immigrants who are entering a school in Manhattan. The signs show their Chinese names and their American names (1964).

Observers have noted that after these changes took place, the nation's morality took a downward spiral. The cause of this spiral is probably more complicated than simply two Supreme Court decisions (probably a larger cause is the lack of Bible reading, prayer, and sincere Christian practice in American homes); but the problems in American morality and the lack of recognition of religion in the public arena are no doubt related.

How blessed are the people whose God is the Lord!
Psalm 144:15

★ Assignments for Lesson 127 ★

American Voices Read "Our God, He Is Alive" by A. W. Dicus (page 354).

Bible Read Luke 6:1-11. List the two incidents in this passage in which Jesus challenged traditional religious practices of His day.

Work on memorizing Luke 4:16-19.

Project Work on your project.

Student Review Optional: Answer the questions for Lesson 127.

James Meredith Walking to Class at Ole Miss, Accompanied by U.S. Marshals (1962)

Lesson 128

Civil Rights and Vietnam

In 1960 four black college students sat down at a white-only lunch counter in Greensboro, North Carolina, and asked to be served. They were not served, but soon similar "sit-ins" occurred in dozens of cities across the South. The usual practice was that, if blacks were arrested at a lunch counter, other blacks entered the store, sat at the lunch counters to take their place, and were arrested. Blacks also entered segregated public swimming pools ("wade-ins") and other facilities, hoping to change segregation laws by defying them. Blacks also engaged in peaceful protest marches to call attention to discriminatory laws. Whites often responded with anger. Demonstrators were frequently sprayed with powerful fire hoses and abused by local police. Many whites became more firmly resolved not to give in to blacks' demands, and sometimes they accused blacks of being Communist agitators.

In the fall of 1962, a court ordered the all-white University of Mississippi to allow African American James Meredith to enroll as a student. Governor Ross Barnett refused to let it happen. When Federal marshals went to Oxford to enforce the court order, an angry white mob prevented them from doing so. Attorney General Robert Kennedy dispatched Army troops to the scene, and for several days they camped out on university grounds. Two people were killed in random shootings during the incident and several others were wounded. Meredith was finally able to enroll and eventually graduated from Ole Miss.

Unrest continued the next year. Martin Luther King Jr., now a minister in Atlanta, led demonstrations in Birmingham, Alabama, against segregation and police brutality. Birmingham police Commissioner Eugene "Bull" Connor used attack dogs, tear gas, cattle prods, and fire hoses on the demonstrators; the nation watched it all on the evening news. King was jailed, and from there he released his "Letter from a Birmingham Jail," which stated his reasoning and his purposes for the non-violent resistance he encouraged. FBI director J. Edgar Hoover saw King as a genuine threat to American justice. He ordered wiretaps on King's telephones and encouraged the rumors that King was under Communist influence.

In the late summer of 1963, Alabama governor George Wallace literally stood in the doorway of a building at the University of Alabama when black students approached to enroll. The event was broadcast live on national television. Wallace backed down, however, when Federal marshals insisted that he let the students enter.

On August 28, 1963, about 250,000 people, roughly two-thirds black and one-third white, gathered on the Capitol Mall in Washington for a huge peaceful demonstration for civil rights.

Martin Luther King Jr. electrified the crowd with his memorable "I Have a Dream" speech, delivered from the steps of the Lincoln Memorial. It was the high point of the civil rights movement to that time.

Sadly, the low point occurred two weeks later. A bomb exploded at a Birmingham church on a Sunday morning, killing four young girls who had arrived early. Witnesses were reluctant to give testimony, and no one was charged with the crimes at the time. Evidence collected by the FBI led to later convictions. One man was convicted in 1977, another in 2001, and a third in 2002. All were sentenced to life in prison.

President Kennedy had been slow to act vigorously on the civil rights issue because he feared alienating white southern Democrats. However, he was moved to take a stronger position for equality for African Americans by what he saw happening. Kennedy proposed sweeping new Federal laws protecting the civil rights of all Americans.

Robert C. Henry (pictured below) was the first African American elected as a city mayor in the United States—Springfield, Ohio, in 1966. The next year Carl Stokes in Cleveland, Ohio, and Richard Hatcher in Gary, Indiana, were also elected as mayors.

This aerial view of the March on Washington shows the shadow of the Washington Monument (1963).

Black Violence

Martin Luther King Jr. and the strategy of nonviolent resistance was having an effect on the conscience of the nation. (King was awarded the Nobel Peace Prize in 1964.) A liberal President and a Democratic Congress worked together to fashion landmark civil rights and voting rights legislation in 1964 and 1965. Then in August of 1965, terrible rioting, destruction, and looting by blacks erupted in the black Watts section of Los Angeles. The next summer, violence spread to over forty cities, mostly in the North. More rioting followed in the summer of 1967.

Just as African Americans appeared to be making greater progress than they had in generations, northern urban black communities appeared to be coming apart at the seams. Most black Americans were non-violent, and King rejected the use of violence; but a segment of the black population began to rise up in revolt not so much at discriminatory laws but at what they saw as a discriminatory society.

Young black leaders such as Stokely Carmichael and H. Rap Brown began to talk of racial separation, not integration; of exercising black power to reshape American society; and of the willingness to use violence against whites, white society, and even blacks who did not agree with them. To the radical blacks, even liberal advocates of civil rights such as President Johnson and Vice President Humphrey were seen as part of the problem. Such people were not to be trusted, black power leaders said, because they were white and were part of the establishment that had brought such misery on American blacks.

White Americans who supported greater civil rights for blacks did not quite know what to make of all this. Meanwhile, whites who opposed an end to segregation felt confirmed in their preconceptions. The lines of fear, suspicion, and hatred were drawn more sharply in American society.

Vietnam

As the 1960s progressed, the United States found itself enmeshed in an increasingly difficult situation in Southeast Asia. North Vietnam, led by Ho Chi Minh, still wanted to conquer South Vietnam and bring the entire country under Communist control. The North supplied weapons to Viet Cong guerrillas in the South who continued to fight southern forces. During President Kennedy's time in office, the number of American military advisors in South Vietnam increased from 2,000 to 16,000.

Meanwhile, the South Vietnamese leader, Ngo Dinh Diem, proved to be corrupt and unreliable. Diem, a professed Catholic, persecuted his political enemies as well as Buddhists. American television showed Buddhist monks setting themselves on fire to protest Diem's violence.

Communists also threatened neighboring Laos, and a coalition government was formed there that included the Communists. North Vietnam supplied the Viet Cong and its own forces in the South by means of the Ho Chi Minh Trail, which ran through Laos.

The United States agreed to stand by when a group of South Vietnamese army generals staged a coup to oust Diem. However, the new government was not much stronger or more stable, as the generals who led the coup fought each other for control. The U.S. wanted to support South Vietnam as part of its effort to contain Communism, but the nation's leaders were not reliable allies.

The escalation of American involvement in Vietnam began in August of 1964. President Johnson reported on August 7 that two American vessels were attacked by the North Vietnamese as they stood in the Gulf of Tonkin off the North Vietnamese coast. In response Congress overwhelmingly passed the Gulf of Tonkin resolution, which authorized the President to take all necessary measures to defend United States forces and to stop any further aggression. This was as close to a declaration of war that Congress ever got with regard to Vietnam, but it gave Johnson the freedom he wanted to pursue the conflict as he saw fit.

In 1965 the United States began aerial bombing of North Vietnam; but it appeared to have little effect on the North or on the war effort by the Viet Cong in the South. In March of 1965, the first American combat troops were sent to Vietnam. Over 180,000 went that year, and by the end of 1966 over

President Johnson visited American troops in Vietnam in 1966. In this photo Johnson is decorating a U.S. soldier as the commander of American forces, General William Westmoreland, looks on.

U.S. Navy Seal Team One on a Mission Near Saigon, Vietnam, in 1967

380,000 were in the country. The stated American goal was to contain Communism and to prevent the fall of South Vietnam to the Communists. In addition, the Administration spoke of a possible domino effect in Southeast Asia: if South Vietnam fell, American officials warned, Laos, Cambodia, and perhaps Thailand might fall to the Communists in quick order. More pessimistic observers feared for the freedom of Australia and other countries in the Pacific rim.

The United States government, however, was not prepared to win the kind of war that was going on in Vietnam. First, it was a war without a front. North Vietnamese regulars and Viet Cong guerrillas would appear, make a quick attack against a village or an American position, and then disappear into the jungle. American troops were often victimized and could only respond to being attacked; it was difficult for the Americans to mount a major offensive.

The U.S. never developed an overall strategy for victory, and the war was prosecuted poorly from Washington. This says nothing, of course, about the bravery and dedication of American troops who fought in Vietnam. They did the best they could with the situation they were given.

Second, the goals of the combatants were different. The United States tried to fight a limited war as it had in Korea, simply trying to repel Communist attacks on the South. American leaders believed that U.S. involvement had to be limited in order to avoid bringing China and Russia into the war in greater measure (those countries were already helping North Vietnam). Meanwhile, the Communists put no limits on their goal. They had no concerns about going too far or being too violent. The Communist goal was the complete takeover of South Vietnam and the rest of Southeast Asia.

Third, the role of the United States as protector of other nations came to be seriously questioned in the U.S. Should the U.S. be fighting South Vietnam's war, if the South Vietnamese weren't willing or able to fight it themselves? The Army of the Republic of Vietnam (ARVN) forces were not strong or well-trained. America appeared to be propping up a corrupt government and a weak military in what was in many respects a Vietnamese civil war. Even further, many Americans questioned how valuable the defense of a non-Communist South Vietnam was in America's strategic interests.

At a 1967 antiwar protest in Arlington, Virginia, this young woman offered a flower to a military policeman.

The war dragged on during Johnson's years in office. The military kept giving positive and optimistic reports about the war and the prospects for victory. However, the war effort seemed aimless. Television coverage, available during a war for the first time, brought the fighting into American living rooms each evening. The number of Americans held as prisoners of war in what were known to be barbaric conditions in North Vietnam continued to grow, as bomber pilots were shot down and other Americans were captured. Each Thursday the Pentagon reported the number of American dead and wounded from the previous week as well as the enemy casualty count (which was almost always higher).

At home America was not united in backing the war effort. Most Senators and Congressmen supported the Johnson Administration at first; but as the war continued, more and more leaders in both parties began to raise questions. Most Americans were patriotic citizens who loved their country despite its problems and supported their government. They disliked and distrusted Communism and wanted to see it contained, but they were not sure that American action in Vietnam was right.

The Toronto Anti-Draft Programme helped young men from America move to Canada to avoid the draft.

Antiwar demonstrations began occurring on college campuses in 1965. Students engaged in sit-ins in classroom and administration buildings, sometimes taking over campus offices. Demonstrations against the draft began occurring in several cities, where young men protested by burning their draft registration cards (or photocopies of their draft cards), which was a Federal offense. In late 1966 and even more in 1967, Martin Luther King Jr. spoke out against the war in Vietnam because he saw it taking resources away from critical domestic needs.

Then came 1968.

King at an Anti-War Demonstration in New York City

Then Jesus said to him, "Put your sword back into its place; for all those who take up the sword shall perish by the sword."
Matthew 26:52

★ Assignments for Lesson 128 ★

American Voices — Read the excerpts from "Letter from a Birmingham Jail" and the "I Have a Dream" speech by Martin Luther King Jr. (pages 340-353).

Bible — Jesus accepted people that others rejected. Read these passages to see examples: tax collectors (Luke 5:27-28), Gentiles (Luke 7:2-10), Samaritans (Luke 17:11-19), and a thief (Luke 23:39-43).

Work on memorizing Luke 4:16-19.

Project — Work on your project.

Student Review — Optional: Answer the questions for Lesson 128.

U.S. and South Vietnamese Troops During the Tet Offensive

Lesson 129

1968

Few years in American history have witnessed so many significant events as did 1968. Many trends, policies, and directions came together to produce decisive events in both domestic and foreign policy.

The *Pueblo* and the Tet Offensive

The United States suffered an international embarrassment when an intelligence-gathering vessel, the USS *Pueblo*, and its crew were captured by North Korea on January 23, 1968. The U.S. demanded their release, but North Korea refused. America was caught between (a) going in after the ship and crew and perhaps causing further conflict or the death of the crew, or (b) pursuing release by diplomatic channels and appearing to be powerless. The *Pueblo* incident lingered throughout the rest of the year and became an issue in the election campaign that fall. The crew were released after 11 months on December 23, but North Korea kept the ship.

On January 31, 1968, the Vietnamese new year (called Tet), North Vietnamese army regulars and Viet Cong guerrillas attacked American positions throughout South Vietnam. The Tet Offensive caused significant American losses, but U.S. forces were able to regroup and launch a counter-offensive that inflicted even heavier casualties on the Communists. The Communists actually lost the Tet Offensive; but decisive damage was done to the entire war effort in American public opinion, which began to turn sharply against the war. President Johnson's approval rating stood at 35%.

Peace negotiations between North and South Vietnam and the United States began in May of 1968 in Paris. They bogged down almost immediately with petty disputes. The two sides had a hard time agreeing on the shape of the negotiating table to use. The North Vietnamese did not want to acknowledge the South Vietnamese as a legitimate government, and the South Vietnamese did not want to acknowledge the separatist National Liberation Front (Viet Cong). Talks continued on and off for years while the fighting continued.

Political Trouble for Johnson

Four years after its greatest landslide victory, the Democratic Party began to splinter. Minnesota Democratic Senator Eugene McCarthy announced an almost unprecedented challenge to an incumbent President when he began a bid for the Democratic presidential nomination on a clear antiwar platform. He pledged to end American involvement in Vietnam and to seek terms for peace.

What Else Was Happening?

1961 *The chairman of the Federal Communications Commission calls television a "vast wasteland."*

1961 *An armed Cuban forces an American passenger jet to go to Havana in the first skyjacking.*

1961 *Roger Maris of the New York Yankees hits 61 home runs during the baseball season, breaking Babe Ruth's record of 60 set in 1927. However, Ruth had hit his in a 154-game season while Maris does it in a 162-game season. The commissioner of baseball requires that Maris' record carry an asterisk explaining the difference in the official baseball record book.*

1962 *First lady Jackie Kennedy gives a tour of the White House on national television.*

1963 *The audio tape cassette is patented.*

1963 *C. S. Lewis dies on November 22.*

1964 *Nikita Khrushchev is forced out as the Soviet leader. He is replaced by two men, Aleksei Kosygin, who becomes the Soviet premier, and Leonid Brezhnev, who is named head of the Communist Party.*

1964 *Cassius Clay wins the heavyweight boxing championship for the first time. He becomes a Black Muslim and takes the name Muhammed Ali. In 1967 Ali refuses to respond to the military draft and claims to be a conscientious objector. He is found guilty of draft evasion and sentenced to prison, and his boxing title is stripped from him. His conviction is overturned in 1971. Ali regains the heavyweight title in 1974, then in 1978 he loses it and regains it again.*

1965 *A power failure hits almost the entire northeastern United States for one night.*

1966 Star Trek *debuts on NBC. Canadian actor William Shatner, shown at right, plays the character Captain James T. Kirk.*

1967 *Israel attacks neighboring Arab states, including Egypt, and seizes the West Bank and the Golan Heights in what is called the Six-Day War.*

1967 *South African Dr. Christiaan Barnard performs the first successful human heart transplant.*

1968 *After attempts are made at expanding political freedoms in Czechoslovakia, Soviet tanks roll into Prague to support a takeover of the government by Soviet loyalists.*

1968 *Two African American athletes receiving medals in the Summer Olympic games in Mexico City, during the playing of the "Star-Spangled Banner," raise their fists as a symbol of black power.*

1969 *The New York Jets defeat the Baltimore Colts in Super Bowl III, after Jets quarterback Joe Namath boldly predicts that the upstart AFL team will win over the heavily-favored Colts. The NFL Green Bay Packers had easily won the first two Super Bowl games.*

1969 Sesame Street *premiers on public television.*

McCarthy was not well known before the primary campaign began, but he quickly became the standard bearer for Democrats who were dissatisfied with Johnson's handling of the war. In the New Hampshire presidential primary in early March, Johnson won with 48% of the vote but McCarthy received an astounding 42%. McCarthy's narrow loss was widely seen as a step toward victory.

On Sunday night, March 31, President Johnson made a televised speech. He announced that he was going to curtail American bombing of North Vietnam and to seek a negotiated peace. Military victory was no longer the goal; now the official policy was for the U.S. to get out of Vietnam in the most honorable way possible. The President concluded his speech with a surprise announcement. He said that he would neither seek nor accept the Democratic Party's nomination for another term. The man who had achieved his goal of becoming President and had achieved the most far-reaching legislative agenda since the New Deal had been turned away from seeking re-election by opposition within his own party over the Vietnam War.

The King Assassination

The following Thursday, April 4, Martin Luther King Jr. was assassinated as he stood on the balcony of the Lorraine Motel in Memphis, Tennessee. King had gone to Memphis to intervene in a sanitation workers' strike. Riots broke out following the assassination in sixty American cities as blacks reacted to the death of one of their most respected and eloquent leaders. After a world-wide manhunt, escaped convict James Earl Ray was arrested and charged with the crime. Ray pleaded guilty and was sentenced to 99 years in prison. Once in prison, Ray almost immediately changed his story and said that he was pressured into pleading guilty. Rumors of a conspiracy against King that used Ray as the trigger man have abounded to this day.

The National Civil Rights Museum opened in 1991 at the Lorraine Motel. A wreath marks the spot where Martin Luther King Jr. was killed.

Robert Kennedy and President Johnson (1966)

Robert Kennedy Assassinated

Johnson's withdrawal left the Democratic field wide open. Vice President Hubert Humphrey announced his candidacy for the nomination, but Johnson's record was a huge albatross around his neck. The most excitement was generated by Robert F. Kennedy, the late President's younger brother. Kennedy had been elected to the U.S. Senate from New York in 1964.

Skeptics noted that Kennedy had refrained from a direct challenge to Johnson until McCarthy's performance in New Hampshire had shown that the President was vulnerable. All of the old Kennedy-Johnson rivalry was rekindled with the Senator's candidacy. Senator Kennedy was a huge favorite in Democratic primaries, both for his own stands and as the bearer of his late brother's legacy.

On June 5, Kennedy won the important California Democratic primary which appeared to put him in the lead for the nomination. As he left the victory celebration through the kitchen area of the hotel, he was shot by a young Palestinian, Sirhan Sirhan, who objected to Kennedy's support for Israel. The Senator died the next day.

Robert was the third Kennedy brother to die a violent death. The oldest brother, Joe, whom many believed was the most promising politician in the family, had been killed in World War II. It was somehow ironic that Robert was killed not for his antiwar position nor for his liberal domestic agenda, but for his support of Israel which had become standard American policy supported by both parties.

Chicago Democratic Convention

Kennedy's death put Vice President Humphrey in the lead for the Democratic nomination (McCarthy's campaign had lost momentum when Kennedy entered the race). When the Democrats assembled in Chicago in early August, Humphrey had the nomination sewn up; but he also had serious additional baggage as the representative of the discredited administration. In addition, leftists had targeted the convention for demonstrations. Outside the convention, thousands of demonstrators clashed with thousands of police and National Guardsmen.

After being provoked by demonstrators, the police waded into the crowd and used excessive violence to stop the protests while the marchers chanted, "The whole world's watching," as indeed it was. Chicago Mayor Richard Daley was seen giving orders to the police from the convention floor. Maine Senator Edmund Muskie received the vice presidential nomination.

Nixon's Comeback

Shortly thereafter, a much calmer Miami Beach hosted the Republican convention and witnessed a remarkable comeback with the nomination of Richard Nixon as their presidential nominee. After losing to Kennedy in 1960, Nixon had run for the governorship of California in 1962 but had lost.

Presidential Candidate Richard Nixon with President Johnson (1968)

In his remarks after the defeat, a tired and bitter Nixon said that this was going to be his last press conference because "you won't have Dick Nixon to kick around any more."

Nixon returned to private life, but he supported Barry Goldwater in 1964 and received a positive reception from Republicans around the country. Nixon continued to rebuild his political reputation and decided to try for the presidency again in 1968. Republicans supported him overwhelmingly and he received the nomination. Nixon chose Maryland governor Spiro Agnew as his running mate, primarily because of the tough stance Agnew had taken against demonstrators in Baltimore.

Nixon said that he had a secret plan to end the war in Vietnam, but he did not want to divulge it during the campaign. One of the main themes of the Republican campaign was law and order, which was a response to rising crime rates and widespread looting in cities. Opponents feared that "law and order" actually meant repression and police brutality. Nixon claimed to speak for the silent majority of Americans who did not demonstrate in the streets and who supported their country and their government.

George Wallace Announces His Candidacy (1968)

Hubert Humphrey Giving a Speech (1968)

Wallace's Candidacy

The potential spoiler role in the election was taken by Alabama governor George Wallace. A lifelong Democrat, Wallace ran as an independent in 1968, charging that "there's not a dime's worth of difference" between the Republican and Democratic Parties. In his early political career, Wallace had been a staunch segregationist, claiming, "Segregation today, segregation now, segregation forever." By 1968 he had moderated his position. Wallace ran on a strong defense of states' rights and a pledge to win the war in Vietnam. His running mate was World War II hero and former general Curtis LeMay.

Nixon's Triumph

The contest between Humphrey and Nixon was too close to call before the voting took place. It was not decided until the morning after the election. Out of 73 million votes cast, Nixon had a plurality of about 500,000 votes over Humphrey and a 43.4% to 42.7% margin, with a 301-191 electoral victory. George Wallace received 9.9 million votes, 13.5% of the total, and 46 electoral votes, all from southern states. Humphrey carried most of the Northeast, while Nixon swept almost all of the midsection of the country and the West.

Lesson 129 - 1968

In December 1968, Bill Anders, Jim Lovell, and Frank Borman, the crew of the Apollo 8 mission, became the first humans to orbit the moon. Anders took this photo of "earthrise" over the lunar surface. On Christmas Eve, the crew made a live television broadcast back to Earth. An estimated 500 million people around the world watched. At the conclusion, the astronauts took turns reading from Genesis 1:1-10.

The year 1968 saw America change its goal in Vietnam from finding a way to win to finding a way to get out. Lyndon Johnson went from a huge landslide win in 1964 to not even attempting a re-election bid, while Richard Nixon scored a comeback from previous defeats to be elected President. Two prominent figures were gunned down and sections of dozens of cities were burned down. Protesters criticized the more liberal of the two major parties for not being liberal enough. America seemed shaken to its roots, and now Richard Nixon had the task of leading the country back from some of its darkest days.

"Come now and let us reason together," says the Lord.
Isaiah 1:18

⋆ Assignments for Lesson 129 ⋆

Bible Work on memorizing Luke 4:16-19.

Project Work on your project.

Student Review Optional: Answer the questions for Lesson 129.

Singers Joan Baez and Bob Dylan at the 1963 March on Washington

The Counterculture of Jesus

The America of 1969 was quite different from the America that had existed in 1960. As the American culture changed over the decade, part of the assault on the status quo took the form of what was called the counterculture: musicians, artists, philosophers, writers, and educators who rejected the culture as it was and advocated a new culture devoid of traditional standards and beliefs. One of the most obvious forms of expression by the counterculture was in music.

Music and the Counterculture

In 1961 few Americans had ever heard of John Lennon, Paul McCartney, George Harrison, and Ringo Starr. As of February 1964, when they first appeared on *The Ed Sullivan Show*, few Americans had not heard of the Beatles. The group led what was called the British invasion of rock music, as many British groups and singers became popular in the United States. Coupled with an active American rock music scene that had begun to develop in the 1950s, it made for a musically rich decade. However, some of the songs and the lifestyles of many of the musicians challenged traditional values.

The counterculture of the Sixties culminated in the Woodstock concert in upstate New York in August of 1969, when about a half million people gathered for four days. Much of the music and many of the people involved encouraged immorality and the use of mind-altering drugs. These were the people who made the headlines, although a minority of American teenagers actually experimented with this kind of lifestyle.

The hippies of the counterculture disdained the establishment and the status quo in society, but they did not seek answers within the political system. Instead, they decided to drop out of the system. However, a fair number of those whom we might call hippies in the 1960s grew up and became responsible adults. The Beatles, by the way, were a phenomenon of the 1960s. The group broke up in 1970.

Searching for God

As the counterculture of the 1960s reacted to the society around it, a very different counterculture attempted to rediscover Jesus. Those who took on the appearance of the counterculture but claimed to follow Jesus were called "Jesus freaks." The musical productions *Jesus Christ Superstar* (1970) and *Godspell* (1971) tried to convey the story of Jesus in contemporary terms. The top rock song of 1970 was "Spirit in the Sky" by Norman Greenbaum.

After many Americans had spent years trying to avoid or denigrate Christianity, some of them went back to God and found what they were looking for. They recognized what believers have known throughout the centuries regardless of societal trends—the timeless truth and power of the Lord. History shows us that the way of Jesus has had a profound impact upon the world precisely because it is distinct from the way of the world. Jesus is the leader of the real counterculture, the One who has changed the world for good.

The Hinge of History

In the March 29, 1999, issue of *Newsweek* magazine, Kenneth L. Woodward wrote:

> For Christians, Jesus is the hinge on which the door of history swings, the point at which eternity intersects with time, the Savior who redeems time by drawing all things to himself. . . . But by any secular standard, Jesus is also the dominant figure of Western Culture. . . . Much of what we now think of as Western ideas, inventions and values finds its source or inspiration in the religion that worships God in his name ("2000 Years of Jesus," p. 54).

That a publication such as *Newsweek* would admit to the pervasive influence of Jesus indicates how powerfully Jesus and His followers have influenced history over the last two thousand years.

A young artist drew this picture in 1964 illustrating the seriousness of how we treat each other.

Jesus is the central figure and the central act of God in the history of the world. All of God's work came together for Jesus to be born exactly when and where He was. When Jesus came to earth it was "the fullness of the time" (Galatians 4:4). The Jews, based in Palestine but scattered throughout the world, had spread belief in the one true God. The Greeks had spread a common language throughout the Mediterranean world. The Roman Empire provided a period of relative peace for the early church to grow. All of this helped the spread of the gospel in the first century.

Jesus Challenged the Status Quo

Jesus was the original counterculturalist. He criticized the most powerful people of His day, the religious leaders of Israel (see Matthew 23). Jesus said that the religious leaders gave lip service to God while elevating their traditions above the Word of God (Mark 7:6-8). Jesus did not reject God; instead, He rejected the man-made traditions of religion that kept people from knowing God. Because the religious culture of Israel had left God, Jesus challenged that culture by calling people back to true devotion to God.

Jesus challenged the power structure of His day. The Sadducees were the wealthy political elite, but Jesus pointed out the error of their beliefs (Luke 20:27-40). When someone asked Jesus one of the hot political questions of that day, whether it was right to pay taxes to Caesar, Jesus said that paying taxes to Caesar was not as important an issue as giving to God what belongs to Him, namely ourselves (Luke 20:19-26). After Jesus was arrested, He was taken before the most powerful men in Israel: the high priest, the Jewish Sanhedrin ruling council, Herod, and the Roman governor. As He stood before them, he confessed His own identity, but otherwise He largely ignored their questions and taunts (Luke 22:66-23:12).

Jesus challenged the popular culture of the day. He warned against the common desire to acquire more and more wealth (Luke 12:13-21). He minimized the gifts given by the wealthy out of their excess and praised the poor widow who gave all she had: two small coins (Luke 21:1-4). He taught that marriage was sacred to God. It was not to be taken lightly and ended for any reason, but it could be ended only when the marriage relationship had been already broken by adultery (Matthew 19: 1-9). He showed the preciousness of children when many people treated children as unimportant (Mark 10:13-16). Jesus repeatedly showed compassion for widows, women who had messed up their lives, people of other ethnic groups, and others who were regarded as outcasts by the Jews.

Jesus lived this way and taught these things, not just to be different, but because His way was right. The culture had gotten off course, and Jesus was calling people back to God's way. To do this, He had to challenge the status quo. The status quo is comfortable and often seems right, but it is not necessarily right. We have to test the status quo and our comfort zone by God's truth. When things don't measure up to God's truth, be it our lives or our culture, things need to change.

Woe Unto You, Scribes and Pharisees
James Tissot (French, c. 1890)

After rioting in Washington, D.C., following the assassination of Martin Luther King Jr., this church facilitated a food distribution.

How Jesus and His Followers Changed the World

Jesus did not come to earth just to establish a new religious movement. He came to bring life (John 10:10). The way of Jesus resulted in a revolution because Jesus taught a revolutionary approach to life.

Jesus gave value to the individual. He said that a person was more than simply a member of a family, a tribe, or an ethnic group. Each person has the opportunity to be a child of God, able to call God "Abba" (Aramaic for "Daddy," Galatians 4:6). Each person has worth because Jesus died for each person as an individual, not simply as a member of a group. Everyone can approach God on his own, without a priest or other mediator. The value of the individual is a concept which has influenced Western culture since the first century.

Jesus reintroduced God's definition of what it means to be male and female. Jesus liberated women from the way men usually treated them. Jesus spoke with women publicly and took time for women who were social outcasts (John 4:1-42, John 8:2-11, Luke 7:36-50). At the same time, Jesus taught that manhood was more than might and position. A godly man was humble, considerate, and self-sacrificing (Ephesians 5:25-33).

Jesus influenced society. He had a high view of the family. Marriage was to be held in honor by all (Matthew 5:27-32, Hebrews 13:4). Children were to be loved and trained well. They were not simply objects that could be thrown away, which was the common opinion of the Romans and pagan European tribes.

Followers of Jesus have led movements that have brought great benefit to mankind. William Wilberforce in England and Harriet Beecher Stowe in the U.S., among many others, opposed slavery because of their deeply-held Christian faith. It has been Christian people who have encouraged temperance in the use of alcohol, built hospitals and clinics to help the people of the third world, and been a leading force in encouraging education. Missionaries have not only taken the gospel to other lands; they have also built schools, provided medical care, improved agricultural practices, and created alphabets and written languages for people.

Chaplain Charles Watters from New Jersey served with the U.S. Army in Vietnam. During a battle on November 19, 1967, he faced enemy fire to bring back wounded soldiers from the battlefield for medical care and provided spiritual comfort to them. Watters was killed when an American plane accidentally dropped a bomb on his unit. For his heroism, he was posthumously awarded the Medal of Honor.

Having a deep faith in the reality of the next world, Christians have taken as a cardinal duty working to make life better in this one. Christians have a reason to serve others. They understand why every life is precious and why everyone should have the chance to know God and to live up to their God-given potential. Just as Jesus redefined life, He also redefined death. Death can no longer be seen as the end of the road. It is the gateway to a life of eternal happiness, or it is the start of eternal misery.

One way to understand the impact of Jesus and his followers is to try to imagine what the world would be like without the influence of Christians. It is no longer common, as it was in the Roman Empire, for fathers to throw out unwanted children, especially daughters, who would be left to die or to be picked up by slave traders. We no longer see the human sacrifices practiced by some European tribes. As barbaric as some modern sports may seem, we have not returned to the practice of the Roman Colosseum where crowds watched men being killed for entertainment. We live in a healthier and more literate and more compassionate world because of what Christians have done.

Most significantly, Jesus provided the answers to mankind's most pressing issues: Who am I? Where did I come from? Why am I here? Where am I going? What do I do with the guilt I feel for what I have done wrong? How can I live in hope and not in despair? What will happen when I die? All of these questions can be answered in Jesus.

Everything that happens in this world is to be viewed through the lens of Jesus. Does it further His name? Does it honor Him? Is it in keeping with the pattern of His submission to God's will? Everyone will be judged by Him, and all who will be saved will be saved by Him (Acts 4:12). One day every knee will bow and every tongue will confess that Jesus Christ is Lord (Philippians 2:10-11).

Participants in the 1965 Civil Rights March from Selma to Montgomery, Alabama

Failings

However, the story of those who claim to follow Jesus has a dark side. Followers of Jesus have used His name to justify the ill-conceived Crusades, the cruel Inquisition, slavery, and racial discrimination. The cross has been used as a symbol of political power. Wrong has been done in the name of Jesus, but much more has been done in His name that is right.

The divisions within Christendom have been one reason why more people have not taken the gospel seriously. "If Christians cannot get along with each other," some wonder, "how can I know which brand is right? Why should I bother?"

In some places in the West, the practice of Christianity has been weighed and found wanting. As a result, many of the great cathedrals in Europe are literally monuments to past religious practice. The United States has a greater percentage of church-going people than does Europe, but even at that it is only about 40% of the population and is declining.

Wherever Christianity is practiced superficially and with a secular veneer, the faith will not grow much and will likely turn people off. However, when the call to discipleship is taken seriously and lives are changed by the Good News, then we will see the growth of Christianity. In recent years, Christianity has been growing in Africa and Latin America. A large underground church exists in Communist China. When the Iron Curtain fell, people in the former Soviet Union and Eastern Europe rushed back to churches and begged for teaching from the Bible. Missionaries from these countries are seeing the need to come to the United States to teach us about real faith in Jesus.

The Revolution of Jesus

The world is different because of the life of one Man who had no place to call His own, no place to lay His head (Luke 9:58). The Gospel of Luke presents Jesus as the One who brought a social, cultural, and spiritual revolution. Jesus told the people in His hometown that God blessed non-Israelites, and they ran Him out of town (Luke 4:23-30). He spoke words of blessing to the poor and the outcasts and words of warning to the rich and comfortable (Luke 6:20-26).

Jesus told stories in which the heroes were a Samaritan, a poor beggar, and a wasteful son who repented. He took notice of a blind beggar and a poor widow whom nobody else seemed to care about. He stood toe to toe with the leaders of the religious establishment and told them how they were wrong (Luke 20). Jesus did not come to initiate a merely social and cultural revolution, but the spiritual revolution He brought has created practical effects through the lives of those who follow Him.

Christians in the United States have too often become complacent in a culture that gives tax-exemptions to churches and stamps "In God We Trust" on its coins. America owes much to its spiritual heritage, but unfortunately it has turned away from that heritage in recent years. For every way in which our culture has left God, Jesus offers the countercultural revolution that will bring people back to God.

In Him was life, and the life was the Light of men.
The Light shines in the darkness,
and the darkness did not comprehend it.
John 1:4-5

⋆ Assignments for Lesson 130 ⋆

Bible Recite or write Luke 4:16-19 from memory.

Project Complete your project for the unit.

Student Review Optional: Answer the questions for Lesson 130 and take the quiz for Unit 26.

American Businesses Produced a Variety of Commemorative Items for the United States Bicentennial in 1976

27 The 1970s

Despite the efforts of hundreds of thousands of American soldiers, the United States did not achieve peace with honor in Vietnam. The Watergate scandal resulted in the only resignation of a President in our country's history. The Iranian hostage crisis reminded us that American power and our own belief in the rightness of our nation do not mean that other nations automatically respect us. The country wrestled with several spiritual issues during the 1970s, especially the issue of abortion, which forces us to address questions about the origin, value, and purpose of human life.

Lesson 131 - The Nixon Administration
Lesson 132 - Watergate
Lesson 133 - Ford and Carter
Lesson 134 - Spiritual Issues of the Seventies
Lesson 135 - Bible Study: *Roe v. Wade*

Memory Work

Memorize Colossians 3:8-11 by the end of this unit.

Books Used

The Bible
American Voices
The Giver

Project (choose one)

1) Write 300 to 500 words on one of the following topics:

   - Describe your life today. Use the essay "Confessions of a Baby Boomer" (*American Voices,* pages 407-409) as an example of what you might include. Talk about the things that are truly important to you and the seemingly little things that characterize your days. You will enjoy looking back at this essay in years to come.

   - Write out your position on abortion. Give Biblical reasons for what you believe. This will be helpful to you as you discuss it with others. See Lesson 135.

2) Arrange a tour of a crisis pregnancy center in your community. Find out how the center was started, how it is supported financially, and how it is staffed. Ask what services are offered to women. Find out how Christians in your community can get involved. See Lesson 135.

3) Make a video newscast about the moon landing as if it were broadcast on July 20, 1969, with yourself as news anchor. Make your video at least three minutes long. See Lesson 131.

Literature

The Giver

The Giver by Lois Lowry was published in 1993 and received the Newbery Award for Children's Literature. It is a story about a seemingly perfect society where everything is not perfect. *The Giver* is a sobering book with a mature message. It is a good book to read together as a family and to discuss in the light of God's love and truth. Because this unit deals with the subject of abortion, it is a good time to read a book that makes us think about the value of life and the consequences of wanting everything to be easy. Plan to finish the book by the end of this unit.

President Richard Nixon at a Washington Senators Baseball Game (1969)

Lesson 131

The Nixon Administration

Richard Nixon's election as President in 1968 was the culmination of a career in national politics that had stretched over twenty years. He was a moderate conservative who claimed to speak for the silent majority of Americans who loved their country and respected their government. Nixon promised to reverse the trend of liberalism and an ever-bigger Federal government. However, as chief executive Nixon dealt with numerous problems, some of which he brought on himself, that hampered and eventually derailed his presidency.

Conservative Counterattack

The 1964 election showed broad support for the liberal Johnson and an uneasiness with the conservative Goldwater. By 1968 the pendulum had swung at least partially back toward the conservative side with Nixon's election and George Wallace's showing as a conservative independent candidate.

One attempt by the Nixon White House to encourage its conservative base was a series of speeches by Vice President Spiro Agnew beginning in the fall of 1969 attacking what he called the liberal media. Agnew charged that the media were "nattering nabobs of negativism" and "an effete corps of impudent snobs" that promoted liberalism and slanted news coverage for political purposes. Conservatives cheered the speeches as reflecting what they had thought for some time, while liberals denied the charges and said that such talk only served to polarize the nation. Since licenses for radio and television stations have to be granted and renewed by the Federal government, some observers saw Agnew's attacks as a veiled attempt to hamper free speech by intimidating the media.

The Vietnam Struggle Continues

During the 1968 campaign, Nixon claimed to have a secret plan to end the war in Vietnam, achieve peace with honor, and bring the Americans home. As it was carried out during his presidency, the plan included three main points. First, the U.S. continued to pursue a settlement at the Paris peace talks; but those negotiations accomplished little because of North Vietnam's refusal to withdraw from the South. Second, Nixon announced a policy which he called the Vietnamization of the war. The U.S. turned more and more of the fighting over to the South Vietnamese army. The U.S. trained and equipped the South Vietnamese while American troops were pulled out of the country. From a high of 540,000 servicemen in 1969, the American military presence was reduced to just 50,000 troops by 1973. However, the South Vietnamese army did not fight

My Lai Massacre

It was revealed in 1969 that during the previous year an American unit had intentionally killed several hundred Vietnamese civilians in the village of My Lai (pronounced me-lie). The photo at left was taken in My Lai on the day of the killings.

It was often impossible for Americans to distinguish between Vietnamese civilians and Viet Cong combatants; but the killing of so many innocent civilians, even if it was during a difficult war, went beyond acceptable American military policy. The incident increased American frustrations over the war and intensified the questions of those who wondered why the U.S. was in Vietnam at all.

Several officers were accused of wrongdoing in the incident, but only one was convicted. Lt. William Calley claimed that he was only following orders in doing what he did, but he was convicted of premeditated murder. Calley was sentenced to life in prison; but President Nixon commuted his sentence, and he was paroled. This event sparked a national debate on whether a soldier had the right to disobey immoral orders.

well; and Communist forces made significant gains against them after the Americans left.

The third part of Nixon's plan involved heavier bombing of Communist bases and supply lines. This included air assaults on the North, but it also included Communist positions in the officially neutral neighboring country of Cambodia. The bombing of Cambodia was carried on in secret for several months. When it became known, those who opposed the war were furious at what they termed an escalation of the conflict. The Communists were, of course, already using the country to stage attacks on the South and on American forces.

New protests against the Cambodian incursions, some of which turned violent, erupted on American college campuses in the spring of 1970. All things military were the target of the protesters. At Kent State University in Ohio, rioters burned down the building that housed the Reserve Officer Training Corps (ROTC) program. The ROTC was a military presence on many campuses. Students who enrolled in the program went through training during college and were commissioned as Army lieutenants upon graduation. Many colleges required all of their male students to go through one or two years of ROTC classes and drills.

When the Ohio National Guard was called to Kent State to protect campus facilities and preserve order, protesters attacked the guardsmen. In the tense and chaotic scene, the National Guardsmen, many of whom were young and nervous, opened fire on the protesters. Four students were killed. The horror of uniformed Americans killing other Americans over a difficult war in Southeast Asia deepened the division in the country and raised even more questions about whether the American presence in Vietnam was worth what it was costing.

Then in 1971, former Pentagon employee Daniel Ellsberg made public classified documents that he had stolen from the Pentagon which showed official duplicity and a lack of purpose and strategy in American planning for the war. The Pentagon Papers showed that plans were being made for an escalation of American involvement even while President Johnson was assuring the public that this was not going to happen.

The Paris peace talks bogged down in late 1972, but stepped-up American bombing of the North helped bring about a settlement in January of 1973. A cease-fire was declared and American prisoners of war were released, but thousands of troops remained officially missing. Former President Lyndon Johnson, who had overseen the major buildup of American activity in Vietnam, died that same month.

The End in Vietnam

After the last American troops were pulled out, fighting resumed between the Communists and the South Vietnamese army. The Communists were much better fighters and more highly motivated. The end of South Vietnam came after Nixon left office. A full-scale Communist invasion of the South took place in 1975, and the South Vietnamese military and government collapsed. The South Vietnamese capital of Saigon fell to the Communists on April 30, 1975. The last remaining American officials escaped by helicopter from the roof of the American embassy. A few desperate South Vietnamese scrambled onto the helicopters and were able to get out also. Saigon was renamed Ho Chi Minh City, and the Communists celebrated their goal of achieving a unified Vietnam under their rule.

The U.S. military helped thousands of people from South Vietnam escape to the United States at the end of the war. The photo below is from April 29, 1975. Among those brought to the U.S. were about 3,000 children, some fathered by American soldiers and born to Vietnamese mothers.

The predicted bloodbath followed, as Communists executed thousands of South Vietnamese who had opposed (or who were suspected of having opposed) them. Earlier in April, the U.S.-backed government in Cambodia fell to the Communist Khmer Rouge, led by the ruthless Pol Pot. It is estimated that during Pol Pot's regime, one million Cambodians died as a result of starvation, disease, or execution.

Thus the long and costly American involvement in Vietnam came to an end. What had begun during the Truman Administration as an attempt to contain Communism and to keep at least part of Vietnam free failed in those objectives. Poor American military planning combined with an unreliable South Vietnamese ally and a highly dedicated Communist opposition led to the outcome. The U.S. lost 58,000 dead and many more injured, but the country lost much in other ways also. Vietnam veterans were never given a homecoming to honor their courage and commitment. Many Americans resented those who fought in the war. The veterans, in turn, resented the way that the military and political establishment did not give them the support they needed to achieve complete victory. They also resented the fact that a large part of the American public was against what they were trying to accomplish in Vietnam. The war resulted in the unification of Vietnam, but it led to a divided America that took years to heal.

However, American efforts in Vietnam did accomplish good. It sent the message that the United States was willing to fight to contain Communism. Our sacrifices there helped to bring about the eventual decline of Communism in many countries. Internal pressures inside Communist countries coupled with external resistance from the U.S. and its allies helped to demonstrate the weaknesses of Communism. Even where Communism continues, it is changing. The government in China is allowing a greater measure of capitalism, and relations between the U.S. and Vietnam have improved.

In 1973, reacting to the Vietnam experience which Congress itself had helped escalate with the Gulf of Tonkin resolution, Congress had passed the War Powers Resolution. This law required the President to report to Congress whenever troops were deployed in combat and to withdraw those troops after sixty days unless Congress approved their continued deployment. The President and others saw this as an inappropriate curtailing of the chief executive's role of commander in chief, while defenders of the law said it would keep Congress informed and prevent another Vietnam.

Nixon's Domestic Policies

Republicans complained about the bloated Federal bureaucracy and runaway Federal spending, but the programs begun during Johnson's Great Society continued. The Environmental Protection Agency was created during Nixon's tenure. Both houses of Congress were controlled by the Democrats during all of Nixon's presidency. One change that did take place was what Nixon called a New Federalism, in which some Federal revenues were returned to the states for them to spend as they saw fit. The program was called revenue sharing.

School desegregation progressed during this time, spurred by Federal court orders. The courts sometimes ordered that children be transported by school buses from their neighborhoods to schools across town in order to achieve racial balance. This occurred in northern and southern cities and was met with protests by parents in both regions.

A proposed Equal Rights Amendment (ERA) to the U.S. Constitution passed the House in 1971 and the Senate in 1972 and was sent to the states for ratification. The proposed amendment said, "Equality of rights under the law shall not be denied or abridged by the United States or any State on account of sex." The amendment was supported by the growing feminist movement, but it was opposed by conservative groups, including many conservative women. Opponents feared that numerous problems would arise if the amendment were ratified, including a mandatory policy of women serving alongside men in the military, the forced acceptance of female clergy in churches, and the outlawing of any gender-specific organizations. Thirty states ratified the amendment within a year after the Senate passed it, but it never was ratified by the required 38 states.

Betty Ford, wife of Nixon's successor Gerald Ford, supported ratification of the ERA.

A major domestic problem that extended throughout the decade of the 1970s was a sluggish economy. The costs of the Vietnam War and domestic social programs led to greater Federal spending, which led to deficit spending and an insufficient supply of money for the economy as a whole. The annual rate of inflation had been 3% in 1967, but it hit 9% in 1973; and it got worse in later years. At the same time, unemployment rose as the nation's businesses were not able to offer enough jobs to meet the demands of the public. The U.S. trade deficit increased as the country bought more goods from abroad than it sold abroad. In August of 1971, President Nixon imposed ninety-day wage and price controls, but the cost of living actually rose during the period and the policy was abandoned.

In 1973 the Organization of Petroleum Exporting Countries (OPEC)—mostly Arab nations—used their oil supply as a weapon against the United States' support of Israel. OPEC cut its sales to the U.S. and increased its prices. The result was severe disruption in the U.S. as cheap gasoline became a thing of the past. Prices rose and supplies decreased dramatically. Many cities saw long lines at gas stations as drivers waited to buy gasoline that rose in price from about 25 cents per gallon to about a dollar a gallon over a few months. Consumption of gasoline declined over the period as Americans started to conserve energy. Smaller, fuel-efficient foreign cars became much more popular as American car makers struggled to change from the tradition of producing larger, gas-guzzler models. The Arab oil embargo ended in March of 1974.

Man on the Moon

The competition between the United States and the Soviet Union for pre-eminence in space continued through the 1960s, culminating in the U.S. finally achieving what it saw as victory.

In May of 1961, astronaut Alan Shepard became the first American in space with a fifteen-minute sub-orbital flight. He went far enough up into space to achieve weightlessness and then returned to earth, splashing down in the Atlantic Ocean. With this small beginning, President Kennedy on May 25, 1961, called for the U.S. to set a goal of sending a man to the moon and returning him safely by the end of the decade. NASA got into high gear and received ample funding from the U.S. government to achieve this goal. Other sub-orbital flights by American astronauts followed.

The first communication satellite, *Telstar*, was launched in July of 1962. It enabled the first live television broadcast from Europe to the United States. On February 20, 1962, John Glenn became the first American to go into orbit, as he went on a mission that took him around the earth three times. These first American manned space flights were called the Mercury program. The U.S. then began preparing two-man crews for the Gemini orbital program. The first Gemini flight took place in July of 1965.

Following the Gemini program, NASA began working on three-man Apollo missions that were designed eventually to take men to the moon. The American space program suffered a great tragedy in January of 1967, when the three astronauts who had been chosen to fly in Apollo I (an earth-orbit mission) died in a fire inside an Apollo capsule during a training exercise. This delayed the Apollo program as new safety features were added to the Apollo spacecraft. The first Apollo craft to achieve lunar orbit was launched in January of 1968.

Then on July 20, 1969, in fulfillment of President Kennedy's goal, the United States landed the first men on the moon. Neil Armstrong was the first man to step on the moon, saying, "That's one small step for man, one giant leap for mankind." Buzz Aldrin followed Armstrong out of the Eagle moon landing craft a few minutes later and the two spent several hours on the surface of the moon, taking rock and soil samples and performing experiments. The third Apollo astronaut, flight commander Michael Collins, remained in lunar orbit aboard the command ship Columbia.

The Apollo 11 astronauts spent several days in quarantine in case they had picked up an unknown space bug. President Nixon spoke with them during this time, as shown below. Buzz Aldrin (right) revealed later that he had taken bread and wine with him and had observed communion on the moon.

Returned safely to earth, the astronauts received a ticker tape parade in New York and were given a hero's welcome in many cities in the U.S. and around the world. Manned Apollo missions to the moon continued through 1972.

Foreign Affairs

President Nixon, the opponent of Communism for years, managed to achieve significant breakthroughs with the two largest Communist nations, China and the Soviet Union. At the time, the U.S. recognized the Nationalists on Taiwan as the legitimate Chinese government. In 1972, however, Nixon announced that he was going to visit the People's Republic of China (Communist China) to begin the process of establishing cultural, trade, and diplomatic relations with that government.

Nixon's visit, which took place later that year, began a thaw in Chinese-American relations. The first American liaison in China was George H. W. Bush. The United States supported the change in the United Nations that made the Communist government, not the Taiwanese government, the official representative in the U.N. and on the Security Council. America maintains relations of a sort with Taiwan, but the two-China policy was a recognition of reality and an abandonment of the long-held Nationalist Chinese goal of retaking the mainland.

President Nixon had a practice of wearing a U.S. flag lapel pin whenever he made a public appearance. When he went on television to announce his trip to China, he did not wear the pin. Nixon did wear the pin during his visit to China, as seen here at dinner with the Chinese Premier Zhou Enlai.

In October of 1973, Egypt and Syria launched a surprise attack on Israel on the Jewish holy day of Yom Kippur (Day of Atonement). Israeli forces were able to push both invaders back, and a cease-fire was declared in November. The United States supported Israel in the conflict. The next year Nixon visited the Middle East, stopping in Egypt, Saudi Arabia, and Syria. He then became the first U.S. President to visit Israel. Children greeted his motorcade with American and Israeli flags.

Also in 1972, Nixon became the first American President to visit the Soviet Union. The visit highlighted the new American policy of detente, or an easing of tensions, with the Russians. The two countries agreed to pursue discussions on a treaty to limit and even cut back on the number of nuclear missiles that each country had.

The negotiations led to the Strategic Arms Limitation Treaties (SALT). Many observers noted the irony that a Republican, who had begun his political career as a Communist hunter, was the President who achieved these historic diplomatic steps with the two largest Communist countries in the world.

God made the two great lights, the greater light to govern the day, and the lesser light to govern the night; He made the stars also.
Genesis 1:16

⋆ Assignments for Lesson 131 ⋆

American Voices Read "A Day in July" and "Confessions of a Baby Boomer" by Ray Notgrass (pages 355 and 407-409)

Literature Begin reading *The Giver.* Plan to finish it by the end this unit.

Bible In the Bible study lesson for this unit we will look at the issue of abortion. Read Psalm 139:1-16.

Start memorizing Colossians 3:8-11.

Project Choose your project for this unit and start working on it.

Student Review Optional: Answer the questions for Lesson 131.

The Watergate Complex, Washington, D.C.

Lesson 132

Watergate

In early 1972, the number of American troops in Vietnam was lower than it had been in many years. Bold new initiatives were being taken with Communist China and the Soviet Union. The Nixon Administration opposed the practice of busing to achieve school desegregation, a practice which was unpopular with many Americans. Despite the war in Vietnam and the stagnant economy, President Nixon was a formidable candidate for re-election. The Committee to Re-Elect the President (CRP, sometimes abbreviated CREEP by its opponents) rolled up a record amount of contributions to finance the campaign.

Helping Nixon's chances was the fact that the Democrats were badly divided. They were united in opposing Nixon and the Democrats controlled both houses of Congress, but the liberal, moderate, and conservative segments of the party distrusted each other. Alabama governor George Wallace ran for President again, this time for the Democratic nomination rather than as an independent. He made impressive showings in early primaries outside of the South. However, while campaigning in Laurel, Maryland, on May 15, Wallace was shot by Arthur Bremer, who was mentally unbalanced. As a result of the shooting, Wallace was paralyzed from the waist down. He won the Maryland and Michigan primaries the next day, but his disability forced him to end his campaign.

The liberal wing of the Democratic Party was led by South Dakota Senator George McGovern, a World War II bomber pilot who had received the Distinguished Flying Cross. McGovern earned a Ph.D. in history and taught at Dakota Wesleyan University, his alma mater. McGovern represented South Dakota in the House of Representatives and then in the U.S. Senate. His efforts within the Democratic Party enabled more blacks, women, and young adults to participate in the political process and the national convention; but these changes alienated the old-time Democratic political bosses.

McGovern, strongly opposed to the Vietnam War, received the Democratic nomination and named Missouri Senator Thomas Eagleton as his running mate. However, the Democrats seemed bent on political self-destruction. In addition to nominating the liberal McGovern, the final convention session ran late and McGovern's acceptance speech was delayed until well after midnight. A few days after the convention, the news broke that Senator Eagleton had received psychiatric electric shock treatments in the 1960s. Many Democrats believed that Eagleton should step down from the ticket, but McGovern said that he supported his running mate "one thousand percent." However, the pressure for

Eagleton to withdraw continued to increase; and he eventually stepped down for what he called the good of the party. Eagleton was replaced by Sargent Shriver, who was married to John Kennedy's sister and had been director of the Peace Corps.

The Democrats were divided and in disarray, while the incumbent Nixon had a smooth-running and well-financed campaign. McGovern was perceived as being so far out of the mainstream than even the typically Democratic AFL-CIO labor organization endorsed Nixon instead of the Democrat. The result in November was the biggest Republican landslide to that time: 47.2 million (61%) to 29.2 million (38%) popular votes and 520 to 17 in the electoral count. McGovern only carried the state of Massachusetts and the District of Columbia. However, the Democrats still had majorities in both houses of Congress.

In 1968 73 million voters, about 61% of those eligible, participated in the presidential election. In 1972 over 77 million people voted; but this was only 55% of eligible voters. The difference was that a new pool of potential voters 18 to 20 years of age had been created by the 26th Amendment, which was ratified in 1971. Participation by the new voters was not very high.

The Watergate Break-In

President Nixon could hardly have appeared to be more secure in his position, but such was not the case. During the campaign, Republican political operatives had gone too far in their efforts to insure the President's re-election; and the aftermath of those mistakes and the subsequent revelation of other dirty political tricks eventually drove the President from office.

On June 17, 1972, five burglars were arrested at the offices of the Democratic National Committee in the office and apartment complex in Washington, D.C. known as the Watergate. The men arrested, along with their supervisors Gordon Liddy and Howard Hunt, were employed by the Committee to Re-Elect the President. The men had electronic surveillance equipment on them and were apparently bugging or re-bugging the Democratic offices.

George Wallace

George Wallace (born in 1919) was elected governor of Alabama in 1962 on a segregationist platform. The next year he tried to prevent the integration of the University of Alabama and the Alabama public schools, but he was forced to back down in each case. Wallace was prevented by the state constitution from running for re-election in 1966, so his wife Lurleen ran and won. Everybody understood that George was actually running the state.

George Wallace was re-elected in 1970, 1974, and 1982. After the 1972 assassination attempt, he was confined to a wheelchair. A third run for the presidency in 1976 was short-lived. He is pictured at right with Republican presidential candidate Gerald Ford in 1976.

Despite his early record as a segregationist, Wallace mellowed in later years and received the endorsement of several black leaders and groups in Alabama. He actually appointed more blacks to government positions than any previous Alabama official. Wallace died in 1998.

As the result of a separate investigation, Vice President Spiro Agnew resigned on October 10, 1973, and pleaded no contest to a charge of tax evasion related to bribes he had received from contractors while he was governor of Maryland. Nixon nominated and Congress confirmed Gerald Ford as the first non-elected Vice President chosen under the provisions of the 25th Amendment. This photo shows Richard and Pat Nixon with Betty and Gerald Ford on October 12.

Not much came of the incident during the campaign, and both the White House and the CRP denied any knowledge of or involvement in the burglary. One poll during the campaign indicated that 48% of the public had not even heard of the Watergate incident. The men directly involved in the break-in pleaded guilty and were sent to jail in January of 1973.

The *Washington Post* newspaper investigated the burglary after the election and found a trail of evidence connecting the burglars to both the White House and the Nixon campaign. A special Senate committee also looked into the matter and found additional evidence of wrongdoing at high levels. Aides close to President Nixon resigned in April of 1973 as charges of criminal activity and illegal cover-ups increased. The counselor to the President, John Dean, testified before the special Senate investigating committee in June that the President, his top aides, and the Justice Department had conspired to conceal evidence connected to the Watergate incident and other illegal campaign activity. North Carolina Democratic Senator Sam Ervin chaired the committee hearings and tolerated no compromise with the truth. The highest ranking Republican member of the committee, Howard Baker of Tennessee, repeatedly asked witnesses, "What did the President know and when did he know it?" This turned out to be the crucial question regarding the President's involvement.

The Legal Battle

Nixon consistently maintained his innocence and said that he wanted all wrongdoers brought to justice. Against his wishes, however, Nixon had to appoint a special prosecutor, Archibald Cox, in May of 1973 to look into the growing scandal. A Federal grand jury under Judge John Sirica (Sih-RICK-ah) worked with Cox. A White House aide,

Alexander Butterfield, revealed in his testimony before the Senate committee that a secret taping system was used in the President's Oval Office to record conversations and phone calls.

Cox obtained a court order to gain access to the tapes; but Nixon refused to hand them over, citing executive privilege to keep the tapes from being made public. Cox continued trying to obtain the tapes, so Nixon ordered Cox fired on Saturday, October 20, 1973. The Attorney General, Elliott Richardson, refused to fire Cox and instead resigned. The deputy attorney general, William Ruckelshaus, also refused and was fired. The solicitor general, Robert Bork, was next in line; and he agreed to fire Cox. The incident became known as the Saturday Night Massacre.

In November of 1973, Nixon said in a speech, "I am not a crook." The President released some tapes that he hoped would show his innocence. One tape that was made public had a gap of silence that lasted about 18 1/2 minutes. The gap had apparently been caused by someone erasing the tape. The President's secretary said that she might have accidentally erased the tape while transcribing its contents; but many people believed that the erasure was intentional. A new special prosecutor, Leon Jaworski, continued to seek access to all of the tapes. Judge Sirica ordered that they be turned over, but Nixon continued to refuse.

President Nixon stated in a national broadcast on April 29, 1974, that he was making public edited transcripts of the White House tapes in question.

The End

In July of 1974, the Supreme Court ruled that Nixon had to release the tapes to the special prosecutor. Also that month, the House Judiciary Committee passed three articles of impeachment against President Nixon. The charges claimed that Nixon was guilty of obstruction of justice in helping cover up evidence related to the Watergate investigation, of refusing to cooperate with the Judiciary Committee, and of abuse of power in misusing government agencies to obtain information about private citizens.

Nixon then released transcripts of tape-recorded conversations made just a few days after the Watergate break-in which showed that, although he did not participate in planning the Watergate burglary, he did help conceal evidence and he agreed to mislead the public about his involvement and the involvement of others in his Administration. It was the "smoking gun" evidence that showed the President to be guilty.

Faced with the Democrat-controlled House about to vote on the articles of impeachment and the Democrat-controlled Senate then bound to hold an impeachment trial, President Nixon resigned effective noon, August 9, 1974. He left Washington shortly before noon and became a private citizen while flying back to California. Vice President Gerald Ford was sworn in at noon on August 9 as the first non-elected President.

One month later, President Ford issued a pardon to Richard Nixon for any Federal crimes he might have committed while President. Many people suspected that Nixon had made a deal with Ford before he resigned, but Ford denied any such deal. The new President said that he wanted to move on from Watergate and that putting a former President on trial would not help the country. It was time, Ford said, for the recovery to begin.

At right is President Nixon's letter of resignation. The photo above shows President Ford announcing his pardon of Nixon.

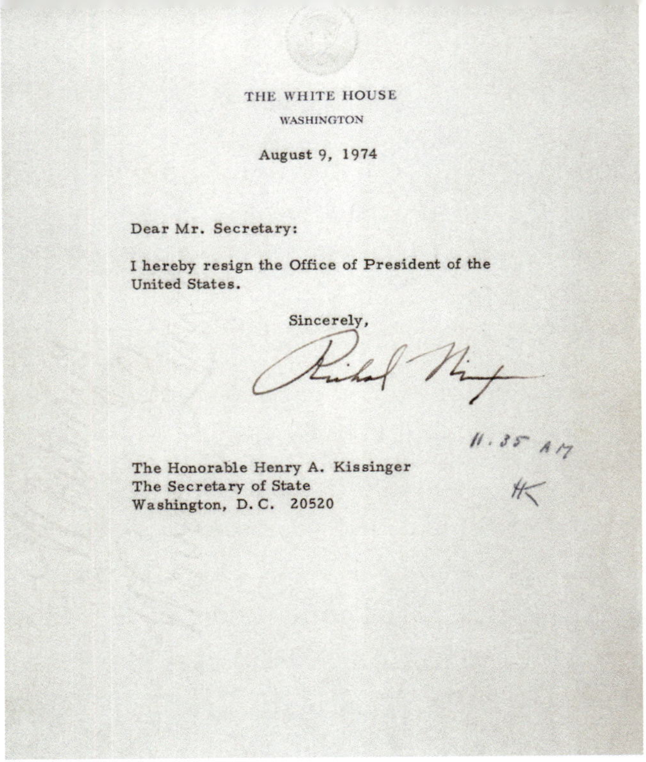

THE WHITE HOUSE
WASHINGTON

August 9, 1974

Dear Mr. Secretary:

I hereby resign the Office of President of the United States.

Sincerely,

Richard Nixon

11.35 AM

The Honorable Henry A. Kissinger
The Secretary of State
Washington, D.C. 20520

HK

In retirement Nixon engineered something of a comeback to respectability. The former President admitted in a 1977 television interview with David Frost that he made mistakes regarding Watergate. Nixon authored several books, mostly on foreign policy, and visited foreign leaders as a private citizen. He died in 1994.

Do not lie to one another, since you laid aside the old self with its evil practices.
Colossians 3:9

★ Assignments for Lesson 132 ★

American Voices Read the remarks Gerald R. Ford made at his swearing-in (pages 363-364).

Literature Continue reading *The Giver.*

Bible Read Luke 1:38-45. The word "baby" used in this passage is the same word used elsewhere in Scripture for a child that has been born. This shows that, in God's eyes, the unborn child is a person.

Work on memorizing Colossians 3:8-11.

Project Work on your project.

Student Review Optional: Answer the questions for Lesson 132.

Jimmy Carter and Gerald Ford Debate During the 1976 Presidential Campaign

Ford and Carter

Gerald Ford was born Leslie King. His parents divorced when Ford was two weeks old. His mother remarried, and her child was adopted and renamed after his stepfather. Leslie King thus became Gerald R. Ford Jr. Ford attended the University of Michigan and played football there. He then went on to Yale Law School. He served in the Navy during World War II. In 1948 he was elected to Congress from Michigan. In 1965 House Republicans chose Ford as minority leader. He had a conservative voting record on issues of defense and on limiting the size of the Federal government, and he generally supported civil rights legislation. Ford continued in the House until he became Vice President in 1973.

A Difficult Presidency

Ford was President during one of the most difficult periods in American history. He had to restore respect for the presidency and lead the nation back from the Watergate scandal. Ford became President three months before congressional elections. Ford's pardon of Nixon was extremely unpopular with many, and the country had high unemployment (it hit 9% during Ford's term), high inflation, and high Federal deficits. That November Democrats widened their majorities in Congress as the Republicans lost five seats in the Senate and 48 in the House. Eight months after Ford took office, South Vietnam fell to the Communists.

Under Ford's leadership, the inflation rate was cut in half. Ford vetoed fifty bills passed by the Democrat-controlled Congress that he thought would increase Federal spending unnecessarily. He encouraged private research into new sources of energy that would be funded by the Federal government. The 1975 Helsinki Agreement was a strong statement in favor of human rights around the world.

President Ford survived two assassination attempts in September of 1975. Lynette "Squeaky" Fromme, a follower of cult leader Charles Manson, pointed a gun at Ford in Sacramento, California, on September 5 but did not fire it. Twenty days later, Sara Jane Moore fired a .38-caliber pistol at Ford, but the bullet was deflected.

The 1976 Election

The Republicans nominated Ford to run for a full term in 1976. Ford chose Senate minority leader Robert Dole to be his running mate. The two made for an able and experienced ticket, but the shadow of Nixon and Watergate hung heavily over them.

Cambodian troops seized the American merchant ship Mayaguez *on May 12, 1975. The incident was reminiscent of the* Pueblo *affair in 1968. However, this time the U.S. conducted a daring rescue mission and recovered the ship and crew. This photo shows U.S. Marines boarding the ship on May 15.*

The Democrats smelled what they believed to be certain victory and had an active primary season. The surprising winner of the Iowa caucuses and the man who became the early front-runner for the nomination was Jimmy Carter of Georgia. Carter had enrolled in the U.S. Naval Academy in 1943 and had served in the Navy until 1953, when he left the service to run the family's peanut farming business in Plains, Georgia. He was elected to the state senate in 1962 and 1964, and then he made an unsuccessful run for the governorship in 1966. It was during this time that Carter had a religious experience and became what he called a born-again Baptist. He ran for governor again in 1970 and was elected to a single four-year term (state law did not permit him to run for re-election).

During his campaign for the Democratic presidential nomination, Carter asked people to trust him. He promised that he would never lie to the American people. He presented himself as an outsider to the typical political activity in Washington. Carter won the nomination and chose Minnesota Senator Walter Mondale as his running mate. Ford and Carter participated in the first televised presidential debates since 1960. In one encounter, President Ford said that he did not believe Poland and the other nations of Eastern Europe were under Soviet domination. He was trying to say that he believed the people of those countries longed for freedom and had not resigned themselves to living under Soviet control forever; but he came across as not having a grasp of the political realities of the world scene.

Only 53.5% of eligible voters turned out on election day, another effect of the Watergate scandal. Carter defeated Ford in a close race, by a margin of 40.8 million to 39.1 million (50.1% to 48%); and he gained a 297 to 240 electoral win. The Democrats continued to maintain sizable margins in both houses of Congress.

Carter's Domestic Policies

The American economy continued to struggle during Carter's term. Unemployment hovered around 7.5%, a new fuel crisis arose in 1979 because of continued unrest in the Middle East, and inflation was a major problem. The annual inflation rate hit 12%, and in some months it was around 18%. Mortgage rates rose to about 15%, and interest on credit cards zoomed to 20%. Loan sharks once got arrested for charging such interest rates, and economists predicted that America would likely never see single digit mortgage rates again. President Carter saw the root problem as one of a national malaise. He urged the American people to stand firm and to be willing to sacrifice, something many voters did not like to hear. Carter's approval ratings plummeted.

Foreign Policy

Carter had more success in some aspects of foreign policy. He advocated limiting American assistance to those countries which had a poor record on protecting human rights. However, the policy was not uniformly followed nor universally appreciated in the U.S. The Carter Administration concluded a treaty that called for the U.S. to relinquish control of the Panama Canal after twenty more years, a move which brought more howls of protest from conservatives who saw the deal as a retreat from American power and influence.

Carter was able to get Egyptian President Anwar Sadat and Israeli Prime Minister Menachem Begin (BAY-gin, hard "g") to sit down at Camp David in 1978 and to reach an agreement to end hostilities between the two countries. They exchanged diplomatic recognition and Israel withdrew its forces from the Sinai Peninsula. Sadat became unpopular with other Arab leaders as well as with some elements in his own country. A group of Islamic fundamentalists in the Egyptian Army assassinated Sadat in 1981.

The United States became involved in a small way with unrest in Afghanistan. The socialist government there was opposed by militant Muslim rebels. The Soviet Union responded to the government's appeal for assistance by sending troops and military supplies into the country. The Russians engineered a coup in 1979 that installed a stronger pro-Soviet government. Russian forces occupied the country. In response President Carter suspended nuclear arms treaty negotiations with the U.S.S.R. and halted grain shipments to Russia.

After the negotiations at Camp David, the leaders met at the White House for a signing ceremony. Seated from left to right are Menachem Begin, Jimmy Carter, Rosalynn Carter, Anwar Sadat, and Aliza Begin. Begin and Sadat returned in March of 1979 to sign a formal peace treaty between Egypt and Israel.

Carter also decided to cancel competition by American athletes at the 1980 Summer Olympic games in Moscow. In response to the widespread boycott of the Moscow Games by the U.S. and other countries, the Soviet Union and its allies boycotted the 1984 Olympic Games in Los Angeles.

The war in Afghanistan continued through the 1980s and became the Soviet Union's Vietnam. Thousands of Russian troops were killed in a no-win situation before Soviet forces withdrew in 1988 and 1989.

The Iranian Hostage Crisis

A tense situation in Iran caused Carter and the United States the greatest embarrassment of his term. In 1979 fundamentalist Muslims ousted the Shah of Iran, a strong dictator who had been a friend of the United States. One reason the Muslims opposed the Shah was his friendship with the U.S., which the Muslims saw as the "great Satan." The spiritual leader of the new Islamic government was the Ayatollah Khomeini. After the Shah was ousted, President Carter agreed for the Shah to come to the United States to receive treatment for cancer.

Saddam Hussein of Iraq (left) and the Shah met in 1975 to sign an agreement between their countries. After the Shah left the United States, he settled in Egypt and died there in July 1980. Saddam ordered an attack on Iran that fall, starting a war that continued for eight years.

Even though the Shah was gone, anger inside Iran against the U.S. increased. On November 4, 1979, a mob invaded the American embassy in Tehran, Iran, and took fifty-three American hostages (one was eventually let go). The Muslim extremists demanded the return of the Shah to Iran and the handing over of his personal fortune. The United States was outraged at this violation of diplomatic rights but took little direct action besides freezing Iranian assets in the United States.

The hostage situation remained largely unchanged day after day and month after month, as the Americans were humiliated by chanting mobs in Tehran. American evening newscasts highlighted the standoff almost daily. President Carter authorized a secret rescue attempt in April of 1980, but it failed when aircraft collided on the ground in their desert staging area and eight American soldiers were killed. Carter canceled the attempt and took full responsibility.

Iranians held the hostages for over a year. As Carter's term neared its end, new diplomatic efforts produced results. Carter agreed to unfreeze the Iranian assets; and Iran, in perhaps a last insult to Carter, released the hostages just as Ronald Reagan was being sworn in as the new President on January 20, 1981.

Disillusionment

The byword in America as 1980 began was disillusionment. The mood had started with John Kennedy's assassination in 1963. The disillusion continued as hundreds of thousands of American troops went off to fight a war in Vietnam that few understood. Race riots and more assassinations followed. Nixon said he would bring a change, but his presidency ended in disgrace. The U.S. economy struggled with recession and inflation. Finally, America was shamed on the world stage once again by militant Muslims who rejoiced at pushing America's face into the dirt. America was disillusioned.

Anti-Iranian Protesters in Washington, D.C., During the Hostage Crisis (1979)

The Lord also will be a stronghold for the oppressed,
A stronghold in times of trouble.
Psalm 9:9

⋆ Assignments for Lesson 133 ⋆

Literature Continue reading *The Giver.*

Bible Read Exodus 4:10-13. Verse 11 teaches us about the worth and identity of an unborn child, even one with physical handicaps.

Work on memorizing Colossians 3:8-11.

Project Work on your project.

Student Review Optional: Answer the questions for Lesson 133.

Muslims Praying in Washington, D.C., (1979)

Lesson 134

Spiritual Issues of the Seventies

Religious and spiritual issues came to the forefront several times during the 1970s. This lesson highlights some of the topics with which Americans grappled. The next lesson deals with the major issue of abortion and the 1973 *Roe v. Wade* Supreme Court decision.

Islamic Fundamentalism

The religion of Muhammed seemed to be of little concern to America for most of this country's existence. The number of Muslims in the U.S. had historically been small, although larger U.S. cities had a Muslim presence, and universities that attracted Muslim students had experience in dealing with individuals professing the Islamic faith. Americans knew that most Arabs were Muslims and that Arabs and Jews did not get along, but even the continuing conflict in the Middle East was not an immediate concern for most people in the U.S.

All of that changed during the Iranian hostage crisis. The television pictures of blindfolded Americans being led past crowds chanting "Death to America" were sobering and infuriating. Americans began hearing strange words such as ayatollah, jihad, and Shi'ite, and wondered what it all meant. The U.S. had gotten used to Russian and Chinese opposition to America, but the virulent hatred of Islamic extremists was a new threat.

The religion begun by Muhammed and his followers in the seventh century AD is based on the belief that Muhammed was the prophet of Allah and that the Koran is the holy book of revelation given through him. Muslims spread their faith throughout the Arabic peoples, into Turkey and the Balkans, and across northern Africa.

Ruhollah Khomeini was the Supreme Leader of the Islamic Republic of Iran from 1979 until his death in 1989. This photo from 2005 shows a portrait of him in Iran.

The faith also spread east into Iran, Iraq, Pakistan, and neighboring countries. Indonesia has the largest Muslim population of any country in the world. However, as Christians have done, Muslims have divided into different factions. Some are militant fundamentalists who are willing to force their views on others and who want to attack those whom they consider to be their enemies.

The United States is a target of the militants' hatred because they see this country as a political oppressor and as a purveyor of worldliness and immorality. The United States is also a target because of its support of Israel. Most followers of Islam in the Middle East resent the existence of Israel on land that they believe belongs to fellow Muslims.

As Americans saw the impact of religious hatred aimed at them, they began asking serious spiritual questions. Does American toleration of religious differences extend to those who want to do us harm? When does loving your enemy end and national self-defense begin? Can we compare the assaults of the medieval Crusades on Muslims to the aggression of modern Muslims against Christians? Is the United States weaker or stronger because of our desire to keep religion separate from our national policies? The confrontation with militant Islam raised political and religious questions that still challenge us as a nation.

Human Rights

President Carter attempted to implement a new foreign policy that limited assistance to countries with a poor record of protecting human rights. He did this out of a belief in the moral responsibilities that a government has toward its people and the people of the world and out of the hope that the United States could influence other countries for good.

Jimmy and Rosalynn Carter

Jimmy Carter and his wife Rosalynn established the Carter Center in 1982. The Center works in many countries around the world to promote peace, fight disease, and encourage economic growth.

President Carter and The Carter Center have engaged in conflict mediation in Ethiopia and Eritrea (1989), North Korea (1994), Liberia (1994), Haiti (1994), Bosnia (1994), Sudan (1995), the Great Lakes region of Africa (1995-96), Sudan and Uganda (1999), and Venezuela (2002-2003).

The photo above right shows the Carters receiving the Presidential Medal of Freedom from President Bill Clinton in 1999. In 2002 Jimmy Carter received the Nobel Peace Prize, in the words of the committee, "for his decades of untiring effort to find peaceful solutions to international conflicts, to advance democracy and human rights, and to promote economic and social development."

Previous foreign policy focused mostly on political realities and what was in the best interests of the United States. The U.S. didn't ask many questions about Stalin's domestic policies, for instance, when it sought Russia's assistance against the Axis in World War II.

Cults

The 1970s brought disturbing events involving religious cults. Korean businessman Sun Myung Moon established his Unification Church in the United States. Parents of some of those who joined the Church charged that their children had been brainwashed. Moon was known for his pro-American political stances and the mass weddings of thousands of couples, some of whom hardly knew each other.

The Church was also known for its members, whom critics called Moonies, selling tracts or flowers in airports and other public places, sometimes under false pretenses. The Church began the *Washington Times* newspaper in the nation's capital, which takes a decidedly conservative editorial stance in contrast to the liberal *Washington Post*. Moon died in 2012.

In 1978 a shocking story came out of the South American country of Guyana. A California Congressman, Leo Ryan, went to Guyana to investigate a community called Jonestown built by a cult that had been based in Ryan's district. The group was known as the People's Temple. The leader of the cult was Jim Jones.

Jones feared that Ryan would expose the corruption of his operations. As Ryan was leaving, members of the cult, following Jones' orders, gunned down Ryan and his party. Following the shooting, Jones forced all of the cult members in Jonestown to drink Kool-Aid laced with cyanide. Those who refused were killed by Jones' helpers. In all over nine hundred people, including Jones, committed suicide or were killed.

The Unification Church, the People's Temple, and other groups prompted questions about how pervasive cults were and how to identify them. Moon and Jones taught heretical doctrines that had little to do with the truth of Jesus. The rise of cults also led to questions about how far religious freedom should go in the United States. Does a person have the freedom to join a group that might even be dangerous for him or her? Some people became specialists in rescuing (abducting) people from cults at the request of family members and then deprogramming them by talking the person out of going back to the cult.

Entrance to the Jonestown Site in Guyana, the "People's Temple Agricultural Project"

An Insightful Warning

Alexander Solzhenitsyn (Souls-en-EAT-sin) was a Russian author who opposed the Communist government of the Soviet Union. He spent time in Russian prisons because of his criticism of the Soviet system. Solzhenitsyn received the Nobel Prize in Literature in 1970. His book *The Gulag Archipelago* was published in the West in 1974. It was a stinging exposé of how Soviet prisons were used to silence political opponents of the government. Solzhenitsyn was exiled from Russia a few years later and came to the United States.

What Else Was Happening?

1970 *The first Earth Day is observed. U.S. Senator Edward Muskie, author of the Clean Air Act of 1970, speaks at an event in Philadelphia on April 22, as shown at right.*

1970 *The U.S. Post Office Department becomes a quasi-independent agency, the United States Postal Service.*

1970 *Monday Night Football begins.*

1970 *Cigarette advertising is banned from television and radio.*

1971 *The microprocessor is developed, making personal computers possible.*

1972 *The Dow Jones industrial average closes above 1,000 for the first time.*

1972 *The Magnavox Odyssey home video game system, pictured at left, is introduced.*

1972 *The computerized tomography (CT) scanner is invented.*

1972 *At the Summer Olympics in Munich, Germany, Arab terrorists attack the Israeli team. The terrorists kill two members and hold others hostage. After intense negotiations, authorities launch an assault to rescue the hostages. Five terrorists and all eight remaining hostages are killed.*

1973 *The World Trade Center twin towers open in New York and the Sears Tower in Chicago becomes the world's tallest building.*

1974 *Thousands of life-size terra-cotta soldiers are discovered in the burial site of an ancient Chinese emperor.*

1975 *Labor leader Jimmy Hoffa disappears and is never heard from again.*

1976 *The supersonic transport Concorde begins regular service between the U.S. and Europe.*

1976 *Bacteria in a hotel air conditioning system infects 182 American Legion members attending a convention in Philadelphia, killing 29. The disease comes to be known as Legionnaire's Disease.*

1976 *The military academies begin admitting women.*

1978 *Polish Cardinal Karol Wojtyla becomes Pope John Paul II.*

1978 *The Apple II computer comes onto the market.*

1979 *Margaret Thatcher becomes the first female prime minister of Great Britain.*

1979 *A nuclear accident at Three Mile Island near Harrisburg, Pennsylvania, releases nuclear material into the air and forces the evacuation of over 140,000 people. The photo at right shows an anti-nuclear rally after the accident.*

1979 *The Walkman personal stereo system goes on sale.*

Solzhenitsyn was widely known as a critic of the Russian system, but he also pointed out the failings he saw in Western culture. His address at the 1978 Harvard University commencement exercise was a landmark indictment of Western culture. He said that the West was losing its courage in standing for the right and that political freedom had been used to promote evil. He criticized the press for hastiness, superficiality, and sensationalism. He said the spiritual life of the United States suffered because of our prosperity; in other words, we have it too easy. In this sense, both the Communist world and the free world suffer from a crisis of the spirit.

Solzhenitsyn said the standard of success should not be how much one makes or how much one pays for gasoline, but whether the world is better by a person's life. He urged recognition of what he called the "Superior Spirit" above us all. These words, especially coming from a man who had seen the worst side of the Communist system, were a strong indictment of the spiritual failings of the democratic West.

Alexander Solzhenitsyn returned to Russia in 1994 after the fall of Communism. He died in 2008.

I came that they may have life,
and have it abundantly.
John 10:10

⋆ Assignments for Lesson 134 ⋆

Literature Continue reading *The Giver.*

Bible Work on memorizing Colossians 3:8-11.

Project Work on your project.

Student Review Optional: Answer the questions for Lesson 134.

Pro-Abortion Demonstrators in Germantown, Maryland (2011)

Lesson 135 - Bible Study

Roe v. Wade

Imagine a young woman, full of life, with hopes and dreams for the future. She isn't rich; but she comes from a respectable family, with parents who have taught her right from wrong. She is preparing to be married, and then she discovers that she is pregnant. Her fiancé no longer wants her. Friends and family will look down on her, to say the least. What can she do? Run away and raise the child on her own? Try to hide her condition and give the baby away? Should she get an abortion?

Mary of Nazareth might seem like the perfect poster child for the "pro-choice" movement: young, poor, unmarried, from a degraded ethnic group, and to top it all off, she became pregnant when she wasn't planning it. The advocates of free access to induced abortion say that people like Mary the mother of Jesus should be able easily to dispose of an unwanted child. Mary, however, didn't choose that path. When Gabriel announced to her the calling God had given her, Mary didn't fuss and fume and talk about her body, her rights, and her choice. She said, "Behold, the bondslave of the Lord; may it be done to me according to your word" (Luke 1:38).

Legal History

In world history, abortion has not always and everywhere been considered a crime. This is not surprising, considering that most countries have been pagan and have allowed all sorts of gross moral violations. Even after the time of Christ, however, countries that nominally followed Biblical teaching did not necessarily view abortion as a crime. This was especially true before a mother could feel her child move (called "quickening"). When the law declared abortion to be wrong, the act was punished less severely than the murder of an adult.

England introduced a strict anti-abortion law in 1803. The state of Connecticut enacted the first anti-abortion law in the United States in 1821. The American Medical Association came out strongly against abortion in 1859, saying that it was an "unwarrantable destruction of human life." Other states followed with anti-abortion laws during the middle and later part of the 19th century. Evidence is inconclusive, though, that the state legislatures were primarily trying to protect unborn babies. Some states, including Texas, did not prosecute mothers for seeking or inducing abortions, only the doctors who performed them. The laws allowed abortion to save the mother's life, with varying degrees of restrictions on what that meant.

Most of these laws stayed on the books, relatively unchanged, into the middle of the 20th century. Changing attitudes toward abortion led some legislatures to reconsider their laws. England passed a new law in 1967 that allowed abortion in many subjective cases, including when the possibility of physical or mental abnormalities existed in the child. Some American states passed new laws that allowed abortions in more circumstances, but they were often more confusing that the original laws.

Groups of feminists, population control advocates, and others began working to change abortion laws in the U.S. Some of them wanted the laws totally repealed, believing that women had an inalienable right to control their own bodies. Others only wanted to reduce the restrictions on when and why women could obtain abortions. State and Federal courts heard numerous cases about abortion in the 1960s and 1970s, but the one that has become the most widely known began in Texas.

The *Roe v. Wade* Case

Jane Roe was the pseudonym of Norma McCorvey. McCorvey was expecting her third child when she met two lawyers, Sarah Weddington and Linda Coffee. They were looking for a plaintiff to help them challenge the Texas abortion law. In 1970 Norma became part of a lawsuit, filed against the District Attorney of Dallas County, which said that she was unable to obtain a legal abortion. She was joined by a married couple and by a doctor who was under prosecution for performing abortions.

A three-judge panel from the Federal Fifth Circuit Court heard the case initially. That court ruled that the Texas abortion law was unconstitutional, but it did not order Texas to stop enforcing it. Weddington appealed the case to the U.S. Supreme Court because the Circuit Court didn't fully rule in her favor; the state of Texas appealed it because the Circuit Court partially ruled in her favor.

The case was first argued before the Supreme Court on December 13, 1971. Justice Harry Blackmun worked for several months on an opinion in favor of Roe. Disagreement among the justices led them to call for a reargument of the case on October 11, 1972. The justices finally issued their opinions on January 22, 1973. The vote was 7-2 in favor of Roe. Chief Justice Warren Burger (appointed by Nixon) and associate justices Harry Blackmun (Nixon), William Douglas (Roosevelt), William Brennan (Eisenhower), Potter Stewart (Eisenhower), Thurgood Marshall (Johnson), and Lewis Powell (Nixon) concurred in the opinion. Associate Justices Byron White (Kennedy) and William Rehnquist (Nixon) dissented. Five of the seven justices supporting the decision were nominated by Republican Presidents.

The Supreme Court decided that broad criminal abortion laws (such as those in Texas) violate the due process clause of the 14th Amendment to the U.S. Constitution. The Court said that a woman has a qualified right to end a pregnancy as part of the right of personal privacy. Justice Blackmun went on to describe this qualified right. He said that during approximately the first trimester, the abortion decision must be left entirely to the medical judgment of the woman's physician. After the first trimester and before viability, when the child could conceivably live outside the womb, the State may regulate abortion to protect the woman's health. After viability, the State could restrict or even prohibit abortion, except when necessary to protect the mother's life or health.

Sarah Weddington (b. 1945) went on to serve as a Texas state legislator, a member of Jimmy Carter's Administration, and a professor. This photo was taken at the 2004 March for Women's Lives.

Biblical Evidence Against Abortion

Justice Blackmun's opinion stated that the Supreme Court did not need to decide when life begins and that the Constitution does not consider the unborn child to be a person. This in effect said that, under American law, unborn children do not have lives worth protecting. In contrast to this, the overwhelming testimony of Scripture is that unborn children are living human beings who grow and change according to God's design.

The Pentateuch. Genesis 25:22 tells us that Jacob and Esau struggled together within Rebekah's womb. Genesis 38:27-30 tells the interesting story of Perez and Zerah. When the time came for Tamar to deliver, Zerah stuck his hand out, and the midwife tied a scarlet thread on his hand. Then Zerah pulled his hand back; and Perez came out, followed by Zerah. Did Zerah become human for a moment when he stuck his hand out and then become a fetus again before he finally came all the way out? If a baby is a baby at nine months, how can we say it is not at eight, seven, six, five, four, three, two months, or one month?

Exodus 21:22-25 is perhaps the most contested passage in the Law that deals with this issue:

> If men struggle with each other and strike a woman with child so that she gives birth prematurely, yet there is no injury, he shall surely be fined as the woman's husband may demand of him; and he shall pay as the judges decide. But if there is any further injury, then you shall appoint as a penalty life for life, eye for eye, tooth for tooth, hand for hand, foot for foot, burn for burn, wound for wound, bruise for bruise.

Abortion advocates suggest that this passage considers the unborn child to be less than human. They say that the penalty for killing a child *in utero* is simply a fine. However, the plain reading of the text indicates that the penalty is a fine if the child is born prematurely and lives. If the child or mother sustains any injury, the *lex talonis* (e.g., eye for an eye) applies.

Margaret Sanger was a leader in founding Planned Parenthood in the early 1900s to promote the availability of contraception. The organization began receiving government funding for family planning services in 1970, the same year it began offering abortions in New York State, which legalized abortion up to 24 weeks. Planned Parenthood clinics are now the largest provider of abortions in the United States.

The Wisdom Books. In his first lament, Job expresses deep sorrow over the troubles that have befallen him. He asks, "Why did I not die at birth, come forth from the womb and expire?" (Job 3:11). He says that he would have been "like a miscarriage which is discarded, I would not be, as infants that never saw light" (Job 3:16). The Hebrew word for infants here is used several times in the Old Testament when describing judgment against a people, saying that the men, women, and children will be destroyed. It is often used in parallel with the word for a nursing baby, as in Psalm 8:2, "From the mouth of infants and nursing babes You have established strength."

When Job is trying to prove his uprightness, he says concerning his slaves, "Did not He who made me in the womb make him, And the same one fashion us in the womb?" (Job 31:15). Job obviously recognizes God's hand in the formation of children within the womb.

A superficial look at Ecclesiastes reveals a passage (6:3-5) that could be hard to digest:

> If a man fathers a hundred children and lives many years, however many they be, but his soul is not satisfied with good things, and he does not even have a proper burial, then I say, "Better the miscarriage than he, for it comes in futility and goes into obscurity; and its name is covered in obscurity. It never sees the sun and it never knows anything; it is better off than he."

Ellen McCormack ran for the Democratic presidential nomination in 1976. Her main focus was opposition to abortion. She won twenty-two delegates in primaries, but the Democratic National Convention, shown below, adopted a "pro-choice" platform.

Does this passage encourage the abortion of children who might face a difficult life? Didn't Jesus say concerning Judas, "It would have been good for that man if he had not been born" (Matthew 26:24)? God in His providence decides who will be born, when they will be born, and the circumstances in which they will be born. Unless God gives specific instructions otherwise (such as calling Abraham to sacrifice his son Isaac), deciding which children should or should not be allowed to live is not up to us.

The Prophets. Two passages in the prophets add to the overall case. In Isaiah 44:24, God is described as "the one who formed you from the womb." Jeremiah related the word of the Lord that came to him: "Before I formed you in the womb I knew you, and before you were born I consecrated you; I have appointed you a prophet to the nations" (Jeremiah 1:5). Some argue that Jeremiah was a special case since he was called as a prophet. However, even though God does not announce to all of us a special calling, we are all formed by Him to accomplish His purposes.

The New Testament. Like Jeremiah, Paul had a special calling, for he says in Galatians 1:15 that God "set me apart even from my mother's womb and called me through His grace." Hebrews 7:9-10 says, "And, so to speak, through Abraham even Levi, who received tithes, paid tithes, for he was still in the loins of his father when Melchizedek met him." If Levi was in the loins of his great-grandfather Abraham before his grandfather Isaac or his father Jacob had even been born, how much more was Levi a living person worthy of respect when God formed him in his mother Leah's womb?

Paul uses the Greek word *pharmakeia* in Galatians 5:19-20, "Now the deeds of the flesh are evident, which are: immorality, impurity, sensuality, idolatry, *pharmakeia* (translated sorcery), enmities," and so forth. We get from this Greek word the English word pharmaceuticals, meaning drugs. In Paul's time, the use of drugs and potions was related to sorcery, which in turn was related to idolatrous practices. Since immorality was a common part of pagan rituals, they used potions to cause temporary sterility and to induce abortions. The second century gynecologist Soranos of Ephesus used the word *pharmakeia* specifically to describe drugs used to cause abortions.

Jesus

When Gabriel appeared to the young woman Mary, he said, "Do not be afraid, Mary; for you have found favor with God. And behold, you will conceive in your womb, and bear a son, and you shall name Him Jesus" (Luke 1:30-31). Gabriel added, "The Holy Spirit will come upon you, and the power of the Most High will overshadow you; and for that reason the holy Child shall be called the Son of God" (Luke 1:35). When Joseph was thinking about not following through on his marriage to Mary, an angel confirmed to him, "the Child who has been conceived in her is of the Holy Spirit" (Matthew 1:20).

Mary went to see her relative Elizabeth, who was also pregnant. Based on the timing given in Luke, Jesus was probably only a few days old in the womb. When Elizabeth heard Mary's greeting, the unborn John the Baptist leaped in her womb. Elizabeth said to Mary, "Blessed are you among women, and blessed is the fruit of your womb! And how has it happened to me, that the mother of my Lord would come to me? For behold, when the sound of your greeting reached my ears, the baby leaped in my womb for joy. And blessed is she who believed that there would be a fulfillment of what had been spoken to her by the Lord'" (Luke 1:39-45).

Was Elizabeth making a fuss over a blob of tissue? Was Jesus simply a growth in Mary's uterus? Was the Word made flesh an inconvenience that could have or should have been destroyed before He saw the light of day? Even if we had no other medical or historical evidence against abortion, the story of Jesus should convince us that abortion is wrong.

This 1503 painting by Italian artist Mariotto Albertinelli depicts Mary's visit to Elizabeth.

Early Church History

While we do not give leaders in the early church the same authority that we give the writers of Scripture, their testimony provides important insight into how God's teachings influenced the first few generations of believers. Early church leaders spoke out against abortion.

The *Didache* is a second-century document described as the Teaching of the Twelve Apostles. It includes this passage that touches on abortion:

> You shall not kill; you shall not commit adultery; you shall not corrupt youth; you shall not commit fornication; you shall not

steal; you shall not use soothsaying; you shall not practice sorcery; you shall not kill a child by abortion, neither shall you slay it when born; you shall not covet the goods of your neighbor (2:2).

Here are several other quotations from early church documents:

> You shall love your neighbor more than your own life. You shall not slay a child by abortion. You shall not kill that which has already been generated.
>
> *Epistle of Barnabas* 19.5 (c. 125 AD)

Elizabeth Cady Stanton wrote in an 1873 letter to Julia Ward Howe, "When we consider that women are treated as property, it is degrading to women that we should treat our children as property to be disposed of as we see fit." Stanton (left) is pictured below with her co-worker Susan B. Anthony.

> For these women who, in order to hide their immorality, use abortive drugs which expel the child completely dead, abort at the same time their own human feelings.
>
> Clement of Alexandria, *Paedagogus* 2 (c. 175 AD)

> In our case, murder being once for all forbidden, we may not destroy even the fetus in the womb, while as yet the human being derives blood from other parts of the body for its sustenance. To hinder a birth is merely a speedier man-killing; nor does it matter whether you take away a life that is born, or destroy one that is coming to the birth. That is a man which is going to be one; you have the fruit already in its seed.
>
> Tertullian, *Apology* 9.4-6 (c. 200 AD)

> Those who give abortifacients for the destruction of a child conceived in the womb are murderers themselves, along with those receiving the poisons.
>
> Basil, *Canons* 188.2 (c. 360 AD)

Historical Evidence Against Abortion

Abortion techniques have been used for thousands of years. Ancient cultures used herbs and potions that caused a woman to miscarry her child. Some groups approved or at least condoned the practice, while others opposed it on moral or medical grounds.

The Hippocratic Oath. Hippocrates was a Greek doctor who has been called the Father of Medicine. Around 400 BC, a medical oath developed that bears his name. Among its precepts are these:

> I will give no deadly medicine to anyone if asked, nor suggest such counsel, and in like manner, I will not give to a woman a pessary (oval stone) to produce an abortion.

Other Greek thinkers at the time, such as Plato and Aristotle, approved abortion; but the Pythagorean school of philosophy believed that the embryo was alive from conception. In the United States, medical students have taken a form of the Hippocratic Oath for many decades. The modern version does not include a prohibition of abortion.

Feminists. Many modern feminists consider having the option of abortion to be an essential right for women. However, feminist leaders and writers in the 18th and 19th centuries, including Elizabeth Cady Stanton and Victoria Woodhull, generally opposed abortion in strong terms.

Former Abortionists. Dr. Bernard Nathanson was a founder of the National Association for the Repeal of Abortion Laws (NARAL, now known as the National Abortion Rights Action League) and director of one of the largest abortion providers in New York City. Nathanson considered himself personally responsible for 75,000 abortions. Soon after the *Roe v. Wade* decision, ultrasound technology began to offer a new look at unborn children. Though Nathanson was an atheist at the time, he began to distance himself from abortion and then began speaking out against it. He eventually became a believer in Christ and joined the Catholic Church.

After abortion was legalized in the United States, Christians organized crisis pregnancy centers to offer help to women facing unplanned pregnancies. Many centers now offer ultrasounds that let a client see the baby in her womb. These centers outnumber abortion clinics in the United States by a wide margin.

After the Supreme Court decision in her case, Norma McCorvey's life became entwined with abortion, even though she never had one. She began operating an abortion facility in Dallas. Operation Rescue, a pro-life group, moved into an office next door. Their buildings shared a wall. Flip Benham and other people involved with Operation Rescue, including a little girl named Emily who had almost been aborted, befriended Norma and helped her see that pro-lifers were real people, too. The continued friendship from Operation Rescue workers eventually convinced Norma to believe in Jesus. Like Dr. Nathanson, she joined the Catholic Church. McCorvey died in 2017.

Hard Cases

Some who oppose abortion in general favor exceptions in certain cases such as pregnancies caused by rape or incest or those that seem to threaten the mother's life. We should not base our principles on exceptional circumstances, but on occasion we must deal with exceptional circumstances.

No unborn child has ever done anything deserving of death, and he should not be punished for the sins of his father. In cases of rape and incest, the mother should trust that God can use her baby for good. If the life of the mother seems truly threatened, the goal should be to preserve life, both of the mother and of the child. All medical procedures carry risk, but sometimes the potential benefit outweighs the risk. During the conscientious attempt to save mother and child (whether by Caesarean section or some other procedure), God might allow the death of mother or child or both. We cannot fully explain why we face such suffering in this life. Thank God we have hope in Christ for a better future!

What We Can Do

Ending legal abortion in America seems to be a daunting task, but with God all things are possible. We can use our pocketbooks to support noble causes and to avoid companies that promote evil. We can use political means to prohibit government funding of abortion and to close abortion clinics. We can elect honorable representatives to work to protect life. It is possible to end legal abortion, but laws do not stop the unlawful from doing as they please. Getting away with abortion, especially with drugs like the "morning after" pill, will always be easier than getting away with other crimes.

The intentional destruction of a child in the womb is a terrible choice, but women who seek abortions and those who provide them are not the enemy. They need to hear the pro-life message of the gospel, the good news of Jesus Christ that provides the answer for all the problems that can make abortion seem like a valid option.

Believers need to set the example by recognizing children as God's gifts. Churches should be involved in taking care of children who are orphaned or abandoned, and in supporting families who have children with special needs. Children with disabilities are valuable because God made them. "Who has made man's mouth? Or who makes him mute or deaf, or seeing or blind? Is it not I, the Lord?" (Exodus 4:11). Children with few material possessions are valuable because God made them. "Did not God choose the poor of this world to be rich in faith and heirs of the kingdom which He promised to those who love Him?" (James 2:5). All children are valuable because God knits them together and gives them value.

May God grant us wisdom to understand His truth, to value the life He gives, and to do all things for His glory.

My thanks to my son John Notgrass for writing this lesson.

I call heaven and earth to witness against you today,
that I have set before you life and death, the blessing and the curse.
So choose life in order that you may live, you and your descendants.
Deuteronomy 30:19

★ Assignments for Lesson 135 ★

American Voices Read the excerpts from the *Roe v. Wade* Supreme Court decision (pages 356-362) and "In America" by John Notgrass (page 393).

Literature Finish reading *The Giver.* Literary analysis available in *Student Review.*

Bible Recite or write Colossians 3:8-11 from memory.

Project Complete your project for the unit.

Student Review Optional: Answer the questions for Lesson 135 and for *The Giver* and take the quiz for Unit 27.

The Crew of the Space Shuttle Challenger

28 The Reagan-Bush Era

After the Watergate scandal and the difficulties of the Carter years, America was ready for a change. Ronald Reagan offered a return to traditional values and pride in America. He took a firm stance against Communism world-wide, but his Administration stumbled in pursuing a policy that involved fighting Communism in Central America. George Bush continued the Reagan agenda but found the economy, influenced by Reagan-era deficits, a thorny problem. The fall of Communism in Russia and Eastern Europe as well as the Persian Gulf War were international events during Bush's term. In any era, we need to learn that God can bring good out of what is bad.

Lesson 136 - The Reagan Revolution
Lesson 137 - Reagan's Foreign Policy
Lesson 138 - The George H. W. Bush Administration
Lesson 139 - The Persian Gulf War
Lesson 140 - Bible Study: Finding Good in Something Bad

Memory Work Memorize Proverbs 3:11-12 by the end of this unit.

Books Used
The Bible
American Voices

Project (choose one)

1) Write 300 to 500 words on one of the following topics:

- Write a review of your favorite work of fiction of those assigned during this course. Tell what you liked about it and why you thought it was effective. Think of your review as a way to encourage someone else to read the book.

- After you read lessons 136 and 137 and the two speeches by Reagan in *American Voices*, summarize Reagan's approach as a leader and tell why you think he was effective.

2) Make a scrapbook of at least ten pages about your homeschooling experience. See Lesson 138.

3) Write and illustrate a children's book about American fads of the twentieth century. Some have been mentioned in this book, but you might need to do additional research. Include at least ten examples of fads. Your book should be at least twenty pages in length.

Ronald Reagan at a Campaign Rally (1984)

Lesson 136

The Reagan Revolution

In 1980 President Jimmy Carter faced difficulties at home and abroad. High inflation and high interest rates sapped the U.S. economy. American hostages held by Islamic militants languished in Iran. The man who stepped forward to offer new leadership was Ronald Reagan.

Reagan's Background

Ronald Wilson Reagan was born in Illinois in 1911. His mother was a strong spiritual influence on him, and as a young teen Reagan was baptized into Christ and became heavily involved in church activities. He became a radio announcer after graduating from Eureka College, then he moved to Hollywood and began a motion picture acting career in 1937. Reagan was a Democrat who voted four times for Franklin Roosevelt. He served as President of his professional union, the Screen Actors Guild. Reagan eventually became disillusioned with bureaucracy in government and liberal influences in the actors' union. He changed his party registration to Republican in 1962 and gave a stirring television speech on behalf of Barry Goldwater in 1964.

In 1966 Reagan was elected governor of California. He served two four-year terms. Reagan stood for conservative principles, but he learned to work with a more liberal state legislature. He made brief attempts to win the Republican presidential nomination in 1968 and 1976. By 1980 the tide of public opinion had moved closer to Reagan's position.

The 1980 Election

Reagan communicated a sunny optimism about America. He believed in the greatness and the potential of the American people. Reagan opposed abortion and favored the return of prayer to public schools. He favored a stronger military and opposed wasteful Federal programs. Reagan talked about eliminating the Department of Education, which Congress had created during Carter's term. He proposed a large tax cut to stimulate the economy. Reagan's thinking, similar to that of John F. Kennedy and others, was that whatever Federal revenue might be lost from reduced income taxes would be more than made up by people putting that money into the economy in other ways. This approach was called supply-side economics: if you put more money into production (i.e., to increase supply), the demand will follow and result in economic growth.

Reagan's primary challenger for the Republican nomination, long-time public servant George Bush, called Reagan's plan voodoo economics. Out of a crowded Republican field, Reagan emerged with the nomination. He chose former rival Bush to be the vice presidential nominee. The two men were able to put aside their differences about Reagan's economic plan.

President Carter had to endure a primary challenge within his own party from Massachusetts Senator Edward Kennedy. Kennedy portrayed Carter as too conservative and too inept to be an effective leader. Carter defeated Kennedy in the primaries, however, and received the nomination.

As is often the case when times are hard, the incumbent Carter had to defend his record and ask the American people to trust him that things would get better under his continued leadership. Reagan, on the other hand, talked of positive changes he would make and issued sharp criticisms of Carter's record. In their televised debates, Reagan repeatedly asked the American people, "Are you better off now than you were four years ago?"

America was ready for a change. Reagan swept the election by a 44 million to 35 million popular vote margin and enjoyed a 489 to 49 electoral landslide. Carter won only six states. Liberal Republican John Anderson of Illinois ran as an independent and received seven percent of the popular vote. In addition the GOP picked up twelve Senate seats to gain its first majority in the upper house since 1954. The Democrats continued to hold a sizable majority in the House, but conservative southern Democrats who supported Reagan's ideas gave the new President a working conservative majority in the House.

In the election, Reagan benefited from a swing toward traditional values and beliefs. Among those supporting Reagan were conservative Christian voters who had been urged to vote their convictions by people such as Baptist preacher Jerry Falwell. Falwell had formed the Moral Majority, a group that promoted ideals such as traditional family structure, prayer in public schools, and opposition to abortion. The Moral Majority encouraged people to become politically active. This movement by conservative Christians came to be called the Religious Right.

The Reagan Presidency

At 69 years of age, Reagan was the oldest man ever to become President. As he was being sworn into office, the American hostages in Iran were released, ending a 444-day national trauma. Just over two months into his term, Reagan was shot as he came out of a Washington, D.C., hotel after making a speech. He was seriously wounded, as was his press secretary, James Brady. Reagan eventually recovered, but Brady's brain injury was such that he was never able to return to his previous lifestyle. James Brady and his wife lobbied Congress to enact new legislation placing more restrictions on gun purchases; it was called the Brady Bill. The would-be assassin, John Hinckley Jr., was found not guilty by reason of insanity. Though generally confined to a mental institution since then, he has been allowed to leave for visits with his parents.

Every U.S. President elected in a year ending in zero from 1840 to 1960 died in office: William Henry Harrison (elected 1840, died 1841); Lincoln (1860, 1865); Garfield (1880, 1881); McKinley (1900, 1901); Harding (1920, 1923); Roosevelt (1940, 1945); and Kennedy (1960, 1963). Ronald Reagan (1980) broke the string. This photo shows President Reagan waving to crowds immediately before he was wounded in the attempt on his life.

The new President demonstrated his no-nonsense approach in August of 1981 when the Professional Air Traffic Controllers Organization conducted an illegal strike, almost paralyzing the nation's air traffic system. When they defied Reagan's back-to-work order, the President simply fired them all and authorized the training of an entirely new group of air traffic controllers.

Reagan was able to get a large tax cut through Congress in 1981. During his second term, another new law simplified and lowered the tax rates. Inflation was brought under control, but Federal revenues did not increase as much as the President had hoped. As a result, Federal budget deficits skyrocketed during Reagan's term. Republicans had long criticized Democrats for deficit spending, but the Reagan presidency produced the biggest deficits to date in American history. Congress and the President blamed each other.

In December of 1982, the unemployment rate rose to over 10%. Also during 1982, Congress raised some taxes to regain some revenue. Reagan presented the nation's first trillion dollar budget in 1987. He cut back on many government programs but increased military spending. In 1983 a bipartisan plan adopted by Congress enabled Social Security to avoid bankruptcy; but the long-term health of the program is still a subject of debate.

The economy did recover somewhat during Reagan's presidency, even though much of the recovery was on money borrowed to finance the government's deficit spending. A major blow to the economy occurred on October 19, 1987, when the New York Stock Exchange suffered its worst one-day loss in history to that date. The Dow Jones average fell 508 points, losing 22 percent of its value. Some observers speculated that the market was trading too high and that the loss was an appropriate adjustment. A significant part of the loss was blamed on computerized trading, which automatically triggered sell orders when prices fell a predetermined amount. Computer trading practices were changed after the incident.

President Reagan explained his tax cut plan in a 1981 televised address to the nation.

Triumph and Tragedy

In 1981 the first reusable spacecraft, the Space Shuttle *Columbia*, was launched from Cape Canaveral. No spacecraft before this had ever been used more than once. Two years later, Sally Ride became the first woman astronaut when she flew aboard the Space Shuttle *Challenger*. The shuttle program re-ignited interest in American space flight.

However, tragedy struck the shuttle program on January 28, 1986, when the *Challenger* exploded shortly after takeoff. All seven aboard were killed, including New Hampshire schoolteacher Christa McAuliffe. An investigation into what went wrong centered on O-rings on the rocket boosters that failed, causing a fuel leak which led to the explosion.

The temperature on launch day was unusually cold, and engineers had recommended that the launch be delayed. Because of pressure from NASA officials, their advice was ignored. Investigators also identified other equipment problems and mismanagement of the entire program. Shuttle flights were grounded until September of 1988.

Space Shuttle Columbia *launched on its first mission on April 12, 1981, as seen above. The shuttle flew twenty-seven successful missions. On February 1, 2003, it disintegrated during re-entry on its twenty-eighth mission. All seven crew members lost their lives.*

The AIDS Epidemic

The first case of Acquired Immune Deficiency Syndrome (AIDS) was identified in New York in 1979. The number of cases around the world increased dramatically in the early 1980s. Medical researchers determined that the disease was caused by the Human Immunodeficiency Virus (HIV), which apparently first appeared in Africa. The virus attacks a person's immune system, weakening the body's ability to fight off illness. Despite intense and well-funded research, no cure for the disease has been found. However, drugs have been produced that enable a person with AIDS to live with the symptoms for a longer time than was first possible.

The disease is transmitted by contact with the bodily fluids of an infected person. Its incidence is especially high among homosexuals and intravenous drug users. About 80% of cases worldwide are traced to sexual activity. AIDS can be transmitted to a baby born to an infected mother. The disease generated a significant amount of public fear as it became known. Unsupported ideas about how it might be transmitted were commonplace. Before screening tests were put in place for donated blood, some people developed AIDS by receiving transfusions of infected blood.

AIDS raises several moral, legal, and ethical questions. These include whether people should be tested for the disease to obtain employment or a marriage license, whether medical personnel should know if a patient has AIDS, and how much the general public should be able to know about an infected person. The fact that the disease is transmitted especially frequently through immoral behavior raises moral and spiritual issues regarding how such people should be treated and how much their care should be paid for with taxpayer funds.

More than twenty-five million people around the world are estimated to have died of AIDS-related causes since 1981. An additional thirty-three million are estimated to be living with HIV/AIDS, with about two-thirds of those in the part of Africa south of the Sahara Desert. About one million people are living with HIV/AIDS in the United States. The U.S. sees about 50,000 new cases and 15,000 deaths of infected persons per year.

This 1989 poster created by the U.S. Centers for Disease Control warned about the risk of contracting AIDS through sharing needles.

President Reagan salutes D-Day veterans while visiting France on the 40th anniversary of the Allied invasion during World War II.

The 1984 Election

By 1984 the economy was in better shape and the Reagan-Bush team seemed unbeatable. The Democrats nominated Walter Mondale, who had been Vice President under Jimmy Carter. Mondale made history when he selected New York Congresswoman Geraldine Ferraro as his running mate. This was the first time that a woman had been chosen for a national ticket by a major party. However, the election was no contest. Reagan and Bush received 59 percent of the popular vote and carried every state except Mondale's home state of Minnesota and the District of Columbia. It was the biggest Republican landslide in history. Reagan's coattails were relatively short, however, since the Democrats still controlled the House of Representatives. Democrats gained a majority in the Senate in 1986.

During Reagan's tenure in the White House, the economy made significant improvement. Inflation was cut in half, the stock market rose, unemployment fell, and overall economic growth and productivity rates were good. The Federal debt grew significantly because of years of deficit spending, but even that statistic was cast in a new light. Federal spending as a percentage of the economy fell slightly during the Reagan years because the overall economy grew so well. A President often accepts the credit for good economic news and takes the blame in bad times, but the real picture is much more complicated. Other factors, such as the growth of individual investments that helped stimulate the economy, were also at work in the 1980s.

After leaving the White House, the Reagans returned to California. In 1994 Reagan revealed that he was suffering from Alzheimer's disease. He died in 2004 and was mourned by millions who respected him and the principles he defended.

Ronald Reagan was known as the Great Communicator. He had the ability to capture the American mood and the American dream in his speeches. He restored America's faith in itself. As the next lesson shows, he also rebuilt the reputation of the United States in the opinion of the world.

President Reagan received this model in 1996 before construction began on the USS Ronald Reagan *aircraft carrier. It was christened in 2001.*

You younger men, likewise, be subject to your elders; and all of you, clothe yourselves with humility toward one another, for God is opposed to the proud, but gives grace to the humble.
1 Peter 5:5

⋆ Assignments for Lesson 136 ⋆

American Voices Read Ronald Reagan's First Inaugural Address (pages 367-370).

Bible In the Bible study for this unit, we will learn from Paul's letter to the Philippians about finding good in something bad. Read Philippians 1.

Start memorizing Proverbs 3:11-12.

Project Choose your project for this unit and start working on it.

Student Review Optional: Answer the questions for Lesson 136.

Ronald Reagan and Mikhail Gorbachev Meet in Geneva, Switzerland (1985)

Lesson 137

Reagan's Foreign Policy

The Reagan presidency saw dramatic events unfold in many parts of the world. Perhaps the most significant accomplishment of the Reagan term as well as the worst scandal to rock his Administration involved foreign relations.

The Soviet Union

Ronald Reagan had been an ardent opponent of Communism for many years. In a speech delivered early in his presidency, Reagan called the Soviet Union an "evil empire." Critics thought that his use of the phrase might set back any hope for better relations with Moscow, but Reagan believed what he said and had the evidence to back it up. An indication of Soviet intentions took place in 1981 in Poland, where the independent labor union Solidarity challenged the political monopoly of the Communist Party. Solidarity leader Lech Walesa (Wah-LENS-ah) aroused cheering crowds with his calls for greater freedom. The Soviets responded by sending military units to Poland to crack down on Solidarity and to insure the continued authoritarian control of the Communist government.

Russia also opposed a plan by Reagan to build a satellite-based detection system to shoot down incoming missiles aimed at the U.S. The official name of the plan was the Strategic Defense Initiative (SDI), but it was soon dubbed the Star Wars system. Although Congress approved research funding for the SDI, no such system was ever built.

Despite Reagan's firm stance, he did want to pursue better relations with Russia. Soviet leader Mikhail Gorbachev (GORE-bah-chov) also showed himself to be willing to pursue an easing of relations. The two nations pursued several avenues of discussion, and finally in 1987 an Intermediate-Range Nuclear Forces (INF) treaty was concluded that was an historic landmark. The two nations agreed to scrap an entire class of nuclear missiles, those with an intermediate range of 300 to 3,000 miles. The treaty included the right to conduct on-site inspections of the other country's cutback process. About 2,500 missiles were eliminated in all, but this was only a small fraction of the nuclear missile capability of each country.

Reagan played a major part in beginning the end of the Cold War. He believed that Communism was evil and was willing to say so. Reagan authorized a strengthening of the U.S. military that challenged the Soviets to match it, which was difficult for the Russians to do because of their weak economy. The U.S. government helped Solidarity in Poland and other Communist fighters in many countries. Finally, Reagan was determined to negotiate with the Soviets from a position of strength and did not give up any American advantages.

Near the end of his term, Ronald Reagan gave a speech in Berlin in which he said, "Mr. Gorbachev, tear down this wall!" Gorbachev did not tear it down, but he set in motion a chain of events that led to its being torn down. We will discuss changes in the Soviet Union and other Communist countries in the next lesson.

Lebanon and Grenada

In 1983 the Reagan Administration both endured a humiliating setback and enjoyed a stunning victory. The setback came in the country of Lebanon. During this period, Lebanon was torn apart by a chaotic civil war. Muslim and Druse Christian factions, a Palestinian Liberation Organization (PLO) force, Syrians, and Israelis all were involved in one way or another in the fighting.

The Israelis pushed the PLO away from the Lebanon-Israel border as a security move. For a while the PLO held Beirut, but after Israeli bombing attacks the Palestinians gave way to the Israelis. At this point, the Druse attacked Muslims in refugee camps. In an attempt to halt the bloodshed, Italian, French, and American troops took positions in and around Beirut as peacekeepers; but their presence was ineffective. On October 23, 1983, a Muslim suicide bomber drove a truck laden with explosives into the Marine quarters at the Beirut airport. The explosion killed 241 Americans. Reagan ordered the redeployment of the rest of the American force to ships off the coast of Lebanon.

The foreign policy victory came much closer to home. In 1983 the U.S. intervened in the Caribbean island nation of Grenada. The leftist government there was seen by neighboring countries as a threat because of its ties with Cuba. Two days after the suicide bombing in Lebanon, Reagan ordered American troops into Grenada to depose the government and rescue Americans enrolled in a medical school there who were unable to leave the country. The move was a complete success, and by it Reagan gave notice that he might approve U.S. interventions elsewhere in the region.

The Iran-Contra Scandal

The biggest foreign policy blunder of the Reagan presidency involved Central America. The country of El Salvador was enduring a civil war between the right-wing government backed by the military on one hand and Communist revolutionaries on the other. Extreme right-wing death squads roamed the country and were accused of killing thousands of suspected rebels and their sympathizers.

The photo below left shows U.S. Army helicopters preparing to touch down in Grenada. The photo below right shows Americans waiting to be evacuated from the island.

On October 7, 1985, Palestinian terrorists hijacked the Achille Lauro, *an Italian cruise ship in the Mediterranean. The hijackers held the ship for two days. Leon Klinghoffer, a Jewish American onboard who was confined to a wheelchair, was shot to death and thrown overboard.*

Meanwhile, the Communist Sandinista government of neighboring Nicaragua, which was backed by Cuba, gave assistance to the Salvadoran rebels and allowed them to operate from bases in Nicaragua. The Reagan Administration supported the government of El Salvador with aid and military advisors. In addition, the Central Intelligence Agency (CIA) supported Nicaraguan guerrilla groups called Contras (meaning they were "against" the Communists), who struck at the Sandinistas from bases in yet another country, Honduras. The overriding issue for Reagan was his desire to contain the influence of Communism in the region.

At the same time, Muslim neighbors Iran and Iraq were engaged in a protracted war in the Middle East. The United States gave assistance to Saddam Hussein and Iraq because of Iran's opposition to the United States, as evidenced by the hostage crisis in Tehran in 1979-80. In the fall of 1986, it was revealed that people in the United States government had been secretly selling arms to Iran in the hope that Iran would use its influence to help free American hostages being held in Lebanon (the hostages were eventually freed). Part of the profits of the arms sales to Iran were used to help fund the Contras in Nicaragua after Congress cut off money to support them. These activities violated official U.S. policy. Reagan had said previously that he would never negotiate with those holding Americans hostage; and although the arms sales were not direct negotiations, the policy was only one step away. The central figure in the complicated arrangement was Marine Lieutenant Colonel Oliver North, who operated out of the White House basement.

An independent counsel, a special investigative commission, and congressional committees concluded that the plan was guided by two of Reagan's National Security Advisors and the director of the CIA. Reagan himself was kept in the dark about it all, which enabled him to make repeated denials. North was convicted of minor charges, but the convictions were overturned on appeal. National Security Advisor John Poindexter was convicted of obstructing justice and lying to Congress and served six months in jail. Although the majority of Americans wanted to contain Communism, the Administration's deception, Reagan's apparently loose management style, and the complicated dealings involving Iran, hostages in Lebanon, and a civil war in Central America cost Reagan some of his popularity.

The Tower Commission presents its investigative report about the Iran-Contra scandal to President Reagan in 1987.

What Else Was Happening?

1980 The Rubik's Cube, a 3-D puzzle designed by a Hungarian professor, becomes an international craze. Budapest, Hungary, hosted the first Rubik's Cube World Championship in 1982, as commemorated by this Hungarian postage stamp.

1980 Former Beatle John Lennon is shot to death outside of his New York City apartment building on December 8.

1981 Pope John Paul II is wounded in an assassination attempt.

1982 AT&T (sometimes called Ma Bell) spins off the 22 local phone systems it owns (called Baby Bells). It does this to avoid possible monopoly problems as it pursues greater involvement in computer systems.

1983 Soviet fighter planes shoot down an unarmed Korean Air Lines passenger jet with 269 people aboard. The plane apparently strayed into Soviet airspace and did not respond to radio contact from the fighters.

1984 A gas leak from a Union Carbide plant in Bhopal, India, kills 2,000 and injures 200,000.

1985 The Live Aid marathon rock music concert, televised around the world from Philadelphia, raises $70 million for relief of African famine victims.

1985 The wreckage of HMS Titanic *is discovered seventy-three years after its sinking.*

1986 Nintendo introduces a line of video games in the United States.

1986 An explosion at a nuclear power plant in Chernobyl in the Ukraine releases radioactive material into the environment. It is the world's worst nuclear accident. The effects of the accident are still being felt in the region.

1986 Halley's Comet is visible from Earth. Its return every 76 years had been predicted by English scientist Edmund Halley in 1682. The photo at right was taken from Easter Island.

1987 Television evangelist Jim Bakker resigns after admitting an affair with a secretary.

1988 Evangelist Jimmy Swaggart confesses to moral failures. His denomination, the Assemblies of God, orders him to quit preaching for a year; but Swaggart refuses.

1988 On July 3, a U.S. Navy warship mistakenly shoots down an Iranian passenger jet over the Persian Gulf, killing all 290 people on board.

1988 On December 21, Pan Am Flight 103 explodes in mid-air over Lockerbie, Scotland. In addition to the 259 passengers and crew, eleven people on the ground are killed. Two men from Libya were eventually charged with placing explosives on the aircraft. One of the men was imprisoned.

In 1982 Ronald Reagan became the first U.S. President to address the British Parliament.

Or what king, when he sets out to meet another king in battle, will not first sit down and consider whether he is strong enough with ten thousand men to encounter the one coming against him with twenty thousand? Or else, while the other is still far away, he sends a delegation and asks for terms of peace.
Luke 14:31-32

★ Assignments for Lesson 137 ★

American Voices Read Ronald Reagan's Farewell Address (pages 371-375).

Bible Read Philippians 2.

Work on memorizing Proverbs 3:11-12.

Project Work on your project.

Student Review Optional: Answer the questions for Lesson 137.

George H. W. Bush Taking the Oath of Office With His Wife Barbara Beside Him (1989)

Lesson 138

The George H. W. Bush Administration

As President Ronald Reagan neared the end of his term, the heir apparent to his mantle was Vice President George Herbert Walker Bush. Bush was born in Massachusetts and grew up in Connecticut, where his father was a wealthy businessman and United States Senator. George served as a Navy flyer in the Pacific during World War II. In September of 1944, Bush's plane was shot down and the young pilot barely escaped death. He was awarded the Distinguished Flying Cross.

After the war, Bush graduated from Yale University; then he moved to Texas and worked in the oil industry. Bush became involved in politics and won a seat in Congress in the 1960s, although he lost in two attempts to become a U.S. Senator. In 1971 Richard Nixon appointed him as U.S. ambassador to the United Nations. He served as chairman of the Republican National Committee as the Watergate scandal unfolded. Nixon named him as the first American liaison in Communist China before the two countries established full diplomatic relations. Bush then served as head of the Central Intelligence Agency under Ford.

The Vice President turned back a primary challenge from conservative columnist and former Reagan speechwriter Patrick Buchanan to win the Republican nomination. Bush selected Indiana Senator Dan Quayle as his running mate. In Bush's acceptance speech, he said Congress would likely push him to raise taxes to ease the spiraling deficit. Bush declared that he would tell Congress, "Read my lips: no new taxes."

Eight Democrats competed for their party's nod, but in the end Massachusetts governor Michael Dukakis won out. His main challenge was from civil rights advocate Jesse Jackson. Dukakis picked Texas Senator Lloyd Bentsen for the party's second spot.

The campaign was especially vicious. Democrats charged that Bush was involved in the Iran-Contra affair and that Bush would do nothing to solve the problem of deficit spending. Republicans countered with the charge that Dukakis was just another big-spending liberal who was soft on crime. The election showed that the voters were not through with Republicans in the White House, as Bush defeated Dukakis 54 to 46 percent and received a 426 to 111 electoral win. Dukakis carried ten states and the District of Columbia. The Democrats, however, remained in control of Congress.

George H. W. Bush was the first incumbent Vice President to be elected President since 1836, when

Martin Van Buren was elected to succeed Andrew Jackson. Bush was also the last World War II veteran to serve as President. Eisenhower, Kennedy, Johnson, Nixon, Ford, and Carter had all served in uniform during that conflict.

Economic Issues

The major domestic problem that confronted Bush was the sagging economy and the increasing Federal deficit. The national debt had tripled since 1980 and stood at $2.6 trillion. America had a continuing deficit in its balance of trade, as the country bought more from overseas than it sold overseas. The U.S. endured a serious recession in 1990 and 1991. Making the problem worse was the failure of the savings and loan industry.

S&Ls, or thrifts, were competitors with banks in providing mortgage loans and other financial services. Deregulation of the industry during the Reagan term had allowed S&L managers to invest depositors' money in high risk bonds and other speculative ventures. When those investments turned sour, hundreds of S&Ls went broke. Failed institutions were sold, closed, or merged; and the Federal Savings and Loan Insurance Corporation had to pay depositors the money they had lost. All S&Ls eventually closed, and the entire debacle cost taxpayers hundreds of billions of dollars.

Another fallout of the troubled economy was the Federal budget. The Democratic Congress wanted to reduce the deficit by increasing taxes, but Bush refused to go along. Instead, Bush wanted to cut spending programs; but Congress refused to do so. Finally in 1990, Congress and the White House agreed on a plan that cut the deficit and increased taxes over several years. Democrats had no regrets about making Bush renege on his "no new taxes" pledge, and they reminded voters about it whenever they could.

The Rise of Homeschooling

The largest and longest-standing private school tradition in the country are the Roman Catholic parochial schools. During the 1960s and early 1970s, many churches and groups of individual believers organized new private schools. Two main reasons they gave were to provide a better education and to provide a more Christian education. During this period, the quality of public school education was declining and the influence of secular thinking was increasing.

The 1980s and 1990s saw a huge increase in the practice of homeschooling in America. Many of these pioneering parents believed that teaching their children at home would better allow them to carry out their God-given responsibilities. Many states did not know what to do with homeschoolers for several years. State compulsory attendance laws forced many homeschoolers to pursue their choice quietly. Gradually all states passed laws enabling homeschooling, although requirements vary greatly from state to state. Getting an accurate count of the number of homeschooled children is difficult, but a 2013 estimate from the U.S. Department of Education placed the number at 1.7 million.

Homeschool Field Trip to the Charles and Caroline Ingalls Home in De Smet, South Dakota (1996)

The Clarence Thomas Nomination

The Supreme Court's first and only African American Justice, Thurgood Marshall (nominated by Lyndon Johnson), retired in 1991. President Bush named Federal judge Clarence Thomas, another African American, to succeed him. Thomas was a conservative; but despite Democrats' raising many questions about his positions and opinions, the nomination was seen as having a fair chance of being approved. Near the end of the hearings before the Senate Judiciary Committee, however, a female African American professor at the University of Oklahoma Law School, Anita Hill, charged that Thomas had sexually harassed her while she worked with him at the Equal Employment Opportunity Commission when Thomas was chairman. Hill made her accusations during a televised hearing.

Clarence Thomas (2007)

Thomas categorically denied the charges and called it an attempt at a "high-tech lynching." No other evidence or testimony supporting Hill's claims was presented. Supporters of Thomas claimed that liberal groups were trying to derail his nomination. Thomas' opponents said that he was unfit to serve. Either Thomas or Hill was lying, and supporters of each had their minds made up. The Judiciary Committee split 7 to 7 and sent the nomination to the full Senate, where it passed 52 to 48. Hill's defenders believed that she did not receive the treatment she deserved, and the incident sparked a new push for women's rights. Thomas has proved to be a capable and intelligent Supreme Court Justice.

In 1991 an African American motorist, Rodney King, was arrested by Los Angeles police. King, who had a police record, tried to resist arrest. The officers then beat him severely, and their actions were captured on videotape. After the officers were acquitted in 1992, violent riots erupted in Los Angeles. Fifty-three people were killed and millions of dollars in property damage resulted. A burned gas station is shown below. In 1993 two Los Angeles police officers were found guilty of violating King's civil rights.

Conflict With Panama

The dictator of Panama, General Manuel Noriega, was indicted in an American Federal court in 1988 on charges related to international drug trafficking. In late 1989, the Panamanian National Assembly declared war on the United States. The next day, a U.S. Marine was killed in Panama when he and three other off-duty soldiers were stopped at a roadblock.

President Bush ordered 12,000 American troops into Panama. The invasion was designed to capture and remove Noriega, install a government led by Noriega's opponents, move against the drug trade, and insure continued access to the Panama Canal. Noriega sought sanctuary in the Vatican Embassy, but he surrendered a week later. The general was convicted and sent to Federal prison in 1992.

The Fall of the Communist Bloc

During the 1980s, the Communist sphere was beset by a number of problems. Communist economies had suffered for many years because of poor planning and inefficient performance. In addition, rumblings of a desire for democracy appeared from time to time, as had been seen in Poland. In 1989 pro-democracy demonstrations in Communist China were crushed in a bloody confrontation in Beijing's Tiananmen Square.

Soviet leader Mikhail Gorbachev sought to change the way his country operated, both domestically and with other nations. He cut back on central planning and censorship and sought better trade relations in the world market. Many in the Soviet Union responded to this freedom with a desire for more. In 1989 Soviet troops pulled out of Afghanistan. Also that year, Gorbachev announced that the Soviet Union would no longer feel compelled to intervene in the domestic affairs of other Communist countries.

The Communist governments in Eastern European countries, now without the threat of Russian military might to back them up, fell in short order. Poland, Hungary, and Bulgaria introduced democratic governments. Czechoslovakia cast off its Communist regime and divided into the Czech Republic and Slovakia, a division that was more in keeping with the ethnic makeup of the region. Romania's democratic revolution was more violent. The Communist dictator Nicolae Ceausescu and his wife were put on trial and executed. The Communist Party still functioned in these countries, but it was not the only party allowed.

Dan Quayle and Family Values

In May of 1992, Vice President Dan Quayle stirred a controversy with a speech he gave to the Commonwealth Club of California. Decrying the decline of morality and family life in America, Quayle cited several reasons for the problem and noted how society was negatively affected by troubled families. Among many other factors, he said that it didn't help for TV character Murphy Brown to bear a child out of wedlock on a prime-time situation comedy and call it just another lifestyle choice.

Quayle, who was the target of much ridicule already, was dismissed as being out of touch. In April of 1993, however, (safely after the election) an article in the usually liberal Atlantic Monthly *magazine by a respected researcher showed that divorce and single-parent families had indeed hurt children in many ways. The title of the article was emblazoned on the cover: "Dan Quayle Was Right."*

The most dramatic change took place in Germany, where the gates in the Berlin Wall were opened to allow free travel between east and west. On November 9, 1989, ecstatic Germans tore down the Berlin Wall. Germany was officially reunited the following October, and the Warsaw Pact of Communist countries was dissolved.

Changes also came to the Soviet Union, though not as smoothly. On August 18, 1991, military leaders and hard-line Communists tried to seize power from Mikhail Gorbachev. Gorbachev was then serving as general secretary of the Communist Party of the Soviet Union and as president of the U.S.S.R. The insurgents put Gorbachev under house arrest and took over government buildings in Moscow.

Boris Yeltsin, president of the Russian republic, openly criticized the attempted coup. The rebellion fell apart and dissolved within days. During the tumultuous events, it became clear that Gorbachev's power and influence were declining while Yeltsin's popularity was increasing.

Most of the republics in the U.S.S.R. declared their independence from Moscow. Estonia, Latvia, and Lithuania, Baltic republics that had been swallowed up by the Soviets after World War II, re-established their autonomy. The rest formed the Commonwealth of Independent States (CIS), with Russia as the largest but not the controlling member. Further moves for freedom erupted in regions such as Chechnya that had long been under Moscow's control. Gorbachev resigned as president of the CIS federation in 1991 and Boris Yeltsin replaced him.

President Bush, meanwhile, responded to the changes that were taking place by announcing in 1991 that the United States would dismantle its nuclear weapons in Europe and Asia and seek further reductions in the missile stockpiles of both the United States and the CIS.

The changes in the Communist sphere included a renewed openness to religion. The Russian Orthodox Church regained its stature and power in Russia. The Cathedral of Christ the Savior in Moscow had been destroyed by the Communists in 1931, as seen below left. A new cathedral was built on the same site and consecrated in 2000.

Millions of people in Russia and Eastern Europe who had been spiritually starved for decades eagerly responded to the message of the gospel brought by American missionaries. Russian schools have encouraged the teaching of the Bible and of moral and spiritual truth to their students, even as American schools have tried to limit such teaching.

Lesson 138 - The George H. W. Bush Administration

The threat of Soviet aggression had disappeared, although some feared that Russian weapons might find their way into the wrong hands. Russia declared that it would voluntarily reduce its weapon count. The cold war of forty-plus years had come to an end. China, Cuba, Laos, North Korea, and Vietnam are the only countries that remain under Communist rule.

Portions of the Berlin Wall have been distributed around the world. These segments were brought to Virginia.

The people who were sitting in darkness saw a great light, and those who were sitting in the land and shadow of death, upon them a light has dawned.
Matthew 4:16 (quoting Isaiah 9:2)

★ Assignments for Lesson 138 ★

American Voices Read the praise songs (pages 365-366).

Bible Read Philippians 3.

Work on memorizing Proverbs 3:11-12.

Project Work on your project.

Student Review Optional: Answer the questions for Lesson 138.

U.S. Planes Flying Over Burning Oil Wells During Operation Desert Storm

Lesson 139

The Persian Gulf War

While the world was watching the dramatic fall of Communism, another international event showed that aggression and war were still a real threat. In 1990 the tiny but wealthy country of Kuwait, which lies just south of Iraq on the Persian Gulf, increased its oil production. This caused a drop in world oil prices which hurt the debt-ridden economy of Iraq. When Kuwait refused to give in to the demands of Iraq's dictator, Saddam Hussein, Iraqi forces invaded and took control of Kuwait on August 2, 1990. Saddam declared Kuwait to be a new province of Iraq.

World Response

President Bush mobilized a large coalition of nations, including Russia, which demanded that Iraq withdraw from Kuwait. The United Nations Security Council condemned Iraq in a 14-0 vote. Days after the invasion, President Bush deployed troops and fighter planes to Saudi Arabia in Operation Desert Shield to guard against a possible Iraqi invasion of that country.

A U.N. resolution on November 29 approved the use of force to remove the Iraqi military from Kuwait. Bush believed that he had authority to attack on the basis of that resolution; but he asked Congress for a supporting resolution backing the use of force, which passed both houses of Congress on January 12, 1991.

The American presence in the region eventually exceeded 500,000, well over twice the usual American force that is stationed there. Bush called up Reserve and National Guard units to help in the conflict, and many in both groups filled important roles in Saudi Arabia and Iraq. The military prepared for action while diplomatic negotiations continued.

President Bush visited American troops in Saudi Arabia on Thanksgiving Day, 1990. This photo shows him with General Norman Schwarzkopf.

Operation Desert Storm

The U.N. set a deadline of January 15, 1991, for Iraq to withdraw from Kuwait. Two days after that deadline passed with no action by Iraq, Operation Desert Shield became Operation Desert Storm as coalition missiles and bombers attacked Iraq. The heavy bombardment lasted for several weeks, intending to weaken Iraq's defenses before a ground invasion began. The air attacks knocked out much of Iraq's command and transportation capabilities. Saddam's response to the attacks was to launch inaccurate SCUD missiles, built in Russia, against Israel and against Saudi Arabia. Saddam hoped to provoke Israel to retaliate, which he believed would weaken the coalition arrayed against him. However, the U.S. persuaded Israel to resist striking back at Iraq.

Joint Chiefs of Staff Chairman Colin Powell and the military commander in the field, American General Norman Schwarzkopf, became familiar figures on American television as they led the coalition effort. Iraq made proposals for a conditional cease-fire that the coalition rejected. On February 24, the coalition ground assault entered Iraq. Thousands of Iraqi soldiers surrendered as their route of retreat was cut off, and the invasion then turned to Kuwait and liberated the capital. Bush declared a cease-fire on February 28 after only 100 hours of ground attacks.

Many wanted to see the coalition forces proceed to Baghdad to take out Saddam, but the declared purpose of the invasion was only to free Kuwait. Retreating Iraqi troops torched several oil wells, which caused serious environmental damage besides wasting the precious natural resource. The United States suffered less than 150 battle deaths and about an equal number of non-combat fatalities. The number of Iraqi casualties is unknown. Initial estimates put Iraqi deaths as high as 100,000, though later analysts suggested lower figures.

Colin Powell (b. 1937) was the son of Jamaican immigrants to New York City. He served with distinction in Vietnam and eventually rose to the rank of general. Powell was Chairman of the Joint Chiefs of Staff from 1989 to 1993.

Cease-Fire

The cease-fire that was finally approved called for Iraq to destroy its chemical and biological weapon capabilities and to allow international inspections to verify that this was happening. Some inspectors were allowed in at times, but they were often hampered in their work and Iraq eventually ordered all inspectors out of the country. The coalition established no-fly zones over the northern and southern areas of Iraq to prevent Iraqi warplanes from menacing other countries. Iraqi aircraft occasionally violated the zones and met firm resistance from coalition fighters. The U.N. set up a trade embargo against Iraq. This hurt Iraq, but it was not consistently enforced. Iraq also agreed to pay reparations to Kuwait.

Iraqi Military Vehicles Destroyed During the Conflict

Impact of the War

The war offered the world its first glimpse of the advanced state of American military technology. Its laser-guided missiles and smart bombs, as well as its ground and artillery capabilities, proved far superior to anything that the Iraqis had. The international coalition against what Bush called naked aggression offered hope that future conflicts could be quickly resolved. With Communism falling and international cooperation increasing, the President spoke often about a new world order. He portrayed the conflict as the fight to protect freedom and to stop aggression in the Middle East and around the world.

Unfortunately, the new world order soon came to look much like the old world order, just with different countries fighting each other. Conflict in the Middle East has continued. Much of it still focuses on the existence of Israel and the Arab/ Muslim hatred of that fact. The region is also a major producer of oil, which plays a vital role in the global economy.

Michael "Scott" Speicher was a U.S. Navy pilot who became the first American combat casualty of the Gulf War. Speicher's plane was shot down over Iraq on January 17, 1991. Though he was initially reported as killed in action, rumors developed that he had been captured by the Iraqis. In 2009, eighteen years later, his remains were discovered by U.S. Marines after a tip from a local Bedouin. Speicher's remains were returned to the United States for burial. His wife and two children were finally able to know what had happened to him.

President Bush enjoyed unprecedented job approval during the Persian Gulf conflict. At one point a survey of Americans gave him a 91 percent positive rating. However, Bush found that his popularity as commander in chief in 1991 did not insure him an election victory in 1992.

What Else Was Happening?

1989 *The oil tanker Exxon Valdez strikes a reef off of Alaska and creates a major oil spill. The tanker captain is charged with drinking while on the job.*

1989 *A earthquake measuring 7.1 on the Richter scale strikes the San Francisco Bay area during the World Series. Sixty-two people are killed.*

1990 *Nelson Mandela is released from a South African prison after 27 years. He helps begin the transition from the long-standing government policy of apartheid (segregation). Mandela is elected president of South Africa in 1994.*

1990 *Lech Walesa, leader of the Polish labor organization Solidarity and winner of the 1983 Nobel Peace Prize, is elected president of Poland. He is seen at right meeting with President Bush in 1989.*

An angry man stirs up strife,
and a hot-tempered man abounds in transgression.
Proverbs 29:22

★ Assignments for Lesson 139 ★

Bible Read Philippians 4.

Work on memorizing Proverbs 3:11-12.

Project Work on your project.

Student Review Optional: Answer the questions for Lesson 139.

Coalition Troops from Multiple Countries During Operation Desert Storm

Lesson 140 - Bible Study

Finding Good in Something Bad

During the Persian Gulf War, a soldier stationed in Saudi Arabia heard the gospel from a fellow soldier and was baptized into Christ. That is not supposed to happen in Muslim Saudi Arabia, and it certainly is not something one expects in a war zone. Good, however, came out of a bad situation. That soldier went to a place of death and found new life.

No one can deny that terrible things happen in our world. The horrors of the Holocaust during World War II still astound us. In more recent times, we have witnessed barbaric acts of terrorism that have destroyed thousands of innocent lives. These and other acts of murder and destruction are the embodiment of evil, yet God is able to bring good out of what is bad. He is an expert at it.

Examples from the Bible

The story of Joseph in the book of Genesis, which we discussed in an earlier lesson, is a classic example of how God brought good out of bad. Joseph was sold into slavery by his brothers, lied about and thrown into prison, and forgotten by the man he helped; yet God eventually placed Joseph in a position where he could help his family and many others.

The cross is the ultimate example of God bringing good out of bad. Jesus was the innocent Son of God; but he was betrayed and abandoned by close friends, lied about before the authorities, condemned on trumped-up charges in an illegal series of hearings, and executed by the most cruel method known to the Romans. Out of that horrible event, however, God brought salvation and hope for everyone who comes to Christ in faith.

Recent Times

Times of difficulty bring opportunities for courage and heroism. The annals of war record countless examples of people sacrificing their all for others. Even simple good can come from evil. When America's supply of natural rubber was cut off by Japanese advances in the Pacific during World War II, for instance, American scientists responded by inventing synthetic rubber.

On a more important scale, millions of American men and women who served in the armed forces during World War II went out into a world they knew little about. As they went, Christians saw a world in need of the gospel. After the war, Christian missionaries went back to the countries where they had fought to take the message of Christ. The terrible events of World War II led to one of the greatest missionary thrusts in the history of the church. In recent times, the patriotism and dependence on God that were demonstrated after the terrorist attacks of September 11, 2001, were inspiring. They showed America's best side. God can indeed bring good out of something bad.

The key to finding good in something bad is having the right attitude. Paul shows us this kind of attitude in his letter to the Philippians.

The Right Attitude

In Philippians 1:12-26, Paul explains how he sees the good that has come from the bad things associated with his being in prison. He does this to encourage the Christians in Philippi to find good in their own circumstances. The entire letter of Philippians, in fact, is a lesson on attitude: "Have this attitude in yourselves, which was also in Christ Jesus" (2:5); "Do all things without grumbling or disputing" (2:14); "Finally, my brethren, rejoice in the Lord" (3:1); "Dwell on these things" (4:8). A positive attitude is not just a by-product of positive circumstances. A positive attitude comes from knowing Christ and seeing good even in the midst of the trying circumstances we all face.

As Paul considered his lot, he could have found plenty to complain about:

- He was in jail.
- Some of his Christian brothers were doing the wrong thing at his expense.
- He was even facing the possibility of death.

Yet Paul did not complain. Instead, he revealed a beautiful, positive attitude which showed that he had learned something practical from the Lord about life. Paul learned an insight that had lifted his life out of the realm of the ordinary, the typical, and the mundane. He did not feel the need to gripe and complain about his circumstances. He had discovered an entirely new way of looking at life; he demonstrated an attitude that we need to learn ourselves. Paul had learned to make the best of a bad situation.

"My Being Thrown into Prison Has Helped Spread the Gospel"

Paul says, "My circumstances (of being in prison) have turned out for the greater progress of the gospel" (Philippians 1:12). Here is the greatest spokesman for the gospel in the slammer. It would be easy to think that this would have all but shut down the work of evangelism, not to mention its potential discouragement to Paul himself. How easily he could have thought, "All these years of preaching the gospel, and look where it has gotten me!"

That is not Paul's attitude, however. He goes on to explain how his being in prison has actually served

St. Paul in Prison, *Rembrandt (Dutch, 1627)*

to advance the message of Christ. Paul says, "My imprisonment in the cause of Christ has become well known throughout the whole praetorian guard and to everyone else" (1:13). He had made it known to the guards, other prisoners, and everyone else that he was there because of Christ.

Paul never shied away from telling the story of Jesus to others. Every situation was an evangelistic opportunity for him. You can just imagine Paul tugging on the chain that was held at the other end by a Roman soldier and saying, "Have you ever heard about Jesus?" You can envision him getting into discussions with other prisoners (talk about a captive audience with felt needs!), telling them about the Lord Jesus himself being arrested—and then being executed—and then rising from the dead. That story would have been especially poignant for prisoners.

How differently we view our circumstances today. We are often fearful of being thought of as tacky or a religious fanatic, so we look for reasons why our situation is not an evangelistic opportunity. If advocates of various causes can voice their opinions, certainly we have every reason to put in a good word for Jesus wherever we are. If we are afraid to mention Jesus at a party, what will we do if one day the soldiers arrive at our door to arrest us because of our faith?

Paul's imprisonment helped the gospel spread because it opened up a whole new field in which he could sow the seed of the kingdom. Paul says that his being put in prison had emboldened others to speak the word of God more fearlessly (1:14). Perhaps they saw Paul's self-sacrifice and decided to get serious about the work of the Lord themselves. Maybe they realized that they would have to take up the slack now that Paul was in prison. Paul had lost his physical freedom; but ironically, because of that the word was being proclaimed even more boldly. People were making the best of a bad situation and Paul was thankful for it.

Ruins of Ancient Philippi

"At Least Christ Is Proclaimed, and in That I Rejoice"

Paul shows this same positive attitude about the increased preaching of the gospel that was taking place because of his imprisonment. He reveals that not all of this new fervor by others for preaching the gospel was from pure motives. Nevertheless, Paul finds something good about it. Some, to be sure, were preaching with pure motives, speaking fearlessly with love and good will. Others, however, were preaching more boldly "from envy and strife" (1:15), "out of selfish ambition" (1:16), and in hopes of causing Paul greater anguish in prison (1:16).

We don't know who these people were or what their precise motivation was. We do know that Paul had opponents in the early church. Perhaps these opponents tried to paint Paul as a scoundrel: "See! Your great apostle Paul—in prison! Do you really want a jailbird as your apostle of God? You never know what kind of trouble he's going to get into next!" Perhaps they were wanting their own measure of fame and popular acceptance and were happy to have Paul out of the way. Perhaps some of them thought that their preaching of the gospel in the city of Rome itself might stir up more trouble for Paul. After all, he was already in prison for spreading the gospel. If more preaching took place, Paul might get roughed up further by the authorities for the problem he had caused.

Whatever their precise motivation might have been, Paul says that some were preaching Christ out of poor motives. However, he goes on to say in verse 18 that at least Christ was being proclaimed. At least some lemonade could be squeezed out of this lemon. This passage has troubled people who see it as endorsing envy and selfish ambition in the preaching of the gospel. Nothing could be further from the truth. Paul is not saying that our motives don't matter. Both Jesus (Matthew 5:28, 6:1-18) and Paul (Colossians 3:22) taught the importance of pure motives. Nor is Paul going easy on the teaching of false doctrine. He is simply saying that if the truth of Christ is proclaimed, good is accomplished regardless of the motives of the proclaimer.

Suppose someone preaches the gospel out of a pure love for the Lord and for others, and someone responds to the message and becomes a Christian. That's great! But suppose someone else preaches because he likes being the center of attention or because he wants to appear to be a better preacher than someone else. If this latter person still preaches the truth and someone responds and becomes a Christian, that new believer is no less a Christian. Good has been done even though the teacher had impure motives. Christ can be proclaimed accurately even through an imperfect proclaimer (after all, that is the only kind of proclaimer anyone can be).

This doesn't make envy and other bad motives right. Rest assured that such sin will eventually have its negative consequences. It does, however, mean that good can be accomplished in a less-than-perfect situation. It is in this that Paul could rejoice. We can rejoice, too, knowing that the message and its Subject are more powerful than—and not limited by the weakness of—the clay jars in which the message is carried (2 Corinthians 4:7).

"It's All Going to Turn Out for Good—One Way or the Other"

Paul assures his readers that what was happening would "turn out for my deliverance (literally, salvation) through your prayers and the provision of the Spirit of Jesus Christ" (1:19). In the verses that follow, Paul talks about the life-and-death struggle that is going on in him and around him. He wonders whether it might be better to depart and be with Christ, but he concludes that it would be best for others if he lives on.

Paul realizes that he is going to be saved from prison one way or the other. He is either going to be released from prison or he will be executed and thus released from this life altogether. He's either going to be freed and get to preach again, or he will be executed and get to be with Christ. He can't lose!

The church in Philippi continued to grow after the first century. This mosaic inscription is from a fourth-century building known as the Basilica of Paul.

Paul had learned that one's present situation in this life is never the last chapter. We have no need to despair. Things are never hopelessly and completely out of control. Paul is not going to stay in prison forever. Something is going to change, and Paul knows it will be a change for the better. Paul can see beyond the prison cell. He knows that it will work out for good one way or the other. Sometimes we can't see beyond the immediate crisis—and we aren't even in prison!

Paul admits that he faces a tough choice. He will either be able to associate with his Philippian brethren and others again, or he will be done with all the trials of this life and be with Jesus soon. Either way, he will be happy. He is in a win-win situation.

He knows also that Christ is going to be honored in his life whatever happens, either through further ministry or through martyrdom. If he lives, it will be to exalt Christ. If he dies, it will be to exalt Christ. The reason Paul could look at his seemingly bleak situation with this optimism, and the reason for his great attitude about all of these otherwise terrible events, is the principle stated in verse 21: "For me, to live is Christ, and to die is gain."

It is important for us to see that this truth has application far beyond the choice Paul faced at that moment. This principle is the dynamic that enabled Paul to live as he did and to accomplish what he did. The Greek infinitives "to live" and "to die" can also be translated here as nouns: Life is Christ, and death is gain. For Paul, Christ was what life was all about; and death in any form was a means of gain.

Paul's life was wrapped up in Christ. For him, Christ defined life. Christ was the point of life. Paul's motivation was Christ; his joy was Christ; his success was Christ. For Paul, to be alive was to be living in and for Jesus Christ.

Death, on the other hand, is a proven principle of gain. A grain of wheat that dies, Jesus said, "bears much fruit" (John 12:24). Dying to self is the way to gain Christ. Dying to sin is the way to become more like God. Giving yourself for others is the way to find the richness of life. Physical death for the believer is the way to receive complete, blissful union with the Savior.

Life is Christ, and death is gain. If that was Paul's basic principle of life, certainly it applied when he was facing the possibility of actual physical death. Any principle or belief system that doesn't work when the chips are down isn't worth following. Paul had indeed found something that works in the crunch.

An Attitude that Really Works

It is easy to see how, with this attitude, Paul could praise the Lord despite his circumstances. We can see how he understood his imprisonment as advancing the gospel, how he realized that preaching with bad motives at least got Christ proclaimed, and how he could see either living or dying as victory. Life is Christ and death is gain—what more could you want?

This sounds great when the sun is shining, but someday a major crisis will come into your life that will severely test this principle. The message of Philippians tells us that it is possible to face life's crises in a positive way. If we get into the habit of looking at life with this attitude, when that crisis hits we will be able to say, "Life is Christ—and death is gain."

The Attitude of Self-Sacrifice

Another beautiful attitude that Paul demonstrates in this passage is that of self-sacrifice—his willingness to give up his own ultimate happiness for the betterment of others. He wants to be with Christ. He knows that this would be better for him. But he also knows that it would be better for the Christians at Philippi if he lives on. Realizing this, he is convinced that this is what will happen (Philippians 1:23-26).

What he is willing to have happen is a vivid object lesson for that group of Christians at Philippi who were struggling with selfishness. Individuals focusing on themselves had caused relationships in the body there to be broken. Paul, however, cares about others so much that he is willing to give up being with Christ for a while in order to serve others.

Since the time of Christ, many of those who follow Him have endured intense suffering and faced death because of their willingness to follow Christ's example. One of these was Maximilian Kolbe, a Polish Catholic priest imprisoned in the Auschwitz concentration camp during World War II. In 1941 he volunteered to take a stranger's sentence of death. This stained glass window honoring him is in Hungary.

Giving yourself up brings people together. If in a conflict you can say to the other person, "Whatever is best for you, that is what we'll do," that will pave the way toward harmony.

Finding good is easy in the midst of good circumstances. At some point, however, we will all face bad circumstances. The calling of people of faith is to find good in bad circumstances. We can do this because we have a powerful God who can bring good out of bad and because we have powerful examples of people of faith who have done this before.

For to me, to live is Christ and to die is gain.
Philippians 1:21

⋆ Assignments for Lesson 140 ⋆

Bible Recite or write Proverbs 3:11-12 from memory.

Project Complete your project for the unit.

Student Review Optional: Answer the questions for Lesson 140 and take the quiz for Unit 28.

Hurricane Andrew in the Gulf of Mexico

29 The 1990s

America in the 1990s enjoyed robust economic growth. With the fall of Communism, the United States was the only major military power in the world. Politics in the 1990s were dominated by Bill Clinton, his electoral successes and his moral failures. Republicans gained control of Congress in 1994 for the first time in forty years. The House impeached Clinton for matters related to his affair with a White House intern. The Senate held an impeachment trial and acquitted the President. The impeachment raised questions about the proper connection between public roles of leadership and the private lives of our leaders.

Lesson 141 - Politics and Economics
Lesson 142 - Issues of the 1990s
Lesson 143 - The Clinton Foreign Policy
Lesson 144 - The Impeachment and Trial of Bill Clinton
Lesson 145 - Bible Study: Public Leaders, Private Lives

Memory Work Memorize 1 John 1:5-10 by the end of this unit.

Books Used The Bible
American Voices

Project (choose one)

1) Write 300 to 500 words on one of the following topics:

- Should local, state, and Federal governments in the United States provide education, public health, and other services to illegal immigrants who are here in violation of the law? Should the children of illegal immigrants be denied public services just because their parents brought them here? Does providing these public services encourage more illegal immigration? See Lesson 142.

- Should the United States enact tougher gun control laws? What is the relationship between access to guns and public safety? Does the Second Amendment have limits? See Lesson 142.

2) Create a collection of photos that represent ways that computers and the Internet have changed everyday American life. Compose your photos intentionally and artistically. Your finished project should be in the form of a slideshow on an electronic device, prints of the photographs displayed on a poster, or photos in book form. Include at least fifteen photos. See Lesson 142.

3) Create a model of a U.S. military weapon or vehicle that was used during the 1990s or since. Make your model as close to scale as you can and from the material of your choosing (e.g., wood, cardboard, clay, STYROFOAM™, or LEGO® bricks).

Hillary and Bill Clinton with Daughter Chelsea and Buddy the Dog on Marine One (1998)

Lesson 141

Politics and Economics

President George H. W. Bush looked invincible going into the 1992 election year. His approval ratings had been extremely high during the Persian Gulf War. The collapse of Communism left the United States as the only real superpower in the world. Although Bush stood strong on the world stage, the domestic economy worked against him. A serious recession began in 1990 that increased unemployment. The chief cause of the economic slowdown appeared to be the huge annual Federal budget deficits. These deficits required the government to borrow money which could otherwise have gone into the private economy. Bush's reversal on his "Read my lips: no new taxes" pledge hurt him also.

In addition, Bush's position as a moderate conservative did not excite traditional Republicans who longed for the days of Ronald Reagan's decisive leadership and uncompromising stands. The conservatives had no one else to support (except for insurgents such as columnist Pat Buchanan), and the party was not unified going into 1992.

Meanwhile, the Democratic Party, sensing the conservative mood of the country, was becoming more moderate after experiencing losses by liberal presidential candidates Walter Mondale and Michael Dukakis. A leading figure among more moderate Democrats was William Jefferson Clinton.

Clinton's Background

Clinton was born in Hope, Arkansas, in 1946 as William Jefferson Blythe III. His father died in an auto accident three months before his birth. A few years later, Bill's mother married Roger Clinton. When Bill was fifteen, he legally changed his name to William Jefferson Clinton. His mother and stepfather had a stormy marriage, and home life was not pleasant. Young Bill was eager to please and succeed, however. As a teenager he was able to go to the White House and meet President Kennedy. That event confirmed in Bill's mind his desire to move into the White House himself some day.

Bill Clinton achieved a stellar academic record. He attended prestigious Georgetown University in Washington, D.C., and then was a Rhodes Scholar in Oxford, England. While in England he participated in anti-Vietnam War protests and experimented with marijuana (although, he said later, he didn't inhale). Returning from England, Clinton attended Yale Law School. There he met and married fellow law student Hillary Rodham of Chicago.

Clinton returned to Arkansas and pursued his first love, politics. He ran unsuccessfully for Congress in 1974, then was elected state attorney general two years later. In 1978 Clinton was elected governor of

President Jimmy Carter meets with governor-elect Bill Clinton in 1978.

Arkansas. At 32 he was the youngest governor in the country. He pushed through higher highway taxes to pay for his reform program, but this cost him popular support and he lost his 1980 re-election bid. He kept running, however, and was elected again in 1982. Clinton continued to be elected to two-year terms as governor of Arkansas through 1990.

The 1992 Campaign

Clinton ran for and won the Democratic nomination for President in 1992. He selected a fellow southerner, Tennessee Senator Al Gore, as his running mate. Clinton proposed cutting income taxes for the middle-class, raising taxes on the wealthy, and ending Federal budget deficits. He promised to "end welfare as we know it" and to reduce the size and influence of the military. Questions surfaced about how Clinton avoided military service during the Vietnam War (he was quoted as saying once that he loathed the military). Clinton was known as a political wheeler-dealer who was willing to sacrifice any principle to gain a political goal. Even bigger questions arose about Clinton's reputation as a womanizer. When asked on the TV program *60 Minutes* if he had ever been unfaithful to his wife, Clinton dodged the question by saying that his marriage to Hillary had had its problems but was now strong. He didn't admit anything, but neither did he deny anything.

Texas billionaire H. Ross Perot helped organize the Reform Party and became a candidate for President in the 1992 election. Perot wanted to run the government simply and efficiently like a business. He resisted labels such as liberal or conservative. Perot dropped out for a time and then re-entered the race. In the end, Clinton won with only 43% of the popular vote; but he received a 370 to 168 electoral college win over Bush, who got just over 34% of the vote. Perot received 18% but no electoral votes. Democrats retained majorities in both houses of Congress.

Republican Resurgence

Once in office, Clinton pursued a more liberal agenda than he had indicated in the campaign. One of his first actions was to lift the ban on homosexuals serving in the military. This was later refined as a policy of "don't ask, don't tell." Military leaders strongly opposed the policy, saying that it would hurt morale among the enlisted personnel.

Clinton's biggest priority was to try to revamp the nation's health care system to produce a program of socialized medicine overseen by the Federal government. He named his wife as chairman of a commission to draw up a plan to submit to Congress. The centerpiece of the proposal was the provision for government health insurance for every American.

Ross Perot

Speaker of the House Newt Gingrich, Vice President Al Gore, and President Bill Clinton Singing the National Anthem at Clinton's Second Inauguration in 1997

However, the plan met stiff opposition in Congress and among the public. The medical, pharmaceutical, and insurance industries opposed the idea of a government takeover. Small business owners did not like the added expense of helping to pay for medical coverage for employees. Many Americans simply did not like the idea of bureaucratizing medical care any more than it already was. By the middle of 1994, the proposal was dead in Congress; and Clinton dropped it.

The 1994 congressional election gave people a chance to vote on Clinton and the Democrats. Republican candidates for the House of Representatives signed on to an agenda called the Republican Contract With America that promised to cut the size of the House bureaucracy, vote on family-friendly legislation such as a child tax credit, and consider term limits for Congressmen.

The majority party normally loses ground in non-presidential election years, but the Democratic losses that year were huge. Republicans captured both houses of Congress, the first time since 1952 that the GOP had accomplished this. No Republican incumbent was defeated, and many new Republicans were elected. The party also picked up several governorships and gained control of more state legislatures. The election was a thorough repudiation of Clinton and the Democratic Congress. New Republican House Speaker Newt Gingrich of Georgia began work on the proposals in the Contract With America the day he took office. The House passed several bills in keeping with its Contract promises, but few of these became law because of the Senate's reluctance to go along.

The 1994 election also showed the power of the Religious Right. The most prominent group in this movement was the Christian Coalition, which had begun in 1989 as the heir to Jerry Falwell's Moral Majority.

Of Taxes, Trade, and Welfare

Soon after taking office, Clinton abandoned his promise of a middle class tax cut. Instead, he sought to balance the Federal budget by a combination of spending cuts and tax increases. He was able to get his plan through Congress on a close vote, and the annual Federal deficit began shrinking. The fiscal 1998 Federal budget showed a surplus for the first time since 1969. The government was even able to pay back some of the Federal debt, which is the accumulation of years of overspending by Washington.

Clinton gained approval of the North American Free Trade Agreement (NAFTA) that had been negotiated with Canada and Mexico by the Bush

Debates about the effects of NAFTA generated controversy for many years. The sign above left appeared at a protest in 2006 regarding a proposed immigration bill. Above right is a NAFTA commemoration ceremony in 2012.

Administration. The free trade zone that NAFTA created among the countries of North America is the largest free trade zone in the world. Clinton, most Republicans, and some Democrats supported it because of its encouragement of free trade and wider business markets. Opponents feared the loss of jobs in the U.S. as companies did move their production to Mexico where wage scales are lower than in this country. The agreement went into effect January 1, 1994. After NAFTA was passed, much production by U.S. companies moved to Mexico.

In 1996 the Republican Congress passed the first major overhaul of the welfare system in decades. States now were to receive grants from Washington to run their own welfare programs. The new plan limited the time that people could receive welfare and required that welfare recipients enroll in a job training program. The law cut food stamps, aid to families with dependent children, and other welfare programs. Liberal Democrats didn't like it, but Clinton knew that it matched the mood of the country.

The 1996 Election

Despite Clinton's stumbles, he easily won renomination in 1996 and never lost his lead in the polls. The Republican nomination was captured by seventy-three-year-old Senate majority leader Bob Dole. Dole was a wounded and honored veteran of World War II. He was the last veteran of that war to run as a major party candidate. Dole had sought the GOP nomination before and had been Gerald Ford's vice presidential running mate in 1976.

Clinton was re-elected with 49% of the vote and a 379 to 159 electoral victory. Dole received 41%, and Ross Perot garnered 8%. The Republicans maintained control of both houses of Congress.

The Economy

The growing American economy contributed to Clinton's win. The reduction in Federal deficits helped the boom, which was marked by low unemployment and negligible inflation. A major factor in the economic life of the country was the money pumped into businesses by American workers making contributions to investment and tax-sheltered retirement accounts. These accounts purchase stock in companies through mutual funds. Mutual funds are run by managers who pool investments from many individuals. The managers of the funds buy stock, which provides money to businesses. The businesses then invest the money in new production. This increased investment in

American business stimulated growth and caused the stock market to rise to new heights.

The Dow Jones Industrial Average (DJIA), the best-known measure of the health of American business, achieved unprecedented growth during the 1990s. The DJIA is a reading of the value of stock based on the stocks of thirty of America's largest and most important businesses, such as Exxon Mobil, Walmart, and AT&T (companies included on the list change from time to time).

The Dow closed over 100 for the first time in 1906. It passed 1,000 at closing for the first time in 1972. The average hit 2,000 in 1987, then 5,000 in 1995 and 10,000 in 1999. The close at the end of 1999 was 11,497, a 25% increase over the close just a year earlier.

Another factor in the strong economy was the role of the Federal Reserve Board and its chairman, Alan Greenspan. Greenspan sought to control the economy and hold down inflation by adjusting the discount rate it charged member banks for money. When the Fed lowered the rate it charged banks, loans for business and home buying were more affordable. If the economy got too active, the Fed held steady or increased the discount rate. The Fed's goals have been to control inflation and to keep the economy growing at a strong but moderate rate.

I know how to get along with humble means,
and I also know how to live in prosperity;
in any and every circumstance
I have learned the secret of being filled and going hungry,
both of having abundance and suffering need.
I can do all things through him who strengthens me.
Philippians 4:12-13

⋆ Assignments for Lesson 141 ⋆

American Voices	Read the Republican Contract With America (pages 376-377).
Bible	Start memorizing 1 John 1:5-10.
Project	Choose your project for this unit and start working on it.
Student Review	Optional: Answer the questions for Lesson 141.

Search and Rescue Efforts After the Oklahoma City Bombing (1995)

Lesson 142

Issues of the 1990s

A new wave of immigrants entered the U.S. in the 1980s and 1990s. Some seven million came into the United States during the 1980s, and a similar number entered over the following decade. These numbers, however, only reflect the legal immigrants; obtaining a count of illegal immigrants is impossible. Latin Americans made up the largest number of newcomers. Asian immigration also increased rapidly, while only 12 percent of the immigrants were from Europe. By 2000 over 28 million people in the U.S. (about ten percent of the population) were born in another country, about half of them in Latin America. Most of these immigrants settled in California, Texas, Florida, New York, Illinois, and New Jersey. Miami, Florida, and San Antonio, Texas, are two cities where a majority of the population is Hispanic.

Americans have struggled to accept and assimilate these newcomers into society. Many cities and towns have faced questions about how to help, educate, and employ large numbers of people who don't speak English. Some Americans have reacted with the same nativist prejudice and hatred that were displayed in previous generations; but legitimate concerns have been voiced about whether local, state, and Federal governments should be expected to provide services to illegal immigrants who do not pay income taxes.

One story highlighting the complexity of immigration policy mesmerized the country in late 1999 and the first half of 2000. Around Thanksgiving Day, 1999, six-year-old Elian Gonzalez, his mother, and ten other refugees escaped Cuba in a small boat heading for Florida. The boat sank and the other refugees drowned. Elian was picked up floating in an inner tube and taken to relatives living in Miami. The boy's father, still in Cuba, insisted that he be returned. Elian's relatives in Miami refused to give him up.

Many Republicans and most Cuban-Americans believed the boy should be allowed to remain in the United States, but most Democrats and many others believed that international law supported the father's rights. Early on the morning of April 22, 2000, armed Federal agents entered the house where the boy was staying and took the child from his relatives to reunite him with his father. The Supreme Court refused to review the case, which left Elian in his father's custody. Father and son flew back to Cuba and were welcomed as heroes.

Militia Movements and Domestic Terrorism

Many Americans are skeptical of the efficiency and trustworthiness of government bureaucracy.

Some groups in the 1990s took this skepticism to the level of open and violent hostility toward the Federal government. They showed their opposition in ways ranging from refusing to pay taxes to setting up armed camps to resist any Federal intrusion into their lives. White supremacists coupled this fear of government with a resentment toward non-whites whose numbers were growing rapidly. Another set of fringe groups involved those with unorthodox religious beliefs.

Randy Weaver of Idaho had attended meetings of a white supremacist group but was not a member. In 1992 federal agents surrounded the Weaver home on Ruby Ridge after Randy failed to attend a court appearance. During the confrontation, federal agents shot and killed Weaver's son and wife, even though they were not accused in the investigation. Weaver was later acquitted of all charges against him except his failure to appear in court. He later received a settlement from the government.

The next year, a religious group in Waco, Texas, called the Branch Davidians, led by David Koresh, was rumored to be stockpiling weapons, engaging in child abuse, and holding people against their will. When agents of the Federal Bureau of Alcohol, Tobacco, and Firearms tried to serve a warrant at the group's compound, people inside the compound fired on the agents. Four agents and two cult members were killed and several others were wounded.

The FBI began a siege of the compound the next day, which lasted for a total of fifty-one days. It was a situation that appeared to be bound for tragedy, and tragedy eventually occurred. Federal agents decided to move in with armored vehicles and tear gas on April 19, 1993. The compound burst into flames, and almost eighty people were killed. Anti-government groups saw the Ruby Ridge and Waco incidents as proof that the Federal government was their real enemy.

Two years to the day after the Waco debacle, on April 19, 1995, a huge truck bomb exploded outside of the Alfred P. Murrah Federal Building in downtown Oklahoma City, tearing the front off of the nine-story building. The blast killed 168 people, including nineteen children in a daycare center in the building, and injured 600 others. The nation was shocked and saddened at this act of domestic terrorism.

Timothy McVeigh and Terry Nichols were arrested in the ensuing investigation. Both men were part of a militia group that feared the government and that hated what had happened at Ruby Ridge and Waco. McVeigh was convicted of Federal murder charges in June of 1997 and was executed in June of 2001 showing no remorse. Nichols was also convicted in 1997 of charges related to the bombing and was sent to prison.

Janet Reno became the first female Attorney General in U.S. history in 1993. She is shown below left (in the red dress) touring the chapel at the U.S. Air Force Academy. Madeline Albright became the first female Secretary of State in 1997. She is shown below right meeting with NATO officers.

Columbine Memorial in Littleton, Colorado

School Shootings

Violence occurred in the nation's public schools at a new level in the 1990s. In incidents in Paducah, Kentucky; Jonesboro, Arkansas; and Springfield, Oregon, students brought guns to school and opened fire on teachers and classmates. The student in the Paducah incident was a high school freshman. The boys in Jonesboro were 13 and 11 years old, and the Oregon shooter was 15.

Then on April 20, 1999, eighteen-year-old Eric Harris and seventeen-year-old Dylan Klebold killed twelve students and a teacher at Columbine High School in Littleton, Colorado. They also wounded thirty others before finally taking their own lives. Investigators found a videotape in which Harris and Klebold predicted their murderous spree. President Clinton and others called for tougher gun control laws in an effort to stop the violence.

The Computer Age

The 1990s saw a dramatic increase in the use of computers in every walk of life. The first electronic computer was invented in 1944. Its circuits filled an entire room. Its memory capacity was small and its capabilities slow compared to today's standards. The invention of the transistor in 1947 that enabled electrical relays to be made with much smaller equipment than large vacuum tubes began a huge revolution in all kinds of electronic equipment.

Computers became much faster, but programming involved the use of cumbersome punch cards. When this author was in college in the early 1970s, student registration for the upcoming semester was handled by a computer that filled a large room. Each class required a separate punch card, and the machine had to be operated carefully so that it didn't overheat.

The microprocessor or microchip was invented in 1971. It enabled computers to be much smaller and to be used in household appliances, automobiles, and many other everyday applications. The first personal computer was created in 1975, and the development of this hardware and related software (programs that enable the computer to do word processing, calculating, and other tasks) brought the revolution to homes and to just about every business. Computers became smaller and smaller, going from desktop to laptop to palmtop.

One of the main reasons why computers have become so popular is because they are able to perform many different functions. Not too long ago, a person would use different equipment to write a letter, perform numerical calculations, design a building, or play games. Today one computer can do all of these tasks and much more.

The Internet is a vast network of computer networks that enables a personal computer to do even more functions and to connect an individual with the world. In 1969 an agency of the Defense Department created a four-computer network. Two years later, about two dozen computers at fifteen sites were connected. The National Science Foundation and government agencies created networks that linked even more computers.

The first browser for what came to be called the World Wide Web was unveiled in 1991. Companies, government agencies, organizations, and individuals created web sites or web pages to provide information about themselves. Today the Internet offers over two billion websites and enables e-mail, audio, and video communication. Web users can place orders for merchandise, research just about any topic, carry out banking functions, and do many other tasks with their computer.

Intel Corporation has been a leading manufacturer of computer microprocessors. This Intel 486 chip was popular in the 1990s.

Members of the U.S. Army Using Computers (1996)

The Internet has enabled the dot-com economy, which attracted many new companies and investors in the 1990s. However, many online businesses failed as the supply of them exceeded consumer demand and some businesses (such as online ordering of groceries) did not generate enough interest. The boom times of the 1990s began to wane in the last years of the decade. Many companies downsized by laying off thousands of workers.

Not to be lost in the emphasis on computers is the vital role that telephone lines play in this revolution. Phone lines enable networking and provide access to the Internet, as well as the use of fax machines. Cell phones now enable phone contact without actual lines. Alexander Graham Bell probably never dreamed what his invention would one day be able to do.

Computers are tools, in themselves neither good nor bad. They have enabled much good, such as helping in the teaching of the gospel and allowing missionaries to stay in better touch with supporters in the U.S. However, computers have also enabled easier access to much that is bad such as pornography and gambling. Computer viruses that destroy data and disable computers have been spread by e-mail. As we are able to have more and do more, we have to be sure that we are good stewards of these resources.

In 1994 Jeff Bezos started planning an online store to take advantage of the growth of the Internet. He decided that selling books over the Internet would be a good place to start. Bezos and his wife MacKenzie raised money from family and friends and started the business in their garage. Within a month after launching the site in 1995, Amazon.com had sold books in all fifty states and forty-five countries. Time *magazine named Jeff Bezos its 1999 Person of the Year. The company has continued to grow and diversify, becoming one of the biggest retail businesses in the world.*

The exercise of justice is joy for the righteous,
But is terror to the workers of iniquity.
Proverbs 21:15

⋆ Assignments for Lesson 142 ⋆

American Voices Read "Defense of Conservatism" by Clarence Thomas (pages 378-385).

Bible Work on memorizing 1 John 1:5-10.

Project Work on your project.

Student Review Optional: Answer the questions for Lesson 142.

U.S. Troops Awaiting a Visit from the President Watch as Air Force One Lands in Haiti (1995)

Lesson 143

The Clinton Foreign Policy

The Clinton Administration faced difficult situations in many parts of the world. In general, the President wanted to support democracy and peace; but his government never formulated any more specific overall policy goals than that. This made American policy appear inconsistent and uncertain. Some of these international hot spots saw a temporary easing of tensions but no long-range solutions.

Somalia and Haiti

When Clinton became President, a chaotic situation existed in Somalia, East Africa, where political anarchy had led to widespread starvation. President Bush gained U.N. backing for American troops to go into the country to restore order and to assist the civilian population. In 1993 international forces began entering the country and American forces withdrew. The American presence helped the immediate crisis, but the basic problem of political instability continued.

The intervention in Somalia was an effort by the American military to carry out a policy called nation building. Debate arose in the U.S. over whether nation building was a proper role for the U.S. military, which is primarily trained to fight and win wars. The policy could lead to American troops being made vulnerable as they try to enforce a peace without clear front lines and with various domestic factions fighting each other. Amid continued fighting and instability, Somalia formed a new government in 2004.

Closer to home, the Caribbean island nation of Haiti was in turmoil. In 1990 former priest Jean-Bertrand Aristide was elected president after a period of military rule. However, Aristide was soon overthrown by another military coup.

In 1994 President Clinton presented the Medal of Honor (posthumously) to the widows of two soldiers killed during a battle in Somalia in 1993. Stephanie Shughart (left) received the medal for her husband, SFC Randall D. Shughart. Carmen Gordon received the medal for her husband, MSG Gary I. Gordon, with their three-year-old daughter Brittany.

Haitian refugees began fleeing to Florida in small boats. Clinton permitted former President Jimmy Carter to negotiate with the military junta, which agreed to relinquish power. Aristide returned to power in Haiti in 1994, and American forces sent there to support his presidency were eventually withdrawn.

Aristide could not legally succeed himself in 1995, but he was re-elected to the presidency in 2000. Opposition parties claimed that the election was rigged and did not participate. Another uprising drove Aristide from power and into exile in 2004. Aristide's successor was re-elected president in 2006, but the country's political situation remained unsettled.

The Middle East

Israel and the Arab nations around her have been at war for decades. Complicating the matter is the Palestinian Authority, which claims to govern the Palestinian Muslims living on the West Bank of the Jordan River and in other regions around Israel.

President Clinton urged that the Palestinian Liberation Organization (PLO) be brought into the on-and-off Middle East peace talks. An agreement reached in Oslo, Norway, in 1993 called for Israel to allow Palestinian self-rule in the Gaza Strip south of Israel and in Jericho on the West Bank. In return for this concession, the PLO promised to reduce the level of violence against Israel.

President Clinton with Yitzhak Rabin (left) and King Hussein at the Signing of the Israel-Jordan Peace Treaty

This arrangement is called land for peace: giving control of land to the Palestinians in exchange for greater security for Israel against Muslim attacks. Israeli prime minister Yitzhak Rabin and PLO leader Yassir Arafat shook hands at a meeting with Clinton at the White House in December of 1993 when the Oslo Accord was signed. In October of 1994, Jordan and Israel signed a peace agreement. Jordan's King Hussein wanted to end the strife in the region.

However, continued violence between Israelis and Palestinians threatened the trend toward peace. Palestinian suicide bombings, for instance, kept Israelis off-balance and defensive. Domestic politics within Israel are not simple either. Israel's prime minister Rabin was assassinated in November of 1995 by a disgruntled Israeli who did not like Rabin's moves for peace. The following January, Yassir Arafat was elected president of the new Palestinian Authority, which functions as a government for the Palestinian people. Many in Israel feared and resented this development, because it appeared that the Palestinians were that much closer to becoming an independent state, something the government of Israel had opposed.

Benjamin Netanyahu was elected prime minister of Israel in 1996 on a platform opposing the land for peace approach. Netanyahu proposed building new Jewish settlements in the West Bank, thus reclaiming the area for Israel. He wanted to retake the Golan Heights from Palestinian control, and he opposed statehood for Palestine. Netanyahu's hard-line ideas found favor with the Israeli voters after Rabin's policies appeared not to bring the region any closer to a permanent and workable peace.

In October of 1998, Clinton, Hussein, Arafat, and Netanyahu met at Wye Mills, Maryland, and worked out a new land for peace deal. However, Netanyahu lost an election in Israel the next year to Ehud Barak, who promised to resume the peace efforts of the late Rabin. Clinton tried hard during

After the attack on the USS Cole, *the damaged ship was towed out to sea, as shown above. It was then carried back to the United States for repair aboard a Norwegian heavy transport ship.*

his last year in office to achieve some kind of Mideast settlement, but he was unsuccessful. Egypt withdrew its ambassador to Israel in 2000 because of dissatisfaction with Israel's handling of the conflict with the Palestinians.

Long-time military and political leader Ariel Sharon won a landslide victory over Barak in February 2001, returning Israel to a more confrontational position against the Palestinians. Palestinians responded by stepping up their terrorist attacks in Israel. Israel, in return, conducted military strikes on Palestinian positions in the West Bank region.

Terrorism

Terrorists attacked United States interests several times during the Clinton years. In what we now see as a haunting preview of September 11, 2001, a bomb exploded in the underground garage of the World Trade Center in New York City in February 1993. Six people were killed. Explosions at U.S. installations in Saudi Arabia in 1995 and 1996 killed a total of 26. In a coordinated attack on the same day in August of 1998, bombs placed outside of the U.S. embassies in Kenya and Tanzania took the lives of a total of 220 people. After these attacks, the U.S. struck terrorist sites in Afghanistan and the Sudan with single missiles; but otherwise the American response was muted.

On October 12, 2000, the American naval destroyer USS *Cole* was refueling at a port in the Arab nation of Yemen when a small boat approached. As it reached the side of the *Cole*, a bomb on the boat went off and blew a huge hole in the destroyer. Seventeen Americans were killed and thirty-nine were injured. The attack was linked to Osama bin Laden, but no military retaliation was made. Terrorists apparently came to believe that the U.S. would not make any significant response if they targeted Americans.

What Else Was Happening?

1994 *Major league baseball players go on strike in August. The World Series is canceled that year, and the strike is not resolved until the following April.*

1995 *The Clinton Administration re-establishes diplomatic relations with Vietnam.*

1995 *Former football star O. J. Simpson is found not guilty in the 1994 deaths of his former wife, Nicole Brown Simpson, and her friend Ronald Goldman. Simpson is later found guilty in a wrongful death civil suit brought by the Brown family.*

1996 *The line-item veto is passed by Congress. The Supreme Court strikes it down as unconstitutional in 1998.*

1997 *Hong Kong, pictured at left, is returned to China after being a British colony for 156 years.*

1997 *Bobbi McCaughey (pronounced McCoy) gives birth to septuplets (7 babies) in Des Moines, Iowa.*

1997 *Diana, Princess of Wales, is killed in a car wreck in Paris, France. As seen at right, Diana had met with Hillary Clinton in Washington, D.C., a few weeks before.*

1998 *Mark McGwire hits 70 home runs in a major league baseball season, breaking Roger Maris' single season record.*

1998 *John Glenn, the first American to orbit the earth and now a United States Senator, returns to space aboard the shuttle* Discovery.

1998 *Tobacco companies reach a settlement with 46 states and the District of Columbia to pay $206 billion over several years for the public health costs of smoking.*

The Balkan Peninsula

Yet another trouble spot in which the United States became involved during Clinton's presidency was the Balkan peninsula. The political and ethnic issues in the region are complex. The former Yugoslavia splintered in 1991 after the end of Communist rule. Slovenia, Croatia, Macedonia, and Bosnia-Herzegovina, which had been parts of Yugoslavia, declared their independence.

This left only Serbia and Montenegro making up Yugoslavia. Serbian minorities caused ethnic conflict in Bosnia and Croatia. The Serbs there received aid from Yugoslavia, which has a Serbian majority, and its Serbian president, Slobodan Milosevic (SLO-bo-dahn Mi-LO-seh-vich). The Serbs were especially cruel to Muslims in Bosnia, driving them from their homes and making them refugees. The Serbs killed over 7,000 Muslims in the Bosnian town of Srebrenica (Sreb-re-NEET-za).

For a time, American assistance was limited to humanitarian aid to the Bosnians. Eventually, the United States and other NATO countries established a military presence that include enforcement of

U.S. Air Force EF-111 On a Mission During NATO Operation Deny Flight (1995)

a no-fly zone and air support for UN troops. In 1995 the parties in the conflict signed the Dayton (Ohio) Accord, which divided Bosnia into a Muslim Croat federation comprising 51% of the land and a Bosnian-Serb republic that controlled the other 49%. The accord was to be enforced by 60,000 NATO troops, 20,000 of whom were Americans. A cease-fire was signed in October of that year to end the conflict.

Trouble in the Balkans erupted again in 1998, this time in the Yugoslavian province of Kosovo. After a period of Kosovar autonomy, in 1998 Milosevic reasserted Serbian control; and Serbian troops practiced ethnic cleansing against the Albanian Muslim majority who long for independence. Many Albanian Muslims in Kosovo fled to Macedonia and Albania.

The remains of over 6,000 victims have been recovered from mass graves and buried at the Srebrenica Genocide Memorial in Bosnia-Herzegovina.

The U.S. requested that NATO forces attack Yugoslavia and weaken its military structure to ease the pressure on Kosovo. NATO approved the move; and for the first time in its history, NATO forces launched an attack against a sovereign country. NATO air strikes, mostly flown by American and British planes, pummeled Yugoslav military facilities. German forces participated in the strikes, the first time German planes had flown in combat since World War II. After 72 days of attacks, Milosevic accepted terms for peace. Kosovo was granted limited autonomy. As Muslim Kosovars returned, Serbians in the province feared retaliation attacks.

Milosevic was defeated in an election in the fall of 2000, but he remained in the presidential palace even after falling from power. Yugoslav security forces arrested him in 2001, and he was then taken to appear before the U.N. War Crimes Tribunal at The Hague in the Netherlands to face charges related to alleged war crimes in Bosnia. During the trial, Milosevic continued to be defiant toward world opinion and his accusers. Before a verdict was reached, Milosevic was found dead in his prison cell in March of 2006.

Serbia and Montenegro are now independent republics. Kosovo became a largely autonomous region in Serbia. It declared independence in 2008.

In June of 1995, an American F-16 fighter plane was shot down over Bosnia-Herzegovina. The pilot, Scott O'Grady, survived the crash and hid for six days before he was rescued by U.S. Marines. O'Grady (at center above after his rescue) is a strong believer in Christ and has credited the Lord as the key factor in his survival.

Now the deeds of the flesh are evident, which are . . .
enmities, strife, jealousy, outbursts of anger,
disputes, dissensions, factions . . .
and things like these.
Galatians 5:19-21

⋆ Assignments for Lesson 143 ⋆

Bible	Work on memorizing 1 John 1:5-10.
Project	Work on your project.
Student Review	Optional: Answer the questions for Lesson 143.

Tickets Given to Gerald and Betty Ford

Lesson 144

The Impeachment and Trial of Bill Clinton

A few months after Bill Clinton took office in 1993, an independent counsel was appointed by the Justice Department to look into the involvement of Clinton and his wife during the late 1970s with the Whitewater Development Company, which had been formed to build a resort on the White River in Arkansas. Bill Clinton had been governor of Arkansas at the time; his wife Hillary Clinton was a partner in a Little Rock law firm.

The company proved to be a fraud, the project fell through, and the Clintons lost money on the scheme. However, a savings and loan that had invested in the project had misused funds from a Clinton gubernatorial campaign; and investigators wanted to know if the governor, now the President of the U.S., had been involved in any criminal wrongdoing. In addition, it was later discovered that Mrs. Clinton had done some legal work for the Whitewater project while her husband was governor, which might have constituted a conflict of interest. Kenneth Starr was named Whitewater independent counsel in 1994.

Also in 1994, former Arkansas state employee Paula Jones filed a suit against the President, charging him with making unwanted advances toward her. Clinton denied the accusations. Jones' lawyers, while trying to collect evidence of a pattern of misconduct by Clinton, discovered evidence of an immoral relationship between the President and White House intern Monica Lewinsky. The news of this alleged affair became public in late January of 1998. That month, the President gave a deposition under oath to investigators on the Jones case and withheld information about Lewinsky.

Charges and Denials

Starr pursued the matter over the next several months. Meanwhile, the President vehemently denied charges of the affair. At one point, he wagged his finger at his audience and the television camera and said that he did not have sexual relations with "that woman, Ms. Lewinsky." During an interview on television, Hillary Clinton accused what she called a "vast right-wing conspiracy" of fabricating the story to discredit her husband. The President's defenders vilified Starr, who is a Christian and had always been seen as a fair and impartial attorney. In public opinion polls, most people said that an affair was wrong; but the majority also continued to approve of Clinton's job performance as President.

On August 6, 1998, Monica Lewinsky appeared before a grand jury investigating Whitewater and

In August of 1998 the United States launched missiles against alleged terrorist locations in Afghanistan and Sudan. The image above is a surveillance photo of Zhawar Kili, a suspected al Qaeda base. Some saw these attacks as an attempt to divert attention from the Lewinsky scandal.

Clinton. She agreed to testify when promised immunity from prosecution. The former intern admitted to an affair with the President but said that she was never asked to lie about it. Eleven days later, President Clinton became the first chief executive to give testimony to a grand jury, when he answered questions for six hours about his relationship with Lewinsky. His answers were evasive (noting at one point that his reply to a question depended on what the definition of "is" is). However, he did admit to having intimate relations with Lewinsky. That evening, Clinton went on national television and admitted that the affair had taken place. His previous denials, meant to protect his family and to protect himself from embarrassment, were not true. The President was defensive about being forced to discuss such personal matters, and he condemned those who pursued the charges against him.

So the President had lied to the American public; he had apparently lied to the Paula Jones grand jury; and when he finally admitted the truth, he blamed the trouble on other people. The next month, Starr submitted to Congress a 445-page report. Starr said that Clinton had not only lied under oath, but that he also might have obstructed justice by suggesting to his secretary and others an outline of events involving Lewinsky that was not true (for example, telling his secretary that she had always been present whenever Lewinsky was with him).

When public opinion condemned the President's defensive posture in his televised speech, Clinton backpedaled and began expressing more contrition for his actions. He began meeting regularly with well-known ministers in a kind of accountability group. Skeptics, however, wondered if Clinton was really sorry or if he had just changed his tune to try to win back some public support. (In November of 1998, Clinton agreed to an $850,000 out-of-court settlement in the Paula Jones case. He neither admitted guilt nor made an apology.)

Impeachment Procedures

The House Judiciary Committee, which has the responsibility of initiating impeachment procedures, voted along party lines to recommend a full investigation that might lead to possible impeachment charges against Clinton. The full House voted on October 8, 1998, to conduct such an investigation, with 31 Democrats voting in favor of the inquest. The Judiciary Committee carried out the inquiry and submitted four articles of impeachment to the House on December 12, 1998. Two charges involved lying under oath during grand jury testimony, and two others charged Clinton with obstruction of justice and lying to Congress. The House passed one perjury charge and the obstruction of justice charge, but they voted down the other two.

On January 7, 1999, the second impeachment trial of a President in American history began in the United States Senate. Chief Justice of the Supreme Court William Rehnquist presided. No witnesses were called, just as no witnesses had been called by the House Judiciary Committee during its hearings on the articles of impeachment; but three videotaped depositions, including one by Lewinsky, were shown to the Senators. Thirteen House managers presented the case against the President, while attorneys for Clinton defended him against the charges. Prosecutors pointed out the serious nature of perjury and obstruction of justice. Clinton's defenders admitted that what the President had done was morally wrong but claimed that it did not rise to the level of "high crimes and misdemeanors."

Many Democrats said that a better course would be to pass a censure resolution against the President, but Republicans allowed no such resolution to be considered by either house. Critics of impeachment said that the Republicans were trying to do with impeachment what they had not been able to do at the polls, namely remove Clinton from office.

The impeachment trial lasted five weeks, but the outcome was never really in doubt. Democrats were going to support the President as much as they could, and Republicans did not pursue the case as vigorously as they could have. As much as the Republicans disliked the President and what he had done, public opinion and political will did not support removing Clinton from office. Sixty-seven votes were needed in the Senate to remove the President from office. On February 12, 1999, the perjury charge was defeated 45 to 55, while the Senators split 50-50 on the obstruction of justice charge. Responding to the votes, Clinton said he was profoundly sorry for what he had done.

On January 19, 2001, Clinton's last full day in office, the President made a deal with Robert Ray, Starr's successor as independent counsel. Clinton admitted that certain statements he had made in the January 1998 deposition for the Paula Jones case were false. The President agreed to pay a $25,000 fine to the Arkansas Bar Association and to forfeit his law license for five years. In return Ray agreed that Clinton would not be indicted on criminal charges once he left office.

Republican Fall-Out

Republicans had little to crow about in Clinton's disgrace. House Speaker Newt Gingrich announced on November 6, 1998, that he would resign as both Speaker and member of the House at the end of his term. The party had not done well in the election three days earlier, and these results were taken as a rebuke of the party's pursuit of impeachment. Gingrich had earlier been reprimanded by the House for misusing donations to a foundation he had begun. In addition, Gingrich's personal life was in disarray. The Speaker had shown that he was more effective in opposition than in leadership.

Later that month, House Republicans chose Bob Livingston of Louisiana to succeed Gingrich as Speaker. However, on December 17, as the House debated the impeachment of Clinton, Livingston admitted to having an extra-marital affair several years earlier. On December 19, Livingston said that he would not seek the Speakership and would himself resign from the House.

Illinois Republican Dennis Hastert, shown at right, was elected Speaker of the House on January 6, 1999. On leaving that post in 2007, he was the longest-serving Republican Speaker in history.

Ray filed his final report on the Lewinsky affair in March of 2002. The report stated that the office of independent counsel had gathered enough evidence to indict and probably convict Clinton on perjury and obstruction of justice charges in a regular court.

The Lewinsky scandal cost Clinton much respect and influence during his last three years in office, but that was the least important of its effects. The President of the United States committed immorality and then lied about it to his family and to the American people. He abused the power of his office and the trust of the American people, and he took advantage of a young female intern (something the President's liberal defenders never discussed much). He acted as though he believed that he was above the law. However, Congress stopped short of taking the serious step of removing him from office.

He who walks in integrity walks securely,
but he who perverts his ways will be found out.
Proverbs 10:9

⋆ Assignments for Lesson 144 ⋆

Bible Work on memorizing 1 John 1:5-10.

Project Work on your project.

Student Review Optional: Answer the questions for Lesson 144.

Secretary of State-Nominee Hillary Clinton and Bill Clinton on Barack Obama's First Inauguration Day (2009)

Lesson 145 - Bible Study

Public Leaders, Private Lives

Bill Clinton is an intelligent, eloquent man who generates widespread admiration. As a Democratic President, he accomplished what Republicans only talked about for years: bringing the Federal budget into balance and reforming the welfare system (although, of course, he had a Republican-led Congress helping on these issues). However, Clinton was shown to have serious moral failings in his personal life.

Richard Nixon was popular with millions of Americans. He helped end American involvement in Vietnam, and he opened diplomatic contact with Communist China. Nixon, however, was apparently deeply suspicious of his opponents, used government agencies to gather information about people, and agreed to help cover up the Watergate scandal.

Jesse Jackson built a loyal following as a leading spokesman for civil rights. However, Jackson admitted to fathering a child out of wedlock; and the record-keeping of his tax-exempt organization has left many questions about where the money he receives winds up. After a short period of repentance about his adultery, Jackson returned to his public role apparently little changed.

Newt Gingrich verbalized the frustrations of many Americans with government and liberalism, and he led an amazing Republican resurgence in 1994. On the other hand, Gingrich also showed indiscretion with money and in his personal life.

How should we view public leaders who espouse ideas we believe in but whose personal lives are lacking? The dilemma extends beyond the field of politics into many walks of life. The great writer Charles Dickens had serious marital problems. Many books and CDs and movies in American homes were produced by people who have had questionable moral lives. What is the proper division, if any, between public figures and their private lives? Should it make a difference if the plumber we hire does good work but cheats on his wife?

All Have Sinned

In one important sense, the only choices we have for leaders, actors, and plumbers are imperfect people. Paul reminds us that "all have sinned and fall short of the glory of God" (Romans 3:23). Everyone has flaws and failings. In addition, Jesus warned us of the danger of judging or condemning others. "By your standard of measure, it will be measured to you," He said (Matthew 7:2). He told his disciples to take the log out of their own eyes before trying to remove the speck from another's eye (Matthew 7:3-5). Our first concern should be our own sin, not that of someone else.

However, no one should use the reality of sin as an excuse. Christians should be putting to death the deeds of the body by the power of the Holy Spirit, not making excuses for them (Romans 8:13). If we start making excuses for sin, our perception becomes clouded. A person who condemns an immoral Democrat but defends an immoral Republican because the latter agrees with his political stance is using a double standard. If you ever decide that wrong behavior in another person's life is not a problem, you can easily make the leap to thinking that wrong behavior is not a problem in your own life.

Defenders of President Clinton often said that his personal moral failings should not be taken into account when considering the job he was doing as President. This, of course, was an excuse for defending someone they agreed with politically. Imagine that a high elected official in Washington was found to be engaged in an adulterous affair about which he lied to the American people and to a grand jury. Now imagine that this official had been not Bill Clinton but Dan Quayle or Ronald Reagan. One can only imagine the howls of protest demanding his resignation from liberals who defended Bill Clinton for precisely the same behavior. This is the bind we get into when we use a double standard to judge the actions of others.

Such a double standard creates a situation in which some sins are considered worse than others. Clinton's personal sins, his defenders claimed, did not affect his ability to perform his duties. This is probably not true, but suppose for the moment that it were true. If his personal sin had been alcoholism, it clearly would have affected his ability to carry out his responsibilities. Who can say which sins have adverse effects and which do not? The Bible does not make such distinctions. "The wages of sin is death" (Romans 6:23).

Another dilemma involves what to do about past sins of which a person has repented. Is it fair to hold against someone sins for which that person

King David exhibited genuine repentance after the prophet Nathan confronted him about David's sin against Bathsheba and Uriah. This illustration is from a tenth-century Byzantine manuscript.

has genuinely repented? Forgiving a person means releasing your hurt and not wishing the other person harm, and this needs to happen. However, it seems fair to ask if the other person is bearing the fruits of repentance before entrusting that person with responsibility (Matthew 3:8). This will require wisdom and discretion, but it is possible. Jesus accepted Peter after that disciple had denied knowing Him on the night He was betrayed (John 21:15-19). Perhaps the best guide on what to do in this situation is the golden rule: how you want others to treat you is the way you should treat others (Matthew 7:12).

Toward a Solution

My first responsibility is to make sure that my life is acceptable to God. I must not make excuses for my sin, but I must be growing in Christ and becoming more like Him (1 John 3:2-3).

Second, I must be aware of my influence on others. Something might not be wrong in itself, but it is wrong if my doing it causes someone else to stumble into sin (1 Corinthians 10:23-24). To stumble is not the same as not liking something. In the context of 1 Corinthians, to cause someone to stumble is to influence a person to do something that violates his or her conscience and thus to sin.

Third, public leaders, like everyone else, are accountable for their personal lives. We cannot compartmentalize our lives because God holds us responsible for everything we do. I must use as consistent a standard as possible when appraising the lives and positions of political leaders. If, for instance, I don't like something about a candidate from one party, then I must be fair enough to disapprove of the same trait when I see it in a candidate from another party (John 7:24). We will always support and vote for imperfect people. Sometimes we have to decide between two or more unpleasant alternatives. We can either hold our noses and vote for the least bad one or choose not to vote at all in that particular race (I have done both.) The problem with merely accepting bad choices, however, is that it lowers the standards and allows some degree of bad to carry the day.

How to handle a good, upbuilding artistic work by a person with a questionable life is a bit more complicated. I can appreciate a poem, a song, or a book for its own value apart from the one who created it. God can use even a broken vessel to teach truth; after all, broken vessels are all He has to use in our world. I have a harder time, however, with a work by a greatly flawed vessel that attempts to teach spiritual truth. I would find it difficult to learn from a preacher, for instance, whose life I knew to be a failure and who was unrepentant and unwilling to change.

Georgia businessman Herman Cain was briefly a leading contender for the Republican presidential nomination in 2011. Allegations of sexual misconduct, which Cain denied, contributed to the suspension of his campaign.

In the last analysis, we all have to answer to God individually for our lives and the choices we make. We must make our personal and political decisions wisely and prayerfully, determining how we can best promote good. A person must always respect his or her conscience. A person should not support a candidate or buy a book or CD just because it is the popular thing to do if such an action violates his or her conscience. We can learn from what others tell us, but we must avoid being swayed just by what our friends think or by what is popular or easy. We must ask, "Is this going to honor God and help me and others, or am I going to compromise what I know to be true and right?"

Jesus said that we must cut out of our lives whatever causes us or others to sin, even if it is a hand, an eye, or a foot. It is better to be maimed and go to heaven, He said, than to be whole and go to hell (Mark 9:43-48). Eyes, hands, and feet, of course, do not cause us to sin; but our thoughts do. Wanting to be popular, or wanting to appear intelligent or in the know, or wanting to do what others do and have what others have, can cause us to sin.

These desires can be as much a part of us as a hand, foot, or eye. If we want to honor God with our lives, we must cut out and throw away these thoughts, even at the risk of appearing to be socially or culturally maimed. This means that we must sometimes make hard choices, but someone who is going against the tide of the world by seeking to follow God will have hard choices to make. The goal we are seeking, however, is worth everything it might cost us in this life (2 Timothy 2:11-13).

If we say that we have no sin, we are deceiving ourselves and the truth is not in us. If we confess our sins, He is faithful and righteous to forgive us our sins and to cleanse us from all unrighteousness.
1 John 1:8-9

⋆ Assignments for Lesson 145 ⋆

Bible Recite or write 1 John 1:5-10 from memory.

Project Complete your project for the unit.

Student Review Optional: Answer the questions for Lesson 145 and take the quiz for Unit 29.

Memorial Service for Conner T. Lowry, a U.S. Marine Killed in Afghanistan (2012)

30 The New Millennium

A statistical snapshot of the country from the 2000 census and other sources reveals much about who we are. The presidential election of that year was one of the most controversial in our nation's history. The terrorist attacks on September 11, 2001, renewed our patriotism and revived the recognition by many Americans of our dependence on God. Republican George W. Bush and Democrat Barack Obama were each elected President twice. We conclude our study with an overview of the story of American history.

Memory Work Memorize 2 Corinthians 5:14-15 by the end of this unit.

Books Used

The Bible
American Voices

Project (choose one)

1) Write 300 to 500 words on one of the following topics:

   - Should the electoral college be changed, abolished, or kept as it is?
   - Write an essay in which you share three things you love about the United States and three things you would like to be different.

2) Make a poster timeline of key events in American history. Include at least twenty-five events. Be creative in the way you present and illustrate the information.

3) Plan a family field trip to an historically significant site in your area that you have never visited before. Prepare yourself to be the family tour guide. Be able to explain how and why this place had an impact on American history.

New York City With the World Trade Centers in the Foreground

Lesson 146

America in 2000

People around the world recognized the year 2000 as a milestone. The information in this lesson, gathered from U.S. Census Bureau data and other sources, gives a snapshot of the United States for that year.

Population

The official population of the United States on April 1, 2000, as determined by the Census Bureau, was 281,421,906. This was an increase of 32.7 million people or 13.2% over 1990, which was the largest growth for a decade in the nation's history. The West and the South were the areas showing the most population increase. The nation recorded about 4 million babies born and 2.4 million deaths in 2000.

Census returns for 2000 indicated that the population was 75.1% white, 12.3% black, and 3.6% Asian. The rest of the population was made up of groups with smaller percentages and those who indicated a background of two or more racial groups. The number of Americans who indicated more than one race in their ethnic background was 2.4% of the total. The Hispanic population, which is a different category from race, totaled 13%. The primary countries of origin for Hispanics in the U.S. were Mexico, Puerto Rico, and Cuba. Half of the Hispanic population lived in Texas and California.

California was the most populous state, with 33.9 million residents. Texas was second with 20.9 million, followed by New York with 19 million. Wyoming was the least populous state, with just under 500,000 people. The five largest cities in order were New York City, Los Angeles, Chicago, Houston, and Philadelphia.

The Census Bureau defines urban areas as Metropolitan Statistical Areas (MSAs), which include major cities and the surrounding population. The five largest MSAs were New York City (including parts of New York, New Jersey, Connecticut, and Pennsylvania) at 21.2 million, Los Angeles at 16.4 million, Chicago with 9.2 million, Washington, D.C.-Baltimore at 7.6 million, and San Francisco-Oakland-San Jose with 7 million. The nation had fifty MSAs of one million or more people, which accounted for over half of the country's population.

In terms of counties, Douglas County, Colorado, near Denver, grew 161% between 1990 and 2000. Las Vegas, Nevada, was the fastest growing metropolitan area, increasing its population 83% during the decade. Maricopa County, Arizona (the Phoenix area), grew by almost one million people between 1990 and 2000. Los Angeles County had 9.5 million residents. Cook County, Illinois

(Chicago), counted 5.1 million. The smallest county population was Loving County, Texas, with sixty-four people.

Eighty percent of the U.S. population (226 million) lived in metropolitan areas of 600,000 or more, while the other 20% (55.4 million) lived in non-urban or rural areas.

New Citizen Celebration in Seattle

Demographics

In 2000 America had 143.4 million women and 138.1 million men. The average American at birth was expected to live 76.7 years (73.9 years for men, 79.4 years for women). The median age (half of the population older, half younger) was 35.3 years. This was the highest median age ever and was the result of the baby boomers getting older and relatively fewer babies being born.

Twenty-eight million people living in America in 2000 were born in another country. The most common country of origin was Mexico, with 7.2 million. The Philippines were the homeland of 1.5 million; and China, Vietnam, and Cuba gave us just under one million each. The number of legal immigrants who entered the country in 2000 was 841,002.

Family Life

The nation registered 105.5 million households in 2000. The average size of a household was 2.59 persons. Married couple households accounted for 52% of the total (54.5 million), down from 74%

Members of the U.S. Olympic Team at the 2000 Summer Games in Sydney, Australia

in 1960. Single person households, including young adults on their own and single elderly people living alone, made up 26% of the total. Children 18 and under were present in 36% of American homes.

Twelve percent of American homes were headed by a woman without a husband present, and four percent were headed by a man with no wife. The number of households with unmarried partners reached 5.5 million, or 1.9% of the total.

Seventy-five percent of white children 18 and under lived in a home with two parents, down from 90% in 1970. Sixty-five percent of Hispanic children lived in such homes, down from 78% in 1970. For black children eighteen and under, the percentage living in a home with two parents was 38%, down from 59% in 1970.

The Economy

The United States had a gross domestic product in 2000 of about ten trillion dollars. The three largest segments of the economy were service; financial, insurance, and real estate; and manufacturing. The average unemployment rate for the year was 4% (5.7 million people), while 134 million people sixteen and over were working. The Consumer Price Index rate of inflation for the year was 3.4%. Over 600 million computers were in use in the world, some 180 million of them in the United States.

The U.S. had 2.2 million farms, down from over 6 million farms in 1940. A total of 943 million acres were in production, and the average size of a farm was 434 acres. Only about 2.5% of the American labor force worked on farms. By contrast 72% of workers earned a living on farms in 1820. The leading crops in 2000 were corn, peanuts, soybeans, and wheat.

Religious Membership

The largest single religious group in the United States in 2000 was the Roman Catholic Church with 62.4 million members. The largest single Protestant denomination was the Southern Baptist Convention, which had 15.9 million. Other Baptist groups claimed a total of another 14 million members. The United Methodist Church accounted for 8.4 million adherents, the Lutherans 8.5 million (divided into the Evangelical Lutheran Church in America, 5.1 million; the Lutheran Church Missouri Synod, 2.6 million; and other smaller Lutheran groups, about 800,000).

The Church of God in Christ claimed 5.5 million members. The Presbyterian Church USA claimed 3.6 million communicants, with other Presbyterian bodies totaling about 500,000-600,000. Assemblies of God registered 2.6 million, while Episcopal Church membership was 2.3 million. A large number of Americans were part of many smaller church groups, especially Bible churches, community churches, and house churches; but a national total of these groups would only be an estimate. Around forty percent of Americans attended a church service on a typical Sunday.

Many other religious groups also claimed a large number of adherents in the U.S. The followers of Islam numbered about 5.8 million in the United States in 2000. Mormons totaled 5.2 million. About 4.4 million people of the different branches of Judaism lived in America, as did 1.3 million Hindus.

Michael Farris, founder of the Home School Legal Defense Association, also founded Patrick Henry College. Located in Purcellville, Virginia, near Washington, D.C., the school welcomed its first class in the fall of 2000.

Update from 2010

The official 2010 census count showed 308,745,538 persons living in the United States. This was a 9.7% increase over 2000, which was the second-lowest growth rate over a decade since 1900. Many people assumed that illegal, uncounted immigrants pushed the actual total number of people living in the United States higher.

The West and Southwest regions contributed most to the nation's population growth during the first decade of the twenty-first century. The four fastest-growing states—Nevada, Arizona, Utah, and Idaho—were all in the West. Population growth in just two states, California and Texas, accounted for one-fourth of the increase for the decade. The Northeast and Midwest had been losing population for several years.

Hispanics made up over half of the country's population increase for the decade. About one in six Americans are Hispanic. Ethnic minorities accounted for ninety percent of the growth during the decade, as a result of immigration and of births among Latinos. Asian Americans had a larger numeric growth than African Americans during the period.

The trends of increasing urban population and decreasing rural population continued. As of 2010, only 16% of Americans lived in rural areas. Urban centers increased both in population and in the size of the geographical areas they covered. The effects of this trend toward urbanization include the closing of businesses and schools in rural areas. More women than men were getting college degrees in 2010. The nation counted about two million stay-at-home dads that year.

As of 2010 less than half (48%) of households included married couples, which was down from 78% in 1950. Only about one-fifth of households were made up of married couples with children eighteen or under living at home. Several factors influenced this latter statistic, including an increase in older couples ("empty nesters") and an increase in single-parent households.

In 2010 barely one-half (51%) of adults eighteen and older were married, down significantly from 72% of adults who were married in 1960. The median age for a first marriage was at an all-time high, just over twenty-six years for women and just under twenty-nine years for men. However, the trend still indicates that the overwhelming majority of adults will be married at some point during their lives.

The country recorded about 2.1 million marriages and 1.1 million divorces in 2010. This might look like the divorce rate was about 50%, but that is not the case. The number of divorces granted in a year is about half the number of marriages that take place in a year, but the divorces take place among all already-married couples. Since married couple households totaled about 58.5 million in 2010, only about 2% of all marriages ended in divorce that year.

The geographic center of population is the point on which the United States would be balanced as a plane if every person weighed the same. It reflects the distribution of people throughout the country. The first center of population in 1790 was just east of Baltimore, Maryland. It has continually moved west since then. The 2010 geographic center of population was the town of Plato (population 109), in south-central Missouri, over one thousand miles west of Baltimore. The center of population moved about thirty miles southwest during the decade. This trend toward the southwest reflects the growth of population in the West and Southwest and the relative decline of population in the Northeast and northern Midwest.

It was estimated that the number of personal computers in use around the world surpassed one billion in 2008. The Pew Internet and American Life Project indicated that one in three American adults owned a tablet computer in 2013.

The Pew Research Center reported in 2012 that membership in traditional mainline Protestant denominations was less than one-half of the population. This was partly the result of people leaving those churches and many becoming members of independent congregations. A significant number of people considered themselves to be "nones," or members of no church, although many still confessed a personal faith in God.

The new home of the National Museum of American Jewish History opened in 2010 in Philadelphia.

Ascribe to the Lord, O families of the peoples,
Ascribe to the Lord glory and strength.
Psalm 96:7

⋆ Assignments for Lesson 146 ⋆

English Begin writing a 300-word review of your favorite non-fiction book that you read while studying this curriculum (*Narrative of the Life of David Crockett, Narrative of the Life of Frederick Douglass, Co. Aytch, Up from Slavery,* or *Miracle in the Hills*). Among other things, tell what it taught you about history. Finish this review tomorrow.

Bible In the Bible study lesson for this unit, we will step back to get some perspective on the overall story of American history as we look at it through the eyes of faith. Read Romans 8:18-25. This passage reminds us that the eternal plan of God gives us a different perspective on the sufferings of the present time.

Start memorizing 2 Corinthians 5:14-15.

Project Choose your project for this unit and start working on it.

Student Review Optional: Answer the questions for Lesson 146.

President George W. Bush Boarding Air Force One

Lesson 147

The Presidency of George W. Bush

In 2000 the nation was at peace, the economy was strong, and the Federal budget was running a surplus. However, the shadow of scandal from the Clinton years hung over the election campaign.

Vice President Al Gore was the Democrats' candidate for President. Gore selected Connecticut Senator Joseph Lieberman for the second spot. Lieberman was the first Jewish major party candidate for President or Vice President.

Texas governor George W. Bush, son of former President George H. W. Bush, gained the Republican nomination. For his running mate, Bush chose former Congressman and former Secretary of Defense Richard Cheney. Bush was a recovered alcoholic who had made a commitment to Christ. In answer to a question during the campaign, Bush said that his favorite philosopher was Jesus Christ.

In the campaign, Bush promised to restore dignity to the office of President. He proposed a large tax cut to let people keep more of their money. Bush promoted increased Federal funding for education, and he also wanted to make schools accountable to the Federal government for how well they educated children. Meanwhile, Gore had to strike a balance between claiming success for the strong economy during Clinton's term and distancing himself from Clinton's moral failures. He promised never to let the American people down.

Election Night and Dimpled Chads

On election night, Florida, where Bush's brother Jeb was governor, became the pivotal state in an extremely close contest. The television networks first called the state for Gore, then retracted that call. In the early morning hours, the networks declared that Bush had won Florida and the election. Gore called Bush to concede. As Gore was driving to the venue where he was to make his concession speech, he received word that the vote count in Florida was tightening and that the networks again retracted their call. Gore phoned Bush to retract his concession.

Weeks of legal wrangling by both sides followed. The automatic machine recount showed Bush ahead by 327 votes. Democrats sued to have manual recounts in a few selected counties. The main point of contention was whether punch card ballots were being read accurately. The Democrats said that even though the chads (the little pieces of paper that were to be punched out) might not be completely detached from the card, election officials should count "dimpled chads" that might have been indented by the stylus used in voting. Republicans argued that people might have started to vote for Gore and then changed their minds; thus dimpled chads were not an accurate reflection of voter intent.

While lawyers for the two parties argued in state and Federal courts for and against manual recounts, Florida election officials spent long hours holding punch cards up to the light to try to determine voter intent. Democrats wanted a new standard created, while Republicans claimed that doing so would be changing the rules after the vote was taken.

Finally!

The Florida Supreme Court ruled that more time be given for recounts. However, on December 12, the Federal deadline for states to choose their electors, the U.S. Supreme Court in a 5-4 decision reversed the Florida Supreme Court ruling. The Florida legislature (with a Republican majority) voted that day to certify the Bush electors. The final official total showed Bush winning Florida and its twenty-five electoral votes by a margin of 537 popular votes out of over six million cast. Several months after the election, news organizations went through the impounded ballots and confirmed that Bush had indeed won.

Out of over 101 million votes cast nationally, Gore won the popular vote by over 500,000 votes (50,996,582 to 50,456,062). However, Bush received the decisive electoral majority of 271 to 266. One Gore elector from the District of Columbia submitted a blank ballot to protest the lack of congressional representation for the District.

Map of Electoral Votes in the 2000 Election

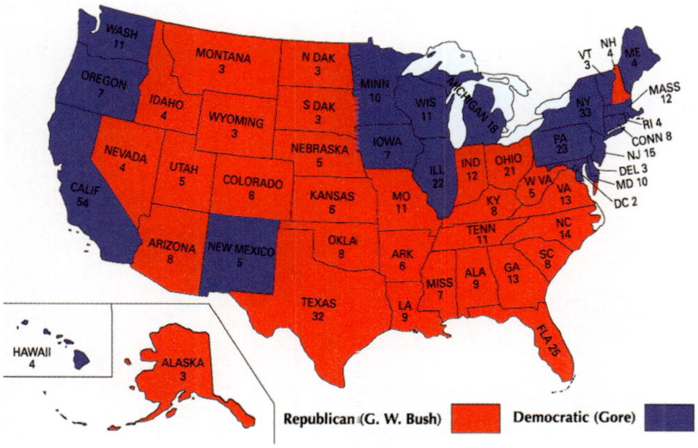

Outside the Florida Supreme Court During the Recount Battle

The election showed a closely-divided nation. Gore carried New England and the large industrial states of New York, Pennsylvania, New Jersey, Michigan, Illinois, and California. Bush swept the South (including Gore's home state of Tennessee and Clinton's home state of Arkansas), the rest of the Midwest, and the mountain states. Gore carried the cities 71% to 25%, while Bush received 60% of the rural and small town vote.

Because of the color-coding used by television networks when they declared that a candidate had won a state, Republican-leaning states came to be called red states while Democratic-leaning states became known as blue states.

The Governing Begins

The 107th Congress that convened in January of 2001 also reflected the even political split of the nation. The Senate was divided 50-50; but with Vice President Cheney voting as a tie-breaker, the Republicans controlled the Senate. However, the Republicans lost control of the Senate in June of 2001 when Vermont Republican Jim Jeffords declared himself an independent and said that he would vote with the Democrats to reorganize the Senate. The GOP had a nine-seat margin in the House.

Secretary of State Condoleezza Rice

President Bush selected Colin Powell, former chairman of the Joint Chiefs of Staff, to be the first African American Secretary of State. Following Powell's retirement at the end of Bush's first term, the President named National Security Advisor Condoleezza Rice to take Powell's place. Rice became the first female African American to serve as Secretary of State.

A tax cut to be phased in over ten years passed Congress in 2001. The next year, Congress enacted a campaign finance reform bill, which outlawed so-called soft money (certain kinds of contributions to political parties) and regulated the kind of ads that could run for a certain period before election day. However, the law did not apply to the 2002 congressional election.

Congress passed and in January of 2002 Bush signed the No Child Left Behind Act. The new law increased Federal involvement in education by requiring local school districts to meet certain benchmarks for student achievement. When schools failed to meet these benchmarks, parents could enroll their children in another school. Critics charged that the law set higher standards for schools but provided insufficient funding to help schools meet these requirements.

After September 11, 2001, the war against terrorism dominated the Bush presidency. The President's policies and proposals in foreign and domestic fields were influenced by the realities of the war on terror, which we will discuss in the next lesson.

The 2001 tax cuts, followed by increased expenditures for the war on terrorism and a decline in the economy caused at least in part by the war on terror, resulted in huge Federal deficits under Bush. This occurred after a tax increase and a strong economy had resulted in budget surpluses in the last years of the Clinton Administration, which had reversed a long pattern of Federal deficits.

Republicans made significant gains in the 2002 congressional election. Usually the party in the White House loses ground in mid-term elections, but support for Bush and the Republicans in Congress enabled the GOP to regain control of the Senate and to strengthen its hold in the House. After the election, Republicans held fifty-one Senate seats compared to the Democrats' forty-eight and one independent. In the House, the margin was 229-205 for the Republicans with one independent.

The 2004 Election

In 2004 Massachusetts Senator John Kerry won the Democratic presidential nomination. Kerry had served in the Vietnam War and was awarded three Purple Hearts and other combat medals, but some fellow veterans questioned the truthfulness of what Kerry claimed about his service record. After Kerry had served only a few months in Vietnam, he returned to the States and became a highly visible and vocal opponent of the war. Kerry was first elected to the U.S. Senate in 1984.

Kerry chose Senator John Edwards of North Carolina to be his running mate. Edwards had been a contender for the Democratic presidential nomination. President Bush and Vice President Richard Cheney were renominated by the Republicans for a second term.

During the campaign, Kerry criticized Bush's handling of the war in Iraq, calling it "the wrong war in the wrong place at the wrong time." Kerry said that he would have spent more time building a coalition of nations to oppose Saddam Hussein and that he would seek the support of other nations before launching similar attacks in the future. Kerry's critics called him weak on defense and accused him of flip-flopping on the issues. The Democrat had voted against U.S. military involvement in the 1991 Persian Gulf War, in favor of the 2002 resolution concerning the use of force in Iraq, and both for and against (at different times) a large appropriation measure for the war effort in Iraq. Kerry also criticized Bush's handling of the economy.

Bush defended the effort in Iraq and said that the U.S. and the world were safer with the Taliban ousted in Afghanistan; Saddam out of power in Iraq; many terrorist leaders killed, captured, or on the run; and security measures strengthened in the United States. The President also called the No Child Left Behind Act the first significant educational reform in a generation. Bush recognized that the economy had endured difficult times but pointed to indicators that showed a rebound was occurring.

President Bush visited troops in Baghdad, Iraq, on Thanksgiving Day in 2003.

Temporary Facade During Construction at the U.S. Department of Education Headquarters (2005)

The election was a more decisive victory for Bush and the Republican Party than most observers expected. The President received 51% of the popular vote, about 60.6 million total, which was the most votes that any candidate had ever received for President up to that time. Kerry received 48%, or about 57.3 million votes. Bush's electoral win was 286 to 252. No serious voting irregularities were reported anywhere in the country on Election Day.

The Republicans once again increased their margin of power in Congress. The GOP controlled the Senate fifty-five to forty-four with one independent. Among the election losers was Senate Democratic leader Tom Daschle of South Dakota, who was defeated by Republican John Thune. Daschle had been in the Senate since 1987 and had been Democratic leader since 1995. The Republicans controlled the House 232 to 201 with one independent and one seat vacant after the death of a Congressman following the November election.

Political analysts saw the election results as indicating that a majority of Americans supported the policies of President Bush and the stance of the Republican Party on defense, moral, and economic issues. The Republicans also did an excellent job of getting out their voters, especially in Florida and Ohio. Many voters perceived Kerry as being indecisive on the issues and not the person they wanted to lead the country.

President Bush Takes the Oath of Office for His Second Term (2005)

Bush's Second Term

In August of 2005, Hurricane Katrina devastated New Orleans and much of southern Louisiana and Mississippi. Levees that had held back water from New Orleans broke, causing even more flooding. The response of local, state, and Federal emergency agencies was slow and confused. Many people sought shelter in the Superdome and other public facilities. Thousands who were able to do so moved away from the area altogether. The erratic governmental response led many to criticize the Bush Administration. New Orleans and the surrounding region slowly began to recover, but Louisiana lost tens of thousands of people who decided not to return there to live.

Bush had two Supreme Court nominations confirmed by the Senate. In 2005 Sandra Day O'Connor announced her resignation. Bush nominated D.C. Circuit Court of Appeals judge John Roberts to replace her. Then Chief Justice William Rehnquist died, and Bush asked the Senate to consider Roberts to be the new Chief Justice. The Senate confirmed Roberts in September of 2005, just before the Supreme Court session began in October. To replace O'Connor, Bush nominated Samuel Alito, a judge on the U.S. Third Circuit Court of Appeals. Alito was confirmed on January 31, 2006, and was sworn in the next day.

The 2006 Election

As the congressional mid-term election approached, many observers assumed that the Republicans would lose ground in Congress. The President had lost much of his popular support, in large measure because of perceptions that the war in Iraq was going badly. Even though the GOP had controlled Congress for most of the time since the 1994 election, Federal spending had continued to increase.

In November voters gave the Republicans what President Bush subsequently called a "thumping." Democrats took control of the House 233 to 202 and chose Nancy Pelosi of California as the new Speaker, the first woman ever to hold that position.

Flooding in New Orleans After Hurrican Katrina

In the Senate, the party split was 49-49; but two independents voted with the Democrats to organize the Senate. No Democrat-held seat in Congress was taken away by the Republicans in 2006. Secretary of Defense Donald Rumsfeld, a prominent member of the Administration's war effort, resigned immediately after the election.

In the final months of the Bush presidency, the worst economic downturn since the Great Depression overshadowed all other issues. We will discuss the Great Recession in Lesson 149.

Nancy Pelosi visited soldiers from California in Iraq in 2009

How blessed are those who keep justice,
who practice righteousness at all times!
Psalm 106:3

⋆ Assignments for Lesson 147 ⋆

English Complete your review of your favorite non-fiction book that you read while studying this curriculum.

Bible Work on memorizing 2 Corinthians 5:14-15.

Project Work on your project.

Student Review Optional: Answer the questions for Lesson 147.

The World Trade Center Buildings After the Attacks

Lesson 148

September 11, 2001, and the War on Terror

Tuesday, September 11, 2001 was pleasant on the east coast of the United States. New York City was having a primary election for mayor and other city offices. President Bush was in Florida visiting a school and promoting his education agenda.

Around 8:00 a.m. (all times Eastern), four flights took off from east coast airports. American Airlines Flight 11 and United Airlines Flight 175 left Boston for Los Angeles. United Flight 93 took off from Newark, New Jersey, heading for San Francisco. American Flight 77 left Dulles Airport near Washington, D.C., for Los Angeles. The planes had relatively few passengers but full fuel loads for their transcontinental journeys.

The Attacks Begin

Soon after the flights were airborne, on each plane passengers attacked the flight crew, took control of the plane, and changed course. At 8:48 a.m., American Flight 11 slammed into the 110-story North Tower of the World Trade Center (WTC) in New York City. Billows of smoke rose from the tower, people on the sidewalks and in nearby buildings watched in horror, workers in the tower hurried down the staircases, and police and firefighters rushed to the scene. News cameras transmitted pictures of the burning building around the world. Speculation immediately began as to whether it was a horrible accident or something else.

Then at 9:30 a.m., before a live world television audience, United Flight 175 crashed into the South WTC Tower. A fireball erupted and a second huge plume of smoke rose skyward. Evacuation began in the second tower, and people began realizing that these events were no accidents. Because of procedures implemented after the 1993 bombing in the WTC underground garage, thousands of people were able to get out of the buildings quickly. However, people in the floors above where the planes hit had no chance of escape.

At 9:37 a.m., American Flight 77 from Dulles, which had turned back toward Washington, crashed into the Pentagon building in Arlington, Virginia, just across the Potomac River from Washington. Another huge fire broke out. The section of the Pentagon where the plane hit had been under renovation, so relatively few people were in it. As news of the three incidents spread, the Capitol and White House were evacuated. Other Federal buildings closed down, and traffic out of the city became snarled.

At 9:59 a.m., the South WTC Tower collapsed from structural damage caused by the intense heat of the impact. United Flight 93 from Newark crashed in rural western Pennsylvania at 10:10 a.m. while on a route that was taking it toward Washington. Passengers on the plane had been in contact with people on the ground by cell phone and knew about the other incidents. When Flight 93 was taken over, some of the passengers decided to intervene. Passenger Todd Beamer's last words heard on the phone were, "Let's roll." The hijackers likely intended to strike another target in Washington, such as the White House or the Capitol.

At 10:28 a.m., about an hour and forty minutes after the nightmare began, the North WTC Tower, the first building hit, also collapsed. Later government investigations indicated that a total of nineteen hijackers had been directly involved.

America Reacts

President Bush was informed of the events as they unfolded. He was in continuous telephone contact with his staff and other officials all day. Air Force One left Florida with Bush aboard and followed a zigzag course, trying to avoid a possible attack on it. Bush was flown first to a military base in Louisiana, then to a base in Nebraska. Finally that evening the President returned to Washington. The government grounded all commercial aviation in the U.S., the first time in history that this had happened. Air service resumed later in the week. No other incidents were known to have been avoided by the grounding.

The United States was in a state of shock. The loss of life, devastation of property, disruption of society, and fear of further incidents were overwhelming. Friday, September 14, was declared a national day of mourning. A memorial service was held at the National Cathedral in Washington. The New York Stock Exchange, not far from the WTC, suspended trading on September 11 until the following Monday. When the market opened, stock prices plummeted out of fear of the unknown.

Some 2,973 victims died on September 11, not including the hijackers. This figure includes 246 passengers and crew on the four airliners, 125 people at the Pentagon, and 2,602 people in New York City. Those who died in New York included some 400 firefighters and policemen who were killed when the towers collapsed on them as they selflessly worked to rescue others. People from some sixty-two nations died in the WTC.

In addition to those who died that day, some people died well after the attacks because of injuries or illnesses caused by the tragedy (for example, lung disease brought on by inhaling dust that day). Over the years, New York City officials have announced that over 150 additional people have died due to causes related to the attacks.

Search and rescue operations continued for days at both the Pentagon (left) and the World Trade Center site (right).

The Culprit

On September 12, Secretary of State Colin Powell named Osama bin Laden as the chief suspect behind the attacks. Bin Laden denied any involvement at first, although he admitted to being happy about the incidents. However, on a videotape captured later, bin Laden described the attacks and clearly indicated that he was behind the plot.

Bin Laden was born in Saudi Arabia in 1957, the 17th of 50 children fathered by the wealthiest construction contractor in the country. Upon his father's death in 1968, Osama inherited a huge fortune. He joined the fight of Islamic rebels in Afghanistan in the 1980s against Soviet troops who had been sent there to shore up a puppet government loyal to the U.S.S.R. Bin Laden later returned to Saudi Arabia and fiercely opposed Saudi cooperation with the United States during the Persian Gulf War. Because of his opposition to the Saudi monarchy, bin Laden was exiled from the country in 1991. He went to Sudan and reportedly established terrorist training camps there. Diplomatic pressure by the United States led to Sudan expelling bin Laden. His family disowned him.

Bin Laden eventually went back to Afghanistan and was protected by the government that was led by the Islamic Taliban faction (the word *taliban* means learner). He set up additional training camps there for the al-Qaeda terrorist network (*al-qaeda* means "the base"). Evidence linked bin Laden to the 1993 bombing in the WTC garage, the killing of eighteen U.S. soldiers in Somalia, the bombing of U.S. embassies in Kenya and Tanzania in 1998, and the attack on the USS *Cole* in Yemen in October of 2000.

The September 11 attacks caused Americans to debate again whether Islam was a religion of peace or of war. Muslims have a record of armed action in the name of their faith, and the Qur'an does talk about *jihad* or holy war. However, many Muslim leaders denounced the terrorist attacks.

The Flight 93 National Memorial is located at the site of the crash in Stonycreek Township, Pennsylvania. A white marble wall containing the names of those who died in the crash was dedicated in 2011.

President Bush at Ground Zero, September 14, 2001

Renewed Patriotism

The response of Americans to the attack was overwhelming. In addition to public acknowledgement of God, a surge of patriotism developed unlike anything since World War II. American flags were emblazoned on homes, businesses, cars, lapels, sports uniforms, and other places. "God Bless America" appeared on numerous outdoor store signs. Citizens donated about one billion dollars to various charities for relief efforts and for the families of victims. Firefighters became national heroes. President Bush visited the WTC Ground Zero site on September 14 to thank the recovery workers. He promised to strike back at the people behind the attack.

America became used to being at war. Airport security was tightened, and armed National Guardsmen went on routine patrol at the nation's airports for a time. Sky marshals began riding on many flights. Airlines improved cockpit security. Bush named Pennsylvania governor Tom Ridge to head the new Office of Homeland Security, which later became a Cabinet department. The government froze the assets of terrorist groups and their accomplices in American banks. The Justice Department detained hundreds of people suspected of being involved in terrorism.

U.S. Army Paratroopers in Afghanistan Moving Toward Observation Post Chuck Norris (2007)

International Military Response

President Bush announced that war had been declared on the United States and that the U.S. was declaring war on terrorism. He warned that it was going to be a long fight. Congress immediately voted billions of dollars in additional military funding for the war. NATO for the first time ever invoked the mutual defense provision of the NATO Charter, which says that an attack on one member is considered to be an attack on them all. Great Britain and Prime Minister Tony Blair offered strong support to the U.S. Russia and China also pledged assistance. Pakistan agreed for American troops to use their country as a base for attacks on terrorist positions in neighboring Afghanistan. All countries except Pakistan withdrew diplomatic recognition of the Taliban government in Afghanistan.

The al-Qaeda camps and the Taliban-led government in Afghanistan were the first targets of the war on terrorism. American military retaliation began October 7 with intense bomb and missile attacks on Afghanistan, followed by an invasion of coalition ground forces working with Afghan groups that opposed the Taliban. The Taliban government fell and a new government was installed. America also airlifted a large amount of food into Afghanistan for the people, since the war was not aimed at them. President Bush encouraged the children of America to donate money for relief of the children of Afghanistan. The President received high approval ratings for his handling of the war. However, bin Laden remained at large.

The U.S. military dropped leaflets like this in Afghanistan, threatening U.S. strikes. The front and back panels are shown with text reading, "Taliban, do you think that you are safe . . . in your tomb?"

U.S. Marines Escort Prisoners of War to a Holding Area in Iraq (2003)

The War in Iraq

The dictator of Iraq, Saddam Hussein, had been widely regarded as an international outlaw for years. His government used chemical weapons against the ethnic Kurds in the northern part of Iraq. Iran and Iraq engaged in a protracted and costly war during the 1980s. The Iraqi invasion of the tiny but wealthy neighboring country of Kuwait precipitated the 1991 Persian Gulf War. When U.S. and other forces moved against Iraq in that war, Iraq sent missiles against Israel, a country which played no active role in the conflict. Saddam's government tortured and killed many political opponents within Iraq.

Many world leaders believed that Iraq had a program to develop weapons of mass destruction (chemical, biological, and nuclear weapons that could be used against large numbers of innocent civilians; abbreviated WMD). After the Persian Gulf War, the United Nations set up an inspection program to locate these weapons in Iraq. However, Iraq never fully complied with the terms that the U.N. set for the inspections. In addition, Saddam's regime harbored and encouraged Islamic terrorists.

On October 8, 2002, the United States Congress voted to give the President the authority to use force against Iraq. The next month, the United Nations Security Council passed a resolution warning Iraq of "serious consequences" if it did not disarm. Again Saddam refused to comply with the resolutions.

In early March 2003, President Bush demanded that Saddam leave Iraq or face the consequences. When the ultimatum was ignored, a coalition of countries led by the United States and Great Britain began a military assault on Iraq on March 20, 2003. It was widely believed that the Iraqi military would offer stiff resistance to the invaders and that they might even use WMD. However, the invasion was overwhelmingly successful. Many Iraqi soldiers gave up without a fight or simply quit wearing their uniforms and melted into the civilian population. Coalition forces took the Iraqi capital of Baghdad and the Saddam government ceased to function, though Saddam himself was not accounted for. On May 1, 2003, President Bush declared major combat to be over.

Coalition forces controlled large areas of Iraq, and many if not most Iraqis welcomed the promise of a new day of freedom. Workers built new schools and hospitals. The shadows of the oppressive Saddam regime began to fade. An interim Iraqi government was formed, and a national election was set for January 2005 to create an assembly that would name a provisional executive council and write a

U.S. forces in Iraq sought to build good relationships with civilians, including children. This soldier colored with an Iraqi girl in 2011 as part of Iraqi Kids' Day.

new Iraqi constitution. The election took place with minimal violence, and a large majority of eligible voters participated. Special polling places were set up in the U.S. for Iraqis living in this country.

However, anti-American insurgents in Iraq conducted a war of terror against coalition troops, civilians from other countries who were in Iraq to help with rebuilding, and pro-coalition Iraqis. Insurgents kidnapped and brutally executed some individuals.

The coalition effort did enjoy many successes, including the capture of Saddam Hussein in December of 2003. Saddam was tried by an Iraqi court and found guilty of charges related to the deaths of some of his political opponents. He was executed by hanging on December 30, 2006.

Continued insurgent attacks, however, caused many American casualties and led opponents of Bush's policies to question the benefit of a continued American presence there. Bush's approval ratings and the support of Americans for the war in Iraq declined in opinion polls as the conflict continued. It turned out that no WMDs were found in Iraq, although evidence showed that they had been there at one time.

Further Developments

In Afghanistan, American and allied forces sought to capture or kill terrorists and to support the pro-American government. In Iraq, American troops supported the pro-Western government and fought against internal opposition to that government. Barack Obama was elected President in 2008 pledging to end American involvement in Iraq and to concentrate our forces in the battle against terrorism in Afghanistan. Obama began withdrawing American troops from Iraq in 2009, and the American military effort there ended in December of 2011. The American military presence in Afghanistan continued, but Obama planned to reduce it dramatically by the close of 2014. Both

During the raid on Bin Laden's compound, an overhead drone provided a video feed of the operation. President Obama gathered with other government officials at the White House to watch.

Iraq and Afghanistan had governments that were friendly to the United States, but neither country was free from civil strife as some groups in both places opposed the American presence.

A few other smaller terrorist attacks took place in various places around the world in the years following September 11, 2001; but the number of attacks almost certainly was lower as a result of American anti-terrorist operations around the world. Many terrorist leaders were captured or killed in the war on terror.

The greatest accomplishment of years of fighting terrorism occurred early on May 2, 2011 (still May 1 in the United States), when Navy SEAL special operation forces invaded a compound near a military academy in Pakistan and killed Osama bin Laden. As President Obama said in announcing the successful raid, "Justice has been done." The operation took only a few minutes to complete, and no Americans were killed or injured.

The terrorist attacks of September 11, 2001, changed our perspective on life in America and in the world. The American government and American military forces responded to the threat with determination and dedication. As God gives us days, may we continue to grow in our faith in God and in our desire to help our country honor Him.

A memorial to the victims of September 11 was built on the site of the former World Trade Center towers. Two large square waterfalls fill the areas where the towers once stood. A museum is located near the waterfalls. A new office tower called One World Trade Center, shown at left, was completed nearby in 2014.

The Lord is my light and my salvation; whom shall I fear?
The Lord is the defense of my life; whom shall I dread?
Psalm 27:1

⋆ Assignments for Lesson 148 ⋆

American Voices Read George W. Bush's National Day of Prayer and Remembrance speech and Address to a Joint Session of Congress and the American People (pages 386-392).

English Imagine that you are contributing to a book about American history sometime in the future. You want the readers to understand what is happening in America now. Today, begin writing a 300-word essay about a current issue in which you explain the significance of that issue and how it affects people's lives. Finish this essay tomorrow.

Bible Work on memorizing 2 Corinthians 5:14-15.

Project Work on your project.

Student Review Optional: Answer the questions for Lesson 148.

President Obama Delivers His First Inaugural Address (2009)

Lesson 149

The Administration of Barack Obama

Economic woes beset the last part of the George W. Bush presidency. It became common to pay over $3.00 for a gallon of gasoline. Factors for the sharp increase in prices included instability in the Middle East, the loss of production and refining capacity in the U.S. following Hurricane Katrina, and increased demand for fuel caused by a growing U.S. and world economy. Meanwhile, oil companies reported record profits during the period. Nevertheless, until late 2007 the American economy continued to grow at a respectable pace despite the increased cost of gasoline.

The Great Recession

A more pervasive economic issue was the credit crunch that climaxed in the fall of 2008. Much of the problem was related to a dramatic increase in the number of home mortgage failures. During the previous few years, many lenders had approved mortgages for people who had less than excellent (often called subprime) credit histories. Prominent political leaders in both parties had encouraged the mortgage system (local banks backed by Federally-created agencies) to loosen its credit approval standards. These subprime mortgages were risky loans, but many experts believed that any problems that might result from mortgage defaults would be minimal. These mortgages were bundled together as investments and sold to large banks and investment companies. The mortgages were supposed to serve as assets that allowed the financial institutions to make other loans to businesses.

However, many mortgage holders began to default on their loans because they could not afford their mortgage payments. When this happened, the growing number of houses on the market caused house prices to fall; and the mortgages became liabilities. This prevented banks from making loans to businesses that the businesses needed in order to pay for their regular operations. Companies began laying off employees. Several major banks and Wall Street investment firms went bankrupt or had to be bought by other companies. Auto dealers sold fewer new cars. Effects of this collapse rippled through the economy.

The Federal government took several steps to try to ease the financial crisis. First, the government borrowed money to send economic stimulus payments to taxpayers beginning in May of 2008, encouraging people to spend the money to increase economic activity. Then the U.S. government became involved in the financial markets in unprecedented ways. Several mortgage and investment companies received bailouts from

The number of U.S. properties facing foreclosure increased dramatically in 2007 and peaked in 2010.

the Federal government, although one major investment firm, Lehman Brothers, was allowed to go bankrupt. In October 2008, Congress approved a $700 billion plan for the government to buy up risky mortgages in order to take them off the books of financial institutions so loans could once again be made to businesses.

Late in 2008, the Federal Reserve System lowered a benchmark interest rate for its loans to banks to between zero and .25 percent to help money keep circulating in the economy. Yet another stimulus package that called for additional significant Federal spending was approved by Congress in early 2009. During 2008 and into early 2009, the Dow Jones Industrial Average lost over half of its value from its all-time high in 2007. Some banks failed as their liabilities exceeded their assets. Many state governments, which are heavily dependent on sales tax revenues, faced budget deficits as consumer sales slumped. Unemployment began to rise as business conditions worsened. Many economists described the situation as the worst financial crisis since the Great Depression. As these developments occurred, the 2008 presidential election took place.

The 2008 Election

Illinois Senator Barack Obama won the Democratic Party's presidential nomination in a close contest with New York Senator Hillary Clinton. Senator Joe Biden of Delaware was nominated for Vice President. The Republicans chose Vietnam War veteran and Arizona Senator John McCain. In a surprise move, McCain tapped Alaska governor Sarah Palin as his running mate. Both presidential candidates said that they would accept public funding for their campaigns, but Obama later reversed his position. This enabled him to raise money without the restrictions that come

Sarah Palin and John McCain at a Rally in 2008 with Palin's Husband, Todd, and McCain's Wife, Cindy

with accepting public funds, which enabled him to collect much more money.

Obama defeated McCain with 52.7% of the popular vote (67 million) and achieved a 365-173 electoral vote victory. The Democrat won all of the states that Kerry had carried in 2004 plus key states that Bush had won such as Florida, Virginia, and Ohio. The Democrats gained a 57-41 majority in the Senate, plus two independents who generally sided with the Democrats. Democrats controlled the House 257 to 178.

The GM assembly plant in Janesville, Wisconsin, opened in 1919. It ceased operations in 2009.

Health Care and the Economy

During the campaign, Obama had said that passage of a comprehensive health care law would be a top priority of his Administration. The Patient Protection and Affordable Care Act (often called "Obamacare") passed Congress in early 2010.

The law requires every American to have health insurance or pay a fine, but it also provides government subsidies for individuals with lower incomes. All but the smallest businesses must provide health insurance coverage to employees or pay a fine. The law makes it illegal for insurance companies to deny coverage to individuals based on pre-existing conditions. The complicated law has many other provisions that increase the Federal government's involvement in the healthcare sector.

Opposition to the bill while Congress was considering it was a key factor in the development of the Tea Party movement among conservatives. No Republican member of Congress voted for the bill when it passed. Some Republicans in Congress continued to work on efforts to modify or repeal the law. As the healthcare program began, the system was plagued by changing rules and a malfunctioning website where people tried to sign up for the health insurance exchange or marketplace.

Critics charged that the law was an unconstitutional takeover of one-sixth of the nation's economy, although Federal involvement in and regulation of healthcare was already extensive. The law was upheld by the U.S. Supreme Court in 2012.

Recovery from the recession was slow. Unemployment, which averaged 4.6% of the workforce in 2006 and 2007, increased to 5.8% in 2008. Then in 2009, it jumped to 9.3% and increased to 9.6% in 2010. The rate began to fall in 2011, averaging 8.9% that year, 8.1% in 2012, and 7.4% in 2013.

Meanwhile, the Federal government continued to spend beyond its means. The budget deficits were $161 billion in 2007 and $458 billion as the recession began to take hold. For 2009 through 2012, the deficit ran over one trillion dollars each year, as the government faced lower revenue because of the sluggish economy but spent more money to stimulate economic activity. The deficit for fiscal 2013 fell to $680 billion as the economy improved. When Obama took office in 2009, the national debt was $10.6 trillion. By May of 2014, it had increased sixty-four percent to $17.4 trillion. Inflation was not a serious problem in the first years of the twenty-first century.

In 2009 both General Motors (GM) and Chrysler declared bankruptcy. The Federal government provided financial assistance to both companies. In the case of GM, the Federal government bought a majority of the company's stock. Both companies became profitable and were able to repay most of the assistance they received. The bailouts cost the Federal

Mitt Romney (left) spoke at the 2012 Republican National Convention. His father George Romney addressed the 1964 Republican National Convention. The elder Romney failed to capture the Republican nomination in 1968.

government money, but some observers believe that the cost was worth it to avoid the failure of either or both companies and the resulting negative impact on the economy.

The National Bureau of Economic Research, a private, non-profit, non-partisan research organization that studies economic cycles, said that the country entered a recession in December of 2007 and emerged from the recession in June of 2009.

By 2010 many voters resented the sluggish economy and growing national debt. Many also disapproved of the Affordable Care Act. In the off-year congressional election, Republicans gained sixty-four seats in the U.S. House, giving them a 242-193 majority. This was the largest turnover since the Democratic victory in 1948. Republicans also picked up six seats in the Senate, cutting the Democratic majority to 51-47 with two independents.

President Obama took the oath of office for his second term in 2013 as his wife Michelle and daughters Malia and Sasha watched.

2012 Election

In 2012 Obama and Biden ran for re-election against Republican candidates Mitt Romney and Paul Ryan. Romney was the son of the late George Romney, who had served as governor of Michigan. Mitt Romney, a businessman, headed the organizing committee for the 2002 Salt Lake City Winter Olympics and later served as governor of Massachusetts. Ryan was a Congressman from Wisconsin who had become an expert in fiscal issues. Romney was the first Mormon to be nominated for President by a major political party.

Obama defeated Romney 51% to 47% (65.9 million votes to 60.9 million). The electoral vote count was 332 to 206. The Democrats picked up two seats in the Senate and eight in the House. Neither presidential candidate accepted public funds, and each party raised over one billion dollars for the campaign, which made it the most expensive in American history.

"The Fiscal Cliff"

In 2011 Republican leaders in the House threatened to shut down the Federal government. They did not want to raise the debt ceiling without a commitment from the President to cut the deficit. The two sides avoided a shutdown then, but a partial shutdown did occur in the fall of 2013 because of differences over budget and funding questions before an agreement was reached. The threat or reality of a government shutdown has been used by Republicans several times since the mid-1990s, but the tactic has never gained wide popular support or been effective in significantly changing the course of Federal spending.

Following the 2012 election, the President and his fellow Democrats had another conflict with Republican leaders over what to do about tax increases and spending cuts that were scheduled to take effect on January 1, 2013. The impact of these changes was described as a "fiscal cliff," a term which suggested that the legally-required changes would have a serious negative impact on the government and the economy.

A last-minute deal allowed for the tax cuts passed by Congress ten years earlier to be continued (something that Obama had said he would not agree to), payroll tax cuts to be ended, and spending on Federal programs to continue.

Controversial Issues

During Obama's first term, Congress, the President, and top military leadership ended the policy of "Don't ask, don't tell" with reference to homosexuals in the military. With the change, an individual's sexual orientation could not be considered with regard to his or her fitness to serve. In 2012 Obama stated that he believed marriage should be permitted between persons of the same sex. Since the Constitution does not give the Federal government any authority with regard to marriage laws, the issue has long been considered a matter for states to decide. Several states have legalized same-sex marriage.

In 2012 an official of the Internal Revenue Service (IRS) admitted that the agency applied unusually intense scrutiny to applications of politically conservative groups for tax-exempt status. Obama called the actions "misconduct" and "inexcusable." He requested and received the resignation of the acting commissioner of the IRS.

Also in 2012, it was revealed that the Obama Administration had requested a court order to have access to the records of phone lines used by Associated Press (AP) reporters as part of an investigation into a news leak regarding a terrorist plot, without notifying AP. The Associated Press said that this was a serious violation of the freedom of the press. The same year, National Security Agency (NSA) records showed that the Obama Administration had required a communications company to turn over metadata (including numbers called and length of calls) from many of its subscribers' phones. Also disclosed was the existence of a program that gathered personal information from companies such as Google, Facebook, and Microsoft for the NSA and the FBI.

Several tragic shootings that received national attention renewed debate about gun control legislation. In January 2011 a gunman seriously wounded Arizona Democratic Congresswoman Gabrielle Giffords in an assassination attempt. He killed six other people and wounded thirteen. Giffords made a remarkable and courageous recovery from a brain injury; saw her husband, astronaut Mark Kelly, command the final flight of the Space Shuttle *Endeavor*; and resumed her seat in Congress before retiring in January of 2012.

The NSA Headquarters in Fort Meade, Maryland, is active twenty-four hours a day, seven days a week. Running its array of advanced computer equipment makes it the largest consumer of electricity in the State of Maryland.

President Obama and Representative Giffords at the 2012 State of the Union Address

A shooting at a movie theater in Aurora, Colorado, in July of that year left twelve dead, while an attack in December resulted in the deaths of twenty students and six adults at a school in Newtown, Connecticut.

International Relations

During his first year in office, while dealing with the financial crisis, President Obama made overtures to a few other countries suggesting he wanted the United States to have a different relationship with them. In December 2009 Obama was awarded the Nobel Peace Prize "for his extraordinary efforts to strengthen international diplomacy and cooperation between peoples," as the prize citation expressed it. Many observers believed that the award was intended to be an after-the-fact condemnation of President George W. Bush, since Obama had not yet actually accomplished much for world peace.

Revolutions in several Muslim countries in the Middle East and northern Africa, often called the Arab Spring, forced the United States government to consider carefully what its role should be in those situations. The U.S. government announced its support of pro-democratic efforts and even provided military assistance to rebels fighting the government of dictator Muammar Gaddafi in Libya. During Obama's second term, Russia's role in the separation of Crimea from the Ukraine and its annexation to Russia caused another foreign policy crisis.

The most troubling event in the region for Americans took place on September 11, 2012, the eleventh anniversary of the terrorist attacks in New York City and Washington, D.C. On that day the American diplomatic post in Benghazi, Libya, was attacked. Ambassador Chris Stevens and three other Americans were killed. The official explanation was that the attack was a spontaneous riot that occurred in reaction to an anti-Muslim movie that had been produced in the United States. As time went on, however, evidence came to light that the incident was a premeditated terrorist attack and that officials in the Obama Administration had tried to cover up the real nature of the incident.

Conclusion

The election of Barack Obama was an historical milestone in that he was the first African American to be elected President. Evaluations of a President's legacy often change over the decades and centuries of history. Hindsight gives us a different perspective on choices made in the past. Each President of the United States is a fallible human being who must

President Obama met with President Hamid Karzai of Afghanistan and President Asif Ali Zardari of Pakistan at the White House in 2009.

make momentous decisions based on the always incomplete information and experience available to him. And even when that person makes decisions with which we disagree, each President of the United States deserves the prayers of God's people.

President Obama at a White House Meeting (2009)

Render to all what is due them: tax to whom tax is due; custom to whom custom; fear to whom fear; honor to whom honor.
Romans 13:7

⋆ Assignments for Lesson 149 ⋆

American Voices Read Barack Obama's "Remarks at the 70th Anniversary of D-Day" (pages 410-413).

English Complete your essay for readers in the future about a current issue in which you explain the significance of that issue and how it affects people's lives.

Bible List three ways in which you have come to see more clearly the importance of faith in understanding American history by studying *Exploring America*.

Work on memorizing 2 Corinthians 5:14-15.

Project Work on your project.

Student Review Optional: Answer the questions for Lesson 149.

Lesson 150 - Bible Study

Rescue Workers at the Pentagon Pause for a Moment of Silence on September 14, 2001, a National Day of Prayer and Remembrance

Putting American History into Perspective

Our journey through the story of America has now come to our own time. In this lesson we identify some key ideas in the story as we consider the past and look toward the future.

The Role of Faith

The Christian religion has been a major influence in America since the founding of the country. It motivated many of the settlers and is the basis for our laws and our social structure. We can see the influence of faith in the value placed on individual lives and in the basic decency that characterizes most of our social interactions. The belief that people are worth our best has time and again motivated the courage and sacrifice that Americans have shown for a cause greater than themselves. The response of the nation to the terrorist attacks of September 11, 2001, is a demonstration of this basic goodness and of our country's foundation of faith.

However, the influence of the Christian faith has lessened in recent years. The evidences of this change include the increase in abortions, the widespread use of pornography, the troubling frequency of sexual and physical abuse, and the debased material distributed through the media. If we can ever recapture the idea that all we are and all we have is from God, we will be a better country.

This is not to say that everything was great in the good old days. America has too often witnessed hatred, prejudice, worldliness, and injustice practiced by Christian people who should have known better. Such people were more influenced by the thinking of the times than they were by the thinking of Christ. American Christians today need to learn from these mistakes of the past so that they don't happen again.

Christianity has never been the official national religion of this country. We know that having an established state church leads to numerous problems and is not what Jesus wanted. What we would like to see instead is the Christian faith respected and obeyed voluntarily. The best way for this to happen is for those of us who are Christians to follow Him without compromise. What we called the civil religion of the United States has helped to keep God in our national consciousness, but it has also hurt the cause of Christ by leaving the impression that a person can be pleasing to God simply by being an American. Christians should guide their lives not by how widely Christianity is accepted in society but by the example Christ set, regardless of what others do.

Whether we live in a religiously tolerant culture or a religiously oppressive culture, we must choose to follow the truth. The danger of living in Communist China is that a person might be tempted to deny his faith in the face of persecution. The danger of living in the United States, on the other hand, is that one may become a cultural Christian and never understand the cost of being a disciple of Jesus. The greatest spiritual danger presented by American culture is ease, not hardship. This might well be changing in our day. Perhaps the turn away from traditional Christian values in our country will challenge us to have a firmer grasp of what it really means to be a Christian.

The Value of Freedom

We have a precious gift in our personal, political, and religious freedom in the United States, a gift that we often take for granted. Perhaps the best way to appreciate this gift is to visit another country where people do not have our freedoms. These freedoms have enabled Americans to accomplish great things by unleashing the potential of the individual. Our freedom has taught us to be tolerant of those who differ with us and to try to convince others with love and by example rather than by force.

Some people have abused our freedoms. Freedom of speech has enabled the expression of wrong and terrible thoughts. Free market capitalism has done much good; but it has also sometimes been used to justify taking advantage of workers or damaging the environment. An open society such as ours has dangers and risks, but they are preferable to the dangers and risks we would face in a closed society that did not have our freedoms. Our freedom is worth defending, even if it means extending it to those with whom we disagree.

In March of 1776, the newly-established Continental Navy and Marines made a raid in the Bahamas in an attempt to capture British ammunition stored there. This 1973 painting is by artist V. Zveg.

Always value freedom. One way to distinguish between politicians is this. One says that he knows best how everyone ought to live, so if we elect him he will take care of us. The other says that each individual knows best how to live, so if we elect him he will protect our freedom to make our own decisions. The latter position gives each person a chance to become what God can make him instead of limiting him to what those in government want him to be. Always value freedom.

The Constitution and the Political System

The United States Constitution is a remarkable document. It created a system of government that has worked well for over two hundred years with only relatively minor changes. Our form of government has survived a civil war, difficult economic times, the explosive period of the 1960s, and blatant corruption. It works because we still hold the basic assumptions that lay behind it: limited government, divided power, trust in the many as opposed to the few, and respect for the rights of the individual.

With this continuity has come change. The way we go about governing and selecting representatives has changed from the early days of the nation. Over time more people (notably women and people of color) have been included in the political process. The Federal government has taken more power than was originally thought to be best, which makes us more dependent on Washington. Both of the two major political parties enjoy having power and criticizing the other party, sometimes at the expense of standing for principle and taking positive action.

Presidential campaigns consume media attention for months as candidates vie for coverage. The 2016 campaign saw many twists and turns.

In this 1910 cartoon from Puck *magazine, artist Udo Keppler suggests that both major political parties obstruct the view of their most ardent partisans, preventing them from clearly seeing the full light of Patriotism, described as "the greatest good for the greatest number." Keppler's father, an Austrian immigrant to the U.S., was also a cartoonist.*

President Donald Trump speaks to a joint session of Congress in 2017. Behind him are Vice President Mike Pence (left) and Speaker of the House Paul Ryan.

Bernie Sanders, an independent U.S. senator from Vermont, challenged Hillary Clinton for the Democratic nomination. Clinton, who had served as First Lady, U.S. Senator, and Secretary of State, won the nomination, becoming the first female presidential nominee of a major party. Donald Trump, a businessman with no political experience, gained the Republican nomination. Trump went on to win the election, becoming the 45th President of the United States.

Politics can be surprising, confusing, and often disappointing and divisive. Americans look at the same Constitution and come to very different conclusions about what it means today. But the foundation of our country remains strong, and citizens have the opportunity to participate in the political process for good.

Changes in American Society

Whereas America was defined by the farm and small town until the early twentieth century, today our nation is defined by the city. The media and the Internet, along with our busy and separated lives, have made it easier for us to know what is happening across the country than to know what is happening across town. We still have local and regional differences, but increasingly our lives are shaped by national standards and practices—at least, the standards and practices that are presented in movies, magazines, and television programs.

We are influenced by our increased ability to travel and communicate. The world is more available to us. This gives us the opportunity to do more good, but it also presents the temptation to engage in more evil. Television can be educational and beneficial, but Americans have far too often also accepted the insipid and often immoral television programming dished out to us. Our responsibility is to be good managers of the resources available to us.

Much of what we have in the U.S. is the envy of the world. Our medical technology is second to none (more due to the absence of government regulation than to the presence of it). Our standard of living is higher than that of almost every other nation. People from all over the world come here to get an education and to get a new start economically because they know that this is the place where they will most likely find what they want.

Four Generations of a Family from the Coast Salish Tribe of the Northwestern United States (c. 1906)

People admire what we have, but our higher calling is for them to be able to respect who we are. We must continue the progress that has been made in race relations. We must use our financial resources for good and not for selfish purposes. We must devote our minds to that which is good as opposed to that which is popular or easy. One positive example of Americans giving their best for others is the way that American missionaries have taken the gospel of Christ around the world.

American families are not as strong as they once were. This is the result of many factors, including the trend of husbands and wives failing to be careful to nurture family relationships. The main reason that families are not as strong as they once were is that too many families have not made the decision to be strong and as a result they have let the world tear them apart.

The breakdown of the family has consequences for individual lives and for society. If you doubt this, talk to a social worker with your state's family services department or to a policeman or district attorney who has dealt with several generations of lawbreakers from the same family. Strong families are good for a society.

The Threat of Terrorism

We have long faced threats from the outside. For forty-five years after World War II, the United States faced the threat of Communism. That menace has faded, only to be replaced by the threat of Islamic terrorism. Godless Communism has been supplanted by extremists from a non-Christian religion who have shown their willingness to do us harm.

Both Communism and Islamic terrorism are examples of the desire for power and control; they just wear different masks. Communism threatened us in the name of the state, while Islam threatens us in the name of Allah. In an earlier generation, the masks were those of Naziism and Japanese imperialism. Muslim terrorists have already caused us harm, but they will not bring us down as long as the American people decide that opposing them is worth the fight. We must not think, however, that our security ultimately resides in military might or diplomatic skill. God alone holds the future, and our only lasting security is in Him.

Back to Notgrove

We began exploring the story of America by visiting the village of Notgrove, England, in 1490. Little had changed in the thousand years before then; but much has changed in the five hundred years since then, especially in the last sixty years.

Notgrove is an actual village in England. Our family came to know Notgrove on a trip to England in 1998. Notgrove was once a manor owned by an English lord. In Notgrove we drove past some twenty small houses and then we arrived at the manor house and the old stone chapel. Near the manor house we saw men using large, modern earthmoving equipment as they worked on a project. We heard that, a few years earlier, the new owner of the manor house had the gravestones in the churchyard bulldozed because he thought they were old and unattractive.

As we were looking around, we met an older man and his middle-aged son who were visiting the church building. The older man's late wife had helped sew a beautiful tapestry that hung behind the altar. They told us that during the German bombing of England in World War II, an ancient stained glass window in the building was removed and buried for safekeeping (it had since been put back in its place). The church building has a history of grandeur, but now rain water seeps into it and a puddle stands in one corner on the floor. Services are held there only once a month.

What we saw in this small English village was an illustration of the past meeting the changing present. The modern world has come even to Notgrove.

History and Eternity

Thinking about the little village of Notgrove and the changes that have taken place there prompts us to think about the changes that have taken place in America and about where we are headed, as individuals and as a nation.

We must remember two important facts. First, the most important factor in understanding and evaluating the course of human events accurately is to remember that human events are not the only reality. The story of mankind does not just involve this physical world. "Our struggle is not against flesh and blood," Paul said, but "against the spiritual forces of wickedness in the heavenly places" (Ephesians 6:12). As Christians, we are involved in a much greater battle than just what happens to the American nation. It was for this greater battle that Christ came. As C. S. Lewis observed in a 1945 address called "Membership":

> There will come a time when every culture, every institution, every nation, the human race, all biological life is extinct and every one of us is still alive. Immortality is promised to us, not to these generalities. It was not for societies or states that Christ died, but for men (originally published in *The Weight of Glory* in 1949; this edition New York: Macmillan, 1980, p. 117).

The Ziggurat of Ur, pictured in the background, was built around 2000 BC, close to the time Abraham lived. During the war in Iraq, four thousand years later, American troops occupied the area. These children, growing up under a new Iraqi government, are celebrating the return of the Ziggurat to Iraqi control in 2009.

Second, just as we must keep the individual events of history in perspective by considering the entire story of history, we must keep human history itself in perspective by remembering eternity. We must remember that, in terms of eternity, the United States is temporary whereas every individual is eternal. In a 1942 radio address, C. S. Lewis also noted:

> If individuals live only seventy years, then a state, or a nation, or a civilization, which may last for a thousand years, is more important than an individual. But if Christianity is true, then the individual is not only more important but incomparably more important, for he is everlasting and the life of a state or a civilization, compared with his, is only a moment (originally published in *Mere Christianity* in 1952; this edition London: Harper Collins Fount, 1977, p. 70).

The eyes of faith will help us to keep the proper perspective on our world, our nation, and ourselves. "The righteous will live by his faith," said the prophet (Habakkuk 2:4). God spoke these words to a prophet trying to understand history, current events, and the future. The words still apply to us as we try to understand the same issues: history, current events, and the future. The best and only accurate way to see the past, present, and future is through the eyes of faith.

The story of America is not finished. The lessons in this curriculum only bring you to today, and history continues to be made every day we live. You are participating in the story of this great and blessed nation. You are receiving the heritage of previous generations; and I pray you will pass on what is of value to the generations that will follow you, as God gives us days and years. May your life and the lives of those you touch be better by what you continue to learn through a lifetime of exploring America.

For the things which are seen are temporal,
but the things which are not seen are eternal.
2 Corinthians 4:18b

⋆ Assignments for Lesson 150 ⋆

History/English Make a list of one period in American history, one event in American history, one person in American history, and one author (whose work you read in this course) about which or about whom you would like to learn more. Note how you would like to do this (read a book, watch a video, visit an historic site, or some other way).

Bible Recite or write 2 Corinthians 5:14-15 from memory.

Project Complete your project for the unit.

Student Review Optional: Answer the questions for Lesson 150, take the quiz for Unit 30, and take the sixth history exam, English exam, and Bible exam.

Celebrate finishing Exploring America!

Detail from Cousin Reginald Spells Peloponnesus (Spelling Bee), *Norman Rockwell (American, 1918)*

Image Credits

Images marked with one of these codes are used with the permission of a Creative Commons Attribution or Attribution-Share Alike License. See the websites listed for details.

CC-BY-2.0	creativecommons.org/licenses/by/2.0/
CC-BY-3.0	creativecommons.org/licenses/by/3.0/
CC-BY-SA-2.0	creativecommons.org/licenses/by-sa/2.0/
CC-BY-SA-2.5	creativecommons.org/licenses/by-sa/2.5/
CC-BY-SA-3.0	creativecommons.org/licenses/by-sa/3.0/
CC-BY-SA-3.0 DE	creativecommons.org/licenses/by-sa/3.0/de/
CC-BY-SA-3.0 NL	creativecommons.org/licenses/by-sa/3.0/nl/

Uncredited images are in the public domain in the United States, taken from Wikimedia Commons and other sources.

v	Library of Congress
vi	Library of Congress
vii	NASA
viii	Brad Hagan (bradhoc) / Flickr / CC-BY-2.0
423	Jim Bowen (jimbowen0306) / Flickr / CC-BY-2.0
426t	Library of Congress
427	U.S. Army Corps of Engineers / Flickr / CC-BY-2.0
428l	Cornell University Collection of Political Americana, Cornell University Library
429	Library of Congress
431	Orange County Archives / Flickr / CC-BY-2.0
432	Library of Congress
433	Library of Congress
436	Library of Congress
437	Library of Congress
438	Brandon Grossardt / Wikimedia Commons / CC-BY-SA-3.0
439	Library of Congress
440	Library of Congress
441	Library of Congress
442	Library of Congress
443	Library of Congress
444	Library of Congress
445	Library of Congress
446	Boise Metro Chamber of Commerce / Flickr / CC-BY-2.0
447	Charlene Notgrass
448	Charlene Notgrass
449	Charlene Notgrass
450	Matt Rafferty / Flickr / CC-BY-2.0
451t	Charlene Notgrass
451b	Angell Williams / Flickr / CC-BY-2.0
452	Charlene Notgrass
453	Library of Congress
455	Florida Keys--Public Libraries / Flickr / CC-BY-2.0
456	anyjazz65 / Flickr / CC-BY-2.0
457	Kheel Center, Cornell University
458	Library of Congress
459	Cliff (cliff1066™) / Flickr / CC-BY-2.0
460	Library of Congress
461	National Library of Ireland
463	Library of Congress
464	Kheel Center, Cornell University
465	Library of Congress
467b	Library of Congress
468	Library of Congress
469	Library of Congress
470	Kheel Center, Cornell University
471	Library of Congress
472	Library of Congress
473t	Eugene Kim (eekim) / Flickr / CC-BY-2.0

474 Carol M. Highsmith Archive, Library of Congress
475t Carol M. Highsmith Archive, Library of Congress
476 Library of Congress
477 Jean-Christophe BENOIST / Wikimedia Commons / CC-BY-3.0
478 Kheel Center, Cornell University
479 Simon Allardice / Flickr / CC-BY-2.0
480 Kheel Center, Cornell University
481 Library of Congress
483r Library of Congress
484 Library of Congress
485 Library of Congress
486 Keene Public Library / Flickr / CC-BY-2.0
487 Library of Congress
488 Library of Congress
489 Library of Congress
490 Library of Congress
491 Library of Congress
492 Library of Congress
493 Library of Congress
497 Library of Congress
498 Library of Congress
499 Library of Congress
500 Library of Congress
501 Library of Congress
502 Library of Congress
503 Zagalejo / Wikimedia Commons
504t Library of Congress
504b Smithsonian Institution Archives
505 Library of Congress
507 University of Michigan Special Collections Library
508 Daniel Ramirez / Flickr / CC-BY-2.0
509 Library of Congress
510r National Archives and Records Administration
511 The National Guard
512 Library of Congress
513t Library of Congress
514 Library of Congress
515 Library of Congress
517 Prince Roy / Flickr / CC-BY-2.0
521 Library of Congress
522 Library of Congress
523t OSU Special Collections
523b Library of Congress
524 Nyttend / Wikimedia Commons
526 Library of Congress
528 Architect of the Capitol
529 Library of Congress
531 Cornell University Library
532 Library of Congress
534 Lance Cheung / U.S. Department of Agriculture
535 Library of Congress
536 Library of Congress
537 Library of Congress
538t Charlene Notgrass
538b Library of Congress
540 Brian Gratwicke / Flickr / CC-BY-2.0
542 Library of Congress
543t University of Texas Libraries, The University of Texas at Austin
543b Library of Congress
544 Library of Congress
546 Library of Congress
547 Library of Congress
548t Library of Congress
549 Chris Pruitt / Wikimedia Commons / CC-BY-SA-3.0
551 Library of Congress
553 Library of Congress
554 Library of Congress
555 Library of Congress
556 Library of Congress
557 Library of Congress
558 Library of Congress
560 National Archives and Records Administration
561b Library of Congress
562t Bundesarchiv, Bild 183-R05148 / Unknown / CC-BY-SA-3.0 DE
562b Bibliothèque Nationale de France
564 Library of Congress
565 Library of Congress
566 Library of Congress
567t U.S. Department of Defense
567b Library of Congress
568 U.S. Army
569t National Archives and Records Administration
569b Library of Congress
570 Sgt. Tatum Vayavananda / U.S. Department of Defense
571 Tipoune / Wikimedia Commons
572t Library of Congress
574t National Library of Ireland
575 Library of Congress
577 Copyright Elin B @ Nordic Touch, www.nordictouch.co.uk / Flickr / CC-BY-2.0
578 Library of Congress
579 Library of Congress
580 Valdete Hasani / Wikimedia Commons / CC-BY-SA-3.0
581 Library of Congress
583 Library of Congress
585t Library of Congress

585b The Children's Museum of Indianapolis / CC-BY-SA-3.0
586 Library of Congress
587 Library of Congress
589 Library of Congress
590 Library of Congress
591 Library of Congress
593 Library of Congress
594 Library of Congress
595 Library of Congress
596 Library of Congress
597 Library of Congress
598 Ray Notgrass
599t Library of Congress
599b Federal Bureau of Investigation
600t Library of Congress
600bl Library of Congress
600br Momos / Wikimedia Commons
602b Library of Congress
604 Library of Congress
605t National Archives and Records Administration
605b Phillip / Flickr / CC-BY-2.0
606 Library of Congress
607 Library of Congress
608 Library of Congress
610 Smithsonian Institution Archives
611 Library of Congress
612 Smithsonian Institution Archives
613 Ray Notgrass
614 Library of Congress
615 Carol M. Highsmith Archive, Library of Congress
617 Carol M. Highsmith Archive, Library of Congress
618 Library of Congress
619 Library of Congress
620 National Archives and Records Administration
621 Library of Congress
622tl Library of Congress
622tr Library of Congress
622b Gary Bridgman, southsideartgallery.com / Wikimedia Commons / CC-BY-SA-3.0
623 Library of Congress
624 Lewis Hine / National Archives and Records Administration
625 Library of Congress
626 Library of Congress
627 Library of Congress
628 Library of Congress
629 Library of Congress
630 Fibonacci Blue / Flickr / CC-BY-2.0
631 Library of Congress
632 Library of Congress
633 Library of Congress
634 Library of Congress
635t Bundesarchiv, Bild 183-G00630 / CC-BY-SA-3.0 DE
635b National Archives and Records Administration
636 Library of Congress
637t Library of Congress
637b National Council of American-Soviet Friendship
638t Library of Congress
638b stooart / Flickr / CC-BY-2.0
639 Library of Congress
640t Library of Congress
640b Bundesarchiv, Bild 183-L15327 / CC-BY-SA-3.0 DE
641l Bundesarchiv, Bild 183-H12751 / CC-BY-SA-3.0 DE
641r Ministry of Information (UK)
642t Library of Congress
642b America First Committee
643 Library of Congress
644 National Archives and Records Administration
645 National Archives and Records Administration
646 Library of Congress
649 Library of Congress
650 Bundesarchiv, Bild 101III-Duerr-053-29 / Dürr / CC-BY-SA-3.0 DE
651 Carol M. Highsmith's America, Library of Congress
653 U.S. Navy
654 Franklin D. Roosevelt Presidential Library and Museum
655 Library of Congress
656l Empire of Japan
656r U.S. Navy
657 Library of Congress
658 Library of Congress
659 Library of Congress
660t Library of Congress
660b U.S. Coast Guard
661t Library of Congress
661b Ministry of Information (UK)
662 U.S. Army Signal Corps
663 National Archives and Records Administration
664t Forrest R. Whitesides / Wikimedia Commons / CC-BY-SA-3.0
664b National Archives and Records Administration
665t Library of Congress
665b Manhattan Project
666 U.S. Army Signal Corps
667t U.S. Army
667b U.S. Marine Corps
668l Library of Congress
668r U.S. Army
669 National Archives and Records Administration
670 Notgrass Family Collection

671 Notgrass Family Collection
672 Notgrass Family Collection
673 Notgrass Family Collection
674 Notgrass Family Collection
675 Notgrass Family Collection
676 Notgrass Family Collection
677 Notgrass Family Collection
678 Franklin D. Roosevelt Presidential Library and Museum
679 Library of Congress
680 Notgrass Family Collection
681 U.S. Air Force
683 USAID / Flickr / CC-BY-2.0
684 User:GrahamColm / Wikimedia Commons / CC-BY-SA-3.0
686 Hynek Moravec / Wikimedia Commons / CC-BY-3.0
687 U.S. Air Force
688t U.S. Air Force
688b User:maix and User:Alphathon / Wikimedia Commons / CC-BY-SA-3.0
689 U.S. Army
690 Library of Congress
691 Library of Congress
692t User:Cmglee / Wikimedia Commons / CC-BY-SA-3.0
692b Library of Congress
694 Library of Congress
695 PFC James Cox / National Archives and Records Administration
696 U.S. Army Signal Corps
697t Sgt. Riley / U.S. Army
697b F. Kazukaitis / U.S. Navy
698 Stefan Krasowski / Flickr / CC-BY-2.0
699 The National Guard
700t National Archives and Records Administration
700b Library of Congress
701 U.S. Air Force
702 U.S. Information Agency
703 Veterans Administration
704t Library of Congress
704b Harry S. Truman Library and Museum
705 Library of Congress
706t Tinou Bao / Flickr / CC-BY-2.0
706b Charles Ayoub / Wikimedia Commons
707b israeltourism / Flickr / CC-BY-2.0
708 Library of Congress
709t Library of Congress
709b Billy Graham Evangelistic Association
710 Library of Congress
711 Mary Evelyn McCurdy
713 National Archives and Records Administration
714b Dwight D. Eisenhower Presidential Library and Museum
715l Zaereth / Wikimedia Commons
715r NASA
716l The United States Army Band / Flickr / CC-BY-2.0
716r SSG Chris Branagan / U.S. Army
717 Charlene Notgrass
718l National Archives and Records Administration
718r U.S. Navy
719 Library of Congress
720l Library of Congress
720r National Archives and Records Administration
721 Library of Congress
722 Library of Congress
724 Library of Congress
725t Eisenhower Presidential Library
725b Central Intelligence Agency
726 Earth Science and Remote Sensing Unit, NASA Johnson Space Center
727tr U.S. Air Force
727bl Eisenhower Presidential Library
727br USAID
728 Library of Congress
729t NASA
729b Gregory R Todd / Wikimedia Commons / CC-BY-SA-3.0
730t NASA JPL-Caltech
730b User:Victor-ny / Wikimedia Commons / CC-BY-SA-3.0
731t RIA Novosti archive, image #159271 / V. Malyshev / CC-BY-SA 3.0
731b John Notgrass
732t Jamling Tenzing Norgay / Wikimedia Commons / CC-BY-SA-3.0
732m John F. Kennedy Presidential Library
732b Frederick Dennstedt / Flickr / CC-BY-SA-2.0
733 Library of Congress
734t National Archives and Records Administration
734b Nyttend / Wikimedia Commons
735 Rex Gray / Flickr / CC-BY-2.0
736 Library of Congress
737 National Archives and Records Administration
738 Library of Congress
739 Library of Congress
741 John F. Kennedy Presidential Library
742 National Archives and Records Administration
743 National Archives and Records Administration
744t Library of Congress
744b National Archives and Records Administration
745 National Archives and Records Administration
746 National Archives and Records Administration

747 LBJ Presidential Library
748 Cecil Stoughton / LBJ Presidential Library
749 Library of Congress
750t Library of Congress
731b User:Marathona / Wikimedia Commons / CC-BY-SA-3.0
751 Library of Congress
752 Library of Congress
753 Library of Congress
754 Library of Congress
755t Library of Congress
755b User:Morhange / Wikimedia Commons / CC-BY-SA-3.0
756 LBJ Presidential Library
757 National Archives and Records Administration
758t National Archives and Records Administration
758b Laura Jones www.baldwinstreetgallery.com / CC-BY-SA-3.0
759 Library of Congress
760 U.S. Marine Corps
761 NBC
762 Carl Wycoff / Flickr / CC-BY-2.0
763t National Archives and Records Administration
763b LBJ Presidential Library
764t Kheel Center, Cornell University Library
764b Library of Congress
765 NASA
766 U.S. Information Agency
767 Karen Martin / Library of Congress
769 Library of Congress
770 U.S. Army Chaplains Museum
771 Peter Pettus / Library of Congress
773 Gerald R. Ford Presidential Library
775 Nixon Presidential Library
776 Ronald L. Haeberle / U.S. Army
777 U.S. Navy
778 Karl Schumacher / Gerald R. Ford Presidential Library
779 NASA
780 Nixon Presidential Library
781 Nixon Presidential Library
782 Ian Mackenzie / Flickr / CC-BY-2.0
783 Library of Congress
784 Gerald R. Ford Presidential Library
785 National Archives and Records Administration
786 National Archives and Records Administration
787 Gerald R. Ford Presidential Library
788 U.S. Marine Corps
789 Jimmy Carter Library
791 Library of Congress
792t Library of Congress
792b Mr.minoque / Wikimedia Commons / CC-BY-3.0
793 Rick Diamond / The Carter Center
794 Jonestown Institute
795t Earth Week Committee of Philadelphia / CC-BY-SA-3.0
795b National Archives and Records Administration
796 Fotocollectie Anefo Bert Verhoeff / Dutch National Archives / CC-BY-SA-3.0 NL
797 Debra Sweet / Flickr / CC-BY-2.0
798 Patty Mooney of San Diego, California / Wikimedia Commons
799 Fibonacci Blue / Flickr / CC-BY-2.0
800 Library of Congress
802 Library of Congress
803 stmaryathens / Flickr / CC-BY-2.0
805 NASA
807 Ronald Reagan Presidential Library
808 Ronald Reagan Presidential Library
809 Ronald Reagan Presidential Library
810 NASA
811t SPC 5 Vincent R. Kritts / U.S. Army
811b U.S. Centers for Disease Control
812 Bernard A. Cardali / U.S. Navy
813 Ronald Reagan Presidential Library
814l SPC Douglas Ide / U.S. Army
814r TSGT M. J. Creen / U.S. Air Force
815t D. R. Walker / Wikimedia Commons / CC-BY-SA-3.0
815b Ronald Reagan Presidential Library
816t Post of Hungary
816m User:Squelle / Wikimedia Commons / CC-BY-SA-3.0
816b W. Liller / NASA
817 Ronald Reagan Presidential Library
818 Library of Congress
819 Notgrass Family Collection
820t Steve Petteway, Collection of the Supreme Court of the United States
820b Spirit of America / Shutterstock.com
821 U.S. Department of Defense
822br User:Alvesgaspar / Wikimedia Commons / CC-BY-SA-3.0
823 Carol M. Highsmith Archive, Library of Congress
824t U.S. Air Force
824b George Bush Presidential Library
825 Russell Roederer / U.S. Army
826t Staff Sgt. Dean Wagner / U.S. Department of Defense
826b Mass Communication Specialist 1st Class Leah Stiles / U.S. Navy
827 George Bush Presidential Library
828 D. W. Holmes / U.S. Navy
830 User:Marsyas / Wikimedia Commons / CC-BY-SA-3.0
832 User:Marsyas / Wikimedia Commons / CC-BY-SA-3.0
833 Primaryspace / Wikimedia Commons

835 NOAA
837 Ralph Alswang / William J. Clinton Presidential Library
838t National Archives and Records Administration
838b Allan Warren / Wikimedia Commons / CC-BY-SA-3.0
839 MSGT Fernando Serna / U.S. Air Force
840l Jim Winstead / Flickr / CC-BY-2.0
840r Bexar County Economic Development Department / Flickr / CC-BY-2.0
842 FEMA
843l Eugene Chavez / U.S. Air Force
843r BasilioC / Wikimedia Commons
844 Denverjeffrey / Wikimedia Commons / CC-BY-3.0
845t Sergeant Angel Clemons / U.S. Army
845b Uberpenguin at the English language Wikipedia / CC-BY-SA-3.0
846 James Duncan Davidson / Flickr / CC-BY-2.0
847t SSGT James D. Mossman / U.S. Army
847b Jerome Howard / U.S. Army
848 Government Press Office (Israel) / CC-BY-SA-3.0
849 Sgt. Don L. Maes / U.S. Marine Corps
850l MIKI Yoshihito / Flickr / CC-BY-2.0
850r The White House
851t SRA Tana R. Hamilton / U.S. Air Force
851b Michael Büker / Wikimedia Commons / CC-BY-SA-3.0
852 SRA Tana R. Hamilton / U.S. Air Force
853 Gerald R. Ford Presidential Library
854 U.S. Department of Defense
855 U.S. House of Representatives
857 TSgt Suzanne M. Day / U.S. Air Force
858 Paris Psalter / Wikimedia Commons
859 Gage Skidmore / Wikimedia Commons / CC-BY-SA-3.0
861 Sgt. Jacob Harrer / U.S. Marine Corps
863 Carol M. Highsmith Archive, Library of Congress
864t Seattle Municipal Archives / Flickr / CC-BY-2.0
864b Tech. Sgt. Rick Sforza / U.S. Air Force
865 Patrick McKay (DebateLord) / Wikimedia Commons / CC-BY-SA-2.5
867 Beyond My Ken / Wikimedia Commons / CC-BY-SA-3.0
868 Keith Wright
869t Village Square / Flickr / CC-BY-2.0
869b National Atlas of the United States
870 U.S. Department of State
871t User:Raul654 / Wikimedia Commons / CC-BY-SA-3.0
871b Staff Sgt. Reynaldo Ramon / U.S. Air Force
872t Tech. Sgt. Kevin J. Gruenwald / U.S. Air Force
872b Petty Officer 2nd Class Kyle Niemi / U.S. Coast Guard
873 U.S. Army
874 Library of Congress
875l TSGT Cedric H. Rudisill / U.S. Air Force
875r Journalist 1st Class Preston Keres / U.S. Navy
876t National Park Service
876b George W. Bush Presidential Library and Museum
877t Sgt. Brandon Aird / U.S. Army
877b U.S. Department of Defense
878t Lance Cpl. Brian L. Wickliffe / U.S. Marine Corps
878b Pfc. Nikko-Angelo Matos / U.S. Army
879 Pete Souza / White House
880l Tanenhaus / Flickr / CC-BY-2.0
880r Bruce Dall / Flickr / CC-BY-2.0
881 Senior Master Sgt. Thomas Meneguin / U.S. Air Force
882t Jeff Turner / Flickr / CC-BY-2.0
882b Mason Votes - Rachael Dickson / Flickr / CC-BY-2.0
883 Cliff / Flickr / CC-BY-2.0
884tl Mallory Benedict - PBS NewsHour / Flickr / CC-BY-2.0
884tr Library of Congress
884b Sonya Hebert / White House
885 National Security Agency
886 Pete Souza / White House
887 Pete Souza / White House
888 Jocelyn Augustino / FEMA News Photo
889 U.S. Naval History and Heritage Command
890 Library of Congress
891 Shealah Craighead / White House
892 Library of Congress
893 Maj. Myles Caggins / U.S. Army

Detail from The Iceberg, *Frederic Edwin Church (American, 1891)*

Index

Pages 1-422 are in Part 1. Pages 423-934 are in Part 2.